# Rajasthan, Delhi & Agra

Abigail Hole

Martin Robinson, Sarina Singh

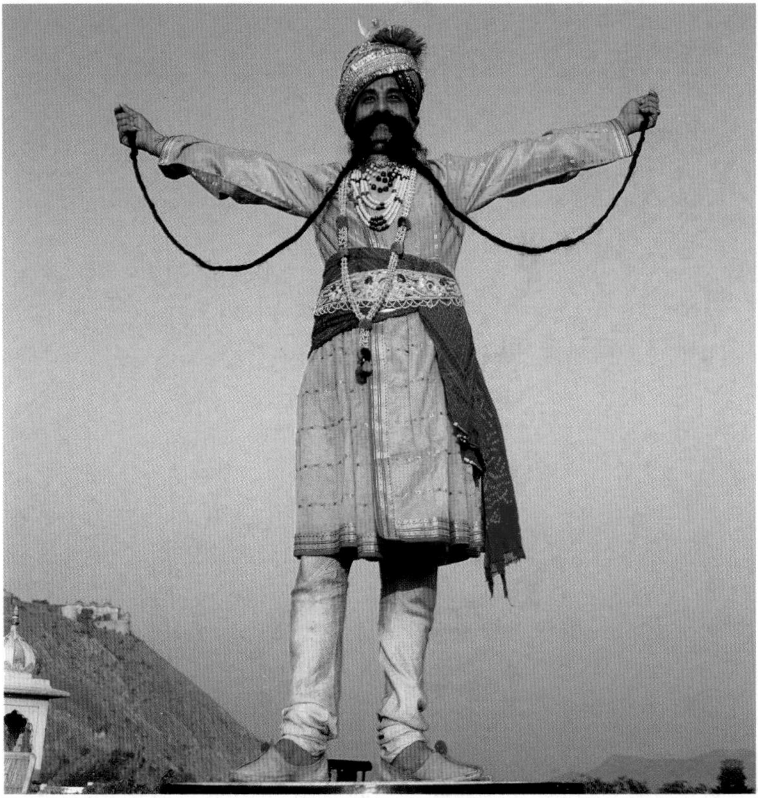

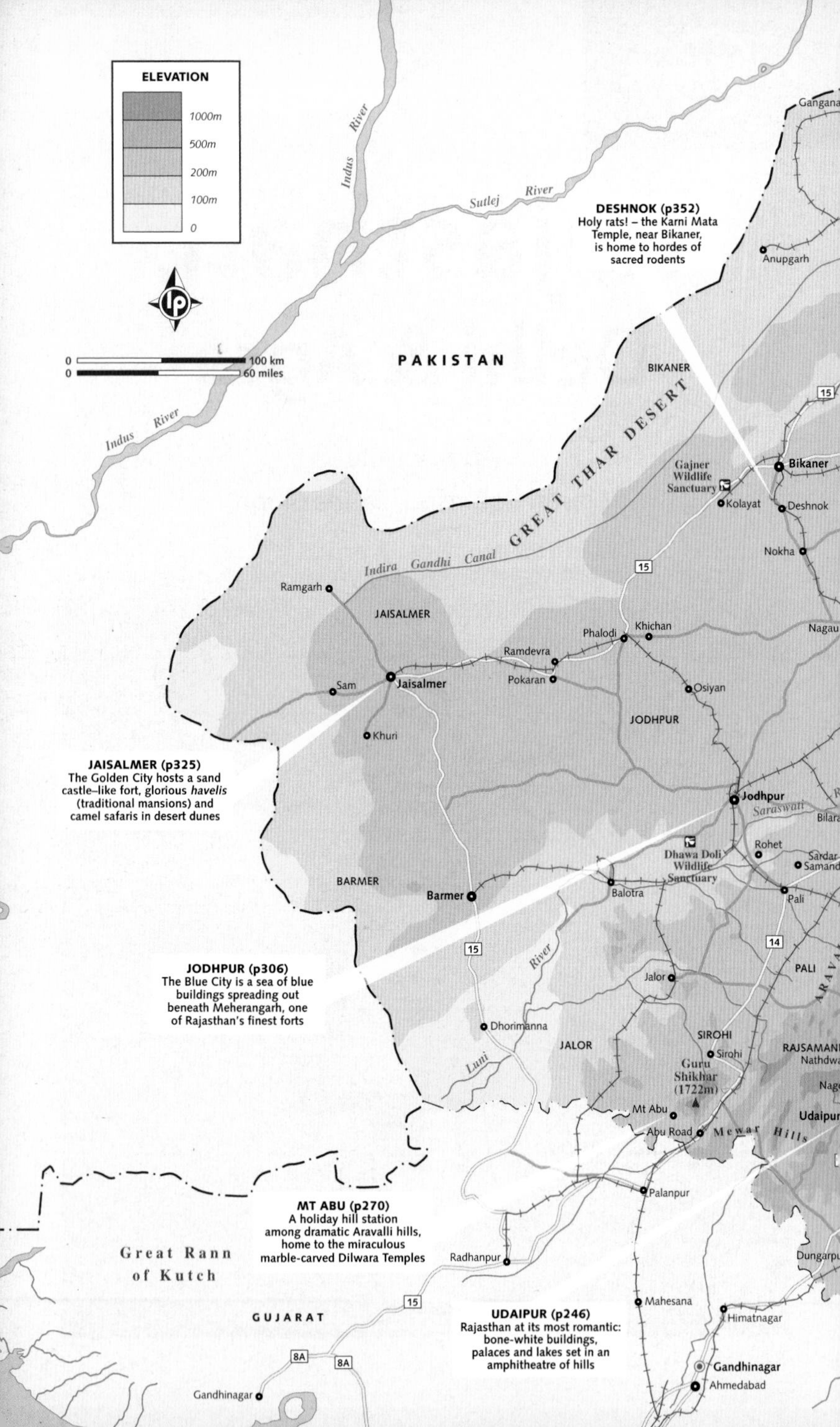

ELEVATION
1000m
500m
200m
100m
0
0 100 km
0 60 miles
PAKISTAN
Indus River
Sutlej River
DESHNOK (p352)
Holy rats! – the Karni Mata Temple, near Bikaner, is home to hordes of sacred rodents
Gangana
Anupgarh
BIKANER
GREAT THAR DESERT
Gajner Wildlife Sanctuary
Bikaner
Kolayat
Deshnok
Nokha
Indira Gandhi Canal
Ramgarh
JAISALMER
Khichan
Phalodi
Nagau
Ramdevra
Pokaran
Jaisalmer
Sam
Osiyan
JODHPUR
Khuri
JAISALMER (p325)
The Golden City hosts a sand castle–like fort, glorious *havelis* (traditional mansions) and camel safaris in desert dunes
Jodhpur
Saraswati
Bilara
Rohet
Dhawa Doli Wildlife Sanctuary
Sardar Samand
BARMER
Barmer
Balotra
Pali
14
15
JODHPUR (p306)
The Blue City is a sea of blue buildings spreading out beneath Meherangarh, one of Rajasthan's finest forts
River
Jalor
PALI
Dhorimanna
SIROHI
JALOR
Sirohi
RAJSAMAND
Nathdwa
Luni
Guru Shikhar (1722m)
Nago
Mt Abu
Udaipur
Abu Road
Mewar Hills
Palanpur
MT ABU (p270)
A holiday hill station among dramatic Aravalli hills, home to the miraculous marble-carved Dilwara Temples
Great Rann of Kutch
Radhanpur
Dungarpu
Mahesana
UDAIPUR (p246)
Rajasthan at its most romantic: bone-white buildings, palaces and lakes set in an amphitheatre of hills
GUJARAT
Himatnagar
8A
Gandhinagar
Ahmedabad

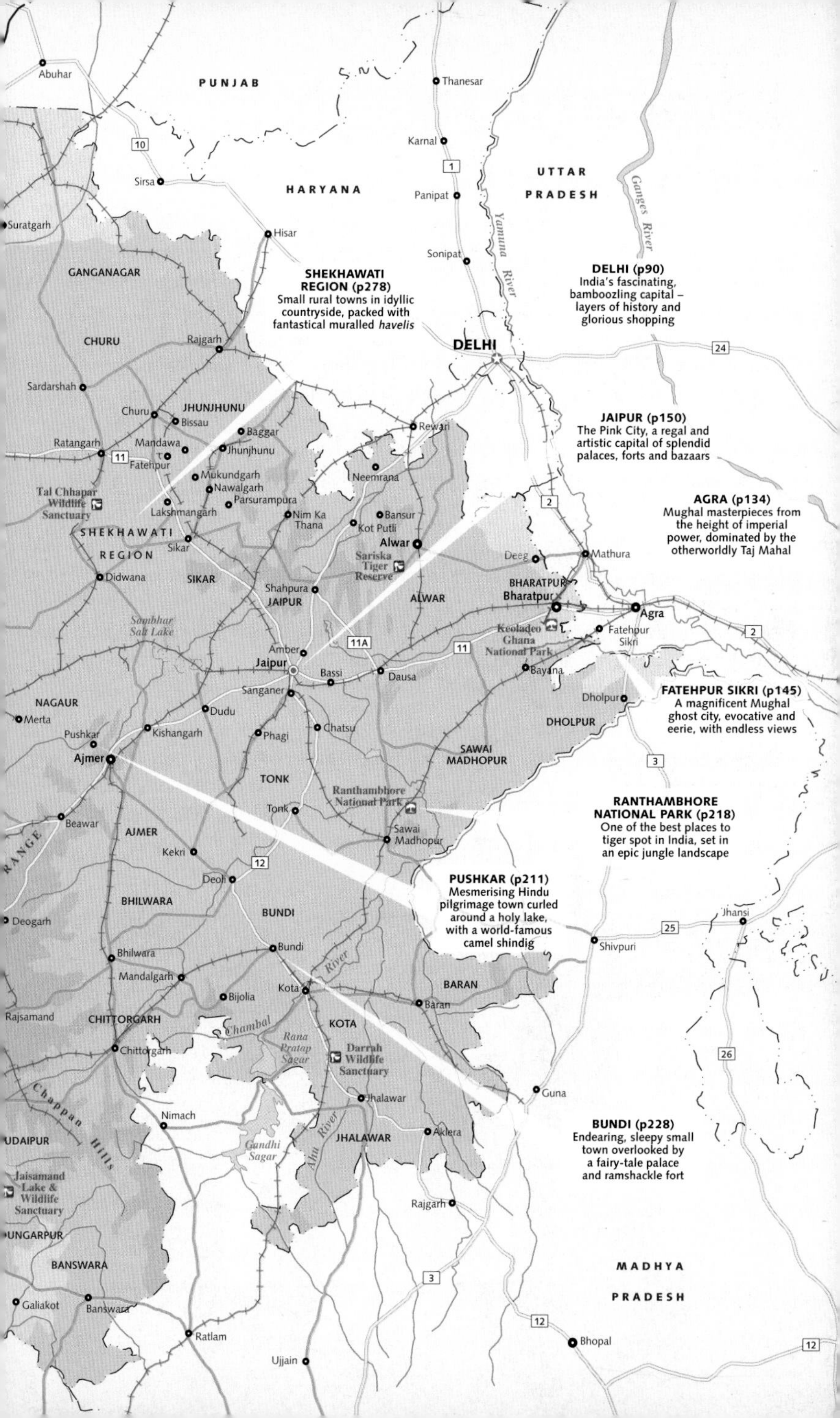
SHEKHAWATI REGION (p278)
Small rural towns in idyllic countryside, packed with fantastical muralled havelis
DELHI (p90)
India's fascinating, bamboozling capital – layers of history and glorious shopping
JAIPUR (p150)
The Pink City, a regal and artistic capital of splendid palaces, forts and bazaars
AGRA (p134)
Mughal masterpieces from the height of imperial power, dominated by the otherworldly Taj Mahal
FATEHPUR SIKRI (p145)
A magnificent Mughal ghost city, evocative and eerie, with endless views
RANTHAMBHORE NATIONAL PARK (p218)
One of the best places to tiger spot in India, set in an epic jungle landscape
PUSHKAR (p211)
Mesmerising Hindu pilgrimage town curled around a holy lake, with a world-famous camel shindig
BUNDI (p228)
Endearing, sleepy small town overlooked by a fairy-tale palace and ramshackle fort
PUNJAB
HARYANA
UTTAR PRADESH
MADHYA PRADESH
DELHI
Jaipur
Agra
Ajmer
Alwar
Bharatpur
Kota
Bundi
Pushkar
Sawai Madhopur
Fatehpur Sikri
Jhansi
Bhopal
Ujjain
Ratlam

# Destination Rajasthan, Delhi & Agra

A young girl dressed up in traditional clothes, serious-eyed, spins in the dust for some passing tourists. A little way away sits her cross-legged brother/father/uncle, accompanying her on off-toned strings. A fort, painted a dull parchment pink, and its crazy array of hat-like cupolas, towers and carved window screens, thrust out of a hillside against a hot sky. A group of farmers crouch under a tree, their turbans blobs of colour resembling a cluster of sweets. A camel stops at the traffic lights, hemmed in by cars, its cart full of grass, its gait strangely dignified. A brilliantly lit festival float booms along the street, with a generator balanced on a rickshaw as its tail. An elephant, patterned in paints as bright as a kite, ambles up to Amber Fort in the hills above Jaipur, Rajasthan's capital. Pilgrims bathe in a holy lake, a pearly sky reflected on its murky surface.

Startling images and heart-stopping beauty are just as likely to be found in everyday Rajasthani life as in the state's marvellous, fantastical, famous forts, palaces and temples. But anywhere that contains a blue city (Jodhpur), a pink city (Jaipur) and a golden city (Jaisalmer) has to be extraordinary. And let's not forget the state's unparalleled contributions to the art of the moustache: tradition dictates this should be groomed, thick, kinkily curved and stiffly gesturing skywards.

The best approach to the state is from Delhi, India's bamboozling yet fascinating capital, which is chock-full of ancient sights, the mad mayhem of daily life and glorious shopping emporiums bursting at the seams with this inspiring nation's astounding creativity. And the final third of this exotic, amazing triptych is Agra, home of the Taj Mahal, one of the few remaining wonders of the world. Enough said.

SARA-JANE CL

# The Golden Triangle

CHRIS MELLOR

The massive Lahore Gate heralds the entrance to Delhi's Red Fort (p98)

PAUL BEINSSEN

Jaipur's honeycombed Hawa Mahal (p160) tiptoes to an effervescent height of five storeys

Early-morning sunlight highlights the luminous beauty of Agra's Taj Mahal (p137)

RICHARD I'ANSON

# The Great Cities

DALLAS STRIBLEY

The utterly romantic Lake Palace Hotel (p259) seems to float on Udaipur's Pichola Lake

The hyacinth-blue buildings of Jodhpur (p306) spread like wild flowers over the landscape

CHRIS MELLOR

Golden tones and vivid skies surround the sandstone city of Jaisalmer (p325)

DAVID TI

# Shekhawati

PRAMOD MISTRY

A multitude of intricate murals decorate the *havelis* (mansions; p282) of Shekhawati

Shimmering gold leaf adorns the many paintings within Sone ki Dukan Haveli (p295) in Mahansar

CHRIS BEALL

A flame-thrower breathes fire at one of the region's startling festivals (p279)

PRAMOD MISTRY

# Forts, Palaces & Temples

MARK ANDREW KIRBY

The mighty Meherangarh (p309) stands sentinel over Jodhpur

Brilliant murals enrich the walls of Bundi Palace (p229)

MONIQUE CHOY

MONIQUE CHOY

An intensely carved temple in Chittorgarh (p241) juts sharply into the sky

JANE SWEENEY

A hidden gateway leads to the splendours of Jaisalmer Fort (p328)

Guards pose proudly in front of the glorious Peacock Gate at the City Palace (p157), Jaipur

LIZ THOMPSON

An enchanting marble pavilion offers a cool retreat within Amber Fort (p179)

RICHARD I'ANSON

# Religious Sites

DALLAS STRIBLEY

Pilgrims flock to the holy town of Pushkar (p211), home to 400 whitewashed temples and sacred waters

LIZ THO

The radiant Chaumukha Mandir at Ranakpur (p266) features 1444 uniqu designed pillars

The towering Buland Darwaza provides entry to Fatehpur Sikri's Jama Masjid (p145)

RICHARD I'ANSON

# Wildlife & Adventure

DANIEL BOAG

A black-faced langur relaxes among the branches of a flame tree in Ranthambhore National Park (p218)

ANTHONY PLUMMER

A camel safari (p374) is an adventurous way to experience desert life

More than 7000 elegant demoiselle cranes winter each year near Khichan (p322)

HIRA PUNJABI

# Festivals

PAUL BE

Heavily decorated pachyderms star at Jaipur's colourful Elephant Festival (p151)

STEPHEN SAKS

Well-groomed camels steal the show at the epic Pushkar Camel Fair (p212)

ANDERS BLOMQVIST

Revellers cut loose at the festival of Holi (p365), in celebration of the coming of spring

# Contents



Lonely Planet books provide independent advice. Lonely Planet does not accept advertising in guidebooks, nor do we accept payment in exchange for listing or endorsing any place or business. Lonely Planet writers do not accept discounts or payments in exchange for positive coverage of any sort.

लोनली प्लैनेट द्वारा प्रकाशित पुस्तकों में निष्पक्ष सूचना दी जाती है। लोनली प्लैनेट अपनी मार्गदर्शिकाओं में कोई विज्ञापन नहीं छापते। हम किसी व्यवसाय और किसी जगह का समर्थन करने या उनको अपनी सूची में सम्मिलित करने के लिए कोई धनराशि भी स्वीकार नहीं करते। लोनली प्लैनेट के सभी लेखक किसी स्थान के बारे में सकारात्मक सूचना देने के एवज़ में किसी तरह की छूट या रुपया-पैसा स्वीकार नहीं कर सकते।

# Regional Map Contents

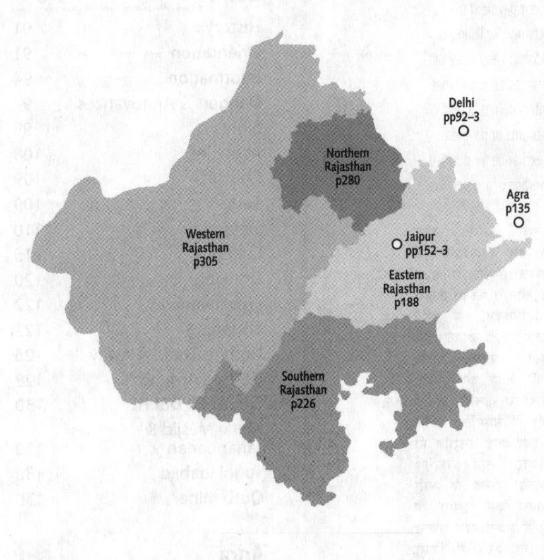

# The Authors

## ABIGAIL HOLE **Coordinating Author, Jaipur & all Rajasthan chapters**

Abigail first visited India over 10 years ago, which was also her first chance to visit Rajasthan. From London, she moved to Hong Kong in 1997, travelling to many parts of Asia during the three years she lived in the region. As well as this book, she has researched and written the Rajasthan and Gujarat chapters for the last two editions of Lonely Planet's *India*. Other far-flung assignments have taken her to Mali, Mauritania, Egypt and Tunisia. She currently lives in Rome.

**My Rajasthan**

I love the backwater of Shekhawati (p278), with its forgotten-feeling towns filled by frescoed *havelis* (mansions). Kolayat (p352), a temple town around a holy lake and top haunt of sleepy sadhus, is a beguiling spot. Jaisalmer (p325), with its sand-castle architecture rearing out of the desert, bedazzles me every time. The soaring and falling mountain landscape around Mt Abu (p270) is another favourite place, and I'd also recommend the remote grandeur of Kumbalgarh (p265) and Abhaneri (p184) – vastly different, splendid sites. Pilgrimage town Pushkar (p211) has a strange otherworldliness that's never overwhelmed by its commercialism, and I'd like to settle down for some slow, slow living in blue-painted Bundi (p228).

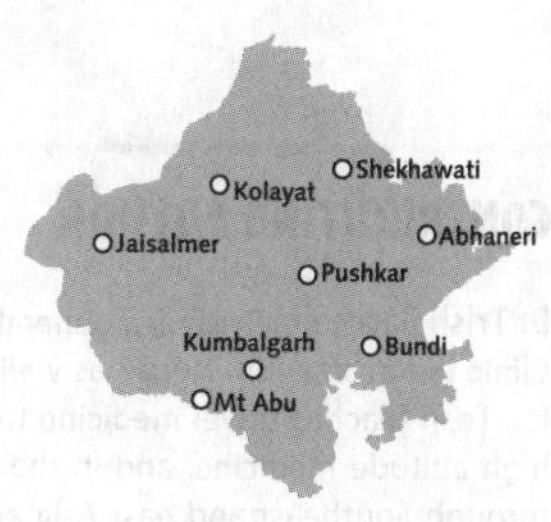


## MARTIN ROBINSON **Agra**

Born and brought up in England, Martin taught his way around Asia for five years and has visited over 50 countries, writing about his travels for newspapers and magazines. He now lives in New Zealand with his wife when not hurrying around our patchwork planet with a notebook in his hand. This was his fourth trouble-free trip to India, and other Lonely Planet titles he has contributed to include *Korea* and *New Zealand*.

**LONELY PLANET AUTHORS**

Why is our travel information the best in the world? It's simple: our authors are independent, dedicated travellers. They don't research using just the Internet or phone, and they don't take freebies in exchange for positive coverage. They travel widely, to all the popular spots and off the beaten track. They personally visit thousands of hotels, restaurants, cafés, bars, galleries, palaces, museums and more – and they take pride in getting all the details right, and telling it how it is. For more, see the authors section on www.lonelyplanet.com.

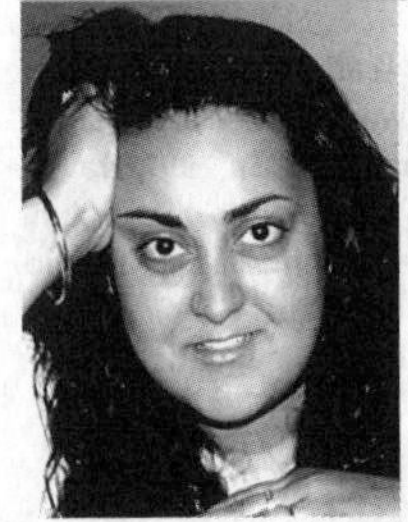

## SARINA SINGH **Delhi**

After finishing a business degree in Melbourne, Sarina bought a one-way ticket to India where she completed a corporate traineeship with the Sheraton. She later ditched hotels for newspapers, working as a freelance journalist and foreign correspondent. After four years in India, Sarina returned to Australia, pursued postgraduate journalism qualifications and wrote/directed *Beyond the Royal Veil*, a television documentary about contemporary Indian 'royalty'. She has worked on almost 20 Lonely Planet books including five editions of *India*, two editions of *Rajasthan*, *North India* and *Pakistan & the Karakoram Highway*. Sarina has also contributed to various international publications such as the *Sunday Times* and *National Geographic Traveler* and is the author of *Polo in India*.

## CONTRIBUTING AUTHOR

**Dr Trish Batchelor** Trish is a general practitioner and travel medicine specialist who works at the Ciwec Clinic in Kathmandu, Nepal, as well as being a medical advisor to the Travel Doctor New Zealand clinics. Trish teaches travel medicine through the University of Otago, and is interested in underwater and high-altitude medicine, and in the impact of tourism on host countries. She has travelled extensively through Southeast and east Asia and particularly loves high-altitude trekking in the Himalaya.

# Getting Started

Rajasthan holds India's greatest wealth of places to visit, and is conveniently adjacent to the wonders of Delhi (most people's starting point) *and* Agra. This area of India is relatively accessible and easy to travel around, with good bus and train connections that make all sorts of routes feasible. The only problem you may face is deciding how many of Rajasthan's extraordinary towns you can fit into your visit. While puzzling this out, make sure you allow some time to visit out-of-the-way places too, as your experience in a rural hamlet or little-visited village will be a world away from that in the fabulous hubbub of the major sites.

Rajasthan suits all budgets – you can travel on a threadbare shoestring, emulate the maharajas or go for a middle-ground sojourn, and in each case have an astonishing, romantic time, staying in fantastic places that evoke the region's past in varying degrees of luxury.

Travel in India can be stressful, so choose your companions with care. Women travelling alone will encounter some hassle (see p378 for more information) but this is irritating rather than dangerous – it's generally a safe place to travel solo whatever your sex. Travel with children is rewarding here, too. In such a family-centred society, children are fêted everywhere and will be your ticket to feeling welcome wherever you go! That said, it's much harder in the hectic cities, so you'll need to plan your route carefully to allow lots of respite on the way. For more information, see p358.

For disabled travellers, India is challenging – crowds, uneven surfaces, lack of adequate facilities, and toilets (often of the squat variety) that test the most able-bodied are all hurdles for any traveller. However, the advantage with travelling here is that you can always find easy help at hand to assist with lifting, carrying or just about anything. With planning and research there's no reason to rule Rajasthan out because you have a disability. See p362 for more details.

You can choose to get around by train, plane, bus or taxi. Many travellers, particularly those short of time, choose to travel solely by taxi – this allows you complete flexibility, and means you can cover a lot of ground and visit out-of-the-way places with ease. Part of the joy of travel, however, can be to take buses and trains – always an experience in itself and a good way of mingling with others. If it suits your needs, trip and budget, the most flexible and rewarding way to get around is a mishmash of methods – taking the occasional train, buses when it suits, and taxis for the more inaccessible places or when you're just a bit tired. For more discussion of the pros and cons of different forms of transport, see p382.

## WHEN TO GO

See Climate Charts (p359) for more information.

Rajasthan is at its best in the balmy winter months (November to March), when the days are warm and sunny (average temperatures across the state are around 25°C), and the nights are cool. However, as this is when most people go, hotel prices are at their highest and you'll also have to plan ahead a little more if you want to stay in the better-known midrange and top-end hotels – the palaces, *havelis* (traditional mansions) and hunting lodges for which Rajasthan is famous – as many will be fully booked. In March and in the postmonsoon season from mid-September to the end of November, it's a bit hotter, but still fine to visit, with average maximum temperatures in October of around 35°C and an average minimum of around 20°C. These periods are also good as places won't be so busy and rooms at those charismatic hotels will be easier to find just by turning up or ringing to book the night before.

Another factor you must watch out for is travelling during Indian holiday times. If you want to catch a train during the Diwali holiday (p366), for example, you'll need to book your ticket weeks in advance. Otherwise you can usually book train and plane tickets just a few days in advance to be assured a place.

Rajasthan is a startlingly vibrant state, and some of its most colourful festivals, such as the Desert Festival in Jaisalmer (p306) and the famous Pushkar Camel Fair (see p212), take place in winter. In October/November it's Diwali, the festival of lights, when people go crazy with fireworks and candles, and oil lamps line the streets. In late February/early March there's Holi (p365), India's most exuberant festival – a child's dream event – when everyone throws coloured powder at each other. Rajasthan's own Gangaur festival (see p151) is celebrated in March/April, as is Udaipur's Mewar Festival (see Festivals in Southern Rajasthan, p227). Jaipur's Elephant Festival (see Festivals in Jaipur, p151) is held in March. For more on festivals, see the boxed text at the beginning of each regional chapter and p363.

Winter is also a good time to visit Rajasthan's best-known wildlife sanctuaries: Keoladeo Ghana National Park (p191), Ranthambhore National Park (p218) and Sariska Tiger Reserve (p201).

If a summer visit is your only option, be aware that it will be horrendously hot. Premonsoon, which extends from April to June, is the hottest season, with temperatures ranging from 32°C to 45°C. There is little relief from the scorching onslaught, particularly in the arid zone to the west and northwest of the Aravalli Range, where temperatures often climb above 45°C. Mt Abu registers the lowest temperatures at this time. The monsoon is a welcome arrival in late June in the eastern and

**DON'T LEAVE HOME WITHOUT...**

If you're backpacking and taking in a number of destinations, the usual rule applies – bring as little as possible. It's much better to buy something you've left behind than lug around an unwieldy pack weighed down with things you'll never use.

Handy items to pack for your trip:

- Sleeping-bag sheet – good if you're unsure about the hotel linen and essential if you're travelling overnight on a 2nd- or 3rd-class sleeper train.
- Packets of wet wipes can be very useful.
- Tampons are available in main tourist centres, but it's worth bringing your own stock.
- Condoms – the quality of local brands is variable.
- High-factor sunscreen is widely available, but it's *expensive*!
- A universal sink plug can be useful in cheap hotels.
- Insect repellent – you can buy this in Rajasthan, but it's not the really good stuff.
- A voltage stabiliser – essential if you are bringing sensitive electronic equipment.
- A spare set of glasses and your prescription – if you wear contact lenses, bring enough solution to last your trip.
- A water bottle – if you use water-purification tablets or filters (see Drinking Water, p398) you'll avoid adding to Rajasthan's alarming plastic waste problem.

southeastern regions of the state, finally falling in mid-July in the desert zones. It is preceded by dust and thunderstorms. Unless the rains are insubstantial, the monsoon is accompanied by a decrease in temperatures, with average maximums dropping to 29°C to 32°C in the south and southeast of Rajasthan, and an average of above 38°C in the northern and northwestern regions. But take comfort in the fact that hotel prices will be at their lowest, you won't have to book ahead anywhere, and plan on taking it easy and doing your sightseeing early or late in the day – you'll still have a good time.

## COSTS & MONEY

Prices vary depending on the season and adjust according to how busy a place is – they shoot up when demand is high and plummet during slack times. In the low season, or even on an off day during the high season, you can get big discounts. Costs also escalate during festivals or other special events. Costs in the larger cities (such as Jaipur, Delhi and Agra) and popular tourist destinations (such as Jaisalmer and Udaipur) are often higher, though accommodation is often cheap at these places because of all the competition.

Costs also vary depending on whether you are travelling solo or in a group. It's more economical travelling with one or more people, as you can save money by sharing hotel rooms, taxis, rickshaws and car hire.

Whatever budget you have, you'll get so much more for your money than in most other countries – Rajasthan is amazing value.

That said, during the high season, prices for top-end hotels can vie with similar places elsewhere in the world. If you stay in luxurious converted forts and palaces, fly between the main cities of Rajasthan, and buy exquisite arts and crafts, you can sail through enormous amounts of cash. It's easy to blow US$200 a night in a swanky palace hotel without even poking your nose out the door.

If you stay in dormitories or the cheapest hotels, travel on public buses, and subsist on dhal and rice, you could see Rajasthan on about US$20 a day.

If you're looking for something between these extremes – or something of a seesaw between the two, mixing budget places with splurges – for US$35 to US$60 a day on average, you'll stay in midrange hotels, eat in good restaurants and take autorickshaws rather than buses.

**HOW MUCH?**

Internet access per hr Rs 20-60

Rajasthani puppet Rs 30-500

Kurta pyjamas Rs 300

Camel safari per day Rs 450

Henna painting per hand Rs 80

### Admission Fees

Most tourist sites have an admission fee, and most levy a fee for the use of cameras and videos. Many sites charge a lower admission fee for Indian residents than they do for foreigners. In case you're wondering, if you're of Indian descent (but not an Indian resident), the foreigners' rate officially applies, although you may escape detection or even be knowingly offered the lower local rate.

In late 2000 the Archaeological Survey of India announced new admission fees for non-Indian tourists at 72 of India's national monuments. The admission price for all World Heritage sites was increased. Admission to the Taj Mahal now costs Rs 750 for foreigners, but most other places are nowhere near as expensive, averaging around Rs 250 for major sites.

## TRAVEL LITERATURE

Robyn Davidson's *Desert Places* is an amazing account of the author's journey by camel with the Rabari (a nomadic tribal group) on their annual migration through the Great Thar Desert. It offers compelling

## TOP EXPERIENCES

### Festivals

Rajasthan is alive with festivals year-round and the following are our top 10 picks (for more on the wealth of festivals and events in Rajasthan, see p363).

- Jaisalmer Desert Festival (p306) in January and February in Jaisalmer
- Holi (p227) in February and March in Udaipur
- Gangaur (p151) in March and April in Jaipur
- Teej (p151) in July and August in Jaipur
- The Urs (p187) in August in Ajmer
- Ramdevra Fair (p306) in August and September in Ramdevra
- Dussehra (p227) in October and November in Kota
- Pushkar Camel Fair (p212) in October and November in Pushkar
- Kolayat Fair (p306) in November in Bikaner
- Ghans Bheru Festival (p227) in October and November in Bharodia, near Bundi

### Romantic Spots

Take time out to enjoy some of the region's most spectacularly romantic sites and experiences.

- *The* monument to love – the Taj Mahal (p137)
- On a rooftop with a view of Lake Pichola (p249), Udaipur
- The narrow mellow-yellow streets of Jaisalmer (p325)
- A night on the dunes, under the stars on camel safari outside Jaisalmer (see Jaisalmer Camel Safaris, p334), Khuri (p342), Bikaner (see Bikaner Camel Safaris, p348) or Osiyan (p322)
- Sunrise or sunset overlooking Pushkar from Saraswati Temple (p212)

### Shop-Till-You-Drop Opportunities

Return home with your bags full of souvenirs and goodies – Rajasthan and Delhi provide some thoroughly fabulous shopping prospects.

- Delhi (p122) is full of amazing emporiums selling goods from all over India.
- Jaipur (p175), Rajasthan's craft capital, is packed with beguiling bazaars and boutiques.
- Udaipur (p262) offers miniature paintings, jewellery and much, much more.
- Jaisalmer (p339) is the best place in Rajasthan to buy mirrorwork.
- Pushkar (p217) has a laid-back bazaar packed with jewellery, CDs, books and bits.

### Gorgeous Hotels

Whether it's an old fort or a luxury tent in the outdoors, you'll sleep well in our top hotel picks.

- Samode Haveli (see The Author's Choice, p171) – a wonderful, rambling *haveli* (traditional mansion) in Jaipur's old city. It offers a great pool and some magnificent suites.
- Connaught House (p274) – evocative and cosy English cottage atmosphere in lush gardens
- Neemrana Fort Palace (p201) – a glorious, out-of-the-way, multilevel fortress
- Devi Garh (see The Author's Choice, p259) – stunningly original hotel with contemporary designs offsetting a beautiful old *haveli*
- Aman-i-Khás (p222) – incredibly luxurious tented camp in the remote Aravalli hills

insight into the plight of the nomads, as well as telling reflections of the solo woman traveller in Rajasthan.

*Rajasthan Stories*, Rudyard Kipling's tales about the state, make for an old-fashioned good read; the three slim volumes are available in bookshops in Jaipur (p155).

Aldous Huxley's *Jesting Pilate – An Intellectual Journey* is his account of travels in India, Burma and Malaya in the 1920s, with observations on British rule, Delhi social life, Indian art and Rajasthan's sights.

*No Full Stops in India*, by BBC correspondent Mark Tully, is a fascinating read that details his travels around India and puts forward some interpretations of contemporary Indian society.

*In Rajasthan*, by Royina Grenal, is part of Lonely Planet's travel literature series and gives a different slant on solo female travel – from a local (if privileged middle-class) perspective.

*Holy Cow*, by Sarah MacDonald, is a lightweight, funny book about the author's travels around India and her cursory investigations of different religions – her conclusions feel a bit glib, but it's very entertaining on the way.

**'Holy Cow is a funny book about the author's travels around India and her investigations of different religions'**

*Scoop-wallah*, by Justine Hardy, follows the author's work on the *Indian Express* in Delhi. It's a tantalising glimpse into the world of Indian journalism that journeys through the author's frustrations and her canny observations of contemporary Delhi.

*City of Djinns*, by William Dalrymple, is a fascinating book about Delhi – its history intertwined with the author's personal struggles to get to grips with the city. It also records a visit to the Sufi shrine at Ajmer during pilgrimage time.

## INTERNET RESOURCES

There are zillions of websites on India and Rajasthan, but you'll find that many are nothing more than glossy, inaccurate public-relations puff. Not all, though. Many local newspapers and current-affairs magazines have useful sites:

**Hindu** (www.thehindu.com) The website of this quality broadsheet.
**Hindustan Times** (www.hindustantimes.com) Another reasonable broadsheet with another reasonable website.
**India Today** (www.india-today.com) A popular magazine on India's current affairs.
**Indian Express** (www.indianexpress.com) Useful coverage on this popular broadsheet's site.
**Times of India** (www.timesofindia.com) National coverage with a tabloid feel, and a curious selection of international news.

The state tourism authority's website **Rajasthan Tourism Development Corporation** (www.rajasthantourismindia.com) offers some useful information on what's happening in Rajasthan.

And for those of you seeking the perfect Indian name for your unborn child, you may want to check out www.indiaexpress.com/specials/babynames/. Good luck!

# Itineraries

## CLASSIC ROUTES

### THE GOLDEN TRIANGLE

**This route covers around 700km, not counting detours to Fatehpur Sikri and Bharatpur. Agra, Jaipur and Delhi have great road and rail connections, and you could do this in a week, though it deserves more time. Try to work in some days of relaxation.**

One route is so well loved it even has a special name: the Golden Triangle – the classic Delhi–Agra–Jaipur trip.

Spend a day or two in **Delhi** (p90) finding your feet and seeing some of the sights, such as the magnificent Mughal **Red Fort** (p98) and **Jama Masjid** (p100), India's largest mosque. Then catch a convenient train to **Agra** (p134) to spend a day being awed by the mighty **Agra Fort** (p139) and the world's most extravagant monument to love, the **Taj Mahal** (p137). Only an hour away is **Fatehpur Sikri** (p145), the beautiful Mughal city dating from the apogee of Mughal power that's amazingly well preserved, which deserves another day.

If you have time, go for some rural respite – **Keoladeo Ghana National Park** (p191), one of the world's greatest bird reserves, is a relaxing, beautiful and intriguing place to visit even if you don't like bird-watching. Having chilled, you can train it to **Jaipur** (p150) for a couple of days in and around Rajasthan's twinkling dusky-pink capital, seeing the **City Palace** (p157) and **Amber Fort** (p179), and stocking up on blue pottery, Rajasthani puppets and other delights before heading back to Delhi.

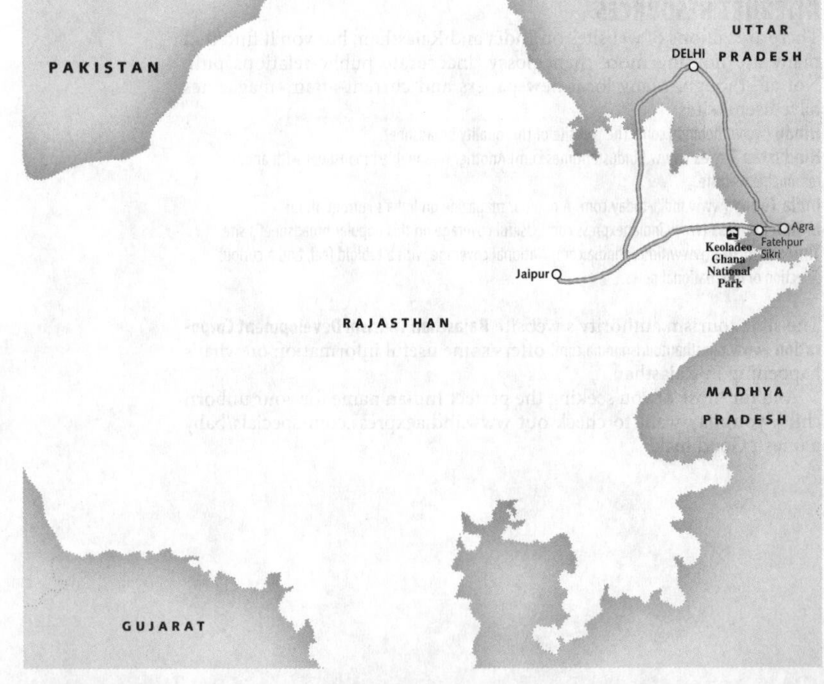

## THE BIG FOUR: JAIPUR, UDAIPUR, JODHPUR & JAISALMER

With a fortnight to spare, you can forget triangles and go all out for a rectangle taking in Rajasthan's four most spectacular cities.

Again, start from **Delhi** (p90) and make your way to gorgeous **Jaipur** (p150), possibly fitting in a side trip to **Agra** (p134) on the way.

From Jaipur, take a long trip to the romantic lake town of **Udaipur** (p246), stopping for a couple of days of rest and relaxation (visiting the fine **City Palace**, p252, and the impressive **Jagdish Temple**, p253, doing some shopping and taking lots of time out on rooftops) before travelling to the extraordinary, bustling, blue city of **Jodhpur** (p306). On your way to Jodhpur, take time to stop at the milk-white Jain temple complex of **Ranakpur** (p266) and the isolated, dramatic fortifications of **Kumbalgarh** (p265), one of Rajasthan's most remote and impressive forts. As they are fairly close together you can visit them comfortably en route in a day. In Jodhpur itself, visit the spectacular **Meherangarh** (p309), a fort that glowers over the city like a shipwrecked spaceship.

Next take an overnight train to the Golden City, **Jaisalmer** (p325), a hallucinatory sand castle in the desert, with its beautiful Jain temples and exquisite merchants' *havelis* (traditional, ornately decorated mansions). Take a short camel safari through magnificent desertscapes if you get a chance, and break your journey back to Delhi with a stop in the less-visited desert city of **Bikaner** (p343), which is home to the fine (yet very different) **Junagarh fort** (p345).

**This whopping 2000km route would be feasible in a fortnight, if you take trains. Again it deserves much more time – you could spend at least a month on this journey, and should factor in a stay in one of the many fantastic palaces deep in Rajasthan's countryside.**

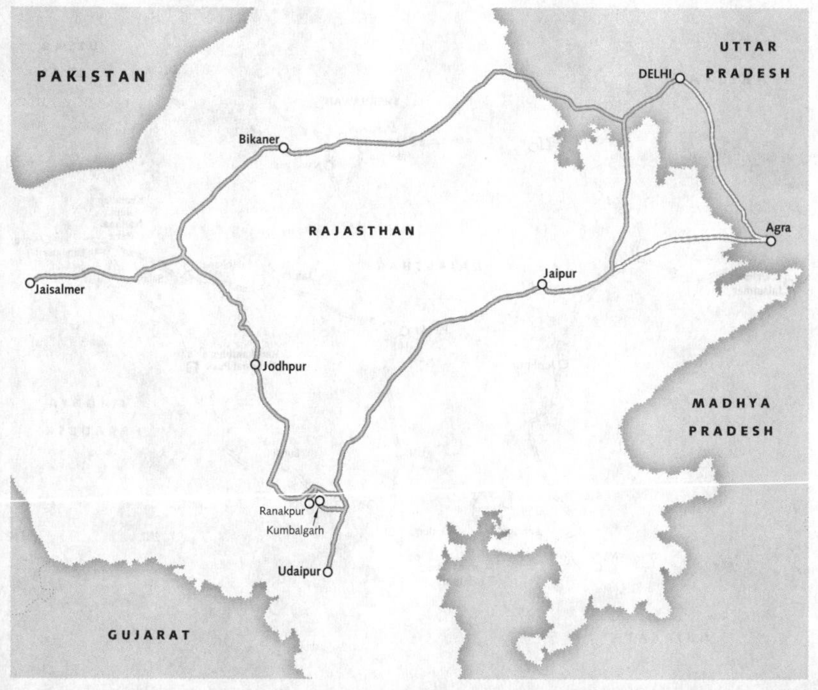

## A MONTH-LONG CIRCUIT

**This circuit is around 2500km to 2600km whether you go via Ranthambhore and Bundi or via Jaipur and Pushkar. It could be done in a month, or, you could take longer. Don't forget to work in rest days, and head off the beaten track – take time to stay in some of the magnificent, beguiling palace hotels.**

With **Agra** (p134) as your first stop after **Delhi** (p90), head to **Fatehpur Sikri** (p145) and the World Heritage–listed bird-watching paradise **Keoladeo Ghana National Park** (p191), followed by **Ranthambhore National Park** (p218) if tigers are your bag.

If they're not, on the road between Bharatpur (for Keoladeo) and Jaipur, stop at **Balaji Temple** (p184) to see the extraordinary exorcisms, and at the incredible step-well at **Abhaneri** (p184). After **Jaipur** (p150) go to the magical pilgrimage town of **Pushkar** (p211) to relax for a few days, before heading to the romantic lake town of **Udaipur** (p246) via the imposing fort at **Chittorgarh** (p241).

If you've chosen the Ranthambhore route, you may want to take the train southwest to Kota for a stop at the charming small town of **Bundi** (p228), then take the train on to Udaipur (stopping at Chittorgarh if you like).

From Udaipur it's worth side tripping to **Mt Abu** (p270) to see the magnificent **Dilwara temples** (p272) before going north to **Jodhpur** (p306), or travel directly to Jodhpur, stopping at **Ranakpur** (p266) and **Kumbalgarh** (p265) on the way. From Jodhpur it's an easy overnight train ride to **Jaisalmer** (p325), the golden desert town, from where you can take a camel trek into the desert. After Jaisalmer, bus to **Bikaner** (p343). Then, if you have time, relax and explore rural **Shekhawati** (p278) for a few days, visiting such towns as **Mandawa** (p299), **Nawalgarh** (p283) and **Fatehpur** (p296), with side trips to other smaller towns, before returning to Delhi.

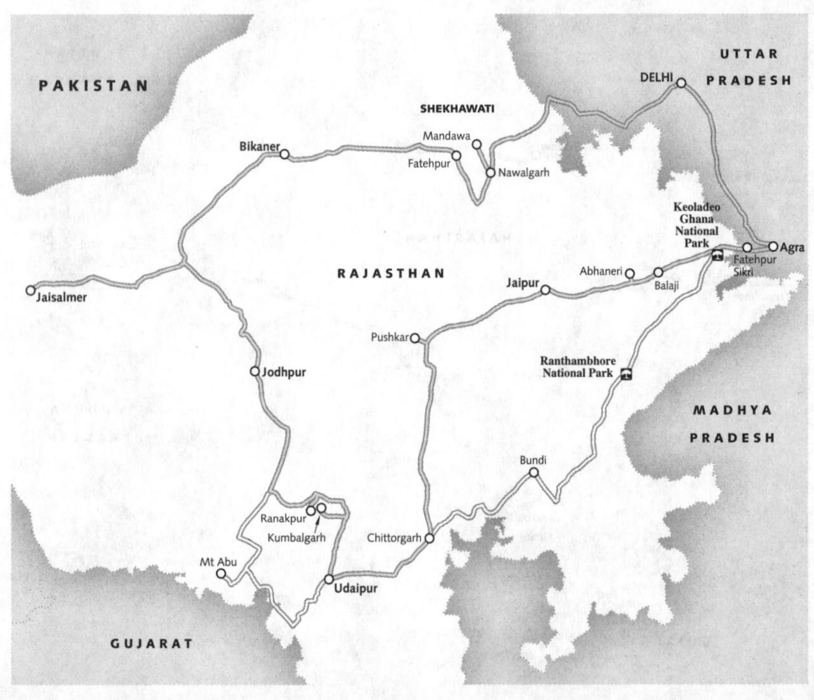

# TAILORED TRIPS

## UNDISCOVERED RAJASTHAN

Many out-of-the-way places in Rajasthan don't see that many tourists – amazing when you consider how many visitors the state receives, and wonderful when you want to escape from the major tourist haunts and see an entirely different side of the state.

Our top recommendations include the Shekhawati region with its colourful *havelis* and rural pace. Mandawa aside, the area has escaped much tourist action and seeking out the amazing murals in its small towns is like a treasure hunt. Some towns worth discovering are **Nawalgarh** (p283), **Fatehpur** (p296), **Dundlod** (p289) and **Mahansar** (p295). Other lesser-known places include: **Kolayat** (p352), a remote town around a holy lake near Bikaner; **Osiyan** (p321), an ancient desert town filled with fine Jain temples; some of the sights around Sariska, such as the ghost town of **Bhangarh** (p202); **Dungarpur** (p269), a royal town with an eccentric empty palace and serene lake; **Jhalawar** (p238), near a magnificent remote fortress and the ancient City of Temple Bells; and **Karauli** (p223), which is adorned by a beautiful, worn palace.

Other wonderful escapes are the countryside around **Udaipur** (p246), with its undulating hills and tiny villages, trekking in the hills around **Mt Abu** (p270) or **Kumbalgarh** (p265), and the pastoral landscape surrounding **Pushkar** (p211).

## ARTS & CRAFTS

Rajasthan's barren landscape seemingly galvanises its inhabitants to produce some of India's most vivid paintings, textiles and jewellery.

Shekhawati's small towns are packed with brilliantly painted *havelis*; in **Nawalgarh** (p286) you can attend craft workshops, and you can take painting lessons at **Jhunjhunu** (p293).

**Jaipur** (p150) is the artistic nerve centre, with some wonderful shops and opportunities to see artisans, particularly jewellers, at work. Nearby is **Sanganer** (p182), where you can visit workshops specialising in papermaking and block printing, and take block-printing or pottery **lessons** (p166). Nearby also is the woodcarving centre of **Bassi** (p240). **Kishangarh** (p209) is renowned for its production of miniature paintings.

Around **Jodhpur** (p306), workers produce woollen *dhurries* (rugs).

**Udaipur** (p246) is another major centre for the arts – a splendid place to buy miniatures, textiles, woodcarving and jewellery, take lessons in painting and see traditional dance. Outside the city is **Shilpgram** (p254), which displays, demonstrates and sells regional creations.

In the west, **Barmer** (p342) is another place to see block printers at work, and in **Bikaner** (p343) you can see artisans producing *usta* (gold-painted camel leather) work.

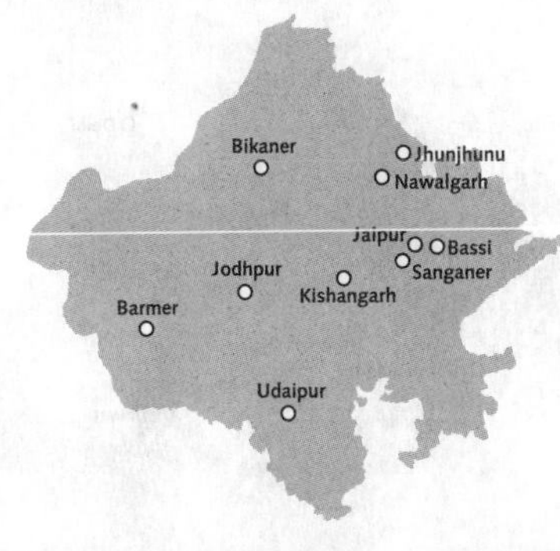

## ANIMALS & BIRDS

You can wildlife-spot till you drop in Rajasthan's beautiful sanctuaries, commune with tamer creatures at festivals or ride them out on safari.

World Heritage site **Keoladeo Ghana National Park** (p191) is one of the world's foremost bird sanctuaries. Rambling **Ranthambhore National Park** (p218) is one of the best places in India to spot tigers. It's trickier to see tigers at **Sariska Tiger Reserve** (p201), but this is another scenic sanctuary protecting leopards, hyenas, bluebulls and lots of bird life.

Catch up with the latest in camel fashion at the epic **Pushkar Camel Fair** (see Pushkar Camel Fair, p212) or the more business-oriented version at **Nagaur** (see Festivals in Western Rajasthan, p306) in January/February. To get even closer to Rajasthan's ships of the desert, take a camel safari from **Jaisalmer** (see Jaisalmer Camel Safaris, p334), **Khuri** (p342), **Osiyan** (p322), **Pushkar** (p214) or from **Bikaner** (see Bikaner Camel Safaris, p348).

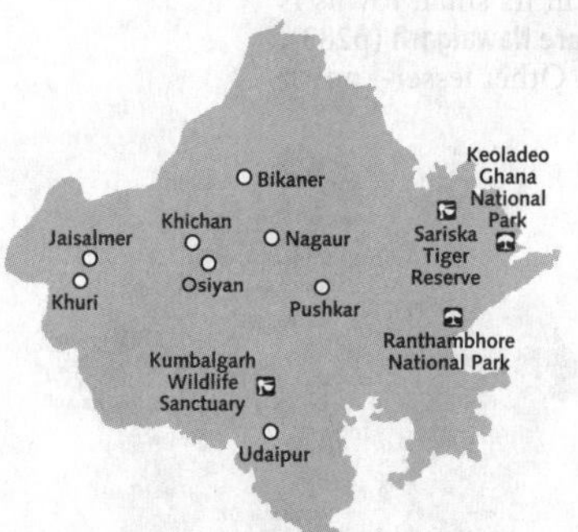


Horse riding around **Udaipur** (p255) is a wonderful way to take in the countryside and some rural life. Between Udaipur and Jodhpur, **Kumbalgarh Wildlife Sanctuary** (p266) has fantastic scenery and is famous for its wolves.

Finally, don't miss **Khichan** (see The Demoiselle Cranes of Khichan, p323), between Jaisalmer and Nagaur, where you can see the spectacular sight of around 7000 demoiselle cranes descending to feed on grain spread around for them by villagers.

## FORT-HOPPING

Water may be a problem, but one thing Rajasthan's not short of is forts. You'll definitely want to work a few of these wonders into your trip.

Delhi is a good place to start on your fort-finding mission, with the city-centre Mughal **Red Fort** (p98). To the east, in Agra, is its red-sandstone cousin, **Agra Fort** (p139), which contains some exquisite Mughal buildings. For something completely different, visit **Ranthambhore Fort** (p220), deep in tangled, hilly jungle. At Sariska Tiger Reserve is **Kankwari Fort** (p202) – a fortified pipsqueak compared to many others, but one that offers superb views. **Taragarh** (p230) at Bundi is overgrown, crumbling and a fantastic place for a ramble. Plateau-top **Chittorgarh** (p241) is Rajasthan's most legendary fort, containing palaces, temples and a mass of myths. Even more spectacular is **Kumbalgarh** (p265), a noble, remote edifice between Udaipur and Jodhpur. Near Jhalawar is little-visited **Gagron Fort** (p240), which towers over the confluence of two rivers.

Most dramatic of all is **Meherangarh** (p309) in Jodhpur, rising from a crag like a mirage. Even more striking is **Jaisalmer** (p328), the golden fort that's still alive, while Bikaner's **Junagarh** (p345) claims the region's most spectacular interiors.

# Snapshot

Rajasthan is both blessed and cursed. The land is harsh and the climate harsher. In recent years the monsoon has become more and more unpredictable, and the desperate dearth of rain ruins people's livelihoods – this in a state where three-quarters of the population are employed on the already inhospitable land. It's a battle for survival. The state's feudal burden also slows development, and in many respects – women's rights, health, education – Rajasthan lags behind India's other states.

The position of women – especially rural women – is a particular cause for concern. In rural areas female education is not rated, largely because of the expense of sending girls to school. But it's also because women have a low status (for more on this, see p41). Population growth is currently over 2% – the number of people living here has quintupled since 1951. Access to education, nutrition, and health resources and services is affected by gender, caste and class far more than elsewhere in the country.

It's not all doom and gloom though. The figures for literacy are encouraging: at around 61% (44.2% for women) this has doubled since 1991 and is a world away from the 8% at the time of Independence. Statistics also indicate a decline in poverty. Rajasthan still falls down, however, on major health indicators – maternity mortality ratios and infant mortality rates are among the highest in India.

As well as underpinning the status quo, feudalism has left Rajasthan some splendid legacies: of pride, colourful traditions, magnificent palaces and forts, and stunning handicrafts and fine arts developed through patronage of the former kings. It's ironic that while holding the state back, the feudal system has also formed the framework for its wonders. These draw in the lucrative tourist trade – 40% of all visitors to India come to Rajasthan, bringing with them cash, providing jobs, affording its magnificent heritage to be maintained, encouraging the region's splendid arts and provoking cultural exchange.

But an economy reliant on tourism quivers in response to current events. Whenever India–Pakistan tensions crank up a notch, Rajasthan, stretched along the India–Pakistan border, feels it first, though the military muscle stationed in the west of the state doesn't impinge on daily life apart from the occasional boom of a military jet. In 2001 Rajasthan received a double whammy: terrorist attacks on the Indian parliament lead to soured relations with Pakistan, and then there was 9/11. People cancelled their holidays, and the economy took a serious dip. But of late things have been much better: there has even been talk of reopening a train link (closed since 1965) running from Rajasthan northwards over the border.

Like elsewhere in India, the state faces some serious environmental issues (see p71). There are the pressures of population, and problems with plastic waste. Marble mines have ruined large swathes of countryside. Deforestation has not helped the drought situation. Multiplying livestock are not matched by multiplying grazing grounds. In 2005 reports suggested, horrifyingly, that all the tigers at Sariska Tiger Reserve had been poached. Rajasthan sometimes seems at risk of eating itself.

With its heritage, arts, tourist trade, encouraging literacy figures, low unemployment, increased prosperity and peaceable temperament, the state's future is in many ways bright. However, threatening shapes lie on the horizon. Like the nonexistent rain clouds and the long shadows of tradition, they are hard to ignore, and harder to address.

**FAST FACTS**

Population: 56.5 million

GDP: Rs 100,094 crore

Inflation: 5%

Unemployment: 0.4%-1.8%

Per capita income: Rs 14,748

Birth rate: 30.6 per 1000

No of camels: 500,000 (half of India's camel population)

# History

Invasions, famines, civil war, colonial rule, Partition and unification – India's complex civilisation has come through a remarkable history. The most extraordinary player in this has been Indian culture itself, or its mass of cultures, strong enough to adapt and provide continuity amid the change. Invaders tended to become largely assimilated, and features from outside were absorbed into Indian life while not shaking its foundations. Rather like today, when you can spot totems of Westernisation – coffee bars and burgers, jeans and mobile phones – but they are superficial, and confined to city life. All the while, life in rural India has changed little in many places for centuries.

Uniquely in India, Rajasthan has never been directly ruled by any foreign invader or power.

Rajasthan has had to cope with more invaders than most other areas of India, being situated in the geographically vulnerable northwest. Its proximity to Delhi and Agra has also played its part. Agra was one of the Mughal seats of power (briefly the capital), and though Delhi has not always been the capital of India, it has always been important. Its turbulent history has led the city to be rebuilt at least nine times.

For many centuries the Rajasthani princely kingdoms, ruled by warrior tribes, were fiercely independent of attempts at central government, and of each other. This has left a legacy unlike anywhere else in the country.

## ANCIENT TREES, EPICS & TRIBES

The most ancient relics in Rajasthan are found in the desert near Jaisalmer, in the west, where it's possible to visit the site of Akal Wood Fossil Park (p342), where fossilised trees – remnants of a huge 180-million-year-old forest – indicate a very different climate to the Great Thar Desert of today.

As far as civilisation goes, the spread of settlements around the region can be dated from around 3000 BC. At Kalibangan, near Ganaganagar in northern Rajasthan, 5000-year-old terracotta pottery and jewellery have been discovered. Kalibangan was later absorbed into the Bronze-Age Harappan civilisation, which had trade links with Mesopotamia and a taste for fine art. Why the settlements declined in the 2nd millennium BC is mysterious – it's suggested the exodus might have been a result of flooding in the Indus Valley, or perhaps climatic change.

The website www.harappa.com provides an illustrated yet scholarly coverage of everything you need to know about the ancient Indus Valley civilisations, including the significance of recent archaeological finds.

Certainly civilisation around 1500 BC began to centre on the area between the rivers Yamuna and Ganga (Ganges), with (it's thought) the migration of Indo-European–speaking seminomads, Aryans (Sanskrit for 'noble') who spoke an early form of Sanskrit. From the Aryans came the roots of Hindu culture, and the social structure that was to develop into the caste system. In Aryan society the birth of a son was fêted, there was a dowry system, and widows committed ritual suicide on their husband's death. It's interesting to see that only the last of these has disappeared (and, even so, there have been occurrences as recently as the 1980s).

Alwar, in northeastern Rajasthan, is possibly the oldest kingdom in kingdom-studded Rajasthan. In 1500 BC it formed part of the Matsya territories of Viratnagar (present-day Bairat), which also encompassed Bharatpur, Dholpur and Karauli.

TIMELINE

**c 2200 BC**
Indus Valley (Harappan) civilisation develops in northern India

**c 1500 BC**
Vedic-Aryan Period forms the foundations of the caste system and the basis of Hinduism

Little is known of Rajasthan's development at this time, but leaping into the mystical realm, Rajasthan made its mark in ancient Hindu scriptural epics – the Mahabharata and Ramayana mention both the holy pilgrimage site of Pushkar and Chittorgarh (Chittor), later the site of Rajasthan's most famous fort. The earliest known incarnation of Delhi – Indraprastha, known to be around 3000 years old – is also mentioned. In the ancient kingdom of Matsya, the Kauravas went cattle rustling, precipitating the war between them and their kinsfolk, the Pandavas – the great battle that forms the basis of the Mahabharata. Krishna was born in Mathura, just over the border in Uttar Pradesh.

*The Wonder That Was India*, by AL Basham, offers detailed descriptions of the Indian civilisations, major religions, origins of the caste system and social customs – a good thematic approach that brings the disparate strands together.

Back in the land of historical fact, after the fall of the Indus Valley civilisations, the Bhil and Mina tribes next settled the area and developed terminally squabbling small kingdoms, commencing the long local history of argumentative neighbours.

The area remained untouched by the great empires, which were consolidating their hold on the subcontinent. Alexander the Great came and went, leaving the Indus in 326 BC after his troops refused to advance beyond the Beas River in Himachal Pradesh. The Mauryan empire (321–185 BC), whose most renowned emperor, Ashoka, converted to Buddhism in 262 BC, also had minimal impact. Ashoka declared Buddhism the state religion, but it later faded and was incorporated into Hinduism – an example of Indian culture's absorbent capabilities. You can see Buddhist caves and stupas (Buddhist shrines; see p240) near Jhalawar, in southern Rajasthan; Ashoka's several rock-cut edicts at Bairat (see p203), an ancient Buddhist site near Sariska; and a 13m-high pillar he inscribed in Delhi (in Firoz Shah Kotla, p108).

Emperor Ashoka's ability to rule over his empire was assisted by a standing army consisting of 9000 elephants, 30,000 cavalry and 600,000 infantry.

## RAJPUTS ON THE RAMPAGE

The time of the emergence of the Rajput clans was Rajasthan's most influential era, its legacies still powerful today.

After the Mauryas and before the rise of the Guptas, there was no central power in India, but it was a prosperous, if fragmented, era. Trade with China and the Romans was already going on in the 1st century BC. The Gupta empire was the next to dominate, and it held sway in northern India for nearly 300 years until the early 5th century AD. It was a period of calm and stability, particularly in the north, during which Hindu culture became firmly established and the arts flourished. The empire's disintegration, caused by attacks from Huns in the north, was followed by a touch of chaos in many areas, including Rajasthan, as various local chieftains tussled to gain supremacy. Stability was only restored with the emergence of the Gurjara Pratiharas, the earliest of the Rajput (from Rajputra meaning 'Sons of Princes') dynasties that were later to reign throughout Rajasthan.

The Rajput warrior clans emerged in the 6th and 7th centuries. From these clans came the name Rajputana, as the princely states were known during the Muslim invasion of India. The Rajputs fled aggressors in their homelands in Punjab, Gujarat and Uttar Pradesh to settle in Rajasthan, trampling over the indigenous tribes, the Bhils and Minas. Evidence suggests that some of the Rajput clans can trace their emergence to the arrival of foreign invaders, such as the White Huns, and other invaders and settlers from Central Asia.

**c 1000 BC**
Indraprastha, Delhi's first incarnation, is born

**c 321–185 BC**
Period of the Mauryan empire

But who needs historical origins when you can have a complex mythological genealogy? The Rajput ancestry can be divided into two main branches: the Suryavansa, (Race of the Sun), which claims direct descent from Rama; and the Induvansa (Race of the Moon), which claims descent from Krishna. Later a third branch was added, the Agnikula (Fire Born). This group claims it was manifested from the flames of a sacrificial fire on Mt Abu. From these three principal races emerged the 36 Rajput clans.

As they were predominantly of lower castes, the Rajputs should not have aspired to warrior status – an occupation reserved for high-caste types. Celestial origins, however, enabled them to claim descent from the Kshatriyas (warrior caste), which in the caste hierarchy falls just below that of the Brahmins (priest caste).

The paradoxically fearsome, beautiful weapons of Indian warriors, especially of the Rajputs, are lovingly detailed in *By My Sword and Shield* by E Jaiwant Paul.

Wherever they came from, the Rajputs' bravery and sense of honour were unparalleled. They resembled the medieval European knights or the Japanese samurai in their fierceness, coupled with strict adherence to tradition and codes of conduct. Rajput warriors would fight against all odds and, when no hope was left, chivalry demanded that *jauhar* (mass suicide) take place – women and children committed suicide by immolating themselves on a huge funeral pyre, while the men donned saffron robes and rode out to confront the enemy and certain death. It's unsurprising that Akbar was keen to have the Rajputs lead his army, nor that subsequent Mughal emperors had such difficulty controlling this part of their empire.

The Rajput clans gave rise to great dynasties, such as the Chauhans, Sisodias, Kachhwahas and Rathores.

The rulers of Udaipur, the world's oldest ruling dynasty, span some 76 generations – read about their highs and lows in the well-researched *Maharana* by Brian Masters.

Chauhans of the Agnikula race, particularly renowned for their valour, emerged in the 12th century. Their territories included the Sapadalaksha kingdom, which encompassed a vast area, including present-day Jaipur, Ranthambhore (part of Mewar), the western portion of Bundi district, Ajmer, Kishangarh and even at one time, Delhi. Chauhan branches also ruled the territories known as Ananta (in present-day Shekhawati) and Saptasatabhumi.

The Sisodias of the Suryavansa race, originally from Gujarat, migrated to Rajasthan in the mid-7th century and reigned over Mewar, which encompassed Udaipur and Chittorgarh.

The Kachhwahas, from Gwalior in Madhya Pradesh, travelled west in the 12th century. They built the massive fort at Amber, and later shifted the capital to Jaipur. Like the Sisodias, they belonged to the Suryavansa race. They had a talent for war and alliances of convenience, so the dominion of the Kachhwahas spread, eventually encompassing a large area abutting the kingdoms of Mewar (Udaipur region) and Marwar (Jodhpur region).

To gem up on the history of royal Jodhpur, read the approachable *House of Marwar*, by Dhananajaya Singh, which covers events from the 13th century to Independence and beyond.

From the same race, the Rathores (earlier known as Rastrakutas) travelled from Kannauj, in Uttar Pradesh. Initially they settled in Pali, south of present-day Jodhpur, but later moved to Mandore in 1381 and ruled over Marwar, the largest kingdom in Rajputana and the third largest of the Indian kingdoms, after Kashmir and Hyderabad. In 1459 Rao Jodha, the Rathore leader, shifted the capital about 9km to the south and founded the city of Jodhpur, where he built the stunning Meherangarh (p309). The desert city of Bikaner was founded by one of Rao Jodha's sons, following a schism in the ruling Rathore family.

**262 BC**
Mauryan empire is briefly converted to Buddhism under Ashoka

**c AD 321**
The stable Gupta empire helps arts flourish

The Bhattis, who belong to the Induvansa race, were driven from their homeland in the Punjab by the Turks, and installed themselves at Jaisalmer in 1156. They remained more or less entrenched in their desert kingdom until they were integrated into the state of Rajasthan following Independence.

While the clans forged temporary alliances and marriages of convenience, pride and independence were always paramount. Much of their energy was spent fighting among themselves and the resultant weakness eventually led to their downfall.

## THE COMING OF ISLAM

The Prophet Mohammed introduced Islam into Arabia in the early 7th century. Under its banner, the Arabs took over Sindh in 713, and began to eye the Rajput territories. However, they were repulsed by the Gurjara Pratiharas, and the Rastrakutas, who when not battling the outsiders, were busy tearing each other to shreds.

By the third decade of the 8th century a new external threat was emerging to distract from inter-Rajput squabbles – the newly converted Muslim Turks, who had occupied Ghazni in Afghanistan.

Around AD 1001 the army of Afghan Mahmud of Ghazni (AKA 'the Sword of Islam') descended upon India, destroying infidel temples and taking everything of value that could be carried – from 1001 to 1017 he raided India 17 times seeking plunder for his capital. Rajasthan's wealth was a favourite target. In response, a confederation of Rajput rulers assembled a vast army and marched northwards to meet the advance. Unfortunately it was too little, too late, and they were crushingly vanquished. The Pratiharas, then centred at Kannauj, fled the city before the Turks arrived, and in their absence the temples of Kannauj were sacked and desecrated, as were so many others in northern India.

Towards the end of the 12th century, Mohammed of Ghori invaded India to take up where Mahmud of Ghazni had left off. He met with a confused defence shield of princely states. Although initially repulsed, Ghori later triumphed, and Delhi and Ajmer were lost to the Muslims. Ajmer remained a Muslim stronghold for much of its history, apart from a brief period when it was retaken by the Rathores. Here you can visit India's most important Muslim place of pilgrimage – the dargah of Khwaja Muin-ud-din Chishti (p205).

## THE SULTANATE OF DELHI

Mohammed of Ghori was killed in 1206, and his successor, Qutb-ud-din, became the first of the sultans of Delhi. Within 20 years, the Muslims had brought the whole of the Ganges basin under their control. The sultanate of Delhi was under persistent and varied attack from outside, and it was a rule of intrigue, treachery and violence – 19 out of its 35 sultans were assassinated.

William Dalrymple's *City of Djinns* is a wonderful book, chronicling the fascinating histories of Delhi in its many incarnations.

In 1297 Ala-ud-din Khilji (who had built Siri, a new capital on the Delhi site) pushed the Muslim borders south into Gujarat. He mounted a protracted siege on the massive fort at Ranthambhore, ruled at the time by the Rajput chief Hammir Deva. Hammir was reported as dead (although it's unknown if he did die in the siege) and upon hearing of

**AD 500–600**
Emergence of the Rajputs – warrior tribes descended from the sun, moon and fire (so they say)

**700**
Arrival of Islam

their chief's demise, the women of the fort collectively threw themselves on a pyre – the first instance of *jauhar* in the history of the Rajputs. In 1303 Ala-ud-din went on to sack the fort at Chittorgarh, held by the Sisodia clan. According to tradition, he had heard of the great beauty of Padmini, the consort of the Sisodian chief, and resolved to carry her off with him (see Death before Dishonour, p244). Like Ranthambhore before it, Chittorgarh fell to the Muslim leader.

## MUGHAL RISE

Mohammed Tughlaq, Ala-ud-din's successor, decided to move the capital from Delhi in 1324, and marched the entire population south – a mistake as many died along the way and he ended up having to return. Delhi regained its splendour, and in the mid-14th century, under Firoz Shah, Delhi was one of the world's most glorious cities, by this time called Firozabad. However, Firoz Shah died in 1388, and the arrival of the Mongol scourge Timur Lenk (Timur the Lame – in the West he is known as Tamerlane), put paid to this, vanquishing the Delhi sultanate and laying waste to the capital.

When Timur sacked Delhi, he spared all the builders so that they could build him a city in Samarkand.

Babur, whose fearsome lineage included Timur and Genghis Khan, marched into Punjab from his capital at Kabul in Afghanistan in 1525 and defeated the sultan of Delhi at Panipat to become the first Mughal ruler. He then focused his attention on the Rajput princely states, many of which, anticipating his designs, had banded together to form a united front under Rana Sangram Singh.

The Rajputs had been taking advantage of the troubles in Delhi to claw back and expand their territories. The kingdom of Mewar, ruled by the Sisodias under the leadership of Rana Sangram Singh, gained preeminence among the Rajput states, pushing its boundaries far beyond its original territory and posing a formidable threat to the new Mughal empire.

The Rajputs, however, were defeated by Babur and sustained great losses, with many Rajput chiefs falling in the fray, including Rana Sangram Singh, who reputedly had 80 wounds on his body gained during this and previous campaigns.

The defeat shook the foundations of the princely states. Mewar's confidence was shattered by the death of its illustrious leader, and its territories again shrank following subsequent attacks by the sultan of Gujarat.

## AKBAR – MASTER OF DIPLOMACY

Babur's successor, Humayun, was forced into exile by Afghan Sher Shah (who built Purana Qila) in 1539, but returned to power in 1555. He died only a year later (you can visit his magnificent tomb in Delhi, p101), so his son Akbar, only 13 years old, came to the throne. He was the most renowned of the Mughal emperors and reigned for 49 years.

Now Marwar, under its ruler Maldeo, emerged as the strongest of the Rajput states – it had fought and beaten Sher Shah. None of the Rajputs, however, were able to withstand Akbar.

Recognising that the Rajputs could not be conquered by force alone, Akbar arranged a marriage alliance with a princess of the important Kachhwaha clan, which held Amber (and later founded the city of Jaipur). The

Kachhwahas, unlike the rest of the Rajputs, aligned themselves with the powerful Mughals, and even sent troops to aid them in times of battle.

Akbar also used more conventional methods to assert his dominance – namely war. At the age of 15 he conquered Ajmer, and in 1567 to 1568 he took the mighty forts of Chittor and Ranthambhore.

In 1571 he began to build his great Mughal capital at Fatehpur Sikri (p145) – you can visit this fascinatingly complete Mughal city, near Agra – it was, however, short-lived, moving to Lahore in 1585 and Agra in 1599.

All the important Rajput states eventually acknowledged Mughal sovereignty and became vassal states, except Mewar (with its capital at Udaipur), which fiercely clung to its independence, refusing to pay homage to the Mughals. Akbar married a Hindu Rajput princess and encouraged good relations between Hindus and Muslims, consolidating his power and encouraging growth and stability. He gave Rajputs special privileges so that they were embraced within his empire, and encouraged intermarriage between Mughals and Rajputs. Akbar was an extraordinarily balanced and far-sighted ruler, who also discouraged child marriage, banned *sati* (ritual suicide of a widow on her husband's funeral pyre) and arranged special market days for women (who were usually enclosed at home) in Delhi. His reign and those of his descendants were times of unprecedented economic boom and development in art and architecture – comparable to the contemporary European Renaissance. You can visit monuments instigated by Akbar all over this area of India – he began Agra Fort (p139) in 1565, and in Agra you can also see his mausoleum (p140), which he planned himself. In Ajmer there is a mosque (p206) and a palace (p207) built by the emperor, who made an annual pilgrimage to the saint's tomb there.

**'Akbar discouraged child marriage, banned *sati* and arranged special market days for women'**

His descendants' greater emphasis on Islam, however, began to rock the relative peace.

## MORE MUGHALS, THE TAJ & AURANGZEB

Within Agra Fort you can visit the luxurious Jehangir's palace (p140), which Akbar built for his son. Jehangir was the next emperor, and he ruled alongside his adored Persian wife, Nur Jahan, who wielded considerable power and brought Persian influences to the court. She commissioned the beautiful Itimad-ud-Daulah (p140) in Agra for her father and mother. This Mughal masterpiece was the first structure built in marble, and is nicknamed 'Baby Taj' because of its inlay work.

The Rajputs continued to maintain mainly cordial relationships with the Mughals; they even took sides in Mughal family feuds – Udai Singh of Udaipur gave Prince Khurram shelter on Jagmandir island when he was escaping his father's wrath.

On Jehangir's death, Prince Khurram took over, taking the title Shah Jahan. His reign was the pinnacle of Mughal power. Like his forefathers, he was a patron of the arts, and some of the finest Mughal miniatures and art were produced at this time, not to mention the Taj Mahal (p137), a work of extreme refinement and beauty, but also of obscene extravagance. He also commenced work on Delhi's seventh incarnation, Shahjahanabad, constructing the Red Fort (p98) – this new city roughly corresponded to the extent of Old Delhi. But he never managed to move here from Agra

**1525**
Rise of the mighty Mughal empire

**1571**
Mughal Emperor Akbar moves his capital to Fatehpur Sikri

as he was deposed by his son Aurangzeb. Shah Jahan bled the country as huge resources were required to back his military ambitions. He was imprisoned by Aurangzeb at another Agra site, the beautiful Musamman Burj (p139), where he died eight years later.

*White Mughals*, by William Dalrymple, tells the true, tragic love story of a British East India Company soldier who fell in love with and married an Indian Muslim princess. It's interwoven with harem politics, intrigue and espionage.

The Rajputs and the Mughal emperors seemed resigned to accept each other as unsatisfactory bedfellows, until the reign of Aurangzeb (r 1658–1707), the last great Mughal emperor, when relations descended into out-and-out hostility.

Even more than Shah Jahan, Aurangzeb devoted all his resources to extending the Mughal empire's boundaries. Punitive taxes, which he levied on his subjects in order to pay for his military exploits, combined with an overextended empire and more than a dash of religious zealotry, eventually secured his downfall. His government's emphasis on Islam alienated his Hindu subjects. Aurangzeb banned the building of new temples, even destroying some, and forbade music and ceremonies at court. Challenges to his power mounted steadily as people reacted against his dour reign. In 1678 he claimed rights over Jodhpur and relations with the Rajputs turned into full-scale war.

The Rajputs were united in their opposition to Aurangzeb, and there were revolts from the Rathores and Sisodias. Before long there was insurgency on all sides and, with his death in 1707, the Mughal empire's fortunes rapidly declined.

*Plain Tales from the Raj*, by Charles Allen (ed), is fascinating reading, consisting as it does of a series of interviews with people who played a role in British India on both sides of the table.

## MARATHA MACHINATIONS

The Marathas rose to prominence with heroic warrior Shivaji, who between 1646 and 1680 dominated central India through guerrilla tactics, taking the unassuming title 'Lord of the Universe' in 1674. The Maratha empire continued under the Peshwas, hereditary government ministers who became the real rulers. They gained a stranglehold on the weakening Mughal empire, first by supplying troops and then by taking control of Mughal land. When Delhi was collapsing under Afghan onslaught, the Marathas were able to move in and help, before themselves being defeated by the Afghans (who later withdrew due to internal rebellions). Both armies robbed the city of countless treasures – the Persians stole the Mughal Peacock Throne, originally in Agra, in 1739, and the Marathas stole the Red Fort's silver ceiling.

The Rajputs were, as usual, busy fighting among themselves. The Marathas conducted numerous raids against the weakened and divided Rajputs, winning copious victories and gaining land. This led to the inevitable decline of the Rajput states.

*Maharanis: the Lives and Times of Three Generations of Indian Princesses*, by Lucy Moore, opens up the largely unexplored world of India's royal women during the great moments in British India.

## HERE COME THE BRITISH

India's next major invaders came by sea. The British East India Company, a London trading company, wanted a slice of the spice trade (having seen how well the Portuguese were doing) and got its first trading foothold in India in 1612. It then set about extending its influence – extraordinarily enough, this commercial company ended up nominally ruling India for 250 years.

The Indians welcomed the new influx of Europeans, hoping that they would help them against the Portuguese. The early English agents became

**1599**
Akbar builds his capital at Agra

**1612**
British establish first trading post in Surat, Gujarat

well assimilated in India, learning Persian and intermarrying with local people, which gave them an edge over other European hopefuls.

At this time the French and British were vying for supremacy, each backing their own local candidates in order to gain influence. However, the French had to back down, as their government felt they were spending too much time politicking and not enough trading.

Struggling with a local nawab for dominance over Bengal, British victory in the Battle of Plassey (1757), near Calcutta (later Kolkata), established their power in the east. They were aided in their moves by disgruntled local forces and merchants who had an eye on British trading opportunities – it was these local contacts that made the British spread of power possible.

Captain James Tod's *Annals & Antiquities of Rajasthan* (published in 1829–32) is a classic, with the captain's fascinating observations on the state.

After the collapse of the Mughal empire and during the ensuing chaos, they made their move, filling the power vacuum and taking over through a series of battles and alliances with local rulers. By the early 19th century India was effectively under British control. From 1784 onwards the British government in London began to take a more direct role in supervising affairs in India, although the territory was still notionally administered by the British East India Company until 1858.

The stable days of the Mughals were over. Dacoits (bandits) terrorised rural areas, and towns had fallen into decay. The Marathas continued to raid the Rajputs, and the British at first ignored the feuding parties. They eventually stepped into the fray, negotiating treaties with the leaders of the main Rajput states. British protection was offered in return for Rajput support. Weakened by habitual infighting and ongoing skirmishes, one by one the princely states forfeited their independence in exchange for protection. British residents were installed in the princely states. The British ultimately eliminated the Maratha threat, but in the process the Rajputs were effectively reduced to puppets – Udaipur was annexed completely in 1852.

Read *A Princess Remembers*, by Gayatri Devi and Santha Rama Rauthe, the maharani of Jaipur's fascinating memoirs, which offer intriguing insights into the bygone days of Rajasthani royalty.

The British had a notion of their own superiority that was to have a lasting impact on India. The colonisers felt that it was their duty to civilise the nation – unlike the first agents of the British East India Company they could not see the value in India's alien culture. Their capital was at Calcutta, ending centuries of Delhi dominance. During the first half of the 19th century the British imposed some radical reforms, for example, banning *sati*. They also introduced education in English, and English replaced Persian as the language of politics and government. New road and canal systems, as well as schools and universities introduced by the British in the 1850s, still form the basis of institutions and systems in existence today. But they also attacked the foundations of Indian society in an unprecedented way.

*The Proudest Day – India's Long Road to Independence*, by Anthony Read and David Fisher, is an engaging account of India's pre-Independence period.

New British bureaucracy was introduced, but with it came punitive taxes on landowners, and as raw materials from India were used in British textile mills, cheap British-produced goods began to destroy local livelihoods. Anger in the country began to rise. This anger found expression in the 1857 Indian Uprising, which was sparked by annexation in 1856 of Oudh, a wealthy Mughal princely state, and rumours that the British were using rifle cartridges greased with animal fat, which was offensive to the religious beliefs of Muslims and Hindus in the forces. Soldiers and peasants took over Delhi for four months and besieged the British Residency in Lucknow for five months before they were finally suppressed. There were also uprisings in Rajasthan among the poor and middle classes, but the Rajput royals supported the British and were rewarded for their loyalty by retaining their titles after the British government assumed control of the country in 1858.

## RAJPUT POMP REPLACES POWER

Pomp and circumstance began to replace real power for the Rajputs; consumption took over from chivalry, so that by the early 20th century many of the maharajas spent much of their time travelling the world with scores of retainers, playing polo and occupying entire floors of expensive Western hotels. Many maintained huge fleets of beautiful cars, which form museums today (the finest is in Udaipur, see p254). While it suited the British to indulge them, the maharajas' profligacy was economically and socially detrimental to their subjects, although there were still a few capable rulers, such as Ganga Singh of Bikaner. When India gained Independence, Rajasthan had one of the subcontinent's lowest rates of life expectancy and literacy.

The magnificently illustrated *A Desert Kingdom: the Rajputs of Bikaner*, by Naveen Patnaik, has an interesting analysis of the reign of Maharaja Ganga Singh of Bikaner, one of Rajasthan's better rulers.

Remnants of the Raj (the British government in India before 1947) can be spotted all over Rajasthan, from the railways, to Mayo College in Ajmer and colonial villas in Mt Abu. Chummy Anglo-Rajput hunting expeditions are documented in the stiff-posed black-and-white photographs that deck any self-respecting heritage hotel.

In the latter days of the Raj British attitudes in India become increasingly insular, exclusive and xenophobic. The 1857 Indian Uprising was a precursor to widespread opposition to British rule that occurred throughout India. In 1885 the Indian National Congress formed – giving form to the resistance – the precursor of today's Congress Party.

Mahatma Gandhi argued that the leader of the Muslim League, Mohammed Ali Jinnah, should lead a united India, if that would prevent Partition.

## INDEPENDENCE & PARTITION

In 1905 the English instigated the partition of Bengal for administrative reasons, which sparked a boycott of British goods and widespread violence. One response was the formation of the Muslim League to promote Muslim political interests. In 1911 the partition was reversed and a new capital began to be built in Delhi – New Delhi, with all its Lutyens buildings – an expression of permanence that was premature.

The tense situation eased somewhat during WWI, when India contributed enormously to the British war effort, with around 1.3 million Indians serving in the forces. Heavy casualties coupled with punitive taxes, however, meant Indians had yet more reasons to resent the British, laying more foundations for Independence.

You've probably seen *Gandhi*, starring Ben Kingsley, Candice Bergen, John Gielgud and 300,000 extras, before, but see it again because few movies capture the grand canvas that is India in tracing the country's path to Independence.

India's road to Independence was an extraordinary one, due to the influence of one man – it was Mohandas Gandhi, later known as Mahatma (Great Soul) Gandhi, who galvanised the peasants and villagers into the nonviolent resistance that was to spearhead the nationalist movement. He caused chaos throughout the country through his urging of people to refuse to pay taxes, and boycott British courts, institutions and products. He was imprisoned until 1924. On his release, he continued to campaign for the Dalits (the 'Untouchables' whom he called the children of god) and for the rural poor, capturing the public imagination through his approach, example and rhetoric.

**1800s**
British take control of the administration

**1911**
New Delhi constructed by the British

The Labour Party, who saw Indian independence as inevitable, came to power in Britain in 1945. Within India, however, a major problem had developed: the large Muslim minority had realised that an independent India would also be a Hindu-dominated India. The country was divided along religious lines, with the Muslim League, led by Mohammed Ali Jinnah, speaking for the Muslims, and the dominant Congress Party, led by Jawaharlal Nehru, representing the Hindu population.

*The Great Indian Middle Class* is Pavan K Varma's powerful and often cutting social history of India's most influential socioeconomic group and its descent into cynicism and materialism.

Gandhi was absolutely opposed to severing the Muslim-dominated regions from the prospective new nation. However, Jinnah was intransigent. The country was sliding towards civil war, and the decision was reluctantly made to divide the country. Independence was finally instituted on 15 August 1947, with the concomitant partitioning of the nascent country – unleashing chaos and horrendous bloodshed as refugees struggled to the appropriate side of the border. Delhi burned. It was predominantly Muslim before the exodus; after Partition their place (around 300,000 had fled) was mainly taken by Punjabi Hindus.

The end result was a Hindu-dominated India and a Muslim-dominated West and East Pakistan. Gandhi had, in his attempts to keep the country together, suggested Jinnah as leader of India. A Hindu extremist, unable to countenance such Muslim-friendly talk, assassinated the Great Soul on 30 January 1948, in New Delhi, which put a stop to any euphoria over Independence. You can visit the memorial museum to Gandhi (p101) in Delhi, and a memorial marks the place where he was shot.

*India: from Midnight to the Millennium*, by Shashi Tharoor, is one of the best accounts of the successes and failures of independent India, although it was written prior to the most recent developments.

## SINCE INDEPENDENCE

Since Independence, Delhi has maintained its position firmly at the heart of things as the seat of governmental power. The first government established the secular constitution that still holds today, with the first prime minister, Jawaharlal Nehru, instigating far-reaching reforms. India clashed with Pakistan in 1965 and 1971, first over the disputed border territory of Kashmir and second over Bangladesh. There was also a border war with China in 1962, over territory in Ladakh. On Nehru's death in 1964, his daughter Indira Gandhi was elected. She faced unrest in 1975, and called a state of emergency – the only time that India's democracy has faltered – but what became known as the Emergency came to an end in 1977 when she called a general election (she lost). Gandhi regained power, but was assassinated by one of her Sikh bodyguards in 1984, in retaliation for her decision to send troops into their holiest shrine, the Golden Temple. Her son Rajiv was next elected to head Congress. In turn, he was assassinated by Sri Lankan terrorists in 1991. Narasimha Rao, who followed, became entangled in corruption scandals, and in 1996 the Hindu-revivalist Bharatiya Janata Party (BJP) won power. A coalition briefly followed, but BJP came to power with a majority in 1998, and promptly caused an international scandal by detonating nuclear devices in the Rajasthan desert (see Nuclear Sabre-Rattling, p324), prompting Pakistan to conduct its own nuclear tests. In 2004 the Congress Party regained power, with Rajiv's Italian-born widow, Sonia Gandhi, at its head – but Manmohan Singh as prime minister. Relations with Pakistan are more cordial than they have been for a while, but the issue of Kashmir is eternally contentious.

*The Nehrus and the Gandhis* is Tariq Ali's astute portrait-history of these families and the India over which they cast their long shadows.

| 1947 | 1952 |
|---|---|
| Partition (creation of Pakistan), Independence and Gandhi's assassination | Rajasthan's first elections held |

The run of Nehru's descendants who have held power in India goes to show that it may be one of the world's most impressive democracies, but politics is still a dynastic game.

## RAJASTHAN IS BORN

In India's first post-Independence elections in 1951 to 1952, the Congress Party won 364 of 489 seats, but took just 45% of the popular vote.

At Independence, India's ruling Congress Party had to make a deal with the nominally independent Rajput states so they'd agree to join the new India. The rulers were allowed to keep their titles and property holdings, and they were paid an annual stipend.

The new state of Rajasthan formed gradually. In 1948 it comprised only the southern and southeastern states of Rajputana. When Mewar joined, Udaipur became Rajasthan's capital. The maharaja of Udaipur became *rajpramukh* (head of state). Manikya Lal Varma was appointed prime minister of the new state, which was inaugurated on 18 April 1948.

Almost from the outset, the prime minister clashed with the *rajpramukh* over the constitution of the state government ministry. Varma wanted to form a ministry of all Congress members, while the *rajpramukh* wanted to invite his buddies from among the *jagirdars* (feudal lords). *Jagirdars* traditionally collected rent and produce from the peasants, to deliver to the princely ruler. They were symbols of the old feudal order, under which millions of Rajputana inhabitants had been held in serfdom. Varma was keen to abolish the age-old system of *jagirdari* and, with Nehru's support, installed his own Congress ministry.

Political Resources – India (www.politicalresources.net/india.htm) contains extensive links to the major players and political parties in India.

Jaipur and the kingdoms of Bikaner, Jodhpur and Jaisalmer were still independent from India. From a security point of view, it was vital to the new Indian Union to ensure that these borderlands were integrated into the new nation. The Rajput rulers were offered fat privy purses, or ongoing government stipends, to sweeten the deal. The princes finally agreed to sign the Instrument of Accession, and the four kingdoms were merged in 1949. The maharaja of Jaipur, Man Singh II, was invested with the title of *rajpramukh*. Jaipur became the capital of the new state of Rajasthan. Heera Lal Shastri was installed as Rajasthan's first premier.

Later in 1949 the United State of Matsya (the former kingdoms of Bharatpur, Alwar, Karauli and Dholpur) was incorporated into Rajasthan. The state burgeoned to its current dimensions in November 1956, with the additions of Ajmer-Merwara, Abu Road and a part of Dilwara, originally part of the princely kingdom of Sirohi that had been divided between Gujarat and Rajasthan. Today it is India's largest state.

In 1997 KR Narayanan became India's president, the first member of the lowest Untouchable Hindu caste to hold the position.

## CONTEMPORARY RAJASTHAN

The first election in Rajasthan was only held in 1952 – the state's first taste of democracy. Since Independence, it had been under monarchical rule – executive and legislative powers were wielded by the *rajpramukh*, Man Singh II of Jaipur, who was assisted by the state ministry, members of which he appointed himself.

Since Rajasthan has had an elected government, it has been ruled by Congress, the Janata People's Party, and by a coalition of the BJP and the Janata Dal. At various times it has also been subjected to President's Rule (if the situation in a particular state is deemed to be unmanageable, the central government has the right to assume power there).

**1956**
State of Rajasthan reaches its current dimensions

**1971**
Privy purses for the maharajas abolished

During the 1990s India was swept up in a wave of Hindu nationalism, and Rajasthan was no exception. In 1990 the state government was won by a coalition of the Janata Dal and the staunchly Hindu revivalist BJP. They retained state power until the elections in 1998 when they lost control to the Congress; however, in the same year the BJP assumed power nationally when Congress suffered a humiliating defeat. In 2004 Congress swung back into power nationally, while Rajasthan continued its reverse trend – the BJP regained power in the state. The BJP chief minister, Vasundhara Raje, is from a noble family, and married to the former maharaja of Dholpur, Hemant Singh.

For a well-written survey of how Rajasthan has developed since Independence, read *Rajasthan: Polity, Economy & Society* by BL Panagariya and NC Pahariya.

As for the former rulers themselves, Indira Gandhi abolished the privy purses and privileges granted to the Rajasthan princes in 1971 – a massive shock to those at the top of the pile. But many continue to use the title of maharaja (or a similar title) for social purposes. The only power it holds today is as a status symbol, but a very good one: the ex-royal families still command enormous respect.

While a handful squandered their family fortunes, others refused to surrender their heritage, and turned to politics (see The Rani of Rambagh, p163), business or other vocations. You can see the accessories of royal power in museums all over Rajasthan, which house elaborate armour, weaponry, costumes and parade paraphernalia. After losing their privy purses, many princes converted their palaces into hotels, the revenue from which enables the maharajas to maintain their properties, sustain traditions and continue to live in the manner to which they are accustomed.

*Conflict Unending*, by Sumit Ganguly, takes an in-depth look behind the India–Pakistan hostilities since 1947, including an analysis of nuclear experiments and the repercussions of 9/11.

Nothing evokes the essence of the Rajputs quite as much as a stay in palatial splendour surrounded by vestiges of the regal age: places such as the Lake Palace Hotel (p259) in Udaipur, the Rambagh Palace (p171) in Jaipur and the Umaid Bhawan Palace (p315) in Jodhpur. Not all the princes' palaces are on the tourist circuit; many Rajput palaces and forts are decaying, empty and full of bats.

**1998**
Nuclear tests at Pokaran prompt tests by Pakistan and bring international condemnation

**2004**
National elections put the Congress Party in power after six years of BJP rule

# The Culture

## RAJASTHANI IDENTITY

Like elsewhere in India, people in Rajasthan are inquisitive, warm and sometimes helpful beyond anything you'll have encountered anywhere. If you have a problem with your train ticket, a crowd will throng to help (or at least to see what's going on). If it turns out you have no reserved seat, people will move to make room for you. Generous, curious and hospitable, these qualities are part of the Indian character.

But the Rajasthani identity is unique. It is partly shaped by geography. The characteristics of the land – arid and harsh – breed resilience; the flat, unforested terrain has fallen prey to centuries of invaders, and this has long been border country.

For a comprehensive historical and cultural analysis of Rajputana, read the scholarly *Cultural History of Rajasthan* by Kalyan Kumar Ganguli.

No other area of India has had the same culture of militarism and chivalry. Tales of valour – true or not – are sewn into Rajasthan's fabric. The impressive moustaches you see around the state are not just a fashion choice: locals speak of an issue of 'moustache' when something is a question of honour.

The Rajputs lie close to the heart of the Rajasthani identity. Their legendary status is a romantic cliché, bumped up by storytellers, art and their position as Rajasthan's top dogs right up till Independence. But however much it may be a mythology, the nobility of the Rajputs has created the state's sense of self today. For support, the Rajput rulers relied on feudal systems that rested on tiers of servitude. Feudalism was the name of the game till Independence, and it's still prevalent, resulting in a fiercely traditional society, unusually in thrall to the past. Caste is still very important here, as is class.

Rajasthan is also India's most touristed area, with 40% of all people visiting India coming here. This exposure means the state is, in places, strikingly cosmopolitan. It's not uncommon to meet a Jaipur rickshaw driver who speaks four or five languages. The inevitable effect is that the tourism frontline is mostly about money: people have little time to win those tourist dollars, and some have developed a battering-ram charm as a means to get them. But scratch the surface, and a more gentle and hospitable people you will rarely meet, who have a sense of history underlying everything they do.

*The Idea of Rajasthan*, edited by Karine Schomer et al, consists of contemporary essays on the historical and cultural influences that have formed Rajasthani identity.

## DAILY LIFE

### Contemporary Culture

Rajasthan's a barren-landed state, where 70% of the population is nevertheless stoically employed in agriculture. Villages nestle close to water sources, small, isolated communities that come together for trade in a frenzy of colour at local markets and melas (fairs).

Although TV pumps in the outside world, daily life remains unchanged by it. Women prepare meals with the aid of a *chakki* (handmill), an *okhli* (mortar) and a *moosal* (pestle), and carry them out to the men working in the fields, where women also help at harvest time. In many ways village life feels like it hasn't changed for hundreds of years.

Like elsewhere in the world, however, there's much urban migration. Around 40% of young men in Rajasthan quit their villages to work in India's big cities. It's often a question of resources – there's not enough land to go around – if a farm has to be split between sons, it will soon shrink to the size of a stamp.

Post-Independence, Rajasthan was one of India's poorest states, a situation exacerbated not only by its feudal legacy, but also by periodic droughts. Currently, the per capita income (Rs 14,748) is still below the national average (Rs 20,989). That said, it has made enormous strides since Independence: the literacy rate in 1951 was just 8%, rising to 38.6% in 1991 and 61% in 2001 (slightly behind the national average of 65.4%). Female literacy was still low at 44.2% (the national average was 54.5%), but this had doubled since 1991.

Average monthly earnings are dependent on profession, and women tend to be paid less than men. Per month, a construction worker earns Rs 600 to 2500, hotel workers Rs 1000 to 3000, and a managing accountant up to Rs 25,000.

Poverty, drought and unemployment have led to problems, such as increases in indebtedness, drug abuse and alcoholism. In certain tribal communities (such as the Bishnoi), opium is offered to guests – this has long been a ceremonial practice. Now, however, the trend is towards secular drug use, and the use of heroin rather than traditional drugs.

**STATUS OF WOMEN**

Men are the kings in the land of kings. The birth of a male child is greeted with great rejoicing and celebration, while the birth of a female child is a cause for commiseration.

There are several reasons for this, the most significant of which is the dowry system. Although illegal, this is entrenched in Rajasthan, and the parents of female children can be plunged into terrible debt trying to maintain their honour by sending their daughter to her in-laws' home with appropriate gifts of cash, jewellery and electrical goods.

If the bridegroom's family believes that the dowry is inadequate, further demands can be made on the bride's family. As in other parts of India, the deaths of new brides in 'stove fires' are not uncommon, allowing the husband to remarry and claim another dowry.

The sex ratio is imbalanced, indicating the presence of female infanticide – the number of women per 1000 men was 922 in 2001. This is still better than in some more prosperous states, such as Punjab, which had a ratio of 874 women per 1000 men.

The birth of a female child is not always considered a calamity. There are several communities, mostly belonging to the Scheduled Castes & Tribes, which demand a *reet* (bride price) on the marriage of their daughters. Young men unable to pay *reet* are either condemned to bachelorhood, or are compelled to exchange their sisters or female cousins in a multiple marriage transaction.

Things are changing fast in urban areas, where women are making inroads into the professions. But it's a different story in the countryside;

For fascinating insights into the position of women in India, particularly rural women, read *May You Be the Mother of One Hundred Sons* by Elizabeth Bumiller.

*Sati: a Study of Widow Burning in India*, by Sakuntala Narasimhan, looks at the startling history of *sati* on the subcontinent.

**AIDS IN INDIA**

After South Africa, India has the world's highest number of HIV-positive cases; in 2005 there were 5.1 million reported cases in India. Apart from sex workers, truck drivers and intravenous drug users also fall into the high-risk category.

In a country of over one billion people, health officials warn that unless the government radically increases educational programmes (especially promotion of condom use) the number of HIV-positive cases could climb to at least 12 million by 2010. Condom sales in urban India plummeted from 530 million in 2001–02 to 476 million in 2003–04.

See also p395.

rural women in Rajasthan are severely disadvantaged, unable to hold property, and receive little, if any, education. You'll often see rural women covering their faces on the approach of a stranger – some women only show their faces to their close family.

Mala Sen's *Death by Fire: Sati, Dowry Death & Female Infanticide in Modern India* is a disturbing and impassioned account, written from the perspective of three different women.

Numerous development programmes run by the central and state governments, as well as Non-Governmental Organisation (NGOs) and donor countries, attempt to address the status of women. Voluntary organisations are also working towards female economic and social empowerment. The Barefoot College (see p210), Urmul Trust and Seva Mandir all run important programmes – for volunteer opportunities see p375.

### TREATMENT OF GAYS & LESBIANS

Homosexuality is not countenanced in Rajasthani culture, although a 2004 report estimated that Indian has about 70 million gay, lesbian and transgender people.

Deepa Mehta's 1998 film *Fire* stunned the country with its sensitive and realistic portrayal of a lesbian relationship between two women trapped in unhappy marriages.

Homosexual relations between men are illegal, although there's no law against lesbian relations. Most people stay in the closet; they otherwise risk being disowned by their families and society. The subject is not entirely hidden: Deepa Mehta's film *Fire* shocked India and prompted violent demonstrations by hardliner Hindu group Shiv Sena.

*Hijras* are transvestites and eunuchs who dress in women's clothing. They're a kind of third sex – some are gay, some hermaphrodite; and others were kidnapped and castrated. They work as uninvited entertainers at weddings and celebrations of the birth of male children, and as prostitutes.

## Traditional Culture

### MARRIAGE & DIVORCE

*The Invisibles: a Tale of the Eunuchs of India*, by Zia Jaffrey, is a book that fills in background on the *hijras*.

Marriages are usually arranged by parents. Cross-caste marriages, once socially taboo, are now performed occasionally (usually in urban areas), and are generally the result of a love match.

Although outlawed by the government, rural child marriages are not uncommon. The United Nations Children's Fund (Unicef) estimates that 82% of girls in Rajasthan are married before they turn 18, and 48% by the age of 15. The Sahariya tribal people arrange marriages while the child is still in the womb. Often a group of children is married simultaneously, to reduce costs, although the newlyweds return to the family home until they reach maturity. On attaining puberty, girls are given gifts by their parents and then dispatched with due ceremony to their in-laws' homes.

Traditionally, among the Jats, Gujjars and Scheduled Castes & Tribes, a woman is permitted to remarry following the death of her husband. However, the new husband has to pay compensation to the relatives of the former husband and to the bride's parents. Remarriage of widows was once forbidden by the upper castes, but is becoming slightly more prevalent. Divorce, also once forbidden, is now also more common among these castes, though it still carries a stigma.

### DEATH

Twelve days after cremation, if the deceased was the male head of the family, a symbolic turban-tying ceremony is performed, in which his successor is recognised by his family and the community.

In rural areas, a death feast known as *mosar*, *barwa*, *kariyawar* or *terwa* is held 12 or 13 days after death. The mourning relatives are reminded of their obligations to perform a death feast by community leaders, regardless of the family's financial position. Frequently these unwelcome visitors are conveniently accompanied by the *bohara* (village moneylender).

## DOS & DON'TS

India has retained many time-honoured traditions and while you won't be expected to get everything 'right', common sense and courtesy will take you a long way. If in doubt about how you should behave (eg at a temple), watch what the locals do, or simply ask.

Dressing conservatively (women *and* men) wins a warmer response from locals (women should also read p377). Refrain from kissing and cuddling in public as this isn't condoned by society.

### Religious Etiquette

Whenever visiting a sacred site, always dress and behave respectfully – don't wear shorts or sleeveless tops (this applies to men and women) and don't smoke. Loud and intrusive behaviour isn't appreciated, and neither are public displays of affection or kidding around.

Before entering a holy place, remove your shoes (tip the shoe-minder a few rupees when retrieving them) and check if photography is allowed.

Religious etiquette advises against touching locals on the head, or directing the soles of your feet at a person, religious shrine or image of a deity. It's also offensive to touch someone with your feet and to touch a carving of a deity.

Head cover (for women and sometimes men) is required at some places of worship. There are some sites that don't admit women and some that deny entry to non-adherents of their faith – inquire in advance. Women may be required to sit apart from men. Jain temples request the removal of leather items and may also request menstruating women not to enter.

### Eating & Visiting Etiquette

If you're lucky enough to be invited to someone's home it's considered good manners to remove your shoes before entering the house and to wash your hands before the main meal. Wait to be served food or until you are invited to help yourself – if you're unsure about protocol, simply wait for your host to direct you.

It's customary to use your right hand for eating and other social acts such as shaking hands; the left hand is used for unsavoury actions such as toilet duties, removing grotty shoes etc. When drinking from a shared water container, hold it slightly above your mouth (thus avoiding contact between your lips and the mouth of the container).

### Photography Etiquette

Exercise sensitivity when taking photos of people, especially women, who may find it offensive – obtain permission in advance.

Taking photos inside a shrine, at a funeral, at a religious ceremony or of people publicly bathing (including in rivers) can be offensive – ask first. Flash photography may be prohibited in certain areas of a shrine, or may not be permitted at all.

### Other Travellers Tips

To increase your chances of receiving the most accurate response when seeking directions, refrain from posing questions in a leading manner. For instance, it's best to ask, 'Which way to the museum?' rather than pointing and asking, 'Is this the way to the museum?'

It's also worth noting that the commonly used sideways wobble of the head doesn't necessarily mean 'no'. It can translate to: yes, maybe, or I have no idea.

Some people celebrate the *mosar* feast in their lifetime, in case their relatives fail to honour them after their death. The state government has enacted laws to limit the guests at a feast, with little success.

### SATI

The practice of *sati*, voluntary self-immolation by a widow on her husband's funeral pyre, is named after Shiva's wife Sati, who immolated herself when her father insulted Shiva by refusing to invite him to a feast. In Rajasthan there historically have been numerous instances of *sati*, especially among the ruling Rajputs by maharajas' wives – to honour their dead husband, and to avoid the ignominy of widowhood.

There are several examples in Rajput's history of *jauhar* – *sati* performed on a mass scale (see Death Before Dishonour, p244).

In 1846 the princely state of Jaipur was the first state in Rajasthan to outlaw *sati* after prompting by the British government, soon followed by other states. Mewar resisted the ban, and in 1861 Queen Victoria issued a proclamation forbidding the practice of *sati*. Intermittent cases of *sati* have taken place since, the most recent known case being in 1987, after which there was further legislation against *sati*.

The often shocking and sad story of India's tribal people is laid bare in *Tribes of India – the Struggle for Survival* by Christoph von Führer-Haimendorf.

## POPULATION

Rajasthan has increased its population by 42 million since 1951. There are various reasons for this phenomenal multiplication. Despite the spectre of drought, improved infrastructure enables the distribution of aid and so increases chances of survival. Ironically, Rajasthan's poverty encourages growth – the perpetual desire for 'an heir and a spare' encourages parents to keep trying for two male offspring.

### ADIVASIS OF RAJASTHAN

Adivasi (tribal) groups were the original inhabitants of the area now called Rajasthan.

#### Bhils

The Bhils are an important group, traditionally inhabiting the southeastern corner of the state – although the largest concentrations of Bhils are found in neighbouring Madhya Pradesh.

Legend has it that the Bhils were fine archers, hence their name, from the Tamil *vil*, meaning 'bow'. The Mahabharata and the Ramayana both mention Bhil bowmen. They were highly regarded as warriors, and the Rajput rulers relied on them to thwart the invading Marathas and Mughals. Some scholars suggest that the Rajputs owe their warrior propensities to the example of the Bhils.

Although originally food gatherers, these days the Bhils have taken up small-scale agriculture, or abandoned the land and headed for the cities. The literacy rate of the Bhils, particularly the women, used to be one of the lowest in the country, which made them prime targets for exploitation and bonded labour. This trend is now being reversed and Bhil fortunes are improving. Several Bhils, including one woman, have even entered state parliament.

Witchcraft, magic and superstition are deeply rooted aspects of Bhil culture. Those Bhils who can afford it engage in polygamy, and love marriages are the norm.

The Baneshwar Fair (see Festivals in Southern Rajasthan, p227) is a huge Bhil festival. Holi is another important time for the Bhils.

#### Minas

The Minas are the second-largest tribal group in the state after the Bhils, and most widespread. They live in Shekhawati and eastern Rajasthan. Scholars still disagree as to whether the Minas are an indigenous tribe, or whether they migrated here from Central Asia. The name Mina is derived from *meen* (fish), and the Minas claim descent from the fish incarnation of Vishnu. Originally they were a ruling tribe, but their downfall began with the rise of the Rajputs and was completed when the British government declared them a 'criminal tribe' in 1924, mainly to stop them trying to regain their territory from the Rajputs. The Minas resorted to means such as demanding protection money from villagers to curtail their dacoit (bandit) activities.

Rajasthan's population is overwhelmingly rural, with the lowest population density in the desert areas.

## RELIGION

Hindus represent around 89% of the state's population, a little over the national average. Jains number around 1.8%. Less than 10% of Rajasthan's population is Muslim, most of whom are Sunnis. There is a small affluent community of Shi'ia Muslims, the Bohras, in southeastern Rajasthan.

Less than 2% of the population professes Sikhism, with most Sikhs clustered in Ganganagar district. There is a tiny population of Christians, amounting to around 0.1%, predominantly in Ajmer and Jaipur. The Buddhist population is barely visible, representing only 0.01%.

Look up the website of the BBC (www.bbc.co.uk/religion/religions) for a concise rundown of the world's major religions and some interesting links.

### Hinduism

Hinduism is one of the oldest extant religions, with firm roots extending back to beyond 1000 BC.

Hindus believe in Brahman. Brahman is eternal, uncreated and infinite; everything that exists emanates from Brahman and will ultimately return to it. Gods and goddesses are merely manifestations of this formless phenomenon.

Shakunthala Jagannathan's *Hinduism – an Introduction* unravels the basic tenets of Hinduism. If you have no prior knowledge of the subject, this book is a terrific starting point.

Following Independence, their ignominious criminal status was lifted, and they took to agriculture. However, their culture was by this time largely destroyed, and they are now protected as a Scheduled Tribe.

As with the Bhils, the literacy rate among the Minas has been very low, but is improving.

Marriage is generally within the tribe, arranged by the parents, and takes place when the bride and groom are children.

#### Gaduliya Lohars

Originally a Rajput tribe, nowadays the Gaduliya Lohars are nomadic blacksmiths. Their traditional territory was Mewar (Udaipur) and they fought with the maharaja against the Mughals. With typical Rajput chivalry, they made a vow to the maharaja that they'd only enter Chittorgarh (Chittor) after he had won. As he died without achieving this, the clan was forced on the road. When Jawaharlal Nehru was in power he led a group of Gaduliya Lohars into the fort at Chittorgarh, with the hope that they would then resettle there, but they preferred to retain their nomadic lifestyle.

#### Garasias

The Garasias are a small Rajput tribe who are found in the Abu Road area of southern Rajasthan. It's thought that they intermingled with the Bhils tribal group, as bows and arrows are also widely used by the Garasias.

Garasia marriages are curious: the couple elope, and money is paid to the father of the bride. If the marriage fails, the bride returns home with some money to give to the father. Widows are not entitled to a share of their husband's property, and so they generally remarry.

#### Sahariyas

The Sahariyas are thought to be of Bhil origin, and live in southeast Rajasthan. They are one of India's least-educated tribes and have been cruelly exploited.

As all members of the clan are considered to be related, marriages are arranged outside the tribe. Their food and worship traditions are closely related to Hindu customs.

In Hinduism, the 'three' shape of Om symbolises the creation, maintenance and destruction of the universe (and thus the Trimurti – Brahma, Vishnu and Shiva).

Hinduism has no central organisation, but spiritual leaders hold a great deal of authority. Beliefs and practices vary widely, but there are several unifying factors, including common beliefs in samsara (reincarnation), karma (conduct or action) and dharma (appropriate behaviour for one's station in life), as well as the caste system.

Living a righteous life and fulfilling your dharma will enhance your chances of being born into a higher caste and better circumstances. If you've been bad enough to accumulate serious negative karma, you may be reborn as an animal. It's only as a human that you can gain sufficient self-knowledge to escape the cycle of reincarnation and achieve moksha (liberation). Traditionally, women are unable to attain moksha. The best they can do is fulfil their dharma and hope for a male incarnation next time around.

A sadhu is someone who has surrendered all material possessions in pursuit of spirituality through meditation, the study of sacred texts, self-mortification and pilgrimage.

## CASTE

In the Hindu religion that dominates India, there are four distinct castes, each with their own special rules of conduct. These, in order of hierarchy, are said to have come from Brahma's mouth (Brahmins; the priest caste), arms (Kshatriyas; the warrior caste), thighs (Vaisyas; the caste of tradespeople and artisans) and feet (Sudras; the caste of farmers and peasants). Within these groups are hundreds of interdivisions. The Rajputs are warriors within Rajasthan's caste system. Below the

### HINDU GODS & GODDESSES

According to the Hindu scriptures there are around 330 million deities in the Hindu pantheon. All of these are regarded as a manifestation of Brahman, and the particular object of veneration is often a matter of personal choice or tradition at a local or caste level. Brahman is often described as having three main representations, which are known as the Trimurti: Brahma, Vishnu and Shiva.

#### Brahma & Saraswati

The only active role that Brahma plays is during the creation of the universe. The rest of the time he is in meditation and is therefore regarded as aloof. His vehicle is a swan and he is sometimes shown sitting on a lotus that rises from Vishnunavel, symbolising the interdependence of the gods. See also Dreamer of the Universe, p214.

Saraswati, goddess of learning, is his porcelain-skinned consort and is considered to be the most beautiful goddess.

#### Vishnu & Krishna

The preserver or sustainer, the god Vishnu is associated with 'right action' and behaves as a lawful, devout Hindu. He is enormously popular, protecting and sustaining all that is good in the world. He is usually depicted with four arms, each arm respectively holding a lotus (the petals symbolise the unfolding of the universe); a conch shell (as it can be blown like a trumpet, the conch symbolises the cosmic vibration from which all existence emanates); a discus (which represents the sun, in reference to Vishnu's origins, and is also a handy instrument that aids in the removal of obstacles to enlightenment); and a mace (a reward Vishnu received for conquering Indra, the god of battle). His consort is Lakshmi, the goddess of wealth. His vehicle is Garuda, who is half-bird, half-beast, and he dwells in a heaven called Vaikuntha. Vishnu has 22 incarnations, including Rama, Krishna and Buddha. He is also known as Narayan, and Lakshmi is also known as Mohini.

Krishna is hugely popular in Rajasthan. In this incarnation, Vishnu was sent to earth as Krishna to fight for good and combat evil. His alliances with the *gopis* (milkmaids) and his love for Radha (a married woman) have inspired countless paintings and songs.

Rajputs, the Vaisyas in Rajasthan can be divided into two groups: those who profess Jainism, and those who profess Vaishnavism (worship of the god Vishnu).

Beneath all the castes are the Dalits and Scheduled Castes (formerly known as Harijans and Untouchables), who have no caste and traditionally do all the dirty work. Hindus cannot change caste – they are born into it and stuck with it.

According to Hindu belief, the lotus flower emerged from the primeval waters connected to the mythical centre of the earth through its stem.

### DARSHAN & PUJA

*Darshan* is an important concept in Hinduism. When devotees visit a temple, they hope to receive *darshan* from the temple god or by visiting their guru. It means glimpse, or sight, and is the religious experience gained by seeing and being in the presence of a god.

Most Hindus perform *puja* regularly – this involves prayer and visiting a shrine or temple for *darshan* and to make offerings. Often the performing of *puja* has a specific purpose, such as to gain good luck in business or family matters.

### SACRED TEXTS

Hindu sacred texts fall into two categories: those believed to be the word of god (shruti, meaning 'heard') and those produced by people (smriti, meaning 'remembered').

#### Shiva & Parvati

Although known as the destroyer, creation could not have occurred without Shiva. Shiva's creative role is symbolised by his representation as the frequently worshipped lingam (phallus). With 1008 names, Shiva takes many forms, including Pashupati, champion of the animals, and Nataraja, lord of the *tandava* (cosmic dance), who paces out the creation and destruction of the cosmos. He has two sons, the elephant-headed Ganesh and six-headed Kartikiya.

Shiva is also characterised as the lord of yoga, a Himalaya-dwelling ascetic with matted hair and a naked, ash-smeared body; a third eye in his forehead symbolises wisdom. Sometimes Shiva has snakes draped around his neck and is shown holding a trident (representative of the Trimurti) while riding Nandi, his bull, who symbolises power, potency, justice and moral order.

Shiva's consort is Parvati, the beautiful, who in her dark side appears as Durga, the terrible, holding weapons in her 10 hands and riding a tiger. As Kali, the fiercest of the gods, she demands sacrifices, wears a garland of skulls, and handles the destructive side of Shiva's personality.

#### Ganesh

The jolly, pot-bellied, elephant-headed Ganesh is held in great affection. He is the god of good fortune, prosperity and patron of scribes (the broken tusk he holds is the one he used to write sections of the Mahabharata). He rides a ratlike creature. How Ganesh came to have the head of an elephant is a story with many variations. One legend says that Ganesh was born to Parvati in Shiva's absence and grew up without knowing his father. One day, as Ganesh stood guard while his mother bathed, Shiva returned and asked to be let into Parvati's presence. Ganesh refused. Enraged, Shiva lopped off Ganesh's head, only to discover he had slaughtered his own son! He resolved to replace Ganesh's head with the head of the first creature that he saw. As Ganesh is good at removing obstacles, he's frequently spotted above doorways and entrances.

#### Hanuman

Hanuman is the hero of the Ramayana and Rajasthan's most popular god. He is the loyal ally of Rama and embodies the concept of bhakti (surrendering to the gods; faith). Images of Rama and Sita are emblazoned upon his heart. He is king of the monkeys, therefore assuring them refuge at temples across the country, but he is capable of taking on any form he chooses.

The Vedas, introduced to the subcontinent by the Aryans, are regarded as shruti knowledge and are considered the authoritative basis for Hinduism. The oldest of the Vedic texts, the Rig-Veda, is over 3000 years old.

There are masses of smriti texts, which include expositions on things domestic as well as government, economics and religious law. Among the better-known works contained within this body of literature are the Kamasutra, the Ramayana, the Mahabharata and the *Puranas*. Unlike the Vedas, the *Puranas* are not limited to initiated higher-caste males and so have wider popular appeal. Big crowd pleasers are the Mahabharata and the Ramayana, which drew an estimated audience of 80 million when serialised by Indian state television in the 1980s.

There are around 330 million deities in the Hindu pantheon; those worshipped is a matter of personal choice or tradition at a local/caste level.

### The Mahabharata

This rip-roaring epic centres on conflict between the gods – the heroes (Pandavas) and the demons (Kauravas). Overseeing events is Krishna in human form. Krishna acts as charioteer for the Pandava hero, Arjuna, who eventually triumphs in a great battle with the Kauravas. The book includes the Bhagavad Gita (in which Krishna advises Arjuna before a great battle).

The Mahabharata is the world's longest work of literature, eight times longer than the Greek epics the *Iliad* and the *Odyssey* combined.

### The Ramayana

Composed around the 3rd or 2nd century BC, the Ramayana tells of Rama, an incarnation of Vishnu, who assumed human form to overthrow the demon king of Lanka (Sri Lanka), Ravana. Rama won the hand of the princess Sita in a competition and was chosen by his father to inherit the kingdom. But at the last minute Rama's stepmother intervened and demanded that her son take Rama's place. Rama, Sita and Rama's brother, Lakshmana, were exiled and went off to the forests where Rama and Lakshmana battled demons and dark forces. Ravana's sister attempted to seduce Rama, but she was rejected and in revenge, Ravana captured Sita and spirited her away to his palace in Lanka. Rama, assisted by an army of monkeys led by Hanuman, eventually found the palace, killed Ravana and rescued Sita. All returned victorious to Ayodhya where Rama was crowned king. This story forms the basis for the important Hindu Dussehra Festival (see p365).

For easy-to-understand depictions of the Hindu holy texts, read Amar Chitra Katha's colourful comic-book style versions of the Ramayana and Mahabharata. Other titles in this children's series include *Ganesh*, *Krishna* and *Hanuman*.

## Islam

Islam was founded in Arabia by the Prophet Mohammed in the 7th century AD. The Arabic term *islam* means surrender, and believers undertake to surrender to the will of Allah (God). The will of God is revealed in the Quran. God revealed his will to the Prophet Mohammed, who acted as his messenger. Muslims are required to pray five times a day. They don't have to pray at a mosque, but wherever prayer takes place, it must follow precise rules.

Islam is monotheistic; God is unique and has no equal. Everything is believed to be created by God and is deemed to have its own place and purpose within the universe. Only God is unlimited and self-sufficient. Although God never speaks to humans directly, his word is conveyed through messengers called prophets, who are never themselves divine. Mohammed is the most recent prophet.

In the years after Mohammed's death a succession dispute split the movement; the legacy today are the Sunnis and the Shi'ias. The initial split stems from the beginnings of Islam, just after the death of the Prophet, when there was a political division over succession. The Sunnis recognised the Medinan (later Ummayad) Caliphs (Islamic leaders) as authorities. The other group, the Shi'ias, believed that power belonged to the descendants of Mohammed, starting with Ali, his son-in-law (Shi'at Ali means 'the party of Ali' in Arabic). Although the original division was political, over the centuries many differences in interpretation and ritual have evolved. Around 90% of the world's Muslims are Sunnis.

Most Muslims in Rajasthan are Sunnis, apart from a small community of Shi'ia Muslims, known as Bohras, in southeastern Rajasthan. The most important pilgrimage site for Muslims in Rajasthan is the extraordinary dargah (burial place) of Khwaja Muin-ud-din Chishti (p205) at Ajmer.

## Jainism

The Jain religion bears many similarities to both Buddhism and Hinduism. It was founded around 500 BC by Mahavira, the 24th and last of the Jain *tirthankars* (path finders; Jain teachers). The Jain religion originally evolved as a reformist movement against the dominance of priests and the complicated rituals of Brahmanism, and rejected the caste system. Jains believe that the universe is infinite and was not created by a deity. They also believe in reincarnation and eventual moksha through following the example of the *tirthankars*.

Try the Jain World website (www.jainworld.com) for Jain philosophy, texts, literature, recipes and links, including information in different Indian and other languages.

### RAJASTHAN'S FOLK GODS & GODDESSES

Folk deities and deified local heroes abound in Rajasthan. Every family also pays homage to a *kuldevi* (clan goddess).

The deified folk hero Ramdev has an important temple at Ramdevra (p323), near Pokaran in western Rajasthan.

Pabuji's is a particularly violent and chivalrous tale: Pabuji entered a transaction with a woman called Devalde, in which, in return for a mare, he vowed to protect her cows from all harm. The time to fulfil this obligation came, inconveniently, during the celebration of Pabuji's own marriage; however, Pabuji immediately went to the aid of the threatened livestock. During the ensuing battle, he, along with all the male members of his family, perished at the hands of a villain by the name of Jind Raj Khinchi.

To preserve the family line, Pabuji's sister-in-law cut open her own belly and produced Pabuji's nephew, Nandio, before committing *sati* on her husband's funeral pyre. An annual festival is held at Kodumand, in Jaisalmer district, the birthplace of Pabuji, at which Bhopas (professional storytellers) perform *Pabuji-ka-phad*, poetry recitations in praise of Pabuji.

Gogaji was a warrior who lived in the 11th century and who could cure snakebite – today victims are brought to his shrine by Hindu and Muslim devotees. Also believed to cure snakebite is Tejaji. According to tradition, while pursuing dacoits who had rustled his father-in-law's cows, Teja was confronted by a snake poised to strike. He pleaded with the snake to let him pass so that he could recover the cows, and promised to return later. The snake relented, and Teja duly returned, bloody and bruised from his confrontation with the dacoits. The snake was reluctant to bite Teja on his wounds, so Teja offered his tongue. So impressed was the snake that it decreed that anyone honouring Teja by wearing a thread in his name would be cured of snakebite.

Goddesses, generally incarnations of Devi (Shakti) the Mother Goddess, include the fierce Chamunda Mata, an incarnation of Durga; Sheetala Mata, the goddess of smallpox, whom parents propitiate in order to spare their children from this affliction; Kela Devi; and Karni Mata, worshipped at Deshnok (see The Temple of Rats, p353), near Bikaner.

Women who have committed *sati* on their husband's funeral pyre are also frequently revered as goddesses, such as Rani Sati, who has an elaborate temple in her honour in Jhunjhunu (p290), in Shekhawati.

Barren women pay homage to the god Bhairon, an incarnation of Shiva, at his shrines, which are usually found under khejri trees. In order to be blessed with a child, the woman is required to leave a garment hanging from the branches of the tree, and often these can be seen fluttering over shrines to Bhairon.

The Jains have an influence disproportionate to their numbers. They are strict vegetarians and revere all forms of life. There are two main sects. Svetambaras (White Clad) wear unsewn white garments and their monks have their mouths covered so as not to breathe in insects and brush their path before they walk it so as not to crush any small creature. The other sect is the Digambaras (Sky Clad), whose monks go naked. The most important rule in Jainism is to avoid intentional harm to others. They are markedly successful in banking and business, as Jains consider these to be nonviolent professions.

# ARTS

Rajasthani culture celebrates beauty, and elaborately decorates everything from walls, to clothes and weapons. (For more on Rajasthani handicrafts see p58.)

## Architecture

The magnificence of Rajasthan's architectural heritage is astounding, and the state is home to some of India's best-known buildings. They reflect the state's long history, the oldest being the Buddhist caves and stupas (shrines) dating from the 5th century BC. You can see some ancient Buddhist caves, statues and stupas near Jhalawar (p240), and some other relics at Bairat (p203) near Alwar, including the remains of a Buddhist monastery. Most spectacular, however, are the Rajput fairy-tale forts and palaces, and the region's Jain temples.

### TEMPLES

Indian temples haven't changed much in shape from the earliest surviving examples. However, decoration and ornament have morphed according to fashion, and as building techniques have developed, temples have sometimes become larger and grander.

Discover more about India's diverse temple architecture (and other temple-related information) at Temple Net (www.templenet.com).

Rajasthan's earliest surviving temples date from the Gupta era – a time of relative peace and order around the 4th to the 6th centuries AD. Sheetaleshvara Temple (p240) at Jhalrapatan is a good example. Gupta temples tend to be harmonious, restrained and small.

In the 8th and 9th centuries, temple architecture developed, and buildings from this time feature stunning sculptural work, such as at Osiyan (p322) and Chittorgarh (p243). Temples usually taper into a single *sikhara* (spire), and there's often a sculpted *mandapa* (pillared pavilion before the inner sanctum); sometimes the main temple is surrounded by a series of small and finely sculpted shrines.

The Dilwara complex (p272) at Mt Abu, dates from the 11th century, and has marble carving that reaches unsurpassable heights of virtuosity.

Solanki kings spent lavishly on architecture, and the five Kiradu Temples, west of Barmer, built between the 10th and 12th centuries, conform to the Solanki style, with intricate carving and plays on light and shade. Most inspiring is Someshvara Temple, which has a fine sculpted frieze and a multitiered spire. Vimal Vasahi at Mt Abu is also built in Solanki style.

Of the later temples, the 15th-century Jain temples at Ranakpur (p266), 60km from Udaipur, are the finest. In Jaisalmer there is another beautiful group of Jain temples, this time carved from soft, golden sandstone, but with similar frenzied ornament to the temples at Dilwara and Ranakpur.

### FORTS, PALACES & PUBLIC POMP

Rajasthani opulent secular architecture is as inspiring as its religious architecture, with rulers building ever more lavishly to show their status.

Sometimes the beauty was doubled by having the palace reflected in an artificial pool or tank (reservoir), as at Deeg (p197) and Alwar (p199). The apogee of Rajput building was from the 15th to the 18th centuries, which coincided with the time of Mughal power, and a time of relative calm for the Rajputs. In the later palaces, the Rajputs often borrowed architectural inspiration from the Mughals, for example, the *sheesh mahal* (mirror palace) is a Mughal innovation. Magnificent examples of Rajput architecture across the state include Amber Fort (p179) and the Hawa Mahal (p160) in Jaipur, and the City Palace (p252) in Udaipur.

At the end of the British era, a novel style emerged known as Indo-Saracenic, which blended Victorian and Indian elements into a highly wrought, frilly whole. Some striking buildings were produced in this style, including Albert Hall (p161) and Jai Mahal (now a hotel, p171) in Jaipur, Lalgarh Palace (p347) in Bikaner and Mayo College (p205) in Ajmer.

The well-photographed *Forts of India* by Virginia Fass provides lots of background information on India's grandest defences.

#### HAVELIS

Rajasthani merchants built ornately decorated residences called *havelis*, and commissioned masons and artists to ensure that they were constructed and decorated in a manner befitting the owners' importance and prosperity. The Shekhawati district of northern Rajasthan is riddled with *havelis* that are covered with extraordinarily vibrant murals (see An Outdoor Gallery, p282). There are other beautiful *havelis* in Jaisalmer, constructed of sandstone, featuring the fine work of renowned local *silavats* (stonecarvers). The *haveli* was not just a building, but a structure built to contain a certain way of life, with interconnecting courtyards for different functions, and separate areas for men and women.

Fascinating and detailed, *The Royal Palaces of India*, by George Michell with photographs by Antonio Martinelli, provides a comprehensive guide, including some archaeological maps.

#### WELLS & TANKS

Given the importance of water here, it's unsurprising that the architecture of wells and reservoirs (often known as tanks or *sagars*, meaning 'lakes'), rival temples. The most impressive *baoris* (step-wells) in Rajasthan are Raniji-ki-Baori (p230) in Bundi and the extraordinary Chand Baori (p184) at Abhaneri (near Jaipur). For more information see The Step-wells of Rajasthan, p230.

#### CHHATRIS

*Chhatris* (cenotaphs) are a statewide architectural curiosity, built to commemorate maharajas, and, as is the case in the Shekhawati district, wealthy merchants such as the Poddars and Goenkas. In rare instances, *chhatris* also commemorate women, such as the Chhatri of Moosi Rani (p199) at Alwar. Although built in honour of Maharaja Bakhtawar Singh, his consort is also commemorated here as she earned herself a degree of immortality with the highest sacrifice – committing herself to the flames of her husband's funeral pyre in an act of *sati*.

*Chhatri* translates as 'umbrella', and you can see why: these structures comprise a central dome, supported by a series of pillars on a raised platform, with a sequence of small pavilions on the corners and sides.

## Painting

The fragments of paintings found on pottery shards recovered from Kalibangan show that the pictorial art tradition stretches back at least as far as Harappan times (2500–1700 BC).

Fresco painting, developed in Italy, arrived with the Mughals, and its finest examples can be seen in Shekhawati, with its multimuralled *havelis*. Other painted houses may be seen in tribal communities, whose *pithoras* (murals – white-painted simple designs on mud walls) are appealing naive designs that keep away evil spirits and bring luck.

### MINIATURE PAINTING

Rajasthan is famed for its miniatures – small-scale paintings crammed with delicate detail. In some towns it seems like you can barely move for them.

*Ateliers of the Rajput Courts,* by Raj K Tandan, contains beautiful loose-leaf colour plates of Rajasthani miniatures, part of the Lalit Kala Akademi series (portfolio No 39), ideal for framing and hanging on your wall.

Various schools of the art emerged in the 17th century. Although employing common themes, different regions had distinct styles. The most important regional schools of painting were those of Mewar (Udaipur), Marwar (encompassing Bikaner, Jaisalmer and Jodhpur), Amber (Jaipur; known as the Dhundhar school), Kishangarh (see p209) and Hadoti (divided into the Bundi and Kota schools; see The Mini Masterpieces of Kota & Bundi, p233).

In Mewar, royal patronage afforded a fertile environment for miniatures, and the area is famous for its paintings, produced for the various maharajas from the early 18th century, depicting court life, festivals, ceremonies, elephant fights and hunts.

The paintings of Jodhpur, belonging to the Marwar school, featured distinctive vivid colours and heroic, bewhiskered men accompanied by dainty maidens. The paintings of Bikaner were greatly influenced by the Mughals, as many master Mughal painters, known as Ustas, were encouraged to attend the Bikaner court.

For all you need to know about 7th- to 19th-century Mewar Art, get the lavishly illustrated *Arts & Artists of Rajasthan* by RK Vashistha.

The Rajasthani painters used colours derived from minerals, ochres and vegetables. The vibrant colours, enduring in miniatures and frescoes in some of the royal palaces, were derived from crushed semiprecious stones, while the gold and silver colouring is finely pounded pure gold and silver leaf. Many were painted on handmade paper, but also on ivory, marble, wood, cloth and leather.

### PORTRAIT & COURTLY PAINTING

Rajput mingling with the Mughals in the first half of the 17th century influenced the decorative arts, and in painting gave rise to a new form: the royal portrait. Throughout the subsequent evolution of Rajasthani painting, while the Rajputs borrowed from the Mughals and adapted their themes, their paintings remained much more idealised, abstract and stylised than those of their more naturalistic Mughal counterparts.

The 18th century saw painting become more secular. Paintings commonly depicted maharajas engaged in various typical activities, including hunting, fighting, chasing women, visiting the zenana (women's quarters), and attending the durbar (royal court). Mewar became the main centre for the production of these courtly themes.

For historical and visual background to Udaipur's Mewar paintings, read the *City Palace Museum Udaipur*, by Andrew Topsfield with photographs by Pankaj Shah.

A distinct difference between the paintings of the Rajputs and those of the Mughals was the use of colour. While the Mughals used muted colours to give a sense of shadow and depth, the Rajputs used bold primaries, which rendered their paintings two-dimensional and abstract. It's not unusual to see Rajasthani miniatures of this period in which the subjects appear to 'float', captured in limbo between the foreground and background.

The 19th century heralded a decline in portraiture in Rajasthan, perhaps reflecting the fading power of the maharajas as the British began to erode their dominance.

### CLOTH PAINTING

The town of Nathdwara, 48km from Udaipur, is the centre for *pichwai* paintings (see p264), religious works on home-spun cloth hung behind images of Krishna (who in Nathdwara is worshipped as Sri Nathji). The paintings were introduced by members of a Vaishnavite sect known as the Vallabh Sampradhya.

Another form of cloth painting is the *phad*, a painted scroll used by the nomadic Bhopas to illustrate the legends of the deified hero Pabuji. The storytelling Bhopa travels from village to village, dancing, singing and pointing to sections of the scroll to assist the narrative.

*Indian Art*, by Roy Craven, provides a sound overview of India's art history, tracing its early beginnings in the Indus Valley, to the development of various forms of Hindu, Islamic and Buddhist art.

## Sculpture & Stonework

Fine marble and sandstone from Rajasthan has bred a state of stonemasons and sculptors. Some of the more famous quarries include those at Makrana, from where the marble used in the Taj Mahal was mined. The impressive Dilwara Jain temples (p272) at Mt Abu also used marble from these mines, which was carried over the hills on elephant back.

The quarries of Dungarpur yield a soft stone used for carving images of the deities that when oiled becomes a rich, lustrous black. Due to their divine subject matter, sculptors producing these images are required to work according to guidelines laid down in the *Shilpa-Shashtra*, an ancient Hindu treatise on sculpture and architecture. In most cases, producing an image of a deity entails the work of two or more sculptors. An apprentice is responsible for carving the crude image, while the fine work is finished off by a master sculptor.

The finest sculptors of the day were commissioned to work on the beautiful temples of Rajasthan, and some of the best work can be seen in the Jain temples. Dilwara Temples at Mt Abu, the Jain temples within Jaisalmer Fort (p328), the ancient temples at Osiyan (p322) and the beautiful 15th-century Jain temples at Ranakpur feature the finest work.

## Literature

For a long time Rajasthan's storytelling tradition was solely oral. *Khuman Raso* (Songs of Khuman), the 9th-century tale of a Mewari hero, by Dalapat Vijaya, is the earliest known written work, and the epic *Prithviraj Raso* (Songs of Prithviraj), which celebrates the life of Maharaja Prithviraj Chauhan, was written by Chand Bardai in the medieval period. While Rajasthan has produced talented writers in the post-Independence period, few of their works have been translated into English.

Marwari is the dialect most commonly used by Rajasthani writers. A form of literary Rajasthani, known as Dingal, evolved in the 15th century for the communication of poetry and ballads telling of heroic exploits.

### MUMAL & MAHENDRA

It was love at first sight for Mahendra of Umarkot. Every night he raced to beautiful Princess Mumal's chamber, borne by a swift camel named Chekal. As Mahendra had to travel at night to visit Mumal in the distant village of Lodhruva, near Jaisalmer, he had little energy left to perform his husbandly duties to the satisfaction of his eight wives. Suspecting his nocturnal visits to the princess, the aggrieved wives ferociously beat Mahendra's trusty camel Chekal, and Mahendra had to use a less-competent camel, which subsequently lost its way.

In the meantime, Mumal's sister Sumal, of more homely appearance, decided to pay a visit to her sister. Sumal was in the habit of wearing men's clothes, and fell asleep next to Mumal. When he finally reached Mumal's apartment, Mahendra was confronted by the sight of her lying next to another man. He fled from the chamber, vowing never to lay eyes on her again, and bitterly cursing the inconstancy of women. Mumal waited every night for him, finally pining away with grief. When Mahendra heard of her death, and realised his misunderstanding, he went mad.

Popular literature is embodied in folk tales, songs and ballads related by bards. Subjects include heroic tales, religious legends and tragic love stories such as those of Dhola Maru (see The Legend of Dhola Maru, p287) and the princess Mumal (see Mumal & Mahendra, p53). The folk literature of Rajasthan, which glorifies heroism, chivalry, virtue and honourable death and sacrifice, has helped to purvey the image of the brave Rajput warrior.

As far as contemporary literature goes, *Raj*, by Gita Mehta, is the convincingly told story of a young Rajput princess contracted in marriage to an arrogant prince, and *Inside the Haveli*, by Rama Mehta, is about a girl from Mumbai who marries into a conservative family in Rajasthan. *The Storyteller*, by Adib Khan, set in the Delhi backstreets, centres on a storytelling outcast dwarf and delves into Delhi's dark side, peopled by pimps, pickpockets and *hijras*. *Delhi: a Novel*, by Khushwant Singh, is funny and irreverent, exploring Delhi's history through the experiences of several generations of inhabitants. These contemporary books are easy to find in English translations.

## Dance, Puppetry & Acrobatics

### DANCE

Each region of Rajasthan has its own dance specialities.

The *ghoomer* (pirouette) is performed by tribal women at festivals or weddings, and varies in communities and regions – in Udaipur, the dancers join a circle and carry sticks that they rhythmically knock together.

The Bhil tribal people perform a special dance, known as the *gir*, during the festival of Holi in February/March. It's performed by men only, who also beat sticks together.

If you combine these, you get a *gir-ghoomer*, one of the few dances men and women perform together. The women, in a small inner circle, are encompassed by the men in a larger circle, who determine the rhythm by beating sticks and striking drums.

Delve into India's vibrant performing arts scene – especially Indian classical dance – at Art India (www.artindia.net).

The *dandiya* forms part of the exuberant Holi celebrations: it's a speciality of Jodhpur district. Participants make a circle and beat together those sticks again – this time small ones. Also performed during Holi, in eastern Rajasthan, is the *gindar*, which is danced throughout the night. In an unusual show of tolerance, caste Hindus perform this dance with Dalits.

The *neja* is danced by the Minas of Kherwara and Dungarpur just after Holi. In this entertaining dance, a coconut is placed on a large pole, and while the men endeavour to dislodge it, the women rhythmically beat sticks and strike the men with whips.

A form of the classical *kathak* dance, more commonly associated with Lucknow in Uttar Pradesh, is performed in Jaipur. Traditionally it was only performed by men, but today it is danced by a mixed crowd, with the women dressed as men. *Kathak* interprets through dance the stories of Krishna and his consort Radha and entails dramatic facial expressions. You can learn the art of *kathak* in Jaipur (see p166).

Rajasthan's cultural heritage is examined in *Folklore of Rajasthan*, by DR Ahuja, with chapters on folk music and dance, customs and traditions, and myths and mythology.

In the *terahtal* (from the Hindi word for 'thirteen') women are covered in 13 cymbals, which they strike using other cymbals held in their hands. The clashing is accompanied by male singers and drummers. The women sometimes also hold a sword between their teeth or dance with lamps on their heads. It can be seen at the Ramdevra Festival (see Festivals in Western Rajasthan, p306).

A nomadic tribal people who are traditionally associated with snake charming, the Kalbelias often complement their performances with dances such as the *shankaria*, which portrays a romantic tale. The Siddha Jats of Bikaner are renowned for their spectacular fire dance, performed

**INDIAN CINEMA**

A visit to see a Bollywood blockbuster in a local cinema is an experience, best of all at Jaipur's Raj Mandir Cinema (p174), which fully deserves its name (King Temple).

India has the world's biggest film industry. Movies are the nation's cheapest and most popular form of entertainment – the formula of love, action, songs, long-lost relatives and wet saris is a fantastic form of escapism for a few hours. It's hard not to get swept away by the sheer ludicrousness of it all. On the surface it may seem like Rambo with a complex family history and a dash of romance, but the subtext is likely to be the Mahabharata, dharma and social justice.

There are no explicit sex scenes in Indian films made for the local market. Kissing creeps in occasionally but rarely on the mouth, and established actresses will not be kissed on screen. However, the sexual element is very much present, with lots of bumping, grinding, and heroines writhing in the rain.

Not all films are throwaway – in recent years some fabulous epics have received critical as well as popular acclaim, such as the cricket extravaganza *Lagaan*, *Devdas* (starring Shah Rukh Khan and former Miss World Aishwarya Rai), *Veer-Zaara* (directed by acclaimed director Yash Chopra, also starring Shah Rukh Khan) and *Swadesh* (yes, also starring Shah Rukh Khan, as most films seem to).

Watch out also for the quality films of Satyajit Ray *(The Apu Trilogy* and *Charulata)*, Mira Nair (*Salaam Bombay*, *Mississippi Masala*, *Kama Sutra*, *Monsoon Wedding* and *Bride & Prejudice* – the latter also stars Aishwarya Rai) and Deepa Mehta (*Earth* and *Fire* – see p42).

on hot coals that reputedly leave no burns. The *chari* dance – from Kishangarh – dices with danger too, as it involves dancing with a lighted pot on the head.

Good places to see traditional dance are Udaipur (see p262) and Chokhi Dhani (see p174).

Stay tuned with the latest Bollywood gossip by reading Bollywood World (www.bollywoodworld.com) and Stardust (www.stardustindia.com).

**PUPPETRY**

Traditional puppeteers, known as *kathputlis* or *putli*-wallahs, originally came from Nagaur. They emerged in the 19th century, travelling from village to village and relaying stories through narration, music and dance. The *kathputlis* are among the most impoverished of Rajasthan's traditional entertainers, and are often compelled to work as farm labourers.

The puppeteer is usually a man, but he is generally assisted in his performance by his wife, who plays the *dholak* (a small drum) and sings. Today there is less demand for the *kathputlis* – although the regions of Lunicha, Kuchaman and Khakholi, on the eastern fringes of the Great Thar Desert, still have a lively tradition of *kathputli* performers – so they have to go further afield in search of paying audiences, making long journeys throughout northern India in the winter months. Up to a dozen families may set out on these journeys, pitching tents at night and carrying all their possessions on their backs.

The Barefoot College (see p210) in Tilonia makes use of traditional puppetry to spread useful information on health, education and human rights.

Legendary 1970s film *Sholay* is a Bollywood classic, so successful it ran in Mumbai for five years. It's about two guys, one girl and dacoits on the loose, and stars Amitabh Bacchchan.

**ACROBATICS**

Like Rajasthan's puppeteers, its acrobats, who belong to the Nat community, are poor and often have to resort to begging. The itinerant Nats travel around the countryside performing acrobatic feats such as tightrope walking and balancing on long bamboo poles. There is still a substantial community of Nats in Chittorgarh district. You can see Nats at Chokhi Dhani (see p174) near Jaipur.

## Music

Like anywhere else in India, you'll hear Hindi pop songs crackling joyfully out of speakers all over the place. But in Rajasthan, folk music is also a vital, living part of traditional culture, engendering a spirit of identity and providing relief from the daily grind.

Rajasthani folk songs are commonly ballads that, like its literature, relate heroic deeds or love stories, and religious or devotional songs known as *bhajans* and *banis*. They tend to sound either desperately haunting and mournful or ebulliently upbeat. Percussion instruments such the *ektara* (a gourd with a skin stretched over it, which is beaten with a finger or a stick of bamboo) or the *dholak* (a small goatskin drum; one end is beaten by hand, the other with a stick) usually keep the beat. Various communities specialise in professional singing, such as the Dhadhis, the Dholis, the Mangamars and the Nats, among others. Musicians are often Muslim. Hindu prostitutes (Patars) and Muslim prostitutes (Kancharis) are renowned for their singing, as are the Muslim Mirasis, who specialise in folk songs called *mands* that almost approximate classical singing.

**'folk music is a vital, living part of traditional culture'**

Good places to see traditional folk musicians are at festivals, in Jaisalmer (where virtuosos often play outside the City Palace within the fort, p328), at Shilpgram (p254) in Udaipur, and at Chokhi Dhani (p174) outside Jaipur. Sometimes on camel safari you'll be treated to folk songs by your camel drivers. In Jaisalmer, the Artist's Hotel (p333) is run by a musicians union, and is a good place to hear concerts. You can buy a good selection of traditional music in Pushkar (see p217).

### PERCUSSION INSTRUMENTS

The most common village instrument is the *dhol* (drum), with a smaller version, the *dholak*, which is one of the most common instruments of northern India.

*Matas* are played in pairs by two musicians. Adapted from the kitchen, the *mata* is an earthenware pot with a skin stretched over the opening. The *chara* is another earthenware pot with an open mouth into which the musician sometimes blows, creating a deep, resonant, booming sound.

The *naupat* is played during marriage ceremonies, and consists of two drums – a *nagada*, the male form of the drum, and the *jheel*, the female form. The *chang* is a large drum played generally by one, but sometimes two, musicians. It's often played during the festival of Holi. Another Holi favourite is the *duff*, a kind of tambourine.

The *nagada* (not to be confused with the male form of the *naupat*) consists of two different-sized drums played together, traditionally beaten during battles. The *khanzari* is a small drum encircled with brass or iron bells, played by Kalbelias. The famous tabla is a pair of drums, played by classical musicians throughout India – tabla lessons are offered in Udaipur (see p255), Pushkar (see p213) and Jaipur (see p166).

### STRINGED INSTRUMENTS

A common stringed instrument is the *sarangi*, and there are various types: the *sindhi sarangi* and the smaller *gujratan sarangi*, both played by Sarangiya Langas, Muslim singers. Another type is the *jogiya sarangi*, favoured by snake charmers from Barmer and Jodhpur.

The five-stringed *tandoora* is played by plucking the strings and beating the rhythm on the bowl of the instrument. It is often used to accompany the *terahtal* dance (see p54).

With four strings, the *tambura* provides a secondary melody, which gives musicians a constant reference point to follow.

The sitar is a classical instrument as opposed to a folk instrument. It dates from the 12th century and was introduced to India by the Muslims. You can learn the sitar in Udaipur (p255), Pushkar (p213) or Jaipur (p166).

#### WIND INSTRUMENTS

Rajasthani wind instruments include the *kariya*, a brass instrument once played in the royal courts and on the battlefield.

The *narh* is a four-holed flute made from a type of desert grass known as kangore, and was traditionally played by shepherds to pass the time on lonely vigils. Kangore was once obtained from Pakistan, but hostilities have made it hard to obtain and there are few Rajasthani *narh* players left.

Another type of wind instrument is the *satara*, consisting of two flutes played simultaneously. One flute has holes, the other doesn't and provides a steady drone. Popular with the Bhils and Meghwals, it's also played by shepherds.

One of the most well-known instruments of the desert is the *poongi* (also known as the *murli*), the traditional snake charmers' flute; the bulge in its centre is formed by a gourd. Reeds of different lengths produce different pitches.

Musafir is a group of singers, dancers, instrumentalists, fakirs, and Sapera snake charmers who play Indian folk – listen to their Romany Indian rhythms on the fabulous albums *Gypsies of Rajasthan* or *Dhola Maru*.

# Rajasthani Handicrafts

The most vivid impression that visitors to Rajasthan take away with them is that of colour: searingly bright tribal dress, bubble-gum pink turbans, lovingly painted trucks, and camels dressed to impress in a rainbow hotchpotch of bobbles and tassels.

The local people have a passion for decoration, and historically they have taken full advantage of their position on trade routes to learn new skills of artistry from other places. These are evident in the painted houses of Shekhawati in northern Rajasthan, in turbans, in the long skirts known as *ghagharas* worn by Rajasthani women, in their *odhnis* (or headscarves), right down to the brilliant embroidered details on their leather jootis (traditional pointy-toed leather shoes) – Rajasthanis celebrate life by dyeing and embellishing everything in their daily lives. Nowhere is this more apparent than in the lively markets and bazaars, where the skills of the artisans are on display. In a land characterised by desert wastelands and sandy monotone landscapes, the people of Rajasthan have created beauty amid the starkness, with the everyday dressed in a fanfare of colours that challenges the bleached, arid terrain.

To find out more, read *Arts & Crafts of Rajasthan*, edited by Aman Nath and Francis Wacziarg, a beautiful, informative and well-illustrated hardback.

India's handicrafts tradition is also fabulous because it is thriving. It's astonishing to see so much work accomplished by hand, when in so many countries products are homogenised through the use of machines.

## JEWELLERY

If you're a princely ruler, you need a lot of silver and gold ornaments, usually encrusted with precious and semiprecious gems. The patronage of princes helped crafts such as jewellerymaking and *meenakari* (enamelwork used on ornaments and jewellery; see opposite) to develop and thrive. In *Annals & Antiquities of Rajasthan*, Colonel Tod records that around 80kg of gold bangles and anklets were found on the bodies of the fallen after a siege of Chittorgarh (Chittor). Traditional Rajput finery combined with the influence of Mughal splendour to produce dazzling works of art.

Take a look at the extraordinary opulence of royal ornaments in *Maharajas' Jewels*, by Katherine Prior and John Anderson.

Like other decorative arts in India, jewellery is not purely aesthetic, but also symbolic – often used to mark various stages in life. For example, a child will have its ears pierced to mark its entry into the world, and a married woman will wear various symbols, such as toe rings.

### Gems

Jaipur is renowned as a gem-dealing centre, and has an entire artisans quarter dedicated to cutting and polishing precious stones using simple, unsophisticated machinery – fascinating to see. If you're going to buy, though, you need to know your gems. See p175 for more information.

*Gold, Silver and Bronze from Mughal India*, by Mark Zebrowski, is a stunning, highly illustrated reference book showing how Hindu and Muslim arts mingled in the exquisite metalwork of the period.

### Folk & Silver Jewellery

In even the poorest villages of Rajasthan, women, and often men, can be seen bedecked in elaborate silver folk jewellery – bracelets, rings, earrings, nose rings, toe rings, ankle bracelets, and pendants worn on the forehead and breast. The quality of the jewellery indicates the relative economic status of the wearer or for a woman, more accurately, of her husband – one woman may lug around ornaments weighing up to 5kg.

Very rarely are these objects of pure silver. Usually the silver is mixed with copper to make it more malleable, although it is still high grade –

generally above 90%. As well as wearing markers of various life stages, villagers and tribal groups of different regions can be identified by their ornaments, which also indicate the caste to which they belong.

Traditional chunky silver folk jewellery is sold by weight (by the gram) in the bazaars of towns and cities, and there is often a silversmiths quarter in the main market. Jaipur's silver jewellers ply their trade in Johari Bazaar where there is a mass of shops. Udaipur is another great place to buy silver jewellery. In Ajmer, you can buy other silver items such as cigarette boxes and pill boxes, and several jewellers sell old tribal adornments. Pushkar is another place lined with shops selling silver jewellery, much of it designed with Western tastes in mind.

Feast on a sumptuous exhibition of Mughal jewellery in the glorious illustrated catalogue *Treasure of the World* by Manuel Keane and Salam Kaoukj.

### Bangles

Bangles are another form of symbolic jewellery – it's thought to be inauspicious for women to have their wrists bare. The only women you may see barewristed are widows.

Rajasthan is renowned for lac (resin) bangles and bracelets. In Jaipur, Maniharon ka Rasta (p175) is the centre of the bangle trade – and you can also see these being made in Bundi. Karauli is known for its lacwork too.

The wooden item to receive the lacquer treatment is first rubbed with liquid clay, and then, when dry, the design is stencilled with the aid of charcoal. Liquid clay, applied with very fine brushes of squirrel hair, is then used to trace the design, which becomes raised with each successive layer. The surface is then coated with paint, and gold leaf applied.

Gold is thought to purify all it touches, and is not usually worn on the feet as it is considered a pure metal (though on the ankles is acceptable).

## MEENAKARI

It was the founder of Amber, Maharaja Man Singh I, who introduced the beautiful *meenakari* (enamelwork) to Rajasthan at the end of the 17th century. Man Singh enticed five master *meenakari* workers from Lahore to his royal court, and established a tradition of fine enamelwork that continues in Jaipur to this day.

The oldest extant example of *meenakari* work is the Jaipur Staff. It's 132cm long and comprises 33 segments of gold, each of which features exquisite enamelwork depicting floral and animal designs. The handle of the staff is solid jade. The maharaja bore this staff with him to Delhi when he was summoned to the royal court by Emperor Akbar.

Both silver and gold can be used as a base for *meenakari*. However, only a limited number of colours, including gold, blue, green and yellow,

Stacks of brilliant bangles adorn a woman's wrists

COREY WISE

can be adhered to silver, whereas all available colours can be applied to gold, making it the preferred medium of enamellers.

For a meticulous study of the social meaning of Indian clothing and ornament, with special focus on Rajasthan, turn to *Costumes, Textiles & Jewellery of India* by Vandana Bhandari.

Jaipur enamellers use the *champlevé* method, in which engravings are made on the object to be enamelled; these are then flooded with the enamel colour. Each colour has to be individually fired, so colours most resistant to heat are applied first, because they will be refired with the addition of each new colour. As a rule, white is the first colour applied, and red the last.

The final piece of art is the product of a succession of master artisans: the *sonar* (goldsmith); the *chattera*, who engraves the piece; and the *minakar* (enameller).

*Kundan* jewellery features precious gems on one side and *meenakari* work on the reverse, requiring the expertise of a *kundansaz*, who applies the gems.

The *meenakari* from Jaipur has particularly vibrant colour. The rich ruby red the *minakars* produce is highly prized. Rajasthan's capital is also by far the best place to pick up some *meenakari*, with much on sale in the Johari Bazaar (p175).

## LEATHERWORK

Leatherworking has a long history in Rajasthan. As working with leather is considered 'unclean', it's performed by the lowest caste in the Hindu hierarchy, the Sudras. Tanning is carried out by the Chamar caste. Cobblers belong to a caste known as Mochis. Leather shoes known as jootis *(mojdis)* are produced in Jodhpur and Jaipur, among other centres. Jootis often feature ornate embroidery *(kashida)* – in Jodhpur, the embroidery is applied directly to the leather, while in Jaipur it's usually worked on the velvet the shoes are covered in. Embroidery is always done by women. Other ornamentation includes fancy stitching on the uppers, and appliqué. Strangely to Westerners, there is no 'right' or 'left' foot: both shoes are identical but, due to the softness of the leather, eventually they conform to the shape of the wearer's foot. Jaipur is the best place to buy jootis, with prices ranging from Rs 50 to 700 per pair – try the marvellous Mojari (p176).

In Bikaner the inner camel hide is stretched and scraped until it is almost transparent, before being beaten into shape to form bottles, frames and lamp shades.

Alwar is known for its beautiful leather bookbindings, a craft which flourished under Maharaja Banni Singh in the early 19th century. One of the finest covers, for the famous copy of *Gulistan* (A Rose Garden) by Shekh Muslihud-din-Sadi, can be seen in the Alwar museum (p199). Bikaner is famous for its *usta* (gold-painted camel leather) products, especially *kopis* (water bottles). Some fine examples can be seen in Bikaner's Ganga Government Museum (p347), while trade is centred on Usta St.

## PAINTING

Miniature painting was another craft that flourished under princely patronage. Displaying religious and mythological subjects, as well as lots of courtly love, the delicate paintings were picked out in clear, bright colours. In the past the paints were mineral and vegetable colours, nowadays harsher synthetic pigments are used.

The subjects you see on sale are frequently copies of works seen in the region's palaces. Like many other crafts in Rajasthan, each area has its own distinctive style.

In Udaipur every other shop in the centre seems to be selling miniatures, while Jaipur and Kishangarh are other good places to buy.

The less-diminutive work of talented contemporary artists is also available in Jaipur – try the splendid Juneja Art Gallery (p175).

An intricate mural from a *haveli* in Bissau depicts an episode from the Ramayana
PRAMOD MISTRY

Shekhawati's painted *havelis* (traditional mansions) form an open-air art gallery, with beautiful work in a kaleidoscope of colour and styles. You can learn mural painting yourself in Jhunjhunu (p293).

## PAPERMAKING

The skill of papermaking is centred in Sanganer, near Jaipur, where you can visit several papermaking factories. Papermaking has been based here since the 18th century. Originally the artisans were based at the court in Amber, but water shortages meant they shifted to Sanganer. These factories use discarded rags to create paper, thus not chopping down any trees in the process. The thick, flexible paper is often decorated with petals, glitter or prints, and is on sale in Sanganer (p182). If you don't make it there, Udaipur (p262) is a centre for selling goods made from the paper, with beautiful items such as notebooks, writing paper and photo albums.

## POTTERY

According to tradition, the first potter was created by Shiva, who required a vessel for ceremonial purposes for his wedding to Sati. This potter was named Rudrapal, and it is from him that the potters' caste, known as the Kumbhars, are descended. Many potters today still take the name Rudrapal, in honour of their legendary forebear.

Of all the arts of Rajasthan, pottery has the longest lineage, with fragments of pottery recovered from Kalibangan dating from the Harappan era (around 2500 BC). Prior to the beginning of the 1st millennium, potters in the environs of present-day Bikaner were decorating red pottery with black designs.

Today, different regions of Rajasthan produce different types of pottery, the most famous of which is the blue pottery of Jaipur. Blue-glazed pottery originated in China and later passed to Persia, from where it was introduced to India by the Muslims. The blue-glazed work was first evident on tiles that adorned the palaces and cenotaphs of the Mughal rulers. Later the technique was applied to pottery.

In most centres the production of this highly glazed pottery declined during the era of the Mughal Emperor Aurangzeb. However, the tradition was revived in Jaipur in the mid-19th century and today can be seen all over the place.

A wide range of items is available, including bowls, plates, tiles, vases, incense burners, mugs, door knobs and ashtrays. The pieces are decorated

The Pink City's textiles, arts and crafts are covered in prize-winning *Jaipur: the Last Destination*, by Aman Nath with photographs by Samar Singh Jodha.

Jaipur's unique blue pottery isn't formed from clay, but from a paste made from crushed quartz.

with images representing legends, ornamental devices and floral motifs, and depictions of animals. They are then painted with a coat of cobalt or copper oxide. After receiving a final coat of glaze, they are baked in a kiln for up to three days. See p175 for information on where to buy – Sanganer is another good place to buy blue pottery, and in both Jaipur and Sanganer you can learn to paint similar ceramics yourself, see p166.

Most villages in Rajasthan have their own resident potter, who not only produces domestic vessels, but is required to produce clay images of the deities for ceremonial purposes. The most striking of these sacred images are produced in the village of Molela, north of Udaipur in southern Rajasthan. Here potters work with terracotta formed from clay and donkeys' dung, continuing a tradition that dates back to the Harappan era.

## TEXTILES

Rajasthan is renowned for its blazing textiles, riotously woven, dyed, printed and embroidered. Cotton cloth is produced by the Julaha (weaver) caste.

Textiles and clothes are on sale everywhere you look. Good places to buy are Jaipur, Udaipur, Pushkar and Jaisalmer – all handicraft centres that cater to the tourist trade, where you can buy traditional saris or Indo-Western clothes, or have clothes made for you by the ubiquitous local tailor. You can also seek out the specialist favourites, such as the Kota *doria* (gold) fabric from the village of Kaithoon near Kota (p233). This is woven in silk, cotton and pure gold thread to create exquisite, delicate saris. And where else would you get jodhpurs tailor-made for you but Jodhpur? Well, perhaps Jaipur, where there is a recommended jodhpur tailor (p176).

Rajasthan produces around 16 million kilograms of wool per year – around 40% of India's wool.

### Tie-Dyed Cloth

Of the dyeing processes, the method producing the most intricate and interesting result is that of *bandhani* (tie-dye). Parts of the fabric are knotted, so that when the fabric is dyed the knotted sections retain their original colour.

The intricate work of tying the cloth is the preserve of women and girls. Different patterns are created by different methods. In the *bandhani* form of tie-dye, a pale background is covered with large splotches. This effect is achieved by knotting the dyed cloth and then bleaching it, with the knotted sections retaining their colour. A worker in this form of tie-dye is known as a *bandhej*. The dominant colours used in *bandhani* are yellow, red, green and pink.

Another form of tie-dye, called *loharia* (which translates as 'ripples'), is striped diagonally and is used in saris and turbans. Diagonal patterns of dots are formed by the *jaaldar* and *beldar* processes. *Loharia* pieces are named according to the number of colours employed: for example, *panchrangi* featuring five colours (from *panch*, meaning 'five'); and *satrangi* (from *sāt*, meaning 'seven') featuring seven. The cloth is worn as turbans and saris.

About 10% of the population of Rajasthan are employed in the textile industry, and textiles are the state's main export.

*Ekdali* features small circles and squares; *shikari* employs animal and human motifs, which are drawn before the cloth is dyed. In *tikunthi*, circles and squares appear in groups of three; in *chaubasi*, they appear in groups of four; and in *satbandi*, in groups of seven.

One of the most intricate designs is produced when the cloth is first folded, and then pressed with wooden blocks embedded with nails, which causes raised impressions on the cloth. These raised points are then gathered up and tied, and the cloth dyed. The brilliant results are worn as *odhnis*. *Pomacha* and *shikari-bandhej odhnis* are also highly sought. The

**SHERLOCK THE BLOCK**

These days, printed fabrics are often produced by machine, a cheaper method that threatens the preservation of block printing. Machine prints are even designed to try to imitate the idiosyncrasies of work by hand, in order to fool undiscerning punters. However, it is quite easy to tell handwork from a machine print – look on the reverse side of the print. If it has been made by hand, you will be able to see the block marks at regular intervals. Slightly messy diagonals will run from the corners towards the centre of the piece. Machine prints will sometimes mimic these uneven lines, but the uniformity of colour, and neat print on the reverse side, make it quite simple to spot them as impostors.

former features lotus motifs against a white or pink background. A yellow background indicates that the wearer has recently given birth. If you want to get more detailed, red circles on a yellow background mean she's had a son. *Shikari-bandhej odhnis* are produced in Sikar, in the region of Shekhawati, and feature designs of birds and animals. You can buy tie-dyed cloth in most places in Rajasthan, particularly Jaipur, Udaipur, and Shekhawati. Jodhpur's Handloom House (p316) has a particularly good selection of fixed-price *bandhani*. In Nawalgarh in Shekhawati you can even learn to do it yourself (see p286).

Three metres of cloth may be stamped more than 1000 times to create a colourful design.

## Printed Cloth

There are two forms of printing – block printing, and reverse or resist printing. In block printing, wooden blocks known as *buntis* or *chhapas*, on which incisions form the basic design, are dipped in dye and applied directly to the cloth. In the second mode, resist printing (similar to batik), part of the cloth is covered with a dye-resistant substance such as wax, and the cloth is then dyed. The waxed sections retain their original colour, and the wax is washed off. These original-colour sections are then block printed.

Colour was first applied to cloth by hand, progressing to the use of twigs and brushes, and later developing into the use of carved blocks.

The village of Sanganer, near Jaipur, is famous for its block-printed fabric. The Sanganeri prints, generally featuring floral motifs, are exported around the world. Every day, thousands of metres of fabric can be seen drying in long swathes on the banks of the Saraswati River. Here you can learn traditional block printing yourself (see p166).

You can also see artisans at work in the village of Bagru, near Jaipur, which is also renowned for its block prints, featuring predominantly zigzag motifs. Another place where you can visit workshops is Barmer, in

Detail of a sequined wall hanging

RICHARD I'ANSON

western Rajasthan, which produces resist-printed cloth featuring geometric designs in blue and red on both sides, which is known as *ajrakh*. It is generally worn only by men as shawls and turbans. Jaisalmer specialises in resist printing, but it's a rarefied sport: only executed at night and in the winter months when it is cold enough.

Traditionally Muslim artisans carve the teak blocks for creating block prints, while Hindus print the cloth.

In Nathdwara, in southern Rajasthan, finely printed cloth depicting religious themes (particularly centred on the life of Sri Nathji, the presiding deity) was used to adorn temples, along with *pichwai* (religious paintings on homespun cloth). Today, the tradition continues with pilgrims buying these cloths as religious mementos.

## Dyes

Before the introduction of synthetic dyes, all colours were derived from natural sources such as vegetables, minerals and even insects. Yellow was derived from turmeric and buttermilk; green from banana leaves; orange from saffron and jasmine; black from iron rust; blue from the indigo plant; red from sugar cane and sunflowers; and purple from the kermes insect. Colours were either *pacca* (fast) or *kacha* (fleeting). Fast colours were generally more muted than fleeting colours, consisting of browns, blues and greens, while the vibrant yellows, oranges and pinks were generally *kacha* colours.

*Pichwai* is typical of Rajasthan, representing images of the Lord Krishna on a black base, and you can read about it in the *Artists of Nathadwara*, by Tryna Lyons, a detailed and beautifully illustrated study.

## Appliqué & Embroidery

Embroidery and appliqué usually takes place after the cloth has been printed or tie-dyed. During the period of the Mughals, embroidery workshops known as *kaarkhanas* were established to train artisans so that the royal families would have an abundant supply of richly embroidered

### SMART SHOPPING

Handicraft production is a large sector of the Rajasthani economy, and many people depend on it for their livelihoods. Unfortunately, some artisans are exploited by unscrupulous middlemen who underpay the producers and then sell their work to tourists at inflated prices. However, you can be sure you're putting your money to excellent use by shopping at cooperatives. These have been set up to protect and promote the income of day labourers and handicraft producers at a grass-roots level. For the customer, the quality and price of products on sale is superior to other shops and the prices are fixed so you don't have to haggle.

There are a few outlets in Rajasthan that are particularly concerned with promoting small producers – see the Shopping sections of the regional chapters for full details. In Jaipur, check out Mojari (p176), a fabulous shoe shop producing a wide range of shoes for export. It's a UN-supported project to help poor leatherworkers reach wider markets. Anokhi (p176) is another outlet in Jaipur well worth visiting. This clothing and textile manufacturer produces high-quality items and provides good conditions for its workers. At Ranthambhore National Park, in eastern Rajasthan, the Dastkar Craft Centre (p222) promotes handicrafts produced by low-caste women in local villages.

In Udaipur, you can shop at Sadhna (p262), the outlet for Seva Mandir, an NGO helping rural women since 1969 to support their families by selling good-quality textiles.

Another well-known outlet is the Urmul Trust's Abhivyakti shop (p350) in Bikaner. The trust provides health care and education to remote villages and sells high-quality crafts produced by local artisans through its shop.

Tilonia, near Kishangarh in eastern Rajasthan, is the home of the Barefoot College (p210), another grass-roots NGO that promotes self-reliance, such as the use of solar technology, in poor communities. The showroom offers excellent handicrafts at reasonable prices, with the profits going back to the artisans themselves.

cloth. Finely stitched tapestries were also executed for the royal courts, inspired by miniature paintings.

In Bikaner, designs using double stitching result in the pattern appearing on both sides of the cloth – for quality embroidery in Bikaner head to Abhivyakti (p350), which is run by the Urmul Trust. In Shekhawati, the Jat people embroider motifs of animals and birds on their *odhnis* and *ghagharas*. Chain stitch is employed against a bold background in Alwar district. Tiny mirrors are stitched into garments in Jaisalmer. Beautifully embroidered cloths are also produced for domestic livestock, and ornately bedecked camels are a wonderfully common sight at the Pushkar (see Pushkar Camel Fair, p212), Nagaur, Bikaner and Jaisalmer (see Festivals in Western Rajasthan, p306 for information about the last three fairs) fairs.

Appliqué work involves cut-out shapes of cloth being sewn onto a base fabric to create a pattern. This is often used in bedspreads and cushion covers, and again, you can find examples all over the place, particularly major centres such as Jaipur, Jaisalmer and Udaipur.

Wall hangings made from segments of intricately embroidered fabric (usually pieces of old clothing), some with mirrorwork, are popular buys. Pieces can range from small cushion-sized squares to bedspread-sized pieces. Prices range from a couple of hundred rupees up to several thousand. The best place to buy these is Jaisalmer, which has a splendid selection, but you can find them all over Rajasthan.

### Carpets & Weaving

Before the emergence of the Muslims in India, the tradition of carpet-making was unknown in the country. Floor coverings consisted of small mats, called *jajams*, on which only one person could sit. Carpet weaving took off in the 16th century under the patronage of the great Mughal Emperor Akbar, who commissioned the establishment of various carpet-weaving factories, including one at Jaipur.

There are around 62,000 weavers in Rajasthan, working away on around 33,000 looms.

In Jaipur pile carpets were produced under the tutorship of Persian weavers. Some of these carpets were enormous. Vast looms had to be constructed in order to produce carpets for the royal durbar halls. There is an exquisite collection of carpets both at the museum in the City Palace (p157), and at the Central Museum (p161), both in Jaipur.

In the 19th century, Maharaja Ram Singh II of Jaipur established a carpet factory at the Jaipur jail, and soon other jails introduced carpet-making units. Some of the most beautiful *dhurries* (flat cotton carpets) were produced by prisoners in jails – Bikaner jail is still well known for the excellence of its *dhurries*.

Following the demise of the princely states, both the quality and quantity of carpets declined without the patronage of the royal families. However, recent government training initiatives have seen the revival of this craft, and fine-quality carpets are being produced in Bikaner, Jodhpur, Jaipur, Kota and other centres. In the village of Salawas (p320), near Jodhpur, a cooperative of weavers sells high-quality *dhurries*. Medium-fine quality knotted carpets have 150 to 160 knots per square inch, and cost around Rs 3000 for a 1.3m x 2m carpet.

## WOODWORK

Given the paucity of wood in most parts of Rajasthan, it's unsurprising that stone sculpture is more prevalent than woodcarving. Nevertheless, there is a tradition of woodcarving that dates back many centuries. Unfortunately, few of the medieval pieces have survived – if they didn't disintegrate in Rajasthan's arid climate the termites got them.

A carved wood elephant from a *haveli* in Jaisalmer

FRANCES LINZEE GORDON

Shekhawati was an important centre for woodcarving, and here you can see the woodcarvers' talent in fantastically wrought doors, and door and window frames. Artisans in Shekhawati also produced *pidas* – low, folding chairs featuring decorative carving. Bikaner was also an important centre for woodcarving, known for its ornately carved doors and lintels, and particularly for latticed jalis (screen windows).

Wooden boxes featuring several layers of lacquer were popular in the 19th century, a craft that was probably introduced from Sindh.

The heads of puppets were usually carved from wood, and then painted with the requisite (ferocious, heroic or lovelorn) expression. Puppets are prevalently on sale in Jaipur, Jaisalmer and Udaipur.

Bassi, near Chittorgarh, is known for the production of wooden puppets and toys, particularly images of Gan and Gauri (Parvati), which feature in the Gangaur Festival, and the bright *kavads* – wonderful little mini temple/theatres, used by storytellers to relay the tales of the gods. You can buy these in Udaipur for around Rs 100, as well as brilliantly painted tiny Hindu gods, standing around 5cm high and costing about Rs 20 apiece.

Carved wooden horses, honouring the trusty steed of the deified hero, Ramdevji, are offered at his temple during the annual Ramdevji Festival when masses of artisans sell the little carvings. The woodcarvers of Barmer use sheesham and rohira wood. Rohira, known locally as 'Marwar teak' and possessing excellent qualities for carving, has now unfortunately almost vanished from the desert.

# Environment

## THE LAND

The Aravalli Range splits Rajasthan like a rugged, bony spine, running from the northeast to the southwest. These rolling mountains – at times lush and forested, at others bare and muscular – form a boundary between the Great Thar Desert to the west and the rich vegetation of the east. With an average height of 600m, in places the range soars to over 1050m; the highest point, Guru Shikhar (1721m), is near Mt Abu. It's thought to be the oldest mountain range in the world. A second hilly spur, the Vindhyas, splays around the southernmost regions of Rajasthan.

The state's sole perennial river is the wide, life-giving swell of the Chambal. Rising in Madhya Pradesh from the northern slopes of the Vindhyas, the river enters Rajasthan at Chaurasigarh and forms part of Rajasthan's eastern border with Madhya Pradesh.

The south is drained by the Mahi and Sabarmati Rivers; the Luni, which rises about 7km north of Ajmer in the Aravalli, is the only river in western Rajasthan. Seasonal and comparatively shallow, the Luni sometimes billows out to over 2km wide.

*Mammals of the Thar Desert*, by Ishwar Prakash, has detailed descriptions and field notes, plus line drawings.

The arid region in the west of the state is known as Marusthali or Marwar (the Land of Death), which gives some idea of the terrain. Sprawling from the Aravallis in the east to the Sulaiman Kirthar Range in the west is the Thar Desert, which covers almost three-quarters of the state. It's a barren, dry, inhospitable expanse – the eastern extension of the great Saharo-Tharian desert – forming 61% of the area covered by desert in India.

Low, rugged, barren slopes occasionally punctuate the parched plains. The region is also about 60% sand dunes, which are formed by the erosion of these low hills and from sand blown from Gujarat's vast desert, the Rann of Kutch.

It's hard to believe, but this desolate region was once covered by massive forests and populated by accompanyingly huge animals. In 1996 two amateur palaeontologists working in the Thar Desert discovered animal fossils, some 300 million years old, including dinosaurs and their ancestors. At the Akal Wood Fossil Park (p342), near Jaisalmer, you can visit the incredible remains of fossilised trees that are around 185 million years old. Plant fossils from 45 million years ago show that Rajasthan's metamorphosis into desert is relatively recent – and it's ongoing.

It's hard to make out where the desert ends and becomes semiarid. This latter, lusher area encompasses about 25% of the state, though lush may be overstating it: semiarid means more rock protrusions and a smattering of short watercourses. The semiarid zone nestles between the Aravallis and the Thar Desert, extending west from the Aravallis and encompassing the Ghaggar River Plain, parts of Shekhawati and the Luni River Basin.

Delhi lies on the vast flatlands of the Indo-Gangetic Plain, though the northernmost pimples of the Aravallis amount to the Ridge, which lies west of the city centre. The Yamuna River flows southwards along the eastern edge of the city. To the south, Agra lies on the banks of the Yamuna, in the neighbouring state of Uttar Pradesh.

## WILDLIFE

For a place with so much inhospitable terrain, Rajasthan has an incredible crowd of animals and birds; the stars are tigers and the Unesco-listed bird sanctuary at Keoladeo Ghana National Park (see p191).

## Animals

Arid-zone mammals have adapted to the lack of water in various resourceful ways. For example, some top up their fluids with insects that are composed of between 65% and 80% water, and water-bearing plants, while others retain water for longer periods. Faced with the incredible heat, many creatures burrow in the sand or venture out only at night – tricks travellers in the hot season may feel like emulating.

### ANTELOPES & GAZELLES

The Bishnoi believe they will be reincarnated as deer.

Scarce blackbuck antelopes, with their long spiralling horns, are most common around Jodhpur, where they are protected by local Bishnoi tribes (see Village Activists, p319). Bishnoi conservation has also helped the chinkaras (Indian gazelles). These delicate little creatures (they're only around 1m tall) are very fast and found in small herds.

Also to be seen is the extraordinary nilgai, which is seemingly half horse and half cow. It's a large, stocky animal whose front legs are longer than its rear legs, giving it an ungainly, sloping stance. Nilgai hang around open plains (except in the extreme west) and in the Aravalli foothills.

### CAT FAMILY

*The Tiger's Destiny*, by Valmik Thapar, with photographs by Fateh Singh Rathore, is all about the besieged tigers of Ranthambhore National Park.

Tigers were once found along the length of the Aravallis. However, royal hunting parties, poachers and habitat destruction have decimated the population, and tigers are now only found in Ranthambhore and possibly Sariska National Parks (in 2005 the question was raised as to whether there were any tigers left in the latter; see p202).

The mainly nocturnal leopard, or panther, inhabits rocky declivities in the Aravallis, and parts of the Jaipur and Jodhpur districts.

### DOG FAMILY

Jackals are renowned for their unearthly howling, which enables them to find each other and form packs. Once common in Rajasthan, they were found close to villages, where they preyed on livestock. Habitat encroachment and hunting (for their skins) have reduced their numbers, though it's common to see them in Keoladeo Ghana, Ranthambhore and Sariska.

Desert-dwelling wolves protect themselves from the scorching heat by burrowing in sand dunes.

The wolf once roamed in large numbers in the desert, but farmers hunted it almost to the point of extinction as a pest. Wolves have begun to reappear over recent decades, due to concerted conservation efforts. The sanctuary at Kumbalgarh is known for its wolves.

The sandy-coloured desert fox is a subspecies of the red fox and was once prolific in the Thar Desert. As with wolves, the fox population has shrunk due to human endeavours, but it's quite common to spot a single animal flitting across a desert road.

### RODENTS

Desert gerbils are small, but they're big trouble: they descend on crops in vast numbers, causing untold damage. In the arid zone an incredible 12,000 to 15,000 burrows per hectare have been identified. Each burrow opening shifts 1kg of soil, which is carried by the high-velocity winds, contributing to soil erosion and dust storms.

### MONKEYS

Monkeys seem to be everywhere in Rajasthan. There are two common types: the red-faced and red-rumped rhesus and the brownish-grey, black-faced langur, with prominent eyebrows. Both types are keen on hanging around human settlements, where they can get easy pickings.

## BEARS

In forested regions you might be greeted by a sloth bear – a large creature covered in long black hair that feeds mostly on vegetation and insects but isn't averse to a bit of carrion. The bears are common around Mt Abu and elsewhere on the western slopes of the Aravalli Range.

When the desert gerbil senses danger, it thumps the earth with its hind feet; the entire colony then flees to the burrows.

## BIRD LIFE

The Aravalli forests harbour orioles, hornbills, kingfishers, swallows, parakeets, warblers, mynahs, robins, flycatchers, quails, doves, peacocks, barbets, bee-eaters, woodpeckers and drongos, among others. Birds of prey include numerous species of owls (great horned, dusky, brown fishing and collared scops, and spotted owlets), eagles (spotted and tawny), white-eyed buzzards, black-winged kites and shikras.

The wetlands in eastern Rajasthan include the internationally renowned Keoladeo Ghana National Park. Here, migratory species include spoonbills, herons, cormorants, storks, openbills, ibis and egrets. Wintering waterfowl include the common, marbled, falcated and Baikal teal; pintail, gadwall, shoveler, coot, wigeon, bar-headed and greylag geese; and common and brahminy pochards. Waders include snipe, sandpipers and plovers. Terrestrial species include the monogamous sarus, which inhabits the park year-round, and the beautiful demoiselle crane. Species resident throughout the year include moorhens, egrets, herons, storks and cormorants. Wetland birds of prey include many types of eagles (greater spotted, steppe, imperial, Spanish imperial and fishing), vultures (white-backed and scavenger) and owls (spotted, dusky horned and mottled wood). Other birds of prey include pallid and marsh harriers, sparrowhawks, kestrels and goshawks.

*Bharatpur: Bird Paradise*, by Martin Ewans, with photographs by Thakur Dalip Singh et al, lovingly details the prolific bird life of Keoladeo Ghana National Park.

Common birds of the grasslands include various species of lark, including the short-toed, crested, sky and crowned finch-lark. Quails, including grey, rain, common and bush, can also be seen, as can several types of shrike (grey, rufous-backed and bay-backed), mynahs, drongos and partridges. Migratory birds include the lesser florican, seen during the monsoon, and the houbara bustard, which winters at the grasslands. Birds of prey include falcons, eagles, hawks, kites, kestrels and harriers.

The Thar Desert also has a prolific variety of bird life. At the small village of Khichan, about 135km from Jodhpur, you can see vast flocks of demoiselle cranes descending on fields in the morning and evening from the end of August to the end of March. Other winter visitors to the desert include houbara bustards and common cranes. As water is scarce, water holes attract large flocks of imperial, spotted, pintail and Indian sandgrouse in the early mornings. Other desert dwellers include drongos, common and bush quail, blue-tailed and little green bee-eaters, and grey partridges. Desert birds of prey include eagles (steppe and tawny), buzzards (honey and long-legged), goshawks, peregrine falcons and kestrels. The most notable of the desert and dry grassland dwellers is the impressive great Indian bustard, which stands some 40cm high and can weigh up to 14kg.

## ENDANGERED SPECIES

Some of Rajasthan's wildlife is disappearing due to encroachment on its habitat, but poaching is also a serious problem.

It's estimated that during the 1990s more than 20 tigers were slaughtered at Ranthambhore National Park. After the skin is removed, the bones inevitably find their way to China, where they form the basis of 'tiger wine', believed to have healing properties. The penis is coveted for its alleged

### ANIMAL AID SOCIETY

Praveen and Poonam met Americans Erika and Jim in 2000. Talking about their distress at seeing so many street animals in pain, together they began to realise a dream – to take action and address the problems of destitute animals. In March 2003 they completed a small hospital in Chhota Hawala village, 3km northwest of Udaipur, which now treats around 200 animals per month.

The society's work includes emergency treatment – they have two ambulances, and can pick up and treat animals who have nowhere else to go. Other special projects include spaying street dogs (20 to 40 per week). There are an estimated 10,000 ownerless dogs in the Udaipur district, so this helps keep numbers under control.

They also deliver preventative medicine to village communities who don't have access to veterinary services, providing treatments such as deworming.

If you've noticed donkeys weighed down with mammoth loads, you'll understand the society's particular concern for these diminutive, overworked, long-suffering creatures. The hospital currently cares for 10 to 20 retired donkeys and runs education programmes to prevent ill-treatment. There are plans to open a donkey sanctuary in the future.

Another great project is the Plastic Bag Education Campaign. Cows let loose on the street to graze often end up chowing down on indigestible plastic. The plastic sits in the cow's stomach, causing the animal to believe itself full. This means it will end up starving to death. Street cows who've been operated on have been found to have as much as 36kg of plastic in their gut. The society aims to educate people about the dangers of this kind of waste, to prevent more cows dying a slow and agonising death.

Visitors are welcome at the **hospital** (🕙 10am-5pm), in Chota Hawala village, near Udaipur. The Animal Aid Society relies on donations and volunteer help, so if you can give either money or time you'll be supporting excellent work. You could give a straightforward gift or sponsor a donkey. The society's website gives details of the projects your money could help. Ideally, a volunteer should commit at least two weeks, working four or more hours a day, but if you have less time, the society is happy to make other arrangements. Volunteers don't have to be skilled – you can help by just giving animals the care and attention that can speed recovery. For more details, call ☎ 0294-3114963 or check the website at www.animalaidsociety.org.

aphrodisiac powers. It has been postulated that Sariska's tigers have been recently poached; see The Mysterious Case of the Elusive Tigers, p202.

National parks and sanctuaries are proving to be lucrative hunting grounds for poachers. Frequently, only main roads in parks are patrolled by (often poorly paid) guards, so poachers can trespass without fear of detection. In July 1992 Badia, one of Ranthambhore's more committed trackers, was murdered – allegedly by poachers.

Numbers of the great Indian bustard – the emblem of the state – have dwindled alarmingly due to hunting and because the bird's eggs are trampled by livestock. In Rajasthan, 131 bustards were recorded in 2001, 97 in 2002 and 85 in 2003. However, this is still one of India's largest populations.

Three types of vulture have become endangered over the past few years. Once common, they joined the endangered ranks after the population in South Asia fell by 95%. The cause was exposure to a veterinary drug, which the vultures absorbed while feeding from livestock carcasses. The reduction in vulture numbers has had knock-on ecological and health effects, as the birds once disposed of many carcasses, thus reducing risks of disease.

## Plants

Vegetation in the desert zone is, unsurprisingly, sparse and hardy. Only a limited range of grasses and very slow-growing thorny trees and shrubs can live here. The most common tree species are the ubiquitous khejri *(Prosopis cineraria)* and strains of acacia. Rajasthan also has some dry teak forest, dry mixed deciduous forest, bamboo brakes and subtropical hill forests. Forest stocks are dwindling, however, as inhabitants scour the landscape for fuel and fodder.

The hardy khejri, which is held sacred by the Bishnoi tribes of Jodhpur district (see Village Activists, p319), is drought resistant on account of its very deep roots. No part of the plant goes to waste: the thorny twigs are used to build barriers to keep sheep and goats away from crops, the leaves are dried and used for fodder, and the bean-shaped fruit can be eaten ripe or unripe. The latter, when cooked, is known as *sangri*. The wood is used to make furniture and the branches are burnt for fuel. The khejri twigs are used in the sacred fire that's lit during marriage ceremonies.

*The Flora of the Indian Desert*, by E Blatter and F Hallberg, was first published between 1918 and 1921. This arid-zone flora classic is a trainspotters' technical reference book, but has interesting notes on the traditional uses of Thar Desert plants.

Another arid-zone tree is rohira *(Tecoma undulata)*. Its pods form medicines that relieve abscesses, and its wood is used for furniture. The Central Arid Zone Research Institute (see p75) has had some success with the introduction of faster-growing exotic species to the desert, including various acacias.

## NATIONAL PARKS & WILDLIFE SANCTUARIES

Among its numerous reserves, Rajasthan has some world-renowned wildlife sanctuaries and national parks (see the table, p72). Some of these, such as Ranthambhore, Keoladeo and Sariska, were originally the hunting reserves of the maharajas. Others, such as the Desert National Park in western Rajasthan, have been established to protect and preserve the unique plants and animals found in the arid zone.

*A Guide to the Wildlife Parks of Rajasthan*, by Dr Suraj Ziddi, with photographs by Subhash Bhargava, is a comprehensive guide to Rajasthan's reserves.

## ENVIRONMENTAL ISSUES

> *Oont chhode Akaro, Bakri chhode Kangro*
> The camel consumes everything other than ak (a thorny shrub) but the goat devours even that, leaving only the pebbles
>
> *Marwari proverb*

Rajasthan's challenging climate and human needs are responsible for its major environmental problems of drought, desertification and overgrazing, while Delhi and Agra's big burdens are air and water pollution.

### Drought

Droughts are a recurrent spectre in Rajasthan, due to the unreliability of the monsoon. There have been 84 droughts in the last 100 years, and seven consecutive droughts between 1997 and 2004 – in such years crops don't have a chance.

These droughts highlight the urgent need for water-conservation strategies in the state, and many villages have been making impressive gains by reviving traditional water-harvesting techniques. However, the state still faces a huge water crisis. In western Rajasthan, even in good years, cultivation barely meets subsistence requirements, due to lack of water.

*The Radiant Raindrops of Rajasthan*, by Anupam Mishra, is an excellent look at the ingenious ways Rajasthanis have managed their meagre water supply over the generations. Find it at People Tree bookshop (p94) in Delhi.

Water scarcity has led to clashes between local people and conservationists. When it was suggested that water be diverted from Panchana dam to drought-ravaged Keoladeo Ghana National Park, local farmers threatened to commit suicide.

**MAJOR NATIONAL PARKS & WILDLIFE SANCTUARIES**

| National park/ wildlife sanctuary | Location | Features | Best time to visit |
|---|---|---|---|
| Darrah WS | southern Rajasthan, p237 | leopards, chinkaras, spotted deer, wild boar, wolves, sloth bears | Feb-May |
| Desert NP | western Rajasthan, p341 | great Indian bustards, blackbuck, nilgai, wolves, desert foxes, crested porcupines | Sep-Mar |
| Dhawa Doli WS | western Rajasthan, p320 | blackbuck, nilgai, partridges, desert foxes | Oct-Feb |
| Gajner WS | western Rajasthan, p351 | desert cats, desert foxes, chinkaras | Oct-Mar |
| Jaisamand WS | southern Rajasthan, p268 | crocodiles, leopards, chinkaras, beautiful *chhatris* (cenotaphs) | Nov-Jun |
| Keoladeo Ghana NP | eastern Rajasthan, p191 | 400 bird species, including migratory birds & waterbirds (wetlands) | Oct-Mar, Jul-Aug |
| Kumbalgarh WS | southern Rajasthan, p266 | wolves in packs of up to 40, chowsinghas, four-horned antelopes, leopards, horse riding | Oct-Jun |
| Mt Abu WS | southern Rajasthan, p277 | deciduous & subtropical forest, sloth bears, wild boar, sambars, leopards | Mar-Jun |
| National Chambal WS | southern Rajasthan, p237 | gharials, wolves, chinkaras, blackbuck, wild boar, caracals | Oct-Mar |
| Ranthambhore NP | eastern Rajasthan, p218 | tigers, chitals, leopards, nilgai, chinkaras, bird life, ancient fort | Oct-Apr |
| Sariska Tiger Reserve | eastern Rajasthan, p201 | tigers, leopards, chitals, chinkaras, bird life, fort, deserted city & temples | Nov-Jun |
| Sitamata WS | southern Rajasthan, p269 | ancient teak trees, deer, sambars, leopards, flying squirrels, wild boar | Mar-Jul |
| Tal Chhapar WS | northern Rajasthan, p303 | blackbuck, chinkaras, desert foxes, harriers, eagles, sparrowhawks | Sep-Mar |

### Desertification

Desertification is another ecological threat. This is partly a natural progression, as geological factors have given rise to warmer, drier climates, but it has been exacerbated by more and more humans and animals using fewer and fewer resources. The Thar Desert is the most densely populated desert in the world, with an average of 61 people per square kilometre.

An acute shortage of water, plus the problems of salinity, erosion, periodic droughts, overgrazing, overcultivation and overconsumption of scanty vegetation for fuel and timber all either contribute to or are a consequence of the continuing desertification of Rajasthan. As inhabitants scour the landscape for wood fuel, some species of vegetation face a severe threat. The roots of the phog plant *(Calligonum polygonoides)*, which is one of the few species found on sand dunes, are removed and used for fuel. Once common in Jodhpur district, phog has now completely disappeared. The plant rohira has all but disappeared from the arid zone. Rohira wood, known locally as Marwar teak, is highly prized for furniture construction, and was traditionally used in the carved architraves and window frames of *havelis* (traditional, ornately decorated mansions).

Although it's 10.4% of the total area of India, Rajasthan has only 1% of India's available water resources.

## Pollution

Deforestation and pollution are damaging many parts of Rajasthan, especially the southern region. Industrial waste has caused air, water and noise pollution; this is particularly noticeable around the industrial town of Kota. Marble mining has been particularly harmful. Some areas of Southern Rajasthan, including the region from Kota to Jhalawar, seem to be covered in a thin layer of marble dust, and around Rambagh, near Jaipur, the landscape is scarred by the (now closed) mines.

To address water pollution, the government has introduced policies that restrict building and development around lakes and rivers.

In Delhi, a shocking 10,000 people die of air pollution–related diseases every year. Road traffic is the chief cause of the problem, and it's hoped that recent measures, such as the development of the Metro and the conversion of all rickshaw engines to use compressed natural gas (CNG), may have an impact. The Yamuna river is also horrendously polluted. In Agra, concerns that air pollution was affecting the Taj Mahal led to the designation of a 4km traffic-free zone around the building in 1994. In 1999 polluting factories in the area were closed, and illegal buildings within 500m were torn down (unfortunately, no provision was made for those affected by these rulings). Though Agra is still hardly fragrant, these are all steps in the right direction.

### INDIRA GANDHI CANAL

The Indira Gandhi Canal was initiated in 1957 and is still incomplete. It includes an amazing 9709km of canals, and the main canal stretches 649km. Critics suggest that the massive project, which is connected with the Bhakra Dam in Punjab, was concerned more with economics than with ecological concerns and conservation.

The canal has opened up large tracts of the arid western region for cash crops, but these tracts are managed by wealthy landowners rather than the rural poor. Environmentalists say that the soil in the command areas has been destroyed through over-irrigation, and maintain that the canal has also been a key factor in the introduction of chemical fertilisers and pesticides to regions opened up to agriculture. Indigenous plants have suffered, further adding to the degeneration of the arid zone. Also, sections of the Indira Gandhi Canal are built on traditional grazing grounds, to which graziers are now denied access. It's been suggested that traditional local food crops, which require less irrigation, and *gochars* (traditional grazing grounds) could have been established instead.

The Indira Gandhi Canal has also been blamed for breeding malaria-carrying mosquitoes and for the extinction of the desert lizard, which couldn't cope with the increased moisture in its habitat.

## Plastic Waste

Almost everywhere in Rajasthan, Delhi and Agra, plastic bags and bottles clog drains, litter the city streets and deserts, and even stunt the growth of grass in parks. Of growing concern are the number of cows, elephants and other creatures that consume this plastic waste (see Animal Aid Society, p70). The antiplastic lobby estimates that about 72% of the plastics used in India is discarded within a week and only about 15% is actually recycled.

## Deforestation

There are regular problems between villagers and the authorities running Rajasthan's sanctuaries as they battle over resources. The dense forests that covered the Aravalli Range prior to Independence are thinning rapidly. Before Independence, villagers were forbidden to encroach on these forests, which were the hunting preserves of the nobility. However, following Independence, huge numbers of trees were felled to meet increasing timber, fuel and fodder requirements, and this trend is continuing.

The alarming disappearance of the Aravalli forests has provoked government intervention, and some areas are now closed periodically to enable the forest to regenerate. However, the closed regions are poorly policed, and locals are also entitled to take dry wood from the areas. There is simply not enough wood for everyone, so villagers ringbark healthy trees, returning later to remove the dead timber. Residents of the villages that surround Ranthambhore and Sariska regularly clash

### RESPONSIBLE TRAVEL

You may feel that as an individual you are helpless to prevent environmental destruction, but there's a lot you can do, with little effort.

#### Rubbish Retaliation

Tourism contributes to the massive rubbish problem in Indian cities. In Udaipur the large number of hotels around Lake Pichola has contributed to widespread pollution within and around the lake. Travellers can help by encouraging hotel management to dispose of rubbish in an environmentally friendly manner. You can put similar pressure on the camel-safari operators who dump rubbish in the desert during their tours.

#### Plastic Peril

Many once pristine regions are now vanishing under a sea of abandoned plastic mineral-water bottles. Travellers can make a significant difference by only buying products that use environmentally friendly packaging.

Discarded plastic bags are a very serious problem (see Animal Aid Society, p70). Avoid buying anything in plastic bags and bottles, and if you must buy plastic, reuse it. Other ways of reducing Rajasthan's plastic peril include buying tea in terracotta cups at train stations (or in your own cup) rather than plastic, bringing your own canteen and purifying water rather than buying it in plastic bottles (see p398), and buying soft drinks in (recyclable) glass bottles.

#### Waste Not, Want Not

Traditionally, Rajasthanis use ingenious methods of conserving every drop of water. In Jaisalmer the same water was used to bathe, wash clothes, wash the floor and water the garden. However, today Rajasthan has a water crisis. Across the state many people face a lack of drinking water, while in Jaisalmer increased water usage is causing the fort to crumble. There are a number of reasons for this, but the growing number of tourist facilities, particularly bathrooms, designed in line with Western standards is definitely one of them.

with the conservationists, as these villagers illegally take wood from the protected areas.

## Conservation

The best way to combat desertification is afforestation. Trees provide food, fodder, fuel and timber, and they also stabilise the earth and act as windbreaks, lessening the damage caused by sandstorms.

The first official recognition of the advancement of the Thar Desert and the alarming ramifications of this for the inhabitants of the arid zone occurred in 1951. As a result, in 1952 the Desert Afforestation Research Station was established in Jodhpur to conduct research into the problems of desertification (the research station became the Central Arid Zone Research Institute in 1959). This is the most important institute of its type in south Asia.

Forests cover just over 9% of Rajasthan, mostly east of the Aravallis.

The institute's endeavours include stabilising the shifting sand dunes, establishing silvipastoral (where trees are grown alongside shrubs that can be used for livestock feed) and fuel-wood plantations, planting windbreaks to reduce wind speed and subsequent erosion, rehabilitating degraded forests, and starting afforestation of barren hill slopes.

Some of the institute's work has been criticised by conservationists, who claim that massive attempts to irrigate and afforest the arid zone alter its fragile composition. An afforestation project along the Indira Gandhi Canal has come under attack, as the indigenous phog plant is

You can make a difference by cutting down on the amount of waste water you produce. Washing with a bucket uses around one-third of the water that's required for a shower. Similarly, using Indian rather than Western toilets reduces the amount of water flushed down the drain.

### Animal Welfare

India's ancient reverence for the natural world manifests itself in myths, beliefs and cults that are an intrinsic part of the cultural fabric. But in a country where millions live below the poverty line, survival often comes before sentiment.

The World Society for the Protection of Animals (WSPA) works to raise awareness of cases of cruelty and exploitation. One campaign focuses on dancing bears. Cubs of endangered sloth bears are captured in the wild, and then their muzzles are pierced so lead rope can be threaded through the hole, and their teeth are pulled out. The bears' nomadic handlers ply tourist traps in Agra and Jaipur. According to the WWF, around 70,000 snakes (including the endangered king cobra) perish annually due to the dreadful living conditions they experience in captivity.

If you're concerned about the welfare of animals, don't take an interest in snake charming, bear dancing, photographic monkeys and other sideshow acts that exploit animals – don't take their photographs or give money. You can also help by using modes of transport such as tongas (horse-drawn carriages), which enable the animals to earn a living without the back-breaking labour of carting heavy loads. Tongas are also much kinder to the environment than fossil fuel–powered contraptions. For information on elephant welfare, see The Amber Elephants, p181.

### Monumental Mission

A number of monuments in Rajasthan are suffering irreparable damage from tourism and government indifference. One of the most threatened is Jaisalmer Fort, which has been listed in the New York–based World Monuments Watch list of 100 endangered sites worldwide. See Golden City Blues, p328, for information on how you could help save the fort. Other monuments in dire need of protection include the painted *havelis* of Shekhawati. You can help to reverse the damage by volunteering in conservation and restoration efforts – see p375.

being uprooted and replaced with fast-growing non-native species such as *Eucalyptus hybrid* and *Acacia tortilis*. Such species upset the finely balanced desert ecosystem, are of little nutritional or practical use to villagers, and reduce traditional grazing grounds (animal husbandry is the economic staple and traditional livelihood for most of the inhabitants of the 11 desert districts of Rajasthan). Environmentalists argue that development should promote the generation and conservation of desert species that are finely attuned and adapted to the fragile environment, and provide food, fodder and fuel.

Several organisations work to regenerate the ecosystem and promote environmentally sustainable development. **Tarun Bharat Sangh** (Young India Organisation; ☎ 01465-225043; www.tarunbharatsangh.org; Tarun Ashram, Bhikampura, Via Thangazi, District Alwar 301022) is an acclaimed nongovernmental organisation (NGO) involved in water-harvesting projects. It constructs small dams to collect rainwater using traditional technology and local labour. Since 1974 it has set up more than 4000 structures.

The **Central Arid Zone Research Institute** (CAZRI; ☎ 029-2740584; Light Industrial Area, near ITI, Jodhpur 342003) focuses on the problems of desertification. It has a small pictorial museum with a photographic exhibition illustrating the institute's work.

**Ubeshwar Vikas Mandal** (chand67@bppl.net.in; 125 Priyadarshini Nagar Bedla Rd, Udaipur) is a small NGO studying and promoting sustainable agriculture, focusing on methods such as rainwater harvesting.

In Shekhawati, Ramesh Jangid has pioneered inspirational ecological measures at his resort, Apani Dhani, a unique project in Rajasthan. See p287 for more information.

# Food & Drink

Indian cuisine is as complex and diverse as the country itself. A myriad of delicious tastes, aromas and flavours awaits you, from the sweet deep-fry of a street-food stall, to the cardamom-scented tea on a train station, to the opulence of a centuries-old regal recipe. And food is not just food here. It's bound up with identity, ritual and tradition. Food marks celebrations and festivals, honours guests, unites and separates.

In Rajasthan, the cuisine is born of the climate. Fresh fruit and vegetables are rare commodities in the arid zones, but the state serves up an amazing and creative variety of regional dishes, making the best of cereals, pulses, spices and milk products. In the desert regions, water is so scarce that cooking developed using milk in its place. Local cuisine was also influenced by the area's warlike history – dishes that would last several days, could be eaten on the move and that didn't need heating came in handy.

Gorge yourself by reading about the extravagant royal recipes of Rajasthan in *Royal Indian Cookery* by Manju Shivraj Singh, the niece of the late Maharaja Bhawani Singh of Jaipur.

Rajasthan's regal feasts are the stuff of legend. It's said that the royal cooks went to incredible lengths to impress, and it was not unusual to have live birds fly out of the most spectacular dishes – you may be relieved to hear that this is no longer a common occurrence.

## STAPLES & SPECIALITIES

### Bread

A meal is not a meal in India unless it comes with roti (bread). Roti is a name used interchangeably with chapati to describe the most common variety, the irresistible unleavened bread, flopping hot onto your dish like a pancake, made with fine wholemeal flour and cooked on a *tawa* (hotplate). In Rajasthan you'll also find *sogra*, a millet chapati; *makki ki* roti, a thick cornmeal chapati; and *dhokla*, steamed maize flour that is formed into balls and cooked with green coriander, spinach and mint, and eaten with chutney. *Bhakri* is thick roti made from barley, millet or corn, eaten by working-class Rajasthanis with pounded garlic, red chilli and raw onions (to avoid sunstroke). This may not be the snack to eat before a first date.

On average, Indians eat almost 2kg of rice a week.

A *purat* roti is a type of Rajasthani filo pastry. The roti is repeatedly coated with oil and folded into a delicious, light and fluffy bread, from which you pull delicious strips to dabble in your sauce.

*Puri* is a delicious North Indian snack of deep-fried wholemeal dough that puffs up like a soft, crispy balloon, to be eaten fresh and hot. Kachori is similar, but the dough is pepped up with corn or dhal. Flaky *paratha* is a soft, circular bread, deliciously substantial and mildly elastic, which makes for a delicious morning snack, and is often jazzed up with a stuffing of *paneer* (unfermented cheese), *aloo* (potato) or grated vegetables. True naan has to be cooked along the walls of a *tandoor* (oven). Laced with garlic, naan is difficult to resist; filled with *paneer*, impossible.

To find out more about the evolution of regional cuisines, check out the *Cuisines of India: the Art and Tradition of Regional Indian Cooking*, by Smita Chandra and Sandeev Chandra, which includes recipes.

### Dhal & Cereals

India unites in its love for dhal (lentils or pulses), with around 60 different pulses slipping onto plates across the nation. In Rajasthan, the dhal of choice is *urad*, lentils boiled in water then cooked with *garam* (hot) masala (mixed spices), red chillies, cumin seeds, salt, oil and fresh coriander to make a spicy, fragrant broth.

The state's signature dish is *bati* (baked balls of whole-meal flour). The balls are broken up by hand, soaked in ghee and mixed with a spicy dhal. In the villages, *bati* is prepared with cinnamon and nutmeg and boiled in water, with a dash of turmeric powder. The balls are then roasted until they turn brown and deep-fried in ghee. *Saadi bati* is a baked ball of wheat-flour paste. *Bafle bati* is steamed wheat-flour balls. *Cheelre* is a chapati made with gram (legume) powder paste. *Masala bati* is wheat balls stuffed with masala, peas and peanuts. The all-time classic is *bati* with *churma* (fried wholemeal flour balls pounded with sugar and nuts), making *dhal bati churma* – this was an ideal dish for life on the road.

A speciality of Jodhpur is *kabooli* Jodhpuri, made with meat, vegetables such as cauliflower, cabbage and peas, and fried gram paste balls. *Khichri* is a mix of cereals, including millet, which is added to meat dishes. *Dalia ki khichri* is wheat porridge mixed with masala, a little *gur* (jaggery, a sweetener made from kitul palm sap) and ghee. *Ghaat* is a corn porridge served with yogurt.

Salt is thought to bring good luck, because it mixes well with everything. To renew a broken friendship, people should eat salt together.

*Besan* (gram or chickpea flour) is a staple, and is used to make pakora (fritters), *sev* (savoury nibbles) and other salted snacks generally known as *farsan*. *Besan* also makes *gate ki sabzi* (or *besan gate*) – spiced *besan* dough rolled into snakes, steamed and cooked in spicy gravy to create a delicious, if weighty, dish.

## Meat

The Brahmins and traders in Rajasthan stick mainly to a vegetarian diet, but the Rajputs have a carnivorous history. When they ran out of people to fight, they went hunting: shikars (hunting expeditions) introduced a variety of game to the dinner table, including venison, quail, duck and wild boar, but these aren't found on the menu today. Goat (known as 'mutton' since the days of the British Raj), lamb and chicken are the mainstays; religious taboos make beef forbidden to Hindus and pork to Muslims.

For recipes online, go to www.indiaexpress.com/cooking, www.indiacurry.com and www.thokalath.com/cuisine.

In the deserts of Jaisalmer, Jodhpur and Bikaner, meats are cooked without water, using milk, curd, buttermilk and plenty of ghee. Cooked this way, they keep for days without refrigeration – another example of culinary practicality. For special occasions, some dishes are left to steep for a few days to intensify the flavours. *Murg ko khaato* (chicken cooked in a curd gravy), *achar murg* (pickled chicken), *kacher maas* (dry lamb cooked in spices), *lal maas* (red meat) and *soor santh ro sohito* (pork with millet dumplings) are classic Rajasthani-desert dishes.

*Safed maas* (white meat) is another great regional delicacy. The secret is in the exotic, delectable gravy of onion, ginger, garlic paste, salt, pepper, cashew-nut paste and cardamom. Chunks of mutton (with bones) are cooked in this gravy, and fresh cream is added just before serving.

Monisha Bharadwaj's *The Indian Kitchen* is an excellent introduction to Indian staples and how to identify and store them, as well as 200 simple recipes.

*Maas ka sule*, a Rajput favourite, is a dry dish that can be made from partridge, wild boar, chicken, mutton or fish. Chunks of meat are marinated in a paste of turmeric powder, coriander powder, ginger and garlic paste, salt, red-chilli powder, mustard oil and yogurt. The chunks are cooked on skewers in a *tandoor*, then glazed with melted butter and a tangy moreish masala.

## Fruit & Vegetables

Vegetables are served at every main meal, and *sabzi* (vegetables) is a word recognised in every Indian language. They're generally cooked *sukhi* (dry) or *tari* (in a sauce); within these two categories they can be fried, roasted, curried, stuffed, mashed, combined, wrapped in batter and made into a pakora or *bhajia* (vegetable fritter), or made into a kebab or kofta.

Rajasthan's vegetable dishes have to be admired on inventiveness alone, but they are also deliciously tasty. *Govind gatta* is a lentil paste with dried fruit and nuts rolled into a sausage shape, sliced and deep-fried.

*Papad ki sabzi* is simply a pappadam with vegetables and *masala*, and *aloo mangori* is a ground lentil paste that is dried in the sun and then put in a curry with *aloo* – once rolled by hand, it is now often forced through a machine in the same way as macaroni. A common vegetarian snack is *aloo samosa*, pastry cones stuffed with spicy potato.

*Mogri* a type of desert bean, is made into *mogri mangori*, or a sweeter version called *methi mangori* – *methi* is the leaf of a green desert vegetable. *Kachri* is a type of desert fruit that is made into a chutney. *Dana methi* is made with *dana* (small pea-shaped vegetables) and *methi*, which are boiled and mixed with sugar, masala and dried fruit. *Cheelra ka saag* is a gram-flour paste chapati that is chopped up, fried and then added to a curry.

*Kair sangri* is served with a mango pickle. *Kair* is a small, round desert fruit, which grows on a prickly shrub and is a favourite of camels as well as humans. If you order something that looks like a plate of old dry sticks, these are *sangri* (dried wild desert beans). The seeds and beans are soaked overnight in water, boiled, and then fried in oil with various masalas, dried dates, red chillies, turmeric powder, shredded dried mango, salt, coriander and cumin seeds, and despite the dry-stick look are amazingly tender.

With developments in infrastructure, more vegetable dishes are now available in Rajasthan than during its warrior past. You'll find potatoes popularly cooked with various masalas, with other vegetables, mashed, spiced or fried for the street snack *aloo ki tikki*. Onions are fried with other vegetables, ground into a paste for cooking with meats, and used raw in relishes or as garnish. Heads of cauliflower are usually cooked dry on their own, with potatoes to make *aloo gobi*, or with other vegetables such as carrots and beans. Fresh green peas turn up stir-fried with other vegetables in *pulaos* (aromatic rice casseroles) and biryanis, and in one of North India's signature dishes, *mattar paneer* (peas and fresh cheese). Brinjal (eggplant; aubergine) is often sliced, deep-fried and served as a delicious side dish. Indians are also very fond of *saag* (a generic term for leafy greens), which can include mustard, spinach, fenugreek and white radish.

Fresh fruit is sold in mountains on street stalls at every turn: you'll find oranges (which are yellow-green), tangerines, custard apples, grapes, pink and white grapefruits, kumquats and sweet limes. Bananas are piled high, too, with many distinct varieties, rich in individual flavour. All these sun-ripened, fresh, seasonal fruits are a world away from the imported supermarket fodder that passes for fruit in the West. You'll also find fruit fashioned into a chutney or pickle, or a flavour in kulfi (ice cream) or other sweet treats.

There's no such thing as an Indian 'curry' – the term is an anglicisation of the Tamil word *kari* (black pepper), and was coined by bewildered Brits for any dish that included spices.

*The Anger of Aubergines: Stories of Women and Food*, by Bulbul Sharma, is an amusing culinary analysis of social relationships interspersed with mouthwatering recipes.

## Pickles, Chutneys & Relishes

You're in a pickle without a pickle: no Indian meal is complete without one, and if possible a couple of *chatnis* (chutneys) and relishes, too. A relish can be anything from a roughly chopped onion to a delicately crafted fusion of fruit, nuts and spices. The best known is *raita* (yogurt or curd combined with any number of vegetables or fruit, served chilled), which makes a delicious and refreshing counter to spicy meals. In Rajasthan it may be *bathua raita*, made with *bathua* leaves, which are boiled, rinsed and mixed with the yogurt.

Pickles and chutneys, known as *achars*, include *goonde achar*. *Goonde* is a green fruit that is boiled and mixed with mustard oil and masalas. *Kair achar* is a pickle with desert fruit as its base. *Lahsun achar* is an onion pickle. *Lal mirch* is a garlic-stuffed red chilli. *Kamrak ka achar* is a pickle made from *kamrak*, a type of desert vegetable with a pungent, sour taste.

## Dairy

Milk and milk products make a staggering contribution to Indian cuisine (hence the sanctity of the cow), and in Rajasthan they're even more important: *dahi* (curd) is served with most meals and is handy for countering heat; *paneer* is a godsend for the vegetarian majority; popular *lassi* (yogurt and iced-water drink) is just one in a host of nourishing sweet and savoury drinks; ghee (clarified butter) is the traditional and pure cooking medium (although not used nearly as much in India as in Indian restaurants abroad); and the best sweets are made with milk.

## Sweets & Desserts

Indians have a mind-boggling range of tooth-numbingly sweet *mithai* (sweets), made from concoctions of milk, ghee, nuts, sugar, sugar and more sugar. Rajasthani varieties include *badam ki barfi*, a type of almond fudge made from sugar, powdered milk, almonds and ghee. *Chakki* is *barfi* (milk-based fudge) made from gram flour, sugar and milk cake. Gram flour, sugar, cardamom, ghee and dried fruits combined make *churma*.

Each year, more than 13 tonnes of pure silver are converted into the edible foil that's added to sweets for decoration.

*Ghewar*, a Rajasthani favourite, is a paste of *urad* cereal that is crushed, deep-fried, and dipped in a sugar syrup flavoured with cardamom, cinnamon and cloves. It is served hot and topped with a thick layer of unsweetened cream and garnished with rose petals. Jaipur is famous for it.

*Moong dhal halwa* is a deliciously powdery dessert of finely ground *moong dhal* (mung beans), fried with ghee, sugar, cinnamon and cardamom powder until the mixture turns a light brown. Raisins, chopped cashew nuts and almonds are added before serving. Also look out for *firni*, a ball-shaped sweet made from *urad* cereal, deep-fried and then dipped in syrup. *Sooji halwa* is semolina pudding, *Meetha chaval* is sweet boiled rice, *lapsi* is jaggery with a wheat-flour porridge, and *maalpua* is a small chapati made from wheat flour, rolled in sugar and fried.

*Kheer* is India's favourite dessert. It's a delectable, fragrant rice pudding with a light, delicate flavour of cardamom, saffron, pistachios, flaked almonds, cashews or dried fruit. *Gulab jamun* are deep-fried balls of milk dough soaked in rose-flavoured syrup. If you get the chance to eat kulfi, do. It's a delicious, substantially firm-textured Indian ice cream made with reduced milk and flavoured with nuts, fruits and berries.

Rajputs traditionally swear allegiance, pledge honour and confirm friendship through the acceptance of a gift of *paan*.

There are also simple sweets, such as *jalebis* (orange-coloured whorls of fried batter dipped in syrup), that you will see all over the country – served hot they melt in the mouth and hang heavy on the conscience. *Aloo ki jalebi* is a variety with mashed potato, sugar, saffron and arrowroot. The mixture is made into spirals and fried in hot oil, then soaked in a warm sugar syrup.

### PAAN

Polish off your meal with *paan*, a sweet, spicy and fragrant mixture of betel nut (also called areca nut), lime paste, spices and condiments wrapped up in an edible *paan* leaf and eaten as a digestive and mouth freshener, and peddled by *paan*-wallahs. The betel nut is mildly narcotic and some aficionados eat it the same way heavy smokers consume cigarettes – if you take to it, bear in mind that over the years *paan* rots your teeth and turns them red and black.

There are two basic types: *mitha* (sweet) and *saadha* (with tobacco). Avoid the foul tobacco version, but a parcel of *mitha paan* is an excellent way to finish a satisfying meal. Pop the whole parcel in your mouth and chew slowly, letting the juices secrete around your gob. When you've chewed the flavour completely, spit the remains out (there's really no point in trying to be discreet).

## Thalis

Thalis are the traditional all-you-can-eat meals, which are a combination of veg (and sometimes nonveg) dishes, relishes, pappadams, yogurt, *puris* or chapatis, and rice. Thali is the name of the plate on which the meal is served. In southern Rajasthan, many restaurants serve lightly spiced and sweet Gujarati thalis – one of the most famous and most delicious regional varieties.

For a comprehensive travellers' guide to India's cuisine, see Lonely Planet's *World Food India*.

# DRINKS

## Nonalcoholic Drinks

### TEA & COFFEE

India runs on chai (tea). It's a unique brew, more milk than water, stewed for a long, long time and sugary enough to make your teeth curl. It's usually masala chai (mixed tea), which has a few spices added, such as ginger and cardamom pods, to give it a delicious tang. A glass of steaming sweet, milky, frothy chai is the perfect energiser and antidote to the heat and stress of Indian travel; the disembodied voice droning 'chai, chai garam' (hot tea) will become one of the most familiar and welcome sounds of your trip. At train stations it is often served in small clay pots, which you then smash on the ground when empty. Unfortunately, these days chai-wallahs are increasingly using plastic cups – far less environmentally friendly. Tea oils every meeting, business or otherwise, and punctuates the day.

If you don't like 20 sugars in your tea, in certain places (such as more upmarket hotels) you can ask for 'tray tea' and the tea, milk and sugar will be served separately.

It's becoming more common to be offered coffee in Rajasthan – though it's a challenge to distinguish it from tea, as it's often made from a somewhat similar recipe (lots of milk, instant coffee and heaps of sugar). Good coffee is also becoming more prevalent, however, with some cafés in tourist haunts serving real filter coffee.

Legend says that Buddha fell asleep during meditation, so he cut his eyelids off in penance. The lids grew into the tea plant, which, when brewed, banished sleep.

### OTHER DRINKS

*Masala soda* is the quintessentially Indian soft drink. Available at all drinks stalls, it's a freshly opened bottle of soda pepped-up with a lime, spices, salt and sugar. Orange juice is widely available, but the most popular street juices are made from sweet lemon and sugar cane, which are pressed in front of you by a mechanised wheel complete with jingling bells.

*Jal jeera* is the most therapeutic and refreshing indigenous drink. It's made with lime juice, cumin, mint and rock salt. It is sold in large earthenware pots by street vendors as well as in restaurants. *Faluda* is a rose-flavoured Muslim speciality made with milk, cream, nuts and strands of vermicelli. But the most popular of Indian drinks is a refreshing sweet or salty lassi (yogurt drink). Jodhpur is famous for its sweet *makhania* lassis, delicious thick, creamy lassis flavoured with saffron that are hearty enough to stand in for a meal. *Chach* and *kairi chach* are other Rajasthani specialities – the former is a thin salted lassi and the latter is unripe mango juice with water and salt, widely available in summer and allegedly a good remedy for sunstroke.

For information on water, see Drinking Water, p398.

## Alcoholic Drinks

There's a plethora of local and national brands of beer, but little to tell them apart as most are straightforward pilsners containing around 5% alcohol. Most travellers champion Kingfisher, which is available nationwide; Royal Challenge, Dansberg, Golden Eagle, London Pilsner

Bagpiper is India's largest-selling whisky, and the 14th most popular whisky in the world – even though it's only sold in India.

and Sandpiper are our favourite national brands. Drunk cold they're all palatable enough.

About a quarter of India's drinks market comprises Indian Made Foreign Liquors (IMFLs), made with a base of rectified spirit. Well-known brands taste vaguely familiar yet unpleasant. Whiskies Peter Scott, Antiquity and Solan No 1 – in that order – are the best of them.

In smart hotels, well-known foreign brands of beer and spirits are sometimes available, but are expensive. For information on drinking alcohol in restaurants and hotels, as well as the local alcohol laws, see below.

The website www.indianwine.com is a portal to websites about Indian wine – with notes on manufacturers, information on growing regions and more.

At the other end of the scale, arak is what the poor drink to get blotto, poignantly called *asha* (hope) in the north of India. It's a clear, distilled rice liquor that creeps up on you without warning. Only ever drink this from a bottle produced in a government-controlled distillery. *Never, ever* drink it otherwise – hundreds of people die or are blinded every year in India as a result of drinking arak produced in illicit stills. You can assume it contains methyl alcohol (wood alcohol).

Mahansar in Shekhawati produces a kind of 'wine' that tastes like Greek ouzo – it's homemade so proceed with caution.

## CELEBRATIONS

Although statewide and national festivals are religiously resonant, they are also occasions for a huge nosh up. Each festival has its own special dishes. Sweets are considered the most luxurious of foods and every occasion is celebrated by tucking into particular specialities. *Karanjis*, crescent-shaped flour parcels stuffed with sweet *khoya* (milk solids) and nuts are synonymous with Holi, the most boisterous Hindu festival, and it wouldn't be the same without *malpuas* (wheat pancakes dipped in syrup), *barfis* and *pedas* (multicoloured pieces of *khoya* and sugar). Diwali, the festival of lights, is the most widely celebrated national festival, and every area has specific Diwali sweets. As well as eating particular varieties, people offer special foods to the gods.

For more information on festivals and special events, see p363.

Ramadan is the Muslim month of fasting, when Muslims abstain from eating, smoking or drinking even water during daylight, replenishing themselves only before daybreak and at night. Each day's fast is broken with dates – the most auspicious food in Islam – followed by fruit and fruit juices. On the final day of Ramadan, Eid al-Fitr, an extravagant feast, celebrates the end of the fast with nonvegetarian biryanis and, yes, more sweets.

## WHERE TO EAT & DRINK

There are multitudes of restaurants (known locally as 'hotels'), and their signage identifies them as either 'veg', 'pure veg' or 'nonveg'. Most midrange restaurants serve one of two basic genres; South Indian (which means the vegetarian food of Tamil Nadu and Karnataka) and North Indian (which comprises Punjabi/Mughlai food). You'll also find the cuisines of neighbouring regions and states. Indians frequently migrate in search of work and these restaurants cater to the large communities seeking the familiar tastes of home. Rajasthan is a favourite holiday destination for affluent Gujaratis – from the famously foodie neighbouring state – which means places often specialise in Gujarati thalis. These include a selection of purely vegetarian, subtly flavoured dishes that are a delight to the palate.

*Dhabas* (wayside eateries) are oases to millions of truck drivers, bus passengers and anyone else going anywhere by road. The original *dhabas* dot the North Indian landscape, but you'll find versions of them throughout the country (in Delhi there are even mock versions, to give middle-class families the feel of the *dhaba* without the trek – complete with star-studded ceilings). The rough-and-ready but extremely tasty food served in these hospitable shacks has become a genre on its own known as '*dhaba* food'. In Rajasthan *dhabas* are known as *bhojanalyas*, from *bhojan* (food or meal) and *alya* (place). These simple eateries are great for travellers who are on a tight budget, but make sure you get food that has been freshly cooked, not just reheated.

Madhur Jaffrey is the West's foremost expert on Indian cookery; her books *Indian Cooking* and *A Taste of India* are bibles of subcontinental cuisine.

Look out for bakeries, sweet shops and juice bars in affluent city districts and the ubiquitous milk shop, which sells a wide range of dairy goodies.

In Rajasthan there are hundreds of restaurants catering to the tourist trade. Often more touristy places or large hotels will serve pale imitations of the local food, assuming that foreign palates can't manage anything else. To avoid this situation, head to the authentic joints recommended in this book, or tell your waiter not to spare the spice. Eating in Rajasthan is as much an adventure as the journey itself, and if you play it safe all the time you will miss out on rich experiences.

In 1999 the government of Rajasthan banned the sale of alcohol from the state's restaurants and 74 beer bars, effectively pushing the trade under the table. Officially, only hotels with a horrendously expensive liquor license can serve alcohol, but in practice many smaller eateries are willing to go and fetch you a bottle of beer from the nearest bottle shop. You'll pay for the privilege, though; a bottle of beer costs anything from Rs 60 to 200. Go to nonvegetarian restaurants if you want to imbibe with your meal, as very few vegetarian places will provide for you. Stringent licensing laws discourage drinking in restaurants, but some places that depend on the tourist rupee will covertly serve you beer in teapots and disguised glasses – but don't assume anything, at the risk of causing offence.

In India, search out these recommended (and inexpensive at Rs 189 each) cookbooks, all by Nita Mehta: *Mughlai Khaana*, *Simply Delicious Curries* and *The Best of Chicken & Paneer*.

## Quick Eats

### STREET FOOD

Whatever the time of day, people are boiling, frying, roasting, peeling, juicing, simmering, mixing or baking some class of food and drink to lure passers-by. Small operations usually have one special that they serve all day, while many other vendors have different dishes for breakfast, lunch and dinner. The fare varies as you venture between neighbourhoods, towns and regions; it can be as simple as puffed rice or peanuts roasted in hot sand, as unusual as a fried-egg sandwich or as complex as the riot of different flavours known as *chaat* (any snack foods seasoned with *chaat masala*).

Deep-fried fare is where it's at on the streets, and you'll find samosas (deep-fried pyramid-shaped pastries filled with spiced vegetables and sometimes meat), *aloo tikka* (mashed potato patties) and *bhajia* in varying degrees of spiciness, along with *puris* and kachoris. In most Muslim areas, you'll find kebabs, doused in smooth curds and wrapped in warm bread.

Peanuts in their shells, sold at many a street stall, are named *munfali*, meaning 'pass the time'.

### PLATFORM FOOD

One of the thrills of travelling by rail is the culinary circus that greets you at every station. Roving vendors accost arriving trains, yelling and scampering up and down the carriages; bananas, omelettes and nuts are offered through the grills on the windows; and platform chefs try to lure you from the train with the sizzle of fresh samosas. Frequent rail travellers know which station is famous for which food item: Agra is famous for *petha* (crystallised gourd).

### STREET FOOD DOS & DON'TS

There are obvious risks involved in eating on India's unsanitary streets, but as long as you use your common sense you should be all right. Remember, fortune favours the brave.

- Give yourself a few days to adjust to the conditions and build up slowly.
- You know the rule about following a crowd – if the locals are avoiding a particular vendor, you should too. Also take notice of the profile of the customers – any place frequented by women and families will be your safest bet.
- Check how and where the utensils are cleaned, and how and where the food is covered. If cooking is done in oil, check that it is clean and looks reasonably fresh. If the pots or surfaces are dirty, there are food scraps about or too many buzzing flies, beat a hasty retreat.
- Don't be put off when you select a deep-fried snack and the cook throws it back into the wok. It is common practice to partly cook the snacks first and then finish them off once they've been ordered. Frying them again will kill the germs.
- Avoid meat from the street.
- Sweet lemon and sugar-cane juicers are ubiquitous and can be dubious. It is usually safe if they press the juice in front of you, but never have what is stored in the jug.
- Don't be tempted by the presliced melon and other fruit, which keeps its luscious veneer with the regular dousing of water.

## VEGETARIANS & VEGANS

India produces some of the best vegetarian food you'll find anywhere on the planet. Vegetarian means without eggs, and 'pure vegetarian' reassures that there has been no contact with meat at all. In the holy town of Pushkar, only pure veg is served. However, while vegetarianism is widely understood and admired, veganism is hard to explain. Animal products like milk, butter and curds infuse most Indian dishes, and your first problem may be getting the cook to understand your requirements. Street food may be your best option because at least there you can see what the cook is adding.

The vegan website www.vegan.com offers advice for vegans travelling in India.

## EATING WITH KIDS

In such a family-centred society, children are welcomed everywhere and foreign children fêted, but don't expect special menus: Indian children are weaned on spicy food, so there's never any question of separate dishes for them. You may ask for a child's portion, but you won't get a discount. If your child is happy to experiment, there are many dishes that don't have a spice kick – roti, rice, dhal, curds, soups – ask if you're unsure. Chicken baked in a *tandoor*, with mild spices, is a good bet. Fresh fruit – sold on every street corner – is also very handy for keeping kids well fed.

As Rajasthan is such a popular tourist destination, many places serve Western-style food, such as veggie burgers, pizzas and some excellent pasta dishes, familiar sustenance that will satisfy small bellies.

For more on travelling with children, see p358.

A recommended veggie bible is *Lord Krishna's Cuisine: the Art of Indian Vegetarian Cooking*, by Yamuna Devi, which packs in 500 vegetarian dishes without a whiff of onion or garlic.

## HABITS & CUSTOMS

Three main meals daily is the norm with as many tiffin (snacks) as can be consumed without sabotaging the appetite. Breakfast is a light meal, usually of paratha. Lunch is substantial, usually the local version of the thali. Although a thali provides a great opportunity to explore regional variations, don't leave India until you've sampled the Gujarati version, available in many places in Rajasthan.

Nobody can wait until dinner before eating again, so a substantial tiffin is tucked into at around 5pm. Indians eat their evening meal relatively late, so restaurants are deserted before 9pm. Dinner will usually have fewer dishes than a thali lunch, but bigger portions. Whatever the meal time, dishes are rarely served in courses; rather they're served hot and together. Desserts as we know them don't feature much (sweet treats are eaten more as tiffin or to celebrate a special occasion); if there is a last course, it will usually be a piece of fresh fruit.

Even deities have their favourite dishes. Krishna likes milk products, and Ganesh is rarely seen without a bowl of *modak* (sweet rice-flour dumplings).

## Food & Religion

Most profoundly, food in India is integral to spiritual advancement. Regardless of creed, Indians share the belief that food is just as important for fine-tuning the spirit as it is for sustaining the body.

All Hindus avoid foods that are thought to inhibit physical and spiritual development, although there are few hard and fast rules. The taboo on eating beef is the most rigid restriction, yet some Hindus – especially middle-class Hindus – eat it in restaurants and in non-Hindu homes. Devout Hindus avoid alcohol and foods such as garlic and onions, which are thought to heat the blood and arouse passions. These items are universally banned from ashrams and temples and during most religious feasts. Some foods, such as dairy products, are considered innately pure and are eaten to cleanse the body, mind and spirit. Ayurveda, the ancient science of life, health and longevity, also heavily influences food customs.

Rice is used to symbolise purity and fertility in Hindu wedding ceremonies, and is often offered as *puja* (offerings) in temples.

Muslims have had a great influence on Indian food, and are responsible for most Indian meat dishes. Pork and alcohol are forbidden, and stimulants such as coffee and tea are avoided by the most devout. Halal is the term for all permitted foods, and haram for those prohibited. Fasting is considered an opportunity to earn the approval of Allah, to wipe the sin-slate clean and to understand the suffering of the poor.

Buddhists subscribe to the concept of ahimsa (the philosophy of nonviolence), and most Indian Buddhists are vegetarians, but to varying degrees: some eat fish, some abstain only from beef. Jainism's central tenet is ultra-vegetarianism, and rigid restrictions are in place to avoid even potential injury to any living creature – Jains abstain from eating vegetables that grow underground because of the potential to harm insects during cultivation. They also eat before nightfall, so that they have time to digest properly before sleeping.

Camellia Panjabi's *Great Curries of India* is an extremely popular cookbook with easy-to-follow recipes, sumptuous photographs and cultural insights.

India's Sikh, Christian and Parsi communities have few or no restrictions on what they can eat.

### EATING INDIAN-STYLE

Most Indians eat with their right hand using the tips of the fingers. *Never* eat with your left hand, which is reserved for unsavoury stuff, such as toilet duties. You can use your left for holding drinks and serving yourself from a communal bowl, but never use it to bring food to your mouth.

Before a meal in any home, or as soon as you walk into a restaurant, ask for the basin and wash your hands thoroughly. Immediately after your meal, go and wash again.

Once your meal is served, mix your food up with your fingers until it is thick and sticky. If you are having dhal and *sabzi*, only mix the dhal into your rice and have the *sabzi* in small scoops with each mouthful. If you are having fish or mutton curry, mix the gravy into your rice and take the flesh off the bones from the side of your plate.

Scoop up lumps of the mix and, with your knuckles facing the dish, use your thumb to shovel the food into your mouth. If you can, wait until you've finished eating before washing, but if the mess is putting you off your meal, discreetly wipe your hand on the bread.

## COOKING COURSES

Your visit is a fantastic opportunity to learn about the basics of Indian cooking and there are several places around where you can learn – many budget guesthouses offer informal cookery lessons. In Udaipur several places run cookery lessons (see p255), and you can also learn in Mt Abu at the Shri Ganesh Hotel (see p273). In Jhunjhunu in Shekhawati, Hotel Jamuna Resort (see p293) runs in-depth 10-day courses, with lessons coupled with field visits to different foodie families and establishments.

## EAT YOUR WORDS

### Useful Phrases

**Do you accept credit cards?**
*kyaa aap kredit kaard lete/letee haing?* (m/f)
**What would you recommend?**
*aap ke kyaal meng kyaa achchaa hogaa?*
**I'm (a) vegetarian.**
*maing ... hoong shaakaahaaree*

**I'd like the ..., please.**
*muje ... chaahiye*
**Please bring a/the ...**
*... laaiye*

| | |
|---|---|
| **bill** | *bil* |
| **fork** | *kaangtaa* |
| **glass** | *glaas* |
| **glass of wine** | *sharaab kee kaa glaas* |
| **knife** | *chaakoo* |
| **menu** | *menyoo* |
| **mineral water** | *minral vaatar* |
| **plate** | *plet* |
| **spoon** | *chammach* |

**I don't eat ...**
*maing ... naheeng kaataa/kaatee (m/f)*
**Could you prepare a meal without ...?**
*kyaa aap ... ke binaa kaanaa taiyaar kar sakte/saktee haing?* (m/f)

| | |
|---|---|
| **beef** | *gaay ke gosht* |
| **fish** | *machlee* |
| **meat stock** | *gosht ke staak* |
| **pork** | *suar ke gosht* |
| **poultry** | *murgee* |
| **red meat (goat)** | *bakree* |

**I'm allergic to ...**
*muje ... kee elarjee hai*

| | |
|---|---|
| **nuts** | *meve* |
| **seafood** | *machlee* |
| **shellfish** | *shelfish* |

### Food Glossary

**achar** – pickles and chutneys
**aloo tikka** – mashed potato patty, often filled with vegetables or meat
**appam** – South Indian rice pancake
**arak** – liquor distilled from coconut milk, potatoes or rice
**baigan** – eggplant; also known as brinjal

**barfi** – fudgelike sweet made from milk
**besan** – chickpea flour
**betel** – nut of the betel tree; chewed as a stimulant and digestive in paan; also called areca nut
**bhajia** – vegetable fritter
**bhang lassi** – blend of lassi and bhang (a derivative of marijuana)
**bhelpuri** – thin fried rounds of dough with rice, lentils, lemon juice, onions, herbs and chutney
**biryani** – fragrant steamed rice with meat or vegetables
**bonda** – mashed potato patty
**chaat** – snack
**chai** – tea
**channa** – spiced chickpeas
**chapati** – unleavened Indian bread
**chatni** – chutney
**cheiku** – small brown fruit that looks like a potato, but is sweet
**dahi** – curd
**dhal** – curried lentil dish; a staple food of India
**dhal makhani** – black lentils and red kidney beans with cream and butter
**dhansak** – Parsi dish; meat, usually chicken, with curried lentils and rice
**dosa** – South Indian dish; paper-thin lentil-flour pancake
**falooda** – rose-flavoured Muslim drink made with milk, cream, nuts and vermicelli
**faluda** – long chickpea-flour noodles
**farsan** – savoury nibbles
**ghee** – clarified butter
**gram** – legumes
**gulab jamun** – deep-fried balls of dough soaked in rose-flavoured syrup
**halwa** – soft sweetmeat made with vegetables, cereals, lentils, nuts and fruit
**idli** – South Indian spongy, round, fermented rice cake
**jaggery** – hard, brown sugarlike sweetener made from palm sap
**jalebi** – circular deep-fried orange- or red-coloured squiggly sweet filled with sugar syrup
**kheer** – rice pudding
**khichdi** – heavy rice dish sometimes made with lentils, potatoes and peanuts
**kormai** – currylike braised dish
**kulcha** – charcoal-baked bread
**kulfi** – flavoured (often with pistachio) ice confection, very similar to ice cream
**ladoo** – sweetmeat ball made with *gram* flour and semolina; also spelt as *ladu*
**lassi** – refreshing yogurt and iced-water drink
**masala dosa** – South Indian dish; large lentil-flour crepe (dosa) stuffed with potatoes and cooked with onions and curry leaves
**mattar paneer** – peas and unfermented cheese in gravy
**milk badam** – invigorating morning drink made with saffron and almonds
**mithai** – Indian sweets
**momo** – Tibetan fried or steamed dumpling stuffed with vegetables or meat
**naan** – flat bread
**pakora** – bite-sized piece of vegetable dipped in chickpea-flour batter and deep-fried
**palak paneer** – unfermented cheese in spinach gravy
**paneer** – unfermented cheese
**paratha** – bread made with *ghee* and cooked on a hotplate
**pilau** – rice cooked in stock and flavoured with spices; also spelt as 'pulau'
**puri** – flat dough that puffs up when deep-fried; also spelt as 'poori'
**raita** – mildly spiced yogurt, often containing shredded or diced cucumber, carrot, tomato or pineapple; served chilled
**rasam** – South Indian dish; thin tamarind-flavoured vegetable broth
**rasgulla** – sweet little balls of cream cheese flavoured with rose-water
**rogan josh** – fiery lamb curry
**roti** – bread

**saag** – leafy greens
**sambar** – South Indian dish; dhal with cubed vegetables and purée
**samosa** – deep fried pastry triangles filled with spiced vegetables and/or meat
**sonf** – aniseed seeds; used as a digestive – usually comes with the bill after a meal
**thali** – 'all-you-can-eat' meal; stainless steel or silver plate for meals
**thukpa** – Tibetan noodle soup
**tiffin** – snack; also refers to the meal container, which is often made of stainless steel
**tikka** – spiced, often marinated, chunks of chicken, *paneer*, lamb etc
**vindaloo** – Goan dish; fiery curry in a marinade of vinegar and garlic

# Delhi

JOHN HAY

# Delhi

Delhi, India's fascinating and sometimes frustrating capital, rewards those who refuse to allow its less-lovable elements to overshadow the plus points of this multidimensional metropolis. Broadly speaking, Delhi encapsulates two very different worlds, each presenting deliciously different experiences. Spacious and planned, New Delhi was built as the imperial capital by the British, while action-packed Old Delhi served as the capital of Islamic India. Visitors can effortlessly dip into both worlds, spending half the day soaking up history at the Red Fort, Jama Masjid and medieval-flavoured bazaars of Old Delhi, and the other half reviving themselves over a frothy cappuccino or ice-cold beer in one of central New Delhi's swanky restaurants or bars. Indeed, the hungry traveller will be happy to know that Delhi's global menus offer everything from rich Mughlai curries to crispy wood-fired pizzas.

As one of India's busiest international gateways, with fantastic connections to both Agra and Rajasthan, Delhi is your natural starting and finishing point. As well as its splendid sights, it's the ideal place to shop – it's chock-a-block with handicrafts from all over India.

As India's capital, it's a political and business hub and also home to a throng of semi-permanent foreigners, many of whom work at the numerous embassies based here. Travelling between here and Rajasthan feels like you are going back in time.

## HIGHLIGHTS

- The **Red Fort** (p98), an evocative testament to the Mughal emperors
- The capital's medley of museums and monuments: standouts include the **National Museum** (p104), **Humayun's Tomb** (p101) and the **Crafts Museum** (p105)
- **Jama Masjid** (p100), India's largest mosque, built by Shah Jahan
- Old Delhi's rambunctious **bazaars** (p123, the places to sniff spices, browse for bangles and gobble *jalebis*
- The **Qutb Minar** (p130), a soaring tower built to proclaim the arrival of Islam
- Exotic handicrafts from the **government and state emporiums** (p123) to redecorate your living room
- Delhi's glorious multicuisine **restaurants** (p115) – forget calorie counting and eat like a piggy

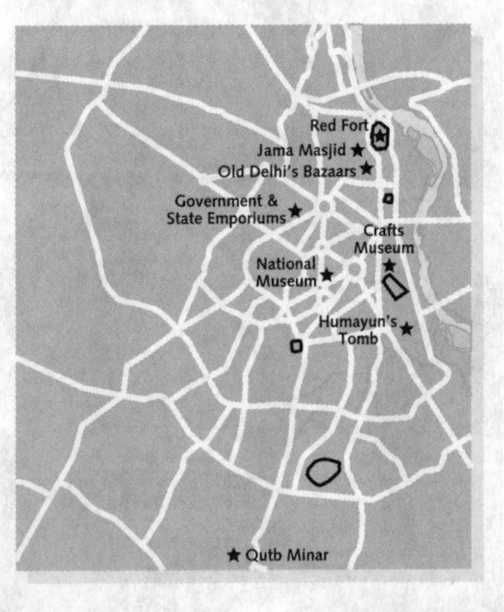


| TELEPHONE CODE: 011 | POPULATION: 12.8 million | AREA: 1483 sq km |
|---|---|---|

**FESTIVALS IN DELHI**

Some of Delhi's festival dates and venues are variable – for this year's details, contact the India Tourism Delhi office (p97).

Delhi celebrates Diwali (p365) and Dussehra (p365) with particular verve. During Dussehra, theatrical renditions of the Ramayana are held – for details and tickets (free) for those festivals visit India Tourism Delhi.

**Republic Day** (26 Jan) At Rajpath, incorporating a military parade.
**Beating of the Retreat** (29 Jan) The closing of the Republic Day celebrations is marked by the Beating of the Retreat, also entailing military pageantry. Tickets (from Rs 25) are essential for both events and are available at India Tourism Delhi.
**Delhi Flower Show** (Jan) This event spans three to four days.
**Mango Festival** (Jun) Running for several days at the Talkatora Gardens, this festival includes awesome mango exhibitions and mango-eating competitions.
**Independence Day** (15 Aug) On this day, when India celebrates its Independence from Britain in 1947, the prime minister addresses the nation from the Red Fort ramparts.
**Qutb Festival** (Oct/Nov) This festival runs for about a week at Qutb Minar, and features classical Indian music and dance performances.

## HISTORY

Delhi hasn't always been India's capital, but it has played a paramount role in Indian history. Many have invaded Delhi, including the Persian Emperor Nadir Shah, who sacked the city in 1739 and carted the Kohinoor Diamond (now part of the British royal family's crown jewels) and the famous Peacock Throne to Iran. The British captured Delhi in 1803, but during the Indian Uprising of 1857 it was a centre of resistance.

There have been at least eight cities founded around modern Delhi. The old saying that whoever establishes a new city at Delhi will lose it has come true every time – most recently for the British, who lasted here only 16 years.

The first four cities of Delhi were to the south, around the area where the Qutb Minar stands. The settlement of Indraprastha, which featured in the epic Mahabharata over 3000 years ago, is the earliest known incarnation of Delhi. It was centred near present-day Purana Qila. At the beginning of the 12th century, the last Hindu kingdom of Delhi was in the vicinity of the Qutb Minar. This was followed by Siri, built near present-day Hauz Khas in the 12th century by Ala-ud-din. The third incarnation was Tughlaqabad, now entirely in ruins. The fourth Delhi, Jahanpanah, dates from the 14th century, and it, too, was a Tughlaq creation. It stood near the Qutb Minar.

The fifth Delhi, Firozabad, was at Firoz Shah Kotla in present-day New Delhi. Its ruins include an Ashoka Pillar, moved from elsewhere, and traces of a mosque where Tinaru prayed during his attack on India.

Emperor Sher Shah created the sixth Delhi at Purana Qila, near India Gate in New Delhi. Emperor Shah Jahan constructed the seventh Delhi in the 17th century, thus shifting the Mughal capital from Agra; his Shahjahanabad roughly corresponds to Old Delhi today and is largely preserved.

Finally, the eighth Delhi, New Delhi, was built by the British. The moving of the capital of British India from Kolkata (Calcutta) – Bengal was championing Indian independence – to Delhi was announced in 1911 but construction was not finished, and the city officially inaugurated, until 1931. In 1947 it became the capital of modern India.

## ORIENTATION

Although Delhi is spread out, it's relatively easy to navigate. In Old Delhi there's the main Inter State Bus Terminal (ISBT) and, to the south, the New Delhi train station. Near this station, acting as a sort of buffer zone between the old and new cities, is Paharganj, packed with cheap accommodation.

New Delhi can be further subdivided into the business and residential areas around Connaught Pl (the city's core; see p107 for information on decoding the confusion of Connaught Pl) and the government areas around Rajpath to the south. Running south from Connaught Pl is Janpath, which has the tourist office, hotels and a shopping strip.

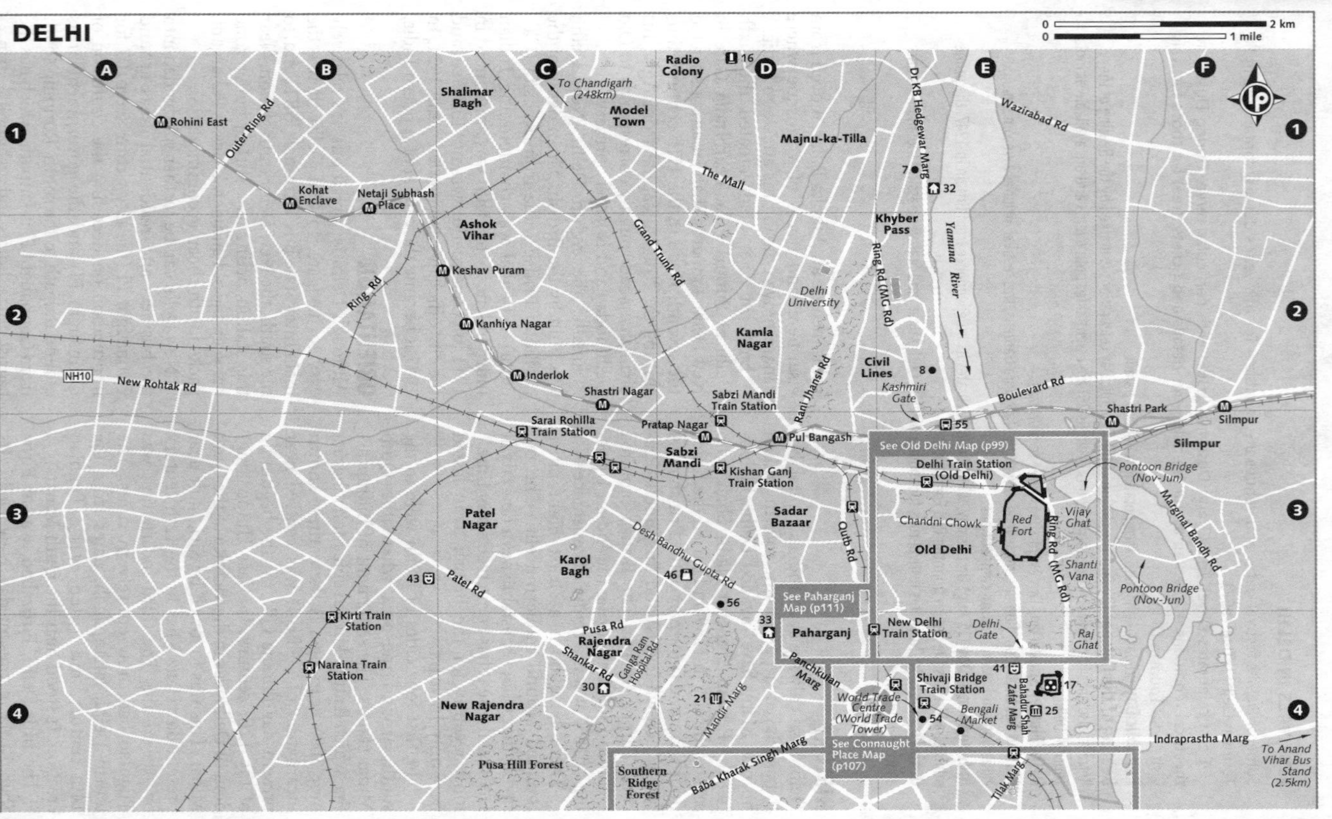
DELHI
0 2 km
0 1 mile
A
B
C
D
E
F
1
2
3
4
Rohini East
Outer Ring Rd
Kohat Enclave
Netaji Subhash Place
Shalimar Bagh
Ashok Vihar
Keshav Puram
Ring Rd
Kanhiya Nagar
Inderlok
Shastri Nagar
Sarai Rohilla Train Station
Pratap Nagar
Sabzi Mandi
Sabzi Mandi Train Station
Kishan Ganj Train Station
Pul Bangash
To Chandigarh (248km)
Model Town
Radio Colony
16
Grand Trunk Rd
The Mall
Majnu-ka-Tilla
Kamla Nagar
Delhi University
Rani Jhansi Rd
Khyber Pass
Ring Rd (MG Rd)
Civil Lines
Kashmiri Gate
8
7
Dr KB Hedgewar Marg
32
Wazirabad Rd
Yamuna River
55
Boulevard Rd
Shastri Park
Silmpur
Pontoon Bridge (Nov-Jun)
Marginal Bandh Rd
To Anand Vihar Bus Stand (2.5km)
Indraprastha Marg
See Old Delhi Map (p99)
Delhi Train Station (Old Delhi)
Chandni Chowk
Old Delhi
Red Fort
Vijay Ghat
Shanti Vana
Raj Ghat
Ring Rd (MG Rd)
Delhi Gate
New Delhi Train Station
Qutb Rd
Sadar Bazaar
See Paharganj Map (p111)
Paharganj
Panchkuian Marg
World Trade Centre (World Trade Tower)
See Connaught Place Map (p107)
Shivaji Bridge Train Station
Bengali Market
54
41
Bahadur Shah Zafar Marg
17
25
Tilak Marg
Baba Kharak Singh Marg
Mandir Marg
21
33
56
Desh Bandhu Gupta Rd
46
Ganga Ram Hospital Rd
Pusa Rd
Rajendra Nagar
Shankar Rd
30
Southern Ridge Forest
Karol Bagh
Patel Nagar
Patel Rd
43
New Rajendra Nagar
Pusa Hill Forest
Kirti Train Station
Naraina Train Station
New Rohtak Rd
NH10

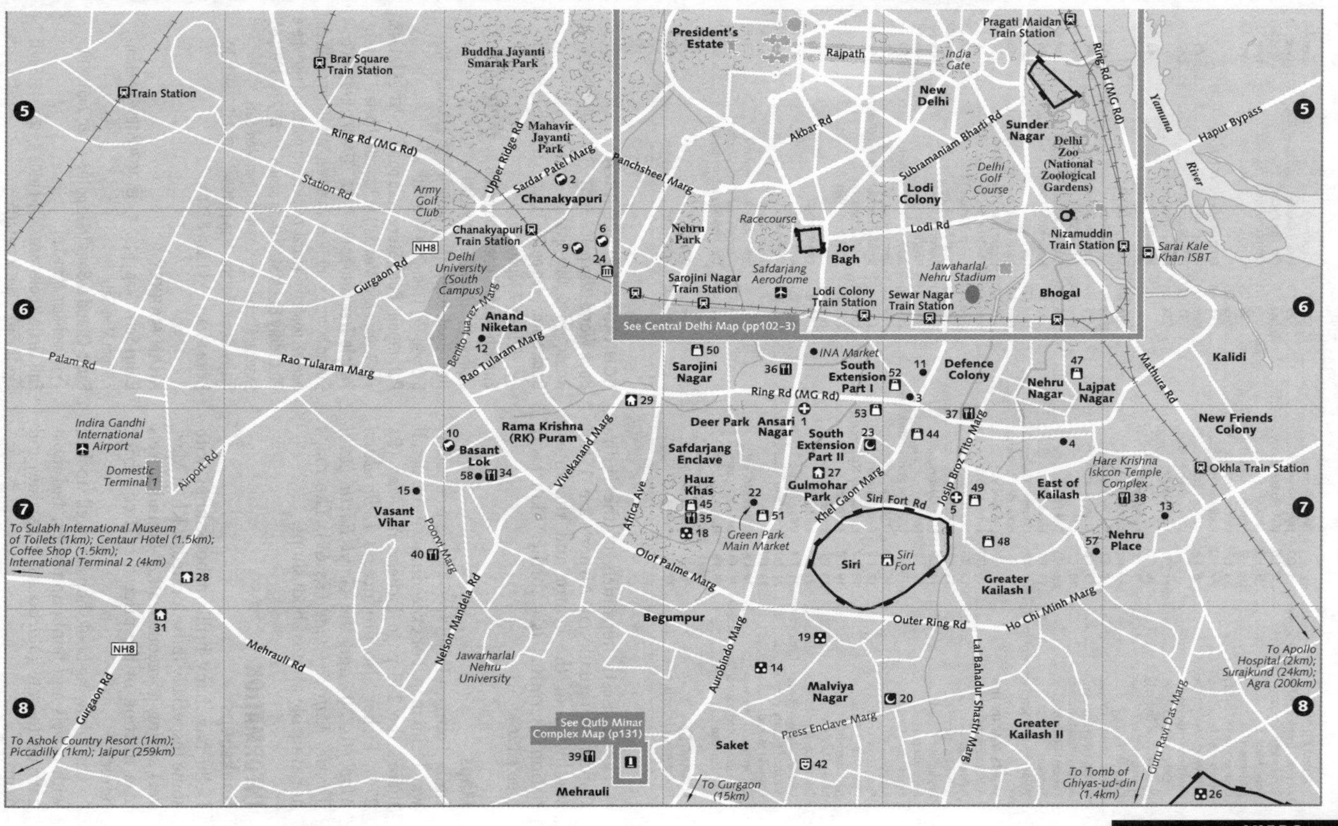
Train Station
Brar Square Train Station
Buddha Jayanti Smarak Park
Mahavir Jayanti Park
Ring Rd (MG Rd)
Upper Ridge Rd
Sardar Patel Marg
Station Rd
Army Golf Club
Chanakyapuri
Chanakyapuri Train Station
NH8
Delhi University (South Campus)
Gurgaon Rd
Anand Niketan
Benito Juarez Marg
Rao Tularam Marg
Palam Rd
President's Estate
Rajpath
India Gate
New Delhi
Pragati Maidan Train Station
Akbar Rd
Subramaniam Bharti Rd
Sunder Nagar
Delhi Zoo (National Zoological Gardens)
Delhi Golf Course
Lodi Colony
Panchsheel Marg
Nehru Park
Racecourse
Lodi Rd
Jor Bagh
Nizamuddin Train Station
Sarojini Nagar Train Station
Safdarjang Aerodrome
Lodi Colony Train Station
Sewar Nagar Train Station
Jawaharlal Nehru Stadium
Bhogal
See Central Delhi Map (pp102–3)
Yamuna River
Hapur Bypass
Sarai Kale Khan ISBT
Sarojini Nagar
INA Market
South Extension Part I
Defence Colony
Nehru Nagar
Lajpat Nagar
Mathura Rd
Kalidi
New Friends Colony
Ring Rd (MG Rd)
Deer Park
Ansari Nagar
South Extension Part II
Josip Broz Tito Marg
Hare Krishna Iskcon Temple Complex
Okhla Train Station
Indira Gandhi International Airport
Domestic Terminal 1
Airport Rd
Rama Krishna (RK) Puram
Vivekanand Marg
Basant Lok
Safdarjang Enclave
Hauz Khas
Gulmohar Park
Khel Gaon Marg
Siri Fort Rd
East of Kailash
Vasant Vihar
Poorvi Marg
Africa Ave
Green Park Main Market
Siri
Siri Fort
Nehru Place
Greater Kailash I
To Sulabh International Museum of Toilets (1km); Centaur Hotel (1.5km); Coffee Shop (1.5km); International Terminal 2 (4km)
Olof Palme Marg
Nelson Mandela Rd
Begumpur
Outer Ring Rd
Ho Chi Minh Marg
Mehrauli Rd
Aurobindo Marg
Lal Bahadur Shastri Marg
Jawaharlal Nehru University
Malviya Nagar
To Apollo Hospital (2km); Surajkund (24km); Agra (200km)
Guru Ravi Das Marg
See Qutb Minar Complex Map (p131)
Press Enclave Marg
Greater Kailash II
Saket
To Ashok Country Resort (1km); Piccadilly (1km); Jaipur (259km)
Mehrauli
To Gurgaon (15km)
To Tomb of Ghiyas-ud-din (1.4km)
DELHI

**INFORMATION**
All India Institute of Medical Sciences....1 D7
Bangladeshi Embassy....2 C5
Book Mark....3 E6
Citibank ATM....(see 34)
Concern India Foundation....4 E7
Dolma House....(see 32)
East West Medical Centre....5 E7
Foreigners' Regional Registration Office (FRRO)....(see 29)
New Zealand Embassy....6 C6
Nirmal Hriday (Missionaries of Charity)..7 E1
Osho World....(see 44)
Shishu Bhavan (Missionaries of Charity).8 E2
Singaporean Embassy....9 C6
South African Embassy....10 C7
Teksons Bookshop....(see 52)
Timeless....11 E6
Wildlife Protection Society of India....(see 48)

**SIGHTS & ACTIVITIES**
Ashoka Pillar....(see 17)
Ashtaang....12 C6
Bahai Temple....13 F7
Begumpur Masjid....14 D8
Beyond Looks....15 B7
Bijai Mandal....(see 14)
Coronation Durbar Site....16 D1
Firoz Shah Kotla....17 E4
Firoz Shah's Tomb....18 D7
Jahanpanah....19 D8
Khirki Masjid....20 E8
Lakmé Beauty Studio....(see 58)
Lakshmi Narayan Temple (Birla Mandir)21 D4
Meghna Beauty Parlour....22 D7
Moth-ki Masjid....23 D7
Rail Transport Museum....24 C6
Shankar's International Dolls Museum.25 E4
Tughlaqabad....26 F8

**SLEEPING**
Home Away From Home....27 D7
Hotel Tarra....28 A7
Hyatt Regency....29 C6
IDA House....(see 32)
Lhasa House....(see 32)
Master Guest House....30 C4
Peace House....(see 32)
Radisson Hotel....31 A8
White House....(see 32)
Wongdhen House....32 E1
Yatri House....33 D4

**EATING**
Arabian Nites....34 C7
Baujee ka Dhaba....(see 35)
Bistro Restaurant Complex....35 D7
Café....(see 29)
Dilli Haat....36 D6
Flavours....37 E7
Gourmet Gallery....(see 53)
Govinda's Sweets....(see 38)
Govinda's....38 F7
Great Kabab Factory....(see 31)
La Piazza....(see 29)
Mohalla....(see 35)
Naivedyam....(see 45)
NYC....(see 31)
O'Briens Irish Sandwich Bar....(see 58)
Olive Bar & Kitchen....39 C8
Park Baluchi....(see 45)
Punjabi by Nature....(see 34)
Roof-top....(see 35)
Sugar & Spice....(see 58)
Tamura....40 B7
Village Bistro....(see 35)
Yo! China....(see 34)

**DRINKING**
Barista (Branch)....(see 44)
Barista (Branch)....(see 58)
Barista (Branch)....(see 53)
Delhi's Devils....(see 53)
Djinns....(see 29)
Geoffrey's....(see 44)
Lizard Lounge....(see 53)
On The Rocks....(see 53)
Opus Lounge....(see 58)
Oxygen....(see 40)

**ENTERTAINMENT**
Dances of India....41 E4
PVR Anupam 4....42 D8
PVR Priya Cinema....(see 58)
Satyam Cineplex....43 B3

**SHOPPING**
Ansal Plaza....44 E7
Delite Jewellers....(see 52)
Ethnic Silver....(see 45)
Fab India....(see 49)
Hauz Khas Village....45 D7
Heritage....(see 52)
Karol Bagh Market....46 D3
Lajpat Nagar Central Market....47 E6
M-Block Market....48 E7
N-Block Market....49 E7
Next Shop....(see 49)
Planet M....(see 53)
Roopak's....(see 46)
Sarojini Nagar Market....50 D6
Soma (Branch)....51 D7
South Extension Market (Part I)....52 E6
South Extension Market (Part II)....53 D7

**TRANSPORT**
Air Canada....54 E4
Air Deccan....(see 57)
Inder Motors....(see 46)
Inter State Bus Terminal....55 E3
Jhandewalan Cycle Market....56 D3
Thai Airways International....57 E7

**OTHER**
Basant Lok....58 C7

The domestic terminals of the Indira Gandhi International Airport are 15km southwest of the centre and the international terminal is a further 8km away (see p126).

## Maps

India Tourism Delhi (p97) has a free foldaway Delhi map. For exceedingly more detail there's the 245-page *Eicher City Map* (Rs 270). Eicher also produces a *Delhi Road Map* (Rs 30) and the *Good Earth Delhi Tourist Map & Guide* (Rs 69). The maps are available at most bookshops.

# INFORMATION

## Bookshops

Delhi has many brilliant bookshops with some (especially those located at Khan Market) selling gorgeous leather-bound novels at a fraction of the price they'd cost back home.

The following bookshops are well stocked with novels and nonfiction titles, and most have up-to-date guidebooks, magazines and maps.

### CONNAUGHT PLACE AREA

**Book World** (Map pp106-7; ☎ 23320128; 7 Palika Bazaar; 10.30am-8pm)
**Bookworm** (Map pp106-7; ☎ 23322260; 29 B-Block; 10.15am-7.30pm)
**English Book Store** (Map pp106-7; ☎ 23415031; 17 L-Block; 10am-7pm Mon-Sat)
**New Book Depot** (Map pp106-7; ☎ 23320020; 18 B-Block; 11am-8pm Mon-Sat)
**Paramount Book Store** (Map pp106-7; ☎ 23321948; 9.30am-8pm Mon-Sat) At Janpath (Tibetan) Market.
**People Tree** (Map pp106-7; ☎ 23744877; Regal Bldg, Sansad Marg; 10.30am-7pm Mon-Sat) Stocks novels and cerebral nonfiction (social, political etc) not found elsewhere.
**Piccadilly Book Stall** (Map pp106-7; ☎ 23413993; 64 Shankar Market; 10am-7.30pm Mon-Sat)
**Rajiv Book House** (Map pp106-7; ☎ 23323692; 30 Palika Bazaar; 11am-8.30pm)

### KHAN MARKET

**Bahri Sons** (Map pp102-4; ☎ 24694610; 11am-7.30pm Mon-Sat)
**Faqir-Chand & Sons** (Map pp102-4; ☎ 24618810; 10am-8pm Mon-Sat)
**Full Circle Bookstore** (Map pp102-4; ☎ 24655641; 10am-7.30pm Mon-Sat)

#### SOUTH EXTENSION

**Book Mark** (Map pp92-4; ☎ 24693216; A2 Ring Rd, Part 1; 🕑 10.30am-7.30pm Tue-Sun) Just outside the market enclave, along the main road.

**Teksons Bookshop** (Map pp92-4; ☎ 24617030; Part 1; 🕑 10am-8pm Tue-Sun)

**Timeless** (Map pp92-4; ☎ 24693257; 46 Housing Society, South Extension Part 1; 🕑 10am-7pm) The beautifully presented Timeless specialises in quality coffee-table books and offers complimentary tea. It's tucked away in a back lane (ask for directions).

#### ELSEWHERE

**Osho World** (Map pp92-4; ☎ 26261616; Ansal Plaza, Khel Gaon Marg; 🕑 11am-8.30pm) Has books (and audio discourses) by and about Bhagwan Shree Rajneesh.

**Tibet House Book Corner** (Map pp102-4; ☎ 24602616; 1st fl, Tibet House, 1 Lodi Rd; 🕑 10am-1pm & 2-5.30pm Mon-Fri) Focuses on Tibetan and Buddhist titles; for spiritual sustenance get *Buddhist Peace Recipes* by Pushpesh Pant.

### Cultural Centres & Libraries

Cultural centres host periodic exhibitions and seminars, and dance, music and theatrical performances (telephone for current happenings).

**Alliance Française** (Map pp102-4; ☎ 51012091; 72 Lodi Estate)

**American Center** (Map pp106-7; ☎ 23316841; 24 Kasturba Gandhi Marg)

**British Council** (Map pp106-7; ☎ 23711401; 17 Kasturba Gandhi Marg)

**Delhi Public Library** (Map p99; ☎ 23962682; SP Mukherjee Marg)

**India International Centre** (Map pp102-4; ☎ 24619431; 40 Max Mueller Marg)

**Italian Institute of Culture** (Map pp102-4; ☎ 26871901; 50E Chandragupta Marg, Chanakyapuri)

**Max Mueller Bhavan** (Map pp102-4; ☎ 23329506; 3 Kasturba Gandhi Marg)

**Rabindra Bhavan** (Map pp102-4; Copernicus Marg) Contains three art academies: Sangeet Natak Akademi (☎ 23387248) for performing arts; Sahitya Akademi (☎ 23386626) for literature; Lalit Kala Akademi (☎ 23384634) for contemporary art.

**World Wide Fund for Nature (India)** (Map pp102-4; ☎ 24616532; 172-B Lodi Estate) Environmental library.

### Internet Access

There are surprisingly few Internet centres in Connaught Pl, but no dearth in other tourist hubs. Most charge Rs 5 to print a page and Rs 25 to scan or write a CD.

**Army Cyber Café** (Map p111; 1057 Main Bazaar, Paharganj; per 30min Rs 10; 🕑 9am-midnight)

**Cyber Graphics** (Map pp102-4; 66A Khan Market; per 30min Rs 25; 🕑 9.30am-8.30pm)

**Cyber Station** (Map p111; Main Bazaar, Paharganj; per 30min Rs 10; 🕑 7-1am) Next to Hotel Star Paradise.

**Dolma House** (Map pp92-4; Majnu-ka-Tilla; per 10/30/60min Rs 10/20/30; 🕑 9am-11.30pm)

#### DELHI IN...

**Two Days**

Step back in time at the exemplary **National Museum** (p104), then grab an autorickshaw southwest to peek at **Safdarjang's Tomb** (p104), before tucking into a scrummy seafood lunch at **Ploof** (p118). Spend the afternoon exploring the sublime **Humayun's Tomb** (p101), which is also in this area.

On day two, ramble around Old Delhi's historic **Red Fort** (p98) and **Jama Masjid** (p100), followed by a stroll through the **bazaars** (see the boxed text, p123). Afterwards, head south to **Connaught Pl** (p107) for a bite to **eat** (p117) and spot of **shopping** (p123) – don't miss the magnificent **government and state emporiums** (p123).

**Four Days**

Follow the itinerary above, and on the third day wander around **Qutb Minar** (p130), then enjoy a languid Mediterranean meal at the nearby **Olive Bar & Kitchen** (see the boxed text, p116). Spend the afternoon in quiet meditation at the **Bahai Temple** (p108). In the evening, watch the mesmerising **Dances of India** (p122), then chill out at one of Delhi's hip **bars** (p120).

On day four, spend the morning at the delightful **Crafts Museum** (p105) and nearby **Purana Qila** (p101). Those keen on doing more **shopping** (p122) can easily devote the rest of the day to doing so, while those who are all shopped out can visit one (or more) of the city's specialist museums – find out which most appeal to you by reading the reviews under Sights (p98).

**DSIDC Cyber Café** (Map pp106-7; N-Block, Connaught Pl; per hr Rs 35; 9am-8pm Mon-Sat)

## Laundry

Dry-cleaning shops are widespread.

**Mercury Drycleaners** (Map pp102-4; 24691352; Khan Market; shirts/trousers Rs 65/90; 10.30am-8pm Mon-Sat) Clothes ready in two days.

**Snowhite Drycleaners** (Map pp106-7; 23418611; 2 K-Block, Connaught Pl; T-shirts/trousers/dresses Rs 60/80/95; 10am-7pm Mon-Sat) Clothes ready in three days (24 hours for 25% extra).

## Media

Information-rich publications (excellent for ascertaining what's happening in town at the time of your visit) include the *Delhi City Guide* (Rs 20) and *Delhi Diary* (Rs 10); both include a Delhi map. *First City* (Rs 30) is a slick monthly magazine with comprehensive listings/reviews of everything from classical dance to in-vogue nightclubs. Sick of the city? Get Outlook Traveller's *Weekend Breaks from Delhi* (Rs 225). Publications are available at most newsstands and bookshops.

## Medical Services

The East West and Apollo get good traveller reports. Pharmacies are found in virtually all markets.

**All India Institute of Medical Sciences** (Aiims; Map pp92-4; 26588700; Ansari Nagar)

**Apollo Hospital** (Map pp92-4; 26925858; Mathura Rd, Sarita Vihar)

**Apollo Pharmacy** (Map pp106-7; 51516149; G8 Connaught Pl; 24hr) Near the Marina Hotel, this is a central pharmacy.

**Dr Ram Manohar Lohia Hospital** (Map pp102-4; 23365525; Baba Kharak Singh Marg)

**East West Medical Centre** (Map pp92-4; 24623738; B-28 Greater Kailash Part 1) An unassuming white building opposite N-Block Market.

## Money

### ATMS

ATMs (24 hours) linked to international networks are plentiful – these are just some possibilities:

**Bank of Punjab** (Map p111; Hotel Ajanta, 36 Arakashan Rd, Paharganj) Visa, MasterCard, Cirrus and Maestro.

**Citibank** Basant Lok (Map pp92-4; Vasant Vihar); cnr C-Block & K-Block (Map pp106-7; Connaught Pl); Jeevan Bharati Bldg (Map pp106-7; 3rd fl, Connaught Pl) Found citywide; takes major cards.

**HDFC** (Map p111; Main Bazaar, Paharganj) Next to Hotel Satyam and near Light Restaurant; Visa, Amex, MasterCard, Maestro and Cirrus.

**HSBC** (Map pp92-4; Basant Lok, Vasant Vihar) Visa, MasterCard, Cirrus and Maestro.

**ICICI** Connaught Pl (Map pp106-7; 9A Phelps Bldg); Paharganj (Map p111; Rajguru Rd) Accepts all major cards.

**UTI** (Map p111; Rajguru Rd, Paharganj) Next to Hotels Roxy and Kelson. Accepts all major cards.

### FOREIGN CURRENCY & TRAVELLERS CHEQUES

The following change major currencies and travellers cheques.

**American Express** (Map pp106-7; 23719506; A-Block, Connaught Pl; 9.30am-6.30pm Mon-Fri, to 2.30pm Sat) Also has an Amex-only ATM.

**Central Bank of India** (Map pp102-4; 26110101, ext 3584; Ashok Hotel, Chanakyapuri; 24hr)

**Chequepoint Foreign Exchange** (Baluja Forex; Map p111; 51541523; 4596 Main Bazaar, Paharganj; 9am-8.30pm) Cash advances on MasterCard and Visa.

**Delhi Tourism & Transport Development Corporation** (Map pp106-7; 23315322; N-Block, Connaught Pl; 10am-6pm Mon-Sat) Has a foreign-exchange counter.

**Thomas Cook** international airport ( 25653439; 24hr); Janpath (Map pp106-7; 23342171; Imperial hotel; 9.30am-7.30pm Mon-Fri, 9am-6pm Sat & Sun); New Delhi train station ( 23211819; 24hr)

### INTERNATIONAL MONEY TRANSFERS

**Thomas Cook** (Moneygram; Map pp106-7; 23342171; Imperial hotel, Janpath; 9.30am-7.30pm Mon-Fri, 9am-6pm Sat & Sun)

**Western Union** (Map pp106-7; 23311133; Sita World Travels, F-Block, Connaught Pl; 9.30am-9pm Mon-Sat, to 6pm Sun) There are numerous citywide branches.

## Photography

Among the usual photographic services (including digital needs), the following snap passport photos (four/10 for Rs 60/100), which take 10 minutes.

**Delhi Photo Company** (Map pp106-7; 23320577; 78 Janpath, Connaught Pl; 9.30am-7pm Mon-Sat)

**Kinsey Bros** (Map pp106-7; 23324446; 2 A-Block, Connaught Pl; 9.30am-7pm Mon-Sat)

## Post & Telephone

Delhi has scores of PCO/STD/ISD telephone kiosks, some offering fax and Internet services.

**DHL** (Map pp106-7; 23737587; Vandana Bldg, 11 Tolstoy Marg; 9.30am-8pm Mon-Fri, to 9pm Sat) International air freight.

**Post offices** Connaught Pl (Map pp106-7; 6 A-Block); New Delhi main post office (GPO; Map pp102-4; ☎ 23364111; Baba Kharak Singh Marg; 🕑 10am-1pm & 1.30-5pm Mon-Sat, 10am-1pm Sun); The main post office is in the middle of a busy roundabout, 500m southwest of Connaught Pl, and has a poste restante facility; ensure mail is addressed to GPO, New Delhi – 110001. The Connaught Pl branch is more conveniently located but has no poste restante.

### Tourist Information

Beware of the many (profit-driven, often substandard) travel agencies and others posing as 'tourist information centres' in Delhi. Do *not* be fooled – the only official one is India Tourism Delhi, listed here.

For contact details of Indian regional tourist offices ask at India Tourism Delhi, or dial the operator on ☎ 197.

**India Tourism Delhi** (Government of India; www.incredibleindia.org) Connaught Pl (Map pp106-7; ☎ 23320008; 88 Janpath; 🕑 9am-6pm Mon-Fri, to 2pm Sat); domestic airport (☎ 25675296; 🕑 8am-last flight); international airport (☎ 25691171; 🕑 24hr) Gives advice as well as a free Delhi map and various brochures. The special branch at 88 Janpath investigates tourism-related complaints.

**Rajasthan tourist office** (☎ 3381884; Tourist Reception Centre, Bikaner House, Pandara Rd, Delhi)

**Student Travel Information Centre** (Map pp102-4; ☎ 23368760; ITDC Hotel Janpath, Janpath; 🕑 9am-6pm Mon-Sat) Renews student cards.

## DANGERS & ANNOYANCES

Following the murder of an Australian female tourist in Delhi in 2004, who'd caught a prepaid taxi from the airport, a special 'tourist police' squad was established. These clearly marked jeeps (each with English-speaking police, including one woman) are stationed at tourist centres, including the international airport, New Delhi train station and Janpath. Seek assistance if you're being badgered by touts or face other problems. Women should also see p377.

### Scams

There are a number of scams operating in Delhi – be extra cautious around tourist hubs.

Touts may come in the form of taxi-wallahs, often at the international airport. Sneaky drivers may try to persuade you that it's mandatory to confirm your hotel booking before actually arriving – this is complete hogwash. The scam goes something like this: you're taken to an office where you phone your hotel (or so you think) and are inevitably told that you don't have a booking. In reality you've been talking to someone in cahoots with the driver. The taxi-wallah will then drop you at the hotel of *his* choice (often in Karol Bagh), where he gets a plump commission and you get a high room rate. Another scam involves the driver scaring you into thinking there are riots in Delhi with the hope of bundling you off to a hotel in a supposedly safe area (again, where he receives commission from the hotel). Alternatively, the driver may claim that he is lost, and stop at a travel agency for directions. The agent (also in on the scam) supposedly dials your hotel and informs you that your room is double booked. The agent promptly finds you another hotel where he and the taxi driver both earn a commission.

Train stations can also attract rapacious tricksters who feed off the tourist traffic. At the New Delhi train station touts may try to stop you from booking tickets at the upstairs (1st-floor) International Tourist Bureau and divert you to one of the (overpriced and often unreliable) travel agencies over the road. Make the assumption that the office is *never* closed (outside official opening hours; see p127), isn't being renovated and hasn't shifted. Other tricksters may insist your ticket needs to be stamped (for a hefty fee payable to them) before it's valid – another scam. Others may try to convince wait-listed passengers that there's a charge

#### DODGING DODGY TRAVEL AGENTS

Regrettably, there has been an alarming increase in the number of travellers who have reported being hoodwinked by unscrupulous travel agents. To avoid grief, always shop around to gauge exactly what's on offer and choose agents who are members of accredited associations such as the Travel Agents Association of India, the Indian Association of Tour Operators and the Adventure Tour Operators Association of India – ask to see their accreditation. Finally, before parting with your hard-earned cash, insist on getting what you've been promised in writing – this will be invaluable if you need to later lodge a complaint with the tourist office.

to check their reservation status – don't fall for it. Once out of the station, avoid overpriced conveyance by heading for the car park's prepaid autorickshaw booth.

The 'shotgun shit on the shoe' scam in Connaught Pl has declined but not disappeared entirely. A shoeshiner grabs your attention by pointing to a brownish splotch on your shoe that wasn't there seconds ago. The seemingly concerned shoeshiner (who is actually responsible for it) offers to remove it (for a ridiculous price). Look out for these tricksters in advance – they have minimal equipment (so they can run fast). Genuine shoeshiners have a box full of shoe-cleaning products, often laid out on the footpath, and charge around Rs 15 to 20.

For shopping scams, see p360.

## SIGHTS

Delhi's major tourist sights are predominantly found in Old Delhi and in the vicinity of New Delhi's Connaught Pl.

Shuttling between attractions is quickest on Sunday, when there's less traffic. Note that many sites are shut on Monday and that US dollar admission charges are payable in the rupee equivalent.

### Old Delhi

The old walled city of Shahjahanabad spreads west from the Red Fort and was at one time surrounded by a sturdy defensive wall, only fragments of which now exist. The **Kashmiri Gate**, at the northern end of the walled city, was the scene of desperate fighting when the British retook Delhi during the 1857 Indian Uprising. West of here is the British-erected **Mutiny Memorial**, dedicated to the soldiers who died during the Uprising. Near the monument is an **Ashoka Pillar**; like the one in Firoz Shah Kotla, it was brought here by Firoz Shah.

#### RED FORT (LAL QILA)

The sandstone walls of the **Red Fort** (Map p99; Indian/foreigner Rs 11/US$2, video Rs 25; sunrise-sunset Tue-Sun) extend for 2km and vary in height from 18m on the river side to 33m on the city side. Shah Jahan began construction in 1638 and it was completed in 1648. Shah Jahan never completely moved his capital from Agra to his new city of Shahjahanabad in Delhi because he was deposed and imprisoned in Agra Fort by his son Aurangzeb.

The Red Fort dates from the very peak of Mughal power. The Mughal reign from Delhi was a short one, however; Aurangzeb was the first and last great Mughal emperor to rule from here.

The Yamuna River used to flow right by the eastern edge of the fort, and once filled the 10m-deep moat.

Tickets to the fort are available from the ticket kiosk (Map p99), opposite Lahore Gate (the main gate).

##### Lahore Gate

The fort's **main gate** (Map p99) takes its name from the fact that it faces towards Lahore, now in Pakistan. You enter the fort through here and immediately find yourself in the vaulted arcade known as the **Chatta Chowk** (Covered Bazaar; Map p99). The arcade of shops here once sold items that the royal household might have fancied – silks, jewellery and gold.

The arcade leads to **Naubat Khana** (Drum House; Map p99), where musicians used to play for the emperor. There's an **Indian War Memorial Museum** (Map p99; admission Rs 2) upstairs. The open courtyard beyond the Drum House formerly had galleries along either side, but these were removed by the British army when the fort was used as its headquarters. Other reminders of the British presence are the monumentally ugly, three-storey barrack blocks that are situated to the north of this courtyard.

##### Diwan-i-Am

The **Hall of Public Audience** (Map p99) was where the emperor would sit to hear complaints or disputes from his subjects. His alcove in the wall was marble panelled and set with precious stones, many of which were looted following the 1857 Uprising. This elegant hall was restored following a directive from Lord Curzon, the viceroy of India between 1898 and 1905.

##### Diwan-i-Khas

The **Hall of Private Audience** (Map p99), which is constructed of white marble, was the luxurious chamber where the emperor would hold private meetings. The centrepiece (until the Persian invader Nadir Shah carted it off to Iran in 1739) was the magnificent solid-gold and jewel-studded Peacock Throne.

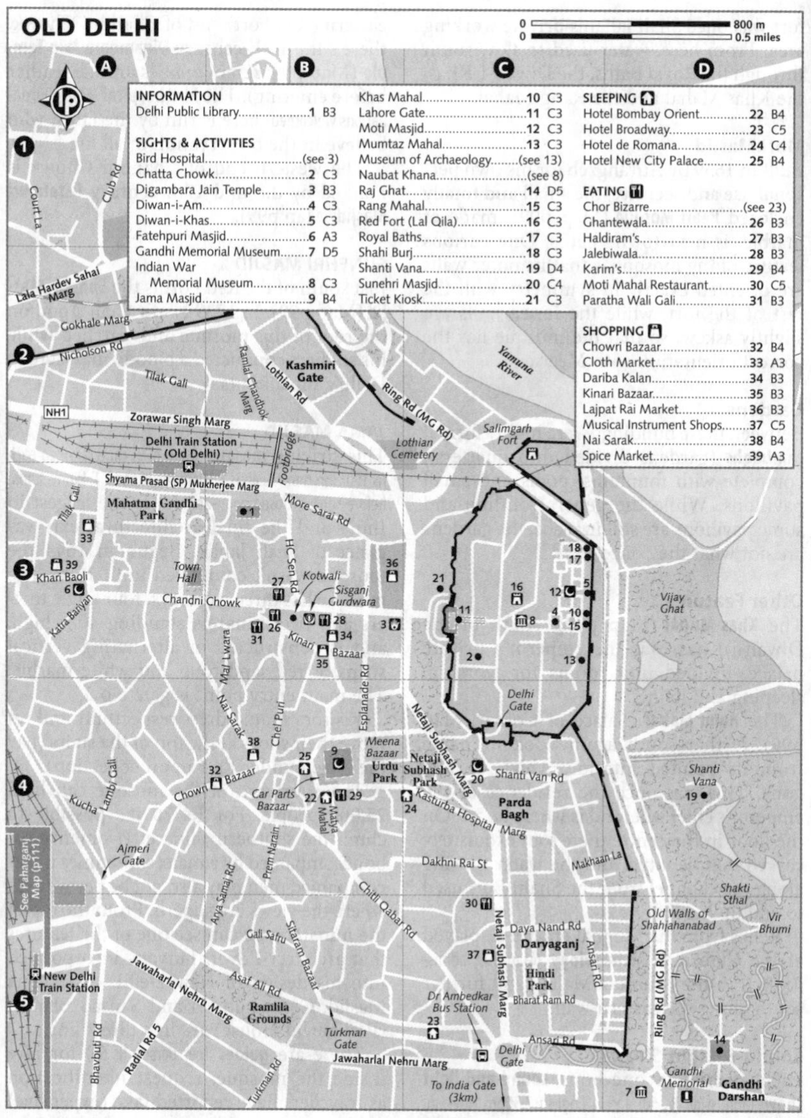


In 1760 the Marathas also removed the silver ceiling from the hall, so today it's a pale shadow of its former glory.

### Royal Baths

Next to the Diwan-i-Khas are the **hammams** (baths; Map p99), three large rooms surmounted by domes, with a fountain in the centre (one was set up as a sauna). The floors were once inlaid with *pietra dura* (marble inlay), and the rooms illuminated through panels of coloured glass in the roof.

### Shahi Burj

This modest, three-storey, octagonal **tower** (Map p99) at the northeastern edge of the fort was once Shah Jahan's private working area. From here, water used to flow south through the Royal Baths, the Diwan-i-Khas, the Khas Mahal and the Rang Mahal.

### Moti Masjid

Built in 1659 by Aurangzeb for his own personal use and security, the small and totally enclosed **Pearl Mosque** (Map p99), made of marble, is next to the baths. One curious feature of the mosque is that its outer walls are oriented exactly in symmetry with the rest of the fort, while the inner walls are slightly askew, so that the mosque has the correct orientation with Mecca.

### Gardens

Between these buildings were highly formal **charbaghs** (gardens divided into quarters), complete with fountains, pools and small pavilions. While the general outline and some pavilions are still in place, the gardens are not what they once were.

### Other Features

The **Khas Mahal** (Map p99), south of the Diwan-i-Khas, was the emperor's private palace, divided into rooms for worship, sleeping and living.

The **Rang Mahal** (Palace of Colour; Map p99), further south again, took its name from its painted interior, which is now gone. This was once the residence of the emperor's chief wife, and is where he ate. On the floor in the centre there's an exquisitely carved marble lotus, and the water flowing along the channel from the Shahi Burj used to end up here.

Relics from the Mughal era are displayed at the **Museum of Archaeology** (Map p99; admission Rs 2) in the Mumtaz Mahal, still further south along the eastern wall.

### Sound-&-Light Show

Each evening a one-hour **sound-and-light show** (admission Rs 50; 🕓 in English 7.30pm Nov-Jan, 8.30pm Feb-Apr & Sep-Oct, 9pm May-Aug) re-creates events of India's history, particularly those associated with the Red Fort. Tickets are available from the ticket kiosk at the fort.

## CHANDNI CHOWK

Old Delhi's main thoroughfare is the chronically congested **Chandni Chowk**, which is best negotiated by cycle-rickshaw. At the eastern (Red Fort) end of Chandni Chowk, there's the 16th-century **Digambara Jain Temple** (Map p99; remove shoes and all leather before entering). The **bird hospital** (Map p99; donations welcomed) here is run by the Jains, who believe in the preservation of all life.

The western end of Chandni Chowk is marked by the mid-17th-century **Fatehpuri Masjid** (Map p99).

## SUNEHRI MASJID

Just south of the Red Fort is the **Sunehri Masjid** (Map p99). In 1739 Nadir Shah stood on the roof of this mosque and watched while his soldiers conducted a bloody massacre of Delhi's inhabitants.

## JAMA MASJID

This striking **mosque** (Map p99; camera/video each Rs 150; 🕓 non-Muslims 8.30am-12.30pm & 1.45pm-30min before sunset, closed noon-2pm Fri) is the largest in India and the final architectural extravagance of Shah Jahan. Begun in 1644 the mosque wasn't completed until 1658. The mosque has three gateways, four angle towers and two minarets standing 40m high, and is constructed of alternating vertical strips of red sandstone and white marble. The main entry point is gate No 3.

Visitors should dress respectfully and remove their shoes at the top of the stairs (pay the shoe minder Rs 5 upon collection).

The courtyard of the mosque can hold 25,000 people. For Rs 20 it's possible to climb the southern minaret (women must be accompanied by a male; sometimes unaccompanied men may also not be permitted), where the views are superb. From the top of the minaret, you can see one of the features that architect Edwin Lutyens incorporated into his design of New Delhi – the Jama Masjid, Connaught Pl and Sansad Bhavan (Parliament House) are in a direct line.

There are **guides** (per person Rs 50) for hire inside the mosque; request identification as travellers have reported fake (expensive) guides, some of whom try to fool visitors into paying an entry fee (mosque admission is free).

## RAJ GHAT

South of the Red Fort, on the banks of the Yamuna, a simple black marble **platform** marks the spot where Mahatma Gandhi was cremated following his assassination.

Jawaharlal Nehru, the first Indian prime minister, was cremated just to the north, at **Shanti Vana** (Forest of Peace; Map p99) in 1964. Nehru's daughter, Indira Gandhi, who was assassinated in 1984, and grandsons Sanjay (d 1980) and Rajiv (d 1991) were also cremated in this vicinity.

The Raj Ghat area is now a beautiful park. The **Gandhi Memorial Museum** (Map p99; ☎ 23311793; admission free; ⌚ 9.30am-5.30pm Tue-Sun) contains various memorabilia, including photos.

## Central Delhi

### RAJPATH

Immensely broad **Rajpath** (Kingsway) is another focus of Lutyens' New Delhi. The Republic Day parade is held here on 26 January and thousands gather for this spectacle.

At the eastern end of Rajpath is India Gate, while at the western end is Rashtrapati Bhavan, which is flanked by the two large Secretariat buildings. These three buildings sit upon a small rise, known as Raisina Hill.

**India Gate** (Map pp102–4), a 42m-high memorial arch, bears the names of around 90,000 Indian army soldiers who died in WWI, the Northwest Frontier operations of the same time and the 1919 Afghan fiasco.

**Rashtrapati Bhavan** (President's House; Map pp102–4), the official residence of the president of India, was completed in 1929. The palacelike building exhibits a blend of Mughal and Western architectural styles. To the west of the building is a **Mughal garden** (admission free, photography prohibited) that occupies 130 hectares. This garden is only open to the public on a certain number of days between mid-February and early March – for dates contact India Tourism Delhi (p97).

Prior to Independence, Rashtrapati Bhavan was the viceroy's residence. At the time of Mountbatten, India's last viceroy, the number of servants needed to maintain the 340 rooms and its extensive gardens was enormous. There were 418 gardeners alone – 50 of them were boys whose sole job was to chase away the birds.

The north and south **Secretariat buildings** (Map pp102–4) are on either side of Rajpath on Raisina Hill. These imposing buildings, topped with small domes, now house government ministries.

Standing at the end of Sansad Marg is **Sansad Bhavan** (Parliament House; Map pp102–4). The building is a circular, colonnaded structure, 171m in diameter. Sansad Bhavan's relative physical insignificance in the grand scheme of New Delhi shows how the focus of power has shifted from the viceroy's residence, which had been given pride of place during the British Raj when New Delhi was conceived.

### PURANA QILA

With massive walls and three gateways, **Purana Qila** (Old Fort; Map pp102-4; ☎ 24353178; Mathura Rd; Indian/foreigner Rs 5/US$2, video Rs 25; ⌚ sunrise-sunset) was the site of Indraprastha (see p91). The Afghan ruler Sher Shah, who briefly interrupted Mughal sovereignty by defeating Humayun, completed the fort during his reign (1538–45), before Humayun regained control of India.

Entering from the south gate you'll see the small, octagonal, red-sandstone tower, the **Sher Mandal**, later used by Humayun as a library. It was while descending the stairs of this tower in 1556 that he slipped and sustained injuries from which he later died. Just beyond it is the **Qila-i-Kuhran Mosque** (Mosque of Sher Shah).

There's a small **archaeological museum** (admission Rs 2) just inside the main gate, and there are good views of Delhi from atop this gate.

The **sound-and-light show** was not operating when we visited, but reportedly it may resume.

### HUMAYUN'S TOMB

Built in the mid-16th century by Haji Begum, Persian-born senior wife of the second Mughal Emperor Humayun, this **tomb** (Map pp102-4; Indian/foreigner Rs 10/US$5, video Rs 25; ⌚ sunrise-sunset), off Mathura Rd, is a superb example of early Mughal architecture. Elements in its design – a squat building with high arched entrances that let in light, topped by a bulbous dome and surrounded by formal gardens – were to be refined over the years to eventually create the magnificence of Agra's Taj Mahal. Haji Begum is buried in the red-and-white sandstone and black-and-yellow marble tomb.

The octagonal tomb of Isa Khan is located through a gate to the left of the entrance and is a fine example of Lodi architecture.

# CENTRAL DELHI

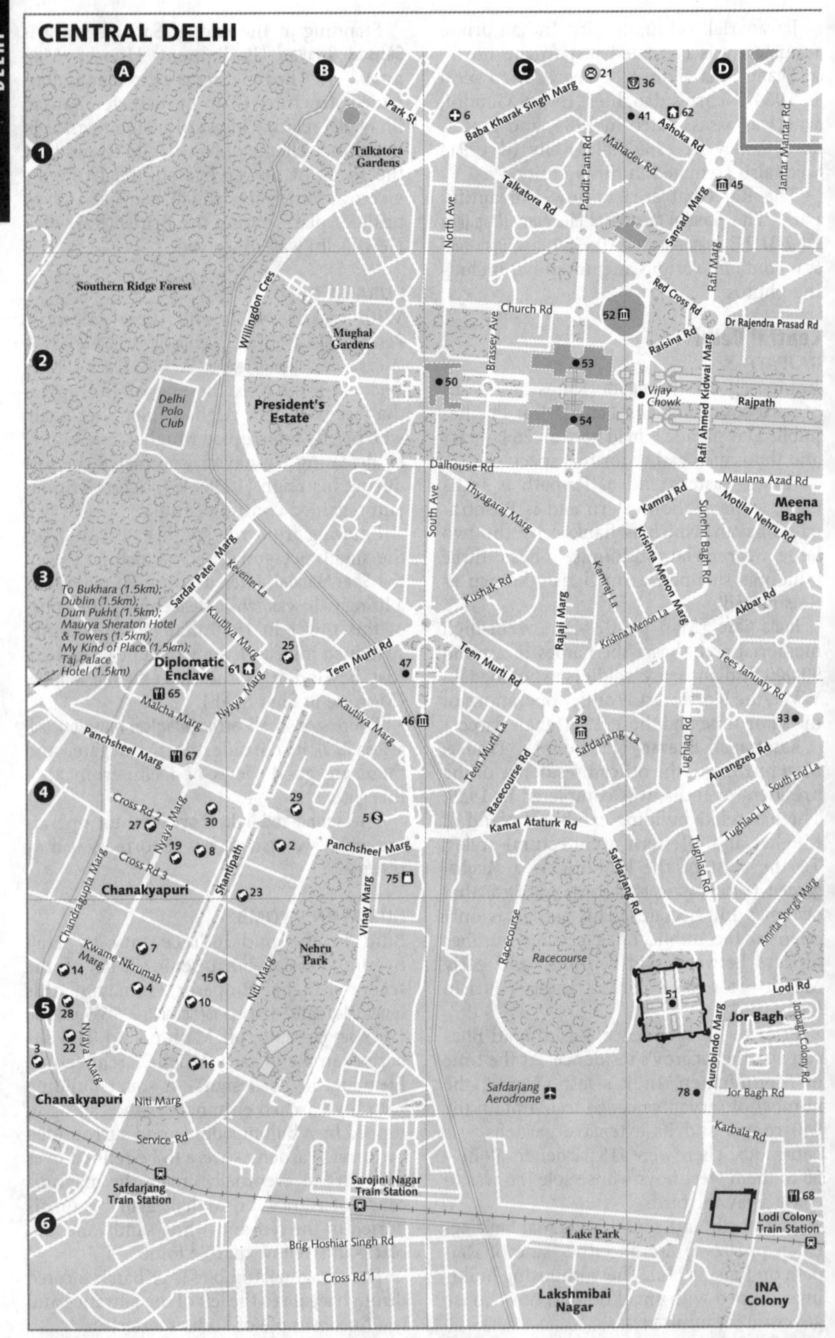

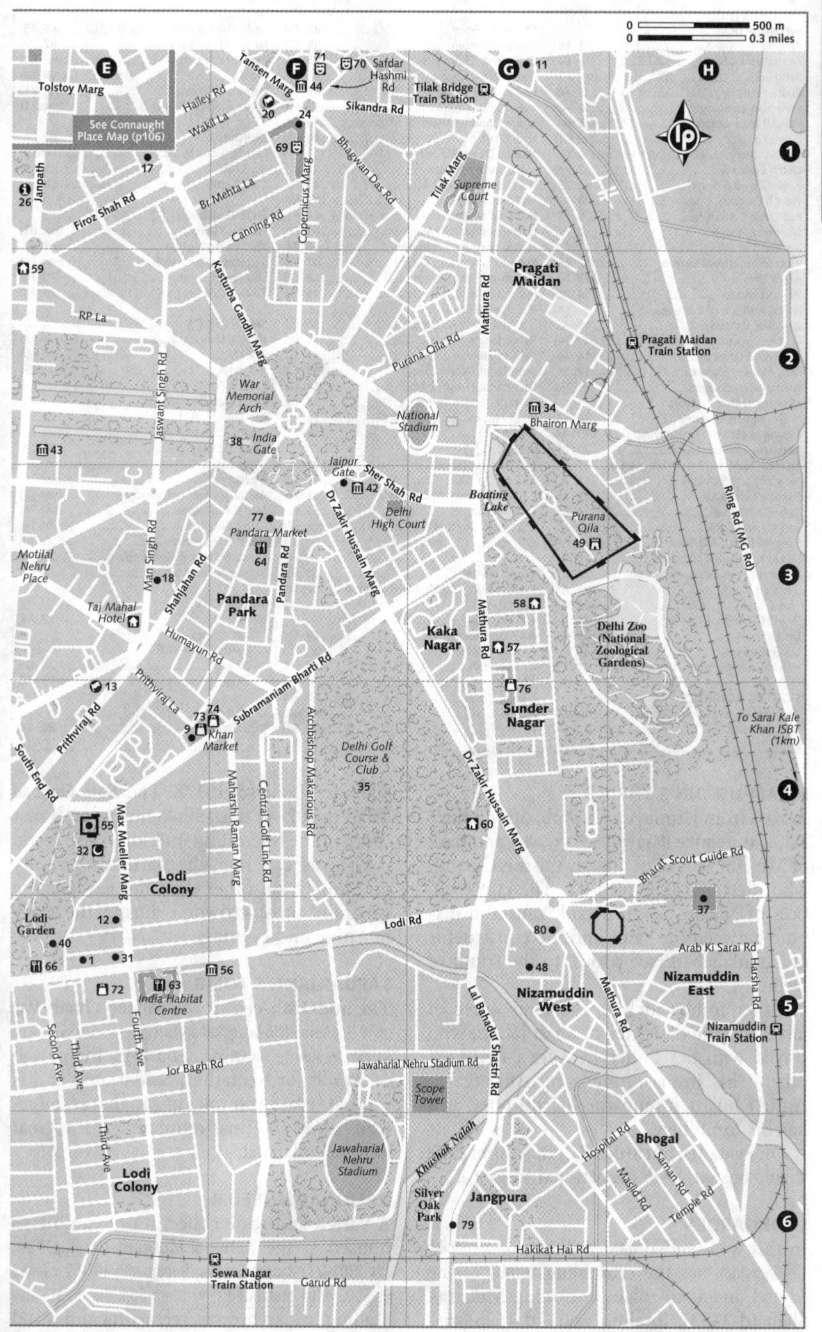

0 500 m
0 0.3 miles
E
F
G
H
1
2
3
4
5
6
Tolstoy Marg
Tansen Marg
Safdar Hashmi Rd
Tilak Bridge Train Station
Hailey Rd
Sikandra Rd
Wakil La
See Connaught Place Map (p106)
Janpath
Firoz Shah Rd
Br Mehta La
Canning Rd
Copernicus Marg
Bhagwan Das Rd
Tilak Marg
Supreme Court
Kasturba Gandhi Marg
Pragati Maidan
Mathura Rd
RP La
Purana Qila Rd
Pragati Maidan Train Station
Jaswant Singh Rd
War Memorial Arch
National Stadium
Bhairon Marg
India Gate
Jaipur Gate
Sher Shah Rd
Boating Lake
Delhi High Court
Purana Qila
Pandara Market
Pandara Rd
Dr Zakir Hussain Marg
Motilal Nehru Place
Man Singh Rd
Shahjahan Rd
Pandara Park
Taj Mahal Hotel
Kaka Nagar
Delhi Zoo (National Zoological Gardens)
Ring Rd (MG Rd)
Humayun Rd
Subramaniam Bharti Rd
Prithviraj La
Prithviraj Rd
Khan Market
Sunder Nagar
To Sarai Kale Khan ISBT (1km)
South End Rd
Archbishop Makarious Rd
Delhi Golf Course & Club
Maharshi Raman Marg
Central Golf Link Rd
Max Mueller Marg
Lodi Colony
Bharat Scout Guide Rd
Lodi Garden
Lodi Rd
Arab Ki Sarai Rd
Harsha Rd
Nizamuddin East
Nizamuddin West
Lal Bahadur Shastri Rd
India Habitat Centre
Nizamuddin Train Station
Second Ave
Third Ave
Fourth Ave
Jor Bagh Rd
Jawaharlal Nehru Stadium Rd
Scope Tower
Jawaharlal Nehru Stadium
Khushak Nalah
Hospital Rd
Bhogal
Saman Rd
Masjid Rd
Temple Rd
Silver Oak Park
Jangpura
Hakikat Hai Rd
Sewa Nagar Train Station
Garud Rd

**INFORMATION**

Alliance Française 1 E5
Australian Embassy 2 B4
Bahri Sons (see 73)
Bhutan Embassy 3 A5
Canadian Embassy 4 A5
Central Bank of India 5 B4
Cyber Graphics (see 73)
Dr Ram Manohar Lohia Hospital 6 C1
Dutch Embassy 7 A5
Faqir-Chand & Sons (see 73)
French Embassy 8 A4
Full Circle Bookstore 9 E4
German Embassy 10 A5
Income Tax Office 11 G1
India International Centre 12 E5
Israeli Embassy 13 E4
Italian Embassy 14 A5
Italian Institute of Culture (see 14)
Japanese Embassy 15 A5
Lalit Kala Akademi (see 24)
Malaysian Embassy 16 A5
Max Mueller Bhavan 17 E1
Mercury Drycleaners (see 73)
Ministry of Home Affairs (Foreigners Division) 18 E3
Myanmar (Burma) Embassy 19 A4
Nepalese Embassy 20 F1
New Delhi Main Post Office (GPO) 21 C1
New Zealand Embassy 22 A5
Pakistani Embassy 23 B4
Rabindra Bhavan 24 F1
Sahitya Akademi (see 24)
Sangeet Natak Akademi (see 24)
Sri Lankan High Commission 25 B3
Student Travel Information Centre 26 E1
Swiss Embassy 27 A4
Thai Embassy 28 A5
Tibet House Book Corner (see 56)
UK Embassy 29 B4
US Embassy 30 A4
World Wide Fund for Nature (India) 31 E5

**SIGHTS & ACTIVITIES**

Archaeological Survey of India (see 43)
Bara Gumbad 32 E4
Claridges Hotel 33 D4
Crafts Museum 34 G2
Delhi Golf Club 35 F4
Gurdwara Bangla Sahib 36 D1
Humayun's Tomb 37 H5
India Gate 38 F2
Indira Gandhi Memorial Museum 39 C4
Lodi Garden 40 E5
Morarji Desai National Institute of Yoga 41 D1
National Gallery of Modern Art 42 F3
National Museum 43 E2
National Museum of Natural History 44 F1
National Philatelic Museum 45 D1
Nehru Memorial Museum 46 B4
Nehru Planetarium 47 B3
Nizam-ud-din's Shrine 48 G5
Purana Qila 49 G3
Rashtrapati Bhavan (President's House) 50 C2
Safdarjang's Tomb 51 D5
Sansad Bhavan 52 C2
Secretariat (North Block) 53 C2
Secretariat (South Block) 54 C2
Sikander Lodi's Tomb 55 E4
Tibet House 56 F5

**SLEEPING**

Hotel Samrat (see 5)
Jukaso Inn 57 G3
La Sagrita Tourist Home 58 G3
Le Meridien 59 E2
Maharani Guest House (see 57)
Oberoi 60 G4
Ten (see 58)
Youth Hostel 61 B3
YWCA Blue Triangle Family Hostel 62 D1

**EATING**

All American Diner 63 E5
Basil & Thyme (see 75)
Chicken Inn 64 F3
Chona's (see 9)
Fujiya 65 A4
Gulati (see 64)
Ichiban (see 64)
Lodi, The Garden Restaurant 66 E5
New Sikkim House 67 A4
Pindi Restaurant (see 64)
Ploof 68 D6
Rampur Kitchen (see 73)
Sugar & Spice (Branch) (see 74)

**DRINKING**

Barista (Branch) (see 9)
Big Chill (see 9)
Café Turtle (see 9)

**ENTERTAINMENT**

Habitat World (see 63)
Kamani Auditorium 69 F1
Sangeet Natak Akademi (see 24)
Shri Ram Centre 70 F1
Triveni Kala Sangam 71 F1

**SHOPPING**

Anokhi (Branch) (see 73)
Anokhi (see 75)
Art Indus (see 75)
C.Lal & Sons (see 72)
Delhi Cloth House (see 74)
Jor Bagh Market 72 E5
Kastro's (see 75)
Khan Market 73 E4
Lotus Eaters (see 75)
Mercury (see 74)
Mittal Tea House (Branch) (see 68)
Mittal Tea House (see 76)
Music Shop 74 F4
Regalia Tea House (see 76)
Santushti Shopping Complex 75 B4
Sunder Nagar Market 76 G4

**TRANSPORT**

Bikaner House 77 F3
Indian Airlines (Safdarjang Airfield Office) 78 D5
Metropole Tourist Service 79 G6

**OTHER**

SOS Childrens Village 80 G5

## NIZAM-UD-DIN'S SHRINE

Across from Humayun's Tomb, off Mathura Rd, is the **shrine** (Map pp102-4; 24hr) and tank of Muslim Sufi saint Nizam-ud-din Chishti, who died in 1325, aged 92. The construction of Nizam-ud-din's tank caused a dispute between the saint and the constructor of Tughlaqabad (see p130), to the south of Delhi.

Other tombs include the later grave of Jahanara, the daughter of Shah Jahan, who stayed with her father in Agra's Red Fort during his imprisonment by Aurangzeb. Amir Khusru, a renowned Urdu poet, also has his tomb here.

On Friday (from around 2pm to 8pm), the shrine has *qawwali* (devotional singing).

## LODI GARDEN

In this well-tended **garden** (Map pp102-4; Lodi Rd; 6am-8pm) are the crumbling **tombs** of the Sayyid and Lodi rulers, including Mubarak Shah (d 1433), Ibrahim Lodi (d 1526) and Sikander Lodi (d 1517). The **Bara Gumbad** (Map pp102-4) is a 15th-century tomb that sports some interesting interior plasterwork.

Crowds can mar the garden's serenity on Sunday; on other days the gardens are generally most crowded during the early morning and evening.

## SAFDARJANG'S TOMB

The mid-18th-century **Safdarjang's Tomb** (Map pp102-4; Aurobindo Marg; Indian/foreigner Rs 5/US$2, video Rs 25; sunrise-sunset) was built by the nawab of Avadh for his father, Safdarjang, and is one of the last examples of Mughal architecture before the final remnants of the great empire collapsed.

## NATIONAL MUSEUM

A varied and wide collection of exhibits is housed at the **National Museum** (Map pp102-4; ☎ 23019272; Janpath; Indian/foreigner Rs 10/150, camera Rs 300, video prohibited; 10am-5pm Tue-Sun), including Indian bronze, terracotta and wood sculptures dating back to the Mauryan period, exhibits from the Vijayanagar period in South India, miniature and mural paintings, musical instruments, manuscripts, tapestries, tribal masks, swords, spears and much, much more. There are free one-hour guided tours at 10.30am, 11.30am, noon, 2pm and 3.30pm. At least half a day is required to fully appreciate this commendable museum.

Next door is the **Archaeological Survey of India** (Map pp102-4; ☎ 23010822; Janpath; 9.30am-1.30pm & 2-6pm Mon-Fri). Publications available at this office cover all the main sites in India.

### GURDWARA BANGLA SAHIB

This prominent **Sikh temple** (Map pp102-4; Ashoka Rd; sunrise-sunset), with its striking golden domes, is constructed at the site where the eighth Sikh guru, Harkrishan Dev, stayed when he visited Delhi in 1664. The temple tank contains water believed to have healing properties. Dress conservatively.

### NATIONAL PHILATELIC MUSEUM

This **museum** (Map pp102-4; ☎ 23036727; Sadar Patel Chowk, Sansad Marg; admission free, photography prohibited; 10am-5pm Mon-Fri) is tucked away in the Dak Bhavan post office. There are over 1600 stamps, all post-Independence.

### NATIONAL GALLERY OF MODERN ART

This **gallery** (Map pp102-4; ☎ 23382835; Jaipur Gate; Indian/foreigner Rs 10/150, photography prohibited; 10am-5pm Tue-Sun), formerly the maharaja of Jaipur's Delhi residence, displays more than 300 contemporary paintings by Indian artists.

### NEHRU MEMORIAL MUSEUM & PLANETARIUM

Teen Murti Bhavan, the former residence of Jawaharlal Nehru (India's first prime minister), just off Teen Murti Rd, has been converted into a **museum** (Map pp102-4; ☎ 23016734; admission free; 9am-5.15pm Tue-Sun). The photographs and newspaper clippings offer an insight into the Independence movement.

In the grounds there is also a **planetarium** (Map pp102-4; ☎ 23014504; 45min show Rs 15; in English 11.30am & 3pm).

### TIBET HOUSE

Tibet House contains a small **museum** (Map pp102-4; ☎ 24611515; 1 Lodi Rd; admission Rs 10, photography prohibited; 10am-1pm & 2-5.30pm Mon-Fri), exhibiting ceremonial items brought out of Tibet when the Dalai Lama fled following Chinese occupation. Pieces include sacred manuscripts and *thangkas* (Tibetan cloth paintings).

Apart from books, the Tibet House Book Corner (p95 sells Tibetan CDs, including Buddhist chanting (Rs 250), postcards (Rs 10), incense (from Rs 25) and prayer flags (Rs 70).

### CRAFTS MUSEUM

Near Pragati Maidan is this tranquil **museum** (Map pp102-4; ☎ 23371817; Bhairon Marg; admission free; 10am-5pm Tue-Sun), containing a collection of traditional stalls displaying various crafts, such as textiles, woodwork and ceramics. There are craft demonstrations, and artisans sell direct to the buyer. It's part of a contrived, yet still very impressive, 'village life' complex.

There's a fantastic indoor museum with several well-kept galleries housing a wide array of clearly labelled items from around India, including old wooden animals, string puppets, masks, paintings, tribal objects and terracotta figures. Photography is only granted with prior permission. A high-quality craft shop sells tempting fare.

### INDIRA GANDHI MEMORIAL MUSEUM

The former residence of Prime Minister Indira Gandhi has been converted into a **museum** (Map pp102-4; ☎ 23010094; 1 Safdarjang Rd; admission free; 9.30am-4.45pm Tue-Sun). On show are some of her personal belongings, including the sari (with blood stains) she was wearing at the time of her assassination, as well as newspaper clippings, letters and photos. On the way out, you'll pass an enclosed garden containing a pathway – this path was where Indira Gandhi walked moments before she was shot by two of her Sikh bodyguards. The path has been covered in crystal – the clear glass portion marks the spot where she collapsed.

### NATIONAL MUSEUM OF NATURAL HISTORY

Although nothing to rave about, this **museum** (Map pp102-4; ☎ 23314849; 2nd fl, FICCI Auditorium, Tansen Marg; admission free; 10am-5pm Tue-Sun), opposite the Nepali embassy, houses some noteworthy fossils such as the 160-million-year-old femur of an Indian sauropod.

 



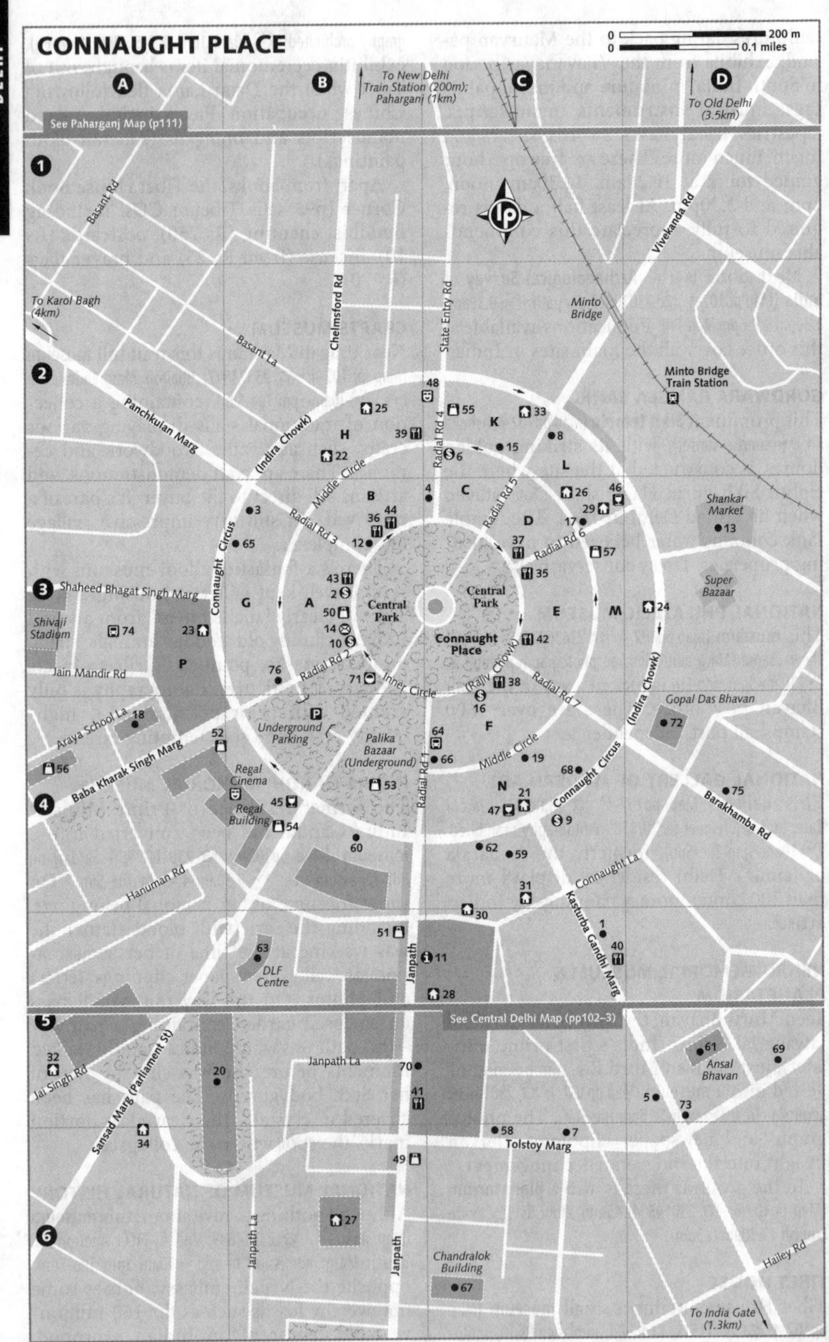
CONNAUGHT PLACE
0 200 m
0 0.1 miles
To New Delhi Train Station (200m); Paharganj (1km)
To Old Delhi (3.5km)
See Paharganj Map (p111)
Basant Rd
To Karol Bagh (4km)
Basant La
Chelmsford Rd
State Entry Rd
Vivekanda Rd
Minto Bridge
Minto Bridge Train Station
Panchkuian Marg
(Indira Chowk)
Middle Circle
Radial Rd 4
Radial Rd 5
Radial Rd 3
Radial Rd 6
Connaught Circus
Shankar Market
Super Bazaar
Shaheed Bhagat Singh Marg
Shivaji Stadium
Central Park
Connaught Place
Jain Mandir Rd
Radial Rd 2
Inner Circle
(Rajiv Chowk)
Radial Rd 7
(Indira Chowk)
Gopal Das Bhavan
Araya School La
Underground Parking
Palika Bazaar (Underground)
Radial Rd 1
Baba Kharak Singh Marg
Regal Cinema
Regal Building
Barakhamba Rd
Hanuman Rd
Connaught La
Kasturba Gandhi Marg
DLF Centre
Janpath
See Central Delhi Map (pp102–3)
Jai Singh Rd
Sansad Marg (Parliament St)
Janpath La
Ansal Bhavan
Tolstoy Marg
Chandralok Building
Hailey Rd
To India Gate (1.3km)

Other exhibits include stuffed armadillos and a Tibetan yak.

## Connaught Place Area

### CONNAUGHT PLACE (CP)

The geographical heart of New Delhi is the vast traffic circle known as **Connaught Pl** and the seven streets that radiate out from it, which are divided into blocks. It has a uniform series of colonnaded buildings devoted to shops, banks, restaurants, hotels and offices.

Often creating confusion, the outer circle is technically called 'Connaught Circus' (divided into blocks from G to N) and the inner circle 'Connaught Pl' (divided into blocks from A to F). On top of that there is also the 'Middle Circle', but most people invariably refer to the *whole* complex as Connaught Pl. Adding to the confusion, in 1995 the inner and outer circle were renamed Rajiv Chowk and Indira Chowk respectively (in honour of Indira Gandhi and her son), but few people use these newer names. To keep things simple, we've just used 'Connaught Pl' in addresses throughout this chapter. Connaught Pl addresses have a block letter and a number, but these are not always presented in a uniform way: some use '50N Block', while others adopt 'N-50' or other variations. In this chapter, we've presented the letter and number in the same way that the individual businesses use them.

### JANTAR MANTAR

Just a short stroll from Connaught Pl, the collection of salmon-coloured structures is the **Jantar Mantar** (Map pp106-7; Sansad Marg; Indian/foreigner Rs 5/US$2, camera/video Rs 4/25; 9am-sunset), one of Maharaja Jai Singh II's amazing observatories. Constructed in 1725 it's dominated by a huge sundial known as the Prince of Dials. Other instruments plot the course of heavenly bodies and predict eclipses.

**INFORMATION**

American Center......1 C5
American Express......2 B3
Apollo Pharmacy......3 B3
Book World......(see 53)
Bookworm......4 C3
British Council......5 D5
Citibank ATM......6 C2
Citibank ATM......(see 60)
Delhi Photo Company......(see 11)
DHL......7 C6
DSIDC Cyber Café......(see 19)
DTTDC Foreign-Exchange Counter......(see 19)
English Book Store......8 C2
Hong Kong & Shanghai Bank......9 C4
ICICI ATM......10 B3
India Tourism Delhi (Government of India)......11 C5
Kinsey Bros......(see 10)
New Book Depot......12 B3
Paramount Book Store......(see 51)
Piccadilly Book Stall......13 D3
Post Office (Branch)......14 B3
Rajiv Book House......(see 53)
Snowhite Drycleaners......15 C2
Thomas Cook (Moneygram)......(see 27)
Thomas Cook......(see 27)
Western Union......16 C4

**SIGHTS & ACTIVITIES**

Ashok Travels & Tours (Indian Tourism Development Corporation)......17 C3
Delhi Tourism & Transport Development Corporation (Branch)......18 A4
Delhi Tourism & Transport Development Corporation (DTTDC)......19 C4
Jantar Mantar......20 A5

**SLEEPING**

Central Court Hotel......21 C4
HK Choudhary Guest House......22 B2
Hotel Alka......23 A3
Hotel Blue......24 D3
Hotel Fifty Five......25 B2
Hotel Jukaso Inn......26 C3
Imperial......27 B6
Janpath Guest House......28 C5
Nirula's Hotel......29 C3
Ringo Guest House......30 C5
Sunny Guest House......31 C4
YMCA Tourist Hostel......32 A5
York Hotel......33 C2
YWCA International Guest House......34 A6

**EATING**

Banana Leaf......(see 21)
Berco's......35 C3
Café 100......36 B3
Embassy......37 C3
Host......38 C3
Kwality Restaurant......(see 54)
Nirula's Ice-Cream Parlour......(see 29)
Nizam's Kathi Kabab......39 B2
Parikrama......40 C5
Sagar Ratna......(see 33)
Saravana Bhavan......41 B5
Saravana Bhavan (Branch)......(see 23)
Spice Route......(see 27)
United Coffee House......42 C3
Wenger's......43 B3
Zen......44 B3

**DRINKING**

1911......(see 27)
Barista......(see 21)
Café Coffee Day......(see 21)
DV8......45 B4
Pegasus......46 C3
Regent's Blues......47 C4
Spirit......(see 35)

**ENTERTAINMENT**

PVR Plaza Cinema......48 C2

**SHOPPING**

Berco's Melody House......(see 35)
Central Cottage Industries Emporium......49 B6
Dhoomimal Art Centre......50 B3
Handloom House......(see 14)
Handpaper World......(see 51)
Jain Super Store......(see 53)
Janpath (Tibetan) Market......51 B5
Khadi Gramodyog Bhawan......52 A4
Music Street......(see 4)
Music World......(see 48)
New Prominent Tailors......(see 55)
Palika Bazaar......53 B4
People Tree......54 B4
Rangarsons Music Depot......(see 33)
Rikhi Ram......(see 3)
Soma......55 C2
State Emporiums......56 A4
Vedi Tailors......57 C3

**TRANSPORT**

Aeroflot......58 C6
Air France......59 C4
Air India......60 B4
British Airways......(see 72)
Budget......61 D5
Delhi Transport Corporation......62 C4
El Al Israel Airlines......(see 69)
Emirates......63 B5
Ex-Servicemen's Air Link Transport Service......64 C4
Gulf Air......65 B3
Indian Airlines......66 C4
Jagson Airlines......(see 7)
Japan Airlines......67 C6
Jet Airways......68 C4
KLM – Royal Dutch Airlines......69 D5
Kumar Tourist Taxi Service......(see 33)
Lufthansa Airlines......70 B5
Malaysian Airlines......(see 75)
Pakistan International Airlines......(see 1)
Prepaid Autorickshaw Booth......71 B3
Prepaid Autorickshaw Booth......(see 11)
Qantas Airways......(see 72)
Royal Nepal Airlines Corporation......(see 41)
Sahara Airlines......72 D4
Scandinavian Airlines......73 D5
Shivaji Stadium Terminal......74 A3
Singapore Airlines......75 D4
Sri Lankan Airlines......76 B3

**OTHER**

Malhotra Building......(see 66)

## Other Areas

### CORONATION DURBAR SITE

North of Old Delhi, in a desolate **field** (Map pp92–4), stands a lone *obelisk* – this is the site where, in 1877 and 1903, the great theatrical durbars, featuring the full set of Indian rulers, paid homage to the British monarch. It was also here that, in the year 1911, King George V was declared emperor of India.

### FIROZ SHAH KOTLA

The ruins of Firozabad (the fifth city of Delhi), erected by Firoz Shah in 1354, can be found at **Firoz Shah Kotla** (Map pp92-4; Indian/foreigner Rs 5/US$2, video Rs 25; sunrise-sunset), just off Bahadur Shah Zafar Marg. In the fortress-palace is a 13m-high sandstone **Ashoka Pillar** inscribed with Ashoka's edicts (and a later inscription). The remains of an old mosque and a well can also be seen in the area, but most of the ruins of Firozabad were used for the construction of later cities.

### LAKSHMI NARAYAN TEMPLE (BIRLA MANDIR)

West of Connaught Pl, with soaring domes, the large Orissan-style **Lakshmi Narayan Temple** (Map pp92-4; Mandir Marg; 6am-9pm) was erected in 1938 by the rich industrialist BD Birla. The main temple is dedicated to Lakshmi, the goddess of wealth.

### RAIL TRANSPORT MUSEUM

Housing almost 30 locomotives and some interesting old carriages, railway buffs will enjoy the **Rail Transport Museum** (Map pp92-4; 26881816; Chanakyapuri; admission Rs 10, video Rs 100; 9.30am-5pm Tue-Sun Oct-Mar, to 7pm Apr-Sep). Exhibits include an 1855 steam-engine, still in working order, and various oddities such as the skull of an elephant that charged a mail train in 1894, and lost.

### HAUZ KHAS VILLAGE

This urban 'village' surrounded by parkland (and the nearby Deer Park) was once the reservoir for the second city of Delhi – Siri – which is situated slightly to the east. Today, Hauz Khas is a chic south Delhi suburb, with fashionable restaurants, art galleries and boutiques.

The area has a number of crumbling tombs, including **Firoz Shah's Tomb** (Map pp92–4). Also part of the former old city of Siri, just east of Hauz Khas Village, is the **Moth-ki Masjid** (Map pp92–4), said to be one of the finest mosques in the Lodi style.

### BAHAI TEMPLE

This contemporary **Bahai Temple** (Map pp92-4, 26444029; Kalkaji; 9.30am-5.30pm Tue-Sun), stunningly shaped like a white lotus, is especially spectacular at dusk when it's floodlit. The 1986 temple is set among pools and well-tended gardens, and welcomes adherents of all faiths to pray or meditate silently according to their own religion. Principles inherent to the Bahai faith include elimination of prejudice and universal peace.

Remove your shoes before entering and, turn off mobile phones and refrain from speaking. Photography is prohibited inside.

### SULABH INTERNATIONAL MUSEUM OF TOILETS

Southwest of the city centre, this quirky **museum** (Off Map pp92-4; 25053646; Sulabh Complex, Mahavir Enclave, Palam Dabri Rd; admission free; 10am-5pm Mon-Sat) houses a small, intriguing collection of toilet-related paraphernalia (from 2500 BC to modern times). Request a guided tour (free), as these bring the loos to life.

### SHANKAR'S INTERNATIONAL DOLLS MUSEUM

Boasting almost 6500 dolls from around 85 countries, **Shankar's International Dolls Museum** (Map pp92-4; 23316970; Nehru House, 4 Bahadur Shah Zafar Marg; admission Rs 10; 10am-6pm Tue-Sun) is certainly impressive. Apart from its immense international collection, there are also Indian dolls, including brides.

## ACTIVITIES

### Beauty Treatments

Pedicures, plucking and other primping is possible at Delhi's plentiful beauty parlours. Deluxe hotel parlours are the most luxurious but they charge at least double that of independent operators.

Some parlours offer *mehndi* (henna 'tattoos') but the pavement *mehndi*-wallahs at markets (eg Paharganj and Lajpat Nagar) are much cheaper.

**Lakmé Beauty Studio** (Map pp92-4; 26140584; 13 Basant Lok, Vasant Vihar; manicure/pedicure Rs 150/200, facial Rs 450-750; 10am-7pm)

**Meghna Beauty Parlour** (Map pp92-4; 26513149; Green Park Main Market; manicure/pedicure Rs 70/90; 9.30am-9pm Wed-Mon) Not as slick as Lakmé, but cheap

**Princess Beauty Parlour** (Map p111; ☎ 23581930; Prince Polonia hotel, 2325 Tilak Gali, Paharganj; manicure/pedicure Rs 150/200; ⌚ 9.30am-6.30pm) Paharganj's most salubrious beauty parlour; upper-lip threading (plucking using thread) is Rs 10.

### Golf

**Delhi Golf Club** (Map pp102-4; ☎ 24362768; Dr Zakir Hussain Marg; weekdays/weekends US$35/40, caddies Rs 100; ⌚ sunrise-sunset) has scenic grounds; on weekends it can get crowded.

### Massage & Ayurvedic Treatments

**Ashtaang** (Map pp92-4; ☎ 24101802; E-2 Anand Niketan; ⌚ 9am-6pm), opposite Delhi University (South Campus), offers authentic Keralan Ayurvedic treatments, such as *sirodhara* (warm oil drizzled on the forehead; 45 minutes costs Rs 1000) and *pzhichal* (oil-intensive body massage; 1¼ hours costs Rs 1200). A head and foot massage costs Rs 350.

**Beyond Looks** (Map pp92-4; ☎ 26141517; lower ground fl, 15 Poorvi Marg, Vasant Vihar; ⌚ 8.30am-8.30pm) is located in a large apartment complex. Services offered include an olive/coconut oil massage (one hour costs Rs 400), shiatsu (one hour costs Rs 600) and *sirodhara* (1½ hours costs Rs 500). Beauty treatments (facials, waxing etc) also possible.

### Swimming

Deluxe hotels have the best pools but they're restricted to guests. Some of the more modest upmarket hotels permit outsiders (for a stout amount). Try **Centaur Hotel** (Off Map pp92-4; ☎ 25696660; National Hwy 8; per person Rs 165), **Claridges Hotel** (Map pp102-4; ☎ 23010211; 12 Aurangzeb Rd; per person Rs 900) and **Hotel Samrat** (Map pp102-4; ☎ 26110606; Chanakyapuri; per person Rs 300).

## COURSES

See p96 for publications containing up-to-the-minute details about various courses.

The **Central Hindi Directorate** (Ministry of Human Resource Development; ☎ 26100758; West Block VII, RK Puram) offers basic Hindi courses but only operates with minimum numbers. The cost is Rs 6000 for 60 hours (two hours a day, three days a week).

### Meditation & Yoga

Telephone for session timings and, if not stated below, venues. Where there are no fees, donations are appreciated.

**Ashtaang** (Map pp92-4; ☎ 24101802; E-2 Anand Niketan; 1hr Rs 150) Beginner and advanced hatha yoga.

**Dhyan Foundation** (☎ 26464174) Meditation classes plus one-day workshops introducing participants to *sanatan kriya* (rotation exercises, yoga and meditation).

**Morarji Desai National Institute of Yoga** (Map pp102-4; ☎ 23721472; www.mdniy.nic.in; 68 Ashoka Rd) Includes pranayama and hatha yoga (one hour Rs 100), meditation (one hour Rs 100) and stress-management courses (Rs 500).

**Studio Abhyas** (☎ 26962757) Yoga classes (1¼ hours) combine asanas (fixed body positions), pranayama and meditation. There's Vedic chanting on some evenings.

**Tushita Meditation Centre** (☎ 26513400) Twice-weekly Tibetan/Buddhist meditation sessions.

## TOURS

Delhi is a spread-out city so taking a tour makes sense, although they can be somewhat hurried. Sunday is particularly good because there's less road traffic, but avoid Monday, when various sites are closed.

The India Tourism Delhi office (p97) can arrange multilingual, government-approved guides. The charge is Rs 350/500 for a half-/full day (maximum five people), Rs 500/630

#### COOL RETREATS

If you find yourself frazzled by Delhi's oppressive heat (outside winter), traffic snarls, pesky touts and other vicissitudes of life on the road, there are some scenic spots to steal solace. In the cooler months, chill out in the pleasant grounds of **Humayun's Tomb** (p101), **Qutb Minar** (p130), **Safdarjang's Tomb** (p104), **Lodi Garden** (p104), **Hauz Khas** (opposite), **Raj Ghat** (p100) and **India Gate** (p101).

During hotter months, **top-end hotels** (p115) – with their powerful AC and comfy interiors – offer revitalising havens. Their coffee shops aren't a bargain, but certainly won't break the bank (unless you go on a feeding frenzy) and are relaxing places to hang for a while. If you're cashed up, these hotels also have plush fine-dining possibilities.

Delhi's modern AC **cineplexes** (p122) are also terrific spots to beat the summer heat without spending a fortune. Movie tickets range from Rs 50 to 150, and that all-important popcorn-and-fizzy-drink combo will set you back around Rs 75.

(maximum 14) and Rs 630/975 (maximum 35). Higher charges apply for tours beyond the city's limits.

Admission fees to the various sites and camera/video charges are not included in tour prices and rates are per person. Bookings should be made at least a day in advance as minimum numbers may be required for them to run.

**Ashok Travels & Tours** (Indian Tourism Development Corporation; Map pp106-7; ☎ 23412336; L-Block, Connaught Pl; ⌚ 6.30am-8.30pm) Near Nirula's Hotel, but you can book at India Tourism Delhi (p97) or at any Indian Tourism Development Corporation (ITDC) hotel. Tours include a morning (8am to 1pm) excursion of New Delhi and an afternoon (2pm to 5.15pm) tour of Old Delhi; each costs Rs 200. A tour of both Old and New Delhi is Rs 300 (8am to 5.15pm). Same-day trips (Saturday to Thursday) to Agra are Rs 850.

**Delhi Tourism & Transport Development Corporation** (DTTDC); Baba Kharak Singh Marg (Map pp106-7; ☎ 23365358; ⌚ 8am-9pm); domestic airport (☎ 25675609; ⌚ 9am-11pm); international airport (☎ 25691213; ⌚ 24hr); N-Block (Map pp106-7; ☎ 23315322; ⌚ 10am-6pm Mon-Sat); New Delhi train station (Map p111; ☎ 23742374; ⌚ 7am-9pm); Nizamuddin train station (Map pp102-4; ☎ 5547065; ⌚ 7am-9pm); Old Delhi train station (Map p99; ☎ 23961083; ⌚ 7am-9pm) Has a morning tour (9am to 2pm) of New Delhi, and an Old Delhi tour that runs from 2.15pm to 5.15pm; each costs Rs 103 and together (same day) cost Rs 202. Same-day trips to Agra (Rs 850) run thrice-weekly while three-day tours of Agra and Jaipur (Rs 3200) operate twice-weekly.

**Hotel Broadway** (Map p99; ☎ 23273821; 4/15 Asaf Ali Rd; Rs 495) Operating from the hotel (p113), two-hour 'gastronomic walking tours' of Old Delhi include lunch at Chor Bizarre (see p115).

**Master Guest House** (Map pp92-4; ☎ 28741089; R-500 New Rajendra Nagar) This guesthouse (p113) offers personalised tours – such as 'Hidden Delhi' (includes Old Delhi) – with a knowledgeable guide. Tours cost the rupee equivalent of US$15, which includes breakfast and snacks.

## SLEEPING

It's wise to book a room in advance as Delhi's most salubrious places can fill up in a flash, leaving new arrivals easy prey for commission sharks (see p97). Most hotels offer pick-ups from the airport (see p128) with advance notice.

Checkout at most hotels is noon (but always ask ahead so you aren't unknowingly charged an extra day) and luggage storage is usually possible (often Rs 3 to 5 per day at budget accommodation).

During the low season (around mid-April to mid-August) room discounts of at least 20% are negotiable.

Hotels with a minimum tariff of Rs 500 charge a 12.5% luxury tax and some places also whack on an additional service charge (of 6% to 10%). Taxes aren't included in the reviews in this chapter unless indicated and all rooms have private bathrooms unless otherwise stated.

Street din can be diabolical – to snooze soundly, request a quiet room and keep earplugs by your bed.

### Budget

Delhi's budget bunch of places to stay is decidedly lacklustre; rooms are typically small and dreary, and the service is rather patchy. Rock-bottom places are desperate for a fresh lick of paint, new mattresses and a bathroom blitz. On the plus side, rooms are not as expensive as they could be for a capital city.

Most backpackers base themselves in Paharganj, a bustling, tourist-oriented pocket near the New Delhi train station. For something much more mellow (but not nearly as central), try Majnu-ka-Tilla.

Room quality within hotels can vary dramatically so inspect a few first. Some places lock their gates after 10pm, so warn them if you'll be back late.

In the following budget listings, only the cheapest, non-AC room rates have been given; the AC rooms, where available, cost around several hundred rupees more.

#### NORTH DELHI

#### Old Delhi

Few travellers stay in Old Delhi but for those who wish to, there are reasonable hotels near the Jama Masjid. Solo women may be viewed with curious disdain.

**Hotel Bombay Orient** (Map p99; ☎ 23286253; fax 23262446; s/d Rs 350/450) The most appealing choice in the area, but ensure you get one of its newer rooms (No 118 is good).

**Hotel New City Palace** (Map p99; ☎ 23279548; s/d Rs 200/250; ❄) Claustrophobic rooms but still better than most other Old Delhi cheapies.

**Hotel de Romana** (Map p99; ☎ 30981216; s/d Rs 410/560; ❄) Down a lane behind the Jagat Cinema, it's characterless but satisfactory if you can't find a room at the above hotels.

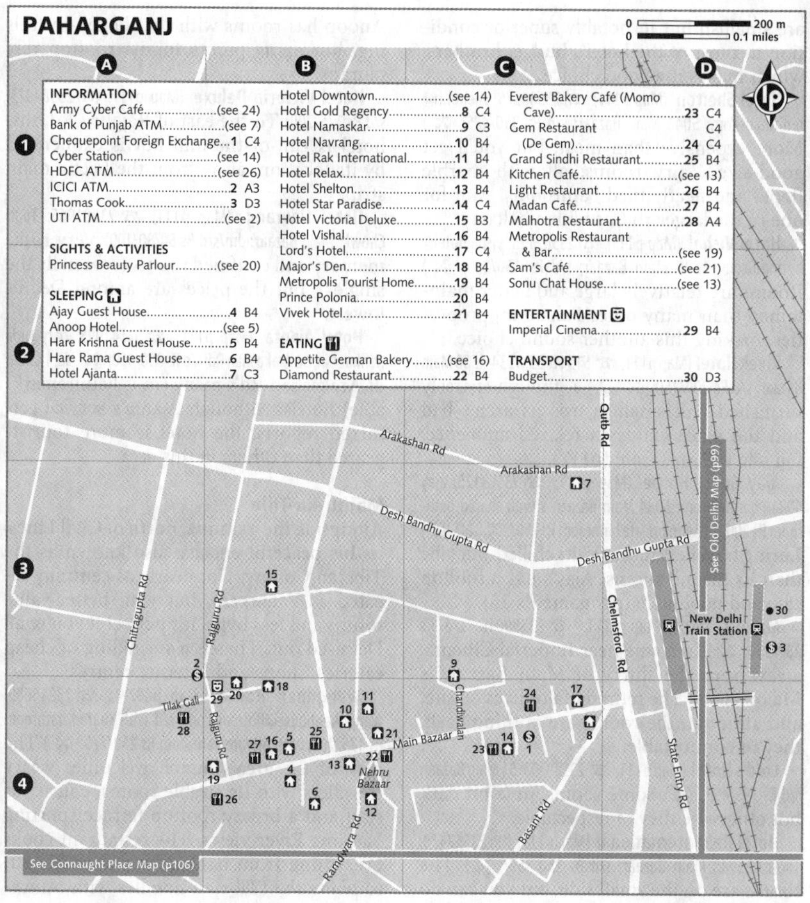


## Paharganj Area

Bursting with budget accommodation, eateries, shops and human traffic, Paharganj isn't everyone's cup of tea. Indeed, many Delhiites regard it as a downright seedy place on account of its reputation for drugs and very shady characters. On the upside, it's in walking distance from the New Delhi train station (handy if you've got an early-morning departure) and it's *the* place to tap into the busy backpacker network. Although Paharganj has some of Delhi's cheapest beds, be prepared for nondescript, often poorly ventilated and sun-starved rooms.

Most hotels are on the main drag of Main Bazaar, with many freckling the numerous (nameless) alleys snaking off it. Since Main Bazaar is so congested during the day, taxi-wallahs may (understandably) refuse to deposit you right at your hotel's doorstep; this is not really a problem as most hotels are a short walk away.

**Hotel Namaskar** (Map p111; ☎ 23583456; namaskarhotel@yahoo.com; 917 Chandiwalan, Main Bazaar; d from Rs 250; ❄) The star attractions of this hotel are its two very helpful brothers, who, apart from dispensing useful advice, can arrange car hire in and beyond Delhi and in Rajasthan. Most of the 32 simple rooms are painted in a cheerful shade of pink.

**Hotel Downtown** (Map p111; ☎ 51541529; fax 51541528; 4583 Main Bazaar; s/d Rs 200/250) The rooms are smallish but in notably superior condition to most of the hotel's budget brothers, which makes it a good choice.

**Hotel Shelton** (Map p111; ☎ 23580575; sheltonh@rediffmail.com; 5043 Main Bazaar; s/d Rs 350/475; ) More expensive than most, but you'll get good-sized, airy rooms, all with marble floors and neatly tiled bathrooms. Aim for one of the larger rooms with a balcony.

**Hotel Vishal** (Map p111; ☎ 23562123; vishalhotel@hotmail.com; 1575 Main Bazaar; s/d Rs 150/250; ) Rooms are relatively large and better maintained than many other Paharganj properties, making this another sound choice.

**Vivek Hotel** (Map p111; ☎ 51541435; 1534-1550 Main Bazaar; s/d Rs 200/250; ) Although sparsely furnished and smallish, rooms aren't bad and the place exudes a relaxed ambience. On site is Sam's Café (p117).

**Ajay Guest House** (Map p111; ☎ 23583125; ajay5084@hotmail.com; 5084 Main Bazaar; s with shared bathroom Rs 200, s/d with private bathroom Rs 250/300; ) Luring travellers more for its chilled-out vibe than its insipid rooms, Ajay's has a rooftop café and pool table (per game Rs 25).

**Major's Den** (Map p111; ☎ 23589010; s/d Rs 280/350; ) In a lane near Imperial Cinema, away from the flurry of Main Bazaar, is Major's Den. The retired Major lives on site, and although the rooms are nothing flash, they're comfortable.

**Lord's Hotel** (Map p111; ☎ 23588303; 51 Main Bazaar; s/d Rs 395/495; ) Some rooms are a bit dark but otherwise they're respectable.

**Hotel Rak International** (Map p111; ☎ 23562478; Tooti Chowk, Main Bazaar; s/d Rs 250/350; ) The rooms are on the small side, but you can do star jumps on the restaurant terrace while gazing at the masses below.

**Hare Rama Guest House** (Map p111; ☎ 23561301; harerama_2000@hotmail.com; T-298 Main Bazaar; s/d Rs 180/230; ) Rooms have cool tiled walls and floors, but some are notably sunlight deprived.

**Hare Krishna Guest House** (Map p111; ☎ 51541340; harekrishnagh@hotmail.com; 1572 Main Bazaar; s/d Rs 200/250) Apart from being smallish, the rooms are in pretty good shape (for Paharganj) and there's a rooftop restaurant.

**Hotel Star Paradise** (Map p111; ☎ 23561597; starview@vsnl.com; 4582 Main Bazaar; s/d Rs 300/400; ) The rooms aren't spacious but are otherwise acceptable.

**Anoop Hotel** (Map p111; ☎ 51541390; anoophotel@hotmail.com; 1566 Main Bazaar; s/d Rs 220/350; ) Anoop has rooms with that boxed-in feeling, but earns points for its rooftop restaurant.

**Hotel Victoria Deluxe** (Map p111; ☎ 23584413; s/d Rs 175/200) To the east of Rajguru Rd, this hotel is run-of-the-mill but is exonerated by its location, away from the hectic main strip.

**Hotel Navrang** (Map p111; ☎ 23581965; Tooti Chowk, Main Bazaar; dm/s/d Rs 50/80/100) Very rudimentary and confined rooms (especially the singles), but the prices are among Delhi's lowest.

**Hotel Ajanta** (Map p111; ☎ 51541995; ccity@nda.vsnl.net.in; 36 Arakashan Rd; s/d Rs 350/450; ) One of Arakashan Rd's many (mostly unremarkable) hotels. Although Ajanta's service gets mixed reports, the hotel is more tourist-geared than others in this area.

### Majnu-ka-Tilla

Alongside the Yamuna, north of Civil Lines, is this peaceful enclave also known as the Tibetan Colony. Not nearly as centrally located as Paharganj, but with better-value rooms and less hype, it's perfect if you're all Delhi-ed out. There's a sprinkling of cheap eateries, shops and Internet centres.

**Wongdhen House** (Map pp92-4; ☎ 23816689; wongdhenhouse@hotmail.com; s/d with shared bathroom Rs 175/200, with private bathroom Rs 250/275; ) The pick of the area's bunch welcomes weary travellers with its sizable rooms, courteous staff and a breezy rooftop terrace sporting Yamuna River views. The restaurant cooks everything from banana pancakes (Rs 30) to *phing sha* (Tibetan noodles with mincemeat, Rs 45).

**Peace House** (Map pp92-4; ☎ 23939415; d 4th/3rd/2nd/1st fl Rs 175/275/325/325) Offers plain but neat rooms and whenever hunger strikes, a plate of steamed *momos* (Tibetan dumplings, Rs 20) is not far away.

Other recommendations:

**IDA House** (Map pp92-4; ☎ 23813960; d Rs 250)
**Lhasa House** (Map pp92-4; ☎ 23939888; d Rs 350; )
**White House** (Map pp92-4; ☎ 23813999; d Rs 250; )

## CENTRAL DELHI

The YWCA Blue Triangle Family Hostel (p114) also has dorm beds.

### Chanakyapuri

**Youth Hostel** (Map pp102-4; ☎ 26116285; yhostel@del2.vsnl.net.in; 5 Nyaya Marg; dm Rs 60, with AC Rs 250, s/d with shared bathroom Rs 450/650; ) Soothing setting but lackadaisical service. The dormitory is good value for members (nonmembers pay an extra Rs 250 and receive membership, which is valid for one year).

### Connaught Place Area

This area's hotels won't exactly make you jump for joy – you're essentially paying for the central location, not the room quality or service, which is, frankly, so-so.

**Central Court Hotel** (Map pp106-7; ☎ 23315013; N-Block; s/d with shared bathroom Rs 700/900, with private bathroom Rs 1000/1250; ) Roomy and with an old-world flavour, this is the most atmospheric budget choice in Connaught Pl. Rooms can be noisy so choose prudently.

**Janpath Guest House** (Map pp106-7; ☎ 23321935; janpathguesthouse@yahoo.co.uk; 82-84 Janpath; s/d Rs 425/485; ) The carpeted rooms can be dark and dank but the prices are fair. It's conveniently close to the tourist office and a prepaid autorickshaw booth.

**HK Choudhary Guest House** (Map pp106-7; ☎ 23322043; harsh@del3.vsnl.net.in; 35/3 H-Block; s with shared bathroom Rs 300, s/d with private bathroom Rs 550/660; ) Near the PVR Plaza Cinema, there are seven rooms that are humdrum but still reasonably priced for this area (some bigger and brighter than others). There's a small outdoor terrace.

**Hotel Blue** (Map pp106-7; ☎ 23416666; hotelblue@indiatimes.com; 2nd fl, M-126; s/d with shared bathroom Rs 600/800, with private bathroom Rs 900/1200; ) Hotel Blue's rooms are looking distinctly tired, but the terrace is good for a spot of sunbathing.

**Ringo Guest House** (Map pp106-7; ☎ 23310605; ringo_guest_house@yahoo.co.in; 17 Scindia House, Connaught Lane; dm Rs 90, s/d with shared bathroom Rs 125/250, d with private bathroom Rs 350) Down a side street near the India Tourism Delhi office, the rooms are poky and elementary but you can't shake a finger at the price.

**Sunny Guest House** (Map pp106-7; ☎ 23312909; sunnyguesthouse.123@hotmail.com; 152 Scindia House; dm Rs 90, s/d with shared bathroom Rs 125/250, d with private bathroom Rs 350) Near Ringo, Sunny is fractionally less impressive.

### AIRPORT AREA

**Hotel Tarra** (Map pp92-4; ☎ 26783677; A-72, St No 2, Mahipalpur Extension, National Hwy 8; s/d Rs 450/495; ) The best budget choice in the area, with comfortable rooms, Tarra is 6km from the international airport, tucked away on a small lane off the main road (follow the signs).

For passengers who have a confirmed departure within 24 hours of arriving by plane, there's accommodation at the retiring rooms of the **domestic terminal** (☎ 25675126, ext 2208; dm/d Rs 450/650; ) and **international terminal** (☎ 25652011, ext 2157; dm Rs 90, with AC Rs 250; ) at the Indira Gandhi International Airport.

## Midrange

### NORTH DELHI

### Old Delhi

**Hotel Broadway** (Map p99; ☎ 23273821; broadway@oldworldhospitality.com; 4/15 Asaf Ali Rd; s/d Rs 1295/1535; ) Broadway's Chor Bizarre restaurant (p115) and 'gastronomic tour' (p110) are more thrilling than the dated rooms.

### Paharganj Area

**Metropolis Tourist Home** (Map p111; ☎ 23561794; metravel@bom9.vsnl.net.in; 1634 Main Bazaar; s/d incl tax Rs 700/800; ) Good rooms (some with balcony) that receive more natural light than most other Paharganj hotels. There's also a pleasant rooftop restaurant (p116).

**Prince Polonia** (Map p111; ☎ 23581930; polinter@del3.vsnl.net.in; 2325 Tilak Gali; s/d Rs 900/1000; ) The standard rooms are OK, but it's worth paying an extra Rs 100 to upgrade to a bigger room with balcony. Extras include a beauty parlour (nonguests are welcome; see p109).

**Hotel Relax** (Map p111; ☎ 23562811; vidur109@hotmail.com; Nehru Bazaar; d Rs 1000; ) Comfortable, albeit slightly kitsch, rooms (request one with a balcony). From the rooftop, watch the scurrying humans and ponder the meaning of life over a cup of lemon tea (Rs 15).

**Hotel Gold Regency** (Map p111; ☎ 23562101; info@goldregency.com; 4350 Main Bazaar; s/d with breakfast Rs 950/1200; ) Rooms are a bit dowdy but fairly commodious.

### West of Paharganj

**Yatri House** (Map pp92-4; ☎ 23625563; www.yatrihouse.com; 3/4 Panchkuian Marg; s/d Rs 1000/1200, with AC Rs 1200/1500; ) Away from the madness of Main Bazaar, on a lane off Panchkuian Marg, is this guesthouse with a green lawn, open-air courtyard and seven well-kept rooms.

### Rajendra Nagar Area

**Master Guest House** (Map pp92-4; ☎ 28741089; www.master-guesthouse.com; R-500 New Rajendra Nagar; s/d with shared bathroom Rs 800/900; ) You'll have no hassles whatsoever at this calm residential guesthouse, located near the Shankar and Ganga Ram Hospital Rds crossing. Run by a friendly couple, there are just four homely rooms, all clean and comfortable. Avnish runs tours (see p110).

## CENTRAL DELHI

### Ashoka Road

**YWCA Blue Triangle Family Hostel** (Map pp102-4; ☎ 23360133; ywcadel@yahoo.co.in; Ashoka Rd; dm Rs 275, with AC Rs 325, s/d Rs 950/1650; ) Open to both sexes, you must become a temporary member (Rs 20, valid for one month) to stay. The dormitory is commendable, if a tad tightly packed, and the private rooms are also nice, despite a lingering hint of fragrance à la mothball. For solo travellers, room 108 is recommended. All rates include tax and breakfast.

### Sunder Nagar

The leafy, upmarket suburb of Sunder Nagar is about 3km southeast of Connaught Pl.

**La Sagrita Tourist Home** (Map pp102-4; ☎ 2435 8572; lasagrit@del3.vsnl.net.in; 14 Sunder Nagar; s/d Rs 1790/2290; ) Smallish rooms but they're comfortable, cosy and fairly priced.

**Jukaso Inn** (Map pp102-4; ☎ 24350308; jukaso@hotmail.com; 49-50 Sunder Nagar; s/d Rs 3000/4000; ) Also appealing – one of its best standard rooms (with a marshmallow-soft bed) is No 506.

**Maharani Guest House** (Map pp102-4; ☎ 24359521; mgh@vsnl.com; 3 Sunder Nagar; s/d Rs 1800/2400; ) Good rooms, although a smidgen small.

**Ten** (Map pp102-4; ☎ 24355047; fax 51507155; 10 Sunder Nagar; s/d Rs 1800/2000; ) Has just five rooms; Nos 105 (double) and 106 (single) share a courtyard.

### Connaught Place Area

**Hotel Jukaso Inn** (Map pp106-7; ☎ 23415450; jukaso@vsnl.com; L-Block; s/d Rs 1800/2500; ) Connaught Pl's most modern and comfortably appointed midrange choice.

**Nirula's Hotel** (Map pp106-7; ☎ 23417419; delhihotel@nirulas.com; L-Block; s/d Rs 2850/3000; ) A three-star hotel with tidy rooms, although some can be gloomy.

**York Hotel** (Map pp106-7; ☎ 23415769; hotelyork@yahoo.com; K-Block; s/d Rs 1800/2950; ) Plain but presentable rooms (avoid the noisy roadside ones).

> **THE AUTHOR'S CHOICE**
>
> **Imperial** (Map pp106-7; ☎ 23341234; www.theimperialindia.com; Janpath; d US$250-1800; ) Gracefully appointed, with a central location, pillared verandas and an avenue of palms, this eclectic Raj-era property, built in 1931, has hosted everyone from royalty to rock stars. Indeed, it's said that Gandhi, Nehru, Jinnah and Mountbatten met here to discuss the thorny matter of India's partition.
>
> Beautifully refurbished, the property amalgamates multiple styles – from classic Victorian to colonial and Art Deco – and exhibits some stunning artwork, including rare 18th- and 19th-century pieces. The 234 soundproofed rooms are attractively furnished, with no trace of the carbon-copy designs found at international chains. There are two bars, a patisserie and four appealing restaurants, including the Spice Route (south and Southeast Asian cuisine), plus a holistic spa complex.

**Hotel Fifty Five** (Map pp106-7; ☎ 23321244; bookings@hotel55.com; H-55; s/d Rs 1300/1800; ) A popular hotel with obliging staff and reasonable rooms (and tariffs).

**Hotel Alka** (Map pp106-7; ☎ 23344328; hotelalka@vsnl.com; P-Block; s/d Rs 1800/2700; ) Some rooms are space-deprived but otherwise agreeable. There's a reputable vegetarian restaurant.

**YMCA Tourist Hostel** (Map pp106-7; ☎ 23361915; ymcath@ndf.vsnl.net.in; Jai Singh Rd; s/d with shared bathroom Rs 630/1230, s/d with private bathroom Rs 1000/1780; ) The hostel takes both genders (Rs 30 membership; valid for one month); see several rooms as some are dingy. The Rs 100 charge (per guest per stay) to use the pool (April to October) is rather cheeky. All rates include tax, breakfast and dinner.

**YWCA International Guest House** (Map pp106-7; ☎ 23361561; www.ywcaindia.org; 10 Sansad Marg; s/d incl tax Rs 1078/1350; ) Has the same institutional feel as the YMCA.

## SOUTH DELHI

**Home Away from Home** (Map pp92-4; ☎ 26560289; 1st fl, D-8 Gulmohar Park; s/d Rs 800/1400, with AC Rs 900/1500; ) This stylish residential apartment offers home-style accommodation and gives discounts to those who stay at least a month. Meals are available with advance notice and the price includes breakfast. Owned by Mrs Kamte – who lives on site and keeps the place in tiptop condition – there are just two rooms, each tastefully furnished. Hush and Puppy, the pet basset hounds, appreciate a tummy tickle.

## Top End

Delhi has many top-end hotels – these are just some of the possibilities.

### CENTRAL DELHI

**Maurya Sheraton Hotel & Towers** (Off Map pp102-4; ☎ 26112233; reservations.maurya@welcomgroup.com; Sardar Patel Marg; s/d US$275/300; ) This world-class hotel has carved a name for itself as one of Delhi's finest. There are 515 luxurious rooms and a range of top-notch facilities, including a health club, beauty parlour and efficient business centre. There are also some exceptional restaurants, including Bukhara and Dum Pukht (see p118).

**Oberoi** (Map pp102-4; ☎ 24363030; reservations@oberoidel.com; Dr Zakir Hussain Marg; s/d US$250/275; ) On the edge of the Delhi Golf Club, the Oberoi scores high marks. Discerning service, elegant rooms and amenities such as a 24-hour state-of-the-art business centre make this hotel especially popular with visiting business people.

**Taj Palace Hotel** (Map pp102-4; ☎ 26110202; palace.delhi@tajhotels.com; Sardar Patel Marg; s/d US$210/235; ) Apart from ritzy, typically five-star-chain rooms, there are four restaurants, a health club and a smooth nightclub, My Kind of Place (p122). The Taj's staff have clearly gone through rigorous training workshops; however, their icy professionalism can sometimes make you feel more like a number than a name.

**Le Meridien** (Map pp102-4; ☎ 23710101; info@lemeridien-newdelhi.com; Windsor Pl, Janpath; s/d US$160/180; ) This glassy high-rise hotel has immaculate, contemporary-style five-star rooms and perks such as a beauty parlour, gymnasium, enticing shopping arcade and four restaurants, including a round-the-clock coffee shop.

### SOUTH DELHI

#### Bhikaiji Cama Place

**Hyatt Regency** (Map pp92-4; ☎ 26791234; india.reservations@hyattintl.com; Bhikaiji Cama Pl, Ring Rd; s/d US$160/170; ) The Hyatt Regency delivers the high standard of comfort-packed rooms and slick service that has made it shine throughout the world. Facilities include a gymnasium, sauna, tennis court and one of Delhi's coolest night spots, Djinns (p121), as well as some sterling dining options (see p119).

#### Airport Area

**Radisson Hotel** (Map pp92-4; ☎ 26779191; www.radisson.com/newdelhiin; National Hwy 8; d US$225; ) If you're seeking creature comforts in the airport locale, this is your best bet. Apart from its 256 stylish rooms, there's a fitness centre and a clutch of smart restaurants (see p120).

**Ashok Country Resort** (Off Map pp92-4; ☎ 2506 4590; www.ashokcountryresort.com; Rajokri Rd; s/d Rs 3500/4500; ) It's not nearly as snazzy as the Radisson Hotel, but the price doesn't pack as much of a punch. Set in secluded green grounds, the Ashok's comfortable, unpretentious rooms make a welcoming retreat.

# EATING

Catering to most palates and pockets, eating out is a Delhi highlight. There are some sublime home-grown restaurants, while those homesick for familiar fast food will find ever-multiplying chains, including McDonald's, Pizza Hut, Subway and TGI Friday's.

Most midrange and all upmarket restaurants attract a service tax of around 10%. Drinks can suck a further 20% to 25% (alcoholic) or 12% (nonalcoholic) tax from your moneybelt.

## North Delhi

### OLD DELHI

#### Restaurants

**Karim's** (Map p99; ☎ 23269880; mains Rs 75-180; noon-3pm & 6pm-midnight; ) Down a lane across the south gate of the Jama Masjid, iconic Karim's has been delighting Delhiites since 1913 with its flavoursome, predominantly nonvegetarian, Mughlai cuisine. During Ramadan, it opens after sunset.

**Chor Bizarre** (Map p99; ☎ 23273821; Hotel Broadway, 4/15 Asaf Ali Rd; mains Rs 115-250, veg/nonveg thalis Rs 260/325; 7.30-10.30am, noon-3.30pm & 7.30-11.30pm; ) Wonderful Kashmiri and Mughlai fare in quirky surrounds – there's a vintage car that serves as a salad bar, and even a four-poster bed as a table. The *sharabi kababi tikka masala* (gravy-based chicken flamed in brandy, Rs 250) is as good as it sounds. Reservations are recommended.

**Moti Mahal Restaurant** (Map p99; ☎ 23273661; 3704 Netaji Subhash Marg, Daryaganj; mains Rs 60-225; 11am-midnight; ) Noted for its very tasty butter chicken (half/full bird Rs 140/265), there's live *qawwali* Wednesday to Monday (from 8.30pm). Reservations are recommended on weekends.

### Quick Eats

Little stalls set up in the evening (many on the south side of the Jama Masjid) doing cheap kebabs, fried fish and more. You can fill up for Rs 40.

**Haldiram's** (Map p99; Chandni Chowk; samosas/pakoras Rs 5/6, barfi per kg from Rs 100) Where the hoi polloi congregate for a salty or sweet Indian fast-food hit.

**Ghantewala** (Map p99; Chandni Chowk; Indian sweets per kg around Rs 80) Near the Sisganj Gurdwara, this simple sweetery has been in business since 1790 and, although facing stiff competition from Haldiram's (opposite), it still has a loyal following.

**Jalebiwala** (Map p99; Chandni Chowk; jalebis per 500g from around Rs 50) Also near the Sisganj Gurdwara, Jalebiwala is *the* place to sink your chompers into fat, syrupy fried *jalebis*.

**Paratha Wali Gali** (Map p99; parathas Rs 10-40) In a lane just behind Ghantewala, off Chandni Chowk, come here to feast on *parathas* (Indian flat bread) flipped fresh off the *tawa* (hotplate); some are stuffed with fillings such as spiced *aloo* (potato) and *paneer* (unfermented cheese).

### PAHARGANJ AREA

Paharganj menus are of the bamboozling have-a-go-at-anything variety, with hit-and-miss recipes presumably passed on by travellers. All of the following places are along or just off Main Bazaar.

**Malhotra Restaurant** (Map p111; mains Rs 30-125; 7am-11pm) Gets kudos from travellers for its delish Indian, Chinese and Continental food. Eat eggs or muesli and yogurt for breakfast, and for lunch and dinner there's everything from cheese macaroni to tandoori chicken. Delhi belly? Try the mashed potato.

**Metropolis Restaurant & Bar** (Map p111; Metropolis Tourist Home, 1634 Main Bazaar; mains Rs 85-250; 8am-11pm) A relaxing rooftop restaurant with decent lasagne, sweet-and-spicy salmon fillets, tandoori capsicum and more. The wicked walnut brownie with hot chocolate sauce (Rs 125) is almost as good as, well, you know what.

**Kitchen Café** (Map p111; Hotel Shelton, 5043 Main Bazaar; mains Rs 60-110; 8am-11.30pm) Another travellers' favourite, this easy-going rooftop restaurant is a formidable place to fuel up on a 'Spanish Breakfast' (omelette, toast, hash brown and tea or coffee, Rs 65), pizzas (Rs 70 to 110), spinach-mushroom cannelloni (Rs 80) and the like.

**Diamond Restaurant** (Map p111; mains Rs 30-100; 7.30am-11.30pm) Diamond shines when it comes to pasta, but its Indian, Chinese,

### THE AUTHOR'S CHOICE

**Olive Bar & Kitchen** (Map pp92-4; ☎ 26642552; Haveli 6-8, One Style Mile, Kalka Dass Marg, Mehrauli; mains Rs 325-595; noon-2.30pm & 8pm-midnight; ) A hidden gem, this elegant yet earthy restaurant is just the place to cool your heels after stomping around Qutb Minar (p130). Mirroring a Mediterranean villa, you can sit out in the banyan-tree shaded courtyard or at one of the sun-washed indoor tables. After dark the place twinkles with candlelight, making it ideal for a romantic tryst. The restaurant has a smart-casual dress code and advises advance reservations.

Olive's often-changing menu has a Mediterranean focus. Friday-lunch diners get a complimentary 'hot stone therapy' massage, while on Sunday there's a picnic-theme buffet brunch (12.30pm to 2.30pm). On the last Wednesday of each month, it's flea-market night (from 8pm), with budding artists assembling stalls in the courtyard. All-day coffee, dessert and wood-fired pizza is also available outside of lunch and dinner hours.

To find this (unsigned) restaurant from the Qutb Minar exit (with your back to Qutb Minar) head left (towards Mehrauli) and walk about 200m. Look to your right for the white building with blue gates, signed 'One Style Mile'.

Continental and Israeli dishes can yield wobbly results.

**Sam's Café** (Map p111; Vivek Hotel, 1534-1550 Main Bazaar; mains Rs 60-110; 7.30am-11pm) Operating on the Vivek Hotel's ground and top floors, settle back with a masala chai or strawberry lassi before diving into the avocado salad, spaghetti bolognaise or roast chicken.

**Light Restaurant** (Map p111; mains Rs 7-25; 11am-midnight) If you're strapped for cash, make a beeline for this *dhaba*-style eatery. It's nothing fancy, but its bean or eggplant curry and rice pudding are a tiny Rs 7 (each), meaning you can fill your belly without emptying your pockets.

**Sonu Chat House** (Map p111; mains Rs 25-100; 8am-10pm) Cooks up South Indian fare – by golly, there's even a chocolate banana dosa (Rs 40) – as well as Chinese and Continental dishes.

**Appetite German Bakery** (Map p111; mains Rs 45-80; 7am-11pm) By the Hotel Vishal, Appetite is good for a slice of cake (cheesecake is Rs 35) and cup of lemongrass tea (Rs 8).

**Madan Café** (Map p111; mains Rs 20-45; 7am-11pm) This small vegetarian Indian, Chinese and Continental café is of particular appeal for its low prices. Thalis start at just Rs 25, and banana curd (yogurt) is Rs 15.

**Gem Restaurant** (Map p111; De Gem; mains Rs 40-200; 9am-midnight) Has an ambitious spectrum of menu items, from banana porridge (Rs 35) to fish curry (Rs 85). Go upstairs for more character and to catch a cricket match on the wide-screen TV.

**Everest Bakery Café** (Map p111; Momo Cave; mains Rs 30-90; 7am-11pm) Opposite the Hotel Star Paradise, this diminutive café boasts particularly enticing teas (mint tea Rs 7). It also does pizza, pasta and assorted snacks.

**Grand Sindhi Restaurant** (Map p111; mains Rs 30-75; 6am-11pm) Lacks oomph, but is OK for a grilled tomato-and-cheese sandwich (Rs 12) on the run.

## Central Delhi

### CONNAUGHT PLACE AREA

#### Restaurants

**United Coffee House** (Map pp106-7; E-Block; mains Rs 65-220; 11am-11pm; ) With old-world charm and pleasing meals, this is a splendid spot to slow the pace. The assorted kebab platter (veg/nonveg Rs 155/215; feeds two) gets a round of applause, but the caramel custard does not.

**Saravana Bhavan** (Map pp106-7; 46 Janpath; dosas Rs 34-70, thalis Rs 65; 8am-11pm; ) Great-value dosas, *idlis* (South Indian rice dumplings) and other southern specialities. When it comes to 'Rice of the Day', Friday (tamarind) and Monday (lemon) get gold stars, as do the inventive sweets (cucumber-seed *ladoo* – gram flour and semolina sweetmeats – is Rs 165 per kilogram). Saravana also has a branch at 15 P-Block, Connaught Pl.

**Kwality Restaurant** (Map pp106-7; 7 Regal Bldg, Sansad Marg; mains Rs 85-180; lunch noon-3.30pm, snacks 3.30-7pm, dinner 7-11pm; ) Feeding Delhi for nearly 70 years, Kwality's tables may be rather tightly packed, but this venerable restaurant's food (especially the Indian dishes) is praiseworthy. Try the *shahi paneer* (unfermented cheese in a creamy tomato sauce, Rs 110).

**Banana Leaf** (Map pp106-7; 12 N-Block; dosas Rs 40-75, thalis Rs 50-70; 10.30am-11pm; ) Apart from some top-notch South Indian standards, there are some more-obscure options such as the dry fruit masala dosa and *bisi bela bath* (spiced rice and lentils, Rs 40).

**Sagar Ratna** (Map pp106-7; 15 K-Block; dosas Rs 32-50, thalis Rs 60; 8am-11pm; ) Another dosa dreamland, Sagar Ratna's *uttapams* (crisp-collared rice-flour and coconut-milk pancakes from Rs 32) also deserve special merit. The cooling *dahi idly* (*idly* dunked in yogurt, Rs 33) is especially mollifying for raw tummies.

**Zen** (Map pp106-7; 25 B-Block; mains Rs 100-450; noon-midnight; ) Quintessentially Chinese, soothing Zen also offers Japanese alternatives. The crispy sesame lamb (Rs 175) is worth a try, as are the honey-drizzled date pancakes (Rs 85). For lunch there's a decent economical set meal (veg/nonveg Rs 195/225).

**Berco's** (Map pp106-7; 8 E-Block; mains Rs 90-270; 12.30-11pm; ) Hot sellers at this popular Chinese restaurant include the Szechwan chicken and sweet chilli tofu.

**Embassy** (Map pp106-7; 11 D-Block; mains Rs 90-200; 10am-midnight; ) Dimly lit, Embassy does a scrummy *palak paneer* (unfermented cheese in spinach sauce, Rs 105) or, for the more adventurous, there's the brain curry (Rs 140).

**Parikrama** (Map pp106-7; 23721616; 22 Kasturba Gandhi Marg; mains Rs 140-400; lunch 12.30-3.30pm, snacks 3.30-7.30pm, dinner 7.30-11pm; ) A revolving restaurant on the 24th floor where you can enjoy Indian or Chinese food while oh-so-slowly spinning (one revolution takes 1½ hours). The views are superlative, especially during the day.

**Café 100** (Map pp106-7; 20 B-Block; mains Rs 80-190; 11am-11pm; ) Easy-going and with a varied menu, kick off with masala fish fingers (Rs 170) and wind up with chocolate mud pie (Rs 60).

**Host** (Map pp106-7; 8 F-Block; mains Rs 90-215; 10am-11.30pm; ) Daydreaming waiters in crumpled bow ties are part of this restaurant's faded appeal. Its Indian food is best.

### Quick Eats

**Wenger's** (Map pp106-7; A-Block) The legendary Wenger's bakes cakes (Rs 23 per slice; birthday cakes from Rs 260 per kilogram), savouries (veg/chicken baguettes Rs 32/37) and bread (German rye Rs 25 per loaf). Cookies, muffins, marzipan and almost 30 different types of homemade chocolates make perfect midnight snacks.

**Nirula's Ice-Cream Parlour** (Map pp106-7; L-Block; ice cream around Rs 35) Scoops up luscious ice cream – try stopping at just one cone.

**Nizam's Kathi Kabab** (Map pp106-7; H-Block; kebabs from Rs 55) Yummy takeaway kebabs. Note that it's only open from 5pm on Sunday (12.30pm other days).

### DIPLOMATIC ENCLAVE & CHANAKYAPURI AREA

**Bukhara** (Off Map pp102-4; ☎ 26112233; Maurya Sheraton Hotel & Towers, Sadar Patel Marg; mains Rs 495-695; 12.30-2.45pm & 7-11pm; ) Award-winning Bukhara does (meat-dominated) Northwest Frontier–style cuisine with aplomb. Reservations are essential and taken between 7pm and 8pm daily.

**Dum Pukht** (Off Map pp102-4; ☎ 26112233; Maurya Sheraton Hotel & Towers, Sadar Patel Marg; mains Rs 680-1000; 7.30-11.30pm Mon-Fri, 12.30-2.45pm & 7.30-11.30pm Sat & Sun; ) The delectable dishes are covered by a pastry cap while cooking so the food is steamed as much as anything else. Reservations (taken any time) are advised.

**Fujiya** (Map pp102-4; 12/48 Malcha Marg Market; mains Rs 85-210; 11.30am-11.15pm; ) Friendly Fujiya serves Chinese and some Japanese dishes. Whether it's Peking lamb or roast bean curd with vegetables, diners are rarely disappointed. There's a first-in-first-served policy – arrive early!

**New Sikkim House** (Map pp102-4; 14 Panchsheel Marg, Chanakyapuri; mains Rs 50-150; 8-10.30am, 12.30-4pm & 7-11pm) Hot-value Chinese and (some) Tibetan dishes. Although the *thukpa* (Tibetan noodle soup) won't win any prizes, it still hits the spot.

**Basil & Thyme** (Map pp102-4; Santushti Shopping Complex, Chanakyapuri; mains Rs 235-265; 10.30am-6pm Mon-Sat; ) Hobnob with Delhi's society ladies, who drop into B&T for blueberry crepes and coffee in between shopping.

### LODI COLONY

Coordinate a meal here with a visit to Safdarjang's Tomb (p104), Lodi Garden (p104) or Humayun's Tomb (p101).

**Ploof** (Map pp102-4; ☎ 24649026; 13 Main Market, Lodi Colony; mains Rs 225-590; 12.30-3pm & 7-11pm; ) Delectable deep-sea delights, including grilled lobster, beer-battered fish and chips, pan-seared salmon steak and baked crab.

**All American Diner** (Map pp102-4; India Habitat Centre, Lodi Rd; mains Rs 125-195; 7am-midnight; ) Decked out in true diner style and serving US classics, from buttermilk pancakes and peanut-butter malts to hot dogs and onion rings. Homesick Americans can seek solace in 'Mom's apple pie'.

**Lodi, The Garden Restaurant** (Map pp102-4; Lodi Rd; mains Rs 165-400; 12.30-11.30pm; ) Its Continental, Mediterranean and Lebanese cuisine gets varied reports, but this pleasant eatery, with a garden setting, is a handy sustenance stop after a power-walking session at nearby Lodi Garden.

### PANDARA MARKET

Pandara Market contains a cluster of restaurants that make a convenient lunch stop for those sightseeing at Humayun's Tomb (p101), Purana Qila (p101) or Safdarjang's Tomb (p104).

**Chicken Inn** (Map pp102-4; mains Rs 100-300; noon-1am; ) Offers good *saag* chicken (curried chicken and spinach, Rs 140) and *jal jeera* (lime, cumin, mint and salt beverage, Rs 30).

**Gulati** (Map pp102-4; mains Rs 100-300; noon-1am; ) Does a fine job of *tangri* kebab (spiced charcoal-grilled chicken drumsticks, Rs 210) and *bhutta* capsicum masala (capsicum in tomato-masala sauce, Rs 140).

**Ichiban** (Map pp102-4; mains Rs 100-300; noon-1am; ) If you're all curried-out, Ichiban specialises in Chinese and Japanese food –

try the *yaki tori* (chicken, Rs 125) and, for dessert, the crispy noodles in honey sauce (Rs 80).

**Pindi Restaurant** (Map pp102-4; mains Rs 100-300; noon-1am; ) Has particularly gratifying butter chicken (Rs 180) and *mattar paneer* (peas and cheese in gravy, Rs 120).

## South Delhi

### KHAN MARKET

There are also two excellent cafés in Khan Market: Big Chill (p120) and Café Turtle (p120).

**Chona's** (Map pp102-4; Khan Market; mains Rs 90-160; 11.30am-11pm Mon-Sat, 12.30-11pm Sun; ) Linger over satiating Indian, Chinese and Continental dishes, or chow down a 'cha-chow chilli chicken hot dog' (Rs 70) if you're on the dash.

**Rampur Kitchen** (Map pp102-4; Khan Market; mains Rs 125-300; 11.30am-3.30pm & 7-11.30pm; ) Lip-smacking tandoori fare (kebab platters are Rs 300) and biryani (veg/nonveg Rs 125/180).

### HAUZ KHAS AREA

**Naivedyam** (Map pp92-4; ☎ 26960426; Hauz Khas Village; dosas Rs 50-75, thalis Rs 90; 11am-11pm; ) A delightful, snug, South Indian restaurant that has a small but great-value menu and happy atmosphere.

**Park Baluchi** (Map pp92-4; ☎ 26859369; Hauz Khas Village; mains Rs 220-530; noon-midnight; ) Set in restful green grounds, you can devour the succulent tandoori chicken (wrapped around a burning sword! Rs 270) in the smart indoor section or out by the garden.

**La Piazza** (Map pp92-4; ☎ 26791234, ext 1310; Hyatt Regency, Bhikaiji Cama Pl, Ring Rd; mains Rs 310-780; noon-3pm & 7-11.30pm; ) Long acclaimed for its high-quality Italian food.

**Café** (Map pp92-4; ☎ 26791234, ext 1306; Hyatt Regency, Bhikaiji Cama Pl, Ring Rd; 24hr) Downstairs from La Piazza, Café offers affordable five-star 'semibuffets', such as its laudable salad buffet (Rs 395), which includes salads, soups, cold cuts (sliced meat, cheese and so on) and often seafood (even prawns). An extra Rs 50 throws in all-you-can-eat dessert.

**Bistro Restaurant Complex** (Map pp92-4; ☎ 26853857; Hauz Khas Village) includes **Mohalla** (Map pp92-4; mains Rs 90-290; noon-3pm & 7pm-midnight; ) for gravy-based curries – try also the *dum ki khumb* (a mushroom-based dish, Rs 175); **Roof-top** (Map pp92-4; mains Rs 145-550; ) for Indian; **Village Bistro** (Map pp92-4; mains Rs 125-290; 11am-11pm; ) for Continental and Indian; and **Baujee ka Dhaba** (Map pp92-4; mains Rs 225-350; 11.30am-3.30pm & 6.30-11.30pm; ) for Northwest Frontier food – don't miss the *murg dhaba* (chicken in 'special sauce', Rs 250).

### VASANT VIHAR

#### Restaurants

**Tamura** (Map pp92-4; ☎ 26154082; D-Block Market, Poorvi Marg; mains Rs 120-380; noon-3pm & 6-10.30pm; ) Armed with a Japanese chef, Tamura creates an authentic repertoire, from miso soup and mixed sushi rolls to *satsumaage* (minced fish cake). Reservations are recommended (request a downstairs table if you can).

**Punjabi by Nature** (Map pp92-4; ☎ 51516665; 11 Basant Lok; mains Rs 225-395; 12.30-3.30pm & 7.30-11.30pm; ) Supremely delicious North Indian food, including a scrumptious spicy lamb korma (Rs 295). Mop up flavour-packed curry sauces with piping-hot tandoori roti (Rs 40).

**O'Briens Irish Sandwich Bar** (Map pp92-4; 32 Basant Lok; sandwiches Rs 70-145; 11am-11pm; ) Wholesome made-to-order sandwiches and more substantial meals such as Irish veg stew. Sensational coffee and fat-free smoothies.

**Yo! China** (Map pp92-4; 7 Basant Lok; mains Rs 80-135; noon-11pm; ) Wok-tossed favourites from shredded crispy lamb to Szechwan vegetables.

#### Quick Eats

**Arabian Nites** (Map pp92-4; 59 Basant Lok; mains Rs 40-200) It may be tiny but it does mighty-good doner platters (veg/nonveg Rs 90/110) and falafel rolls (Rs 40).

**Sugar & Spice** (Map pp92-4; 48 Basant Lok) This place serves takeaway cakes, cookies, bread and savouries. The walnut tarts (Rs 35), muffins (Rs 20) and tandoori chicken sandwiches (Rs 45) are winners, but steer clear of the desert-dry croissants and doughnuts. There's also a branch of Sugar & Spice at Khan Market.

### DEFENCE COLONY & SOUTH EXTENSION AREA

**Flavours** (Map pp92-4; ☎ 24645644; 51-54C Moolchand Flyover Market, Ring Rd; mains Rs 150-310; noon-11pm; ) The Italian owner/chef ensures you eat the *real* thing, whether it's bruschetta, wood-fired pizzas, gourmet sandwiches (with ciabatta), risotto or, of course, pasta. Dessert connoisseurs will appreciate the custard crème caramel, 'an honest home-made dessert fresh by the hour'. You can eat in the attractive restaurant or out by the garden.

**Gourmet Gallery** (Map pp92-4; South Extension Part II; noon-11pm; ) Houses two stylish restaurants: Tasveer (mains Rs 110 to 220) for Indian, and Whispering Bamboo (mains Rs 130 to 370) for Chinese. It's also home to On the Rocks (opposite) or, for something groovier, wiggle your way to the nearby Lizard Lounge (opposite).

**Dilli Haat** (Map pp92-4; Aurobindo Marg; admission Rs 10; 10.30am-10pm Oct-Mar, to 9.30pm Apr-Sep) Although this open-air food-and-crafts market is rather contrived, it does offer the opportunity to sample regional Indian cuisine, even Manipuri veg thalis (Rs 60). Avoid the weekends, which can get frightfully busy. It's opposite the INA Market.

#### EAST OF KAILASH

**Govinda's** (Map pp92-4; Hare Krishna Iskcon temple complex, East of Kailash; buffet Rs 175; 12.30-3.30pm & 7-10pm; ) Promising a 'transcendental dining experience', Govinda's pure-veg (no onion or garlic) Indian buffet is indeed otherworldly. Every Sunday, there are no less than 56 dishes (around 25 on other days), all blissfully delicious.

**Govinda's Sweets** (Map pp92-4; ladoo per kg Rs 140; 9am-1pm & 2-9pm) Next door to Govinda's. Sells takeaway *mithai* (Indian sweets).

#### AIRPORT AREA

**NYC** (Map pp92-4; 26779191; Radisson Hotel, National Hwy 8; mains Rs 265-425; 24hr; ) A glam but pricey coffee shop – keep things cheap by opting for an entrée (spinach-and-broccoli soup is Rs 145) or settling for a cappuccino (Rs 95).

**Great Kabab Factory** (Map pp92-4; 26779191, ext 648; Radisson Hotel, National Hwy 8; 7.30-11.30pm Mon-Sat, 12.30-2.30pm & 7.30-11.30pm Sun; ) Spectacular kebab meals (veg/nonveg Rs 650/750); book ahead (especially at weekends).

**Piccadilly** (Off Map pp92-4; Ashok Country Resort, Rajokri Rd; mains Rs 125-225; 24hr; ) Lacks the wow factor, but at least you won't have to dig deep to fill up on its multicuisine fare.

**Coffee Shop** (Off Map pp92-4; Centaur Hotel, National Hwy 8; mains Rs 100-225; 24hr; ) Sure, it may have as much charisma as a kitchen sponge, but a chicken-salad sandwich here costs the same as a cappuccino at the Radisson.

## DRINKING

From chilled-out bars to perky cafés, Delhi has something to please boozers and teetotallers alike.

### Cafés

Caffeine addicts won't suffer withdrawal symptoms from lack of a *real* cup of coffee thanks to Delhi's blossoming café scene.

**Barista** (Map pp106-7; 16 N-Block, Connaught Pl; snacks Rs 32-60; 9am-1am; ) Hip and happening, Barista serves comforting fare, from smoked-chicken sandwiches to chocolate-chip muffins and, of course, foamy cappuccinos (Rs 30). Branches include Khan Market (Map pp102–4), South Extension Part II (Map pp92–4), Basant Lok (Map pp92–4; Vasant Vihar) and Ansal Plaza (Map pp92–4).

**Café Coffee Day** (Map pp106-7; 11 N-Block, Connaught Pl; snacks Rs 30-50; 9am-midnight; ) Less swish but a whisker cheaper than nearby Barista is this chirpy café, where the icy granitas (Rs 45) are sure to quench the most savage summer thirst. The sandwiches and focaccias aren't bad either, although getting the waiter's attention for that all-important second caffeine fix can involve some serious arm waving.

**Big Chill** (Map pp102-4; Khan Market; mains Rs 60-190; noon-11pm; ) Serves outrageously divine smoothies (Rs 70) and homemade ice cream, including a chocolate-chip-cookie-dough flavour (Rs 50 per scoop). Meals are also rewarding – let us know if the penne with vodka is as intoxicating as it sounds. The 'squidgy chocolate mousse cake' washed down with a hot cuppa is sheer magic.

**Café Turtle** (Map pp102-4; 2nd fl, Full Circle Bookstore, Khan Market; mains Rs 75-250; 10am-7.30pm Mon-Sat; ) Perfect for a languid cinnamon tea and a wedge of orange poppy-seed cake. Savoury eats include quiche, salads and sandwiches. Sit inside or out on the breezy balcony.

### Bars

Thirsty travellers can get sozzled on a multitude of domestic or imported beverages, but it's the taxes that will really make you dizzy (alcoholic drinks 20% to 25%, nonalcoholic 12%; not included below unless otherwise indicated).

Many bars double as music-pumping nightclubs any time after 8pm, drowning out any hope of conversation. A smart-casual dress code applies at the more upmarket places.

Five-star hotels have Delhi's most svelte (but wallet-wounding) bars: **Dublin** (Off Map pp102-4; Maurya Sheraton Hotel & Towers, Sardar Patel Marg; 6pm-1am; ) and **Djinns** (Map pp92-4; Hyatt Regency, Bhikaiji Cama Pl, Ring Rd; 6pm-1am; ) were the trendsetters during our visit (see also p122).

### PAHARGANJ

These licensed establishments offer good drinking possibilities in this area. Unlicensed eateries may also serve beer in a teacup if you're discreet about it.

**Metropolis Restaurant & Bar** (Map p111; Metropolis Tourist Home, 1634 Main Bazaar) Pricier than Hotel Gold Regency and Gem, but Metropolis has more pizzazz and you can even sip Henekell Trocken (German sparkling wine; Rs 1000 per bottle). See p116 for a review of the restaurant.

**Hotel Gold Regency** (Map p111; 4350 Main Bazaar) Sells cheap beer (a bottle of Kingfisher is Rs 72, including tax) at its bar and has live Indian music nightly.

Low-cost beer can also be found at the Gem Restaurant (p117).

Those nursing hangovers can get a vitamin C boost at one of the **juice stalls** (small/large glass Rs 10/20) dotted around Main Bazaar.

### CONNAUGHT PLACE AREA

**DV8** (Map pp106-7; 13 Regal Bldg; 11am-midnight Mon-Sat, 6pm-midnight Sun; ) If it's been one of *those* days, the 'Resurrection' (Bacardi, gin and vodka–based cocktail, Rs 200) should put the fizzle back into fizzled-out souls. Or perhaps the time has come for a 'Brain Haemorrhage' (Baileys, peach schnapps and grenadine, Rs 250)? This sophisticated, stress-banishing bar also offers nonliquid goodies, from pork spare ribs to lobster bisque (Rs 150 each).

**1911** (Map pp106-7; Imperial hotel, Janpath; noon-1am; ) Just the place to recharge your batteries after haggling hard at the nearby Janpath (Tibetan) Market. Named after the year in which Delhi was proclaimed British India's capital, this grand bar claims to have over 500 beverages, from brutally good Bloody Marys (Rs 425) to no-nonsense grapefruit juice (Rs 80).

**Regent's Blues** (Map pp106-7; 18 N-Block; noon-midnight; ) Dimly lit and with a cool vibe, Regent's Blues is a relaxed place for a mug of draught beer (Rs 135). After 8pm a couples-only policy applies, along with a cover charge of Rs 200. Happy hour is between 4pm and 8pm.

**Spirit** (Map pp106-7; 34 E-Block; noon-midnight; ) A cosmopolitan bar-restaurant with a particularly pleasing wine list (Californian and Australian bottles for around Rs 1700); by the glass it's Rs 300/200 for foreign/domestic wine. There's a good menu specialising in Lebanese.

**Pegasus** (Map pp106-7; L-Block; 11am-1am; ) Jolly Pegasus has an old-fashioned pub ambience with happy hour from 3pm to 7pm. Draught beer is Rs 110 (per mug), or for more kick there's Kingfisher Strong (Rs 175 per bottle).

### SOUTH DELHI

**Lizard Lounge** (Map pp92-4; ☎ 23048061; 1st fl, E5 South Extension Part II; mains Rs 150-295; noon-midnight; ) A world away from the rat race, this funky yet suave lounge is a desirable place to unwind over a Heineken (Rs 200 per can) or, if the mood is right, bubbly (Dom Perignon is a cool Rs 12,000). The food is also recommended: graze on a vegetarian meze platter (dips, olives, fetta, Arabic salad and pita bread, Rs 295) or, for more volcanic stomach rumblings, try the hearty Egyptian-inspired 'Lahem Stew' (Rs 275). Dinner reservations advised.

**On the Rocks** (Map pp92-4; Gourmet Gallery, South Extension Part II; noon-11pm; ) Dares you to 'Smooch the Witch' (vodka, Kahlua and chocolate-syrup cocktail, Rs 250).

**Delhi's Devils** (Map pp92-4; 3rd fl, E3 South Extension Part II; 5pm-1am Mon, noon-1am Tue-Sun; ) Above Planet M, this cavernous, party-geared bar is OK for a quick quaff of imported bourbon (Rs 225) in between window-shopping at South Extension. Salsa nights (Thursday after 9pm) are a blast.

**Geoffrey's** (Map pp92-4; Ansal Plaza, Khel Gaon Marg; 12.30pm-midnight; ) If you're in the area, English-themed Geoffrey's is recommended for a drop of Grover's Estate wine (Rs 195 per glass) accompanied by asparagus spears wrapped in smoked salmon (Rs 270).

**Opus Lounge** (Map pp92-4; 47 Basant Lok, Vasant Vihar; noon-midnight; ) Handy for a pre- or postmovie (at PVR Priya Cinema, below) glass of wine and mini Thai spring rolls (each Rs 150).

**Oxygen** (Map pp92-4; D-Block Market, Poorvi Marg, Vasant Vihar; noon-midnight; ) Roll into Oxygen for a late-night cognac (Hennessy Rs 200) after dining at Tamura (p119), next door.

## ENTERTAINMENT

### Cultural Programmes

To access Delhi's dynamic cultural scene, peruse local newspapers and magazines – *First City* is especially good (see p96). Dance, theatrical and music venues:

**Dances of India** (Map pp92-4; ☎ 23289464; Parsi Anjuman Hall, Bahadur Shah Zafar Marg; tickets Rs 200; 6.45pm) A one-hour performance of regional dances that includes *bharatanatyam*, *kathakali* and Manipuri. Tickets are sold on site.

**Habitat World** (Map pp102-4; ☎ 24682222; India Habitat Centre, Lodi Rd)

**India International Centre** (Map pp102-4; ☎ 24619431; 40 Max Mueller Marg)

**Kamani Auditorium** (Map pp102-4; ☎ 23388084; Mandi House, Copernicus Marg)

**Sangeet Natak Akademi** (Map pp102-4; ☎ 23387246; Rabindra Bhavan, Copernicus Marg)

**Shri Ram Centre** (Map pp102-4; ☎ 23714307; 4 Safdar Hashmi Rd)

**Triveni Kala Sangam** (Map pp102-4; ☎ 23718833; 205 Tansen Marg)

### Cinemas

Consult newspapers for session details – the PVR cinemas also have details (and online bookings) at www.pvrcinemas.com.

Most cinemas feature Bollywood films but you can catch a Hollywood blockbuster at a handful of modern cineplexes. Cultural centres (p95) also occasionally screen international films.

**Imperial Cinema** (Map p111; ☎ 55396702; Rajguru Rd, Paharganj) Strictly Bollywood.

**PVR Anupam 4** (Map pp92-4; ☎ 51000458; Saket Community Centre, Saket)

**PVR Plaza Cinema** (Map pp106-7; ☎ 51513391; H-Block Connaught Pl)

**PVR Priya Cinema** (Map pp92-4; ☎ 9810708625; 61 Basant Lok, Vasant Vihar)

**Satyam Cineplex** (Map pp92-4; ☎ 25797387; Patel Rd, Patel Nagar)

### Nightclubs

The hippest nightclubs are at five-star hotels, which is where you'll rub shoulders with Delhi's beautiful people. Prices are ugly, though, with drink taxes as high as 30%. Entry to hotel nightclubs can be hit-and-miss, with priority given to members and hotel guests. Couples and women stand a better chance of being admitted than unaccompanied men. Don't rock up in shorts and a T-shirt.

What's hot and what's not can change in the blink of an eye. To stay tuned into Delhi's fickle club scene, ask around and read *First City* (p96). At the time of writing, the 'in' places were **Dublin** (Off Map pp102-4; ☎ 26112233; Maurya Sheraton Hotel & Towers, Sardar Patel Marg; 6pm-1am; ) and **Djinns** (Map pp92-4; ☎ 26791122; Hyatt Regency, Bhikaiji Cama Pl, Ring Rd; 6pm-1am; ), both of which transform from bars to nightclubs as the evening unfolds. Djinns has a live band most nights.

A perennial favourite among Delhi's party-going expats is **My Kind of Place** (Off Map pp102-4; Taj Palace Hotel, Sadar Patel Marg; 6.30pm-1am Wed-Sat; ), especially popular on Friday and Saturday nights.

## SHOPPING

Delhi has marvellous shopping opportunities and its emporiums mean you can find items from all over India. There's also a magnificent mix of markets, from cheap clothing bazaars to designer shopping enclaves.

Apart from the emporiums and other fixed-price shops, bargain hard and beware of scam merchants (see p361). Some taxi and autorickshaw drivers earn juicy profits (from you) via the commission racket – politely decline their shopping suggestions.

There are oodles of eye-popping handicrafts to buy, including textiles, brassware, woodwork, jewellery, leatherwork, carpets and metalwork, as well as *agarbathi* (incense), spices and tea. The capital also has some of India's most phenomenal bookshops (p94).

Top-end hotels have glitzy shopping arcades selling quality, if often overpriced, products, while at the other end of the spectrum you'll find indefatigable street hawkers flogging everything from squeaky toys to fake beards.

Pickpocketing is more prevalent wherever there's a jam-packed crowd – always

**OLD DELHI'S BUZZING BAZAARS**

Getting lost in the old city's colourful, convoluted bazaars (Map p99) is half the fun of shopping here. These frenetic bazaars are busiest (and best avoided) on Monday and Friday and during other afternoons. Come at around 11.30am when most shops have opened and the jostling is bearable. For organised jaunts around Old Delhi, see p109.

For silver jewellery (and some gold) head for Dariba Kalan, near the Sisganj Gurdwara. Nearby Kinari Bazaar has a focus on bridal gear, from fancy sari borders to iridescent tinsel decorations. The cloth market, not surprisingly, sells uncut material, as well as bed linen and towels, while electrical gadgets are the speciality of Lajpat Rai Market. Chowri Bazaar is the wholesale paper and greeting-card market. Nearby, Nai Sarak deals in wholesale stationery and books and also has a portion devoted to saris.

Near the Fatehpuri Masjid, on Khari Baoli, is the aromatic Spice Market, ablaze with fiery-red chilli powders and burnt-orange turmeric, as well as pickles, tea and nuts. Being a wholesale market, spices here rarely come hermetically sealed – for these, go to Roopak's (p124) in Karol Bagh.

stash your valuables in a well-concealed inner pocket or moneybelt.

## Government & State Emporiums

Although the prices at these fixed-price emporiums can be marginally higher than elsewhere, you're assured of quality and don't have to haggle. If time permits, scout emporiums to get an idea of prices before exploring the markets – you can always return later if you didn't find comparable products at better prices in the bazaars.

**Central Cottage Industries Emporium** (Map pp106-7; ☎ 23326790; Janpath; 🕑 10am-7pm) This multilevel store is filled with India-wide handicrafts, including woodcarvings, silverware, jewellery, pottery, papier-mâché, brassware, textiles and loads more. The Darjeeling green tea shower gel (Rs 120) makes a nice gift.

**State Emporiums** (Map pp106-7; Baba Kharak Singh Marg; 🕑 10am-6pm Mon-Sat) This string of state government emporiums showcases authentic products from around the nation. Set aside several hours to do them justice.

## Markets & Shopping Complexes

Apart from the emporiums (above), there are some other fine shopping options in the markets and shopping complexes around the city. Many markets are closed once a week (indicated below), with most operating from roughly 10am to 5.30pm.

### ANSAL PLAZA

A modern shopping mall on Khel Gaon Marg, **Ansal Plaza** (Map pp92-4; 🕑 11am-8.30pm Mon-Fri, 8.30am-9.30pm Sat & Sun) squarely targets Delhi's well-to-do (not tourists), with shops selling designer fashion, foreign-brand cosmetics and the like.

### CHANDNI CHOWK

Pure pandemonium, **Chandni Chowk** (Map p99; 🕑 Mon-Sat) is Old Delhi's famous shopping street (note that some of the shops open from around 10am to 7pm and others are open from noon to 9pm). Wending your way through the old city's jumble of chaotic bazaars is a head-spinning assault on all the senses – see the boxed text, above for more information.

### CONNAUGHT PLACE AREA

#### Connaught Place

Recent legislation allows shops at Connaught Pl, including Palika Bazaar and Janpath (Tibetan) Market, to remain open every day; however, many shops still choose to stay shut on Sunday. Among Connaught Pl's tourist-oriented shops are some great standouts.

**Khadi Gramodyog Bhawan** (Map pp106-7; Regal Bldg, Sansad Marg; 🕑 10am-7.45pm) Best known for its *khadi* (homespun cloth), but also ventures beyond textiles, with items such as handmade paper and delicately scented glycerine soaps (the neem leaf and herbal honey soaps are favourites, priced at Rs 42 each).

**Handloom House** (Map pp106-7; 9 A-Block; 🕑 10.30am-7.30pm) Stocks quality hand-loom (handmade) textiles, from cotton to silk.

**People Tree** (Map pp106-7; Regal Bldg, Sansad Marg; 🕑 10.30am-7pm) The easy-to-miss People Tree sells excellent avant-garde T-shirts (around Rs 170), many with socio-political messages, as well as books (see p94) and some costume jewellery.

**Soma** (Map pp106-7; 1st fl, 44 K-Block; 10am-7pm) Opposite the PVR Plaza Cinema, Soma has block-printed textiles from oven mitts and aprons, to shirts and scarves. It also has a branch at E13 Green Park (Map pp92-4).

**Dhoomimal Art Centre** (1st fl, 8 A-Block; 11am-7pm) Houses some interesting contemporary paintings by Indian artists; prices start at Rs 3000.

### Janpath (Tibetan) Market

This buzzing tourist strip, running north of the Imperial hotel, beckons tourists with its shimmering mirrorwork textiles, shiny brass Oms, psychedelic Ganesh T-shirts, dangly earrings and trinkets galore. Haggle hard. For quality handmade paperware, visit **Handpaper World** (Map pp106-7; 12B Janpath Market; 10am-7.30pm).

### Palika Bazaar

This is a bustling underground bazaar with competitively priced consumer goods (especially clothing) aimed at local clientele. Tourists are invariably quoted higher prices, so don't be shy to bargain. The **Jain Super Store** (Map pp106-7; shop 172; around 10.30am-7.30pm) stocks 250 locally made perfumes and 100 essential oils; the jasmine oil (Rs 1000 per 10g) is to die for, but if it blows the budget try the juniper berry, geranium and rosemary (Rs 60 per 10g).

### DILLI HAAT

Located on Aurobindo Marg, stalls at **Dilli Haat** (Map pp92-4; admission Rs 10; 10.30am-10pm Oct-Mar, to 9.30pm Apr-Sep) sell regional handicrafts, such as shawls and woven baskets, but they're nothing to write home about. It's more recommended for its food (see p120).

### HAUZ KHAS VILLAGE

Nestled in a green belt of south Delhi, the fashionable **Hauz Khas Village** (Map pp92-4; Mon-Sat) has art galleries, boutiques and furniture shops geared to society's upper crust. For affordable silverware, try **Ethnic Silver** (9A Hauz Khas Village; noon-9pm), which has earrings from Rs 200.

### JOR BAGH MARKET

After sightseeing at Safdarjang's Tomb (p104), drop into **C.Lal & Sons** (Map pp102-4; 9/172 Jor Bagh Market; 9.30am-7.30pm), run by the lovely Mr Lal, at the **Jor Bagh Market** (Map pp102-4; Mon-Sat). This humble little 'curiosity shop' is especially popular with expats for its charming Christmas-tree decorations (from Rs 65). The handicrafts (cheaper than those at touristy markets) include papier-mâché (a painted egg is Rs 15), blue pottery, candles, marble, sandalwood, soapstone, scarves and even coconut-carved monkeys.

### KAROL BAGH MARKET

Popular for its competitively priced clothing, shoes, homeware and general consumer goods is **Karol Bagh Market** (Map pp92-4; Tue-Sun). To cook the perfect curry back home, get happy at **Roopak's** (Map pp92-4; 6/9 Ajmal Khan Rd; 10am-8pm), two shops side by side that sell a similarly priced range of excellent, well-packed spices, most for less than Rs 100 per 100g. They also sell pickles, nuts and sonf (aniseed mouth fresheners). Their *namkin* (savoury nibbles) make an ideal snack for long train journeys – a healthy alternative to the mostly fried mixes are the roasted green lentils (Rs 30 per bag).

### KHAN MARKET

Popular with diplomats and well-heeled locals, **Khan Market** (Map pp102-4; Mon-Sat), apart from its sensational bookshops (p94) and tailors (p126), has shops devoted to fashion wear, sunglasses, CDs/DVDs, homeware and accessories for the pampered pooch. Small grocery stores overflow with imported edibles, from Australian oranges to Swiss chocolates. Avoid Khan Market on Saturday when the huge crowds can be exasperating.

### LAJPAT NAGAR CENTRAL MARKET

This **market** (Map pp92-4; around 11am-9pm Tue-Sun) attracts bargain hunters on the prowl for household goods, clothing and jewellery. If you've fallen in love with those colourful jangly bangles widely worn by Indian women, you can get them here for around Rs 50 per two dozen.

### MAIN BAZAARMAP

Geared for backpackers, Paharganj's bubbly **Main Bazaar** (Map p111; Tue-Sun) abounds with cheap T-shirts, shawls, leatherware, costume jewellery, essential oil, incense, bindis and even bongs. Although officially closed on Monday, many shops remain open, especially during the tourist season.

#### M-BLOCK & N-BLOCK MARKET

This **shopping enclave** (Map pp92-4; Greater Kailash 1; ⏰ Wed-Mon) is best known for its garment, fabric and furnishings store **Fab India** (Map pp92-4; N-Block Market; ⏰ 10am-7.30pm); *dhurries* (cotton rugs) range from Rs 105 to 15,000. Also worth a look is the **Next Shop** (Map pp92-4; N-Block Market; ⏰ 10am-7pm), which has pretty home accessories and giftware.

#### SANTUSHTI SHOPPING COMPLEX

**Santushti** (Map pp102-4; ⏰ Mon-Sat), opposite the Ashok Hotel in Chanakyapuri, is a small oasis, sprinkled with à la mode boutiques catering to wealthy Delhiites. Cigar aficionados will appreciate **Kastro's** (Map pp102-4; ⏰ 10am-6.30pm) – 'purveyor of fine cigars and cigar accessories' – where Cuban cigars range from Rs 110 to 2000 and Davidoff mini-cigarillos are Rs 950 for a pack of 20. **Lotus Eaters** (Map pp102-4; ⏰ 10am-6pm) has sublime old gold and silver pieces (silver frames from Rs 2100). Request a peek of the intriguing *itar dani*, an 80-year-old lotus-shaped perfume contraption that's not for sale. **Art Indus** (Map pp102-4; ⏰ 10am-6pm) sells paintings by renowned Indian artists such as Haku Shah, Vinjender Sharma and Shuvaprasanna. **Anokhi** (Map pp102-4; ⏰ 10am-7pm) specialises in block-printed textiles, including tablecloths, garments and toiletry bags. There's also an Anokhi branch at Khan Market (Map pp102–4).

#### SAROJINI NAGAR MARKET

This **market** (Map pp92-4; ⏰ around 11am-9pm Tue-Sun) is good for cheap Western-style clothes, which have been dumped here either because they were an export surplus or are from a cancelled line. Check for holes, faulty zips, crooked seams, stains and missing buttons. Bargain hard. Avoid Sunday (especially afternoons), when the place swarms with elbowing shoppers.

#### SOUTH EXTENSION MARKET PARTS I & II

This is an upmarket **enclave** (Map pp92-4; ⏰ Tue-Sun) selling modish garments, jewellery, shoes and handbags. **Heritage** (Map pp92-4; Part I; ⏰ 10am-2pm & 3-7.30pm) deals in high-quality men's (suits, shirts, ties, cufflinks) and women's (saris, shawls, handbags) attire. **Delite Jewellers** (Map pp92-4; Part I; ⏰ 10.30am-8pm) stocks reasonably priced silver; toe rings start from Rs 40.

#### SUNDER NAGAR MARKET

Just south of Purana Qila, this upmarket **enclave** (Map pp102-4; ⏰ Mon-Sat) specialises in Indian and Nepali handicrafts and 'antiques' (most are replicas). Before purchasing anything, check out all shops (the market is compact) to see what's on offer at the best prices. There are two outstanding teashops here: **Regalia Tea House** (Map pp102-4; ⏰ 10am-7.30pm) and **Mittal Tea House** (Map pp102-4; ⏰ 10am-7.30pm), both offering similar products and complimentary tea tastings; Mittal has also has a **branch** (Map pp102-4; 8A Main Market) at Lodi Colony. There's plenty to choose from, including a dreamy green rose tea (Rs 100 per 100g) and the exquisite Darjeeling Golden Tips (Rs 240 per 100g). The white tea (Rs 340 per 40g) is said to contain even more antioxidants than green tea. Both shops also sell a nifty 12-spice pack (Rs 300).

### Music

#### MUSICAL INSTRUMENTS

For competitively priced Indian instruments, inspect the **musical instrument shops** (Map p99; ⏰ Mon-Sat) bunched along Neetaji Subhash Marg in Daryaganj.

More-upmarket options are to be found in Connaught Pl. **Rikhi Ram** (Map pp106-7; ☎ 23327685; Marina Arcade, 8 G-Block, Connaught Pl; ⏰ 11.30am-8pm Mon-Sat) is patronised by some of India's most-esteemed musicians. Sitars start at Rs 22,000 and tablas are upwards of Rs 4500.

**Rangarsons Music Depot** (Map pp106-7; ☎ 23413831; 12 K-Block, Connaught Pl; ⏰ 10am-5.30pm Mon-Sat) prides itself as being 'leading suppliers to the armed forces'. Items include brass-band instruments (trumpets Rs 2500), tablas (from Rs 1600) and sitars (from Rs 2500).

#### MUSIC CASSETTES & CDS

Music retailers stock stacks of CDs (including tremendous fusion – an innovative blend of Eastern and Western music styles) and a more limited range of cassettes, which are handy if you're hiring a car with driver as almost all hire vehicles are fitted out with cassette players. Many shops also sell English and Hindi DVDs.

**Palika Bazaar** (Map pp106-7; ⏲ around 10.30am-7.30pm) has some good music-store options.

Recommended outlets in Connaught Pl:

**Berco's Melody House** (Map pp106-7; ☎ 23413757; 8 E-Block; ⏲ 10am-7.30pm Mon-Sat)
**Music Street** (Map pp106-7; ☎ 23321171; 29 B-Block; ⏲ 10am-10pm)
**Music World** (Map pp106-7; ☎ 23350061; PVR Plaza Cinema Bldg; ⏲ 11am-9pm Mon-Sat)

At Khan Market, try **Mercury** (Map pp102-4; ☎ 24690134; ⏲ 10.30am-8.30pm Mon-Sat) and the **Music Shop** (Map pp102-4; ☎ 24618464; ⏲ 10.30am-8pm Mon-Sat). South Extension's rocking **Planet M** (Map pp92-4; ☎ 26251620; Part II; ⏲ 11am-8.30pm Tue-Sun) has two floors – 1st/2nd for English/Indian.

### Tailors

Tailors adeptly replicate ready-made garments so bring your favourite party frock. Ultra-cheap tailors can be shoddy – seek recommendations or try the following (reputable) outlets. Always confirm whether quotes include fabric; the following exclude material.

**Delhi Cloth House** (Map pp102-4; ☎ 24618937; Khan Market; ⏲ 10.30am-7.30pm Mon-Sat) Men's boxer shorts cost Rs 150 to 200, long-sleeved shirts are Rs 200 and ankle-length skirts cost Rs 450.
**New Prominent Tailors** (Map pp106-7; ☎ 23418007; 25 K-Block, Connaught Pl; ⏲ 11am-7.30pm Mon-Sat) A skirt (without lining) is Rs 150, men's trousers are Rs 300.
**Vedi Tailors** (Map pp106-7; ☎ 23416901; 60 M-Block, Connaught Pl; ⏲ 11.30am-8pm Mon-Sat) Men's-only tailor. Charges Rs 300/2400 for trousers/suits.

## GETTING THERE & AWAY

Delhi is a major international gateway to India. It's also a centre for domestic travel, with extensive bus, rail and air connections. Note that Delhi's airport is prone to fog in December and January, disrupting airline schedules. For more details of arriving from overseas see p379.

### Air

The domestic terminals (Terminal 1) of the Indira Gandhi International Airport (Map pp92–4) are around 15km from Connaught Pl, and the international terminal (Terminal 2) is a further 8km away. There's a free shuttle bus between the two terminals, or you can use the Ex-Servicemen's Air Link Transport Service (see p128).

For flight inquiries, call the **international airport** (☎ 25652011) or the **domestic airport** (⏲ 25675126).

#### DOMESTIC

##### Arrivals & Departures

Check-in at the airport for domestic flights is one hour before departure. Note that if you've just arrived and have an onward connection within India, it may be with Air India, the country's international carrier, rather than its domestic carrier, Indian Airlines. If this is the case, you must check-in at the international terminal (Terminal 2), not the domestic terminal. For details of flights to Rajasthan, see the table, below.

##### Airlines

The most convenient **Indian Airlines office** (Map pp106-7; ☎ 23310517; F-Block, Malhotra Bldg, Connaught Pl; ⏲ 10am-1.15pm & 2.15-5pm Mon-Sat) is at Connaught Pl. There's also a ticket office at **Safdarjang airfield** (Map pp102-4; ☎ 24631337; Aurobindo Marg; ⏲ 7am-11pm). For Indian Airlines' recorded flight arrival and departure details, dial ☎ 1407.

Other domestic airlines:

**Air Deccan** (Map pp92-4; ☎ 51750000; office 803, 98 Hemkund Tower, Nehru Pl; ⏲ 10am-6.30pm Mon-Sat)

**FLIGHTS TO RAJASTHAN FROM DELHI**

| Destination | Duration (hr) | Airline code | Frequency | Fare (US$) |
|---|---|---|---|---|
| Jaipur | ¾ | CD | 1 daily | 73 |
| | | 9W | 1 daily | |
| | | IC | 1 daily | |
| Jodhpur | 1½ | CD | 1 daily | 115 |
| Udaipur | 2½-3 | CD | 1 daily | 119 |
| | | 9W | 2 daily | |

CD – Alliance Air (Indian Airlines), IC – Indian Airlines, 9W – Jet Airways

**Air Sahara** (Map pp106-7; ☎ 23352771; Gopal Das Bhavan, 28 Barakhamba Rd, Connaught Pl; ⏲ 10am-5.30pm Mon-Sat)
**Jagson Airlines** (Map pp106-7; ☎ 23721594; Vandana Bldg, 11 Tolstoy Marg; ⏲ 9.30am-6pm Mon-Sat)
**Jet Airways** (Map pp106-7; ☎ 51641414; 40 N-Block, Connaught Pl; ⏲ 9am-9pm Mon-Sat, to 6pm Sun)

### INTERNATIONAL

#### Arrivals

The international airport's arrivals hall has 24-hour money-exchange facilities, a prepaid taxi counter and a tourist information counter. There's also a railway booking counter, but at the time of research it only operated from 8am to 8pm (many flights arrive after 8pm).

#### Departures

You *must* have your check-in baggage X-rayed and sealed – don't forget to do this or you'll be sent back. At the check-in counter, ensure you collect tags to attach to your hand luggage (these are mandatory to clear security later).

#### Airlines

**Aeroflot** (Map pp106-7; ☎ 23723241; 15-17 Tolstoy Marg)
**Air Canada** (Map pp92-4; ☎ 51528181; 5th fl, World Trade Tower, Barakhamba Rd)
**Air France** (Map pp106-7; ☎ 23738004; 7 Atma Ram Mansion, Connaught Pl)
**Air India** (Map pp106-7; ☎ 23731225; 2nd fl, Jeevan Bharati Bldg, Connaught Pl)
**British Airways** (Map pp106-7; ☎ 25652078; 11th fl, Gopal Das Bhavan, Barakhamba Rd, Connaught Pl)
**El Al Israel Airlines** (Map pp106-7; ☎ 23357965; room 303, Prakash Deep Bldg, 7 Tolstoy Marg)
**Emirates** (Map pp106-7; ☎ 55314444; 7th fl, DLF Centre, Sansad Marg, Connaught Pl)
**Gulf Air** (Map pp106-7; ☎ 23324293; 12 G-Block, Connaught Pl)
**Japan Airlines** (Map pp106-7; ☎ 23324922; Chandralok Bldg, 36 Janpath)
**KLM-Royal Dutch Airlines** (Map pp106-7; ☎ 23357747; Prakash Deep Bldg, 7 Tolstoy Marg)
**Lufthansa Airlines** (Map pp106-7; ☎ 23724200; 56 Janpath)
**Malaysian Airlines** (Map pp106-7; ☎ 23359711; 10th fl, Ashoka Estate Bldg, Barakhamba Rd)
**Pakistan International Airlines** (PIA; Map pp106-7; ☎ 23737791; Kailash Bldg, 26 Kasturba Gandhi Marg)
**Qantas Airways** (Map pp106-7; 11th fl, Gopal Das Bhavan, Barakhamba Rd, Connaught Pl) British Airways takes care of Qantas flights.
**Royal Nepal Airlines Corporation** (RNAC; Map pp106-7; ☎ 23321164; 44 Janpath)
**Scandinavian Airlines** (SAS; Map pp106-7; ☎ 2335 2299; Ambadeep Bldg, 14 Kasturba Gandhi Marg)
**Singapore Airlines** (Map pp106-7; ☎ 23356283; 9th fl, Ashoka Estate Bldg, Barakhamba Rd)
**Sri Lankan Airlines** (Map pp106-7; ☎ 23731473; 55 G-Block, Connaught Pl)
**Thai Airways International** (THAI; Map pp92-4; ☎ 51497777; Park Royal Intercontinental Hotel, America Plaza, Nehru Pl)

### Bus

Delhi's main bus station is the **Inter State Bus Terminal** (ISBT; Map pp92-4; ☎ 23868836; Kashmiri Gate; ⏲ 24hr), north of the (Old) Delhi train station. It has a 24-hour left-luggage facility (Rs 10 per bag). This station can be chaotic so try to arrive at least 30 minutes ahead of your departure time.

For bookings and information contact **Rajasthan Roadways** (☎ 24864470; counter 36) – bookings are also taken at Bikaner House – or **Uttar Pradesh Roadways** (☎ 23868709; counter 38).

**Bikaner House** (Map pp102-4; ☎ 23383469), located near India Gate, operates comfortable state-operated buses that service Jaipur (Rs 245/425 in deluxe/AC, 5½ to six hours, 5.30am to midnight daily). There are also comfortable private bus services, but their schedules can be erratic (inquire at travel agencies). To Agra (Rs 125/185 in ordinary/deluxe, 5½ hours) buses leave half-hourly from 6am to 10pm.

### Train

For foreigners, it's easiest to make ticket bookings at the **International Tourist Bureau** (Map p111; ☎ 23405156; 1st fl, New Delhi train station; ⏲ 8am-8pm Mon-Sat, to 2pm Sun). Do *not* believe anyone who tells you it has shifted, closed or burnt down – this is a scam to divert you elsewhere (see p97). If making bookings at the International Tourist Bureau, tickets must be paid for in rupees backed up by money-exchange certificates, or in US dollars, euros or pounds sterling; any change is given in rupees. You may be asked to present your passport. Railway porters should charge around Rs 20 per bag. There's also a railway booking counter at the airport – see left.

There are two main stations in Delhi – (Old) Delhi train station (Map p99) in Old Delhi, and New Delhi train station (Map p111) at Paharganj; make sure you know

**MAJOR TRAINS FROM DELHI**

| Destination | Train No & name | Fare (Rs) | Duration (hr) | Departures & station |
|---|---|---|---|---|
| Agra | 2180 *Taj Exp* | 82/266 (A) | 2½ | 7.15am HN |
| | 2002 *Shatabdi Exp* | 370/720 (B) | 2 | 6am ND |
| Ajmer | 2015 *Shatabdi Exp* | 580/1135 (B) | 6½ | 6.10am Thu-Tue ND |
| | 4743 *Dee Cor Exp* | 178/731/1379 (D) (no 3AC available) | 10¾ | 8.50pm SR |
| Alwar | 2015 *Shatabdi Exp* | 335/635 (B) | 2½ | 6.10am Thu-Tue ND |
| Bikaner | 9733 *Shekhawati Exp* | 203/610 (C) (2AC & 3AC not available) | 11 | 11pm SR |
| Chittorgarh | 9020A *Dehradun Exp* | 243/1108/2064 (D) (3AC not available) | 14½ | 9.40pm |
| Jaipur | 2413 *Intercity Exp* | 107/441/665/1244 (D) | 5½ | 5.15am OD |
| | 2015 *Shatabdi Exp* | 465/915 (B) | 4½ | 6.15am ND |
| Udaipur | 9615 *Chetak Exp* | 271/1142/2151 (D) (3A not available) | 19 | 2.10pm SR |

Train stations: ND – New Delhi, OD – Old Delhi, HN – Hazrat Nizamuddin, SR – Sarai Rohilla
Fares: A 2nd class/chair car, B chair car/executive class, C 3AC/2AC/1AC, D sleeper/3AC/2AC/1AC

which station serves your destination (New Delhi train station is closer to Connaught Pl). If you're departing from the Delhi train station you should allow adequate time to meander through the often-snail-paced traffic of Old Delhi.

There's also the Nizamuddin train station (Map pp102–4), south of Sunder Nagar, where various trains start or finish.

Some trains between Delhi and Jaipur, Jodhpur and Udaipur operate to and from Sarai Rohilla train station (Map pp92–4), which is about 4km northwest of Connaught Pl.

There are many more destinations and trains than those listed in the boxed text (above) – consult *Trains at a Glance* (Rs 45), available at most newsstands, or ask railway officials or tourist-office staff.

## GETTING AROUND

City buses can get hopelessly crowded so autorickshaws and taxis are good alternatives. Keep change handy to pay fares.

### To/From the Airport

Airport-to-city transport is not as straightforward as it should be, due to predatory taxi and autorickshaw drivers who often target first-time visitors – see p97.

Many international flights arrive at ghastly hours, making it wise to book a hotel in advance and notify it of your arrival time.

**PREARRANGED PICK-UPS**

Be aware that if you arrange an airport pick-up through a travel agency or hotel (excluding the top-end hotels, which have complimentary shuttles), it's more expensive than a prepaid taxi from the airport. This is because of the time required to organise it, the addition of an airport parking fee (up to Rs 100) and the Rs 50 charge for the person collecting you to enter the airport arrivals hall. It's worth the peace of mind though, and there's nothing more comforting after a long-haul flight than seeing someone holding a placard with your name on it.

**BUS**

The **Ex-Servicemen's Air Link Transport Service** (EATS; Map pp106-7; ☎ 23316530; F-Block, Connaught Pl; 🕑 10am-10.30pm) has a bus service between the airport (both terminals) and its office, near Indian Airlines. The fare is Rs 50, plus Rs 10 per large piece of luggage. The bus will drop you off at most of the major hotels, and at the Ajmeri Gate entrance to New Delhi train station (for Paharganj), en route. There is no set timetable as the bus operates according to flight arrivals.

When leaving the international terminal, the counter for EATS is just to the right as you exit the building. Nearby is a Delhi Transport Corporation (DTC) counter, which also operates frequent buses (Rs 50) into town.

#### TAXI

Look for the Delhi Traffic Police Prepaid Taxi Booth just to the right outside the international terminal entrance, or inside the arrivals hall of the airport (after customs). It costs about Rs 210 to Paharganj; there's a 25% surcharge between 11pm and 5am. If you're arriving at night on your own, you may prefer to prearrange a pick-up for security reasons – see p97.

You'll be given a voucher with the destination on it – insist that the driver honours it and, if not, return to the prepaid booth. Never surrender your voucher until you actually get to your destination; without that docket the driver won't get paid. To lodge complaints contact the **traffic police** (☎ 23378888; 🕑 24hr).

At the domestic airport, the prepaid taxi-booking counter is just inside the terminal.

### Bus

The DTC (Map pp106–7) runs some buses, and others are privately owned, but they all operate along the same set routes. Tickets cost a maximum of Rs 10 for travel within the city precincts. Whenever possible, try to board at a starting or finishing point, such as the **Shivaji Stadium terminal** (Map pp106-7; Connaught Pl), as there's more chance of a seat.

Useful buses:

**Buses 101, 104 & 139** Shivaji Stadium terminal to the Red Fort.

**Bus 505** Janpath (from opposite the Imperial hotel) to Qutb Minar.

**Buses 604, 620, 632 & 641** Connaught Pl (on Sansad Marg) to Chanakyapuri.

### Car

#### SELF-DRIVE HIRE

**Budget** (Map p111; ☎ 23318600; bracindia@hotmail.com; 104 Ansal Bhavan, Kasturba Gandhi Marg; small AC vehicle per day Rs 1870; 🕑 9.30am-5.30pm Mon-Fri, to 1.30pm Sat) hires out cars for a minimum of three days. There's also a **branch** (Map p111; ☎ 30939132) at the New Delhi train station.

#### HIRING A CAR & DRIVER

Numerous operators offer chauffeur-driven cars – for important tips see p385. Hotels can also often arrange cars but choose carefully – one reliable option is the Hotel Namaskar (p111).

The following companies have received good reports from travellers. Each has an eight-hour, 80km limit per day. All offer tours beyond Delhi (including to Rajasthan) but higher charges apply for these. If you plan on hiring a car for touring Rajasthan, shop around. So many travellers end up paying too much when they book a car from Delhi to Rajasthan, as they have often just arrived and don't have a clear idea of prices. For advice and information about booking a car and driver see p385. The rates given below are only for travel within Delhi.

**Kumar Tourist Taxi Service** (Map pp106-7; ☎ 2341 5930; kumartaxi@rediffmail.com; 14/1 K-Block, Connaught Pl; non-AC/AC per day Rs 500/600; 🕑 8am-9pm) Near the York Hotel is this tiny office, run by two brothers, Bittoo and Titoo.

**Metropole Tourist Service** (Map pp102-4; ☎ 2431 0313; metropole@vsnl.com; 244 Defence Flyover Market; non-AC/AC per day Rs 550/750; 🕑 8am-9pm) Under the Defence Flyover Bridge.

### Cycle-rickshaw & Bicycle

Cycle-rickshaws are banned from the Connaught Pl area and New Delhi itself, but they can be handy for commuting between Connaught Pl and Paharganj (about Rs 20). They're recommended in Chandni Chowk (Old Delhi), as the drivers (around Rs 50 per hour) are veritable wizards at weaving through the crowds.

If you want to purchase a bike, the largest range of new and second-hand bicycles can be found at Jhandewalan Cycle Market (Map pp92–4).

### Metro

The first phase (Line 1) of Delhi's Metro system is now operational. This section runs from Barwala to Shahdara. Line 2 is scheduled for completion in late 2005; however, half of this line may be ready by mid-2005. The first half of Line 2 will run from Delhi University to the ISBT; the remainder will continue from the ISBT to the Central Secretariat. The entire Metro network is scheduled for completion some time in 2010.

Tickets are sold at Metro stations and range from Rs 4 to 14. To monitor the latest developments, click on www.delhimetrorail.com or call ☎ 24369912.

### Motorcycle

To purchase or hire motorcycles (including legendary Enfields), head for Karol Bagh – do shop around and seek advice from fellow travellers in order to ensure you get the best deal. **Inder Motors** (Map pp92-4; ☎ 25728579; lallisingh@vsnl.com; 1740-A/55 Basement, Hari Singh Nalwa St, Karol Bagh Market) receives consistently positive reports; for more information see p388.

### Taxi & Autorickshaw

All taxis and autorickshaws are metered but you may find the meters are 'not working' or that drivers will simply refuse to use them (so they can overcharge). Insist on using the meter and if the driver disagrees, look for one who will. From 11pm to 5am, there's a 25% surcharge for autorickshaws and taxis.

To avoid shenanigans, catch an autorickshaw from a prepaid booth:

**India Tourism Delhi** (Map pp106-7; 88 Janpath; 11am-7pm) The booth is just outside the India Tourism Delhi office.

**New Delhi train station car park** (Map p111; 24hr)

**Palika Bazaar's Gate No 2** (Map pp106-7; Connaught Pl; 11am-9pm)

At the time of writing there was no prepaid taxi stand in Connaught Pl, but the New Delhi train station (car park) has a 24-hour counter offering meter-operated taxis.

#### AUTORICKSHAW RATES

To give you an idea of fares vis-à-vis distances, the following are one-way rates departing from the prepaid autorickshaw booth outside the India Tourism Delhi office (Map pp106–7). Taxis charge around double these rates.

| Destination | Fare (Rs) |
|---|---|
| Ansal Plaza | 50 |
| Bahai Temple | 60 |
| Basant Lok (Vasant Vihar) | 60 |
| Crafts Museum | 25 |
| Hauz Khas Village | 50 |
| Humayun's Tomb | 40 |
| Karol Bagh | 25 |
| Majnu-ka-Tilla | 50 |
| National Museum | 17 |
| Old Delhi train station | 40 |
| Paharganj | 17 |
| Purana Qila | 25 |
| Red Fort | 40 |
| Safdarjang's Tomb | 40 |
| South Extension | 50 |

# GREATER DELHI

## KHIRKI MASJID & JAHANPANAH

This interesting **mosque** (Map pp92-4; sunrise-sunset), with its four open courts, dates from 1380. Nearby are remains of the fourth city of Delhi, **Jahanpanah** (Map pp92–4), including the **Bijai Mandal platform** (Map pp92–4), and the **Begumpur Masjid** (Map pp92–4) with its multiplicity of domes.

## TUGHLAQABAD

Crumbling **Tughlaqabad** (Map pp92-4; Indian/foreigner Rs 5/US$2, video Rs 25; 7.30am-5.30pm) was the third city of Delhi. The walled city and fort with its 13 gateways was built by Ghiyas-ud-din Tughlaq. Its construction involved a legendary quarrel between Ghiyas-ud-din and the saint Nizam-ud-din: when the Tughlaq ruler took the workers whom Nizam-ud-din wanted for work on his shrine, the saint cursed the king, warning that his city would be inhabited only by shepherds. Today, this is indeed the case.

The dispute between king and saint did not end with a curse. When the king prepared to take vengeance on the saint, Nizam-ud-din calmly told his followers, 'Delhi is a long way off'. Indeed it was, for the king was murdered on his way from Delhi in 1325.

Janpath's prepaid autorickshaw booth charges Rs 160 for the return trip to Tughlaqabad, including 30 minutes' waiting time (Rs 20 per extra hour).

## QUTB MINAR

The imposing buildings in the **Qutb Minar complex** (Map p131; ☎ 26643856; Indian/foreigner Rs 10/US$5, video Rs 25; 7.30am-5.30pm Tue-Sun) date from the onset of Islamic rule and are fine examples of early Afghan architecture.

The Qutb Minar itself is a soaring tower of victory started in 1193, immediately after the

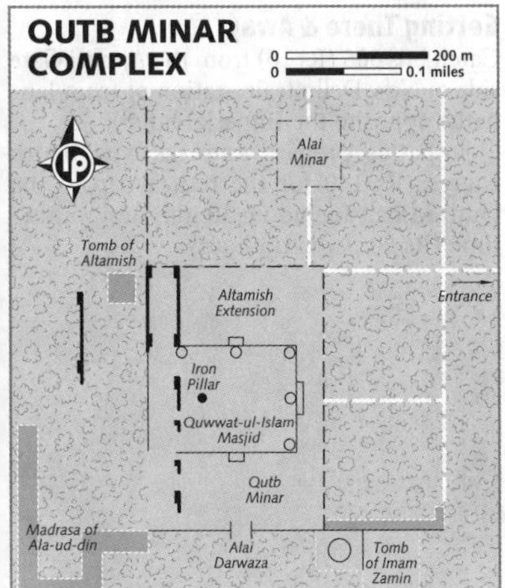


defeat of the last Hindu kingdom in Delhi. It's nearly 73m high and tapers from a 15m-diameter base to just 2.5m at the top.

The tower has five distinct storeys, each with by a projecting balcony. The first three are made of red sandstone, the 4th and 5th are of marble and sandstone. Although Qutb-ud-din began construction of the tower, he only got to the 1st storey. His successors completed it and, in 1368, Firoz Shah rebuilt the top storeys and added a cupola. An earthquake brought the cupola down in 1803 and an Englishman replaced it with another in 1829. That dome was deemed inappropriate and removed some years later.

Today, this impressively ornate tower has a slight tilt, but otherwise has worn the centuries remarkably well. It's no longer possible to climb the tower.

Try to visit Qutb Minar on weekdays, as weekends can get crowded. For a nearby recommended eating spot, check out the Olive Bar & Kitchen (see the boxed text, p116).

## Quwwat-ul-Islam Masjid

At the foot of the Qutb Minar stands the first mosque to be built in India, the **Might of Islam Mosque**. Qutb-ud-din began construction of the mosque in 1193, but it has had various additions and extensions over the centuries. The original mosque was built on the foundations of a Hindu temple, and an inscription over the east gate states that it was built with materials obtained from demolishing '27 idolatrous temples'. Many of the elements in the mosque's construction indicate their Hindu or Jain origins.

Altamish, Qutb-ud-din's son-in-law, surrounded the original mosque with a cloistered court, built between 1210 and 1220. Ala-ud-din added a court to the east and the magnificent Alai Darwaza gateway in 1300.

## Iron Pillar

This 7m-high pillar stands in the courtyard of the mosque and it has been here since long before the mosque's construction. A six-line Sanskrit inscription indicates that it was initially erected outside a Vishnu temple, possibly in Bihar, and was raised in memory of Chandragupta II, who ruled from AD 375 to 413.

What the inscription does not tell is how the pillar was made, for the iron in the pillar is of quite exceptional purity. Scientists have never discovered how the iron, which has not rusted after almost 2000 years, could be cast using the technology of that time.

It was said that if you could stand with your back to the pillar and encircle it with your arms your wish would be granted; however, the pillar is now protected by a fence.

## Alai Minar

When Ala-ud-din made his additions to the mosque, he also conceived a far more ambitious construction programme. He would build a second tower of victory, exactly like the Qutb Minar, except it would be twice as high! By the time of his death the tower had reached 27m and no-one was willing to continue his overambitious project. The incomplete tower stands to the north of the Qutb Minar and the mosque.

## Other Features

Ala-ud-din's **Alai Darwaza** gateway is the main entrance to the whole complex. It was built of red sandstone in 1310 and stands just southwest of the Qutb Minar. The **tomb of Imam Zamin** is beside the gateway, while the **tomb of Altamish**, who died in 1235, is by the northwestern corner of the mosque. The largely ruined **madrasa of Ala-ud-din** stands at the rear of the complex.

There are some **summer palaces** in the area and also the **tombs** of the last kings of Delhi, who succeeded the Mughals. An empty space between two of the tombs was intended for the last king of Delhi, who died in exile in Yangon, Burma (Myanmar), in 1862, following his implication in the 1857 Indian Uprising.

### Getting There & Away

Catch bus 505 (Rs 10) from the Ajmeri Gate side of New Delhi train station or from Janpath (opposite the Imperial hotel).

Janpath's prepaid autorickshaw booth charges Rs 140 for the return trip to the Qutb Minar, including 30 minutes' waiting time (Rs 20 per extra hour).

# Agra

PATRICK HORTON

# Agra

Agra is home to India's most famous monument – the translucent, perfect Taj Mahal, a building that seems to glow with an ethereal light. The city was the Mughal capital from 1526, established by Emperor Babur on the banks of the Yamuna River, and for the next century Agra witnessed a remarkable spate of architectural activity as each emperor tried to outdo the grandiose monuments built by his predecessors – leaving the city with a remarkable collection of Mughal masterpieces.

Today the city is sprawling and industrial, the clamour and hustle a strident contrast to the otherworldly grace of the Taj Mahal. It has a lively but chaotic *chowk* (marketplace) and plenty of places to stay and eat, but the hordes of rickshaw-wallahs, touts and souvenir vendors are as persistent as the monsoon rain and would test even the patience of Buddha.

Many tourists choose to visit Agra on a whistle-stop day trip – made possible by the excellent transport connections between here, Delhi and Rajasthan. However, Agra contains many Mughal wonders other than the Taj Mahal, much more than can be seen in a day, and if you have the time (and patience), you can enjoy several days' sightseeing.

Only an hour away by bus, also in the state of Uttar Pradesh and covered in this chapter, is the deserted city of Fatehpur Sikri, another vestige of the Mughal empire at its peak, eerily well preserved and with stupendous views.

## HIGHLIGHTS

- The **Taj Mahal** (p137), a magical jewel that is the planet's most wondrous sight
- The awesome riverside **Agra Fort** (p139) with its exquisite palaces and mosques
- The fascinating red-sandstone palaces and other buildings in the lost city of **Fatehpur Sikri** (p145)
- A walk through a stunning gateway and a deer park to the **mausoleum of Akbar** (p140), the greatest Mughal emperor, at Sikandra
- Another Mughal marvel, the **Itimad-ud-Daulah** (p140), the so-called Baby Taj, constructed of white marble intricately inlaid with semiprecious stones.

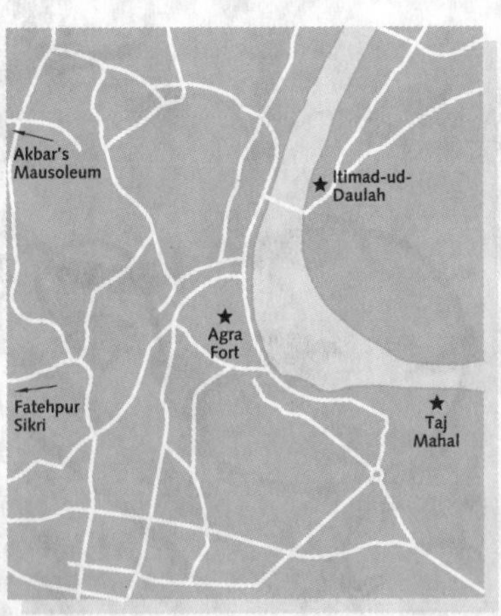


- TELEPHONE CODE: 0562
- POPULATION: 1,321,410

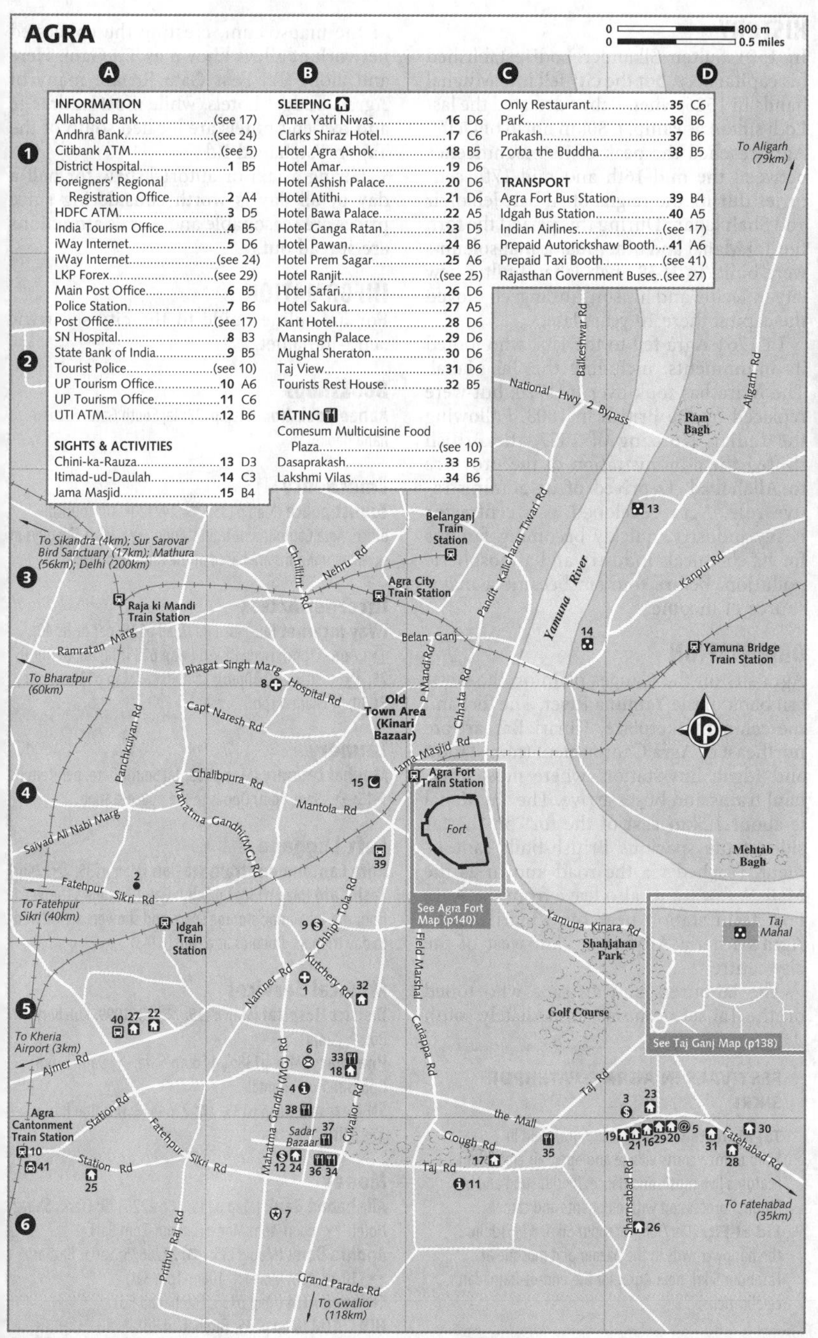
AGRA
0 800 m
0 0.5 miles
A
B
C
D
INFORMATION
Allahabad Bank....................(see 17)
Andhra Bank....................(see 24)
Citibank ATM....................(see 5)
District Hospital....................1 B5
Foreigners' Regional Registration Office....................2 A4
HDFC ATM....................3 D5
India Tourism Office....................4 B5
iWay Internet....................5 D6
iWay Internet....................(see 24)
LKP Forex....................(see 29)
Main Post Office....................6 B5
Police Station....................7 B6
Post Office....................(see 17)
SN Hospital....................8 B3
State Bank of India....................9 B5
Tourist Police....................(see 10)
UP Tourism Office....................10 A6
UP Tourism Office....................11 C6
UTI ATM....................12 B6
SIGHTS & ACTIVITIES
Chini-ka-Rauza....................13 D3
Itimad-ud-Daulah....................14 C3
Jama Masjid....................15 B4
SLEEPING
Amar Yatri Niwas....................16 D6
Clarks Shiraz Hotel....................17 C6
Hotel Agra Ashok....................18 B5
Hotel Amar....................19 D6
Hotel Ashish Palace....................20 D6
Hotel Atithi....................21 D6
Hotel Bawa Palace....................22 A5
Hotel Ganga Ratan....................23 D5
Hotel Pawan....................24 B6
Hotel Prem Sagar....................25 A6
Hotel Ranjit....................(see 25)
Hotel Safari....................26 D6
Hotel Sakura....................27 A5
Kant Hotel....................28 D6
Mansingh Palace....................29 D6
Mughal Sheraton....................30 D6
Taj View....................31 D6
Tourists Rest House....................32 B5
EATING
Comesum Multicuisine Food Plaza....................(see 10)
Dasaprakash....................33 B5
Lakshmi Vilas....................34 B6
Only Restaurant....................35 C6
Park....................36 B6
Prakash....................37 B6
Zorba the Buddha....................38 B5
TRANSPORT
Agra Fort Bus Station....................39 B4
Idgah Bus Station....................40 A5
Indian Airlines....................(see 17)
Prepaid Autorickshaw Booth....................41 A6
Prepaid Taxi Booth....................(see 41)
Rajasthan Government Buses....................(see 27)
1
2
3
4
5
6
To Aligarh (79km)
Balkeshwar Rd
Aligarh Rd
National Hwy 2 Bypass
Ram Bagh
To Sikandra (4km); Sur Sarovar Bird Sanctuary (17km); Mathura (56km); Delhi (200km)
Belanganj Train Station
Chhilint Rd
Nehru Rd
Agra City Train Station
Pandit Kalicharan Tiwari Rd
Yamuna River
Kanpur Rd
Raja ki Mandi Train Station
Ramratan Marg
Belan Ganj
Yamuna Bridge Train Station
To Bharatpur (60km)
Bhagat Singh Marg
Hospital Rd
P Mandi Rd
Chhata Rd
Old Town Area (Kinari Bazaar)
Capt Naresh Rd
Panchkuiyan Rd
Jama Masjid Rd
Ghalibpura Rd
Agra Fort Train Station
Mantola Rd
Mahatma Gandhi (MG) Rd
Fort
Saiyad Ali Nabi Marg
Mehtab Bagh
Fatehpur Sikri Rd
To Fatehpur Sikri (40km)
Chhipi Tola Rd
See Agra Fort Map (p140)
Yamuna Kinara Rd
Taj Mahal
Idgah Train Station
Kutchery Rd
Shahjahan Park
Field Marshal Cariappa Rd
Namner Rd
Golf Course
To Kheria Airport (3km)
Ajmer Rd
See Taj Ganj Map (p138)
Taj Rd
Agra Cantonment Train Station
Station Rd
Fatehpur Sikri Rd
Gwalior Rd
Sadar Bazaar
the Mall
Gough Rd
Fatehabad Rd
Station Rd
Taj Rd
Sharnsabad Rd
To Fatehabad (35km)
Prithvi Raj Rd
Grand Parade Rd
To Gwalior (118km)

## HISTORY

In 1501 Sultan Sikander Lodi established his capital here, but the city fell into Mughal hands in 1526, when Babur defeated the last Lodi sultan at Panipat, 80km north of Delhi. Agra reached the peak of its magnificence between the mid-16th and mid-17th centuries during the reigns of Akbar, Jehangir and Shah Jahan. During this period the fort, the Taj Mahal and other major mausoleums were built. In 1638 Shah Jahan built a new city in Delhi, and his son Aurangzeb moved the capital there 10 years later.

In 1761 Agra fell to the Jats, who looted its monuments, including the Taj Mahal. The Marathas took over in 1770, but were replaced by the British in 1803. Following the Indian Uprising of 1857, the British shifted the administration of the province to Allahabad. Deprived of its administrative role, Agra developed as a centre for heavy industry, quickly becoming famous for its chemicals industry and atmospheric pollution, before tourism became a major source of income.

## ORIENTATION

Agra sits on the Ganges plain on the western bank of the Yamuna River. The fort and the main marketplace, Kinari Bazaar, are northeast of Agra Cantonment train station and Idgah bus station, where most long-haul trains and buses arrive. The Taj Mahal is about 1.5km east of the fort on the far side of the spacious British-built cantonment, reached via the road known as the Mall. A few trains also leave from the Agra Fort train station near the Kinari Bazaar. Agra's Kheria Airport is 7km west of the city centre.

The labourers and artisans who toiled on the Taj set up home immediately south of the mausoleum, creating the congested network of alleys known as Taj Ganj. Here and along Taj East Gate Rd are many of Agra's budget hotels, while most midrange and top-end hotels are located south of the Taj on Fatehabad Rd.

Hiring a taxi or autorickshaw for half a day or all day is worth considering since prices are reasonable and Agra's attractions are spread out.

#### FESTIVALS IN AGRA & FATEHPUR SIKRI

**Taj Mahotsav** (18-27 Feb; Agra) Held in Shilpgram, a crafts village and open-air emporium. Features live music and dance, food tasting and a Mughal procession with elephants and camels.
**Eid al-Fitr** (Dec/Jan; Fatehpur Sikri, p145) Join the happy crowds in the bazaar and mosque at Fatehpur Sikri, near Agra, for the end-of-Ramadan celebrations.

## INFORMATION

For an online guide to the city see www.agra-india.net.

### Bookshops

**Aanee Bookshop** (Map p138; Taj South Gate) Second-hand books.

### Emergency

**Tourist police** (Map p135; ☎ 2421204; UP Tourism office, Agra Cantonment train station; 24hr) The guys in sky-blue uniforms are based at the tourism office.

### Internet Access

**iWay Internet** Fatehabad Rd (Map p135; per hr Rs 40; 7am-11pm); Hotel Pawan (Map p135; Taj Rd; per hr Rs 25; 6.30am-10.30pm); South Gate (Map p138; per hr Rs 30; 8am-11pm)

### Laundry

**Mughal Laundry** (Map p138; Taj South Gate; per item Rs 5-15; 9am-9pm) Opposite the police station.

### Left Luggage

**Agra Cantonment train station** (Map p135; 24hr)
**Yash Café** (Map p138; Taj South Gate) A stone's throw from the Taj Mahal; storage space and showers are offered to day trippers. Doubles as a café (p143).

### Medical Services

**District Hospital** (Map p135; ☎ 2361099; Kutchery Rd; 24hr)
**Pharmacy** (Map p138; Taj South Gate; 9am-11pm) Opposite Hotel Kamal.
**SN Hospital** (Map p135; ☎ 2264428; Hospital Rd; 24hr)

### Money

**Allahabad Bank** (Map p135; ☎ 2226179; Clarks Shiraz Hotel; noon-4pm Mon-Fri, noon-2pm Sat)
**Andhra Bank** (Map p135; ☎ 2226675; Sadar Bazaar; 10am-4pm Mon-Fri, 10am-1pm Sat)
**Citibank ATM** (Map p135; Fatehabad Rd)
**HDFC ATM** (Map p135; Fatehabad Rd)

**LKP Forex** (Map p135; Fatehabad Rd; 9.30am-6pm Mon-Sat) Part of a reliable India-wide chain. Arrive without a rickshaw-wallah in tow.

**State Bank of India** (Map p135; 2252078; 10am-4pm Mon-Fri, 10am-1pm Sat) Off Chhipi Tola Rd.

**UTI ATM** Sadar Bazaar (Map p135); Taj South Gate (Map p135)

### Photography

**Radhey Lal Colour Lab** (Map p138; Taj South Gate) Can handle all your print and digital requirements.

### Post

**Main post office** (Map p135; 2226437; the Mall; 10am-6pm Mon-Sat) The poste restante is not recommended.

**Post office** (Map p135; Clarks Shiraz Hotel; 10am-5pm Mon-Sat)

### Tourist Information

**Foreigners' Registration Office** (Map p135; 2269 563; Fatehpur Sikri Rd; 10am-4pm Mon-Fri)

**India Tourism office** (Map p135; 2226378; www.incredibleindia.org; 191 the Mall; 9am-5.30pm Mon-Fri, 9am-2pm Sat & government holidays) Has brochures on local and India-wide attractions; can fix you up with an official guide (half-/full day Rs 280/400).

**UP Tourism office** Agra Cantonment train station (Map p135; 2421204; 24hr); Taj Rd (Map p135; 2226431; 64 Taj Rd; 10am-5pm Mon-Sat) The train station branch has round-the-clock help and advice, and is the place to contact the tourist police.

## DANGERS & ANNOYANCES

Many hotels, tourist shops and moneychangers pay hefty commissions to taxi drivers and rickshaw-wallahs who bring in customers; if this happens you will pay more in order to cover their commission. Cheap or free rickshaw rides always lead to a gem or souvenir shop. Lots of 'marble' souvenirs are actually soapstone. Keep away from hole-in-the-corner travel agents.

### Scams

Don't fall for the 'gem import scam', which has been conning naive tourists for more than 10 years. Travellers are invited to help a shop avoid import duty by carrying gems back to their home country, where a company representative will reimburse them for their costs plus a tidy profit. The travellers are asked to make a small credit card payment 'as a sign of good faith'. Without exception, the gems are worthless, the representative never materialises and travellers are lumped with a credit-card bill of US$1000 or more. Keep your credit card firmly sheathed! For more information, see A Warning, p361.

In the past, a few Taj Ganj restaurants went to the extent of deliberately poisoning travellers and rushing them off to crooked doctors who then billed insurance companies thousands of dollars. Following police investigations this scam has disappeared, but it could always raise its ugly head again.

## SIGHTS & ACTIVITIES

### Taj Mahal

Described as the most extravagant monument ever built for love, this sublime Mughal **mausoleum** (Map p138; 2330498; Indian/foreigner Rs 20/750, video Rs 25; 6am-7pm, closed Fri) is India's tourist emblem. Many have tried to sum up its beauty – 'a teardrop on the face of eternity' according to Indian poet Rabindranath Tagore, 'the embodiment of all things pure' according to British writer Rudyard Kipling. As an architectural masterpiece it stands alone, head and shoulders above any other contender.

The Taj was built by Emperor Shah Jahan as a memorial for his second wife, Mumtaz Mahal, who died giving birth to their fourteenth child in 1631. The death of Mumtaz left the emperor so heartbroken that his hair is said to have turned grey overnight. Construction of the Taj began in the same year and was not completed until 1653. In total, 20,000 people from India and Central Asia worked on the building. Specialists were brought in from as far afield as Europe to produce the exquisite marble screens and *pietra dura* (marble inlay work) made with thousands of semiprecious stones. The construction bill is believed to have run to Rs 3 million, equivalent to about US$70 million today.

The spectacular World Heritage white-marble mausoleum looks as immaculate today as when it was first constructed, although in recent years there has been growing concern about damage from pollution. Acid rain, produced by sulphur dioxide from vehicle and industrial emissions, has begun to discolour the famous white marble and erode the fine carving and inlays. In an attempt to reduce pollution, new industrial developments in Agra were banned in 1994, and only nonpolluting vehicles are allowed in the immediate vicinity of the Taj.

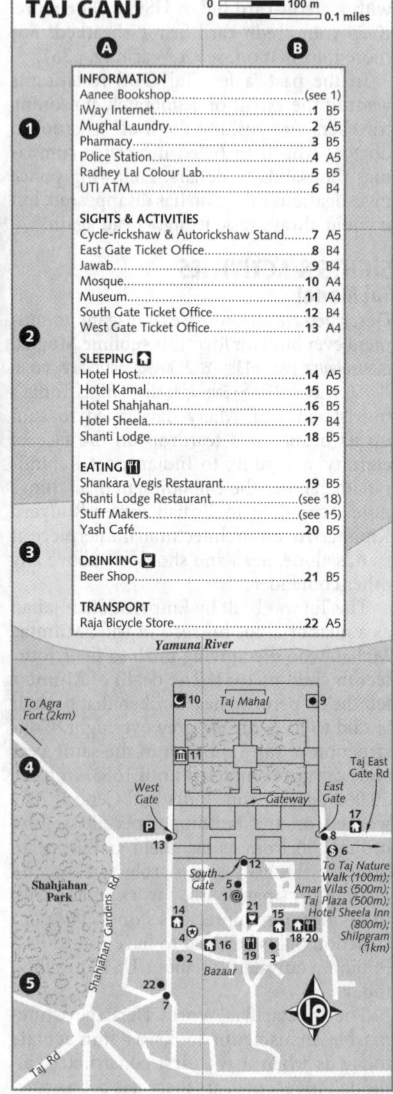


The Taj can be accessed through the west, south and east gates which all lead to an outer courtyard. Prohibited items such as food, tobacco, matches, mobile phones and camera tripods can be left without charge in cloakrooms. Cameras and videos are permitted, but you cannot take photographs of the tombs inside the mausoleum, and areas where you can take your video camera are limited. The top shot of the Taj is of the gem-encrusted building reflected in the watercourse that runs through the gardens. The fountains are often turned off so that the reflection is not spoiled.

Entry to the inner compound is through a 30m red sandstone **gateway** on the south side of the forecourt, which is inscribed with verses from the Quran in Arabic. The **ornamental gardens** are set out along classical Mughal *charbagh* (formal Persian garden) lines – a square quartered by watercourses, with an ornamental marble plinth at the centre.

To the west is a very small **museum** (admission Rs 5; 10am-5pm Sat-Thu). It houses original architectural drawings of the Taj and some nifty celadon plates, said to split into pieces or change colour if the food served on them contains poison.

The Taj Mahal itself stands on a raised marble platform at the northern end of the ornamental gardens. Raising the Taj up means that the backdrop is only sky – a master stroke of design. Purely decorative slender white **minarets** grace each corner of the platform. After more than three centuries they are not quite perpendicular, but they may have been designed to lean slightly outwards so that in the event of an earthquake, they would fall away from the precious Taj. The red sandstone **mosque** to the west of the main structure is an important gathering place for Agra's Muslims. The identical building to the east, the **jawab**, was built for symmetry and was probably used as accommodation for travellers.

The central Taj Mahal structure is made of semitranslucent white marble, carved with flowers and inlaid with thousands of semiprecious stones in beautiful patterns. A perfect exercise in symmetry, the four identical faces of the Taj feature impressive vaulted arches embellished with *pietra dura* scrollwork and quotations from the Quran. The whole structure is topped off by four small domes surrounding the famous bulbous central dome.

Below the main dome is the **Cenotaph of Mumtaz Mahal**, an elaborate false tomb surrounded by an exquisite perforated marble screen inlaid with some 43 different types of semiprecious stones. Beside it, offsetting the symmetry of the Taj, is the **Cenotaph of**

### TAJ BY MOONLIGHT

Moonlight viewings at the Taj Mahal were stopped in 1984 because of security fears. In 2004, moonlight visits to the Taj were again allowed but with many restrictions. A maximum of 400 visitors are allowed on five nights a month (the full-moon night plus two nights before and after), and they can only gaze at the white wonder from some distance away. Visitors are subject to strict security checks and are divided into batches of 50. Each group stays for 30 minutes between 8.30pm and 12.30am. Cameras are allowed but not video cameras. There are no refunds if clouds cover the moon.

**Tickets** (Indian/child aged 3-15/foreigner Rs 510/500/750; 6am-7pm, closed Fri) must be bought at a ticket office at one of the Taj's three gates at least 24 hours before you want to go. All arrangements are subject to the approval of the Supreme Court and could change at any time. To find out full-moon dates view http://aa.usno.navy.mil/data, click on 'Dates of Primary Phases of the Moon' and go to the year and month you require.

All in all it is easier (and cheaper) to view the moonlit Taj from one of the rooftop restaurants in Taj Ganj, or take an autorickshaw to Mehtab Bagh (p140) and enjoy a close-up view of the back of the Taj, which is a mirror image of the front view.



**Shah Jahan**, who was interred here with little ceremony by his usurping son Aurangzeb in 1666. Light is admitted into the central chamber by finely cut marble screens. The real **tombs** of Mumtaz Mahal and Shah Jahan are in a locked basement room below the main chamber and cannot be viewed.

Sunrise is a magical time to visit, as is sunset when the white marble first takes on a rich golden sheen, then slowly turns pink, red and finally blue with the changing light.

## Agra Fort

Construction of the massive red-sandstone **fort and palace** (Map p135; ☎ 2364512; Indian/foreigner Rs 20/300, video Rs 25; sunrise-sunset), on the bank of the Yamuna River, was begun by Emperor Akbar in 1565. Further additions were made, particularly by his grandson Shah Jahan, who added buildings using his favourite building material, white marble. The fort was built primarily as a military structure, but Shah Jahan upgraded it to a palace, and later it became his gilded prison for eight years after his son Aurangzeb seized power in 1658.

The ear-shaped fort's colossal double walls rise over 20m in height and measure 2.5km in circumference. They contain a maze of buildings, forming a city within a city. Many of the structures were destroyed over the years by Nadir Shah, the Marathas, the Jats and finally the British who used the fort as a garrison.

The **Amar Singh Gate** to the south is the sole entry point to the fort and its dog-leg design is meant to confuse attackers.

**Diwan-i-Am** (Hall of Public Audiences) was used by Shah Jahan for domestic government business, and features a throne room where the emperor listened to petitioners. In front of it is the small and rather incongruous **grave of John Colvin**, a lieutenant-governor of the northwest provinces who died of an illness in the fort during the 1857 Uprising. The Moti Masjid (Pearl Mosque) is usually closed to visitors but don't miss the tiny but exquisite **Nagina Masjid** (Gem Mosque), built in 1635 by Shah Jahan for the ladies of the court. Down below was the **Ladies' bazaar** where the court ladies bought goods.

Overlooking the river and the distant Taj Mahal is **Takhti-i-Jehangir**, a huge slab of black rock with an inscription around the edge. This throne was made for Jehangir when he was Prince Salim.

**Diwan-i-Khas** (Hall of Private Audiences) was reserved for important dignitaries or foreign representatives. The famous jewel-encrusted Peacock Throne was housed here until Aurangzeb moved it to Delhi. It was taken off to Iran in 1739 by the Persian plunderer Nadir Shah.

The **Shish Mahal** (Mirror Palace) has its walls inlaid with tiny mirrors, but at the time of research was closed for restoration.

**Musamman Burj** and **Khas Mahal** are the wonderful white-marble octagonal tower and palace where Shah Jahan was imprisoned for eight years and from where he could look out at the Taj Mahal, the tomb of his wife. The **Mina Masjid** was his own private mosque.

In the courtyard of the large harem quarters is **Anguri Bagh**, a garden that has been brought back to life; now it looks like it may have done in Shah Jahan's time.

The huge red-sandstone **Jehangir's palace** was probably built by Akbar for his son Jehangir; the palace blends Hindu and Central Asian architectural styles, a reminder of the Mughals' Afghani cultural roots. In front of the palace is **Hauz-i-Jehangir**, a huge bowl carved out of a single block of stone, which may have been used for bathing.



### Akbar's Mausoleum

This outstanding sandstone and marble **tomb** (☎ 2641230; Indian/foreigner Rs 10/110, video Rs 25; sunrise-sunset) commemorates the greatest of the Mughal emperors. The huge courtyard is entered through a stunning gateway. It has three-storey minarets at each corner and is built of red sandstone strikingly inlaid with white-marble geometric patterns.

The tomb itself lies in the centre of a peaceful garden, where deer graze, monkeys play in the trees and raucous peacocks and parakeets also make their presence felt.

Akbar started the construction himself, blending various elements just as his religious and political philosophy did (see the boxed text, p147).

The mausoleum is located at Sikandra, 10km northwest of Agra Fort. Getting there is tricky but buses (Rs 10, 30 minutes) heading to Mathura from Agra Fort bus station (Map p135) go past the mausoleum. Alternatively, an autorickshaw should cost Rs 120 for a return journey including waiting time. Consider hiring the autorickshaw for longer and visiting other sights on the same trip.

### Itimad-ud-Daulah

Nicknamed the **Baby Taj** (Map p135; ☎ 2080030; Indian/foreigner Rs 10/110, video Rs 25; 6.30am-5.30pm), the exquisite tomb of Mizra Ghiyas Beg is a must-see. This Persian nobleman was Jehangir's *wazir* (chief minister). His daughter Nur Jahan, who married Jehangir, built the tomb between 1622 and 1628, in a style similar to the tomb she built for Jehangir near Lahore in Pakistan. Asmat Begum, Mizra Ghiyas Beg's wife, is buried next to him.

Though it lacks the magic of the Taj, 6km away, many of its design elements foreshadow the Taj. The Itimad-ud-Daulah was the first Mughal structure totally built from marble and the first to make extensive use of *pietra dura*.

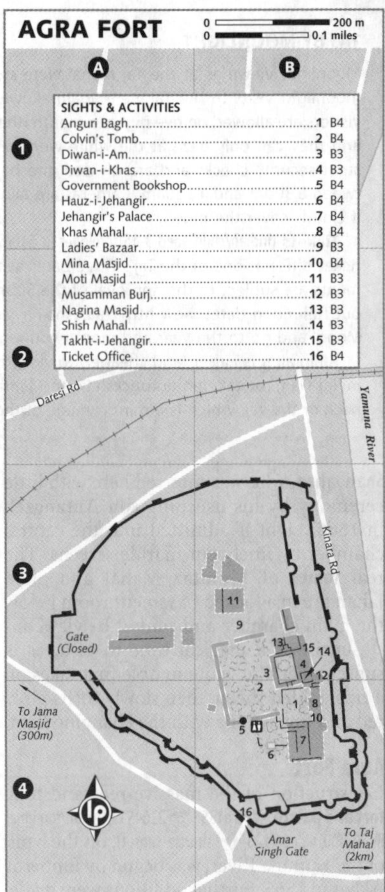


### Chini-ka-Rauza

This is the Persian-style, riverside **tomb** (Map p135; 6am-6pm) of Afzal Khan, a poet and high official in the court of Shah Jahan. It was built between 1628 and 1639. This relatively unknown mausoleum is hidden away down a shady avenue of trees. Bright blue tiles still cover part of the exterior and the interior is painted in floral designs. The upper storey offers fine views.

### Mehtab Bagh

This new **park** (Map p135; Indian/foreigner Rs 5/100) is attempting to recreate a Mughal-style garden. It's well worth coming here to enjoy a wonderful view of the back of the Taj – in some ways a better view than the view from the front. Walk down to the Yamuna River on the path that runs alongside the park and view the Taj without any tourist crowds in a peaceful and natural ambience of buffaloes and wading birds.

### Taj Nature Walk

Follow the stone pathways through this **mini-wilderness** (Off Map p138; Taj East Gate Rd; admission Rs 5; 6am-6pm) for a pleasant nature ramble among birds and butterflies, with the Taj hovering in the background. There are seats and picnic spots, and opposite is a **garden restaurant** (veg meals Rs 20-35).

### Jama Masjid

This fine **mosque** (Map p135), built in the Kinari bazaar by Shah Jahan's daughter in 1648, has no minarets but features striking marble patterning on its domes.

### Swimming

Hotel Amar charges nonguests Rs 175 to use its outdoor pool, Rs 40 to use the gym and Rs 500 for Ayurvedic massages. Other hotels with outdoor pools are Hotel Atithi (Rs 250), Hotel Agra Ashok (Rs 300), Mansingh Palace (adult/child Rs 300/50), Taj View (Rs 345), Mughal Sheraton (Rs 440) and Clarks Shiraz Hotel (Rs 450).

## TOURS

UP Tourism runs **daily tours** (Indian/foreigner incl entry fees Rs 350/1650) that leave Agra Cantonment train station at 10.30am, after picking up passengers arriving from Delhi on the *Taj Express*, which pulls in at 10.07am. The AC coach tour includes the Taj Mahal, Agra Fort and Fatehpur Sikri with a 1¼-hour stop in each place. Tours return to the station so that day-trippers can catch the *Taj Express* back to Delhi at 6.55pm. Contact either of the UP Tourism offices (see p137) to book a seat.

## SLEEPING

### Budget

All hotels have private bathrooms with sit-down flush toilets and hot water except where indicated. In summer, budget hotels tend to provide hot water in a bucket, but in winter it arrives by pipe. The first three hotels are the most modern and clean. The hotels south of the Taj have a wonderful close-up view of the Taj, but from their rooftop restaurants rather than from the rooms.

#### TAJ GANJ AREA

**Hotel Sheela** (Map p138; ☎ 2331194; www.hotelsheelaagra.com; Taj East Gate Rd; d with/without AC Rs 600/350; meals Rs 25-70; ) Despite the lack of Taj views this is the best budget option in Taj Ganj because of the garden that creates an oasis of calmness, the clean, attractive rooms and the helpful staff. The garden restaurant is the perfect spot to sip a mixed fruit lassi. Book ahead.

**Hotel Sheela Inn** (Off Map p138; ☎ 3093437; Taj East Gate Rd; s Rs 300-500, d Rs 400-600, r with AC Rs 700; ) A brand new option that is clean and smart although the rooms are smallish. The rooftop restaurant serves some Nepali items.

**Taj Plaza** (Off Map p138; ☎ 2232515; fax 2368230; Taj East Gate Rd; s/d Rs 350/450, with AC Rs 600/700; ) The simple but bright rooms in this modern hotel have TVs and four of them have a Taj view.

**Hotel Kamal** (Map p138; ☎ 2330126; hotelkamal@hotmail.com; Taj South Gate; r Rs 200-300) The best budget hotel with a rooftop close-up view of the Taj. Ask to see a number of rooms as they vary regarding size, shape and window light. In summer hot water comes in a bucket. Staff are very friendly and the restaurant Stuff Makers (p143) is recommended.

**Shanti Lodge** (Map p138; ☎ 2231973; shantilodge2000@yahoo.co.in; Taj South Gate; s Rs 100-150, d Rs 150-300, r with AC Rs 500; ) Some rooms have TVs and Taj views in this popular and above-average budget hotel. The new section has the best rooms and the rooftop restaurant's Taj view is hard to beat.

**Hotel Host** (Map p138; ☎ 2331010; Taj West Gate; s/d with shared bathroom Rs 100/125, d with private bathroom Rs 150-200) All the rooms have TV, and the owners have made an effort to make them nice. The usual bucket-hot-water system operates in summer. A few rooms have no window, and some have balconies. The Taj can be seen if you perch on the very top of the building.

**Hotel Shahjahan** (Map p138; ☎ 2233071; Taj South Gate; s/d with shared bathroom from Rs 70/100, with private bathroom from Rs 100/200, r with AC Rs 700; ) A real mixed bag of rooms can be found in this rather scruffy hotel, but you might pick up a bargain.

### OTHER AREAS

**Tourists Rest House** (Map p135; ☎ 2363961; dontworrychickencurry@hotmail.com; Kutchery Rd; s Rs 120-300, d Rs 150-350; ❄ 💻) Helpful owners, a homely atmosphere, free pick-ups and spotless rooms grouped around a shady garden that is used for candlelit dinners. This place, near Kavisha Motors, is such a perennial favourite that you usually need to book well ahead. Rooms have hot showers, most have TV, and some have rather odd 'magic marble' décor.

**Hotel Safari** (Map p135; ☎ 2333029; hotelsafari@hotmail.com; Shamsabad Rd; s/d Rs 200/250, with AC Rs 350/400; ❄) All rooms are white and spotless and have TVs in this admirable hotel with the same owners as Tourists Rest House.

**Hotel Sakura** (Map p135; ☎ 2420169; ashu_sakura@yahoo.com; Ajmer Rd; d Rs 200-500; 💻) Another long-running favourite that has a very friendly owner and is close to Idgah bus station, but needs a facelift. The restaurant is recommended – try the butter chicken followed by *kheer* (rice pudding). Internet access is Rs 60 per hour.

**Hotel Pawan** (Map p135; ☎ 2225506; pawotel@sancharnet.in; 3 Taj Rd; s/d Rs 250/350, with AC Rs 800/900; ❄ 💻) Reasonable budget rooms with TVs are available at Hotel Pawan, which is set among the shops and restaurants of the Sadar Bazaar area.

Other recommendations:

**Hotel Ranjit** (Map p135; ☎ 2364446; 263 Station Rd; s/d Rs from 350/500) Within walking distance of Agra Cantonment train station.

**Hotel Prem Sagar** (Map p135; ☎ 2261137; 264 Station Rd; s/d/tr Rs 250/350/450)

**Hotel Bawa Palace** (Map p135; ☎ 2420151; Ajmer Rd; d from Rs 500, with AC Rs 700; ❄) Close to Idgah bus station, the rooms are not as flash as the façade.

## Midrange

Agra has few good midrange hotels; most of them are clustered together in Fatehabad Rd, so look at a few and try bargaining before making your choice. The posher midrange hotels are bordering on top end.

**Hotel Ashish Palace** (Map p135; ☎ 2230032; fax 2330404; Fatehabad Rd; s/d Rs 800/950; ❄) At last someone has realised that Agra is lacking good hotels at this price and has built one. Brand spanking new, the smart rooms have fridges, large-screen TVs and hot showers (complete with shower curtains and even shower caps). Book ahead.

**Hotel Amar** (Map p135; ☎ 2331884; www.hotelamar.com; Fatehabad Rd; s Rs 1400-2700, d Rs 1650-3000; ❄ 🏊) The executive rooms have a touch of maharaja style and there is a restaurant, bar, pool with a small slide, Ayurvedic health club (massages Rs 43 to 500) and gym (Rs 40).

**Hotel Atithi** (Map p135; ☎ 2230040; www.hotelatithi.com; Fatehabad Rd; s Rs 1350-1600, d Rs 1600-2150; ❄ 🏊) The pool and lawn are the main attractions at this hotel. Spacious, well-equipped rooms on each floor are colour-coordinated – choose blue, black, white or the most popular, green. The foyer is a fetching lilac and has a free drinking-water dispenser.

**Amar Yatri Niwas** (Map p135; ☎ 2233030; amaragra@sancharnet.in; Fatehabad Rd; s Rs 950-1200, d Rs 1200-1450; ❄) This is one of Agra's better midrange hotels at this price, although that's faint praise.

**Hotel Ganga Ratan** (Map p135; ☎ 2330329; www.hotelgangaratan.com; Fatehabad Rd; s Rs 900-1500, d Rs 1200-1800; ❄) All rooms have fridges in this hotel, which has Indian artwork on the walls.

**Kant Hotel** (Map p135; ☎ 2331332; www.hotelkantagra.com; Fatehabad Rd; s/d Rs 950/1500, with Taj glimpse Rs 1500/2250; ❄) Rooms are ordinary but have fridges, and you can relax in the pleasant bar.

**Hotel Agra Ashok** (Map p135; ☎ 2361223; sales@hotelagraashok.com; 6B the Mall; s/d/ste Rs 2300/2900/4500; meals Rs 175-450; ❄ 🏊) A pool in the garden, a water feature in the lobby, a plush Chinese restaurant and some stylish rooms are the pluses in this quality but expensive midrange hotel.

**Mansingh Palace** (Map p135; ☎ 2331771; mansingh.agra@mailcity.com; Fatehabad Rd; s/d/ste Rs 3200/3700/6500; ❄ 💻 🏊) Built of red sandstone, this stylish hotel has plush rooms and is crammed with Mughal design themes. The garden has an unusually shaped pool, and the Sheesh Mahal restaurant has live *ghazals* (Urdu songs derived from poetry) nightly at 8pm except Tuesday.

**Clarks Shiraz Hotel** (Map p135; ☎ 2226121; www.hotelclarksshiraz.com; Taj Rd; s Rs 4000-5500, d Rs 4500-5800; ❄ 💻 🏊) Three sections of high-rise executive rooms can be found here, along with live music in the rooftop restaurant, a 'cakes and bakes' area, a gym and Ayurvedic massages. There is also a bank, a post office, shops and airline offices.

**Taj View** (Map p135; ☎ 2232400; www.tajhotels.com; Fatehabad Rd; s/d US$110/120, s/d/ste with Taj glimpse US$135/145/275; ) Cool elegance and Indian style feature in the communal areas with an open-plan foyer, restaurant and bar and a flow through to the outdoor pool. Rooms have been recently renovated but are disappointingly ordinary. Activities for children include a magician.

### Top End

**Amar Vilas** (Off Map p138; ☎ 2231515; www.oberoihotels.com; Taj East Gate Rd; s/d US$425/450, ste US$1350-2400; ) A world-class hotel. The elegant interior is suffused with Mughal style as are the exterior fountain courtyard and the outstanding swimming pool set in a water garden. If you cannot afford to stay, take a look around this modern palace and sip a Kingfisher beer (Rs 125) in the bar.

**Mughal Sheraton** (Map p135; ☎ 2331701; mughal.sheraton@welcomgroup.com; Fatehabad Rd; s/d/ste US$150/160/400; ) This sprawling red-brick luxury hotel is set amid tranquil gardens that include a tree planted by actor Peter O'Toole. Everything is shining and elegant; one of the three restaurants serves Northwest Frontier BBQs. Relax with a game of tennis, badminton or minigolf while the kids enjoy a puppet show.

## EATING & DRINKING

Delicious Agra specialities can be found in the bazaars. *Peitha* (Rs 36 to 44 per kilogram) is a square sweet made from pumpkin and glucose flavoured with rosewater, coconut or saffron. *Dalmoth* (Rs 60 per kilogram, with dried fruit Rs 90 per kilogram) is Agra's famous version of *namkin* (prepackaged spicy nibbles). From October to March look out for *gajak* (Rs 56 to 90 per kilogram), a slightly spicy sesame seed biscuit strip.

The beer shop in Taj Ganj is open from 10am to 11pm – a bottle of Kingfisher or Royal Challenge is Rs 60, while a bottle of Guru is Rs 65.

### Taj Ganj Area

This lively but messy area has plenty of budget rooftop restaurants, where the meals and menus are similar. None are licensed but nearby alcohol shops are open all day every day. Some small eateries serve thalis and big breakfasts for as little as Rs 15.

**Stuff Makers** (Map p138; Hotel Kamal; meals Rs 25-60) Eat downstairs in the thatched hut or join the crowd on the rooftop terrace with its fairy lights and Taj views. The food is reliable but uninspired and includes backpacker items such as honey and banana pancakes.

**Shanti Lodge Restaurant** (Map p138; meals Rs 30-75) The usual menu but the food is reasonable and the rooftop Taj view is special.

**Shankara Vegis Restaurant** (Map p138; meals Rs 25-60) This relaxed rooftop restaurant has no Taj view but does have all the vegetarian favourites as well as music and games like carom.

**Yash Café** (Map p138; meals Rs 30-70, pizzas Rs 65-95) A very laid-back joint with a '60s feel. Yash shows movies in the evening and offers a shower and storage space to day visitors.

### Other Areas

**Zorba the Buddha** (Map p135; Sadar Bazaar; meals Rs 70-90; noon-4.30pm & 6-9.30pm, closed Jun; ) Vases of flowers on neat little tables greet guests at this Osho-inspired bistro-style vegetarian restaurant. The healthy food and herbal teas are designed to nurture your soul as well as your body.

**Comesum Multicuisine Food Plaza** (Map p135; Agra Cantonment train station; meals Rs 35-70; 24hr; ) This is the cleanest and best-looking dining area in any Indian train station. Relax in the fast-food ambience as you scan the plastic replicas of the dosa, thali and burger sets that are on offer. It also has snacks, sandwiches, muffins and desserts. Worth a visit even if you're not travelling by train.

**Dasaprakash** (Map p135; Gwalior Rd; meals Rs 60-105; ) With comfy sofas and cheerful décor, this cubicle-style South Indian restaurant chain has dosas and ice creams for which its fans are willing to fork out Rs 60 or more.

**Only Restaurant** (Map p135; the Mall; veg/nonveg buffet Rs 225/275; ) This bamboo-lined, cosy restaurant with a garden is often packed with happy tour groups and has live music every evening from 7pm.

**Lakshmi Vilas** (Map p135; Taj Rd; meals Rs 32-50; ) A clean popular restaurant with South Indian mains plus desserts like *rawa kesari* (fried semolina and coconut). Over 30 dosa varieties are available including a family dosa that is over a metre long and makes a foot-long Subway look very puny.

**Prakash** (Map p135; Sadar Bazaar; meals Rs 35-70; closed Fri) The special feature here is the Bengali, Punjab and South Indian thalis, but roast chicken and fish and chips are also on the menu.

**Park** (Map p135; Sadar Bazaar; meals Rs 55-175; ) An upmarket restaurant with soft music, Park serves up Indian, Continental and Chinese food.



## SHOPPING

Agra is well known for marble items inlaid with coloured stones, similar to the *pietra dura* work on the Taj. Sadar bazaar (Map p135) and the area around the Taj are full of emporiums of one kind or another, but prices here are more expensive than in the bazaars of the old town area. Prices are set according to the quality of detailed workmanship, not the size of the item. Be careful when buying marble, as fake marble (usually soapstone which scratches easily) is common.

Other popular buys include rugs, leather and gemstones, though the latter are imported from Rajasthan and are cheaper in Jaipur. Gem shops are also some of the worst offenders when it comes to credit-card fraud and other scams (see p361).

Kinari bazaar (Map p135) is crowded but if you brave the mad traffic you can find traditional market stalls selling everything from textiles to fruit. The smaller bazaar south of Taj Ganj is much calmer and tailors there will sew you up a pair of trousers for around Rs 200 or a shirt for Rs 100.

About a kilometre along the traffic-quiet road from Taj East Gate is **Shilpgram** (Off Map p138; 10am-10pm Oct-Mar), an open-air collection of stalls selling handicrafts and artworks that also has a café and bar. Every February a week-long food, craft and culture festival takes place (see p136).

## GETTING THERE & AWAY

### Air

Agra's Kheria Airport is 7km from the city centre. **Indian Airlines** (Map p135; ☎ 2226821; Clarks Shiraz Hotel; 10am-1.15pm & 2-5pm Mon-Sat) flies to Delhi every Monday, Wednesday and Friday.

### Bus

Most long-haul buses leave from **Idgah bus station** (Map p135; ☎ 2366588; Ajmer Rd). Hourly buses run to Delhi's Sarai Kale Khan bus station (Rs 105, five hours) via Mathura (Rs 29, 1½ hours). Hourly buses go to Jaipur (Rs 105, six hours). Frequent buses head off to Fatehpur Sikri (Rs 18, one hour) and Bharatpur (Rs 31, 1½ hours).

From **Agra Fort bus station** (Map p135; Power House bus station; ☎ 2364557) buses also leave for Delhi (Rs 105, five hours) via Mathura (Rs 29, 1½ hours).

Rajasthan government buses (Map p135) depart from Hotel Sakura, which is very close to Idgah bus station. Deluxe buses run hourly to Jaipur (Rs 137, 5½ hours) between 6.30am and 2.30pm, and then at 4.30pm, 5.30pm, 7.30pm, 10pm and midnight. Between March and October AC buses (Rs 228) run three times daily.

### Train

**Agra Cantonment (Cantt) train station** (Map p135; ☎ 2421204) is an important stop on the main Delhi–Mumbai line, with several trains daily from both New Delhi and Nizamuddin train stations. The fastest train to and from Delhi is the daily AC *Shatabdi Express* (Rs 395/760 in chair/executive, two hours). It leaves New Delhi at 6am and departs from Agra for the return trip at 8.43pm, making it ideal for day-tripping.

A cheaper alternative is the daily *Taj Express* (Rs 55/191 in 2nd/chair car, three hours). It leaves Delhi's Nizamuddin train station at 7.15am and departs from Agra for the return trip at 6.55pm. This gives you less time in Agra, but it connects with the daily tour (see p141). Be doubly cautious with your luggage on this route.

The *Marudhar Express* runs west to Jaipur, leaving Agra at 7.25am, reaching Jaipur (Rs 80/277 in 2nd/chair car) at 2am, and Jodhpur (Rs 136/476 in 2nd/chair car) at 9pm.

## GETTING AROUND

### To/From the Airport

To Kheria Airport, taxis should charge about Rs 200 and autorickshaws Rs 100, but initially the drivers will ask for a lot more.

### Autorickshaw

Just outside Agra Cantonment train station is the **prepaid autorickshaw booth** (Map p135; 24hr). It costs Rs 15 for a short 1km ride, Rs 30 to Sadar bazaar and Rs 52 to Taj Ganj. A three-hour tour to the Taj Mahal and Agra

Fort return costs Rs 160, a four-hour tour Rs 200 and an eight-hour tour Rs 300. A round trip including waiting time to Sikandra for Akbar's Mausoleum is likely to cost Rs 120. Autorickshaws are not allowed to go to Fatehpur Sikri, so take a bus or taxi.

### Bicycle
Bicycles can be hired from **Raja Bicycle Store** (Map p138; per day Rs 50; 8am-8.30pm) but the roads are a race track-cum-obstacle course.

### Cycle-rickshaw
Best for short distances, this nonpolluting transport is cheaper than autorickshaws and rides should cost between Rs 20 and 40 depending on the distance travelled.

### Taxi
Just outside Agra Cantonment train station is the **prepaid taxi booth** (24hr). Taxis can take up to four people and the cost to any five-star hotel is Rs 120 (AC Rs 150), while a three-hour tour costs Rs 300 (AC Rs 375) and a four-hour tour is Rs 450 (AC Rs 650). An eight-hour tour is Rs 650 (AC Rs 950) but costs Rs 950 (AC Rs 1400) if it includes Fatehpur Sikri. A four-hour trip to Fatehpur Sikri costs Rs 600 (AC Rs 900). A return trip to the World Heritage–listed Keoladeo National Park at Bharatpur costs Rs 950 including waiting time. Further afield, one way to Delhi is Rs 2500, and Jaipur Rs 2700.

### Other Transport
From the Taj the roads west to Agra Fort and east to Shilpgram are traffic quiet. **Battery-operated buses** (Indian/foreigner Rs 4/free; every 15min 6am-7pm) and tongas, electric *vikrams* (large tempos), camel carts and an elephant provide exotic transport options along these roads. Amar Vilas even has its own electric golf buggies to scoot guests around.

# AROUND AGRA

## FATEHPUR SIKRI

☎ 05613 / pop 28,750

This magnificent fortified ghost city, 40km west of Agra, was the Mughal empire's short-lived capital between 1571 and 1585, during the reign of Akbar. Although brilliant and unusual from an architectural point of view, Akbar's city was erected in an area that suffered from water shortages and it was abandoned shortly after his death. The well-preserved palace buildings and the still-used mosque are the main points of interest, but you can wander round other ruins that are scattered behind the mosque and the mint.

Most people visit this World Heritage site as a day trip from Agra, but you can stay in the nearby town, and the red sandstone palaces are at their most atmospheric at sunset. See p365 for details of the Eid al-Fitr celebrations.

### Orientation & Information
The palace buildings lie on the top of a ridge with the town of Fatehpur Sikri just to the south. The Jama Masjid and the ruins near it and behind the mint can be visited for free. Swarms of unofficial guides pester visitors, demanding a ridiculous fee of Rs 300, but if you want a guide it's best to hire an official one near a ticket office (Rs 50 to 100). The purpose of many buildings is uncertain and much of what the guides say is invented.

### Sights
#### JAMA MASJID
The beautiful **Jama Masjid** (Dargah Mosque), completed in 1571, contains elements of Persian and Hindu design. The main entrance is through the impressive 54m-high **Buland Darwaza** (Victory Gate), perhaps the

#### SAVE THE BEARS
India's first sanctuary for 'dancing' bears was established by the **World Society for the Protection of Animals** (WSPA; www.wspa.org.uk) in 2002 with help from the UP Forestry Department and **Free the Bears** (www.freethebears.org.au). The 8-hectare site is inside the Sur Sarovar Bird Sanctuary, 17km west of Agra. It provides a refuge for up to 90 sloth bears that have been rescued from Kalandar gypsies who force them to 'dance' in return for money from onlookers. This cruel entertainment is illegal in India but still enslaves 1000 bears. To visit the sanctuary, first contact **Wildlife SOS** (☎ 0981-0114563; www.wildlifesos.com). Also see Animal Welfare, p75.

largest in Asia, built to commemorate Akbar's military victory in Gujarat. A Quranic inscription inside the archway quotes Jesus saying: 'The world is a bridge, pass over it but build no house upon it. He who hopes for an hour may hope for eternity', which seems appropriate considering the fate of the city.

Inside the courtyard is the superb white marble **tomb of Shaikh Salim Chishti**, completed in 1581. Inside the mausoleum are brightly coloured flower murals and the canopy is decorated with mother-of-pearl shell. Just as Akbar came to the saint four centuries ago hoping for a son, childless women visit his tomb today and tie a thread to the jalis (marble lattice screens), which are among the finest in India.

### PALACES & PAVILIONS

The first of the **palace buildings** (Indian/foreigner Rs 20/260, video Rs 25; sunrise-sunset) you enter from the south is the largest, the **Palace of Jodh Bai**. Constructed around a courtyard, it blends Hindu columns, Islamic cupolas and blue Persian roof tiles.

The **Palace of the Christian Wife** was used by Akbar's Goan Christian wife Mariam, and you can see the remains of the paintings that used to cover the inside. Mariam married Akbar in 1562, gave birth to Jehangir in 1569 at Fatehpur Sikri and died in Agra in 1623.

**Birbal Bhavan**, ornately carved inside and out, was probably used by two of Akbar's senior wives.

The function of the **Lower Haramsara** is controversial – it may have housed servants but it looks more like stables for the horses, camels and elephants.

The most intricately carved structure is the amazing **Rumi Sultana**, which is covered all over its surface with a mass of exuberant carving.

The whimsical **Panch Mahal** is a five-storey pavilion that was used by the court ladies. Each of the storeys is reduced in size until the top one consists of only a tiny kiosk. The lower floor has 84 columns, which are all different.

The **Treasury** has sea monsters, intended to protect the fabulous wealth once stored

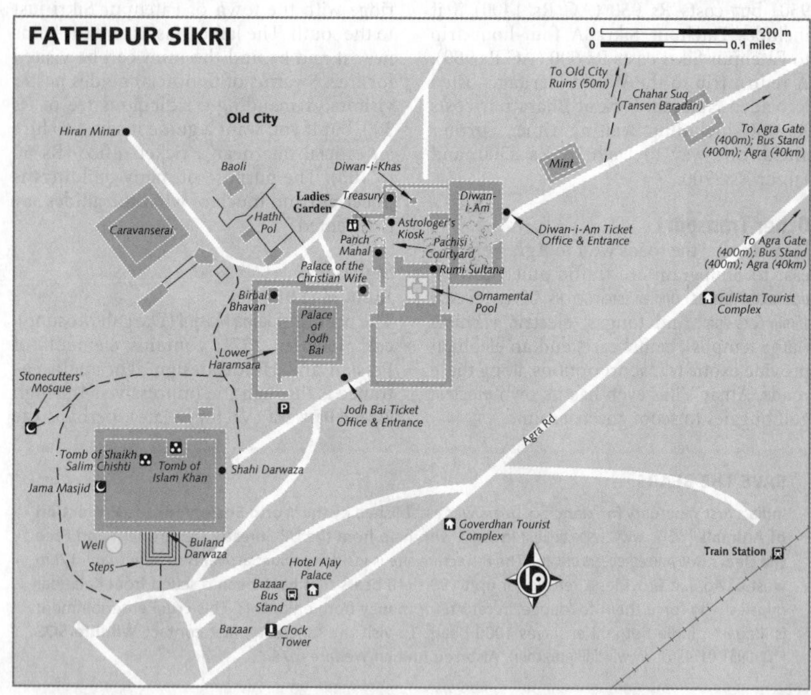

### AKBAR THE GREAT

Regarded as the greatest of the Mughals, Akbar was brought up in Afghanistan and although thrust into power at the tender age of 13, he expanded the Mughal empire to cover most of northern India. A wise and just ruler, Akbar followed a policy of Sulh-i-Kul (Peace for All) and abolished many of the restrictions placed on infidels (nonbelievers), including the very unpopular 'pilgrimage tax' on Hindus.

Although Akbar's military campaigns were as bloody as any in the Mughal era – following his victory at Panipat, he is said to have built a tower of Hindu heads – the great Mughal is best remembered for his tolerance of other religions. Akbar counted Christians and Hindus among his many wives and went on to invent a philosophy known as Din-i-Ilahi (Faith of God), asserting the common truth in all religions.

Honouring the Sufi mystic Shaikh Salim Chishti, whom Akbar credited with bringing him a male heir, a 'perfect city' was constructed in the desert at Fatehpur Sikri, designed as a physical expression of Din-i-Ilahi. A community of intellectuals from many different religions was created to fulfil the emperor's love of debate.

In fact, the perfect city was Akbar's only folly. Built far from the nearest river, Fatehpur was plagued by water shortages and all the ingenious irrigation systems developed by Akbar's engineers were unable to solve the problem. Fatehpur was abandoned shortly after Akbar's death, along with most of his liberal attitudes.



there, carved onto the ceiling struts, while the so-called **Astrologer's Kiosk** in front has its roof supports carved into a serpentine Jain style.

The **Diwan-i-Khas** (Hall of Private Audience) has an ordinary exterior, but the interior is dominated by a magnificently carved stone column in the centre. The pillar flares to create a flat-topped plinth linked to the four corners of the room by narrow stone bridges, from where Akbar is believed to have debated with scholars who stood at the ends of the four bridges. Outside is the **Pachisi Courtyard** where Akbar is said to have played the game pachisi using slave girls as pieces.

The **Diwan-i-Am** (Hall of Public Audience) is where Akbar dispensed justice 'without harshness or ill-will', according to the information board.

Plenty of ruins are scattered behind the mosque, including the **caravanserai**, a vast courtyard surrounded by rooms where visiting merchants used to stay, and the bizarre 21m-high **Hiran Minar** tower that's decorated with hundreds of stone representations of elephant tusks. Badly defaced elephants still guard **Hathi Pol** (Elephant Gate), while the remains of the small **Stonecutters' Mosque** and a **hammam** (bath) are nearby. Other unnamed ruins can be explored north of the mint, including some in the middle of a village.

## Sleeping & Eating

**Hotel Ajay Palace** (☎ 282950; Agra Rd; d with shared/private bathroom Rs 200/300; meals Rs 20-80) Rooms in this small four-room guesthouse have squat toilets, but are neat and clean and the hosts are friendly. Hot showers and a heater are available in winter. The restaurant has the best food in town – especially the fried eggplant, the mango and honey sauce and the *kheer*. Relax downstairs or on the shady rooftop after a hard slog around Akbar's folly. You can also leave your luggage here.

**Goverdhan Tourist Complex** (☎ 282643; www.hotelfatehpursikriviews.com; Agra Rd; d with/without AC from Rs 700/200; ❄ 💻) Some rooms have odd décor, but the hotel has a nice garden and offers free Internet use for 20 minutes. The AC rooms are cleaner and have recently been renovated.

**Gulistan Tourist Complex** (☎ 282490; fax 282840; s/d Rs 525/575, with AC Rs 775/900; ❄) Run by UP Tourism, it has a restaurant and a bar.

Fatehpur Sikri's culinary speciality is *khataie*, which are the biscuits you can see piled high in the bazaar.

## Getting There & Away

Tour buses usually stop for 1½ hours, which isn't long enough. Make a day of it by catching a bus (Rs 15, 1½ hours) from Agra's Idgah bus stand; buses depart every 30 minutes between 6.30am and 7pm. Be sure to get on a small bus to Fatehpur Sikri town and not a big bus going to Bharatpur, which will drop you near Agra Gate, a 1km walk from the monuments. The last bus back to Agra from the bazaar bus stand leaves at 7pm.

Autorickshaws are not allowed to travel from Agra to Fatehpur Sikri; however, a taxi should cost Rs 600 return including waiting time.

Buses from the bazaar bus stand leave regularly for Bharatpur (Rs 12, 30 minutes) and Jaipur (Rs 75, 4½ hours). If you are going on to either of these places, you can store your bags at Hotel Ajay Palace.

# Rajasthan

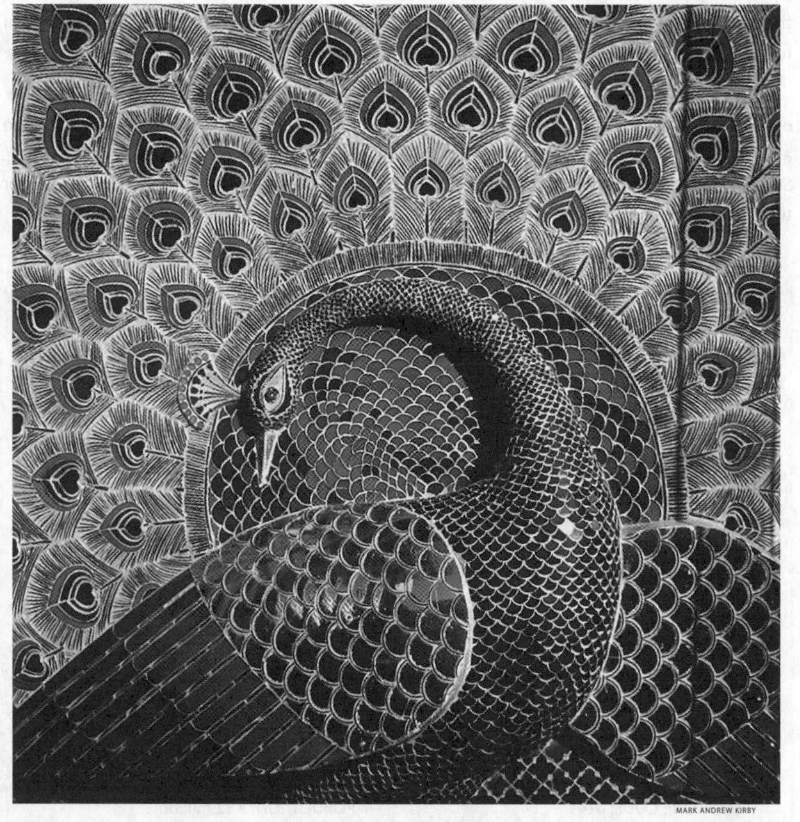

MARK ANDREW KIRBY

# Jaipur



Prepare your senses to be shaken up, blasted and returned to you. Clattering, chaotic, brilliant, dusky and dirty, Jaipur was painted a beguiling shade of pink to welcome the Prince of Wales in 1876, and doesn't look like it's been touched up since (though it's given a fresh coat annually). Acid-bright colours punctuate the streets – crouched porters group by the station in red shirts and turbans, billowing saris catch the eye like butterflies, and shop fronts glitter with fierce fabrics. There's something strangely bygone about the city – perhaps it's the prevalence of camel carts, pigs and cows standing motionless in the middle of the road, around which weave rickshaws, motorbikes, cars and death-defying pedestrians.

Standing amid the mayhem are the splendours of Jaipur's royal past. The city's overlooked by two imposing forts, and its palace spreads across its heart. There are also Jantar Mantar, the royal observatory, a meringue-shaped cinema and grids of enticing bazaars. Just out of town is the faded-rose Amber Fort, which seems to have reared up from a fairy tale.

It's not all fairy tales. Due to rapid expansion, Jaipur suffers problems of unemployment, overcrowding and pollution. As the region's major city, it's a magnet for the rural poor seeking a living; you'll see more people sleeping in the streets here than anywhere else in the state. Some travellers are turned off by this, particularly the hassle factor. But it's good to give Jaipur time: you'll settle in, enjoy its dishevelled romance, and learn to give hustlers the slip.

### HIGHLIGHTS

- Brilliant **bazaars** (p175) – the state's best shopping, with artisans a-go-go and all sorts of crafts
- **City Palace** (p157), a beautiful maze of buildings where you can see how the maharajas lived
- Outsized, out-there astronomical instruments at **Jantar Mantar** (p159)
- **Hawa Mahal** (p160), the Palace of the Winds, a dusky pink honeycomb built for the women of the court
- Jaipur **festivals** (opposite) – the thrill of processions, painted elephants, chandelier carriers and rickety generators
- **Amber Fort** (p179), a delicate Rajput masterpiece, rising from a rocky hill 11km from Jaipur
- A Bollywood blockbuster at the **Raj Mandir Cinema** (p174) – a building somewhere between a temple, a meringue and a nightclub

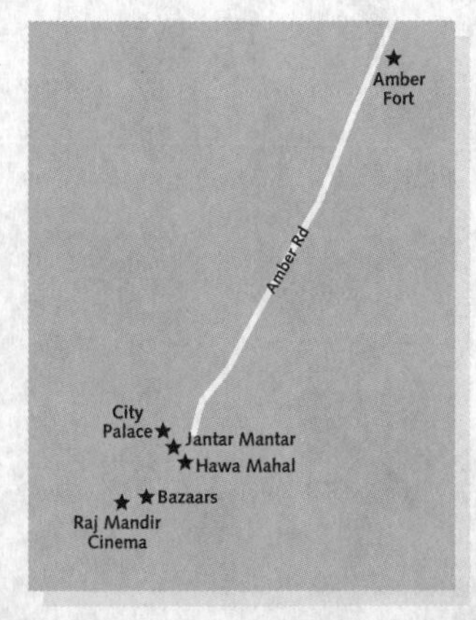


- TELEPHONE CODE: 0141
- POPULATION: 2.32 million

## HISTORY

*Je na dekkhyo Jaipario to kal main akar kaai kario?*
If one has not seen Jaipur, what is the point of having been born?

Jaipur is named after its founder, the great warrior-astronomer Jai Singh II (r 1688–1744), who came to power at age 11 after the death of his father, Maharaja Bishan Singh. The maharaja had been assured by astrologers that the boy would achieve great things in his lifetime, and young Jai (meaning 'victory') received the best education in the arts, sciences, philosophy and military affairs.

Jai Singh could trace his lineage back to the Rajput clan of Kachhwahas, who consolidated their power in the 12th century. Their capital was at Amber, about 11km northeast of present-day Jaipur, where they built the impressive Amber Fort (p179). They had a talent for war and alliances of convenience, so the dominion of the Kachhwahas spread, eventually encompassing a large area abutting the kingdoms of Mewar (in Udaipur region) and Marwar (in Jodhpur region).

The Kachhwaha clan recognised the expediency of aligning themselves with the powerful Mughal empire, and subsequently enjoyed the patronage of the Mughal emperors, which brought them great riches and influence. Raja Bihar Mal led an army for Humayun (second Mughal ruler of India), and was the first Rajput to be presented at Akbar's court. When Akbar visited the

### FESTIVALS IN JAIPUR

Jaipur has some unique festivals, and numerous statewide and national festivals are celebrated with particular vigour and flair here. It's worth visiting for any of these to catch some of the build-up, the dressing up and a few processions. For more information on festivals, see p363.

**Makar Sankranti** (14 Jan) This kite festival is worth catching. It's celebrated all over India, and heralds the transition of the sun into the northern hemisphere. The sky is full of kites, with special displays and kite fights – participants fiercely compete to cut down each others' kites (the strings are dipped in crushed glass) – anyone is fair game.

**Jaipur Heritage International Festival** (www.jaipurfestival.org; 14-23 Jan) In celebration of Jaipur's heritage, this two-week festival aims to revive and conserve the vibrant regional culture and traditions. Performances are held throughout the old city, in atmospheric venues from forts to temples. As well as the usual displays of folk, classical, traditional and contemporary dance, there are theatre, film, music and sport events, as well as concerts, workshops, exhibitions and fashion shows. Contact the Indian National Trust for Art and Cultural Heritage (Intach; ☎ 2228275) for more details.

**Elephant Festival** (Mar) Begins in Phalgun, just before Holi. Elephants painted in amazing patterns and dressed in ribbons and jewellery (spot the females by their jangling anklets) lumber through the streets, along with camels, horses and dancers. Elephantine craziness includes matches of elephant polo at Chaughan Stadium in the old city, elephant races, and a tug-of-war between elephants and humans. There's also colourful Holi on elephants, where players get to throw coloured powder at each other. Readers have found this festival touristy, but it's a lot of fun, tremendously colourful and great for kids.

**Gangaur** (Mar-Apr) Rajasthan's most important festival, especially for women, celebrates the love between Gan (Shiva) and his consort Gauri (Parvati). Parvati symbolises perfection in married life, so it's considered a good move for both unmarried and married women to worship during this festival. It commences on the day following Holi, the first day of Chaitra, and continues for 18 days. Newlywed women should observe the full 18 days following their marriages. Unmarried women usually fast during this period. People make small terracotta images of Gan and Gauri, to dress and worship. Some families have permanent wooden images of Gauri, which are freshly painted. The last three days are the climax of the festival. The terracotta and wooden images are dressed to impress in beautiful costumes and jewels. An elaborately garbed image of the goddess is carried on a palanquin from the Tripolia Gate, at the City Palace, through the streets of the old city. The traditional dish to eat in Jaipur at this time is *ghewar*, a kind of sweet.

**Teej** (Jul-Aug) This is the swing festival, and heralds the onset of the monsoon month, Shravan. It's celebrated across Rajasthan in honour of the marriage of Gan and Gauri, but is at its best in Jaipur. It's another favourite with Rajasthani women, and a chance for them to get dressed up – traditionally they wear green and sing songs celebrating the onset of the rains. Flower-bedecked swings are hung from trees, and in Jaipur there are glittering processions for two days through the streets – floats feature gods and goddesses and wonderful costumes.

## JAIPUR

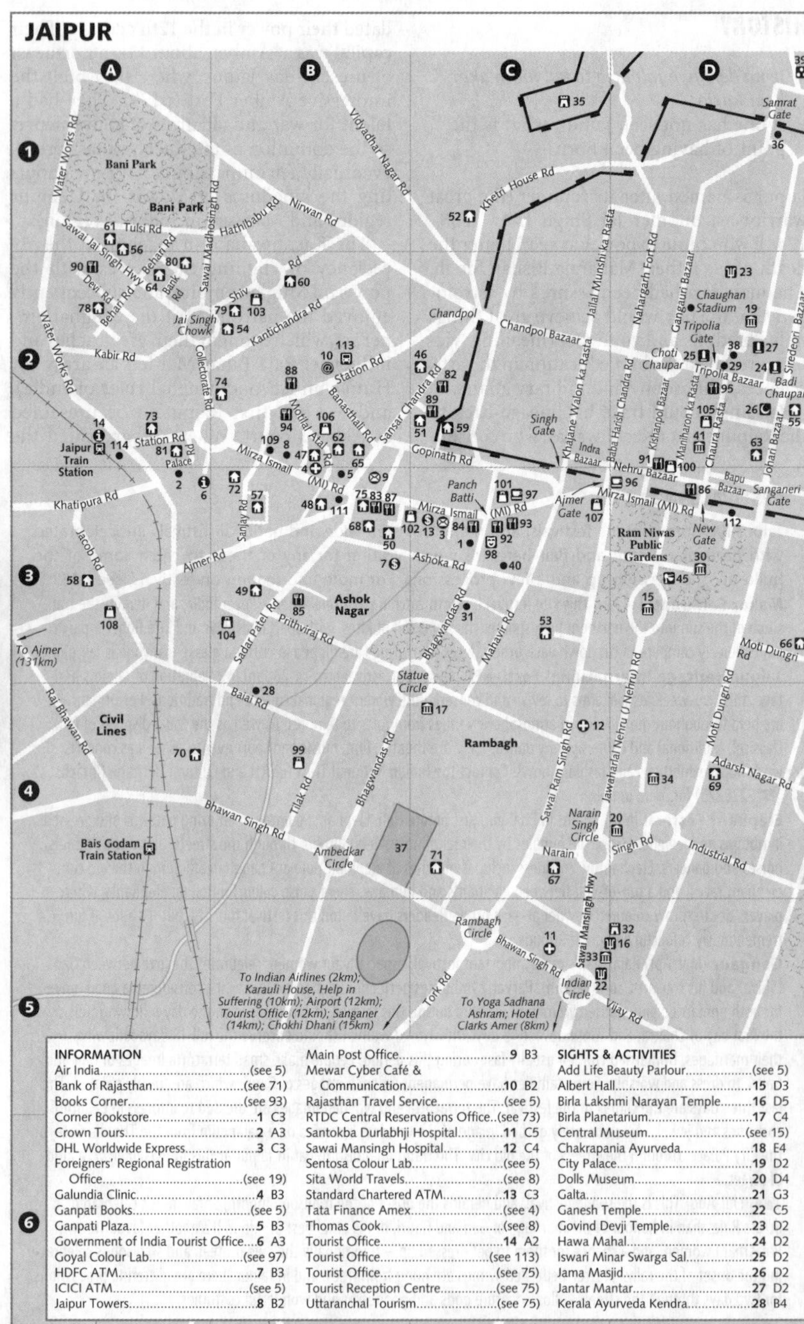
Bani Park
Water Works Rd
Sawai Jai Singh Hwy
Tulsi Rd
Devi Rd
Behari Rd
Bank Rd
Sawai Madhosingh Rd
Hathibabu Rd
Nirwan Rd
Vidyadhar Nagar Rd
Khetri House Rd
Shiv Rd
Jai Singh Chowk
Kantichandra Rd
Collectorate Rd
Kabir Rd
Station Rd
Chandpol
Chandpol Bazaar
Jallal Munshi ka Rasta
Nahargarh Fort Rd
Gangauri Bazaar
Chaughan Stadium
Tripolia Gate
Choti Chaupar
Tripolia Bazaar
Badi Chaupar
Siredeori Bazaar
Samrat Gate
Banasthali Rd
Sansar Chandra Rd
Motilal Atal Rd
Mirza Ismail (MI) Rd
Jaipur Train Station
Palace Rd
Gopinath Rd
Singh Gate
Khajane Walon ka Rasta
Baba Harish Chandra Rd
Kishanpol Bazaar
Maniharon ka Rasta
Chaura Rasta
Johari Bazaar
Indra Bazaar
Nehru Bazaar
Bapu Bazaar
Sanganeri Gate
Panch Batti
Ajmer Gate
New Gate
Khatipura Rd
Jacob Rd
Sanjay Rd
Ajmer Rd
Ashoka Rd
Ram Niwas Public Gardens
Ashok Nagar
Sadar Patel Rd
Prithviraj Rd
Bhagwandas Rd
Mahavir Rd
To Ajmer (131km)
Moti Dungri Rd
Statue Circle
Bajaj Rd
Raj Bhawan Rd
Civil Lines
Rambagh
Sawai Ram Singh Rd
Jawaharlal Nehru (J Nehru) Rd
Adarsh Nagar Rd
Tilak Rd
Bhawan Singh Rd
Narain Singh Circle
Narain Singh Rd
Industrial Rd
Bais Godam Train Station
Ambedkar Circle
Sawai Mansingh Hwy
Rambagh Circle
Tork Rd
Indian Circle
Vijay Rd
To Indian Airlines (2km); Karauli House, Help in Suffering (10km); Airport (12km); Tourist Office (12km); Sanganer (14km); Chokhi Dhani (15km)
To Yoga Sadhana Ashram; Hotel Clarks Amer (8km)

INFORMATION
Air India (see 5)
Bank of Rajasthan (see 71)
Books Corner (see 93)
Corner Bookstore 1 C3
Crown Tours 2 A3
DHL Worldwide Express 3 C3
Foreigners' Regional Registration Office (see 19)
Galundia Clinic 4 B3
Ganpati Books (see 5)
Ganpati Plaza 5 B3
Government of India Tourist Office 6 A3
Goyal Colour Lab (see 97)
HDFC ATM 7 B3
ICICI ATM (see 5)
Jaipur Towers 8 B2
Main Post Office 9 B3
Mewar Cyber Café & Communication 10 B2
Rajasthan Travel Service (see 5)
RTDC Central Reservations Office (see 73)
Santokba Durlabhji Hospital 11 C5
Sawai Mansingh Hospital 12 C4
Sentosa Colour Lab (see 5)
Sita World Travels (see 8)
Standard Chartered ATM 13 C3
Tata Finance Amex (see 4)
Thomas Cook (see 8)
Tourist Office 14 A2
Tourist Office (see 113)
Tourist Office (see 75)
Tourist Reception Centre (see 75)
Uttaranchal Tourism (see 75)

SIGHTS & ACTIVITIES
Add Life Beauty Parlour (see 5)
Albert Hall 15 D3
Birla Lakshmi Narayan Temple 16 D5
Birla Planetarium 17 C4
Central Museum (see 15)
Chakrapania Ayurveda 18 E4
City Palace 19 D2
Dolls Museum 20 D4
Galta 21 G3
Ganesh Temple 22 C5
Govind Devji Temple 23 D2
Hawa Mahal 24 D2
Iswari Minar Swarga Sal 25 D2
Jama Masjid 26 D2
Jantar Mantar 27 D2
Kerala Ayurveda Kendra 28 B4

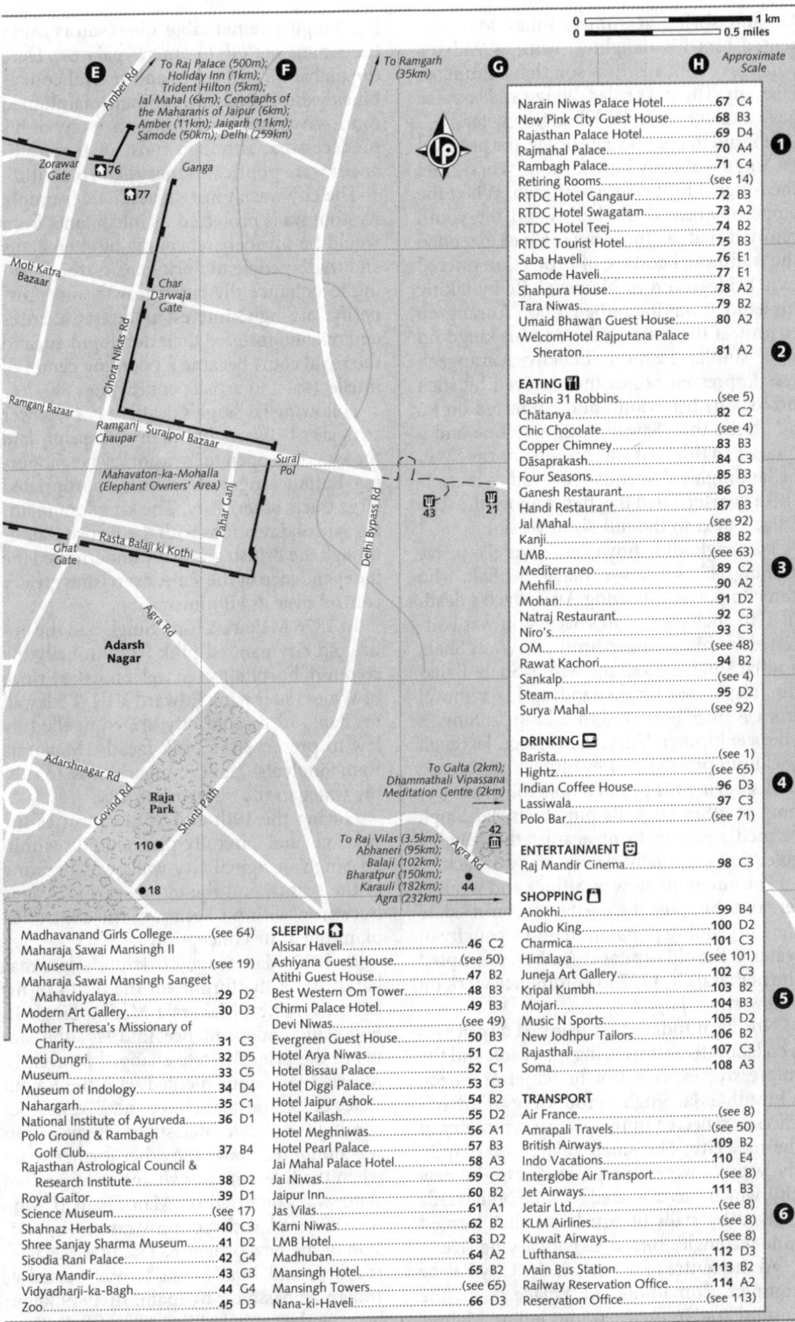
0 1 km
0 0.5 miles
Approximate Scale
E
F
G
H
1
2
3
4
5
6
To Raj Palace (500m); Holiday Inn (1km); Trident Hilton (5km); Jal Mahal (6km); Cenotaphs of the Maharanis of Jaipur (6km); Amber (11km); Jaigarh (11km); Samode (50km); Delhi (259km)
To Ramgarh (35km)
Amber Rd
Zorawar Gate
76
77
Ganga
Moti Katra Bazaar
Char Darwaja Gate
Ghora Nikas Rd
Ramganj Bazaar
Ramganj Chaupar
Surajpol Bazaar
Suraj Pol
Mahavaton-ka-Mohalla (Elephant Owners' Area)
Pahar Ganj
Delhi Bypass Rd
43
21
Ghat Gate
Rasta Balaji ki Kothi
Agra Rd
Adarsh Nagar
Adarshnagar Rd
Govind Rd
Raja Park
Shanti Path
110
18
To Galta (2km); Dhammathali Vipassana Meditation Centre (2km)
42
To Raj Vilas (3.5km); Abhaneri (95km); Balaji (102km); Bharatpur (150km); Karauli (182km); Agra (232km)
Agra Rd
44
Madhavanand Girls College....(see 64)
Maharaja Sawai Mansingh II Museum....(see 19)
Maharaja Sawai Mansingh Sangeet Mahavidyalaya....29 D2
Modern Art Gallery....30 D3
Mother Theresa's Missionary of Charity....31 C3
Moti Dungri....32 D5
Museum....33 C5
Museum of Indology....34 D4
Nahargarh....35 C1
National Institute of Ayurveda....36 D1
Polo Ground & Rambagh Golf Club....37 B4
Rajasthan Astrological Council & Research Institute....38 D2
Royal Gaitor....39 D1
Science Museum....(see 17)
Shahnaz Herbals....40 C3
Shree Sanjay Sharma Museum....41 D2
Sisodia Rani Palace....42 G4
Surya Mandir....43 G3
Vidyadharji-ka-Bagh....44 G4
Zoo....45 D3
SLEEPING
Alsisar Haveli....46 C2
Ashiyana Guest House....(see 50)
Atithi Guest House....47 B2
Best Western Om Tower....48 B3
Chirmi Palace Hotel....49 B3
Devi Niwas....(see 49)
Evergreen Guest House....50 B3
Hotel Arya Niwas....51 C2
Hotel Bissau Palace....52 C1
Hotel Diggi Palace....53 C3
Hotel Jaipur Ashok....54 B2
Hotel Kailash....55 D2
Hotel Meghniwas....56 A1
Hotel Pearl Palace....57 B3
Jai Mahal Palace Hotel....58 A3
Jai Niwas....59 C2
Jaipur Inn....60 B2
Jas Vilas....61 A1
Karni Niwas....62 B2
LMB Hotel....63 D2
Madhuban....64 A2
Mansingh Hotel....65 B2
Mansingh Towers....(see 65)
Nana-ki-Haveli....66 D3
Narain Niwas Palace Hotel....67 C4
New Pink City Guest House....68 B3
Rajasthan Palace Hotel....69 D4
Rajmahal Palace....70 A4
Rambagh Palace....71 C4
Retiring Rooms....(see 14)
RTDC Hotel Gangaur....72 B3
RTDC Hotel Swagatam....73 A2
RTDC Hotel Teej....74 B2
RTDC Tourist Hotel....75 B3
Saba Haveli....76 E1
Samode Haveli....77 E1
Shahpura House....78 A2
Tara Niwas....79 B2
Umaid Bhawan Guest House....80 A2
WelcomHotel Rajputana Palace Sheraton....81 A2
EATING
Baskin 31 Robbins....(see 5)
Chātanya....82 C2
Chic Chocolate....(see 4)
Copper Chimney....83 B3
Dāsaprakash....84 C3
Four Seasons....85 B3
Ganesh Restaurant....86 D3
Handi Restaurant....87 B3
Jal Mahal....(see 92)
Kanji....88 B2
LMB....(see 63)
Mediterraneo....89 C2
Mehfil....90 A2
Mohan....91 D2
Natraj Restaurant....92 C3
Niro's....93 C3
OM....(see 48)
Rawat Kachori....94 B2
Sankalp....(see 4)
Steam....95 D2
Surya Mahal....(see 92)
DRINKING
Barista....(see 1)
Hightz....(see 65)
Indian Coffee House....96 D3
Lassiwala....97 C3
Polo Bar....(see 71)
ENTERTAINMENT
Raj Mandir Cinema....98 C3
SHOPPING
Anokhi....99 B4
Audio King....100 D2
Charmica....101 C3
Himalaya....(see 101)
Juneja Art Gallery....102 C3
Kripal Kumbh....103 B2
Mojari....104 B3
Music N Sports....105 D2
New Jodhpur Tailors....106 B2
Rajasthali....107 C3
Soma....108 A3
TRANSPORT
Air France....(see 8)
Amrapali Travels....(see 50)
British Airways....109 B2
Indo Vacations....110 E4
Interglobe Air Transport....(see 8)
Jet Airways....111 B3
Jetair Ltd....(see 8)
KLM Airlines....(see 8)
Kuwait Airways....(see 8)
Lufthansa....112 D3
Main Bus Station....113 B2
Railway Reservation Office....114 A2
Reservation Office....(see 113)

Muslim shrine at Ajmer, Bihar Mal presented him his daughter, who, as Akbar's wife, gave him his first son, later Emperor Jehangir. The next ruler, Bhagwan Das, also gave a daughter to be Jehangir's wife.

It's said that at 15 years of age, the prodigal Jai Singh – already king for four years – met the Mughal Emperor Aurangzeb. When the emperor grasped the lad's hand the youth retorted that, as the emperor had extended the traditional gesture of protection offered by a bridegroom to his new wife by taking his hand, it was incumbent upon Aurangzeb to protect the young ruler and his kingdom in a similar fashion. Luckily Aurangzeb was impressed rather than peeved by such precocious behaviour, and conferred on Jai Singh the title 'Sawai', meaning 'one and a quarter', a title that was proudly borne by all of Jai Singh's descendants – today there is still a quarter-sized flag flying above the City Palace, next to the full-sized version.

Jai Singh did, however, severely peeve Aurangzeb's successor, Bahadur Shah, who came to power following Aurangzeb's death in 1707. Bahadur Shah's accession was contested by his younger brother, Azam Shah, and Jai Singh backed the wrong Shah. Bahadur responded by demanding his removal from Amber Fort, and installing Jai Singh's younger brother, Vijay, in his place. Jai Singh was unimpressed and eventually succeeded in dislodging his brother. Soliciting the support of other large Rajput states, Jai Singh formed a strong front against the Mughal ruler and eventually clawed his way back.

The kingdom grew wealthier and wealthier, and this, plus the need to accommodate the burgeoning population and a paucity of water at the old capital at Amber, prompted the maharaja in 1727 to commence work on a new city – Jaipur.

Northern India's first planned city, it was a collaborative effort using his vision and the impressive expertise of his chief architect, Vidyadhar. Jai Singh's grounding in the sciences is reflected in the precise symmetry of the new city. The small villages that lay in the vicinity were incorporated into the new city, which was dissected by wide boulevards flanked by stalls of equal size that formed nine rectangles *(mohallas)* of varying size.

At the centre of the grid is the City Palace complex, containing the palace itself, the administrative quarters, the Jantar Mantar (Jai Singh's remarkable observatory) and the zenana *mahals* (women's palaces). Here the maharaja's 28 wives and several concubines were installed. Jai Singh maintained more wives and concubines than any of his predecessors, although most of these alliances were political rather than romantic.

The city wasn't just an aesthetic triumph; its stout walls protected its inhabitants from would-be invaders, encouraging merchants and tradespeople to flock here, further serving to enhance the city's growth and prosperity. Jai Singh's interest in the arts, sciences and religion fostered their development, and the royal court became a booming centre of intellectual and artistic endeavour.

Following Jai Singh's death in 1744, power struggles between his many offspring laid the kingdom open to invasion by neighbouring Rajput kingdoms, which appropriated large tracts of territory. The kingdom maintained good relations with the British Raj, although the British gradually undermined the independence of the state, exercising greater control over its administration.

In 1876 Maharaja Ram Singh had the entire old city painted pink (traditionally the colour of hospitality) to welcome the Prince of Wales (later King Edward VII). Today all residents of the old city are compelled by law to preserve the pink façade. Maharaja Ram Singh also built Ramgarh Lake to supply water to the burgeoning city.

During the 19th and 20th centuries the spacious and carefully planned city within Jai Singh's original city walls was bursting at the seams, and the city began to sprawl outwards, with no notion of the controlled planning at its conception.

In 1922 Man Singh II, Jaipur's last maharaja, took the throne on the death of his adoptive father, Maharaja Madho Singh II. Following Independence in 1947, the status of the princely state changed forever. In March 1949 Jaipur merged with the Rajput states of Jodhpur, Jaisalmer and Bikaner, becoming the Greater Rajasthan Union. Jaipur was honoured above the other former states when the title *rajpramukh*, meaning head of state, was conferred on Man Singh II, who was invested with administrative supervision of the new province. The title was later revoked, and Man Singh II was posted as Indian ambassador to Spain. In 1949 Jaipur became the capital of the state of Rajasthan.

Since 1950 the population has exploded from 300,000 to over two million, and it shows: unplanned urban sprawl has disfigured what was once one of India's most beautiful cities. Such massive growth breeds its own problems; overcrowding, pollution and traffic being the most obvious. The city is prosperous though, with an impressive brand-new Rajasthan Legislative Building, and attracts plenty of investment as a commercial, business and tourist centre.

## ORIENTATION

The walled 'Pink City' (old city) is in the northeast of Jaipur; the new parts have spread to the south and west. The city's main tourist attractions are in the old city, which is partially encircled by a crenellated wall pierced at intervals by gates. The major gates are Chandpol (*pol* means 'gate'), Ajmer Gate and Sanganeri Gate. Broad avenues, over 30m wide, divide the Pink City into neat rectangles, each of which is the domain of a particular group of artisans or commercial activities (see Pink City Walking Tour, p164, for details about the locations of these).

There are three main interconnecting roads in the new part of town – Mirza Ismail (MI) Rd, Station Rd and Sansar Chandra Rd. Along or just off these roads are most of the budget and midrange hotels and restaurants, the main train station, the main bus station, many of the banks and the modern shopping strip. Panch Batti, midway along MI Rd, is a landmark intersection near the southwest corner of the old city.

## INFORMATION

### Bookshops

**Books Corner** (MI Rd; 10am-8pm Mon-Sat) Wide range of English-language books and magazines, and some French-language books; books on India with particular emphasis on Rajasthan. Sells the informative *Jaipur Vision* (Rs 20) and *Jaipur City Guide* (Rs 30).

**Corner Bookstore** (Bhagwandas Rd; 10am-10.30pm) Sells some English books. Housed with a small branch of Barista coffee bar.

**Ganpati Books** (shop 67, ground fl, Ganpati Plaza, MI Rd; 11am-8.30pm Mon-Sat) A good selection of Indian fiction and local-interest books, focusing on Rajasthan.

### Internet Access

Many places throughout Jaipur provide Internet access. The quality of the connections varies greatly – providers with Integrated Services Digital Network (ISDN) lines offer the fastest speeds. However fast or slow, it'll set you back Rs 20 to 60 per hour.

**Mewar Cyber Café & Communication** (Station Rd; per hr Rs 40; 24hr) Near the main bus station, caters for insomniac email-heads.

### Media

*Jaipur Vision* and *Jaipur City Guide* are two useful booklets (available at Books Corner) that feature fairly up-to-date listings, local adverts and features, which are good for scouting out information.

### Medical Services

At **Galundia Clinic** (☎ 2361040; MI Rd), **Dr Chandra Sen** (☎ 9829061040) is on 24-hour call; a normal consultation costs Rs 300 (however, reports suggest that he may recommend a number of consultations). Most hotels can arrange a doctor on site.

Good hospitals:

**Santokba Durlabhji Hospital** (☎ 2566251; Bhawan Singh Rd)

**Sawai Mansingh Hospital** (☎ 2560291; Sawai Ram Singh Rd)

### Money

There are plenty of places to change money, and masses of ATMs, most of which accept foreign cards, including **HDFC** (Ashoka Rd), **ICICI** (ground fl, Ganpati Plaza, MI Rd) and **Standard Chartered** (Bhagwat Bhavan, MI Rd), which are open 24 hours. Moneychangers are faster and more efficient than banks.

**Bank of Rajasthan** (☎ 2381416; Rambagh Palace; 7am-8pm)

**Tata Finance Amex** (☎/fax 2364026; Saraf House, MI Rd; 9.30am-6.30pm Mon-Fri, 9.30am-2.30pm Sat) Represents American Express (Amex).

**Thomas Cook** (☎ 2360940; Jaipur Towers, MI Rd; 9.30am-6pm Mon-Sat) Changes cash and travellers cheques.

### Photography

Both labs listed here develop photos in one hour for around Rs 5 per print. They also sell lithium batteries, memory sticks and compact flash cards. Most photo places around town (there are masses) will save your digital photos onto CD for around Rs 100.

**Goyal Colour Lab** (☎ 2360147; MI Rd; 10.30am-8.30pm Mon-Sat, 10am-4pm Sun)

**Sentosa Colour Lab** (☎ 2388748; ground fl, Ganpati Plaza, MI Rd; 10am-8.30pm Mon-Sat)

 

### Post

**DHL Worldwide Express** (☎ 2362826; www.dhl.co.in; G8 Geeta Enclave, Vinobha Rd) A reliable international courier. Ensure that you ask to pay customs charges for the destination country upfront. Air freight starts at Rs 8101 for a 10kg box and Rs 14,212 for a 'jumbo' 25kg box to Australia (Rs 8034 and Rs 14,788 for Europe, Rs 8339 and Rs 15,609 for the USA).

**Main post office** (☎ 2368740; MI Rd; 8am-7.45pm Mon-Fri, 10am-5.45pm Sat) Efficient and has a parcel-packing wallah (from 10am till 4pm Monday to Saturday) in the foyer, who will pack, stitch and seal your parcels – he asks around Rs 10 to 100 per package, depending on size.

### Telephone

There are plenty of public call offices (PCOs) scattered around Jaipur, which are usually cheaper than the hotels for long-distance calls. The international reverse-charges operator can be reached on ☎ 186.

It is not unusual for telephone numbers to change in Rajasthan. Jaipur has tackled this problem with an excellent automated Jaipur **'changed telephone number' service** (in English ☎ 1952, in Hindi ☎ 1951). For local telephone number inquiries call ☎ 197.

### Tourist Information

The Tourism Assistance Force (police) is stationed at major tourist traps.

**Foreigners' Regional Registration Office** (FRRO; ☎ 2619391; 10am-5pm Mon-Sat) Any applications for visa extensions should be lodged at the FRRO, which is somewhat hard to find (ask around) in the City Palace complex, though the likelihood you'll get an extension on a tourist visa is slight – see p375 for more details.

**Government of India tourist office** (☎ 2372200; 9am-6pm Mon-Fri) Next to Hotel Khasa Kothi. Provides brochures on places all over India.

**RTDC Central Reservations Office** (☎ 2202586; MI Rd; 10am-5pm Mon-Sat) Handles bookings for RTDC hotels around Rajasthan, accommodation in the RTDC tourist village during the Pushkar Camel Fair (see Pushkar Camel Fair, p212) and reservations for the *Palace on Wheels* train (see Palace on Wheels, p390). Behind RTDC Hotel Swagatam.

**Tourism helpline** (☎ 1363)

**Tourist offices** airport (☎ 2722647); Jaipur train station (☎ 2315714; platform 1; 24hr); main bus station (☎ 5064102; platform 3; 10am-5pm Mon-Fri); RTDC Tourist Hotel (☎ 2375466; 8am-8pm Mon-Sat) Several obliging tourist offices around town.

**Uttaranchal Tourism** (☎ 2378892; 10am-6pm Mon-Sat Jul-Apr, 10am-6pm daily May & Jun) Has an office in the RTDC Tourist Hotel compound.

### Travel Agencies

The capital has plenty of travel agencies and most can tailor local sightseeing trips – for a half-day tour it costs around Rs 350/450 for a non-AC/AC car with driver; a full day costs Rs 450/550. You can hire guides for Rs 300/450 per half/full day. See p177 for rates on longer trips. The following agencies can arrange cars and jeep or camel safaris, make hotel reservations and book air tickets.

**Crown Tours** (☎ 2363310) Opposite the Rajputana Palace Sheraton.

**Indo Vacations** (☎ 9414312872; www.indien-reise.com in German; 312-6 Valmiki Rd, Raja Park)

**Rajasthan Travel Service** (☎ 2365408; www.rajasthantravelservice.com; ground fl, Ganpati Plaza, MI Rd)

**Sita World Travels** (☎ 5103434; Jaipur Towers, MI Rd)

## DANGERS & ANNOYANCES

Travellers have reported problems with commission merchants in Jaipur. The town is notorious for gem scams – don't get involved in any get-rich-quick export schemes. So common they even have their own terminology, these *lapkas* (crooked touts) are involved in *dabbabazi* (the business of scamming tourists). The *lapkas'* latest tactic is to accuse you of hating Indians if you refuse to talk to them. They're particularly annoying around the City Palace, at train and bus stations, and at Amber Fort. Usually they'll leave you alone if you steadfastly ignore them, but if this doesn't work you can report them to the tourist police stationed at these places. Often simply threatening to report them is enough to do the trick. For more information, see A Warning, p361.

## SIGHTS

The old city, with its remarkably spacious and harmonious layout, was laid out by Jai Singh and his talented architect according to strict principles of town planning set down in the *Shilpa-Shastra*, an ancient Hindu treatise on architecture. It's a spacious grid, partially encircled by a crenellated wall. Major gates (recently restored) are Chandpol, Ajmer and Sanganeri. Avenues divide the Pink City into neat rectangles, each specialising in certain crafts, as ordained in the *Shilpa-Shastra*. The main bazaars in the old city include Johari Bazaar, Tripolia Bazaar, Bapu Bazaar and Chandpol Bazaar – see p164 or p175 for more details. At dusk the sunset-shaded buildings have a magical glow.

## City Palace

A complex of courtyards, gardens and buildings, the **City Palace** (☎ 2608055; www.royalfamilyjaipur.com; Indian/foreigner Rs 35/180, child aged 5-12 Rs 20/100, camera Indian Rs 50, video Indian/foreigner Rs 100/200; 9.30am-4.30pm) is right in the centre of the old city. The outer wall was built by Jai Singh, but within it the palace has been enlarged and adapted over the centuries. There are palace buildings from different eras, some dating from the early 20th century. Despite the gradual development, the whole is remarkably well balanced, a blend of Rajasthani and Mughal architecture.

The Kachhwaha Rajputs were patrons of the arts and took pride in their collection of valuable artefacts. For a long time there was a private museum here, for viewing by visiting dignitaries, and in 1959 this became a public museum under Man Singh II. His successor, Maharaja Bhawani Singh, took a keen interest in its development and enlarged the museum substantially.

This is a living palace as well as a museum, in that it is still inhabited by the erstwhile royal family. The current maharaja is a great polo chum of Britain's Prince Charles. Beyond the main courtyards is the seven-storeyed Chandra Mahal, which is still his residence and therefore not open to visitors. The rest of the palace is open for viewing, though.

Admission also gets you in to Jaigarh fort (see p181, a long climb above Amber Fort). This is valid for two days.

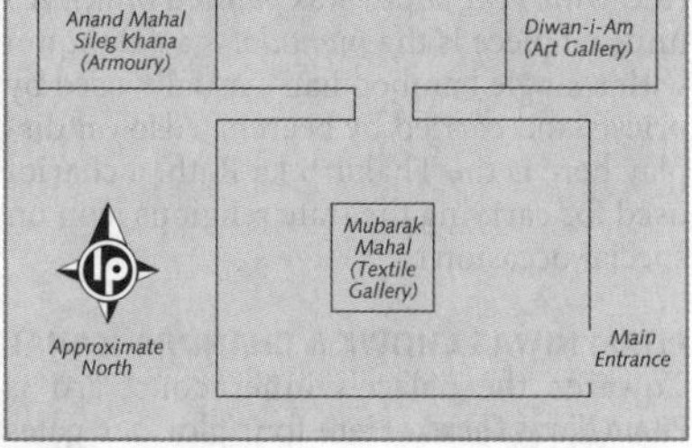

There are two entrances to the City Palace: the main entrance, approached through Virendra Pol, and one through Udai Pol near Jaleb Chowk.

### MUBARAK MAHAL

Entering through Virendra Pol, you'll see the **Mubarak Mahal** (Welcome Palace), a diminutive reception centre strewn with delicate colonnades, used for receiving visiting dignitaries. It was cooked up in an Islamic, Rajput and European stylistic stew by Maharaja Madho Singh II in the late 19th century. It now forms part of the **Maharaja Sawai Mansingh II Museum**, containing a collection of royal costumes and superb shawls, including Kashmiri *pashmina* (wool shawls). The most remarkable exhibit is Madho Singh I's clothing dating from 1760, a loose quilted dress made from silk brocade woven with *zari* (gold embroidery). It has pale yellow cotton lining and is almost 2m long, 3.5m around the chest and almost 7m around the hem. The maharaja was a cuddly 2m tall, 1.2m wide and 250kg. Guides will take great delight in telling you how much he apparently would eat for breakfast. Appropriately for such an excessive figure, he had 108 wives.

Also on display here is Maharaja Pratap Singh's more diminutive wedding dress – a red and gold piece with a massively pleated skirt dating from 1790. There are also several dresses with exquisite gold embroidery, dating from the 19th century, which were worn by royalty around Diwali.

### RAJENDRA POL

North of the Mubarak Mahal is the grand **Rajendra Pol**, flanked by carved elephants with lotus flowers in their mouths – symbolising royalty – that date from 1931. The gate has brass doors and walls embedded with precious and semiprecious stones.

### SARVATOBHADRA (DIWAN-I-KHAS)

Set between the Armoury and the Diwan-i-Am art gallery is an open courtyard known as **Sarvatobhadra**. In the 18th and 19th centuries this was used as the **Diwan-i-Khas** (Hall of Private Audience), where the maharajas would consult their ministers. At its centre is a marble-paved gallery, in which you can see enormous silver vessels, 1.6m tall and each weighing 345kg. These were made by silversmiths in the City Palace, and beaten into shape from silver sheets (each made from 14,000 melted silver coins) without any soldering. They were made for Maharaja Madho Singh II, a devout Hindu, so that he could take sufficient holy Ganges water to England when he visited for Edward VII's coronation in 1902. These enormous vessels each have a capacity of over 9000L, and have been listed in the *Guinness Book of World Records* as the largest sterling-silver objects in the world.

There are a number of crystal chandeliers hanging from the ceiling; they are covered with plastic to protect them and are only uncovered on certain festive occasions.

### DIWAN-I-AM

Contained in the lavish **Diwan-i-Am** (Hall of Public Audience) is the art gallery. Its great array of exhibits includes a touching collection of illustrated manuscripts showing everything from scenes of daily life to the tales of the gods. The hall still has its beautifully preserved painted ceiling, with its barely faded, original semiprecious stone colours, and an enormous crystal chandelier.

Exhibits include a copy of the entire Bhagavad-Gita handwritten in tiny script, and miniature copies of other holy Hindu scriptures, which were small enough to be easily hidden in the event that Mughal zealot Aurangzeb tried to destroy the sacred texts. There are Persian translations of the Ramayana and Mahabharata; the latter was made specially for Akbar, and has illustrations by the greatest Mughal painters. Some beautiful Sanskrit books are also on display, as are early manuscripts on palm leaf, and particularly fine miniature paintings of the Rajasthani, Mughal and Persian schools depicting religious themes. You'll see various ornate howdahs, and exquisitely detailed paper cutouts incised with a thumbnail.

On the walls are some beautiful carpets, made in Lahore in the 17th century and probably bought to decorate the new fort-palace at Amber. One of the carpets is made from *pashmina* wool and is incredibly delicate, decorated with a floral pattern and made either in Kashmir or Lahore.

### THE ARMOURY

The Anand Mahal Sileg Khana – the Maharani's Palace – houses the **Armoury**, which has one of the best collections in the country.

Fearsome daggers are arranged over the entrance to say Welcome. Many of the ceremonial weapons are exquisitely engraved and inlaid as if to belie their real purpose. They include two-bladed steel daggers that at the flick of a catch become scissors inside their victims; walking-stick swords; swords with pistols attached to their blades; and beautiful crystal-, ivory- and silver-handled daggers. There is also armour of chain mail, one complete set of which can weigh up to 35kg. Some pieces have a history attached to them, such as a sword inscribed for Shah Jahan, and a sword encrusted with rubies and emeralds that was presented by Queen Victoria to Maharaja Ram Singh, ruler of Jaipur from 1835 to 1880. Gun-lovers fear not, there is a fine array, including some that also serve as walking sticks; a gun the size of a small cannon for use on camel back; and double-barrelled pistols, which held bullets made of lead, dipped in poison and packed with gunpowder. Smart gunpowder flasks made of horns, leather and seashells, and decorated with inlaid ivory are on display.

If bloody weaponry isn't your bag, however cunningly vicious and finely engraved, the 19th-century mirrored and gold-inlaid ceilings, decorated with a gorgeous floral pattern and women in various moods, are well worth a gaze.

### BAGGHI-KHANA – THE CARRIAGE MUSEUM

The **museum** houses a grand collection of carriages and palanquins, featuring special covered versions for palace women, with the purpose of maintaining purdah (the custom among some Muslims and Hindus of keeping women hidden from men outside their own family). It's interesting also to see 19th-century European cabs adapted to Indian conditions, such as the small Victoria *bagghi* (carriage) given to the maharaja by the Prince of Wales in 1876 (the same year Jaipur was painted pink). An unusual piece is the *mahadol* – a palanquin with a single bamboo bar – usually used by priests and carried by bearers. Also on display here is the Thakurji ka Rath, a chariot used for carrying the state religious icon on special occasions.

### PITAM NIWAS CHOWK & CHANDRA MAHAL

Towards the palace's inner courtyard is **Pitam Niwas Chowk**. Here four glorious gates represent the seasons. The **Peacock Gate** depicts autumn, with zigzagging patterns and peacock motifs – around the doorway are five beautiful repeated peacock bas reliefs in all their feathered glory. The **Lotus Gate**, signifying summer, is as splendid, and is covered in repeated flower and petal patterns. Spring is more subdued, but still beautiful with its simple green design, and winter is embodied by the **Rose Gate**, again with repetitive flower patterns, but more monochromatic than the autumn or summer gates.

Beyond this *chowk* (square) is the private palace, the **Chandra Mahal**, where Iswari Singh – son of Jai – killed himself by a snakebite (see p160). This is where the maharajas still live, a seven-storeyed building with fantastic views over the city from the top floor. Flying above the building, you can see the one and a quarter flags that signify the presence of the maharaja. If he is away, the queen's flag will fly in its place.

#### GOVIND DEVJI TEMPLE

This early-18th-century Krishna **temple** is part of the City Palace complex, though outside the walls. It's decorated with a mixture of European and Indian designs – the chandeliers are European, the paintings Indian. The ceiling is decorated in gold. A popular place of worship, it's set in gardens and was situated so that the maharaja could see the god from his palace, the neighbouring Chandra Mahal. The god is unveiled seven times daily for *aarti* (worshipping ritual).

### Jantar Mantar

Near the City Palace is **Jantar Mantar** (admission Rs 10, free Mon, camera Indian/foreigner Rs 20/50, video Rs 50/100; 9.30am-4.30pm). The name is derived from the Sanskrit *yanta mantr* meaning 'instrument of calculation'. The building, begun by Jai Singh in 1728, is an observatory that at first glance looks like a collection of mammoth, bizarre sculptures. If sensing you've stepped into *Alice Through the Looking Glass* isn't enough, the Rs 150 (half-hour to one hour) guide fee is worthwhile. Guides provide fascinating explanations of how each instrument works, and how, through watching, recording and meticulous calculation, Jai Singh measured time by the sun's shadow falling on the huge sundials, and charted its annual progress through the zodiac.

Jai Singh liked astronomy even more than he liked war and town planning. Before constructing the observatory, he sent scholars abroad to study foreign constructs. He built five observatories in total, and this is the largest and best preserved (it was restored in 1901). Others are in Delhi, Varanasi and Ujjain. The fifth, the Mathura observatory, has disappeared.

Each construction within Jantar Mantar has a specific purpose, for example, measuring the positions of the stars, altitude and azimuth, and calculating eclipses.

The most striking instrument is the **Brihat Samrat Yantra** (King of the Instruments) sundial, a massive yellow edifice to the far right of the observatory complex, with a staircase running to the top. It has a 27m-high gnomon arm set at an angle of 27 degrees – the same as the latitude of Jaipur. The shadow this casts moves up to 4m in an hour, and aids in the calculation of local and meridian time and various attributes of the heavenly bodies, including declination (the angular distance of a heavenly body from the celestial equator) and altitude. It's still used by astrologers and is the focus of a gathering during the full-moon days of June and July, when it helps predict local monsoon rains, and subsequent success or failure of crops. Niches carved into the wall are designed to prevent storms affecting the instrument.

If you tour the *yantras* in a clockwise direction, to the left as you enter the compound is the **Laghu Samrat Yantra**, a small sundial of red sandstone and white marble, inclined at 27 degrees. It does not measure as precisely as the Brihat Samrat Yantra, but does calculate the declination of celestial bodies, and the shadow cast by its gnomon enables local time (which differs from 10 to 40 minutes from Indian Standard Time) to be determined. On either side are two quadrants and local time can be determined by the shadow cast on each quadrant (one for the morning, one for the afternoon). Nearby is the **Dhruva Darshak Yantra**, used to find the location of the Pole Star and the 12 zodiac signs. This is divided according to an ancient system of Hindu measurement, based on breath and known as *prana*. Six *pranas* (breaths) make one *pala*, 60 *palas* equal one *ghatika* and 60 *ghatikas* equal 24 hours.

The large circular object nearby, known as the **Narivalaya Yantra**, is actually two small sundials. The two faces of the instrument represent the northern and southern hemispheres, and enable calculation of the time within a minute's accuracy.

Two large disks suspended from the wooden beams nearby comprise the **Yantra Raj**, a multipurpose instrument that, among other things, can help determine the positions of constellations and calculate the Hindu calendar. A telescope is at the centre. The similar-looking **Unnatansha Yantra** lies in the northeastern corner of the observatory complex. This metal ring is divided into four segments by horizontal and vertical lines. A hole where these lines intersect, in the centre of the instrument, aids in the calculation of the altitude of celestial bodies.

Nearby is **Dakhinovrith Bhitti Yantra**, which serves a similar function to the Unnatansha Yantra in helping to determine the placement of heavenly bodies.

West of the Brihat Samrat Yantra, near the southern wall of the observatory, you come to a cluster of 12 yellow instruments, the **Rashi Yantras**. Each *rashi* (individual instrument) represents one of the 12 zodiac signs. The gradient of each *rashi* differs in accordance with the particular sign represented and its position in relation to the ecliptic.

The **Jai Prakash Yantra**, resembling two huge slotted bowls, was the last instrument installed at the observatory and was invented by Jai Singh, after whom it was named. The instrument is used in celestial observations, but can also verify the calculations determined by other instruments at the observatory. Each of the two cavities is divided into six marble slabs, which are marked with minutes and seconds, and also with signs of the zodiac. The metal ring suspended in the centre represents the sun, and calculations can be made from the shadow cast by it on the marble slabs. This instrument may be used to calculate auspicious days for weddings, business negotiations and so on.

The two other sunken concave structures in the western section of the observatory compound comprise the **Kapali Yantra**. The eastern Kapali Yantra is inscribed with lines to which astronomers refer in their deliberations, and is used for graphical analysis. The western Kapali Yantra is used to determine the position of a celestial body. Between the two bowls stands the **Chakra Yantra**, a pair of metal wheels, which can revolve parallel to the earth's axis, and can be fitted with a brass tube in order to calculate the declination of celestial bodies.

Two other impressive instruments are the **Ram Yantras**, which look like miniature coliseums made of 12 upright slabs and 12 horizontal slabs. They are used in the calculation of the altitude and azimuth of celestial bodies. Between them is another circular instrument, the **Digansha Yantra**, with a pillar in the middle and two outer circles. It's used for calculating azimuth, particularly of the sun. It can also be used to determine the time of sunrise and sunset.



## Hawa Mahal

Jaipur's most distinctive landmark, the **Hawa Mahal** (Palace of the Winds; admission incl museum Rs 5, camera Indian/foreigner Rs 10/30, video Rs 20/70; 9am-4.30pm Sat-Thu) is an extraordinary, fairy-tale, pink-sandstone, delicately honeycombed hive that rises a dizzying five storeys. Constructed in 1799, the building is an amazing example of Rajput artistry, built to enable ladies of the royal household to watch the life and processions of the city. Inside it's barely a building at all, only around one room deep, with narrow, delicately scalloped walkways, under bulbously domed canopies. It's still a great place for people-watching from behind the small broken shutters, which are patterned by light. The top offers stunning views over Jantar Mantar and the City Palace one way, and over Siredeori Bazaar the other. The palace was built by Pratap Singh and is part of the City Palace complex.

There's also a small **museum** ( 9am-4.30pm Sat-Thu), with miniature paintings and some rich relics, such as ceremonial armour, that help evoke the royal past.

Entrance to the Hawa Mahal is from the back of the complex. To get here, return to the intersection on your left as you face the Hawa Mahal, turn right and then take the first right again through an archway.

## Iswari Minar Swarga Sal

Piercing the skyline in this part of town is the unusual **Iswari Minar Swarga Sal** (Heaven-Piercing Minaret; admission Rs 2, camera/video Rs 10/20; 9am-4.30pm), near Tripolia Gate. The minaret was erected by Jai Singh's son Iswari, who later ignominiously killed himself by snakebite (in the Chandra Mahal) rather than face the advancing Maratha army – 21 wives and concubines then did the necessary noble thing and committed *jauhar* (ritual mass suicide by immolation) on his funeral pyre. You can climb to the top of the minaret for excellent views over the old city. The entrance is around the back – take the alley 50m west of the minaret along Chandpol Bazaar.

## New City

By the mid-19th century it became obvious that the well-planned city was bulging at the seams. During the reign of Maharaja Ram Singh (1835–80) the seams ruptured and the city burst out beyond its walls. Civic facilities, such as a postal system and piped water, were introduced. This period gave rise to a part of town very different from the bazaars of the old city, with wide boulevards, landscaped grounds and florid buildings. The maharaja commissioned the landscaping of the **Ram Niwas Public Gardens**, on Jawaharlal Nehru (J Nehru) Rd, and the uproarious splendour of **Albert Hall**, built in honour of the Prince of Wales' 1876 visit, which now houses the Central Museum (right). It was designed by Sir Swinton Jacob, and combines elements of English and North Indian architecture. It was known as the pride of the new Jaipur when it opened in 1887. The gardens were in part a famine-relief project – to provide work for the unemployed.

These civic improvements were continued by Jaipur's last maharaja, Man Singh II, who is credited with the university, the Secretariat, residential colonies, schools, hospitals and colleges. Unfortunately the city has developed wildly outwards, in an unplanned urban sprawl, where private interests and political expediency have outweighed aesthetic considerations.

Opposite Albert Hall is Jaipur **zoo** (admission Rs 10; 9am-5pm Wed-Mon), one of the oldest in India, and housing the usual motley array of disconsolate animals and bird life.

An old theatre houses Jaipur's **Modern Art Gallery** (admission free; 10am-5pm Mon-Sat), on the 1st floor of the Ravindra Manch building, a very peaceful place with some striking contemporary work – well worth a visit.

To the south, looming above J Nehru Rd to the left, is the small, romantic fort of **Moti Dungri**. It has served as a prison, but today remains in the possession of the former royal family, and entry is prohibited.

**Birla Lakshmi Narayan Temple** (J Nehru Rd; admission free; 6am-noon & 3-8.30pm) is a large, splendid, modern marble edifice at the foot of Moti Dungri fort. The wealthy industrialist Birla, born in Palani, Rajasthan, bought the land on which the temple now stands from the maharaja for a token Rs 1. Stained-glass windows depict scenes from Hindu scriptures. Ganesh, the protector of households, is above the lintel, and the fine quality of the marble is evident when you enter the temple and look back at the entrance way – Ganesh can be made out *through* the marble, which is almost transparent. The images of Lakshmi and Narayan were carved from one piece of marble. Many of the deities of the Hindu pantheon are depicted inside the temple, and on the outside walls great historic personages and figures from other religions are shown, including Socrates, Zarathustra, Christ, Buddha and Confucius. There is a small **museum** (J Nehru Rd; admission free; 8am-noon & 4-8pm) next to the temple. The collection includes Birla family household objects and clothing. Parking costs Rs 2.

Just down the street is the popular **Ganesh Temple** (J Nehru Rd; photography prohibited; 5am-9pm Thu-Tue, 5am-11pm Wed). If you don't like crowds avoid the temple on Wednesday (the auspicious day), when there are throngs of devotees. You can buy *ladoos* (ball-shaped sweetmeats) to offer to Ganesh from the sweet stalls outside the temple.

Another construction funded by the wealthy Rajasthani industrialist, **Birla Planetarium** (Statue Circle; admission Rs 17; 11am-8pm, closed last Wed of month) is at the BM Birla Science & Technology Centre, near Statue Circle. Most shows (35 minutes) are in Hindi. An English commentary is only given at the 6pm session. Next door, there's a worthy **science museum** (☎ 2384224; admission Rs 10). Parking costs Rs 5 for a car or autorickshaw.

## Other Museums

The dusty but impressive **Central Museum** (☎ 2570099; Indian/foreigner Rs 5/30, free Mon, photography prohibited; 10am-4.30pm Sat-Thu) is housed in the spectacularly florid Albert Hall, south of the old city. It opened in 1887 and feels its age – a grand old museum with smeared cabinets holding a great array of traditional tribal dress, models of yogis adopting various positions, dioramas depicting various Rajasthani dances, decorative arts, puppets, costumes, carpets, drawings, musical instruments and even an Egyptian mummy.

**Shree Sanjay Sharma Museum** (☎ 2323436; 1670 Maniharon ka Rasta; Indian/foreigner Rs 35/80, photography prohibited; 🕑 10am-5pm) is a fascinating collection, a brilliant jumble of precious objects gathered by the parents of Shree Sanjay Sharma (who died as a boy) in his memory. It includes many rare manuscripts and some wonderful, historic Indian art from around the country. There's a set of 18th-century paintings of yoga postures showing which poses to strike if you're drowning, going deaf or suffering from gas. The collection also features elaborate locks, bookstands, drawings of temple architecture, beautiful royal games, 19th-century paper cutouts, illustrated alchemy books and much more.

The collection of shoes is particularly fascinating: exquisite 18th-century atonement slippers (with only a toe hold), special acupressure slippers and one tiny 17th-century brass pair. All were used by sadhus or maharajas. On an upper floor is an amazing room containing 125,000 manuscripts, dramatically shown off by the curator, but which seem to be slowly disintegrating and turning to dust in their cupboards. The museum is signposted off Chaura Rasta.

The ramshackle, dusty treasure trove of the **Museum of Indology** (Indian/foreigner incl guide Rs 20/40; 🕑 8am-6pm) is another extraordinary private collection. It contains folk-art objects and other pieces – there's everything from a manuscript written by Aurangzeb and a 200-year-old mirrorwork swing from Bikaner, to a glass bed (for a short queen). The museum is signposted off J Nehru Rd, south of the Central Museum. There are plans afoot to move the collection to a new building on Amber Rd, 6km from Jaipur.

Close to the Museum of Indology, in the Deaf, Dumb & Blind compound on J Nehru Rd, is the little **Dolls Museum** (admission by donation; 🕑 9.30am-4.30pm Mon-Sat). The collection includes dolls wearing traditional costumes from around India and the world, including two Irish leprechauns.

## Nahargarh

Built in 1734 and extended in 1868, sturdy **Nahargarh** (Tiger Fort; ☎ 5148044; Indian/foreigner Rs 15/20, camera Rs 10/20, video Rs 20/70; 🕑 10am-5pm) overlooks the city from a sheer ridge to the north. An 8km road runs up through the hills from Jaipur, or the fort can be reached along a zigzagging 2km footpath, which starts northwest of the old city. The views are glorious – it's a great sunset spot, and there's a restaurant that's perfect for a beer. The story goes that the fort was named after Nahar Singh, a dead prince whose restless spirit was disrupting construction. Whatever was built in the day crumbled in the night. He agreed to leave on condition that the fort was named for him.

The fort was built in 1734 by Jai Singh to increase the Amber defences, and was adapted in 1868 to its present form by Maharaja Ram Singh, to house the maharaja's numerous wives. You can visit the **Madhavendra Bhawan**, which has the nine apartments of Maharaja Ram Singh's nine other halves, with a separate suite for the king himself. There are bathrooms, toilets, boudoirs and kitchens with a large chimney.

Doors and windows had coloured panes, of which a few remain. Some of the boudoirs retain Belgian mirrors, and all are decorated with floral and bird motifs.

The rooms are linked by a maze of corridors – used so that the king could visit any queen without the others' knowledge.

You can even stay at the fort (see p170).

## Royal Gaitor

The royal **cenotaphs** (admission free, camera Indian/foreigner Rs 5/10, video Rs 10/20; 🕑 9am-4.30pm), just outside the city walls, are an appropriately restful place to visit and feel remarkably undiscovered. Surrounded by a straggling village, the monuments bear much beautiful, intricate carving. Maharajas Pratap Singh, Madho Singh II and Jai Singh II, among others, are buried here. Jai Singh II has the most impressive marble cenotaph, with a dome supported by 20 carved pillars.

The **cenotaphs of the maharanis of Jaipur** (Amber Rd) are between Jaipur and Amber.

## Jal Mahal

Near the cenotaphs of the maharanis of Jaipur, on Amber Rd, is the red-sandstone **Jal Mahal** (Water Palace; 🕑 closed to public), built in 1799 by Madho Singh as a summer resort for the royal family – they used to base duck-hunting parties here. It's accessible via a causeway, beautifully situated in the middle of the sparkling but stinking watery expanse of Man Sagar, which is choked with hyacinths. Suffering from subsidence, much of the palace is waterlogged and its future is uncertain, though it is pitched to be developed for tourism, in a massive project partly funded by the government that will also mean a massive cleanup of the lake. The lake is home to a variety of migratory and resident birds.

## Sisodia Rani Palace & Vidyadharji-ka-Bagh

Six kilometres from the city, on Agra Rd (leave by the Ghat Gate), are a pair of formal gardens that are enjoyable to wander around and take in a breath of fresh air. The first, grand formal **terraced gardens** (admission Rs 5; 8am-6pm), with fountains and statuary, were built in the 18th century for Maharaja Jai Singh's second wife, a Sisodian princess. They're overlooked by the **Sisodia Rani Palace** (closed to public), whose outer walls are decorated with murals depicting hunting scenes and the Krishna legend.

**Vidyadharji-ka-Bagh** (Agra Rd; admission Rs 5; 8am-6pm), similar in style, was built in honour of Jai Singh's chief architect and town planner, Vidyadhar, and is about 200m before Sisodia Rani Palace.

Regular local buses leave from Ghat Gate for the Sisodia Rani Palace (Rs 5). Ask the bus driver to drop you at the Vidyadharji-ka-Bagh, and then continue on to the palace. An autorickshaw will cost around Rs 150 return from the city centre to visit both.

## Galta & Surya Mandir

Perched between the cliff faces of a rocky valley, **Galta** (Monkey Temple) is a desolate and barren, if evocative, place. At sunset hundreds of monkeys converge on the temple and you can buy peanuts at the gate to feed to them.

### THE RANI OF RAMBAGH

The life story of Gayatri Devi, the celebrated maharani of Jaipur, is an allegory of 20th-century Rajasthan, capturing the state's ambivalence towards its transition from princely rule to part of post-Independence, democratic India.

In her heyday, Gayatri Devi was an icon of royal glamour, adored by gossip columnists and dubbed by *Vogue* magazine as one of the most beautiful women in the world. She was born in 1919, a princess from the small state of Cooch Behar (now in West Bengal). At the age of 19 she fell in love with Man Singh II, the last maharaja of Jaipur. Although Man Singh already had two wives, they were married in 1939 and settled down to the life of luxury enjoyed by Indian royalty of the time. There were polo matches, hunting jaunts, decadent dinner parties and summers in England.

Man Singh converted his former hunting lodge, 3km southwest of the old city, into the magnificent Rambagh Palace for Gayatri Devi. Today the palace is surrounded by Jaipur's sprawling suburbs, but it was once a secluded retreat well beyond the limits of the city centre. Here the couple entertained some of the world's richest and most famous people, including Eleanor Roosevelt and Jackie Kennedy.

By this time, however, the Man Singhs were adjusting to their new role in post-Independence India. Rajasthan's ancestral rulers had been stripped of their powers, but many were still held in high regard by a large proportion of their former subjects. Banking on this support, Gayatri Devi, like many other royals, decided to enter politics. She stood against the Congress Party in the national elections in 1962 and swept the board. Her stunning victory is now listed in the *Guinness Book of World Records* as the largest margin ever recorded (a staggering 175,000 votes) in a democracy. In the 1967 and 1971 elections she retained her seat.

Indira Gandhi's Congress Party, however, was quick to act against the royals who were successfully challenging its hold on power. The privileges that the maharajas were promised following Independence (notably the privy purses or stipends paid to the royals from public funds) were abolished and investigations into their financial affairs were mounted. In the early 1970s Gayatri Devi was convicted of tax offences and served five months in Delhi's notorious Tihar Jail. On her release she penned her fascinating autobiography, *A Princess Remembers*. Now in her 80s, Gayatri Devi retains residential quarters at the Rambagh Palace, which, in 1958 was the first former palace in Rajasthan to be converted into a hotel (see p171).

The temple houses a number of sacred tanks, into which some daring souls jump from the adjacent cliffs. The water is claimed to be 'several elephants deep' and fed from a spring that falls through a space shaped like the mouth of a cow. The walls are decorated with frescoes, although very heavy rains in 1991 destroyed many of the original paintings.

There are some original frescoes in reasonable condition in the chamber at the end of the bottom pool, including those depicting athletic feats, the maharaja playing polo, and the exploits of Krishna and the *gopis* (milkmaids).

On the ridge above Galta is the **Surya Mandir** (Temple of the Sun God), which rises 100m above Jaipur and can be seen from the eastern side of the city. A 2.5km walking trail climbs up to the temple from Suraj Pol, or you can walk up from the Galta side. There are fine views over the humming city.

## ACTIVITIES

### Astrology

Dr Vinod Shastri is the medal-laden general secretary of the **Rajasthan Astrological Council & Research Institute** (☎ 2613338; Chandani Chowk, Tripolia Gate; ⏲ consultations 9am-8pm), who will prepare a computerised horoscope if you have your exact time and place of birth. A detailed five-year prediction costs Rs 1200, while a 30-year prediction is a hefty Rs 3000! Or you can have your palm read – this costs Rs 300 for a simple reading (when you may ask two questions), Rs 900 for a detailed reading or Rs 1800 for even more detail. Dr Shastri can be found in his shop near the City Palace. Though he should know when you're arriving, it's best to make an appointment.

Dr Shastri also conducts astrology lessons for beginners (see p166).

### Ayurvedic Clinics

Is Jaipur making your nerves jangle? Relax at swanky **Kerala Ayurveda Kendra** (☎ 5106743; Bajaj Rd; ⏲ 8am-noon & 4-8pm), which offers Ayurvedic massage and therapy at its professional clinic. Treatments include *sirodhara* (Rs 1800), where 4L to 5L of medicated oil is streamed steadily over your forehead for 1½ hours to reduce stress, tone the brain and help with sleep disorders (Rs 1800). Massages (by male or female masseurs) cost from Rs 500 for an hour.

Or try **Chakrapania Ayurveda** (☎ 2620746; www.chakrapaniayurveda.com; ⏲ 9am-2pm & 3-7pm Mon-Sat, 9am-1pm Sun), where you can get your body type analysed for Rs 200, a massage for Rs 650 and you can have 30 to 45 minutes of *sirodhara* for Rs 400.

If you're seeking treatment for a specific ailment, you can visit the **National Institute of Ayurveda** (Madho Vilas), near Samrat Gate. This government hospital provides free Ayurvedic therapies, including oil massages, steam baths and purification programmes. You first consult a doctor who will determine the appropriate treatment for you.

### Beauty Parlours

Jaipur has plenty of beauty parlours, which usually cater for both women and men.

**Shahnaz Herbals** (☎ 2378444; 50-55 Ashoka Rd, C-Scheme; ⏲ 9.30am-7.30pm) is long-standing and feels it, rather like stepping into a 1940s' beauty parlour. It does good massages (female masseurs for women). The head massage is a 15-minute massage, after which an electric tea cosy is placed on your head to warm the oils. A manicure costs from Rs 80 to 100, a pedicure costs Rs 130, a head/back/body massage cost Rs 80/130/350 and henna costs Rs 80 per hand.

The **Add Life Beauty Parlour** (☎ 2388691; F143 Pt C, Ganpati Plaza, MI Rd; ⏲ 8.30am-6pm), below Pizza Hut, is a much more contemporary place, and offers excellent, soothing massages (Rs 375 to 625), facials (Rs 250 to 600) and face massages (Rs 75 to 300). A manicure costs Rs 100. If it's not hot enough for you outside, there's a sauna (Rs 125).

### Golf

**Rambagh Golf Club** (Bhawani Singh Rd; ⏲ 6am-6.30pm), near the Rambagh Palace, has a scenic 18-hole course that was once part of the polo grounds. There are caddie charges and a small green fee; equipment is available.

## PINK CITY WALKING TOUR

This walking tour will take you through Jaipur's bazaars and the main attractions in the old city. Allow about half a day for the tour (longer if you linger at the sights), and bring a hat, your camera and plenty of water.

Entering the old city from **New Gate (1)**, turn right into **Bapu Bazaar (2)**, on the inside of the southern city wall. In a stark contrast to most Indian cities, the old city is made up of grids of streets such as this, straight and wide and lined with uniformly sized shops. This bazaar also has an added and unusual advantage – it's mostly traffic-free, being barred at one end. Brightly coloured bolts of fabric, leather jootis (traditional, pointy-toed shoes), trinkets and aromatic perfumes make the street a favourite destination for Jaipur's women. At the end of Bapu Bazaar you'll come to **Sanganeri Gate (3)** on your right, but turn left here into **Johari Bazaar (4)**, the jewellery market, one of the city's main shopping strips. Johari Bazaar and the small lanes that dissect it are where you will find jewellers, goldsmiths and silversmiths. Of particular interest are the artisans doing *meenakari* (enamelling). This highly glazed and intricate work, in shades including ruby, bottle green and royal blue, is a speciality of Jaipur. On Johari Bazaar you can also find cotton merchants – cloth here is usually cheaper than at Bapu Bazaar. Interspersed with the uniform shop fronts are the grand pink *havelis* (mansions) of Jaipur's wealthy merchants.

Distance: 4.25km
Duration: three to five hours
Start: New Gate
Finish: Panch Batti

You'll pass the **Jama Masjid (5)** to your left, with its tall minarets, and soon come to the old city's major square **Badi Chaupar (6)**. To the north of the square is **Siredeori Bazaar (7)**, also known as Hawa Mahal Bazaar. The name is derived from the extraordinary **Hawa Mahal** (8; Palace of the Winds; p160), a short distance to the north on the left side of the street. The building's exterior is most spectacular, but it's also worth going inside. It's entered via the rear entrance, which you'll find if you head back to Badi Chaupar and turn right (west) into Tripolia Bazaar and right again down a small lane.

Back on **Tripolia Bazaar (9)**, continue west and you'll be confronted by stall after stall crammed with domestic kitchen utensils, textiles, trinkets and ironware. The stalls are closed on Sunday.

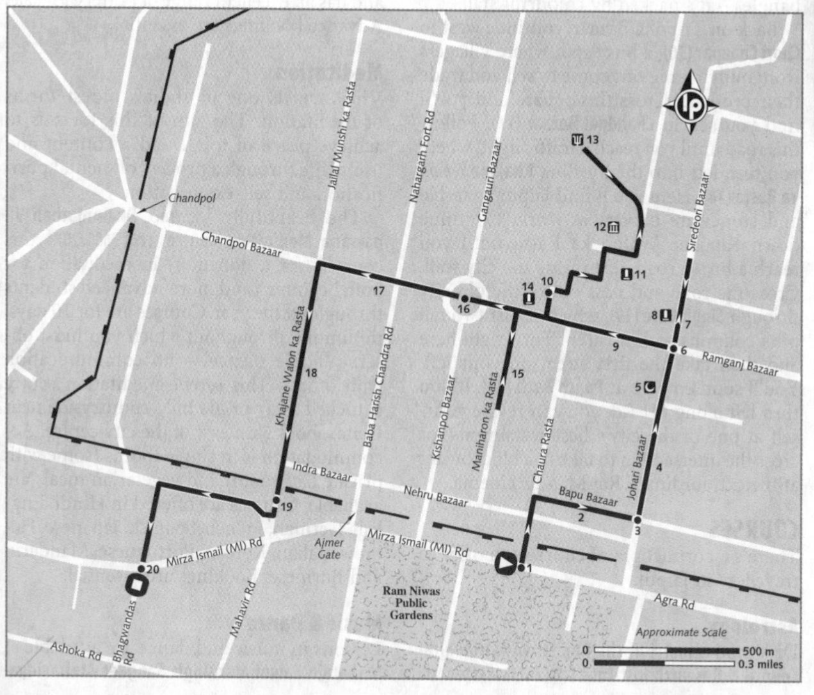


JAIPUR

A few hundred metres along is the triple-arched **Tripolia Gate (10)**, after which the bazaar is named. This is the main entrance to the **Jantar Mantar** (**11**; p159) and **City Palace** (**12**; p157), but only the maharaja's family is may enter here. The public entrance to the palace complex is via the less-ostentatious Atishpol (Stable Gate), a little further along. To the north of the City Palace is the **Govind Devji Temple** (**13**; p159), surrounded by gardens. Here Jai Singh installed an image of Govinda Deva (an incarnation of Krishna), the patron deity of his family. Govinda Deva has a sweet tooth and is unveiled seven times daily to receive treats from devotees.

After visiting the City Palace complex, head back to Tripolia Bazaar and resume your walk west. To your right you'll see the **Iswari Minar Swarga Sal** (**14**; Heaven-Piercing Minaret; p160), the highest structure in the old city. The minaret was erected by Iswari Singh, who succeeded Jai Singh. Cross the road and you'll see a small archway directly opposite the minaret. If you head west from here, the next lane on the left is **Maniharon ka Rasta (15)**, the best place to buy lac (resin) bangles – it's packed by colourful stalls.

Back on Tripolia Bazaar, continue west to **Choti Chaupar (16)**, a busy spot where villagers from outlying regions come to sell and trade their produce. Cross this square and you'll find yourself in **Chandpol Bazaar (17)**. Follow this road until you reach a traffic light, where you turn left into the bustling **Khajane Walon ka Rasta (18)**. Here you'll find Jaipur's marble and stoneware carvers at work. Continue down Khajane Walon ka Rasta until you reach a broad road, just inside the city wall. Cross the road and pass out of the old city through **Singh Gate (19)**, which is just two tall pink columns with no arch. Turn right here and then take the first street on your left. You'll soon emerge at **Panch Batti (20)**. If you turn left along MI Rd, you can revive yourself at one of the city's best restaurants, or cross the intersection to take in a blockbuster at the extraordinary Raj Mandir cinema.

## COURSES

There's a cornucopia of courses on offer to travellers in Jaipur.

### Astrology

Dr Vinod Shastri at the **Rajasthan Astrological Council & Research Institute** (☎ 2613338; Chandani Chowk, Tripolia Gate; consultations 9am-8pm) offers lessons in astrology. The charge is Rs 3000 per person for 15 one-hour lectures, given over a period of five days (a minimum of five people are needed). More-advanced lessons are also available.

### Block Printing, Painting & Pottery

You can do block-printing courses in nearby Sanganer village, around 16km south of Jaipur. **Sakshi** (☎ 2731862; Laxmi Colony; shop 8.30am-8.30pm, factory 9am-6pm) offers three-day basic block-printing or blue-pottery courses (eight hours per day) for US$50. You can also do two- to three-month courses; contact Sakshi for more details.

**Mr Kripal Singh** (☎ 2201127; B18A Shiv Rd, Bani Park) is a highly respected artist offering lessons in Indian painting at Kripal Kumbh (p175). The lessons are free, but you must supply your own materials (Mr Singh can advise on this), and he doesn't accept beginners. You'll need to book eight hours a day for at least a week. He also gives free lessons in pottery (although it's not possible during the monsoon, from late June to mid-September) and has an excellent range of pottery for sale. Advance bookings are essential.

### Meditation

Vipassana is one of India's oldest forms of meditation. The aim of this form is to achieve peace of mind and a content and useful life through a process of mental purification and self-examination.

The beautifully located **Dhammathali Vipassana Meditation Centre** (☎ 2680220) runs courses (for a donation) in meditation for both beginners and more-advanced students throughout the year. Courses are for 10 days, minimum, throughout which you must observe 'noble silence' – no communication with others. This serene meditation centre is tucked away in the hilly countryside near Galta, about 5km east of the city centre. Accommodation is in single rooms (some with private bathroom) and vegetarian meals are available. Courses are offered in Hindi, English, German, French, Spanish, Japanese, Hebrew, Italian, Korean, Portuguese, Mandarin and Burmese. Bookings are essential.

### Music & Dance

Lessons in music and dance are available at **Maharaja Sawai Mansingh Sangeet Mahavidya-**

**laya** (☎ 2611397), behind Tripolia Gate. The sign is in Hindi – ask locals to point you in the right direction. Tuition is given in traditional Indian instruments, such as tabla, sitar and flute. It costs Rs 500 per month in a small group for regular students. Music lessons are held from 8am to 11am, and dance lessons from 3.30pm to 4.30pm and 5pm to 6pm. There is also tuition in *kathak*, the classical Indian dance. Classical Indian vocal tuition can also be undertaken. For details contact the school principal, Mr Shekhawat.

### Yoga

There are several places in Jaipur that conduct yoga classes, including the **Yoga Sadhana Ashram** (Bapu Nagar; 🕑 Wed-Mon), which nestles among trees off University Rd (quite near Rajasthan University). Classes incorporate breathing exercises, yoga asanas (poses) and exercise. Most of the classes are in Hindi, but some English is spoken in the 7.30am to 9.30am class.

Alternatively you could try the casual classes held at **Madhavanand Girls College** (☎ 2200317; C19 Behari Rd, Bani Park), next door to the Madhuban guesthouse. There are free daily classes, in Hindi and in English, from 6am to 7am.

## TOURS

The **RTDC** (☎ 2202586; MI Rd; 🕑 10am-5pm Mon-Sat) offers half-/full-day tours of Jaipur and its surrounds for Rs 100/150. The full-day tours (9am to 6pm) take in all the major sights (including Amber Fort), with a lunch break at Nahargarh. The lunch break can be as late as 3pm, so have a big breakfast. AC bus tours (10am to 5pm) cost Rs 135/180; they don't include Nahargarh. Rushed half-day tours are confined to the city limits (8am to 1pm, 11.30am to 4.30pm and 1.30pm to 6.30pm) – some travellers recommend these, as you avoid the long lunch break. Fees don't include admission charges. Tours depart from Jaipur train station (depending on demand), and pick up from the RTDC Hotel Teej, RTDC Hotel Gangaur and RTDC Tourist Hotel. You are not necessarily immune to prolonged stops at emporiums along the way. Book at the **office** (🕑 7am-8pm) at the RTDC Tourist Hotel.

Approved guides for local sightseeing can be hired through the officer at the **tourist office** (☎ 2375466; RTDC Tourist Hotel, MI Rd; 🕑 8am-8pm Mon-Sat). A half-day tour (four hours) costs Rs 350. A full-day tour (eight hours) is Rs 450. An extra fee of Rs 100 to 150 for both tours is levied for guides speaking French, German, Italian, Japanese or Spanish.

The community group **Jaipur Virasat** (☎ 2367678; Jaipur Virasat Foundation, 9 Sardar Patel Rd, C-Scheme), in association with the Indian National Trust for Art and Cultural Heritage (Intach), organises City Heritage Walks, which are run by volunteers, to increase awareness of the city's fascinating history. The worthwhile two-hour guided walks take you through the walled city and focus on typical Jaipur architecture, local artisans and the homes of famous people. The walks are free (donations appreciated), and leave on Saturday from Albert Hall (the Central Museum) at 8.15am in winter (November to March) and 8am in summer (April to October). Bookings are essential.

**Rajasthan Travel Service** (☎ 2365408; www.rajasthantravelservice.com; ground fl, Ganpati Plaza, MI Rd) has a 'Jaipur by Night' tour for Rs 600 (dinner costs an extra Rs 225).

## SLEEPING

Autorickshaw drivers besiege travellers who arrive by train or bus. If you don't want to go to their choice, many will either refuse to take you or will double the fare. If you do go to their hotel, you'll pay through the nose for accommodation because they will receive a commission of at least 30% of what you are charged (and the charge won't go down for subsequent nights). Some enterprising rickshaw drivers openly declare their financial interest, which at least is honest. Ignore the 'Rs 10 anywhere in Jaipur' crowd – 'anywhere' means the place of their choice or a sudden increase in price.

To avoid such shenanigans, go straight to the prepaid autorickshaw stands at the bus and train stations. Alternatively, some hotels will pick you up if you ring ahead.

From May to September, most midrange and top-end hotels offer bargain rates, dropping prices by 25% to 50%.

All of the rooms listed here have private bathroom unless otherwise indicated. Prices quoted for midrange and top-end options exclude luxury taxes (officially applicable to rooms with rates over Rs 1000).

### Budget

**Hotel Pearl Palace** (☎ 2373700; www.hotelpearlpalace.com; off Ajmer Rd; s/d from Rs 250/350, better r Rs 500/550; ) Here Mr Singh makes vast efforts, constantly upgrading and improving the rooms, which are good, clean and modern, some with balcony. The rooftop restaurant has wrought-iron sculptured chairs, an extraordinary peacock canopy, door and flowerbed decoration, and views over the small Hathroi Fort. The food is tasty and cheap (thalis Rs 40), and the kitchen reassuringly spick-and-span.

**Jaipur Inn** (☎ 2201121; jaipurinn@sancharnet.in; B17 Shiv Rd, Bani Park; camp sites per person Rs 50, dm Rs 100, s/d with shared bathroom Rs 150/250, s/d with air-cooling Rs 400/500, s/d with AC Rs 600/700; ) This is a travellers' favourite, with an excellent range of rooms – more-expensive ones have balconies or open onto small terraces, and walls are printed with repeated motifs. There's lots of blue pottery inside and out, with distinguishing attention to detail. Free meals can be exchanged for creative contributions, including artwork, architectural help, cooking or interior design. Budgeteers can stay in the cramped dorm, featuring a unique tiled roof with mini skylights designed by a Dutch visitor. There's free pick-up from the train or bus station, and you can use the washing machine for Rs 100. The restaurant (p173) has fine views.

**Atithi Guest House** (☎ 2378679; atithijaipur@hotmail.com; 1 Park House Scheme Rd; r Rs 450-850; ) This family-run guesthouse, set between MI and Station Rds, offers strikingly clean, simple rooms around a calm courtyard. It's central but quiet, and big efforts are made to ensure your stay is relaxing. The service is friendly, laid-back and helpful. There's an amiable restaurant (guests only), room service and you can eat on the charming rooftop terrace. Rickshaw drivers don't like it here because the owner won't pay commission (always a good sign). Showers have regular hot water.

**Karni Niwas** (☎ 2365433; karniniwas@hotmail.com; C5 Motilal Atal Rd; s Rs 400-650, d Rs 450-850; ) Tucked behind Hotel Neelam, this has considerable charm, with nicely decorated rooms, often with balconies. There are lots of relaxing plant-decked terraces. It recently added 16 more rooms, and all are spacious with some appealing details. This hotel often receives favourable reports. Free pick-up from the train or bus station is available.

**Hotel Arya Niwas** (☎ 2372456; www.aryaniwas.com; s/d Rs 500/600, with AC Rs 650/800; ) Just off Sansar Chandra Rd, this is a popular travellers' haunt, well run (though impersonal) and well thought-out. There's a long, soothing terrace facing a peaceful grassy patch. It has a self-service veg restaurant and spotless rooms, with notably clean linen, although some are a bit claustrophobic (check out a few). Unfortunately one testament to its success is the barrage of rickshaws at the end of the road, but they're easily ignored.

**Evergreen Guest House** (☎ 2363446; evergreen34@hotmail.com; Chameliwala Market; s/d from Rs 125/150; ) Just off MI Rd, in the backpacking ghetto of Chameliwala Market, is Evergreen – a real backpacking scene. With a shady, atmospheric garden courtyard, it has something of a student-union feel. It has 100 rooms – cleanliness and service are erratic. The courtyard restaurant is a prime place to meet other travellers. Nonguests can use the pool for Rs 100. The AC rooms aren't worth it.

**Ashiyana Guest House** (☎ 2375414; Chameliwala Market; d with shared bathroom Rs 100, with private bathroom from Rs 130) Near the Evergreen, this is small, homey and family run. The grubby-mark-on-wall count is lower than at some other low-end places. Rooms are petite and there's a plant-filled courtyard.

**Devi Niwas** (☎ 2363727; singh_kd@hotmail.com; Dhuleshwar Bagh, Sadar Patel Rd, C-Scheme; s/d Rs 150/300) This paying guesthouse, in a spacious pale-yellow building nestled in the middle-class C-scheme area, has a homier feel than most and is run by an affable family. There are eight rooms – those downstairs are biggest and best. Food is home-cooked and tasty, and there's a small garden.

**New Pink City Guest House** (☎ 2363779; off MI Rd; s/d Rs 200/300) Opposite the main post office, this is tucked off MI Rd, down a lane. The accommodation is fronted by a lawn and garden, and it's surprisingly peaceful considering its central location. Rooms are reasonable value, but reception is somewhat charmless. It's a popular marriage venue, so one to avoid in the wedding season (November to February).

**Hotel Kailash** (☎ 2577372; Johari Bazaar; s with shared bathroom Rs 205-240, d with shared bathroom Rs 240-255, s with private bathroom Rs 270-400, d with private bathroom Rs 300-455) This hotel, opposite the Jama Masjid, is one of the few places to stay within the old city, and is right in the thick of it. It's nothing fancy (the rooms are basic cubbyholes), but it's buoyantly friendly and welcoming. Rooms at the back are quieter.

**RTDC Tourist Hotel** (☎ 2360238; MI Rd; s/d from Rs 200/300) Near the main post office and fronted by lawns, this hotel has a certain faded appeal, though its courtyards feel like a cross between a colonial mansion and a prison yard. Rooms have very high ceilings and are cleanish inside, but outside it's stained with ingrained dirt. Still, it's OK for the price.

**RTDC Hotel Swagatam** (☎ 2200595; Station Rd; dm Rs 50, s/d from Rs 350/450) The closest budget hotel to the train station. It has a rather institutional feel, but is perfectly acceptable, with drab standard rooms or deluxe air-cooled rooms with TV.

**Retiring rooms** (gents-only dm Rs 60, s/d Rs 150/300, r with AC Rs 500; ) At the train station. Handy if you're catching an early-morning train. Make reservations on the inquiries number (☎ 131).

## Midrange

### BANI PARK

The pleasant Bani Park area is green, tranquil and leafy, a 1.5km rickshaw ride from the old city.

**Madhuban** (☎ 2200033; www.madhuban.net; D237 Behari Rd, Bani Park; s Rs 1100-1800, d Rs 1200-2100; ) Madhuban is a smart, quiet heritage place, run by a friendly family (the owners once ruled Patan, 70 miles north-east), that consistently receives rave reviews. It's hassle-free and permeated by calmness. The building is surrounded by plants and decorated with bright frescoes. The restaurant is fine and the small walled-in pool is lit in the evening for nocturnal swimmers. Free pick-up from the bus or train station is offered.

**Jas Vilas** (☎ 2204638; www.jasvilas.com; C9 Sawai Jai Singh Hwy, Bani Park; s/d Rs 1500/1750; ) Next door to Hotel Meghniwas, this house was built by a military man in 1950. Run by a charming family, it offers welcoming, eager-to-please service and a sparkling pool surrounded by wrought-iron chairs set in a romantic courtyard. There are only nine comfortable rooms, alongside the pool courtyard, decked out in traditional furniture and elephant-print bedspreads.

**Shahpura House** (☎ 2203069; www.shahpurahouse.com; D257 Devi Rd, Bani Park; s/d from Rs 1400/1600, ste Rs 1800/2200, royal ste Rs 2400; ) Another prime choice, though lacking the family-run feel you get in some hotels in this category. It's built in elaborate traditional style, and offers immaculate rooms, some with balconies, featuring lots of murals, hanging coloured-glass lamps, ceilings covered in small mirrors (in the suites) and even a durbar hall with huge chandelier. Cushions stand to attention on stiff sofas. There's an elegant rooftop terrace.

**Umaid Bhawan Guest House** (☎ 206426; www.umaidbhawan.com; Behari Rd, via Bank Rd, Bani Park; s/d Rs 1100/1300, ste Rs 2000; ) This heritage guest-house, behind the Collectorate, is efficiently run by a retired air-force officer's family. Rooms are stately, full of carved-wood furniture. Some open out onto balconies and some are echoingly huge. Free pick-up is available from the train or bus station.

**Hotel Meghniwas** (☎ 2202034; www.meghniwas.com; C9 Sawai Jai Singh Hwy; s/d from Rs 1100/1200, apt Rs 1800/2000; ) In a building erected by Brigadier Singh in 1950 and run by his gracious descendants, this has modern rooms, with traditional carved-wood furniture and leafy outlooks. Nos 201 and 209 are like mini apartments – good for long-termers. The pool is in a pleasant lawn area.

**Tara Niwas** (☎ 2203762; www.aryaniwas.com; s/d per 15 days from Rs 4700/5700, with AC Rs 7000/8500; ) Run by the people behind Hotel Arya Niwas, Tara Niwas offers long-stay apartments (minimum stay 15 days) at bargain prices, for roomy, bright accommodation that's well furnished and smart.

**Jai Niwas** (☎ 5124531; www.aryaniwas.com; 3 Jalupura Scheme, Gopinath St; r from Rs 650, s/d with AC Rs 700/850; ) Also under the Arya Niwas umbrella, this modern place is peaceful (fronted by a smart lawn), yet centrally located just off MI Rd. Rooms are spacious and comfortable, if a little functional.

**Hotel Jaipur Ashok** (☎ 2204491; fax 2204498; Jai Singh Circle, Bani Park; s/d/ste Rs 1200/1800/2000; ) About 1km north of the train station, Jaipur Ashok is contemporary but features some traditional design elements. Cheaper rooms are characterless, but the suites are as large as small flats and decorated in Rajasthani style. There're a pool (open to nonguests for Rs 125), a coffee shop, restaurant and bar. It'll drop prices at the drop of a hat.

**ELSEWHERE**

**Narain Niwas Palace Hotel** (☎ 2561291; www.hotelnarainniwas.com; Narain Singh Rd; s/d from Rs 1950/2700; ) In Kanota Bagh, just south of the city, this hotel has a wonderful ramshackle splendour, though a somewhat impersonal feel. There's an old-fashioned veranda, and rooms are varyingly atmospheric – suites are the best. There's a secluded pool and lush rambling gardens.

**Alsisar Haveli** (☎ 2368290; www.alsisarhaveli.com; Sansar Chandra Rd; s/d Rs 2000/2500; ) A gracious 19th-century mansion set in beautiful, green gardens, Alsisar Haveli has quaintly furnished, elegant rooms with lots of arches. This is a winning choice, though again, a little impersonal.

**Best Western Om Tower** (☎ 2366683; ommljaipur@yahoo.com; Church Rd, off MI Rd; s/d from Rs 2160/2750; ) Jaipur's newest landmark rises above the city like a chunky space rocket. Rooms are comfortable and very good value, with better views the higher you go, but the glitz-and-beige design may not be everyone's bag. The revolving restaurant (see p172) is spectacular. The next-door building (also part of the hotel) has a rooftop pool on the 6th floor and a pub-disco-bar.

**Hotel Diggi Palace** (☎ 2373091; www.hoteldiggipalace.com; off Sawai Ram Singh Rd; r with shared bathroom Rs 350, r with private bathroom Rs 500-1500) About 1km south of Ajmer Gate, the splendid former residence of the *thakur* (nobleman) of Diggi is surrounded by gorgeous, serene lawns. Once a budget hotel, it has upgraded to mid-range, though those staying in the cheaper rooms may disagree. The more-expensive rooms are OK, with painted decoration, alcoves and a romantic feel. Management can be grumpy.

**Nana-ki-Haveli** (☎ 2615502; www.dbr.nu/nana-ki-haveli; Fateh Tiba, Moti Dungri Rd; r Rs 1200-1800) Off Moti Dungri Rd is this tranquil, tucked-away, homey place with attractive modern rooms decorated with traditional flourishes (discreet wall painting, wooden furniture). It's operated by a lovely family for whom nothing is too much trouble. It's fronted by a quiet lawn.

**Hotel Bissau Palace** (☎ 2304391; www.bissaupalace.com; outside Chandpol; d with/without AC Rs 1800/990, ste Rs 2800; ) This is worth considering if you want to stay in a palace, but can't afford the higher-priced places. It has charm, and lots of antique furnishings and maharaja mementos, such as moustached photos and hunting paraphernalia. But it feels run-down, tired and a bit slipshod. The biggest suite is definitely not worth considering – it's no better than the smaller ones. There's a swimming pool, but it's a bit murky. You could console yourself, though, in the handsome wood-panelled library and two restaurants (one on the rooftop offering splendid views; guests only), and by hobnobbing with the peacocks.

**Karauli House** (☎ 2211532; www.karauli.com; New Sanganer Rd, s/d Rs 1200/1400; ) This is the modest city pad of the maharaja of Karauli. It's a house set in pleasant gardens, south of town. There are just six airy, well-furnished but unexciting rooms, and good home cooking.

**Nahargarh** (Tiger Fort; ☎ 5148044; d Rs 500) Nahargarh is a romantic choice set high above the old city. There's only one very basic double room, in one of the fort's parapets behind the restaurant – the views from the bed are unparalleled.

**Chirmi Palace Hotel** (☎ 2365063; www.chirmi.com; Dhuleshwar Bagh, Sadar Patel Rd; s/d from Rs 650/750, deluxe Rs 1000/1200; ) Set in a traditional grand family house, Chirmi Palace is run by a grand elderly couple. Rooms are atmospheric with high ceilings and make up in character what they lack in lushness. There are a few cheaper rooms (around Rs 350 to 500 depending on the season) upstairs. The dining room is ornately painted.

**LMB Hotel** (☎ 2565844; info@lmbsweets.com; Johari Bazaar; s/d/deluxe Rs 1125/1425/1825; ) In the old city above the well-known restaurant of the same name. The rooms offer a prime vantage point from where you can check out the mayhem of the bazaars. Rooms are large, but generally grimy, seemingly unchanged since the late 1970s. This is not true of the 3rd floor, however, where rooms are much brighter and cleaner due to recent makeovers. Cheaper rooms have no view and depressingly blocked windows.

**Rajasthan Palace Hotel** (☎ 2611542; 3 Peelwa Garden, Moti Dungri Rd; d with/without AC Rs 700/400; ) This rather forgotten-feeling option has a quiet lawn area, a small pool and keen management. The high-ceilinged rooms are a bit shabby but pretty clean and reasonable value (especially the cheaper ones).

**RTDC Hotel Teej** (☎ 2203199; Collectorate Rd; dm Rs 50, s/d Rs 350/450, deluxe Rs 550/650, with AC

Rs 800/900; ) Located opposite the Moti Mahal Cinema, Hotel Teej is set in a garden, and is better and more welcoming than many RTDC joints. Rooms are spacious, high ceilinged and quite pleasant, though the difference between ordinary, deluxe and superdeluxe seems to be the degree of cleanliness of the carpet. AC rooms are very overpriced.

**RTDC Hotel Gangaur** ( 2371641; Sanjay Rd; s/d from Rs 600/700; ) This option is just off MI Rd and has a crazy-paving exterior, but that's where the madness ends – inside are typically drab but comfortable state-run rooms.

## Top End

Jaipur has plenty of top-notch hotels, from regular plush chains to beautifully restored palaces and *havelis*. At some, however, service leaves something to be desired.

**Raj Vilas** ( 2680101; www.oberoihotels.com; Goner Rd; s/d US$450/475, luxury tents US$570, villas US$1500; ) About 8km from the city centre is Jaipur's most sophisticated hotel. It has 71 rooms, yet a boutique feel and attentive, unobtrusive service. Its terracotta domes are set in more than 32 shady orchard- and fountain-filled hectares. Immaculate rooms, with sunken baths, are subtly and gorgeously decorated. Each villa has its own pool. Guests ride around in golf buggies. Check the website for special offers.

### THE AUTHOR'S CHOICE

**Samode Haveli** ( 2632370; www.samode.com; s/d/ste €110/130/153, Sheesh Mahal or Haveli ste €188; ) The northeast corner of the old city is a charming place to stay, and tucked away is this fantastic 200-year-old building, once the town house of the *rawal* (nobleman) of Samode, Jaipur's prime minister. Several of the suites are astonishingly romantic, covered in intricate, twinkling mirrorwork, ornate paintings, tiny alcoves and soaring arches. The run-of-the-mill suites are also lovely, gracefully large, arched and decked out with big carved beds. Most have private terraces. The rooms are more ordinary. The pool with its bar is an oasis of peace. Lounge-lovers should get up early to get one of the poolside double beds. If rates seem out of reach, note that prices halve from May to September.

**Raj Palace** ( 2634077-9; www.rajpalace.com; Chomu Haveli, Zoramar Singh Gate, Amber Rd; r US$135-165, ste US$275-375; ) A former royal home, Raj Palace was built by Thakur Mohan Singhji of Chaumoo, then prime minister. The imposing building, just north of town on the Amber Rd, overlooks a splendid courtyard and has a fantastic range of atmospheric rooms, such as the romantic white arches of Room 103, or the enormous high bed and Japanese tapestry of Room 304. Room 401 has a view over the impressive courtyard from a tiny window, and access to an amazing rooftop from where you can enjoy a striking Jaipur panorama. There's disabled access.

**Jai Mahal Palace Hotel** ( 2223636; www.tajhotels.com; Jacob Rd; s/d from US$220/230; ) Run by the Taj Group, and located south of the train station, this grand hotel is set in 7 hectares of beautifully manicured Mughal gardens, which most of the swish rooms overlook. The 18th-century building was once the residence of Jaipur's prime minister. Tastefully furnished standard rooms are very comfortable and enhanced by miniature paintings. The suites are stunningly conservative and refined, with some fantastic antique pieces. There's a gorgeous circular pool.

**Rambagh Palace** ( 2211919; www.tajhotels.com; Bhawan Singh Rd; s/d from Rs 10,000/11,000; ) Once the Jaipur pad of Maharaja Man Singh II, set in 19 hectares, this place is now a Taj Group hotel. There are fantastic views across the immaculate lawns. More-expensive rooms are naturally most sumptuous. The maharani still lives in separate quarters in the hotel grounds. Non-guests can dine in the restaurant or take tea on the veranda. At least treat yourself to a drink at the Polo Bar (p174).

**Saba Haveli** ( /fax 2630521; d Rs 4000; ) Near Samode Haveli, in the northeastern part of the town, Saba Haveli is positioned among a warren of narrow, community-feeling streets. It's another 200-year-old *haveli* that's in the process of being converted into a hotel – the top floor is derelict. At the time of research, there were only five beautifully converted rooms that were as fantastic as the smaller suites at Samode Haveli, but lacking the finesse of service and the pool. In the low season (May to September) you'll get discounts of over 50%.

**Chokhi Dhani** (☎ 2225001; www.chokhidhani.com; hut/haveli ste Rs 4000/5000; ) This is a mock-traditional Rajasthani village, 15km from Jaipur, with wonderful restaurants and entertainment in the evenings (see p174). Accommodation is in traditional-style mud huts with untraditional interiors. These are very well appointed, with a bedroom and sitting room decorated with mud walls and mirrorwork. There are also eight big rooms in a *haveli*, all swathed in ruched satin. Additional features are the commodious pool and spacious grounds. It's popular with middle-class Indian families, and a good place to stay if you want something a bit different.

**Rajmahal Palace** (☎ 5105665; www.royalfamilyjaipur.com; Sadar Patel Rd; s/d Rs 1900/2200, superior Rs 2300/2500, ste Rs 3500/3995; ) In the south of the city, this place is a more-modest edifice than the other palace hotels (Rambagh or Jai Mahal), but still ineffably smart. The superior rooms are supremely comfortable, with cool marble floors inside and small patches of lawn to the front. Standard rooms are still good, though less appealing. Built in 1729 by Jai Singh, it was also formerly the British Residency, and temporarily the home of Maharaja Man Singh II and the maharani after their residence, the Rambagh Palace, was converted into a luxury hotel.

**Mansingh Hotel** (☎ 2378771; www.mansinghhotels.com; Sansar Chandra Rd; s/d Rs 3500/4000, ste Rs 4500/5000; ) Just making it into the top-end scale, Mansingh Hotel is very central, just off Sansar Chandra Rd, and has first-class rooms and large two-bedroom suites.

**Mansingh Towers** (☎ 2378771; s/d from Rs 4000/4500, ste Rs 6500-8500; ) Next door to Mansingh Hotel is the even newer and swankier Mansingh Towers, which has a huge atrium and spacious rooms. All rooms have spa baths.

Other plush options:

**Trident Hilton** (☎ 2670101; www.trident-hilton.com; s/d US$100/110; ) About 5km north of the city on Amber Rd, Trident is slick and very well managed, and offers balconies and lingering views. It's opposite the Jal Mahal. Disabled access.

**WelcomHotel Rajputana Palace Sheraton** (☎ 5100100; www.welcomgroup.com; Palace Rd; s/d from Rs 5500/6000; ) Swanky but with a 1970s feel, staffed to the hilt and built around a pool.

**Holiday Inn** (☎ 2672000; r from Rs 2450; ) About 1km north of the city on Amber Rd, this impressive, traditional-style building offers the usual comfortable Holiday Inn standards, and is good value.

**Hotel Clarks Amer** (☎ 2550616; www.hotelclarks.com; s/d US$89/100; ) About 8km south of the city, this 200-room hotel is welcoming, plush and serves very decent food.

# EATING

## Restaurants

### MI ROAD

**OM** (☎ 236683; Church Rd, off MI Rd; dishes Rs 90-250; noon-3.30pm & 7-11pm) Jaipur's newest landmark is a rocket-shaped tower, with a splendid, glitzy, emphatically vegetarian revolving restaurant at 56m. A revolution takes 45 minutes and it's an amazing way to see the city for its clientele of upper-crust Indian families and businesspeople. The cuisine, which features delicious Rajasthani specialities, almost lives up to the view.

**Niro's** (MI Rd; mains Rs 80-290; 10am-11pm) Established in 1949, Niro's is a long-standing bright and cheery favourite. Beneath a mirrored ceiling, throngs tuck into veg and non-veg Indian, Chinese and Continental food. Particular specialities are the *murg malai* (chicken and cheese) kebabs, *raj sulal* (lamb in spices) and *began bharta* (aubergine), which can be enjoyed to an accompaniment of piped 'musak'.

**Sankalp** (MI Rd; dishes Rs 35-90; 9am-11pm) This vivid, popular chain restaurant could win the hot contest for the most waiters on MI Rd. It serves great South Indian dishes to a background of car-chase music.

**Natraj Restaurant** (☎ 2375804; MI Rd; mains Rs 40-160; 9am-midnight) A little further east, towards the old city, is this classy, two-level vegetarian place, which has an extensive menu featuring North Indian, Continental and Chinese cuisine. Diners are blown away by the vegetable bomb curry, and there's a good selection of thalis (Rs 100 to 160) and South Indian food – the *paper masala dosa* (curried vegetables inside a papery thin pancake) is delicious. Décor is beige, a bit 1970s, with *Happy Days*–style booth seating and a Casio-music soundtrack. It's good for takeaway Indian sweets, too.

**Dāsaprakash** (MI Rd; dishes Rs 50-130; 11am-11pm) Part of a sparkling, efficient chain, Dāsaprakash concentrates on yummy South Indian cuisine. After your dosa or your *idli* (rice dumpling), you can choose from some amazing sundaes, such as Gold Rush: 'strike it delicious' (fudge, praline chocolate, coffee and butterscotch).

**Handi Restaurant** (MI Rd; dishes Rs 60-180; noon-3.30pm & 6.30-11.30pm) Handi has been satisfying customers for years and now has two eateries, opposite the main post office. One is the original, tucked at the back of the Maya Mansions, offering scrumptious barbecue dishes and specialising in tandoori and Mughlai cuisine. In the evenings it sets up a cheap kebab stall at the entrance to the restaurant. The newer, pricier AC alternative is decorated with puppets and mirrors on the mud-covered walls.

**Copper Chimney** (Maya Mansions, MI Rd; dishes Rs 65-200; noon-3.30pm & 6.30-11.30pm) Near Handi, Copper Chimney is a smart, classy place with the requisite waiter army and a big rollicking horse mural. It offers veg and non-veg Indian, Continental and Chinese food in a cool, pleasant setting with a window overlooking the mayhem of MI Rd.

**Surya Mahal** (MI Rd; dishes around Rs 40; 9am-10.30pm) Near Natraj Restaurant is this good-value, popular, less-smart option that has prices to match, specialising in excellent South Indian food; try the delicious *masala dosas*, and specials, such as the tasty *makki ki roti sarson ka saag* (mustard vegetables with chickpea flour).

## AROUND MI ROAD

**Four Seasons** (D43A Subhas Rd; mains Rs 45-130; noon-3.30pm & 6.30-11pm) One of Jaipur's best restaurants, a sleek, vastly popular place on two levels, with a glass wall to the kitchens. It's a bit out of the way, but has renowned vegetarian food and a great range of dishes, including tasty Rajasthani specialities. Try a thali (Rs 85 to 100) or the speciality *rawa masala dosa* (South Indian ground rice and semolina pancake with coconut, onions, carrots and green chillies).

**Mediterraneo** (9 Khandela House, behind Amber Tower; dishes Rs 65-195; 8am-11pm) This Italian restaurant offers wood-fired pizzas and pasta dishes – we had both tested by an Italian who pronounced them 'quite good'. The highlight is that it's on a rooftop and candlelit at night – an unusually romantic place to eat for Jaipur.

**Chãtanya** (Sansar Chandra Rd; dishes Rs 30-195; 8am-11pm) A slick vegetarian restaurant, with too many waiters and a central pillar that's inventively painted to look like a tree. Have-a-go cuisine touches on Mexican, Italian and Chinese, but you're best sticking to the superb Indian dishes and excellent breads.

## BANI PARK

**Mehfil** (5B Maharaja Complex, Devi Rd; dishes Rs 50-200; 11am-3.30pm & 7.30-11pm) This is a fine restaurant with innovative North Indian, Rajasthani and Chinese dishes. There are some particularly delicious *paneer* (unfermented cheese) dishes, such as the tandoori *paneer* stuffed with sweet-and-sour chutney. From 8pm there is a *ghazal* (Urdu songs derived from poetry) singer. Décor includes a horrendous rockery, brass pots and velveteen seating, which all looks better after dark.

**Jaipur Inn** (☎ 2201121; B17 Shiv Rd, Bani Park; buffet dinner Rs 100; dinner) This backpackers' favourite hotel has an excellent rooftop restaurant, with superlative views over the capital. It has an Indian veg buffet dinner (nonguests should book in advance) and a bonfire in winter.

## OLD CITY

**LMB** (Johari Bazaar; mains Rs 55-170; 11.30am-3.30pm & 7-11pm) LMB is a *sattvik* (pure vegetarian), AC restaurant in the old city that's been going strong since 1954. A make-over has left it with an Art Deco–meets-disco-inferno look. The menu opens with a warning from Krishna about people who like *tamasic* (putrid and polluted food), which gets you into the *sattvik* mood. Try the thali for a range of Rajasthani tastes and specialities. The *paneer* tikka stuffed with fennel and served with mint chutney is another scrummy choice.

**Ganesh Restaurant** (Nehru Bazaar; dishes Rs 5-80; 9am-11pm) Near New Gate is Jaipur's best-kept secret. This pocket-sized outdoor restaurant is in a fantastic location – on the old city wall. The cook is in a pit on one side of the wall, so you can check out your food being freshly cooked. There's no English menu and not much English is spoken, but if you're looking for a local eatery with fresh tasty food you'll love it. There's a signpost at one end of Nehru Bazaar.

**Steam** (☎ 2325698; Chaura Rasta; dishes Rs 30-70; noon-3.30pm & 7.30-11pm) Steam is quite close to the City Palace and is an open-fronted, cheap-and-not-all-that-cheerfully decorated option, but with friendly staff and reliable veg food – the usual mix of Indian, Chinese and Continental.

**Mohan** (144-5 Nehru Bazaar; dishes Rs 7-40; 9am-10pm) Simple, cheap and popular. The name is in Hindi and it's on the corner of the street, a few steps down from the footpath. The place is grubby, but the food is freshly cooked and flavoursome.

#### ELSEWHERE

**Chokhi Dhani** (☎ 2225001; adult/child aged 3-9 incl dinner Rs 190/100; ) Chokhi Dhani means 'special village' and this neo-Rajasthani village, 15km south of Jaipur, lives up to its name. You can enjoy a delicious Rajasthani thali, while lounging on floor seating. As well as the restaurants there is a bevy of traditional entertainment (see right). It's hugely popular with middle-class Indian families. You can even stay here, in luxurious huts with mud walls and mirrorwork (see p172).

### Quick Eats

**Jal Mahal** (MI Rd; ice creams Rs 12-110) Next door to Surya Mahal is this packed little takeaway ice-cream parlour, with some inventive concoctions, from the 'Earthquake' to the 'After Ate'.

**Chic Chocolate** (MI Rd) Around the corner from Atithi Guest House, Chic Chocolate is a clean pastry shop serving excellent cheese (with onion and peppers) toast (Rs 25). It also bakes its own bread and cakes.

**Rawat Kachori** (Station Rd; sweets Rs 5-10 or per kg Rs 80-300, lassis Rs 22) For great sweets head to the mobbed Rawat Kachori. A delicious milk crown should fill you up for the afternoon.

**Kanji** (Station Rd; sweets per kg Rs 110-300) Across the road from Rawat Kachori, Kanji has a fabulous array.

**Baskin 31 Robbins** (shop 15, Ganpati Plaza, MI Rd; ice creams Rs 33-110) Excellent if you're homesick and hankering for ice cream.

## DRINKING

### Cafés

**Lassiwala** (MI Rd) This famous, much-imitated institution, opposite Niro's, is a simple place that whips up fabulous, creamy lassis at Rs 10/20 for a small/jumbo. Will the real Lassiwala please stand up? It's the one that says 'Since 1944', directly next to the alleyway. Imitators spread to the right as you face it.

**Indian Coffee House** (MI Rd; coffees Rs 10) Off the street, down a sleazy alley, this coffee house offers a decent cup of coffee, and feels like a place for shady deals.

**Barista** (Bhagwandas Rd; coffees around Rs 60) This smart coffee bar is part of a chain that sells great lattes, cappuccinos and espressos. This branch shares its space with a small bookshop.

### Bars

Bars around town tend to be oppressive, all-male affairs; however, most upper-end hotel bars are good for a drink, the choicest among them being Polo and Hightz.

**Polo Bar** (Rambagh Palace Hotel, Bhawan Singh Rd; 11am-midnight) Has arched, scalloped windows overlooking the perfect lawns. A bottle of beer costs Rs 220 and cocktails around Rs 300.

**Hightz** (Mansingh Hotel, Sansar Chandra Rd; 5.30pm-midnight) This is a DJ bar, but not as cool as it sounds (you may find a Hammond organ rather than the promised DJ), though the views are great and cocktail prices begin at Rs 150.

## ENTERTAINMENT

Jaipur isn't a big late-night party town, although many hotels put on some sort of evening music, dance or puppet show. English-language films are occasionally screened at some cinemas in Jaipur – check the local press for details.

**Raj Mandir Cinema** (☎ 2379372; admission Rs 20-80) Just off MI Rd, Raj Mandir is *the* place to go to see a Hindi film in India. This opulent cinema looks like a huge cream cake, with a meringue auditorium and a foyer somewhere between a temple and Disneyland. It's a tourist attraction in its own right and is usually full, despite its immense size. Bookings can be made one hour to seven days in advance (10am to 6pm) at window Nos 7 and 8 – this is your best chance of securing a seat, although forget it in the early days of a new release. Alternatively, sharpen your elbows and join the queue when the current booking office opens 45 minutes before curtain up. Avoid the very cheapest tickets, which are very close to the screen. Films are screened at 12.30pm, 3.30pm, 6.30pm and 9.30pm.

**Chokhi Dhani** (☎ 2225001; adult/child aged 3-9 incl dinner Rs 190/100; ) Around 15km from Jaipur, Chokhi Dhani provides a fantastical, magical evening. It's a mock Rajasthani village, but don't let this put you off. It is mainly gardens, lit by glimmering lamps, with several restaurants serving traditional Rajasthani food (see opposite) that's included in the admission. You can wander around and watch the various entertainment, from the bizarre to the more bizarre: traditional tribal dancers setting fire to their hats, children balancing on poles and dancers dressed in lion costumes lurking in a wood. You can also take elephant or camel rides. Children will adore it.

**Polo ground** (Ambedkar Circle, Bhawan Singh Rd) Maharaja Man Singh II indulged his passion for polo by building an enormous polo ground next to the Rambagh Palace, which is still a polo-match hub today. A ticket to a match also gets you into the lounge, which is adorned with historic photos and memorabilia. The polo season extends over winter, with the most important matches played during January and March – contact the Rajasthan Polo Club (☎ 2385380) for ticket details.

During Jaipur's Elephant Festival in March (see Festivals in Jaipur, p151) you can see elephant polo matches at the Chaughan Stadium in the old city. Contact the Rajasthan Polo Club or **RTDC** (☎ 2202586; MI Rd; ⏲ 10am-5pm Mon-Sat) for details.

Many hotels will let you use their pool for a daily fee. Try the smashing pool at the **Jai Mahal Palace Hotel** (Jacob Rd). The **Jaipur Ashok** (Jai Singh Circle, Bani Park) charges Rs 125 for nonguests to use its pool. At the lowest end of the scale, **Evergreen Guest House** (Chameliwala Market) charges Rs 100.

## SHOPPING

Jaipur is shopping heaven. Buyers come here from all over the world to stock up on the amazing range of crafts that come from all over Rajasthan. You'll have to bargain hard though – shops have seen too many cash-rich, time-poor tourists. Shops around major tourist centres, such as the City Palace and Hawa Mahal, tend to be pricier.

For useful tips on bargaining, see The Art of Haggling, p371. At some shops, ie the government emporium and some upmarket stores, prices are fixed.

Most of the larger shops can pack and send your parcels home for you – although it'll be cheaper if you do it yourself (see p156).

Jaipur is famous for precious and semiprecious stones. There are many shops offering bargain prices, but you do need to know your gems. The main gem-dealing area is around the Muslim area of Pahar Ganj, in the southeast of the old city. Here you can see stones being cut and polished in workshops tucked off narrow backstreets.

The city is still loosely divided into traditional artisans quarters. The Pink City Walking Tour (p164) will take you through some of these.

Bapu Bazaar is lined with saris and fabrics, and is a good place to buy trinkets. **Johari Bazaar** (⏲ closed part of Sun) and Siredeori Bazaar are where many jewellery shops are concentrated, selling gold, silver and highly glazed enamelwork known as *meenakari*, a Jaipur speciality. You may also find better deals for fabrics along Johari Bazaar, where many merchants specialise in cotton.

Kishanpol Bazaar is famous for textiles, particularly *bandhani* (tie-dye). Nehru Bazaar also sells fabric, as well as jootis, trinkets and perfume. MI Rd is another good place to buy jootis. The best place for bangles is Maniharon ka Rasta, near the Shree Sanjay Sharma Museum.

Plenty of factories and showrooms are strung along the length of Amber Rd, between Zorawar Gate and the Holiday Inn, to catch the tourist traffic. Here you'll find huge shops selling block prints, blue pottery, carpets and antiques, but the emporiums are used to busloads swinging in to blow their cash, so you'll need to wear your bargaining hat.

Rickshaw-wallahs, hotels and travel agents will be getting a hefty cut from any shop they steer you towards. Stay clear of friendly young men on the street trying to steer you to their uncle's/brother's/cousin's shop – commission is the name of their game too. Many unwary visitors get talked into buying things for resale at inflated prices, especially gems. Beware of these get-rich-quick scams.

### Arts & Crafts

**Kripal Kumbh** (☎ 2201127; B18A Shiv Rd, Bani Park; ⏲ 9am-5pm) This is a showroom in a private home and a great place to buy Jaipur's famous blue pottery produced by the renowned, multiaward-winning potter Mr Kripal Singh. Now in his 80s, he is an accomplished artist and has some stunningly beautiful artworks for sale. Ceramics go for anything from Rs 10 (for a paperweight) to

JAIPUR

10,000 (for a large vase). You can also learn how to paint or make blue pottery here (see p166). Touts may take you elsewhere and claim that someone else is Mr Kripal Singh, or even that he is dead, so make sure that you are taken to the right place (near the Jaipur Inn).

**Rajasthali** (MI Rd; 11am-7.30pm Mon-Sat) The state government emporium, just opposite Ajmer Gate, is packed with good-quality Rajasthani artefacts and crafts, including enamelwork, embroidery, pottery, woodwork, jewellery, colourful puppets, block-printed sheets, cute miniatures, brassware, mirrorwork and more, but it has an air of torpor that doesn't make shopping much fun. The best reason to visit is to scout out prices, before launching into the bazaar (things can be cheaper at the markets, after haggling, and you'll find more choice).

**Juneja Art Gallery** (6-7 Laksmi Complex, MI Rd; 10am-8pm) This gallery has some striking pieces of contemporary art by Rajasthani artists (Rs 100 to 50,000). There are regular shows of contemporary artists changing almost weekly.



## Ayurvedic Remedies

**Himalaya** (MI Rd; 10am-8pm Mon-Sat) For Ayurvedic preparations, try this place near Panch Batti, which exports internationally, and has been selling herbal remedies and beauty products for 70 years. The products are good value, and can help you with a wide variety of ailments, including diarrhoea, poor memory, acne, hangovers and sexual disorders. There are even treatments for your pet. The shampoos, moisturisers and beauty products are reasonable buys if you don't have anything more serious to treat.

## Musical Instruments

**Music N Sports** (73 Chaura Rasta; 10.30am-8pm Mon-Sat) This store sells a range of musical instruments, including sitars, tablas, hand cymbals (Rs 20 to 200), bamboo flutes (Rs 20 to 2000), dancing bells on ankle cuffs (Rs 90 to 350) and harmoniums (Rs 2000 to 18,000). The staff can recommend music teachers.

**Audio King** (Nehru Bazaar; 9am-9pm) This tiny shop is good for picking up traditional and current Hindi music on CD or tape, and it offers a good selection of film soundtracks, past and present.

## Shoes

**Mojari** (Bhawani Villa, Gulab Path, Chomu House, off Sadar Patel Rd; 11am-6pm Mon-Sat) Calling all foot fetishists! This shop sells fabulous footwear for Rs 400 to 600. Named after the traditional decorated shoes of Rajasthan, Mojari is a UN-supported project that helps 3500 rural leatherworkers' households, traditionally among the poorest members of society. There is a wide range of footwear available, including embroidered, appliquéd and open-toed shoes, mules and sandals. There are also shoes featuring creative stitching, unusual cuts or decoration with bows, bells, beads and sequins. The products meet export-quality standards, but are based on traditional leatherworking skills and design. You may have trouble finding your size. Mojari also has a small collection of covetable leather and felt bags.

**Charmica** (MI Rd; 10am-8pm Mon-Sat) Opposite Natraj restaurant, this small shop is the place for well-made but pricey jootis.

## Tailors

**New Jodhpur Tailors** (9 Ksheer Sagar Hotel, Motilal Atal Rd; 9am-8.30pm Mon-Sat, 9am-5pm Sun) You can have a beautiful pair of jodhpurs (Rs 500) made in preparation for your visit to the Blue City. Or you can just go for a made-to-measure suit (Rs 1800) or shirt (Rs 100).

## Textiles

**Anokhi** (2 Tilak Rd; 10am-7pm) Near the Secretariat, this is a classy, upmarket boutique that's well worth visiting. It sells stunning high-quality textiles, such as block-printed fabrics, tablecloths, bed covers, cosmetic bags and scarves, as well as a range of well-designed, beautifully made clothing that combines Indian and Western influences. The pieces are produced just outside Jaipur at an unusually ethical factory, built on the grounds of an organic farm. Anokhi provides excellent working conditions, including limited working hours, free health care and transport for its 200 workers, as well as a crèche and educational funding for their children.

**Soma** (5 Jacob Rd, Civil Lines; 10am-8pm Mon-Sat, 10am-6pm Sun) This is a chic boutique, which sells first-rate textiles, including bright, fresh block prints and lots of unique furnishings, as well as some lovely children's clothes.

## GETTING THERE & AWAY

### Air

It's possible to arrange flights to Europe, the USA and other places, such as Dubai, all via Delhi. For details of international airlines, see p379. It's best that you book air tickets through travel agencies, where you will usually get a better price than by going directly to the airlines. See p156 for details.

Offices of domestic airlines:

**Indian Airlines** (☎ 2743500; Nehru Place, Tonk Rd)
**Jet Airways** (☎ 2360450; Umaid Nagar House, MI Rd; 9.30am-5.30pm Mon-Sat, 10am-3pm Sun) Opposite Ganpati Plaza.

### Bus

Rajasthan State Transport Corporation (RSTC) buses all leave from the **main bus station** (Station Rd), picking up passengers at Narain Singh Circle (you can also buy tickets here). There is a left-luggage office at the main bus station (Rs 10 per bag for 24 hours), as well as a prepaid autorickshaw stand.

Deluxe or private buses are far preferable to local buses, which stop at every small village and are usually crowded bone-rattlers. Deluxe buses all leave from Platform 3, tucked away in the right-hand corner of the bus station, and seats may be booked in advance from the **reservation office** (☎ 2205790), which is within the main bus station.

For long journeys, private buses can be more comfortable, though the RSTC Silverline luxury services get good reviews. Private companies also often provide sleeper buses over long distances, where you can lie down – ensuring better sleep than a chair service, and are also usually cheaper. Private buses are generally not as reliable, however, when it comes to schedules. There is a cluster of private offices along Motilal Atal Rd, near the Polo Victory Cinema.

There are regular buses to many destinations, including those outlined in the table (p178). Numerous private agencies also operate direct services to these cities.

### Car

There are currently no car-hire operators offering self-drive cars in Rajasthan. You'll have to hire a car in Delhi if you're mad enough to try this – see p129 for details.

You can arrange a car directly with the driver at the taxi stand at the train station. Usually the drivers need only a day's notice for a long trip. A reasonable price is Rs 3.50 per kilometre, with a 250km minimum per day and an overnight charge of Rs 100 per night. See p385 for more information.

For those who prefer booking through a travel agency, **Amrapali Travels** (☎ 2375100; Chameliwala Market; 10am-7pm Mon-Sat), near Evergreen Guest House, offers non-AC cars for Rs 4 per kilometre (minimum 250km per day and Rs 100 per night overnight charge).

**Rajasthan Travel Service** (☎ 2365408; www.rajasthantravelservice.com; ground fl, Ganpati Plaza, MI Rd) hires out vehicles for Rs 4.50/5.50 per kilometre for non-AC/AC (minimum 250km per day and Rs 100 overnight charge).

Rates with the RTDC are from Rs 4.50/6 per kilometre (Rs 100 overnight charge) for a non-AC/AC car, with the usual 250km minimum per day.

#### DOMESTIC FLIGHTS FROM JAIPUR

There are plenty of domestic flights from Jaipur, mostly run by Indian Airlines and Jet Airways, who offer similar prices. Air Deccan, Alliance Air, Jagson Airlines and Air Sahara also offer extremely competitively priced domestic flights serving Jaipur: see p382 for more details. Airline schedules can be erratic, so you'll need to double-check the information here. If you're under 30, you get a 30% discount in price.

| Destination | Fare (US$) | Duration | Frequency |
|---|---|---|---|
| Ahmedabad | 115 | 1hr | 2 weekly |
| Delhi | 55 | 40min | daily |
| Jodhpur | 90 | 40min | daily |
| Kolkata (Calcutta) | 230 | 2hr | 6 weekly |
| Mumbai (Bombay) | 165 | 1½hr | daily |
| Udaipur | 90 | 1¾hr | daily |

JAIPUR

**BUSES FROM JAIPUR**

| Destination | Fare (Rs) | Duration (hr) | Frequency |
|---|---|---|---|
| Agra | 67, AC 227 | 5½ | 12 daily |
| Ajmer | 67, AC 86 | 2½ | 7 daily |
| Bharatpur | 85 | 4½ | 4 daily |
| Bikaner | 80, AC 100 | 8 | hourly |
| Bundi | 105 | 5 | 5 daily |
| Chittorgarh | 116 | 7 | 2 daily |
| Delhi | 281, AC 425 | 5½ | at least hourly |
| Jaisalmer | 236 | 15 | 1 daily |
| Jhunjhunu | 70 | 5 | half-hourly |
| Jodhpur | 142 | 7 | 3 daily |
| Kota | 123 | 5 | 3 daily |
| Mt Abu | AC 302 | 13 | 1 daily |
| Nawalgarh | 51 | 4 | half-hourly |
| Sawai Madhopur | 60 | 6 | 3 daily |
| Udaipur | 202 | 10 | 5 daily |

### Train

The efficient **railway reservation office** (☎ 135; ⌚ 8am-2pm & 2.15-8pm Mon-Sat, 8am-2pm Sun) is to your right as you exit Jaipur train station. It's open for advance reservations only. Join the queue for 'Freedom Fighters and Foreign Tourists' (counter 769). See the table (opposite) for details of routes and fares.

For same-day travel, buy your ticket at the train station on platform No 1, window No 9. The railway inquiries number is ☎ 131.

There's a prepaid autorickshaw stand at the road entrance to the train station, as well as a tourist information office and a cloakroom on platform No 1 – it costs Rs 10 to deposit a bag for 24 hours.

## GETTING AROUND

### To/From the Airport

There are no bus services from the airport, which is 12km southeast of the city. An autorickshaw/taxi costs at least Rs 150/250 for the 15km journey into the city centre, or there's a prepaid taxi booth inside the terminal.

### Autorickshaw

There are prepaid autorickshaw stands at the bus and train stations. Rates are fixed by the government, which means you don't have to haggle. In other cases you should be prepared to bargain hard.

If you want to hire an autorickshaw for local sightseeing, it should cost about Rs 150/250 for a half/full day (including a visit to Amber but not Nahargarh); be prepared to bargain. This price is per rickshaw, not per person, and don't let drivers tell you otherwise. Make sure you fix a price before setting off to avoid a scene later. A slower, but cheaper, and more environmentally friendly option, is to hire a cycle-rickshaw, though it can be uncomfortable watching someone pedalling hard to transport you (however, this *is* how they make a living).

# AROUND JAIPUR

Jaipur's environs contain some fantastic ancient sites and interesting towns and villages that make great day trips. A comprehensive network of local buses makes getting to these regions relatively simple, or it's possible to join an organised tour run by the RTDC that includes a commentary on the various places visited. See p167 for more details.

## AMBER

The delicate, magnificent, pink fort-palace of Amber, an ethereal example of Rajput architecture, rises from a rocky mountainside about 11km northeast of Jaipur. Amber was the ancient capital of Jaipur state.

En route to Amber you can squeeze in visits to Royal Gaitor (p162), the Jal Mahal (p162) and the cenotaphs of the maharanis of Jaipur.

**MAJOR TRAINS FROM JAIPUR**

| Destination | Train No & name | Fare (Rs) | Duration (hr) | Departure |
|---|---|---|---|---|
| Agra | 2308 *Howrah Jodhpur Exp* | 127/356*/570 | 6½ | 11.10pm |
| Ahmedabad | 2958 *Ahmedabad SJ Rajdhani Exp* | 955/1395 | 9¼ | 12.45am (Wed-Mon) |
| | 2916 *Ahmedabad Ashram Exp* | 278/727*/1115 | 11 | 8.55pm |
| Ajmer | 2015 *Shatabdi* | 310/605 | 2 | 10.45pm (Thu-Tue) |
| Bikaner | 4737 *Bikaner Exp* | 119/853 | 9¼ | 10.10pm |
| | 2468 *Intercity Exp* | 122/351 | 6¾ | 3.25pm |
| Delhi | 2016 *Shatabdi* | 505/1020 | 4¼ | 5.45pm |
| | 2957 *Rajdhani* | 530/790 | 5½ | 2.30am |
| | 2414 *Jaipur-Delhi Exp* | 80/277 | 5½ | 4.25pm |
| Jaisalmer | 4059 *Delhi-Jaisalmer Exp* | 256/690* | 12¾ | 12.05am |
| Jodhpur | 2465 *Intercity Exp* | 81/284 | 5½ | 5.10pm |
| | 2461 *Mandore Exp* | 180/450*/679 | 5½ | 2.35am |
| Sikar | 9734 *Shekhawati Exp* | 37/135 | 2¾ | 6.05pm |
| Udaipur | 9615 *Chetak Exp* | 167/748 | 12¼ | 8.40pm |

Rajdhani fares are 3AC/2AC; Shatabdi fares are chair/executive (* = 3AC).

Amber was built by the Kachhwaha Rajputs, who originally hailed from Gwalior, in present-day Madhya Pradesh, where they reigned for over 800 years. They were always adept at diplomacy through marriage, and it was a marital alliance between a Kachhwaha prince Taj Karan and a Rajput princess that resulted in the granting of the region of Dausa to the prince by the princes's father.

Taj Karan's descendants eyed the hilltop that Amber Fort was later built on, recognising its virtue as a potential military stronghold. The site was eventually prised from its original inhabitants, the Susawat Minas, and the Minas were granted guardianship of the Kachhwahas' treasury in perpetuity.

The Kachhwahas, despite being devout Hindus belonging to the Kshatriya (warrior) caste, realised the convenience of aligning themselves with the powerful Mughal empire. They paid homage at the Mughal court, cemented the relationship with marital alliances and defended the Mughals in their various skirmishes. For this they were handsomely rewarded. With war booty they financed construction of the fort-palace at Amber, which was begun in 1592 by Maharaja Man Singh, the Rajput commander of Akbar's army. It was later extended and completed by the Jai Singhs before the move to Jaipur on the plains below.

## Sights

### AMBER FORT

This magnificent **fort** (pronounced 'Amer'; Indian/foreigner Rs 10/50, camera/video Rs 75/150; 7am-7pm) is more of a palace, built from red sandstone and white marble, and divided into four main sections, each with its own courtyard. Entry is through **Suraj Pol** (Sun Gate), which leads to the **Jaleb Chowk** (main courtyard), where returning armies would display their war booty to the populace – women could view this area from the veiled windows of the palace. The ticket office is directly across the courtyard from Suraj Pol.

Hiring a guide (Rs 100 to 150 for 1½ hours, maximum of four people) at the entrance is an asset here as there are few signs, and it would be a pity to get lost in the labyrinthine zenana. The maharaja doubtless knew the route to the woman of his choice each night, but you won't.

From Jaleb Chowk, an imposing stairway leads up to the main palace, but first it's worth taking the steps just to the right, which lead down to the small **Kali Temple** (photography prohibited; 6am-noon & 4-8pm). Every day from the 16th century until 1980 (when the government banned the practice) a goat was sacrificed here. It's a beautiful temple, entered through gorgeous silver doors featuring repoussé (raised relief) work. Before the image of Kali lie two silver lions. According to tradition, Maharaja Man Singh prayed to the goddess for victory in a battle with the ruler of Bengal. The goddess came to the maharaja in a dream advising that if he won the battle he should retrieve her image, which was lying at the bottom of the sea. After vanquishing his foes, the maharaja recovered the statue and installed it in the temple as Shila Devi (*shila* means 'slab' – the image is carved from one piece of stone). Above the lintel of the temple is the usual image of Ganesh, this one carved from a single piece of coral.

Heading back to the main stairway will take you up to the second courtyard and the **Diwan-i-Am** (Hall of Public Audience), which has a double row of columns each topped by a capital in the shape of an elephant, and latticed galleries above. Here the maharaja held audience and received the petitions of his subjects.

The maharaja's apartments are located around the third courtyard – you enter through the fabulous **Ganesh Pol**, decorated with mosaics and sculptures. The **Jai Mandir** (Hall of Victory) is noted for its inlaid panels and multimirrored ceiling. Patterns made with coloured foil and paint are covered in glass. At night this would have been candle-lit and the convex mirrors would have glittered brightly like stars. Regrettably, much of the decoration was allowed to deteriorate during the 1970s and 1980s, but restoration

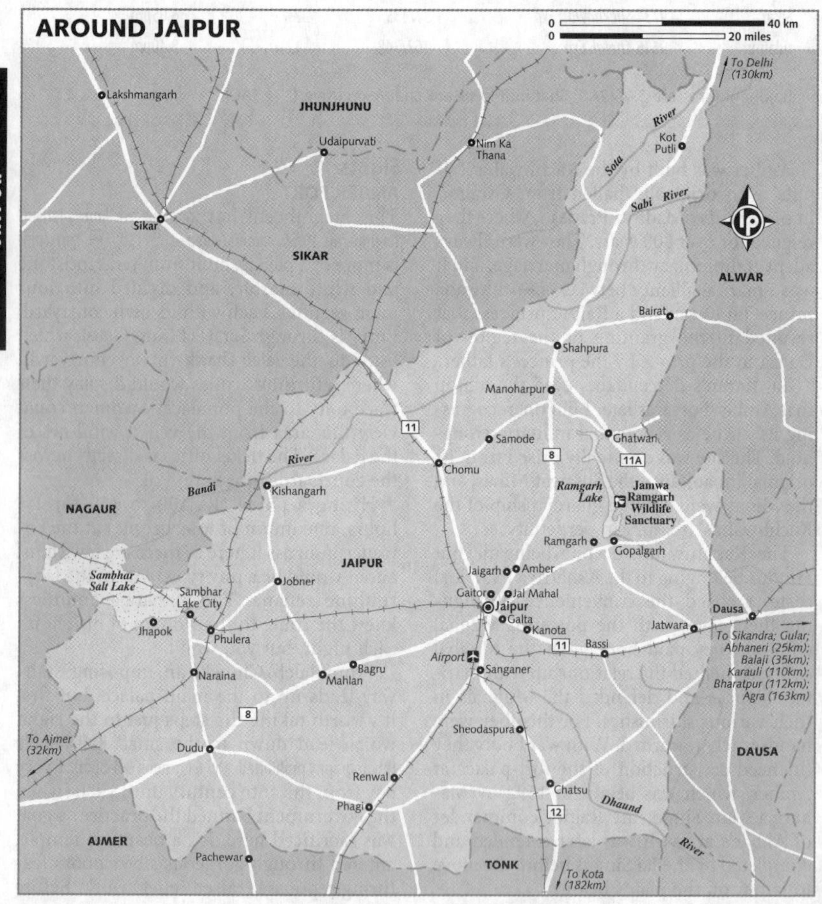

**THE AMBER ELEPHANTS**

If an elephant has its own way, it will live in a hot, wet place, preferably close to a nice deep pool for bathing. Unfortunately, Rajasthan doesn't come up with the goods – it's a long way from the tropics and the elephants that trundle tourists up and down the steep cobbled road to Amber Fort suffer greatly from the hot, dry days and freezing nights of their adopted desert state.

There are around 100 elephants working in rotation at Amber. Every day they have to walk to the fort from their compound, the Mahavaton-ka-Mohalla in Jaipur's old city – a distance of 11km each way. During the hot season temperatures at Amber can reach 45°C, and the elephants suffer from sunburn and cracked feet from walking on the hot bitumen roads. Elephants need to drink around 250L of water a day, most of which they drink while bathing. The Amber elephants used to do this at the lake below the palace – until the water level dropped. They also suffer from foot rot, abscesses and blindness caused by vitamin deficiencies.

Many of the mahouts (elephant keepers) are deeply concerned about the health and welfare of their elephants, but unfortunately some resort to metal goads, which sometimes draw blood, to keep their elephants in line. Often this is linked to the poor conditions of the mahouts themselves – low wages mean that there's a high turnover of new recruits, and the important relationship between elephant and mahout never has a chance to develop.

If you're concerned about the elephants working the tourist trade at Amber, you can write a letter of support to Help in Suffering (see the boxed text, p183). This organisation is lobbying the government to speed up its plans to build an elephant compound with bathing facilities close to Amber Fort, and to address the need for enforceable regulations to protect the animals, as well as better training and pay for the mahouts.

of varying quality proceeds. Carved marble relief panels around the hall are fascinatingly delicate and quirky, depicting cartoonlike insects and sinuous flowers.

Opposite the Jai Mandir is the **Sukh Niwas** (Hall of Pleasure), with an ivory-inlaid sandalwood door and a channel running through the room. It once carried water and acted as an ingenious air-cooling system. Not a single drop of water was wasted, with the overflow passing through conduits to the gardens. From the Jai Mandir you can enjoy fine views from the palace ramparts over picturesque **Maota Lake** below. The lake, at the foot of the hillside, reflects the fort's terraces and ramparts, but it dries up in the winter months. Around July and August, when the lake is full, boats can be hired for around Rs 40 per person for 15 minutes.

The **zenana** are around the fourth courtyard. The rooms were cleverly designed so that the maharaja could embark on his nocturnal visits to his wives' and concubines' respective chambers without the others knowing, as the chambers are independent but open onto a common corridor.

At Amber Fort there's also an **RTDC restaurant** (veg/nonveg thalis Rs 60/90), off the Jaleb Chowk, which has a pleasant garden and a Rajasthali government emporium.

You can climb up to the fort from the road in about 10 minutes (cold drinks are available at the top). A seat in a jeep up to the fort costs Rs 120 return. Riding up on elephants is popular at Rs 450 return (price per elephant; each can carry up to four people). If you don't want to pay this much, you can have a ride around the courtyard for Rs 100. Help in Suffering (see the boxed text, p183) is lobbying the government to speed up plans to build better facilities for these elephants.

## Getting There & Away

There are frequent buses to Amber from near the Hawa Mahal in Jaipur (Rs 8, 25 minutes). An autorickshaw will cost Rs 100 to 150 for the return trip. RTDC city tours (see p167) include Amber Fort.

A good option is to hire a taxi from the stand near Jaipur train station – a round trip covering Amber Fort, Jaigarh and Nahagarh will cost around Rs 450, including waiting time (maximum five people). Try to arrive at Nahagarh in time for a sunset beer overlooking the city.

# JAIGARH

This scrubby green hill – Cheel ka Teela (Mound of Eagles) – tumbles down above

Amber, topped by imposing **Jaigarh** (Indian/foreigner Rs 15/20, camera/video Rs 20/100, admission free with City Palace ticket, car Rs 50; 9am-5pm). This massive fort was planned by Jai Singh I, but what you see today dates from the reign of Jai Singh II. It was only opened to the public in mid-1983 and thus has remained very much intact. Punctuated by whimsically hatted lookout towers, the fort was never captured and is a splendid example of grand 18th-century defences, without the palatial frills that are found in many other Rajput forts. It has water reservoirs, residential areas, a puppet theatre and the world's largest wheeled cannon, Jaya Vana.

During the Mughal empire Jaipur produced many weapons for the Mughal and Rajput rulers. This most spectacular example was made in the fort foundry, which was constructed in Mughal times. The huge cannon dates from 1720, has a barrel around 6m long, is made from a mix of eight different metals and weighs 50 tonnes. To fire it requires 100kg of gunpowder, and it has a range of 30km. It's debatable how many times this great device was used.

Sophisticated rainwater harvesting systems are in place at this fort. Complicated drainage channels, which fed three large tanks, are scattered throughout the fort. The largest has a capacity for 22.8 million litres of water. The fort served as the treasury of the Kachhwahas, and for a long time people were convinced that at least part of the royal treasure was still secreted in this large water tank. The Indian government even searched it to check, but found nothing. These tanks used to provide water for all the soldiers, residents and livestock that lived in the fort.

Within the fort is an **armoury** and **museum**, with the essential deadly weapons collection and some royal knick-knacks, including some interesting photographs, maps of Jaigarh, spittoons and circular 18th-century playing cards. The structure also contains various open halls, including the **Shubhat Niwas** (Meeting Hall of Warriors), which has some weather-beaten sedan chairs and drums lying about.

It's an uphill walk (about 1km) from Amber and offers great views from the Diwa Burj watchtower.

Admission is free if you have a ticket to Jaipur's City Palace that is less than two days' old. Vehicles can drive up to the fort.

## SANGANER & BAGRU

The large village of Sanganer is 16km south of Jaipur, and has a **ruined palace**, a group of **Jain temples** with fine carvings (to which entry is restricted) and two ruined **tripolias** (triple gateways). The main reason to visit, however, is to see its handmade paper and block-printing shops, workshops and factories (most shops can be found on or just off the main drag, Stadium Rd), where you can see the products being made by hand.

Best of all in Sanganer is to walk down to the riverbank to see the brightly coloured fabrics drying in the sun. The block printers of Sanganer are famous for small floral prints, and the prints produced here were traditionally used by the royal court. Traditional papermakers were also brought to the court at Amber in the 16th century, but moved to Sanganer in the late 18th century due to water shortages. Later Gandhi's support helped to develop the industry.

**Salim's Paper** (☎ 2730222; www.handmadepaper.com; Gramodyog Rd; 9am-5pm) is the largest handmade paper factory in India and claims to be one of the biggest in the world. It's well set up for visitors: you can take a free tour to see the paper production process – the paper is not made from trees, but from scrap pieces of fabric, and often decorated with petals or glitter. You'll recognise lots of styles and designs, as they are exported all over the world. The 300 employees produce 25,000 sheets a day. There's also a beautiful range of tree-free paper products for sale in the showroom – great (and light) gifts for friends back home.

Another huge handmade paper manufacturer is **AL Paper House** (☎ 2731706; www.alpaperhouse.com; 9am-5pm), near the tempo stand. The factory is open to visitors.

For block-printed fabrics and blue pottery, there are a number of shops, including **Sakshi** (☎ 2731862; Laxmi Colony; shop 8.30am-8.30pm, factory 9am-6pm). You can see the block-printing workshop here, and try your hand at block printing yourself. It also runs courses in block printing and blue pottery (see p166). There's a tremendous range of blue pottery and block-printed fabrics for sale.

About 20km west of Sanganer is the little village of **Bagru**, also known for its block printing, particularly of colourful designs featuring circular motifs. You won't see as much here as in Sanganer, but it's more off

**HELP IN SUFFERING**

Around 10km south of Jaipur, off the road to Sanganer, **Help in Suffering** (HIS; ☎ 2760803; Maharani Farm, Durgapura; 9am-5pm) is an animal shelter that was founded in 1980 by Crystal Rogers, an English woman who was appalled by the conditions of Jaipur's street creatures. Today this vibrant organisation runs a rabies- and population-control programme for Jaipur's dogs, operates mobile clinics to rural areas, treats the elephants working at Amber and rescues animals in trouble. It's possible to visit the shelter, where delightfully happy dogs wander the grounds, and birds and animals of all descriptions convalesce in the excellent facilities here.

If you find an animal that is in need of some help, you can call HIS. Qualified vets can also volunteer here – see p376 for further details.

Donations to Help in Suffering will be put to good use – contact the **UK office** (member@dharney.freeserve.co.uk; 49 Baring Rd, Beaconsfield, Bucks HP9 2NF), the **Australian office** (Richard & Brenda Glasgow; rnbglasgow@aapt.net.au; PO Box 210, Nana Glen, NSW 2450) or **Animaux-Secours** (info@animaux-secours.com; Refuge de l'Espoir, 74380 Arthaz) in France.

the beaten track. The fabric is dyed with natural colours here and the printers' quarter – full of small family businesses – is a hive of activity.

### Getting There & Away

Buses leave from the Ajmer Gate in Jaipur for Sanganer every few minutes (Rs 10, one hour). To Bagru, there are daily buses from Sanganer (Rs 20, 1½ hours).

## SAMODE

☎ 01423

The small village of Samode is spectacularly set among rugged hills, about 50km north of Jaipur. The only real reason to visit is if you can stay at the **Samode Palace** (admission Rs 100). If you want to be precise, it's not a palace, as it was owned by a nobleman rather than a ruler, but it's certainly palatial enough to get away with the title. Like the Samode Haveli in Jaipur, this building was owned by the *rawal* of Samode, and today it's also run by his descendants.

Mainly dating from the 19th century, it's a fantastical building nestling between the Aravalli hills and built on three levels, each with its own courtyard. The highlight is the exquisite Diwan-i-Khas, which is covered with original paintings and mirrorwork.

Above the palace is the overgrown Samode Fort – ask around and you'll find someone to let you in – where there are great views from the ramparts. This is also good walking country, with paths heading off into the countryside. Beneath the palace is a small village, where locals sell block-printed cloth and glass bangles.

### Sleeping & Eating

**Samode Palace** (☎ /fax 240014/23; www.samode.com; s/d May-Sep €71/91, ste from €130, s/d Oct-Apr €141/177, ste from €212; ) Largely extended in the 19th century, this magnificent place is a gloriously grand hotel decorated in no-holds-barred Rajput splendour, with a great courtyard swimming pool. Suites are particularly atmospheric. The palace admission fee for nonguests is deducted if you have a meal here. You can book through Samode Haveli (p171) in Jaipur. Check the website for special offers.

**Samode Bagh** (☎ 40235; www.samode.com; deluxe s/d May-Sep €70/75, Oct-Apr €83/89; ) Also part of the Samode group, this luxurious tented accommodation (featuring private modern bathrooms complete with sit-down flush toilets and hot water) is a real retreat. It's wonderfully peaceful, set in 8 hectares of land, amid formal gardens and near a 150-year-old pavilion. Samode Bagh is 4km from Samode Palace. You can book through Samode Haveli in Jaipur.

### Getting There & Away

There are a few direct buses to Samode from the main bus station in Jaipur (Rs 35, 1½ hours), or you can hire a taxi for around Rs 800 return.

## RAMGARH

☎ 01426

This green oasis, about 35km northeast of Jaipur, has a pretty, though much shrunken lake, the **Jamwa Ramgarh Wildlife Sanctuary**. In 1982, when the lake was much fuller, some water sports fixtures of the Asian Games

JAIPUR

took place here. The area around here has been scarred by mines – all are now closed as the area is protected. Panthers, hyenas, antelopes and wild boars once roamed the area, as the trophy-laden walls of Ramgarh Lodge testify, but loss of habitat, lack of water and hunting have, understandably, driven the wildlife to more welcoming areas. The scenery, with lush palms, huge banyans, remote villages, and small temples set into craggy rock, make it worth a visit to explore and walk in the area. There's a picturesque **polo ground** (in Jaipur for fixtures ☎ 0141-2374791) and the **Jamwa Maa Di Mandir**, an ancient Durga temple.

**Ramgarh Lodge** (☎ 2552217; www.tajhotels.com; d with breakfast & dinner Rs 3700-4700, ste Rs 6700; ), a one-time royal hunting lodge overlooking Ramgarh Lake, is spectacular, but it's one of those places with zillions of busy staff and immensely slow, offhand service, even when there are only a couple of guests. Inside the lodge are masses of glass-eyed stuffed beasts, saddest of which is a bear holding a tray. Billiards, squash and tennis are available, as well as boating when the lake's water level is high enough. The pool (check it's full) has a great setting, and the most expensive rooms have fabulous views. Jeep safaris to the park cost Rs 1000 per jeep for one hour (maximum six people).

**RTDC Jheel Tourist Village** (☎ 52170; s/d Rs 300/400), further away from the lake, is very peaceful and offers accommodation in small round huts, which are a bit run-down with peeling paint, but fine. The gardens are well kept with colonially trim lawns, and the views across to the remains of the lake are lovely. An extra bed costs Rs 100. There's a small dining area with veg thalis for Rs 55. Boating on Ramgarh Lake can be arranged when the water is high enough (Rs 125 per person per hour). It can also arrange jeep and camel safaris through the park.

Buses travel between Jaipur (from the main bus station) and Ramgarh (Rs 13, one hour).

## ABHANERI

About 95km from Jaipur on Agra Rd, this remote village surrounded by rolling wheat fields is the unlikely location for one of Rajasthan's most awe-inspiring step-wells, the **Chand Baori** (admission free; sunrise-sunset).

With around 11 visible levels of zigzagging steps, this 10th-century water tank is an incredible, geometric sight, 20m deep. Flanking the *baori* is a small, crumbling **palace**, where the royals used to picnic and bathe in private rooms (water was brought up by oxen) – it's now inhabited by pigeons and bats. Next door is the **Harshat Mata Temple**, also dating from the 10th century, which was damaged by Muslim invaders, but retains some beautiful deep relief sculptures in warm orange sandstone. Both are thought to have been built by King Chand, ruler of Abhaneri and a Rajput from the Chahamana dynasty.

From Jaipur, catch a bus to Sikandra (1½ hours), from where you can hire a jeep for the 10km trip to Abhaneri (Rs 250 return, including a 30-minute stop). Alternatively, take a bus to Gular, from where it's a 5km walk to Abhaneri. If you have your own transport, this is a worthwhile stop between Jaipur and Bharatpur or Agra.

## BALAJI

The extraordinary Hindu **exorcism temple** of Balaji, about 102km from Jaipur, is about 3km off the Jaipur to Agra road. People bring their loved ones who are suffering from possession here to have bad spirits exorcised through prayer and rituals. Most exorcisms take place on Tuesday and Saturday. At these times the street outside feels like it's hosting a Hindu rave, and the only people who can get inside the temple are the holy men and the victims – services are relayed to the crowds outside on crackly video screens. The possessed scream, shout, dance and shake their heads. It's an extraordinary experience.

If you wait until the service has finished, you will be able to look inside the temple. You may want to cover your head with a scarf as a mark of respect. No photography is permitted inside. The often-disturbing scenes at this temple may upset some. Believers say you shouldn't take items you buy from around the temple with you – they could bring you bad luck. The number of stands lining the way to the temple indicates that not everyone heeds these solemn warnings.

From the main bus station in Jaipur there are numerous buses to Balaji (local/express Rs 32/50, 2½/two hours).

## SAMBHAR SALT LAKE

The country's largest salt lake, around 60km west of Jaipur, Sambhar Salt Lake's vast 230-sq-km wetland expanse once attracted flamingos, cranes, pelicans and many other waterfowl. According to myth, Sambhar is believed to have been given to local people by the goddess Shakambari some 2500 years ago. Her shrine, **Mata Pahari**, juts into the lake west of Jhapok. The people are certainly making good use of it – around 80 sq km of the lake is used for salt farming. On the eastern end, the lake is divided by a 5km-long stone dam. East of the dam are salt-evaporation ponds where salt has been farmed for the past 1000 years.

Also east of the dam is a railway line, built by the British (before Independence) that provides access from Sambhar Lake City to the saltworks. Water from the vast western section is pumped through gates to the other side when it is saline enough for salt extraction.

Sambhar was designated as a Ramsar site (recognised wetland of international importance) in 1990, because the wetland is a key wintering area for birds that migrate from northern Asia, some from as far as Siberia. Its privileged status, however, has not done it much good in recent years.

Usually the water depth fluctuates from a few centimetres during the dry season to about 3m postmonsoon. The specialised algae and bacteria growing in the lake provide striking water colours and support the lake ecology that, in turn, sustains the migrating waterfowl. Poor monsoons, however, have affected this environment, and the lake has almost completely dried up in places. Check locally about the current situation before heading out here, unless you have a particular interest in salt.

The best way to reach Sambhar from Jaipur is via train to Phulera Junction (Rs 25 in 2nd class, one hour and 10 minutes, two daily), 9km from the lake. From the station you can hire a jeep or rickshaw.

# Eastern Rajasthan

Hilly, with jungle scrub, ravines and rich vegetation, eastern Rajasthan is split from the barren desertscapes of the west by the Aravalli Range, a bony, spiky, purple-shaded backbone – one of the world's oldest mountain systems. The Aravallis cover a vast area, running from around Alwar down to Mt Abu in southern Rajasthan, near the border with Gujarat.

In the east lie Rajasthan's finest nature reserves. World Heritage site Keoladeo's marshlands, crossed with narrow cycling tracks, see thousands of exotic birds descend every winter. South of Keoladeo are the tangled hills of Ranthambhore, a landscape fit for an epic, starring a cliff top, a jungle fort and lots of tigers. Sariska Tiger Reserve has more wonderful scenery and some amazing sights, such as the mysterious ghost city of Bhangarh. The ancient forts and palaces speak of the region's colourful past. Alwar is one of the state's oldest kingdoms, while the power of the Jats was concentrated around Bharatpur and Deeg. Exploring where these powers once held sway gives you the chance to find Rajasthan's little-visited corners, such as the Muslim stronghold of Tonk and the picturesque town of Karauli.

Here also are Rajasthan's most mesmerising pilgrimage sites, among them the Hindu sacred town of Pushkar. Legend has it that its holy lake appeared when Brahma dropped a lotus flower. Pastel-tinted Pushkar is also a magnet for travellers, who come to chill, drown in Hindu mysticism, and get head-to-toe in neo-Indian threads and silver jewellery. Nearby is the dargah of Khwaja Muin-ud-din Chishti, India's most important Muslim site.

## HIGHLIGHTS

- Myriad bird species in Unesco World Heritage–listed **Keoladeo Ghana National Park** (p191)
- The laid-back pastel-coloured pilgrimage town of **Pushkar** (p211), centred on its enchanting holy lake
- Mayhem, hubbub and camels with corn rows at the grand epic **Pushkar Camel Fair** (p212)
- Tiger-spotting in the temple-dotted wild jungle of **Ranthambhore National Park** (p218), overlooked by a clifftop fort
- India's most revered Muslim shrine – the **dargah** (p205) in Ajmer, tomb of an important Sufi
- Little-known sites – temples, forts and a ghost city – in and around **Sariska Tiger Reserve** (p201)

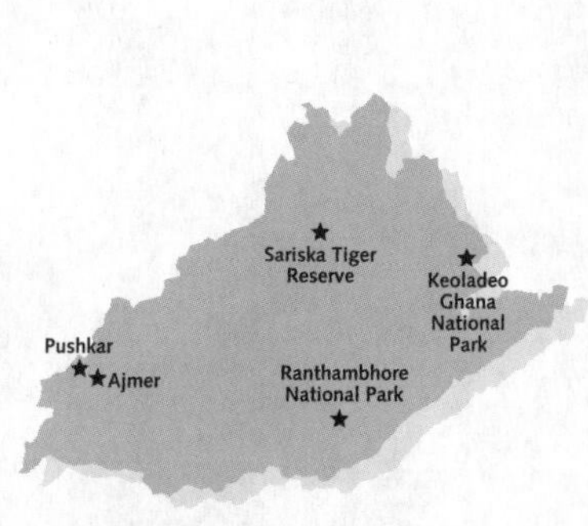

## History

Alwar is perhaps Rajasthan's most ancient kingdom, part of the Matsya kingdom since 1500 BC. It has been much coveted and fought over, due to its position on the strategic southwestern frontier of Delhi. The city of Alwar is believed to have been founded by a member of the Kachhwaha family from Amber, but control was wrested from the Kachhwahas by the Nikumbhas. They in turn lost the city to the Bada Gurjara Rajputs of Machari. It then passed to the Khanzadas, under Bahadura Nahara of Mewat, who converted from Hinduism to Islam to win the favour of Emperor Tughlaq of Delhi. At this time Alwar and Tijara were part of the kingdom of Mewat.

In 1427 descendants of Bahadura Nahara of Mewat bravely defended the fort at Alwar against the Muslims. Although the Mewati leader professed the Muslim faith, he chose to ally himself with the Rajputs as opposed to the Muslims in Delhi. The Mughals weren't at all happy about this and mounted military forays into the region, conquering it after great difficulty. Alwar was later granted to Sawai Jai Singh of Jaipur by Aurangzeb, but the emperor took back his generous gift when he visited the city and saw the strategic virtues of its forts.

The Jats of Bharatpur threw their hat in and briefly overran the region, installing themselves in the Alwar fort. They were evicted by the Lalawat Narukas (the descendants of Naru, the Kachhwaha prince of Amber) between 1775 and 1782 under the leadership of the Naruka *thakur* (nobleman) Pratap Singh. His descendants were great patrons of the arts, commissioning the transcription of numerous sacred and scholarly texts, and encouraging painters and artisans to visit the Alwar court.

In 1803 the British invested the Alwar *thakur* with the title of maharaja as thanks for support in a battle against the Marathas. This friendly alliance was short-lived, however, since the maharaja of Alwar strongly resented the British interference when a British Resident was installed in the city.

After Independence in 1947 Alwar was merged with the other princely states of Bharatpur, Karauli and Dholpur, forming

### FESTIVALS IN EASTERN RAJASTHAN

These festivals are marked on Map p188. For festivals celebrated statewide and nationwide, see p363.

**Brij Festival** (❶; 2-4 Feb; Bharatpur, p189) The Brij takes place over several days prior to Holi (so expect a bit of premature colour to be splashed around). It's known for the *rasalila* dance, which acts out the story of the love between Krishna and Radha, and is a good chance for everyone to get dressed up in colourful finery.

**Alwar Utsav** (❷; Feb-Mar; Alwar, p197) A tourist carnival showcasing cultural activities with a procession, traditional music and dance, a flower show and craft displays.

**Kaila Devi** (❸; Mar-Apr; Kaila, p223) One of eastern Rajasthan's bigger festivals, this huge event is held at the village of Kaila, 24km southwest of Karauli, in the month of Chaitra. The temple of Kaila Devi (also known as Lakshmi, the goddess of wealth) is 2km northwest of Kaila village, and thousands of pilgrims make their way here at this time of year bringing offerings. The devout will cover the distance to the temple wriggling prostrate along the ground, and the very devout won't eat or rest on the journey either. Masses of traders descend to make the most of the festival, selling crafts and souvenirs, and Mina tribespeople perform songs and dance.

**Shri Mahavirji Fair** (❹; Mar-Apr; Chandangaon, p218) This huge Jain fair is held in honour of Mahavir, the 24th and last of the Jain *tirthankars* (teachers), at the village of Chandangaon in Sawai Madhopur district. The Mahavirji temple contains an idol believed to have been dug out from a nearby hillside. Thousands of Jains congregate on the banks of the Gambhir River, to which an image of Mahavir is carried on a golden palanquin (litter) drawn by bullocks.

**The Urs** (❺; Aug; Ajmer, p204) This is the anniversary of Sufi saint Khwaja Muin-ud-din Chishti's death, and signals a huge Muslim pilgrimage to Ajmer.

**Ganesha Chaturthi** (❻; Aug-Sep; Ranthambhore, p218) Celebrated nationwide, Ganesh's birthday is particularly huge at Ranthambhore, which holds one of Rajasthan's most important Ganesh temples. Thousands of devotees make the pilgrimage here.

**Pushkar Camel Fair** (❼; Oct-Nov; Pushkar, p211) Eastern Rajasthan hosts one of India's greatest festivals: a surreal, huge gathering of tribespeople, camels, livestock, horses, tourists, camera crews and touts.

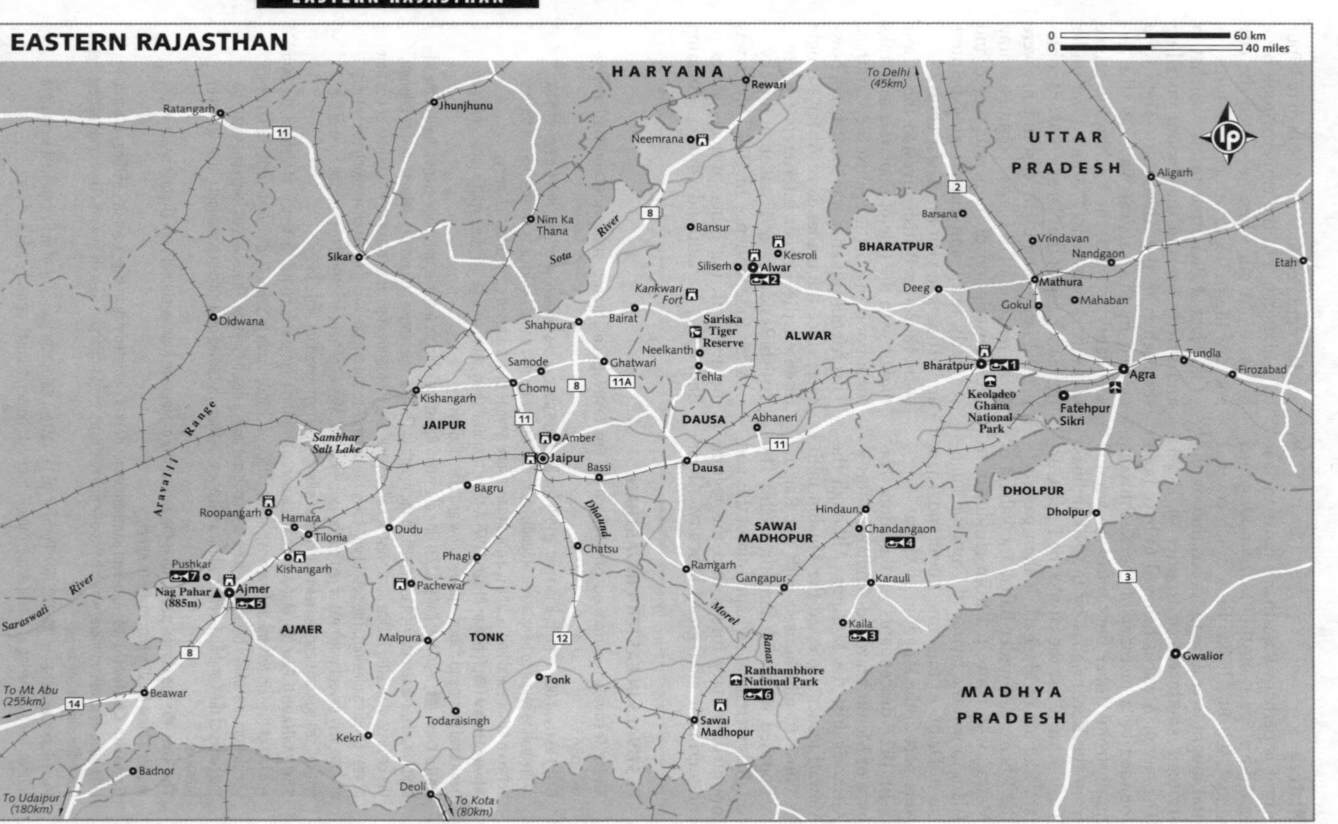
EASTERN RAJASTHAN
0 60 km
0 40 miles
HARYANA
UTTAR PRADESH
MADHYA PRADESH
BHARATPUR
ALWAR
DAUSA
JAIPUR
SAWAI MADHOPUR
DHOLPUR
AJMER
TONK
Rewari
To Delhi (45km)
Ratangarh
Jhunjhunu
Neemrana
Aligarh
Barsana
Nim Ka Thana
Sota River
Bansur
Vrindavan
Nandgaon
Etah
Sikar
Kesroli
Siliserh
Alwar
Mathura
Deeg
Mahaban
Gokul
Kankwari Fort
Bairat
Shahpura
Sariska Tiger Reserve
Didwana
Neelkanth
Tehla
Samode
Ghatwari
Chomu
Kishangarh
Bharatpur
Tundla
Firozabad
Agra
Fatehpur Sikri
Keoladeo Ghana National Park
Abhaneri
Aravalli Range
Sambhar Salt Lake
Amber
Jaipur
Bassi
Dausa
Bagru
Roopangarh
Hamara
Tilonia
Dudu
Dhaund
Chatsu
Hindaun
Chandangaon
Dholpur
Phagi
Pushkar
Kishangarh
Nag Pahar (885m)
Ajmer
Pachewar
Ramgarh
Gangapur
Karauli
Saraswati River
Morel
Kaila
Malpura
Banas
Gwalior
Tonk
Ranthambhore National Park
To Mt Abu (255km)
Beawar
Todaraisingh
Sawai Madhopur
Kekri
Badnor
Deoli
To Udaipur (180km)
To Kota (80km)
2
3
8
11
11A
12
14

the United State of Matsya, a name that reflected the fact that these states all comprised the ancient Matsya kingdom. In 1949 Matsya was merged with the state of Rajasthan.

Bharatpur is another ancient city, traditionally home of the Jats, who settled in this region before the emergence of the Rajputs. The relationship between the Jats, tillers of the soil, and the warrior Rajputs was, at best, uneasy. Marital alliances helped to reduce the friction, but they continually tussled over territory. The differences were only overcome when both groups turned to face the mutual threat posed by the Mughals.

It was Jat leader Suraj Mahl who built Deeg's beautiful palace and gardens, and commenced work on the Bharatpur fort, which was completed in the late 18th century after nearly 60 years of toil. This was time well spent, as the British unsuccessfully besieged the fort for around six months, finally conceding defeat after substantial losses. The rulers of Bharatpur were the first to enter into an agreement with the East India Company.

The huge fort at Ranthambhore, founded in the 10th century by the Chauhan Rajputs, predates that at Bharatpur by many centuries. It's believed to be one of Rajasthan's oldest. Ranthambhore was held in reverence by the Jains, and several temples here were very important spiritually. Over the centuries Ranthambhore was subjected to numerous assaults by the Muslims.

The Mughal Emperor Akbar negotiated a treaty with Surjana Hada, a Bundi ruler who bought the fort of Ranthambhore from Jhunjhar Khan, and the fort passed to Jagannatha, under whose leadership the Jain religion flourished. Aurangzeb took the fort, and it remained with the Mughals until the 18th century, when it was granted to the maharaja of Jaipur.

Ajmer was also founded by the Chauhans, three centuries earlier than Ranthambhore. In the late 12th century it was taken by Mohammed of Ghori, and remained a possession of the sultanate of Delhi until the 14th century. Another strategic jewel, it was fought over by various neighbouring states over subsequent centuries, but was mostly under Mughal rule. It was one of the few places in Rajasthan to be directly controlled by the British, from 1818.

# BHARATPUR

**☎ 05644 / pop 204,456**

Close to Bharatpur is the Unesco-listed Keoladeo Ghana National Park (see p191), an incredible bird sanctuary. Apart from the park, Bharatpur has a few historical vestiges, though it would not be worth making the journey for these alone. The town is dusty, noisy and not particularly visitor friendly.

The town feels more like Uttar Pradesh than Rajasthan. This is partly due to its position nestling near the border and to the dominance of the Jat people here.

## Orientation & Information

Keoladeo Ghana National Park lies 5km to the south of Bharatpur's centre. The fort is on an island in the centre of the old city, which was once surrounded by an 11km-long wall (now demolished). For tourist and other information, see p194.

## Sights

### LOHAGARH

Lohagarh, the early-18th-century Iron Fort, was aptly so named because of its sturdy defences. Today still impressive, though also forlorn and derelict, it occupies the entire small artificial island in the town centre. The main entrance is the **Austdhatu (Eight-Metal) Gate** – apparently the spikes on the gate are made of eight different metals.

Maharaja Suraj Mahl, constructor of the fort and founder of Bharatpur, built two towers, the Jawahar Burj and the Fateh Burj, within the ramparts to commemorate his victories over the Mughals and the British. The fort also contains three much-decayed palaces within its precincts.

One of them, centred on a tranquil courtyard, houses a seemingly forgotten **museum** (admission Rs 3, free Mon, camera/video Rs 10/20; 🕓 10am-4.30pm Sat-Thu). Downstairs is a Jain sculpture gallery that includes some beautiful 7th- to 10th-century sculpture, and most spectacularly, the palace's original *hammam* (bathhouse), which retains some fine carvings and frescoes. Upstairs, dusty cabinets contain royal toys, weapons – such as miniature cannons, some creepy animal trophies, and portraits and old photographs of the maharajas of Bharatpur. It's worth clambering up onto the roof for views across the city and other bird-inhabited palaces.

**Jawahar Burj**

This viewing point is a short walk to the northeast of the museum along a steep path that starts opposite the large water tank. It was from here that the maharajas surveyed their city and it still has fantastic views – great for watching a bit of daily life. It's a peaceful, evocative place capturing the cool breezes in a series of pavilions, the ceilings of which feature badly deteriorating frescoes with scenes of elephants and chariots.

**GANGA TEMPLE**

Not far from the Lohiya Gate is this exquisite red-sandstone two-storey temple dedicated to the goddess Ganga, with elaborately carved stone terraces. Construction started in 1845 during the rule of Maharaja Balwant Singh, but it was not finished until 1937, five generations later, during the reign of Maharaja Brijendra Sawai. Inside is a black-and-white chequered floor. There's a real sense of peace. However, you could shatter it if you go too close to the edges of the terrace on which the temple stands, overlooking the busy streets below – they're not stable.

On the laneway leading up to the temple, vendors sell mattress stuffing that's made of Punjabi wool.

## Sleeping

**Shagun Guest House** (Map p190; ☎ 232455; s/d with shared bathroom Rs 70/80) In the hectic, dusty town, this place is the only reasonable choice,

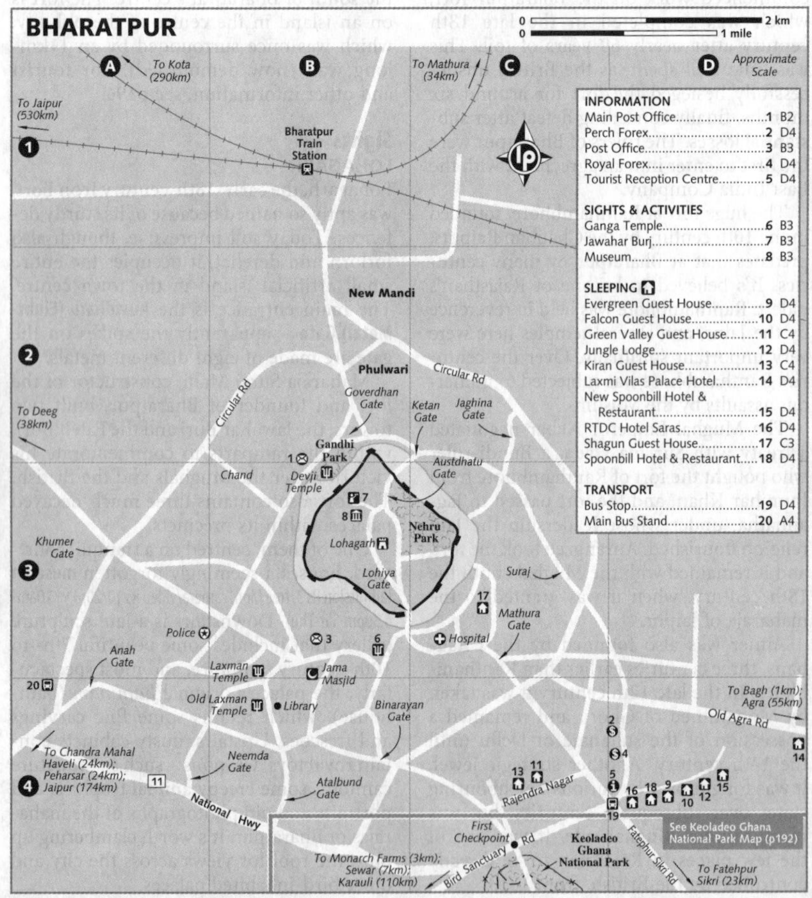

down a lane inside Mathura Gate. Rooms are basic, cell-like and dusty, but it's cheap and fronted by a little tree-shaded courtyard. The friendly owner is knowledgeable about the park and does village tours.

For additional accommodation options, see p194.

## Getting There & Away

### BUS

There are regular buses to various places, including Agra (Rs 31/48 in local/express, 1½ hours), Fatehpur Sikri in Uttar Pradesh (Rs 12, one hour), Jaipur (Rs 76, 4½ hours), Deeg (Rs 14, one hour) and Alwar (Rs 43, four hours). Buses leave from the bus station, but also drop off and pick up passengers at the bus stop at the crossroads by the tourist office.

### TRAIN

The *Janata Express* (Nos 9023/4) departs from Delhi (Rs 54/82 in 2nd class/sleeper) at 1.45pm and arrives in Bharatpur at 6.20pm. It leaves Bharatpur at 7.35am, arriving in the capital at 1.20pm. There are about six trains to Sawai Madhopur (Rs 54 in 2nd class, 182km), which go on to Kota and Mumbai. To Agra, there's a passenger train in the morning and afternoon.

## Getting Around

An auto- or cycle-rickshaw from the bus stand to the tourist office and most of the hotels should cost around Rs 15, and Rs 25 from the train station. An excellent way to zip around is by hiring a bicycle, which can be done at many of the hotels or at the park entrance – see p194 for further details.

# KEOLADEO GHANA NATIONAL PARK

This beautiful **sanctuary** (Indian/foreigner Rs 25/200, video Rs 200; 6am-6pm Apr-Sep, 6.30am-5pm Oct-Mar) ironically originated as a duck-shooting preserve made for Maharaja Suraj Mahl of Bharatpur in the 1850s. He converted a low-lying swamp formed by the confluence of the Gambhir and Banganga Rivers into a reservoir, the Ajun Bund. Flooding during subsequent monsoons soon inundated the surrounding region, creating a shallow wetland ecosystem, the perfect habitat for an astonishing variety of birds. It's named Keoladeo (one of Shiva's many incarnations) after the small temple in the park.

The maharaja was compelled not by conservationist motives but by the fine shooting (and dining) possibilities, and Keoladeo continued to supply the maharajas' tables until as late as 1965. A large tablet near the small temple in the park records that 12 November 1938 was a particularly bad day to be a duck – 4273 were shot, of which the then Viceroy of India, Lord Linlithgo, killed about 2000.

A fence was built around the forests of the wetlands in the latter part of the 19th century to stop feral cattle from roaming through. Between 1944 and 1964 afforestation policies were pursued by means of the planting of acacias.

The post-Independence period was one of great turmoil. Poor local communities were keen to divert the canals, which feed the swamplands, for irrigation and to convert the wetlands into crop lands. Although this tension still exists, the conservationists won the day, and in 1956 the region was made a sanctuary, although hunting was not prohibited until 1972. In 1982 Keoladeo was declared a national park and it was listed as a World Heritage site in 1985. Over one-third of the park is submerged during the annual monsoon.

Today Keoladeo is recognised as one of the world's most important bird-breeding and feeding grounds. It hosts a staggering 364 species within its 29 sq km. Here you can have the rare experience of spotting hundreds of different species within a few days. The marshland patchwork is a vital wintering area for aquatic birds, including visitors from Afghanistan, Turkmenistan, China and Siberia. However, a 1999 UN report found that Keoladeo's fragile ecosystem was being strained by increased tourism and pressure from surrounding villages. It predicted that some species would soon be extinct in the park, including the critically endangered Siberian crane (see p194).

In recent years, Keoladeo has suffered from poor monsoons, and less water has meant fewer birds. In 2004 the park tried to get water diverted from the nearby Panchana dam, in Karauli district, but came up against opposition from local villagers – farmers threatened suicide if the waters were released. It's hoped that a permanent backup source of water will be established, as drought is detrimental to this World

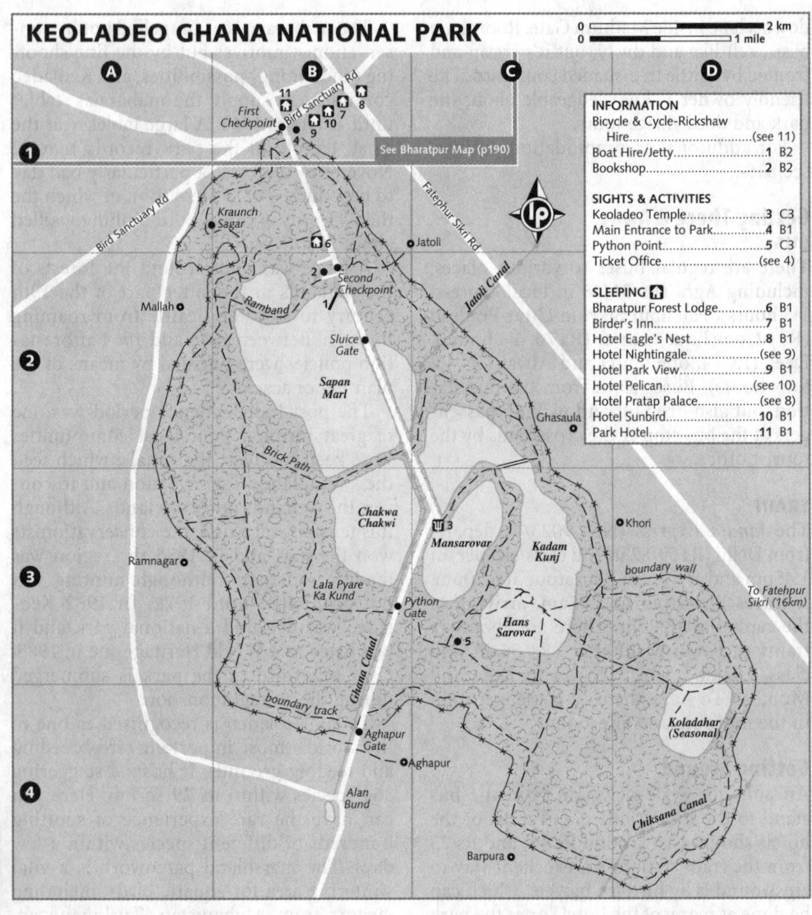


Heritage site. There are plans for a pipeline from the Chambal River, which could solve the problem, but this could take several years.

You can also do your bit to keep the birds happy by disposing of rubbish properly and keeping noise to a minimum.

## Visiting the Park

The best time for visits to this park is from October to February, when you'll see many migratory birds.

Admission entitles you to one entrance per day; if you want to spend the day inside, get your hotel to provide a packed lunch. Carry drinking water, as bird-watching is thirsty work.

One narrow road (no motorised vehicles are permitted) runs through the park, and countless embankments thread their way between the shallow wetlands. Walking or cycling along them affords unique opportunities to observe the rich birdlife at close quarters.

The southern reaches are a web of deserted tangled paths. There's rumoured to be a tigress roaming this area – her realm is even marked on the park map that comes with your ticket – but this is debatable, as no-one appears to have actually seen her.

There are a bookshop and a snack bar near the Keoladeo Temple. You can also get a bite to eat at the Bharatpur Forest Lodge (see p196) in the park.

### GUIDES & CYCLE-RICKSHAWS

Hiring an experienced ornithologist guide will cost around Rs 70 per hour for up to six people and Rs 120 per hour for more than six people. Guides can be hired at the park entrance. Many hotels are run by qualified guides or will arrange guides for you, who charge the same rate. All registered guides provide a good service, but you may find a guide who speaks better English by arranging one through your hotel. If you want a guide who speaks another European language, it's also best to enquire at your hotel.

In slow years, when there have been few travellers about and people's livelihoods have been threatened, the competition among rival Bharatpur guides has become deadly. In February 2002 one man was killed and several others seriously injured when a dispute broke out after tourists, who'd already had their guide arranged by a hotel, were shown around by another guide.

Government-authorised cycle-rickshaws (recognisable by the yellow plate bolted onto the front) only are allowed inside. You don't pay an admission fee for the drivers, but they charge Rs 50 per hour. Some are

### THE BIRDS OF KEOLADEO

During the monsoon period (July to August), and for a month or so following the monsoon, the park is home to vast colonies of birds that come here to breed and feed on the wetland's rich aquatic species.

Some of the species that nest at this time include storks, moorhens, herons, egrets and cormorants.

Keep your eyes peeled for storks spreading their wings to shield their chicks from the hot sun. There are several types: open-bill storks – whose gappy bills are thought to have evolved so that they can eat snails (these are the first migratory birds to arrive) – white-neck storks, black-neck storks and the familiar painted stork.

Three types of cormorants breed at Keoladeo, the biggest being the imaginatively named large cormorant.

The Indian darter is another familiar sight, also known as the snake bird because of the way it looks when swimming. This beautiful silver-streaked black bird spends a lot of time fishing in the water but has to keep coming back to dry land, as its feathers are not waterproof.

There are several types of egret, including the large egret, which is pure white and grows long plumage during the breeding season to attract a partner. The birds greet each other during this season by touching bills and necks.

Saras cranes are the largest birds in the park, and have a unique breeding ritual whereby the male and female hop in front of each other and make trumpeting calls. Numerous herons include the grey, purple and night heron.

You'll also see kingfishers, and the park attracts many birds of prey, including eagles, vultures and owls.

Around October the bird population increases enormously with the arrival of wintering migratory birds, which usually stay until around the end of February; these intervening months are the best time to visit. In October and November the park becomes full of ducks and geese. Pelicans arrive later, when the fish are bigger and make for a more substantial meal. The most famous winter visitor was once the rare Siberian crane (see p194).

The migratory birds have mostly left by the end of March. At the beginning of April, when the waters begin to recede, there is still a substantial population of birds of prey, some kingfishers and smaller birds, such as robins, wagtails and mynahs. Many of these birds feed at the few pools teeming with fish that remain in the park during the dry summer months. During the height of summer, when the waters have all but disappeared, the sanctuary is carpeted in dry grasslands that afford habitat to a variety of fauna, such as deer (spotted, sambar, bluebull), jackals, jungle cats, blackbucks, hares and mongoose.

Pythons are most commonly seen in the winter, when they have to come out from the underground for a sunbath.

The best times for bird-spotting are the early morning and evening.

very knowledgeable. However, these cycle-rickshaws can only travel along the park's larger tracks. A horse-drawn tonga costs Rs 100 per hour (maximum of six people).

**BICYCLES**

It's a good idea to take a rickshaw or guide on your first visit, then strike off on your own later. You get a scrappy but adequate map free with your ticket. An excellent way to see the park is hiring a bike (around Rs 30 per day), at either the park entrance or your hotel. At the entrance you must leave your passport or a Rs 1000 deposit. Having a bike is a wonderfully quiet way to travel, and allows you to avoid bottlenecks, which occur at the nesting sites of the larger birds. It's just about the only way you'll see the numerous kingfishers at close quarters – noise or human activity frightens them away.

The southern reaches of the park are virtually devoid of *humanus touristicus*, and so are better than the northern part for serious bird-watching.

## Orientation & Information

Keoladeo Ghana National Park is 3km south of Bharatpur's centre and easily accessed by cycle-rickshaw. A lot of places offer (slow) Internet access for around Rs 60 per hour.

**Bookshop** (Map p192; ⌚ 6am-6pm) At the second checkpoint, 1.5km from the main gate inside the park. This small place has a selection of titles on Indian animal and bird life, and also sells postcards.

**Main post office** (Map p190; ⌚ 10am-1pm & 2-5pm Mon-Sat) Near Gandhi Park.

**Perch Forex** (Map p190; ☎ 233477; B6 New Civil Lines; ⌚ 5am-11pm) Cash travellers cheques, get credit-card advances or change money here.

**Royal Forex** (Map p190; New Civil Lines; ⌚ 6am-10pm) An alternative to Perch Forex.

**Tourist Reception Centre** (Map p190; ☎ 222542; ⌚ 10am-5pm Mon-Sat, closed 2nd Sat of month) About 700m from the park entrance; has a map of Bharatpur (Rs 10).

## Sleeping & Eating

Don't be pressured by touts at Bharatpur train or bus stations. The following places are all within easy walking distance (within 1km) of the bird sanctuary. All offer binocular (around Rs 50 per day) and bike hire (around Rs 30 per day), and will arrange park guides. Prices fluctuate according to the season. There's greater choice among budget places (which tend to be the best value) than midrange, and there are just a couple of top-end options. All of the rooms listed in this chapter have private bathrooms, unless otherwise noted.

**BUDGET**

The cluster of guesthouses from the Spoonbill to the New Spoonbill are all run by different branches of the same family.

### SO LONG, SIBERIAN CRANES

Park authorities at Keoladeo were concerned when the endangered Siberian crane *(Grus leucogeranus)* failed to appear during two successive winter seasons in 1994 and 1995. In 1996, on the first day of winter, ornithologists around the world heaved a collective sigh of relief when four of these magnificent birds, white-bodied, pink-billed and pink-legged, flew into the park, nearly two months after their usual arrival. In 1998 only one pair came to the park, and this pair has returned each season until 2002. However, in 2003 and 2004 they were nowhere to be seen.

An estimated 100 of these now critically endangered birds have perished over the last 12 years during their 5000km-long journey from the Orb River basin in Siberia over inhospitable terrain. But it's not just the natural rigours of the long migration that are blamed for the critical depletion of Siberian crane numbers, but also hunting in Afghanistan and Pakistan and poisoning by pesticides.

Two other populations of Siberian cranes hail from the Orb River. The most substantial population, numbering almost 3000, winters at the Yangtze River in China, although their habitat is threatened by the Three Gorges dam project and agricultural development. A small population of about a dozen flies to winter grounds along the south coast of Iran's Caspian Sea. The tiny remaining population makes its annual winter journey to Iran and India, and it was part of this group that Keoladeo hosted. About 30 years ago more than 200 'Sibes', as they are known, would spend their winter here, and this sharp drop in numbers raises grave fears about their survival as a species.

Rajendra Nagar, which runs parallel to Bird Sanctuary Rd, just to the north, has some good budget options away from the noise of the main road.

**Jungle Lodge** (Map p190; ☎ 225622; Gori Shankar; r Rs 150-300) Clean, plain, comfortable rooms are set by a lovely jungly garden and open onto a shady veranda. The owner is a naturalist, and the family is warm and welcoming. Tasty home-cooked meals are available. Motorbike hire costs Rs 400 per day.

**Falcon Guest House** (Map p190; ☎ 223815; falconguesthouse@hotmail.com; r Rs 200-500; veg thali Rs 60) In the same area as the Spoonbill, the Falcon is a well-kept, snug place to stay, run by the friendly Mrs Rajni Singh. Her husband, Tej, is an ornithologist and he's happy to answer any bird-related questions when he comes home from work. There are comfortable, good-sized rooms, though more money gets you a softer mattress and private balcony. Flavoursome food is served here.

**Spoonbill Hotel & Restaurant** (Map p190; ☎ 223571; hotelspoonbill@rediffmail.com; dm Rs 50, r Rs 100-500; dishes Rs 30-50) This place is run by a businesslike retired major, and has good-value and clean, if shabby, accommodation; the best room is super-spacious and has a balcony. The cooking is excellent, with curd from the family cow and Rajasthani delicacies such as *churma* (sugar, cheese and dried fruit fried in butter), the royal dish of Rajasthan. There's a campfire in winter, and some mountain bikes are available.

**Evergreen Guest House** (Map p190; ☎ 225917; s/d Rs 100/150) This is a more basic, less outstanding option, but a good cheapie that satisfies customers, with a garden restaurant serving delicious home cooking.

**Green Valley Guest House** (Map p190; ☎ 229576; greenvalleybirdpark@yahoo.com.in; 376 Rajendra Nagar; r Rs 200-300) Recommended by travellers, this has a cosy, family atmosphere and only two rooms – one with a lovely green outlook and the other with its own sitting room. You eat on the rooftop. It's on a quiet road set back parallel to Bird Sanctuary Rd, a short walk from the park. Meals are available – the family makes its own milk, butter and curd.

**Kiran Guest House** (Map p190; ☎ 223845; 364 Rajendra Nagar; s with shared bathroom Rs 80, d with private bathroom Rs 150-300) Managed by eager-to-please brothers, this is homy, welcoming and great value, with its simple rooms and pleasant rooftop where you can eat tasty home cooking. It's on the same quiet road as Green Valley, not far from the park. Free pickup from the Bharatpur train station is on offer.

**Hotel Nightingale** (Map p192; ☎ 227022; d Rs 300) One of the closest hotels to the park, its basic rooms are plain, large and airy, but a touch overpriced. It's set in a eucalyptus grove, so you'll need mosquito repellent.

**Hotel Park View** (Map p192; ☎ 220802; d Rs 200-400) Readers have enjoyed staying at this place, close to the park, with its range of rooms from small and cell-like to spacious and decent – some with freshly tiled bathrooms. The small restaurant is surrounded by greenery.

### MIDRANGE & TOP END

**Birder's Inn** (Map p192; ☎ 227346; brdinn@yahoo.com; Bird Sanctuary Rd; s/d Rs 825/1045; ❄ 💻) Set back from the road, with a little garden at the front, its rooms are appealing, airy and spacious, nicely decorated and with good bathrooms.

**Hotel Sunbird** (Map p192; ☎ 225701; www.hotelsunbird.com; Bird Sanctuary Rd; s/d Rs 700/800, deluxe Rs 950/1050; ❄ 💻) A well-run, popular place further along Bird Sanctuary Rd, with a leafy seating area housing an appealing restaurant with a good range of dishes. Rooms are clean and attractive, similar to the Birder's Inn, but less spacious.

**New Spoonbill Hotel & Restaurant** (Map p190; ☎ 223571; hotelspoonbill@rediffmail.com; r Rs 400-500) Run by the major's son, this recently built place has smart but simple rooms, each with a small terrace. The bigger rooms are great, with lots of windows. The dining room looks onto the garden.

**Monarch Farms** (Off Map p190; ☎ 9414215139; divayog30@yahoo.com.in; Rampura; r Rs 400) This is an unusual opportunity to stay as a guest in a family house, 3km from Bharatpur. The charming upper middle–class family speaks excellent English and dwells inside a huge bungalow surrounded by large grounds, in which it runs a separate restaurant, Cardoman Court.

**Hotel Eagle's Nest** (Map p192; ☎ 225144; Bird Sanctuary Rd; s/d Rs 650/800, with AC Rs 800/1000; ❄ 💻) This smart option, run by a naturalist, has comfortable if unexciting rooms.

**Hotel Pelican** (Map p192; ☎/fax 224221; Bird Sanctuary Rd; s/d from Rs 250/300) This hotel is attractively surrounded by vegetation, but this also suggests potential mozzie hell. Rooms are OK and clean, opening onto a frontside walkway. If you pay around Rs 100 more, you get a better, bigger room. Staff have a somewhat lackadaisical approach.

**Hotel Pratap Palace** (Map p192; ☎ 225093; www.hotelpratappalace.net; Bird Sanctuary Rd; s/d Rs 100/150, ordinary Rs 300/400, deluxe Rs 700/850, with AC Rs 1100/1250; ) This outwardly grand-seeming hotel, built in traditional style, offers spacious but poorly maintained and very faded rooms. There are basic rooms, more accommodating, larger 'ordinary' rooms and better 'deluxe' options. The standard at all levels is variable, so look at a few.

**Bharatpur Forest Lodge** (Map p190; ☎ 222760; s/d Rs 2500/2799) This lodge, run by the Indian Tourism Development Corporation (ITDC), is 1km inside the park and 8km from the Bharatpur train station. It's looking a little faded, and service is typically lax. However, the comfortable, quiet rooms have balconies with swing seats and are surrounded by greenery. The restaurant's handy if you want something to eat while within the park (nonguests are welcome).

**Park Hotel** (Map p190; ☎ 233192; thepark@yahoo.com; d from Rs 750) This is a reasonable midrange option, a kind of low-rent business hotel, popular with Indian tourists. Clean and modern, it offers spacious motel-style rooms that overlook the surrounding well-cut lawns.

**RTDC Hotel Saras** (Map p190; ☎ 223700; cnr Fatehpur Sikri & Bird Sanctuary Rds; dm Rs 50, s/d from Rs 350/450, with AC from Rs 600/700; ) Offers a dusty dorm and shabby rooms, centrally placed at the crossroads just by the tourist office and the bus stop.

**Bagh** (Off Map p190; ☎ 225415; Agra-Achmera Rd; www.thebagh.com; s/d Rs US$80/100; ) A beautiful new hotel, in the former royal orchard 2km from town, this has 14 elegant rooms spread out in separate buildings around the orchard, with antique furnishings but a contemporary, designer feel. The 4-hectare garden is 200 years old and has masses of birds if you're feeling too lazy to go to the park.

**Laxmi Vilas Palace Hotel** (Map p190; ☎ 223523; www.laxmivilas.com; Kakaji-ki-Kothi, Agra-Achmera Rd; s/d/ste Rs 2450/2650/3500; ) This is a heritage hotel on Old Agra Rd, about equidistant between the national park and the town centre, owned by the younger son of Maharaja Jaswant Singh. Arched ceilings and heavy old furniture make for atmospheric rooms, set around a courtyard.

**Chandra Mahal Haveli** (☎ 05643-243238; Peharsar; s/d Rs 1650/2050, ste Rs 2100/2400; ) Good if you are travelling by car, this is an old converted Muslim *haveli* (traditional, ornately decorated residence), in Peharsar village, 23km from Bharatpur, about 1.5km off the Jaipur–Agra Hwy. The grand building, dating from 1850, has charming, simple rooms set around an inner courtyard. Ask for a room with a balcony – some have views over the surrounding countryside. It's very peaceful, and you can visit carpet weavers in the surrounding village.

### Getting There & Around

For travel details, see p191.

## DHOLPUR

Situated almost midway between Agra (in Uttar Pradesh) and Gwalior (in Madhya Pradesh), on an eastward thrusting spur of Rajasthan, is Dholpur. By virtue of its location close to the route from Delhi to Deccan, and to Agra, Dholpur has had a turbulent history and has been plundered and destroyed repeatedly. It was near here that Aurangzeb's sons fought a pitched battle to determine who would succeed him as the emperor of the rapidly declining Mughal empire. Today there are few sights to detain the visitor – the ancient Shergarh fort is now in ruins. There's a palace in the centre of the town, but this is closed to visitors – it's still occasionally inhabited by the royal family (influential folk – Vasundhara Raje, the chief minister of Rajasthan, is married to the maharaja of Dholpur). Worth a look is **Muchkund**, a tank (reservoir) 8km from the town, situated by an impressive red-sandstone temple.

The town has a reputation for its sandstone, used in many forts and palaces across Rajasthan.

There are regular train and bus connections from Agra to Dholpur, as well as from Dausa and Gwalior.

## DEEG

**☎ 0564 / pop 40,826**

Deeg is a small, rarely visited, dusty tumult of a town. At its centre stands an incongruously glorious palace edged by stately formal gardens, famous for their coloured-water fountains (switched on for festivals). Nearby are mighty fortifications. It's about 36km north of Bharatpur, and is an easy day trip (there's nowhere good to stay) from Bharatpur, or from Agra or Mathura, both in the adjacent state of Uttar Pradesh.

Built by Suraj Mahl in the mid-18th century, Deeg was formerly the second capital of Bharatpur state and was the site of a famous battle in which the maharaja's forces withstood a combined Mughal and Maratha army of 80,000 men. Eight years later the maharaja even had the temerity to attack the Red Fort in Delhi, carrying off masses of booty, including an entire marble building, which can still be seen in the palace grounds.

## Sights

### SURAJ MAHL'S PALACE

One of India's most beautiful and carefully proportioned buildings, the **palace** (Gopal Bhavan; admission Rs 200, photography prohibited; ⌚ 10am-5pm) is splendidly preserved. It was used by the maharajas until the early 1970s, and rooms contain their original furnishings, including faded, spilling sofas, huge swing fans, chaises longues, plenty of antiques, a stuffed tiger, elephant-foot stands, and fine porcelain from China and France. In an upstairs room at the rear of the palace is an Indian-style marble dining table – a long, horseshoe-shaped affair raised just 20cm off the ground. Guests sat around the edge, and the centre was the serving area. In the maharaja's bedroom is an enormous, 3.6m by 2.4m bed, made from a single piece of black granite. It's said that the king brought this back as war booty and used it as a bed, but its original purpose was to wash bodies as part of the Parsi death rites.

Built in a mixture of Rajput and Mughal architectural styles, the 18th-century, mostly two-storey palace is three and four storeys high in places. The eastern façade is fronted by imposing arches to take full advantage of the early-morning light. On either side of the palace are two exquisite pavilions. In the northern pavilion is a throne of black marble, while that in the southern pavilion is of white marble.

Two large tanks lie alongside the palace, **Gopal Sagar** to the east and **Rup Sagar** over to the west. The well-maintained gardens and flowerbeds, watered by the tanks, continue the extravagant theme, with monsoon pavilions creating sounds mimicking thunder when it rains – metal balls run around a channel surrounding the building. The **Keshav Bhavan** (Summer Pavilion) is a single-storey edifice with five arches along each side. An arcade runs around the interior of the pavilion over a type of canal with hundreds of fountains, many of which are still functional. They are turned on for local festivals, when paint is used to colour the water. The fountains are worked by hand, and powered by water pressure when plugs are pulled from a rooftop reservoir. Deeg's massive walls (which are up to 28m high) and 12 vast bastions, some with their cannons still in place, are also worth exploring. You can walk up to the top of the walls from the palace.

Along the northern side of the palace grounds is the **Nand Bhawan**, an oblong hall enclosed by a grand arcade.

### LAXMI MANDIR

This ancient **temple** is presided over by a *mataji* (a female priest). There are alcoves on three sides enshrining images of Durga, Hanuman and Gada, and a small shrine to Shiva to one side. The temple is on Batchu Rd, 20 minutes' walk from the palace.

## Sleeping

Few travellers stay in Deeg, and there's only one option available.

**RTDC Midway Deeg** (☎ 2321203; camping per person Rs 100, s/d Rs 300/400; ✖) Near the bus stand, this place and its three scrubby rooms are OK if you must stay. Meals are available; a veg thali costs Rs 55.

## Getting There & Away

The roads to Deeg are rough and the buses crowded. Frequent buses run to and from Alwar (Rs 27, 2½ hours) and Bharatpur (Rs 14, one hour, half-hourly). One direct bus travels to Agra (Rs 50) and one express bus goes to Mathura (Rs 20, 1½ hours).

# ALWAR

☎ 0144 / pop 260,245

Sprawling, dusty Alwar has a fine palace and a museum packed with royal booty, testifying to its former importance as capital of a Rajput state. Alwar is perhaps the oldest of the Rajasthani kingdoms, in 1500

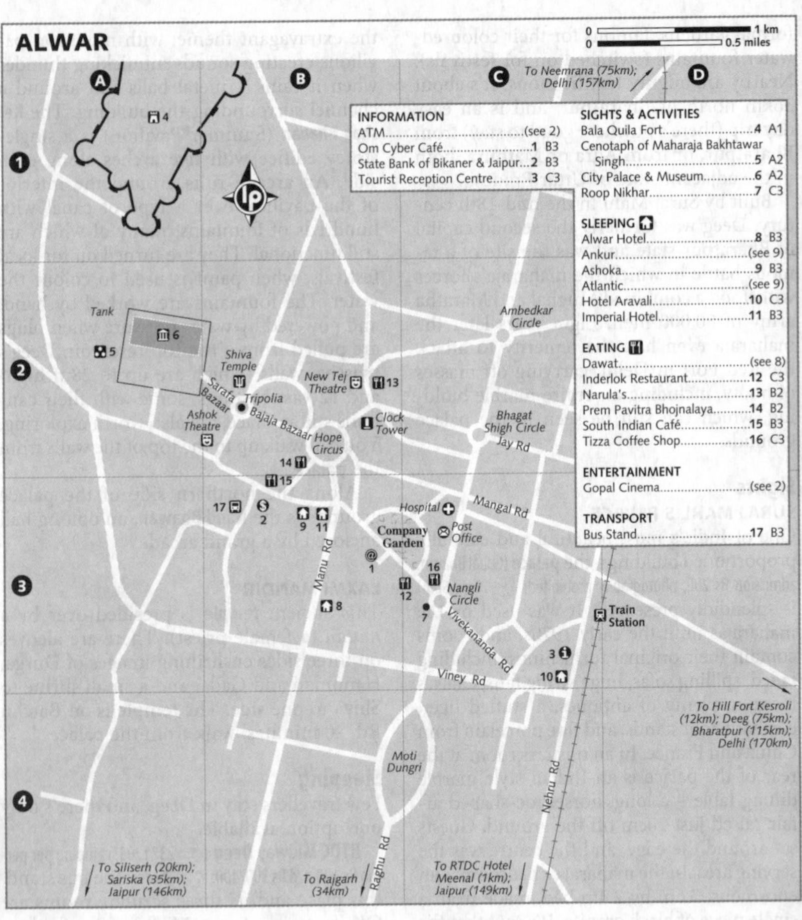


BC forming part of the Matsya territories of Viratnagar. It emerged again in the 18th century under Pratap Singh, who pushed back the rulers of Jaipur to the south and the Jats of Bharatpur to the east, and who successfully resisted the Marathas. It was one of the first Rajput states to ally itself with the fledgling British empire, although British interference in Alwar's internal affairs meant that this partnership was not always amicable.

Not many tourists come here, so there's a refreshing lack of hustle, and there are some colourful bazaars as well as the fine palace. It's the nearest town to Sariska Tiger Reserve, where a grand hunting lodge is another relic of Alwar's royal past.

## Orientation

The city palace and museum are found in the northwest of the city, a steep 1km north of the bus stand. There's a collection of budget hotels a short distance to the east of the bus stand. The main post office is about midway between the bus stand and the train station; the latter is on the eastern edge of the town.

## Information

**Om Cyber Café** (18 Ram Kuteer, Company Bagh Rd; 7am-10pm) One of several places that offer Internet access.

**State Bank of Bikaner & Jaipur** ( 10am-2pm Mon-Fri, 10am-noon Sat) Near the bus stand. Changes travellers cheques and major currencies.

EASTERN RAJASTHAN

**Tourist Reception Centre** (☎ 2347348; Nehru Rd; 🕒 10am-5pm Mon-Sat) Near the train station, not far from the Hotel Aravali. The helpful centre has maps of Alwar and booklets on different aspects of Rajasthani culture.

## Sights

### BALA QUILA

This imposing **fort**, with its 5km of ramparts, stands 300m above the city, its walls clinging to the steep incline. Predating the time of Pratap Singh, it's one of the few forts in Rajasthan built before the rise of the Mughals, who used it as a base for attacking Ranthambhore. Babur and Akbar have stayed overnight here, and Prince Salim (later Emperor Jehangir) was exiled in Salim Mahal for three years. Now in ruins, unfortunately, the fort houses a radio transmitter station and can only be visited with permission from the superintendent of police. However, this is easy to get: just ask at the superintendent's office in the City Palace complex. You can walk up to the fort entrance or take a rickshaw (it's a steep couple of kilometres from town).

### CITY PALACE COMPLEX

Below the fort sprawls the delicately coloured, complicated **City Palace complex**, its massive gates and tank lined by a beautifully symmetrical chain of ghats and pavilions. Today most of the maze is occupied by bustling, overflowing government offices, filled with piles of dusty papers and fluttering pigeons, and splattered with *paan* (a mixture of betel nut and leaves for chewing). You can peer through the offices at the once splendid rooms and marvel at their neglect, and there's an interesting government museum (below), housed in the former city palace. To gain access to the tank and the Cenotaph of Maharaja Bakhtawar Singh, take the steps on the far left when facing the palace. Just outside the palace you will come to clerks busily clacking away on typewriters for their lawyer bosses (who have outdoor 'offices' here). Spot the lawyers by their white shirts and black jackets.

#### Museum

Hidden away in the stunning City Palace is this excellent government **museum** (admission Rs 3, free Mon; 🕒 10am-5pm Sat-Thu). Its exhibits evoke the extravagance of the maharajas' lifestyle, with stunning weapons, royal ivory slippers, miniatures, royal vestments of amazing brocade, stuffed animals (including an enormous bear), Kashmiri lacquerwork and stone sculptures, such as an 11th-century sculpture of Vishnu. There are also some striking views across the complex from some of the windows. Somewhat difficult to find in the Kafkaesque tangle of government offices, it's on the top floor of the palace, up a ramp from the main courtyard. However, there are plenty of people around to point you in the right direction.

### CENOTAPH OF MAHARAJA BAKHTAWAR SINGH

This double-storey edifice, resting on a platform of sandstone, was built in 1815 by Maharaja Vinay Singh in memory of his father. The **cenotaph** is also known as the Chhatri of Moosi Rani, after one of the mistresses of Bakhtawar Singh who performed *sati* (self-immolation) on his funeral pyre – after this act she was promoted to wifely status. Everyday several women can be seen paying homage to the maharani by pouring holy water over raised sculpted footprints of the deceased royal couple. There is fine carving on the interior of the cenotaph (shoes should be removed), but unfortunately the paintings on the ceiling have almost disappeared. It's alongside a beautiful tank, which is lined by a row of temples that also act as houses for local families.

## Activities

### BEAUTY PARLOUR

For a touch of TLC, pop to pint-sized **Roop Nikhar** (☎ 2330868; Nangli Circle; 🕒 10am-8pm), an unsnazzy but reputable women-only beauty parlour offering facials and massages. Ask to see its price list to avoid getting talked into the most expensive option.

## Sleeping

As not many tourists stop here, Alwar's hotels are mostly aimed at budget business travellers, and are mediocre and not particularly good value. Finding a budget place is not a problem, but anything better is scarce. Contact the Tourist Reception Centre (opposite) for details about the houses involved in the Paying Guest House Scheme (Rs 400 to 1200).

There are some splendid choices outside town if you have your own transport.

### BUDGET

**Imperial Hotel** (☎ 2701730; 1 Manu Rd; s/d from Rs 180/250, deluxe Rs 400/750; ❄) This place is at the start of the laneway that leads to budget hotels Ankur, Ashoka and Atlantic, near the bus station. It has musty but large rooms that are pretty clean, and somewhat better deluxe options. Single women will feel awkward here.

Several hotels owned by brothers ring a central courtyard about 500m east of the bus stand, set back from Manu Rd. All have a range of rooms and prices, so it's worth looking at a few. **Ankur** (☎ 2333025; s/d from Rs 150/200; ❄) is friendly, and has passable rooms, though you'll need your own sheets. **Atlantic** (☎ 2343181; s/d from Rs 125/200) has plain, clean rooms, also requiring clean sheets. **Ashoka** (☎ 2346780; s/d from Rs 250/300) offers good rooms, some of which have been freshly painted. The cheaper rooms are less appealing; the priciest have groovy geometric murals and freshly tiled bathrooms.

Dormitory beds are available at the train station for Rs 50.

### MIDRANGE

**Alwar Hotel** (☎ 2700012; 26 Manu Rd; s/d from Rs 400/700, with AC Rs 800/1000) Set in leafy grounds, this hotel has spacious, recently renovated rooms. Staff are helpful. There's a good restaurant, and you can eat in the garden.

**RTDC Hotel Meenal** (☎ 2347352; s/d from Rs 400/500) About 1km south of town, this is a respectable midrange place with tidy rooms and leafy outlooks, though it's a long way from the action.

**Hotel Aravali** (☎ 2332883; www.hotelaravali.com; dm Rs 100, s/d from Rs 250/250, standard Rs 400/450; ❄ 🏊) This is one of the town's better choices, but nevertheless is a bit like *Fawlty Towers* without the humour. Turn left out of the train station and it's about 100m down the road. Request a quiet room, as some are disturbed by the residents' love of full-blast TV. There's a summer-only pool. The restaurant's not great.

## Eating

Alwar has a reasonable selection of restaurants, and is famous for its *palang torh* (milk cake) – not for those watching their weight.

**Prem Pavitra Bhojnalaya** (Old Bus Stand; dishes Rs 20-80; 🕒 11am-10.30pm) Alwar's best restaurant is in the heart of the old town (there's another branch near Moti Dungri) and serves fresh, tasty pure veg food – try the delicious *aloo parathas* (bread stuffed with spicy potato) and *gaajar ka halva* (dessert made with carrots, cardamom and pistachios, topped by curd).

**South Indian Café** (dishes Rs 10-30; 🕒 8am-10pm) This dimly lit place, opposite Gopal Talkies, has a shuffling, half-hearted atmosphere, but it's popular with families and offers cheap, excellent South Indian dishes, such as delicious masala dosas.

**Narula's** (dishes Rs 40-100; 🕒 11am-3pm & 5.30-10.30pm) Tucked away in a basement, Narula's whips up Indian, Chinese and Continental food. A long-established restaurant, it offers a good choice of veg and nonveg dishes.

**Dawat** (Alwar Hotel, Manu Rd; dishes around Rs 50; 🕒 Tue-Sun) Dawat serves pretty good Indian, Continental and Chinese food, and it's possible to eat outside in the pleasant garden.

**Inderlok Restaurant** (dishes Rs 25-90) This hotel restaurant has lots of palatable veg and unusual *paneer* choices. There's a typically hushed ambience in the AC room, which is plain and functional, with a waterfall picture as a concession to design. It's popular with courting couples.

**Tizza Coffee Shop** (Nangli Circle) This small café is a great place to stop. It's a town favourite for its excellent lassis (yogurt and iced water drinks) and coffee.

## Getting There & Away

### BUS

From Alwar there are buses to Sariska (Rs 12/14 in local/express, one/1½ hours, half-hourly 5.15am to 8.30pm), which go on to Jaipur (Rs 68/73, four hours), via Bairat (Rs 25). There are also frequent (bumpy) services to Bharatpur (Rs 43, four hours) for Keoladeo Ghana National Park, and Deeg (Rs 27, 2½ hours). Buses to Delhi take two different routes (Rs 81, via Tijara/Ramgarh four/five hours, half-hourly).

### CAR

A return taxi to Sariska Tiger Reserve (including a stop at Siliserh) will cost you around Rs 700.

### TRAIN

The *Shatabdi Express* (Nos 2015/6) passes through Alwar. It departs for Ajmer (Rs 440

EASTERN RAJASTHAN

in chair class, four hours) at 8.35am and stops at Jaipur (Rs 315, two hours) at 10.40am. For Delhi, it departs at 7.28pm (Rs 350/670 in chair/executive, 2½ hours).

The *Mandore Express* leaves at 11.43pm, arriving in Jodhpur (Rs 884/578 in 2AC/3AC, 465km) at 8am. The *Jaisalmer Express*, leaving at 8.50pm, goes all the way to Jaisalmer (Rs 251/705 in sleeper/3AC, 16 hours, 759km).

### Getting Around

There are cycle-rickshaws, autorickshaws, tempos and some tongas. A cycle-rickshaw from the train station to the town centre should cost about Rs 15. You can hire bicycles near the train station (Rs 25 per day).

## AROUND ALWAR

### Siliserh

For a tranquil breath of fresh air, this fairytale retreat, 20km southwest of Alwar (off the road to Sariska Tiger Reserve), is one of the state's best-kept secrets. Uninhabited wooded hills surround a serene 10.5-sq-km lake. There's not much else here except for a few cheap restaurants and a restored palace, now a hotel. A cream-coloured confection with cupolas, balconies and courtyards, set in a dramatic location overlooking the lake, it was built by the Alwar Maharaja Vinay Singhis in 1845 as a hunting lodge and palace. You can see life from the water by hiring a **paddleboat** (per 30min Rs 60), or roaring around on a **motorboat** (per 15min Rs 300).

The **RTDC Hotel Lake Palace** (☎ 0144-2886322; d from Rs 500, with AC Rs 990), in the palace, is beautiful, with a lot of atmosphere and wonderful lake views. It's a good choice if you overlook the erratic cleanliness and service.

#### GETTING THERE & AWAY

A crowded tempo from Alwar will cost you about Rs 10, or you can hire a car for around Rs 300.

### Kesroli

This pleasant small town, 12km from Alwar, has a rambling 14th-century, seven-turreted fort – now a hotel – sturdily set on a hill overlooking agricultural land. The fort ramparts offer views across the fields, where the working villagers make splashes of colour.

The warm, atmospheric **Hill Fort Kesroli** (☎ 01468-289352; www.neemranahotels.com; r Rs 2000, ste Rs 4000) is run from the Neemrana Fort Palace (below). A bit haphazard, it has 22 comfortable, characterful rooms and is set in marvellously peaceful countryside.

From Alwar you can take a taxi or an autorickshaw to the fort.

### Neemrana

This small, unprepossessing village lies about 75km north of Alwar on the main Delhi–Jaipur Hwy, a short distance to the south of the Haryana border. The reason to visit is the magnificent fortress palace, 2km away. Dating from 1464, it was from here that the Rajput Maharaja Prithviraj Chauhan III reigned, and it's now one of Rajasthan's oldest luxury hotels.

The magnificent, parchment-coloured **Neemrana Fort Palace** (☎ 246007; www.neemranahotels.com; s/d/ste from Rs 1500/2500/3500; ⊠ 🏊) is mounted on a fortified plateau. The fort rises an amazing 10 levels, set in 25 acres among the folded Aravalli hills. Rooms are decorated in a mixture of Rajput and colonial styles, and are massively varied – try to get one with a balcony or terrace – while the fort layout is fascinatingly complex, with mazelike corridors and hidden courtyards and terraces.

#### GETTING THERE & AWAY

Buses on the main Delhi to Jaipur route generally stop at Behror, 14km from Neemrana (from where it's a further 2km to the hotel). A taxi from Behror to the hotel will cost about Rs 200.

## SARISKA TIGER RESERVE

☎ 0144

Surrounded by the dramatic, shadowy folds of the Aravallis, the **Sariska reserve** (Indian/foreigner Rs 25/200, jeep Rs 125, video Rs 200; 🕒 7am-4pm Oct-Mar, 6am-4.30pm Apr-Sep) lies in a wooded valley, a tangle of greenery against red clay, with craggy canyons and dry jungle scrub. It covers 800 sq km (including a core area of 498 sq km), and is home to sambars, spotted deer and wild boars.

Tragically, Sariska has recently been at the centre of a huge wildlife scandal – it seems that poaching may have decimated the park's tiger population. Although Project Tiger has been in charge of the sanctuary since 1979, it appears that there has been a dramatic failure. In 2004 there were an estimated 18 tigers in the park; however, reports in 2005 called this into question, after an investigation by the World Wildlife Fund, and prompted the government to create a task force to discover what has happened at Sariska. See the boxed text, below, for more details.

Tigers or no tigers, Sariska is in any case a fascinating sanctuary to visit. However, without its big stripy crowd pleasers, its popularity will surely take a tremendous dive. Unlike most national parks, it opens year-round, although the best time to spot wildlife is November to March; during July and August your chance of spotting wildlife is minimal, as the animals move on to higher ground. You'll see most wildlife in the evening.

## Sights

Besides wildlife, Sariska has some fantastic sights within the park or around its peripheries, which are well worth seeking out. If you take a longer tour, you can ask to visit one or more of these. A couple of them are also accessible by bus.

### KANKWARI FORT

Deep inside the sanctuary, this imposing small **jungle fort**, 22km away from Sariska, offers amazing views over the plains of the national park, dotted with red mud-brick villages. This is the inaccessible place that Aurangzeb chose to imprison his brother, Dara Shikoh, Shah Jahan's chosen heir to the Mughal throne, for several years before he was beheaded.

### HANUMAN TEMPLE

You can visit a small **Hanuman temple** in the park, deep in the forest. Its recumbent idol, adapted from a rock, is covered in silver paper and shaded by metal umbrellas. People give offerings of incense and receive tiny parcels of holy ash. Indians can enter the park for free between 8am and 3pm Tuesday and Saturday if they're visiting the temple.

### NEELKANTHESHWAR TEMPLE

Around 35km from Sariska is an ancient **temple complex**, up a dramatically winding road that allows fantastic views. This 8th-century complex sits on a small plateau ringed by low hills where the old defensive wall is still visible. It's said that the temples remained preserved because bees chased Aurangzeb away when he tried to attack them. The main temple is dedicated to Shiva (photography prohibited). The small podlike shrines outside the temple are priests' graves. A little bit further away, through a tangle of vegetation (ask locals to point out the right path), is a Jain temple built from orange-red sandstone, with a huge stone statue of the 23rd *tirthankar*, known locally as Nogaza.

### BHANGARH

Around 55km from Sariska, beyond the inner park sanctuary and out in open countryside, is this deserted, well-preserved, notoriously haunted city. It was founded in 1631 by Madho Singh, and had 10,000 dwellings, but was suddenly deserted about

### THE MYSTERIOUS CASE OF THE ELUSIVE TIGERS

Whatever has happened to the tigers at Sariska? News splashed across the press in spring 2005 that the tigers were gone, presumed poached. The news followed a report from the WWF, who had searched areas previously frequented by tigers and found that there was no evidence to indicate any recent tiger activity. They had also learned that no tigers had been sighted in these areas since August 2004. The WWF concluded that something had happened to the tigers between July and December 2004, that previous estimations of numbers of tigers in the park were in any case exaggerated, and if any tigers remained, their numbers were small. According to the WWF, poaching is the most likely cause of the disappearance. The WWF also highlighted the issues of widespread woodcutting and grazing within park boundaries and low morale among staff, and pointed to the regular changes of management as being contributory to the park's problems. And it's not only tigers at risk here – sambars have also been targeted for their horns.

In March 2005 Prime Minister Manmohan Singh ordered an inquiry into the tiger crisis, and further investigations should shed light on whether there are still tigers in the sanctuary.

As things stand, Sariska Tiger Reserve might be due for a name change.

300 years ago for reasons that remain mysterious. However, the favoured explanation is that a magician who loved the queen found his love unrequited and cursed the city. The buildings today, in their wonderful setting of unspoilt countryside, are largely restored, which gives a remarkable sense of the city and its town planning. Temples and *chhatris* (cenotaphs, literally 'umbrellas') dot the surrounding area.

After you enter the main gate, there is a *haveli*, once a grand house, to the right. Beyond it, you can walk through the market area's well-defined and ordered bazaars up to the ruined, evocative palace for long views across the pastoral landscape. Within the complex are two well-preserved, ornate Shiva temples. One has its lingam (phallic symbol – symbol of Shiva) still intact, and lies alongside a green-shaded tank.

Bhangarh can be reached by a bus that runs twice daily through the sanctuary (Rs 25) to nearby Golaka village. Check what time the bus returns, otherwise you risk getting stranded.

## Tours

While it's possible to take private cars into the park, they are limited to sealed roads, minimising the chances of spotting wildlife. The best way to visit the park is by jeep, which can explore off the main tracks. For diesel/petrol jeeps you'll be quoted Rs 600/700 for three hours, or Rs 1500/1800 for a full day. They can take up to five people. It's worth paying the extra for a petrol jeep, as the diesel vehicles are noisier and can scare away the animals. On the days when admission is free for Indians (Tuesday and Saturday) the park gets very crowded. Guides are available (Rs 100 for three hours; maximum five people). It's also possible to arrange guided treks.

Bookings can be made at the **Forest Reception Office** (☎ 2841333; Jaipur Rd), directly opposite the Hotel Sariska Palace, which is where buses will drop you.

## Sleeping

**Sariska Tiger Heaven** (☎ 224815; r Rs 1500, with AC Rs 1800; ) This is an isolated place about 5km west of the bus stop; free pick-up is on offer. Rooms have big beds and windowed alcoves, and are set in five acres of peaceful grounds. It's a tranquil, if overpriced and overstaffed, place to stay. Staff can arrange jeeps and guides to the park.

**Hotel Sariska Palace** (☎ 2841322; r Rs 5000; ) Near the park entrance is this imposing former hunting lodge (not actually a palace) of the maharajas of Alwar. There's a long sweeping driveway leading from opposite the Forest Reception Office. Horses graze in the immaculate grounds, beyond which the views stretch into the mountains. Rooms are disappointing, though those in the new annexe by the swimming pool have better interiors and good views. The drawing room has the usual sorry array of stuffed beasts, and the dining room is stuffed with antiques. It's set in 20 hectares, and it's possible to take short horse and camel rides around the grounds. However, guests have reported being dissatisfied with both rooms and service.

**RTDC Hotel Tiger Den** (☎ 2841342; dm Rs 50, s/d from Rs 600/700; ) Hotel Tiger Den is a quasi-Soviet block, but backed by a green, rambling garden. Rooms are drab and a bit run-down, but they have balconies and occupy a pleasant setting. Bring a mosquito net or repellent.

**Amanbagh** (☎ 065-68873337; www.amanresorts.com; r Feb-Aug US$500-800, Sep-Dec US$550-900) Set some way away, isolated among the Aravalli hills, is this vastly opulent place, a lush walled compound that was once a site for the hunting camps of the maharaja of Alwar. Amanbagh means 'peaceful garden'. The splendid rooms have domed ceilings and huge baths – it's like walking into a very glitzy movie set – and the most expensive have a private pool. The resort is just 10km from Bhangarh.

## Getting There & Away

Sariska is 35km from Alwar, a convenient town from which to approach the sanctuary. There are frequent buses from Alwar (Rs 12/14 in local/express, one/1½ hours, at least hourly) and on to Jaipur (Rs 55/65). Buses stop in front of the Forest Reception Office.

# BAIRAT

Around 25km west of Sariska, 85km north of Jaipur, is the ancient Buddhist centre of Viratnagar, or Bairat, which has a fascinating combination of Mughal and Buddhist relics. Archaeological evidence – ancient coins, the remains of a Buddhist monastery, and several rock-cut edicts, a legacy left by the great 3rd-century BC Buddhist convert, the Emperor Ashoka – indicates that this was once an important centre of Buddhism.

Jaipur to Alwar buses pass through Bairat (to Jaipur Rs 40, 3½ hours; to Alwar Rs 20, 1½ hours).

## AJMER

**☎ 0145 / pop 485,197**

Next to the beautiful calm lake of Ana Sagar, and surrounded by Aravalli hills, Ajmer is a bustling, hectic town around 130km southwest of Jaipur. Ajmer contains one of India's most important Muslim pilgrimage centres – the shrine of Khwaja Muin-ud-din Chishti, a venerated Sufi saint who founded the Chishtiya order, which still exists as the prime Sufi order in India today – and has some superb examples of early Muslim architecture. However, most travellers just use Ajmer as a stepping stone to nearby Pushkar. With Ajmer's combination of high-voltage crowds, commerce and traffic, it's very much a pilgrimage site rather than a travellers' hang-out, which accounts for the dearth of good accommodation. Many people choose to stay in Pushkar and visit on a day trip.

It gets very busy during Ramadan, and the anniversary of the saint's death – the Urs (see p187).

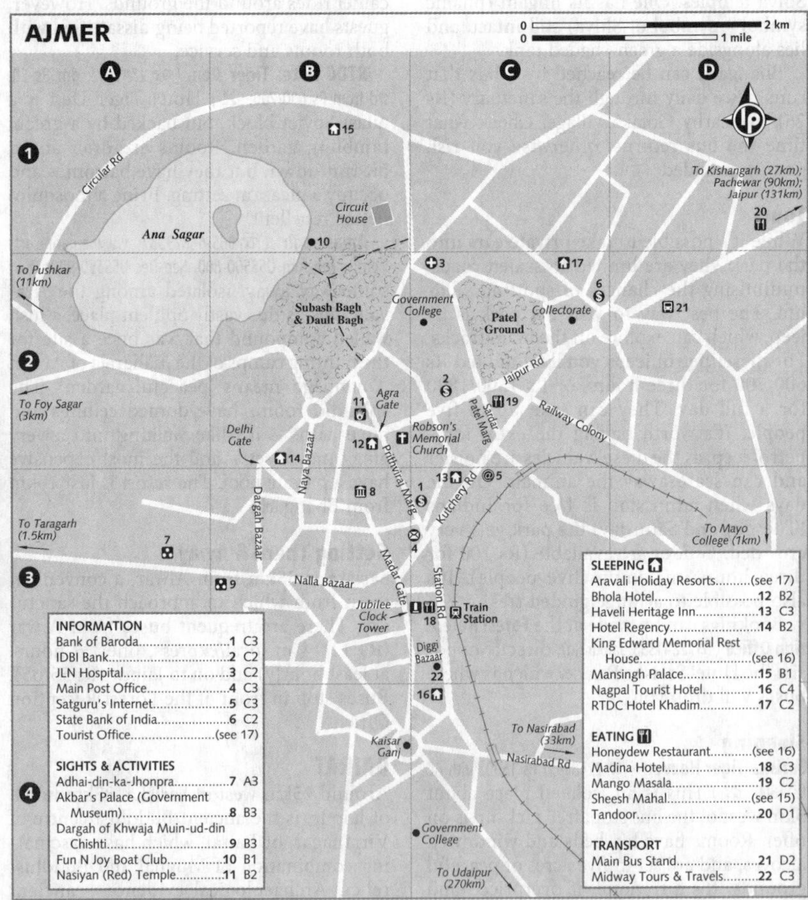

## History

Of strategic importance due to its secure position, protected by the Aravallis, and its location on the major trade route between Delhi and the ports of Gujarat, Ajmer was fought over for centuries. Its significance was such that its rulers, from the time of the Turks until the East India Company, tried to keep Ajmer under direct control. The city is also Rajasthan's most important place in terms of Islamic history and heritage. It was founded in the 7th century by Ajaipal Chauhan, who constructed a hill fort and named the place Ajaimeru (Invincible Hill). Ajmer was ruled by the Chauhans until the late 12th century, when Prithviraj Chauhan lost it to Mohammed of Ghori.

It consequently became part of the sultanate in Delhi. After 1326 Ajmer was continually fought over by surrounding states, including the sultans of Delhi and Gujarat, and the rulers of Mewar (Udaipur) and Marwar (Jaipur).

Later in its history, Ajmer became a favourite residence of the great Mughals. One of the first contacts between the Mughals and the British occurred in Ajmer when Sir Thomas Roe met Emperor Jehangir (who lived here for three years) in 1616.

In 1659 Aurangzeb battled and won here against his brother Dara Shikoh, changing the course of succession and signalling the end of the Mughal empire.

The city was subsequently taken by the Scindias and, in 1818, was handed over to the British, becoming one of the few places in Rajasthan controlled directly by the British rather than being part of a princely state. The British set up Mayo College here in 1875, a prestigious school in an overexcited building, exclusively for the Indian nobility. Today it's open to all boys (whose parents can afford the fees). Other monuments that stand as reminders of Ajmer's colonial past are the Edward Memorial Hall, Ajmer Club and Jubilee Clock Tower.

## Orientation

The main bus stand is close to the RTDC Hotel Khadim on the east side of town. Most of the hotels are west of the train station. Northeast of the main post office is Naya Bazaar (known for its silver jewellery and tie-dyed fabrics) and Agra Gate. Further north is the large artificial lake Ana Sagar.

## Information

Ajmer has several ATMs, including an IDBI ATM in Jaipur Rd.

**Bank of Baroda** (Prithviraj Rd; 🕑 10am-3pm Mon-Fri, 10am-12.30pm Sat) Changes travellers cheques and does credit-card advances.

**Main post office** (🕑 10am-1pm & 1.30-6pm Mon-Sat) Less than 500m from the train station.

**Satguru's Internet** (60-61 Kutchery Rd; per hr Rs 20; 🕑 9am-10pm) Has quite good connections.

**State Bank of India** (☎ 2627048; 🕑 10am-2pm & 2.30-4pm Mon-Fri, 10am-1pm Sat) Opposite the Collectorate, changes travellers cheques and currency.

**Tourist office** RTDC Hotel Khadim (☎ 2627426; 🕑 8am-noon & 3-6pm Mon-Sat); train station (🕑 10am-2pm & 2.30-5pm Mon-Sat)

## Sights

### ANA SAGAR

This large lake, created in the 12th century by damming the River Luni, is set against a blue-grey hilly spine that merges into its surface. On its bank is a delightful park, the **Subash Bagh & Dault Bagh**, containing a series of marble pavilions erected in 1637 by Shah Jahan. There are good views towards Ajmer from the hill beside the Dault Bagh, particularly at sunset. It's a popular place for an evening stroll, though you may get quite a lot of attention. Pedalos and motorboats can be hired from the Fun N Joy Boat Club.

Foy Sagar, 5km west of the city, is an artificial lake built to create employment.

### DARGAH OF KHWAJA MUIN-UD-DIN CHISHTI

> The dargah was packed. Tens of thousands of devotees from all over India and beyond were milling around. Ecstatics and madmen were shrieking to themselves, beating their foreheads against the stone railings on the tomb. Blind beggars stumbled around with their alms bowls. Women discreetly suckled young babies under the folds of their saris.
>
> *William Dalrymple,* City of Djinns

Situated at the foot of a hill and in the old part of town is the **dargah of Khwaja Muin-ud-din Chishti** (www.dargahajmer.com; 🕑 5am-9pm winter, 4am-9pm summer, closed for services 3-4pm & 2.30-3.30pm Thu), India's most important Muslim pilgrimage site.

EASTERN RAJASTHAN

## THE INCLUSIVE SAINT

Born in eastern Persia sometime in 1138 or 1139, Khwaja Muin-ud-din Chishti was orphaned in his early teens and lived on the proceeds of his ancestral orchards. According to legend, a holy man passed his garden and when Khwaja rushed out to greet him, the holy man gave him some food that enlightened him. Khwaja then renounced all worldly goods, became a fakir (Muslim holy man) and began to wander in search of knowledge. He visited Samarkand and Bukhara, great centres of Islamic learning, and absorbed all he could from great Central Asian Sufis – theirs was an Islam with an emphasis on devotion, mysticism and miracles. He then settled in Baghdad, and later made a pilgrimage to Medina for the haj, where he heard a divine voice telling him to go to Hindustan. Now in his 50s, he wandered to India, arriving in Ajmer in around 1190, where he settled on a hill by Ana Sagar. His beliefs and life of meditation and fasting – it's said he only ate one chapati every eight days – had brought him great renown, and people flocked to him to hear his teachings. Even Mohammed of Ghori took time off raiding temples to pay his respects to the holy man.

His preachings were notably generous and inclusive. He spoke to Hindus as much as to Muslims, emphasising that theirs were different approaches along the same path. Hindus could relate to many aspects of Sufism (for example, holy men renouncing everything except faith bears considerable resemblance to Hindu practice). He preached against discrimination and differentiation between believers of different faiths.

In 1236 he died, aged 97, and was buried in his simple brick cell, now covered by its elaborate shrine. In tribute to his teachings and beliefs, it is regarded as a holy place by people of many different faiths.

This is the tomb of a Sufi saint Khwaja Muin-ud-din Chishti, who came to Ajmer from Persia in 1192 and died here in 1236. The tomb gained its significance during the time of the Mughals – many emperors added to the buildings here. Construction of the shrine was completed by Humayun, and the gate was added by the nizam (ruler of Hyderabad). Akbar used to make the pilgrimage to the dargah from Agra every year.

You have to cover your head in certain parts of the shrine, so remember to take a scarf or cap, although there are plenty for sale at the colourful bazaar leading to the dargah, along with floral offerings and delicious Muslim toffees.

The first gate is the Nizam Gate, built in 1915 up some steps to protect it from the rains. The green and white mosque, **Akbari Masjid**, on the right was constructed by Akbar in 1571 and is now Moiniua Usmania Darul-Uloom, an Arabic and Persian School for religious education. The second gate was built by Shah Jahan, and is often called the Nakkarkhana because it has two large *nakkharas* (drums) fixed above it.

In an inner court there is another mosque, built by Shah Jahan. Of white marble, it has 11 arches and a Persian inscription running the full length of the building.

The third gate, Buland Darwaza, dates from the 16th century. It's tall – about 28m high – and whitewashed, and leads into the dargah courtyard.

Flanking the entrance of the courtyard are the *degs*, large iron cauldrons (one donated by Akbar in 1567, the other by Jehangir in 1631) for offerings for the poor. Sometimes someone will sponsor a cauldron and they will be filled with porridge to be distributed to the needy (one *deg* feeds around 70 people). In the past this gave rise to a specialist profession, known as 'looting the *degs*' – people wearing protective clothes would dive into the cauldrons to distribute the food. Today it's more boringly distributed using large ladles.

The saint's tomb has a marble dome, and the tomb inside is surrounded by a silver platform. Pilgrims believe that the saint's spirit will intercede in their behalf in matters of illness, business or personal problems, so the notes and holy string attached to the railings around are thanks or requests.

At the entrance, *khadims* (Muslim holy servants or mosque attendants) wielding donation books will ask you for cash (there are 4000 *khadims* in Ajmer!). It's likely you'll be asked for still more money inside, where you might be blessed with the edge of the tomb blanket. If you don't want to give, just be firm about it or give a small amount.

Despite the hustle, it's a fascinating shrine with a sense of profound significance. It's good to visit in the evening, when it's decorated in twinkling lights and there are Qawali singers, who sing verses in praise of the Prophet and saints. These verses can have a powerful effect – it's said that Khwaja Sahib once heard a verse devoted to the Prophet and was so ecstatic that he fainted and was unconscious for seven nights and days.

Pilgrims and Sufis come from all over the world on the anniversary of the saint's death, the Urs (when William Dalrymple visited). The anniversary is celebrated in the seventh month of the lunar calendar, Jyaistha (the dates are variable, so check with the tourist office). The saint retired to his cloister for a long meditation, and when it was opened six days later he was dead, hence the festival lasts six days. It's an interesting time, but the crowds can be suffocating – praying people line the streets all the way down from the dargah. Many pilgrims also come here in the month of Ramadan.

#### ADHAI-DIN-KA-JHONPRA & TARAGARH

Beyond the dargah, on the town outskirts, are the extraordinary ruins of the **Adhai-din-ka-Jhonpra** (Two-and-a-Half-Day Building) Mosque. According to legend, construction in 1153 took 2½ days. Others say it was named after a festival lasting 2½ days. It was built as a Sanskrit college, but in 1198 Mohammed of Ghori seized Ajmer and converted the building into a mosque by adding a seven-arched wall covered with Islamic calligraphy in front of the pillared hall.

Although it's in need of restoration, it's an exquisite piece of architecture, with soaring domes, pillars and a beautiful arched screen, largely built from pieces of Jain and Hindu temples.

About 3km and a steep 1½-hour climb beyond the mosque, the ancient **Taragarh** (Star Fort) commands a superb view over the city (accessible by car). Built by Ajaipal Chauhan, the town's founder, it saw lots of military action during Mughal times and was later used as a British sanatorium.

#### NASIYAN (RED) TEMPLE

The amazing Jain **temple** (Prithviraj Rd; admission Rs 3; 8.30am-5pm Nov-Mar, 8.30am-5.30pm Apr-Oct) was built in 1865. It's also known as the Golden Temple, due to its unique display – its double-storey temple hall is filled with a huge golden diorama depicting the Jain concept of the ancient world, with 13 continents and oceans, the intricate golden city of Ayodhya, flying swan and elephant gondolas, and gilded elephants with many tusks. The hall is decorated with gold, silver and precious stones. It's unlike any other temple in Rajasthan and is worth a visit. Children will like it, too.

#### AKBAR'S PALACE

Not far from the main post office, Akbar built this imposing palace in 1570 – partly as a pleasure retreat, but mainly to keep an eye on pesky local chiefs. It houses the **government museum** (admission Rs 3, free Mon, camera/video Indian Rs 5/10, foreigner Rs 10/20; 10am-4.30pm Sat-Thu), with a small collection of old weapons, miniature paintings, ancient rock inscriptions and stone sculptures that date back to the 8th century.

### Sleeping

Commission rackets are ingrained in Ajmer: you'll be accosted by cycle- and autorickshaw drivers the minute you step off the bus or train. On top of this, the hotels here offer poor service and soulless atmosphere – typically, there are more budget options than good midrange places. It's a far better idea to stay in nearby Pushkar. You can visit Ajmer on a day trip from Pushkar, or on the way through.

A good and often cheaper alternative to hotels is to stay in one of the homes participating in Ajmer's Paying Guest House Scheme, which gives you the interesting opportunity to stay with an Indian family. Rates range from around Rs 100 to 800 per night depending on the facilities provided. The tourist office (p205) has details about these guesthouses.

#### BUDGET

**Bhola Hotel** (☎ 2432844; Prithviraj Rd; d Rs 150) Opposite the church, southeast of Agra Gate, this hotel is friendly and one of the few habitable budget options, with five nondescript but clean and comfortable rooms. It has a good restaurant.

**King Edward Memorial Rest House** (☎ 2429936; Station Rd; dm Rs 15, s from Rs 65, better s/d from Rs 100/150)

Known locally as KEM, this place is to the left as you exit the train station. Don't let the grand name fool you: it resembles a 19th-century workhouse. It's primarily a pilgrim flophouse, and has run-down, dusty, drab rooms, from very basic cell-like singles to better larger singles and doubles, around a large, scrappy courtyard.

**Nagpal Tourist Hotel** (☎ 2429503; s/d from Rs 250/400; ❄) With a good location next to the Honeydew restaurant and near the train station, this hotel is salubrious and fairly clean but dreary and uninspiring – a typical low-budget Indian business hotel.

### MIDRANGE & TOP END

**Haveli Heritage Inn** (☎ 2621607; Kutchery Rd; r Rs 400-1000) Set in a 100-year-old *haveli*, this is a welcoming city-centre oasis and arguably Ajmer's best choice. The high-ceilinged rooms are quite large, though a bit run-down. There's a pleasant, grassy courtyard and the hotel is infused with a family atmosphere, complete with home-cooked meals.

**Mansingh Palace** (☎ 2425956; Circular Rd; s/d Rs 2500/3000) This modern place, overlooking Ana Sagar, is Ajmer's only top-end hotel. It's rather out of the way, but has attractive and comfortable, though overpriced, rooms, some with views and balconies. There're a pleasant garden, a bar and an acceptable restaurant, the Sheesh Mahal (right).

**RTDC Hotel Khadim** (☎ 2627490; dm Rs 50, d from Rs 300) This option is near the bus stand and has bright, reasonable, unexciting rooms that are good value.

**Aravali Holiday Resorts** (☎ 2627089; d from Rs 350) Next door to Khadim, Aravali is more homy and has eight simple rooms that are clean and comfortable.

**Hotel Regency** (☎ 2620296; s/d from Rs 450/500) Grey and dreary, but close to the dargah, this is a serviceable choice in a town with scarce options.

## Eating

Ajmer's restaurants are much more promising than its accommodation. It has some good options, and there is also a flourishing trade in ice creams and cakes.

**Mango Masala** (dishes Rs 18-90; 🕑 11am-11pm) With dim, bar-like lighting and crèche-style décor, this is where Ajmer's hip crowd hangs out. There's an imaginative menu of pizzas, Chinese food, and North and South Indian vegetarian food – tasty and freshly cooked. The attached sweet shop has cakes, ice cream, floats and crazy mocktails.

**Tandoor** (Jaipur Rd; dishes Rs 30-160; 🕑 9am-10.30pm) Recommended by satisfied customers, it offers good tandoor and nonveg dishes, and, unusually for Ajmer, is set in an appealing garden oasis off the main road, with tables housed in little huts.

**Honeydew Restaurant** (dishes Rs 30-160; 🕑 9am-11pm) This comfortingly staid and gloomy place has long been Ajmer's best, and is the restaurant of choice for Mayo College students' midterm treat. There's a good selection of veg and nonveg Indian, Chinese and Continental food. It's just near the Nagpal Tourist Hotel.

**Bhola Hotel** (veg dishes Rs 15-40; 🕑 11am-10pm) This place (see Sleeping, p207) has a surprisingly serene, appealing and good-value veg restaurant at the top of a seedy staircase. Tasty thalis cost Rs 35.

**Madina Hotel** (dishes around Rs 40; 🕑 9am-11pm) Handy if you're waiting for a train (it's opposite the station), this simple, open-to-the-street eatery cooks up cheap veg and nonveg fare, with specialities such as chicken Mughlai and *rumali roti*.

**Sheesh Mahal** (dishes around Rs 80; 🕑 noon-3pm & 7-10.30pm) This upmarket place, located in the Mansingh Palace, offers Indian, Continental and Chinese dishes that are nothing to write home about but reliably palatable. It overlooks a grassy courtyard and also has a pleasant bar.

## Getting There & Away

### BUS

There are frequent buses going from Ajmer to Pushkar (Rs 8, 30 minutes), which leave from the main bus stand or from by the Nasiyan Temple. Regular RSTC buses go to and from the places listed in the table. The inquiry number is ☎ 2429398.

In addition, there are private buses to these destinations – many companies have offices on Kutchery Rd. If you book your ticket to one of these destinations through an agency in Pushkar, they should provide a free transfer to Ajmer to start your journey.

### TRAIN

There are no tourist quotas for many Ajmer trains, so book early; go to booth 5 at the train station's **reservations office** (🕑 8am-2pm

EASTERN RAJASTHAN

**BUSES FROM AJMER**

| Destination | Fare (Rs) | Duration (hr) |
|---|---|---|
| Agra | 158 | 10 |
| Ahmedabad | 225 | 13 |
| Alwar | 123 | 6 |
| Bharatpur | 129 | 8 |
| Bikaner | 114 | 8 |
| Bundi | 76 | 5 |
| Chittorgarh | 80 | 5 |
| Delhi | 180 | 9 |
| Indore | 215 | 12 |
| Jaipur | 67/AC 86 | 2½ |
| Jaisalmer | 200 | 10 |
| Jodhpur | 88 | 6 |
| Kota | 92 | 6 |
| Udaipur | 120 | 8 |

& 2.15-8pm Mon-Sat, 8am-2pm Sun). **Midway Tours & Travels** (☎ 2628744; anilgujra@yahoo.com; 🕑 8am-8pm) will book sleeper-/upper-class berths for Rs 17/28.

Most trains stop here, as Ajmer is on the Delhi–Jaipur–Ahmedabad–Mumbai line. The *Shatabdi Express* (Nos 2016/5, Thursday to Tuesday) runs between Ajmer and Delhi (Rs 650/1250 in chair/executive class) via Jaipur (Rs 270/545). It leaves Delhi at 6.10am and arrives in Ajmer at 12.45pm. Going the other way, the train leaves Ajmer at 3.50pm, arriving in Jaipur at 5.45pm and in Delhi at 10.20pm. There's also the No 2957 *Rajdhani Express* to Delhi (Rs 655/995, seven hours), which leaves Ajmer at 12.35am.

The *Delhi-Ahmedabad Mail* (Nos 9105/6) departs from Ajmer at 8.28pm and arrives in Delhi (Rs 170/762/476 in sleeper/2AC/3AC, 442km) at 5.20am. Heading for Gujarat, the train leaves Ajmer at 7.40am and arrives in Ahmedabad (Rs 116 in 2nd class, 492km) at 5.30pm.

The *Khandwar Express* (No 9671) leaves at 8.20pm, arriving in Udaipur (Rs 127 in sleeper, 301km) at 7.50am.

### Getting Around

There are plenty of autorickshaws (anywhere in town should cost around Rs 20), as well as cycle-rickshaws and tongas. For longer trips, you can hire a car/jeep for Rs 3.5/4 per kilometre. A half/full day of sightseeing will cost Rs 600/1200.

## AROUND AJMER

### Kishangarh

Kishangarh is 27km northeast of Ajmer, founded in the early 17th century by Kishan Singh, a Rathore prince. Since the 18th century Kishangarh has had one of India's most famous schools of miniature painting. Among its renowned works is the *Bani Thani* painting by Kishangarh master Nihal Chand – a sensual, graceful portrayal of Krishna's consort, Radha, depicted with exaggeratedly slanting, almond-shaped eyes – you'll see this reprinted all over Rajasthan. Today local artists are trying to revive this magnificent school of painting by making copies of the originals on surfaces such as wood, stone and cloth (the originals were done on paper). Kishangarh is also famous for painted wooden furniture.

Kishangarh town is divided into the charming old city and the less-charming new part, which is mainly commercial. Pollution is steadily increasing, along with the growing number of dusty marble factories and textile mills.

#### SLEEPING

**Roopangarh Fort** (☎/fax 01497-220444; www.royalkishangarh.com; s/d Rs 1600/2100, ste Rs 3000; ❄) About 25km out of town, Roopangarh Fort has been converted into an evocative hotel by the maharaja and maharani of Kishangarh. Roopangarh was the capital of this province for about 100 years and was never conquered, despite being repeatedly attacked by its neighbouring states. The fort was founded in 1653 by Maharaja Roop Singh, the fifth ruler of Kishangarh, who was inspired to make this site his capital after watching a mother sheep gallantly protect her lambs from a pack of hungry wolves. Rooms are large, and decorated with lots of traditional furniture. The road to the fort passes through a timeless village, where it seems life has been the same for centuries. The hotel can arrange village tours, bird-watching, and camel, horse or jeep safaris, and if you stay here you can view the maharaja's private collection of miniatures. The fort itself is well endowed with fine paintings.

#### GETTING THERE & AWAY

Frequent daily buses go between Ajmer and Kishangarh (Rs 15).

### Tilonia

In Tilonia village, located about 25km east of Kishangarh and 7km off the Ajmer to Jaipur road, is the inspiringly radical **Barefoot College** (☎ 01463-288204; www.barefootcollege.org); see the boxed text, below. This NGO is run by and for villagers, and uses their skills for development work in the area to address problems of water supply, housing, education, health and employment. Part of the complex is devoted to an impressive showroom where goods made by villagers are on sale – it's a fantastic place to pick up high-quality, reasonably priced souvenirs, including everything from wall hangings to furniture and leather goods. Other great gifts include bell totas (colourful strings of stuffed birds), painted ceramic bowls and wooden toys. All proceeds go towards maintaining and developing rural projects.

#### GETTING THERE & AWAY

The easiest way to get to Tilonia is to hire a taxi, which should cost around Rs 400 to 500 return from Ajmer or Pushkar. From Ajmer you can take a Harmara bus (Rs 20) and ask to be dropped off at Tilonia. There are also buses from Kishangarh (Rs 8). The Barefoot College centre is about 1km from the bus stop.

### Pachewar

This little village, about 90km east of Ajmer, has a lake that attracts migratory birds in winter. It has an impressive fort, once ruled by the Khangarot Rajputs. Thakur Anoop Singh Khangarot captured the fort of Ranthambhore from the Marathas and annexed it to his family allies in Jaipur. To reward him, Maharaja Sawai Madho Singh I of Jaipur granted him the Pachewar territory in 1758.

**Pachewar Garh** (in Jaipur ☎ /fax 0141-2601007; s/d Rs 1450/1600) is a 300-year-old fort. The comfortable rooms have the usual array of antiques, and some are grandly frescoed. It's unpretentious rather than flash, despite the grandeur of the fort's exterior. The hotel can also arrange jeep safaris.

#### BAREFOOT COLLEGE

Barefoot College is an NGO mixing radical change with respect for traditional knowledge. The college emphasizes that it values people without qualifications, degrees, certificates or the usual signals of expertise. It values people who are dispossessed and deprived, and invests in their training in order to benefit the community in which they live. It teaches people new respect for themselves and for their capabilities, as well as humility and openness to new knowledge.

The entire complex is solar powered, and Barefoot has been instrumental in bringing solar power to many communities. It's even pulled women out of purdah to teach them how to become solar-power engineers. Other major projects are the installation of handpumps and the implementation of rainwater harvesting projects. Local people, including significant numbers of women, have been trained to maintain the systems.

Barefoot makes great use of puppet shows in poor rural areas, and has trained 2500 puppeteers to communicate with semiliterate communities, with shows on health, education and human rights. Use of a medium such as puppetry is typical of its work, as it is appropriate to the environment, based on the long Rajasthani tradition of storytelling and education through puppet theatre. Barefoot communicators also include screen-printers, photographers and filmmakers, who help get similar messages across with more modern means.

Officially known as the Social Work & Research Centre, Barefoot College was set up in 1972 and since then has pioneered many creative ideas like this to promote self-reliance in poor communities. Other programmes include night schools that give working adults and children access to education, and a variety of schemes that promote the work of low-caste artisans on fair-trade principles.

The organisation is largely supported by the government and international donors. However, the handicrafts section employs around 300 women – often homebound and unable to pursue other work because of the tradition of purdah – who are able to support their families through their skills. You can support the college's efforts and check out the project by visiting the craft showroom at Tilonia.

## PUSHKAR

☎ 014581 / pop 14,789

Bewitching Pushkar has a magnetism all of its own, unlike anywhere else in Rajasthan. It's a Hindu pilgrimage town, a cluster of pale onion domes, with 400 milky temples, where regular *pujas* (prayers) create the town's episodic soundtrack of chanting, drums and gongs, and devotional songs booming out from crackling speakers. The town curls around a holy lake, said to have appeared when Brahma dropped a lotus flower. It also has one of the world's few Brahma temples (see the boxed text, p214).

Besides pilgrims, travellers have long discovered Pushkar's charms, and small, whitewashed budget guesthouses almost outnumber the temples. Many visitors reach here and grind to a satisfied halt, experimenting variously with spirituality, bhang (hemp) and facial hair. Time can slip by very easily in Pushkar.

The result of this magnetism is a muddle of religious and tourist scenes. The main street is one long bazaar, selling anything to tickle a traveller's fancy, from hippy-chick minidresses to didgeridoos. Despite this commercialism (the banana pancakes and bhang uneasy partners to prayer and pilgrimage) the town remains enchantingly small and extraordinarily mystic. You can preserve the equilibrium that makes it so bewitching by dressing appropriately and abiding by local restrictions (no alcohol, meat or eggs, and no public displays of affection).

Pushkar is world famous for its spectacular camel fair (see the boxed text, p212), which takes place here in the Hindu lunar month of Kartika (October/November). If you're anywhere nearby at the time, you'd be crazy to miss it.

During this period the town is jam-packed with tribal people from all over Rajasthan, pilgrims from all over India, and filmmakers and tourists from all over the world. And there are plenty of camels and other livestock (it's best to arrive a few days before the official start to see serious trading).

Pushkar is only 11km from Ajmer but separated from it by Nag Pahar, the Snake Mountain.

### Orientation

The desert town clings to the side of the small but beautiful Pushkar Lake, with its many bathing ghats and fabulous temples. Pushkar town remains amazingly small despite the constant stream of visitors, and it's a twisting maze of narrow streets filled with interesting little shops, food stalls, hotels and temples. Fortunately, there's virtually no motorised traffic in the main bazaar, making it a pleasurable place to explore at leisure. The town is very tourist-friendly and most people speak some English, so you should have no problem finding your way around.

### Information

Cash and travellers cheques may be changed at places along Sadar Bazaar Rd, but check the commission first. Many places offer Internet services, but they can be painfully slow. Most charge Rs 60 per hour.

**Ganesh Enterprises** (Sadar Bazaar Rd) Quality film processing for Rs 5 per photo.

**Main post office** (🕒 9am-5pm Mon-Sat) Just south of the hospital.

**Post office** (🕒 9.30am-5pm) This convenient, small post office is in the main bazaar.

**State Bank of Bikaner & Jaipur** (☎ 2772006; 🕒 10am-4pm Mon-Fri, 10am-12.30pm Sat) Changes travellers cheques and currency, but is slow.

**Tourist Information Centre** (☎ 2772040; 🕒 10am-5pm Mon-Fri, closed 2nd & 4th Sat of month) Gives out a free map.

### Dangers & Annoyances

Priests – some genuine, some not – will approach you near the ghats and offer to do a *puja* (prayer) for which you'll receive a 'Pushkar passport' (a red ribbon around your wrist). Others proffer flowers (to avoid trouble, avoid taking any flowers that you are offered). In either case you'll be asked to tot up your family members – alive and dead – whose happiness is *surely* worth multiple Rs 100. You could always try denying your family, or massively exaggerating their number to get a reduction on bulk purchase. However, you may choose to avoid encouraging these pushy, unprincipled 'priests' altogether – they can become unpleasantly aggressive. At least don't be bullied and agree on a price beforehand. The priests will suggest anything from Rs 101 to 1001 (Indians add the 1 for luck), and beyond! An offering of Rs 11 or 21 is enough, though you'll probably have trouble getting an unprincipled priest to accept this. Be prepared for an earful of abuse if you don't give the priest as much as they want, and try not to let this spoil your visit to the lake.

You can try reporting people to the tourist office if they get you down. If enough people make a fuss, the tourism authorities may address the problem.

On the other hand, flowers are offered at the Brahma Temple, where there are simply donation boxes. Here you can offer flowers and sacred sweets for the happiness of your friends, family and everyone you've ever known – and still have change for a *masala chai*.

## Sights

### TEMPLES

Pushkar boasts hundreds of temples, though few are particularly ancient, as they were mostly desecrated by Aurangzeb and subsequently rebuilt. Most famous is the **Brahma Temple**, said to be one of the few such temples in the world as a result of a curse by Brahma's consort, Saraswati (see the boxed text, p214). The temple is marked by a red spire, and over the entrance gateway is the *hans* (goose symbol) of Brahma. Inside, floor and walls are engraved with dedications to the dead.

The one-hour trek up to the hilltop **Saraswati Temple** overlooking the lake is best made before dawn, though the views are fantastic at any time of day. The views from the closer **Pap Mochani Temple**, reached by a track behind the Marwar bus stand, are also worth the climb.

About 8km southwest of the town (past the turn-off to Savitri) are a collection of **Shiva temples** near Ajaypal, which make a great trip by motorbike (or bike if you're fit and start early in the day), through peaceful hills and past quiet villages. Be warned: the track is hilly and rocky. Another Shiva temple is about 8km north, tucked down inside a cave, which would make for a good excursion.

### GHATS

Fifty-two bathing ghats surround the lake, where pilgrims bathe in the sacred waters. If you wish to join them, do it with respect; re-

#### PUSHKAR CAMEL FAIR

Come the month of Kartika, the eighth lunar month of the Hindu calendar and one of the holiest, Thar camel drivers spruce up their ships of the desert and start the long walk to Pushkar in time for Kartik Purnima (full moon). Each year around 200,000 people converge here, bringing with them some 50,000 camels and cattle. The place becomes an extraordinary swirl of colour, sound and movement, thronged with musicians, mystics, tourists, traders, animals, devotees and camera crews. It's camel-grooming nirvana, with an incredible array of cornrows, anklets, embroidery and pom-poms.

Trading begins a week before the official fair (a good time to arrive to see the serious business), but by the time the fair starts, business takes a back seat and the bizarre sidelines (snake charmers, children balancing on poles) jostle onto centre stage. Even the tourist board's cultural programme is bizarre: dancing on hot coals, or seeing how many people can balance on a camel.

It's hard to believe, but this seething mass is all just a sideshow. Kartik Purnima is when Hindu pilgrims come to bathe in Pushkar's sacred waters. The religious event builds in tandem with the camel fair in a wild, magical crescendo of incense, chanting and processions to dousing day, the last night of the fair, when thousands of devotees wash away their sins and set candles afloat on the holy lake.

Although fantastical, mystical and a one-off, it must be said that it's also crowded, touristy, noisy (light sleepers should bring earplugs) and tacky. Those affected by dust and/or animal hair should bring appropriate medication. However, it's a grand epic, and not to be missed if you're anywhere within camel-spitting distance.

It usually takes place in October or November:

| 2005 | 2006 | 2007 | 2008 | 2009 |
|---|---|---|---|---|
| 8-15 Nov | 29 Oct-5 Nov | 17-24 Nov | 5-13 Nov | 25 Oct-2 Nov |

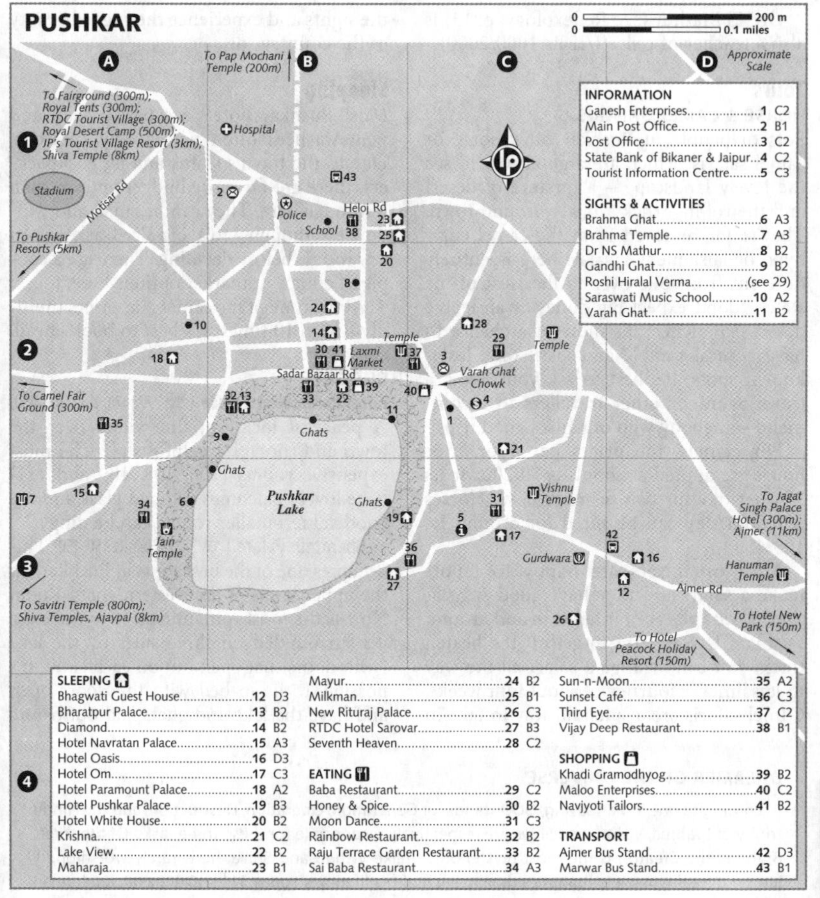


member, this is a holy place. Remove your shoes and don't smoke, kid around or take photographs.

Some ghats have particular importance: Vishnu appeared at **Varah Ghat** in the form of a boar, Brahma bathed at **Brahma Ghat** and Gandhi's ashes were sprinkled at **Gandhi Ghat** (formerly Gau Ghat).

## Activities

### REFLEXOLOGY

**Dr NS Mathur** (☎ 2641185; Shri Raghu Nathji Temple; 🕓 10.30am-6.30pm) provides a toe-challenging reflexology session (Rs 100), which will most certainly take your mind off any pains you might have had. The doctor also teaches reiki.

## Courses

### MUSIC

The excellent **Saraswati Music School** (☎ 2773124; Mainon Ka Chowk; 🕓 10am-10pm) teaches classical tabla (drums), flute, singing and dance *(kathak)*. Birju, who's been playing for over 15 years, charges Rs 200 for two hours, and, for an intensive bout, you can live in for Rs 80 to 200 a night. He often conducts evening performances (8pm to 9.30pm), and also sells instruments.

### YOGA & HEALING

For reiki, yoga and shiatsu, Reiki Master Roshi Hiralal Verma is based at Baba Restaurant (p217). Costs depend on the duration and nature of your session.

Dr NS Mathur (see Reflexology, p213) is also a teacher of reiki (I/II Rs 1000/2000).

## Tours

### HORSE & CAMEL SAFARIS

Lots of people in Pushkar offer horse or camel safaris, which are a good way to see the lovely landscape – a mixture of desert and the rolling, rocky hills – around town. They're far removed from the camel-crazy hype of Jaisalmer. A safari here is entirely different from one over in the west of the state – don't expect big dunes or an iconic desert experience; it's more of a chance to have a rural ramble and visit some little-known spots. It's best to ask your hotel, a travel agent or other travellers to recommend somebody who organises good trips.

For camels, the prices per hour/three hours are quoted at about Rs 70/200, or Rs 350 per day for two or more days. Horses per hour/day can be hired for around Rs 100/450.

Most organisers are happy to tailor-make a safari and they have good suggestions about places of interest in and around Pushkar. If you want to get off the beaten track, you can arrange a safari all the way to Jaisalmer, a journey of about four weeks. Camel safaris are a splendid way to take in the sights and experience the rugged beauty of the countryside.

## Sleeping

Most Pushkar hotels are basic, clean and whitewashed, often with lovely rooftops. Due to the town's status among backpackers, there are far more budget options than midrange here. They can be small and windowless, though – to avoid a cell, ask to see a few rooms before deciding. There are a couple of choice upmarket options here, too.

At the time of the camel fair, prices multiply five to 10 times; it's best to book ahead.

### BUDGET

**Hotel Paramount Palace** (☎ 2772428; d Rs 100-450) A peaceful location, fine views over the town and (notably) helpful staff. The most expensive rooms (106, 108, 109 and 111) have lovely balconies, stained glass and are good value; smaller rooms can be dingy.

**Bharatpur Palace** (☎ 2772320; r Rs 150-450) This occupies one of the best spots in Pushkar, on the upper levels of the western ghats. Room No 1 is the most romantic place to wake up: it's surrounded on three sides by the lake (with doors that open out on each side). It's possible to lie in bed with the doors open and have the lake and ghats laid out before

### DREAMER OF THE UNIVERSE

According to one Indian saying, GOD stands for Generation, Operation, Destruction, and the Hindu trinity of Brahma, Vishnu and Shiva are respectively responsible for these three tasks. Of the three, Brahma, the Creator, is the most mysterious. Unlike Vishnu and Shiva, he is rarely worshipped, although reality itself is Brahma's dream. Each of his lifetimes spans 311,040,000,000,000 human years and corresponds to a great cycle of the universe, at the end of which it is destroyed by Shiva. Then Brahma is reborn to dream it all again.

Brahma is usually depicted with four bearded faces facing the four directions, and four hands, each holding one of the four books of the Vedas (Books of Knowledge). His vehicle is the swan and his consort is Saraswati, the Goddess of Education.

According to legend, the sacred lake of Pushkar sprang up at the spot where Brahma dropped a lotus flower from the sky. Pushkar takes its name from this incident – push means 'flower' and kar means 'hand'. Brahma wanted to perform a *yagna* (holy sacrifice) at the lake on a full-moon night, a ceremony that required the presence of his consort. But Saraswati was late. Irritated, Brahma quickly married a convenient milkmaid named Gayatri, and when Saraswati arrived she discovered Gayatri seated in her own honoured place beside Brahma. Saraswati was understandably furious and vowed that Brahma would be forgotten by the people of the earth. It was a profound curse and the gods pleaded with her to reconsider. Finally she relented, decreeing that he could be worshipped, but only in Pushkar. Since then, the Brahma temple at Pushkar has remained one of the only temples in the world dedicated to Brahma and allegedly the only one in India. Meanwhile, Saraswati and Gayatri receive their *pujas* at separate temples, at opposite ends of the town.

you (with all of the attendant clamour and noise). Even without a bathroom, it's a bargain at Rs 450 (Rs 2000 during the camel fair). Room No 9 is also good, with three doors opening onto the lake. During the camel fair, rates increase around ninefold.

**Diamond** (☎ 2305022; Holi ka Chowk; s with shared bathroom Rs 60, r with private bathroom Rs 90) Tucked away, with a friendly European owner, Diamond has rooms around a small tranquil courtyard. They're tiny but spotless and bright, with alcoves.

**Hotel Om** (☎ 2772672; om_deepak2004@yahoo.com; r Rs 200-250; ) Om has a calm garden with a titchy pool, and views over surrounding hills and fields. Rooms are basic and a bit overpriced, and service receives mixed reports.

**Hotel White House** (☎ 2772147; hotelwhitehouse@hotmail.com; r Rs 150-450) This place is spotless, with airy rooms (more expensive ones have balconies) and fine views from the plant-filled rooftop restaurant. Meals are good. It's efficiently run by a tenaciously businesslike mother-and-son team.

**Lake View** (☎ 2772106; www.lakeviewpushkar.com; r with shared bathroom Rs 70-100, with private bathroom Rs 200-300) Lake View is a long-standing place, wonderfully located above the ghats, with superb views over the lake from the roof. Rooms are simple and run-down, but some doubles (usually those with shared bathroom) have balconies facing the water.

**New Rituraj Palace** (☎ 2772875; r Rs 80-100) This peaceful, tucked-away place has clean, basic rooms and gets good reviews from travellers. There's an attractive garden, and good home-cooked food is available.

**Mayur** (☎ 2772302; mayurguesthouse@hotmail.com; s/d Rs 100/120) A pleasant place, right on the main drag, with neat, simple rooms around a leafy courtyard, a cheerful welcome and a good view from the rooftop.

**Hotel Oasis** (☎ 2772100; r from Rs 200, with AC from Rs 400; ) Right near the bus stop is this big hotel, which is very popular with Israeli tourists. It has large, bare rooms (the larger the more you pay), which open onto long walkways. The best rooms are higher up, if you can be bothered to climb all the stairs. Occasional loud techno might put some off. The pool is popular but tiny.

**Bhagwati Guest House** (☎ 2772423; s/d with shared bathroom Rs 40/50, d with private bathroom Rs 80-250) Near the Ajmer bus stand, this guesthouse is a good option if you're going through a cash crunch. There are small, dingy but cheap rooms and some pricier ones out the back, which open onto a garden. The roof-terrace restaurant is popular and good for overlooking the action of the street.

### THE AUTHOR'S CHOICE

**Seventh Heaven** (☎ 5105455; www.inn-seventh-heaven.com; Chotti Basti; r Rs 300-700) Run by the laid-back Anoop, who's lived in London, this is in the heart of Pushkar and is a perfect place to chill out, with an incense-perfumed courtyard, round a fountain. It's a lovingly converted *haveli*, with traditionally crafted furniture, including swing chairs on the main court, galleries and rooftop. The cool tiled rooms have gorgeously pretty individual touches and blissfully comfy beds, and the rooftop restaurant has wonderful views and scrummy food.

Other good cheapies:

**Krishna** (☎ 2772461; s/d with shared bathroom Rs 100/125, r Rs 250-300) Elaborate, lovely old building with simple, bare rooms. Pleasant garden area.

**Maharaja** (☎ 2773527; Mali Mohalta; r Rs 100) Popular and tucked away, with a restful rooftop.

**Milkman** (☎ 2773452; vinodmilkman@hotmail.com; Mali Mohalta; s/d Rs 50/100) Backstreet location in a family house, with a peaceful rooftop.

### MIDRANGE

Several of these are a bit out of town.

**Hotel New Park** (☎ 2772464; Panch Kund Rd; s/d Rs 450/550, with AC Rs 650/750; ) This is an excellent, quiet, modern hotel, tranquilly located among fields a few kilometres out of town. Smart rooms with balconies overlook chrysanthemum, rose and market gardens against a backdrop of hills. There're a nice pool and restaurant.

**Hotel Navratan Palace** (☎ 2772981; s/d Rs 250/300; ) Close to the Brahma Temple, this hotel has a lovely enclosed garden and reasonable rooms opening onto a long walkway. There's a smashing pool (Rs 50 for nonguests), but check whether it's operational.

**Hotel Peacock Holiday Resort** (☎ 2772093; s Rs 150-550, d Rs 200-600; ) Around 500m southeast of the centre of Pushkar, Hotel Peacock also has a pool (Rs 75 for nonguests), set in a leafy courtyard. The cheapest rooms are shabby and feel grimy, but the pricier ones are better, and some have AC.

**RTDC Hotel Sarovar** (☎ 2772040; dm Rs 50, s/d Rs 350/450, with lake view Rs 550/650, with AC Rs 800/900; ) This hotel, next to Pushkar Palace, is set in spacious grounds and has a great position alongside the lake. It has more character than most RTDC places, with a long arched colonnade, but there's indifferent service and the rooms are nothing special.

**Pushkar Resorts** (☎ 2772017; www.pushkarresorts.com; s/d Rs 2695/3000; ) This resort, 5km out of town, is set in an orchard and has a pool shaded by palms. There are 40 modern, clean and comfortable cottages, but they're a bit worn and characterless.

**JP's Tourist Village Resort** (☎ 2772067; d Rs 750-1200; ) About 3km out of town, JP's has atmospheric small, reed-roofed cottages with elaborate wooden furniture. In the shady, rambling gardens are a tree house (for the brave), a pint-sized pool and a restaurant. It's a good place for families, with lots of exploring potential and kids' play equipment.

### TOP END

**Jagat Singh Palace Hotel** (☎ 2772953; d low/high season Rs 1800/2700; ) This is Pushkar's finest – a lovely heritage hotel in a new but traditional building designed like a fort. It offers romantic bedrooms with carved wooden furniture, balconies and nice bathrooms, overlooking lush large gardens and a gorgeous, secluded-feeling pool (Rs 250 for nonguests) with mountain views. There are tempting low-season discounts.

**Hotel Pushkar Palace** (☎ 2773002; www.hotelpushkarpalace.com; s/d from Rs 2200/2700) Once belonging to the maharaja of Kishangarh, and in a romantic lakeside setting, this is let down by unwelcoming staff. Rooms have wooden furniture and carved beds, but aren't as appealing as those at Jagat Singh. There's a pleasant outdoor eating area overlooking the lake. Only the suites look directly onto the lake; other rooms open onto a lakeside walkway. If you don't want to splash out on staying, nip in for a serene drink.

### TOURIST VILLAGE

During the camel fair, the RTDC and many private operators set up a sea of tents near the fair ground. It can get rather cold at night, so bring something warm. A torch (flashlight) may also be useful. You're advised to book ahead. These all have private bathroom, except for the dorm tents.

**RTDC Tourist Village** (☎ 2772074; dm tents per person Rs 200-350, s tents Rs 3700-4600, d tents Rs 4150-5200, s Swiss tents Rs 2900-5800, d Swiss tents Rs 3200-6350, s huts Rs 3200-6350, d huts Rs 3450-6350) This option has dorms and standard tents, and upmarket Swiss and deluxe huts. Full payment must be received two months in advance. Rates include meals for all except the dorm tents.

**Royal Tents** (tents US$250), owned by the maharaja of Jodhpur, are the most luxurious, and most expensive, tents. The rates include meals. Reservations for the Royal Tents should be made in advance through Jodhpur's **Balsamand Palace** (☎ 0291-2571991).

**Royal Desert Camp** (☎ 2772957; tents US$125) is further away from the fairground than Royal Tents, but is another good option. You can book at **Hotel Pushkar Palace** (☎ 2772001).

## Eating

Pushkar is the kind of place where everyone has their favourite restaurant, and there are plenty of atmospheric eateries, though hygiene standards are sometimes lacking. Strict vegetarianism, forbidding even eggs, limits the range of ingredients, but the cooks (sometimes) make up for this with imagination – eggless omelette, anyone? Western-style dishes are hit and miss.

Buffet meals are popular, with several places offering all-you-can-eat meals for Rs 35 to 45. It's safest to eat buffet meals at the busiest places, where the food is more likely to be freshly cooked for each meal rather than reheated.

**Raju Terrace Garden Restaurant** (dishes Rs 25-60; 10am-10pm) This relaxed place serves unusually good Indian food and lots of dishes for the homesick (for example, shepherd's pie, pizza and baked potatoes). It's on a rooftop that's filled with pot plants and fairy lights, and has great views of the lake.

**Rainbow Restaurant** (mains Rs 25-100; 11am-11pm) On a small rooftop with a lovely view over the lake, and decorated with coloured light bulbs, the Rainbow looks grubby, but stick it out and you can eat great pasta dishes with tangy sauces. The hummus with fresh pita bread is delicious.

**Sun-n-Moon** (dishes Rs 25-125; 8am-10pm) Popular with ultra-chilled neo-hippies, the Sun-n-Moon has a friendly owner and a lovely, quiet courtyard surrounding a bodhi tree, a shrine and happy tortoises. There's a sense of soothing calm, and breakfast for the homesick includes hash browns and hot chocolate, while for others there are sustaining lassis and masala chai.

**Honey & Spice** (Laxmi Market; ⌚ 8am-10pm) Run by a friendly couple who learned their skills in Europe, this has delicious homemade banana cakes, soups and vegetable stew.

**Baba Restaurant** (☎ 2772858; dishes Rs 20-50; ⌚ 8am-10pm) Baba, tucked away near the post office and open to the street, has good food and a chilled atmosphere.

**Moon Dance** (dishes Rs 25-110; ⌚ 8am-10.30pm) This has tables in an inviting twinkly, laid-back garden, and an area with low tables and floor cushions to lounge around on. It feels a bit like it's been made from a backpacker-restaurant kit, but the food, including Indian, Mexican and many Italian dishes, is ace, with impressive pizzas.

**Sunset Café** (dishes Rs 10-110; ⌚ 7.30am-midnight) Right on the eastern ghats, this café has sublime lake views. It offers the usual mongrel menu (the food's not up to much), but there's a German bakery, which serves good cakes. The lakeshore setting is perfect at sunset and gathers a crowd.

**Sai Baba Restaurant** (dishes Rs 15-100; ⌚ 10am-midnight) In a relaxing garden, this offers lots of Indian and Italian dishes. There are regular mesmeric dance displays in the evenings with whirling nomadic dancers.

**Third Eye** (dishes Rs 20-60; ⌚ 10am-11pm) This high up, colourful, funky little place sells Israeli snacks very much aimed at the munchie market, and has lake *and* street views, with chairs tucked into narrow balconies. There's a pool table (Rs 30 per game).

**Vijay Deep Restaurant** (dishes around Rs 30; ⌚ 10am-10pm) A large but cosy local joint with a dirt floor near the Marwar bus stand, it has a simple menu, but is a good spot if you want to get away from the tourist scene.

## Shopping

Pushkar's main bazaar is lined with absorbing little shops and is a fantastic place for picking up gifts. There's plenty of silver and beaded jewellery, much catering to foreign tastes, and some old tribal pieces, too. Coloured glass lamps are another appealing buy (you can ponder over trying to get them home intact), as are embroidered and mirrored wall hangings. The range of Indian-music CDs makes this an excellent place for buying some local tunes, and the shops are packed with Indo-Western clothes – designs born from pieces travellers have asked tailors to create, as well as tribal outfits.

Much of the stock comes from the Barmer district south of Jaisalmer and other tribal areas of Rajasthan. As Pushkar is touristy, you'll have to haggle. Ignore 'last-price' quotes that aren't negotiable – take your time and visit a few shops.

Pushkar is great for stocking up on reading material. Bookshops in the main bazaar sell a tremendous range of second-hand novels, and they'll usually buy them back for around 50% of the price you paid.

Pushkar is also good for getting clothes made. One reliable place with reasonable prices is **Navjyoti Tailors** (Sadar Bazaar Rd). Also recommended is **Maloo Enterprises** (Varah Ghat Chowk), opposite the post office.

**Khadi Gramodhyog** (Sadar Bazaar Rd) is almost hidden on the main street. It's a fixed-price shop for traditional hand-woven stuff – mainly men's shirts, scarves and shawls.

## Getting There & Away

Buses for Ajmer leave from the road heading eastwards out of town; other buses leave from the station to the north. There are frequent buses to/from Ajmer (Rs 8/5 – the difference is the road toll to Ajmer; for cars the toll is Rs 25). It's a spectacular climb up and over the hills, and you never know quite what to expect around each turn.

Local travel agencies sell tickets for private buses – shop around for the best price. These buses generally leave from Ajmer, but the agencies should provide you with free connecting transport. Those that leave from Pushkar usually stop for an hour or more in Ajmer anyway. Be warned that some buses (particularly those travelling via Jodhpur) don't go all the way, in spite of promises; they involve a change of bus *and* an extra fare. Destinations include Jaisalmer (Rs 250, 10½ hours), Jodhpur (Rs 87, five hours), Udaipur (Rs 110, eight hours), Delhi (Rs 180/250 in ordinary/sleeper, 10½ hours), Jaipur (Rs 80, four hours) and Agra (Rs 150/250 in ordinary/sleeper, nine hours). Government buses to various destinations leave from the Marwar bus stand; they're a shade cheaper but less comfortable.

For around Rs 50, some agencies will book train tickets for services ex-Ajmer (including free transfer to Ajmer).

### Getting Around

There are no autorickshaws, but it's a breeze to get around on foot. Another good option is to hire a bicycle (Rs 5/25 per hour/day) or a scooter/motorbike (Rs 150/300 per day). A wallah can carry your luggage on a hand-drawn cart to/from the bus stand for around Rs 10.

## TONK

This town, 95km south of Jaipur, on the way to Ranthambhore National Park, was built in the mid-17th century. It's a quiet place, very much off the tourist trail, and worth a stop to see its beautifully painted mosque, or if you're interested in ancient Arabic and Persian manuscripts.

The town of Tonk was originally ruled by a tribe of Afghani Pathans, and their prosperous Muslim descendants have left a legacy of fine mansions, a testament to the wealth they accumulated when they ruled as nawabs from this region. Tonk also served as an important administrative centre during the era of the Raj, and the British have left behind some well-preserved colonial buildings. Surrounded by rocky hills, one is surmounted by a *chhatri*. This is Rasiya ke Tekri, named for a lover who used to sit up here and sing romantic songs.

Worth seeking out is the early-19th-century **Sunehri Kothi** (Najar Bagh Rd), which is decorated with exquisite coloured glass, inlay work and gilding; however, it may be difficult to find it open. A contrasting but equally beautiful sight is the imposing **Jama Masjid**, Rajasthan's finest mosque. Delicately frescoed inside and out with interlocking patterns, ferns and flowers, and sinuous gold decoration, it's hung with dusty glass chandeliers and busy with elderly men praying. This important place of worship was begun in 1246 by the first nawab of Tonk, Nawab Amir Khan, and completed by his son in 1298.

At the **Arabic & Persian Research Institute** (🕑 10am-5pm Mon-Fri) a rare collection of old Arabic and Persian manuscripts and books is housed, dating from the 12th to the 17th century.

About 22km out of town, by Ranthambhore Rd, is a huge elephant carved out of a single block of stone. This is **Hathi Bhata**, carved in 1200 – the date is given in script on the elephant's right ear.

### Getting There & Away

Many local buses from Jaipur's main bus stand pass through Tonk (Rs 47, 2½ hours) en route to Kota. There are also numerous buses between Tonk and Sawai Madhopur for Ranthambhore National Park (Rs 50, two hours).

## RANTHAMBHORE NATIONAL PARK

☎ 07462

Near the grotty town of Sawai Madhopur, this **park** (Indian/foreigner Rs 25/200; 🕑 Oct-Jun) has fantastically dramatic scenery – wild jungle scrub hemmed in by steep crags, crossed by a system of lakes and rivers, and peppered by crumbling temples, ruined pavilions and *chhatris*. The 10th-century Ranthambhore Fort stands on a rocky outcrop as if left over from an epic *Tarzan* movie. The park was a hunting ground for maharajas till 1970 – a curious 15 years after it had become a sanctuary. You can still see numerous hides where the Jaipur maharajas mounted their elaborate big-game shoots (shikars). The queen and Prince Philip were the special guests at a shikar of Maharaja Man Singh. They stayed in the erstwhile hunting lodge (now a hotel, the RTDC Castle Jhoomar Baori, p222), and the Duke of Edinburgh killed a large tiger.

In 1955 this game park was declared a wildlife sanctuary, and in 1973 became one of nine sanctuaries selected as part of the Project Tiger programme. In 1980 it was designated a national park, and the original area was expanded over subsequent years. The park now covers 1334 sq km.

Ranthambhore is where you are most likely to spot a tiger on safari in India. Traffic into the park is much restricted, and the tigers are so used to being observed that they are not scared away by jeeps and canters (large, open-topped trucks seating 20) – being sociable animals, they are even intrigued by visitors.

The park is one of Project Tiger's greatest conservation successes, though here the project's difficulties have also been thrown into relief, such as when government officials were implicated in tiger poaching for the Chinese medicine trade. In 2000 the visit of then US president Bill Clinton led to growth in the park's popularity, although sadly it also highlighted its problems. Bumbram, the tiger seen by President Clinton, could not be found when the park reopened after the monsoon in October 2000. This lead to fears that the now-famous tiger had been poached, although park authorities denied the reports. Following the worrying revelations about the possible disappearance of the Sariska tigers (see the boxed text, p202), there have been concerns that Ranthambhore may also have been targeted by poachers. Extra guards have been mounted and restrictions imposed on the park.

There is also an annual struggle between local villagers and the authorities over livestock grazing in the area, a problem that has intensified in drought-afflicted years and that threatens the tigers' habitat. Villagers compete for land in both the national park and its buffer zones. They need land for cultivation, grazing and wood-felling. There are 332 villages in and around Ranthambhore, with around 143,500 cows. Most of the villages are directly dependent on the park for fodder. Although it is illegal to graze stock within the core national park area, some villagers have been compelled to break the law as overgrazing has left them with no grazing grounds at all. Despite efforts of ecodevelopment and education within the local villages, the relationship between the villagers and park authorities remains strained.

According to a recent census, the park had 35 to 40 tigers. Seeing one is just a matter of luck; you should plan on two or three safaris to improve your chances. There are

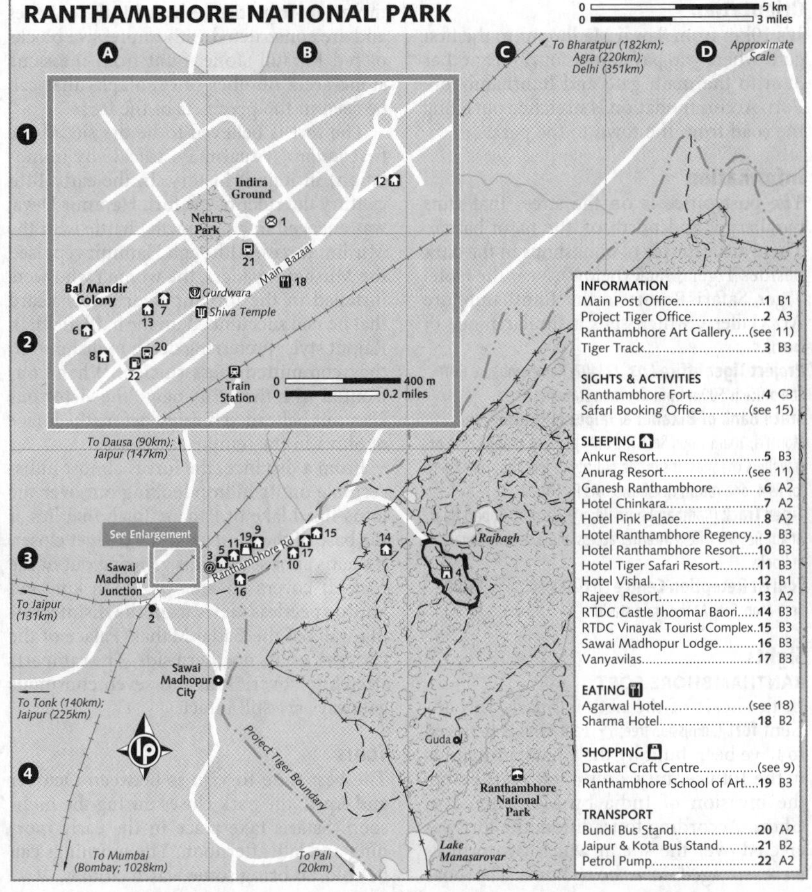

also more than 300 species of birds in the park. Other animals inhabiting Ranthambhore include the endangered caracal, also a member of the cat family, the leopard and the jungle cat; several members of the dog family, such as hyenas, foxes and jackals; the sloth bear; and varieties of deer, including the chital (spotted deer) and the sambar, India's largest deer. There are also two species of antelope: the chinkara (Indian gazelle) and the nilgai (bluebull). However, the park is also worth visiting for the scenery alone, particularly if you walk up to the fort.

Ranthambhore is heavily on the tourist trail, which has led to pressure on resources around the park, and there can be difficulties getting a place in a jeep or canter.

## Orientation

It's 10km from Sawai Madhopur to the first gate, where you pay admission, and another 3km to the main gate and Ranthambhore Fort. Accommodation is stretched out along the road from the town to the park.

## Information

The post office is on the street that runs parallel to, and north of, the main bazaar. There are a couple of bookshops in the park besides Tiger Track (below). Near the Hotel Tiger Safari Resort is the Ranthambhore Art Gallery, which sells a similar range of books.

**Project Tiger office** (☎ 223402; Ranthambhore Rd) The office is 500m from the train station.

**State Bank of Bikaner & Jaipur** (🕑 10am-2pm Mon-Fri, 10am-noon Sat) The only place to change cash or travellers cheques. It's in the old city (a local bus runs there for Rs 4, or a return rickshaw costs Rs 60).

**Tiger Track** (Ranthambhore Rd; 🕑 7am-10.30pm) Near Ankur Resort. Offers Internet access and a useful range of books.

**Tourist Reception Centre** (☎ 2220808; 🕑 10am-5pm Mon-Sat) At the train station.



## Sights

### RANTHAMBHORE FORT

In the heart of the national park, this ancient **fort** (admission free; 🕑 6am-6pm) is believed to have been built by the Chauhan Rajputs in the 10th century, only a few years before the invasion of India by Mohammed of Ghori. According to tradition, the fort was erected over the site at which two princes were engaged in a boar hunt. The boar eluded the princes and dived into a lake. Not to be thwarted, the princes prayed to Shiva to bring back the boar. This Shiva deigned to do, on condition that the princes build a fort in his honour at the spot.

However, it is ever-popular Ganesh who rules the roost at the fort, and a temple to him overlooks its southern ramparts – often busy with pilgrims. Traditionally, when a marriage is to take place, invitations are forwarded to Ganesh before any other guests. The temple at the fort receives hundreds of letters each week addressed to the elephant god, some of which include money to enable him to cover his fare.

There are three Hindu temples inside the fort – besides that dedicated to Ganesh, there are others to Shiva and Ramlalaji. All three date from the 12th and 13th centuries and are constructed with impressive blocks of red Karauli stone. Built from the same stone are a number of cenotaphs that can be seen in the precincts of the fort.

The fort is believed to be the site of the first *jauhar* (ritual mass suicide by immolation) in Rajput history. In the early 14th century the ruler of the fort, Hammir Deva, was engaged in a protracted battle with the Muslim forces. Although Hammir repulsed the Muslim invaders, the women who were installed in the fort for their safety heard that he had succumbed on the battlefield. In Rajput style, preferring death to dishonour, they committed mass suicide. When confronted with the grisly news, the victorious Hammir beheaded himself before the image of Shiva in the temple at the fort.

From a distance, the fort is almost indiscernible on its hilltop looking out over the lotus-filled lake of Padam Talab that lies at the base of the ramparts – as you get closer, it seems almost as if it is growing out of the rock. It covers an area of 4.5 sq km, and affords peerless views from the disintegrating walls of the Badal Mahal (Palace of the Clouds), on its northern side. The ramparts stretch for over 7km, and seven enormous gateways are still intact.

## Tours

The best time to visit is between October and April; the park closes during the monsoon. Safaris take place in the early morning and late afternoon. The mornings can be cold, so bring some warm clothes.

The best way to travel is by jeep, which takes five people. A good network of seven gravel tracks crisscrosses the park, and on each safari jeeps divide among the trails. The jeeps are open-sided. If you've ever been on safari in Africa you might be thinking this is risky, but the tigers appear unconcerned by garrulous tourists toting cameras only metres away from where they're lying. No-one has been mauled or eaten – yet!

Alternatively, you can get a seat in a canter. You still have a good chance of seeing a tiger from a canter, though sometimes passengers can be rowdy, which obviously isn't a great advantage when spotting wildlife.

In 2004 a new system of booking commenced: under this system, seats in both jeeps and canters are allocated on a first-come-first-served basis (previously jeeps had to be booked two months ahead). Demand outstrips supply because the number of motorised vehicles is restricted – only 15 jeeps and 15 canters are allowed inside per session. Although this system is preferable, as it allows people to just turn up and have a chance of a place in a jeep, the change has led to problems, with chaotic queues at the ticket office. Ring the RTDC Vinayak Tourist Complex in advance to check the current situation in case the system has altered again.

A guide is compulsory and is included in the canter ticket price, but will cost an extra Rs 150 if you go by jeep.

Safaris take three hours. From October to February, both canters and jeeps leave at 7am and 2.30pm. From March to June, they leave at 6.30am and 3.30pm. Booking are made at the **RTDC Vinayak Tourist Complex** (☎ 221333; Ranthambhore Rd; Indian/foreigner Rs 25/200, vehicle Rs 125, jeep Rs 1050, canter per person Rs 150, video Rs 200; 🕑 5-7am & noon-2pm). Ask around to check when is best to start queuing for a spot.

If you are taking photos, it's worthwhile bringing some 400 or 800 ASA film, as the undergrowth is dense and surprisingly dark in places. The prime time for photography is May to June, when there are fewer people around. Jeeps are better suited to photography than canters.

## Sleeping & Eating

### BUDGET

Budget travellers will find the cheapest (grimiest and noisiest) lodgings in uninspiring Sawai Madhopur. Many of the hotels offer hefty discounts (up to 50%) during the low season. A straggly town centred on a small bazaar – the road leading from the train station – Sawai Madhopur isn't a particularly friendly place.

**Ganesh Ranthambhore** (☎ 220230; 58 Bal Mandir Colony, Civil Lines; d from Rs 400; ❄) The town's most appealing option: clean and more airy and light than most of the pokey options in Sawai Madhopur. Rooms are cheery, with good bathrooms, and meals are available.

**Hotel Pink Palace** (☎ 220722; plot A1, Bal Mandir Colony; r with shared bathroom Rs 150, with private bathroom Rs 200-400, with AC Rs 450-700; ❄) This option, on the western side of the overpass, is the friendliest and has basic but clean, good-value rooms – more expensive ones open onto a terrace. There's a restaurant.

**Hotel Chinkara** (☎ 220340; 13 Indira Colony, Civil Lines; s/d from Rs 100/200) This place is quiet, with large, dusty, quaint, good-value rooms. It's run by a cheery, family.

**Rajeev Resort** (☎ 221413; 16 Indira Colony, Civil Lines; s with shared bathroom Rs 100, s/d with private bathroom Rs 150/300) Just a few doors away, Rajeev Resort has decent rooms of a better standard than Chinkara's, but less-welcoming staff. It's long had a big *paan*-spitting problem in the hallways, but it seems to have that under control.

**Hotel Vishal** (☎ 220504; s with shared bathroom Rs 60, d with private bathroom Rs 80-150) In the main bazaar, this hotel offers just one dank single and doubles that aren't much better. However, they're acceptable if you're strapped for cash. Some rooms have balconies. You'll need your own sheets.

**Sharma Hotel** (Station Bazaar; dishes Rs 16-60; 🕑 6am-midnight) A basic, open-fronted, pure veg place, this has oily but tasty dishes.

**Agarwal Hotel** (Station Bazaar; dishes Rs 15-60; 🕑 6am-midnight) Next to Sharma Hotel, this small restaurant in the main bazaar has a variety of cheap vegetarian eats that are reasonable enough if you need to fill your belly.

Rooms can also be found at the train station. Dorm beds cost Rs 60, doubles with private bathroom Rs 175.

### MIDRANGE & TOP END

All of the following places offer fixed-price meals, and some also offer an à la carte selection. Many of the places to stay along this strip close when the park is closed.

**Hotel Tiger Safari Resort** (☎ 221137; www.tigersafariresort.com; Ranthambhore Rd; d from Rs 740, cottages Rs 1300; dishes Rs 35-125; ❄) About 4km from the train station is one of the nicest options, a relaxed place that's more personal than some along the strip, though it's pricey for what it offers. The spacious spick-and-span doubles have wall paintings, and are centred on a well-kept garden. The rooftop restaurant is airy and cool, with good views and food.

**Ankur Resort** (☎ 220792; Ranthambhore Rd; s/d from Rs 1200/1800, super deluxe Rs 1200/1800, AC cottages Rs 1600/2200; ❄ 🏊) Ankur Resort, 3km from the train station, is a popular choice, though somewhat overpriced. Rooms are clean, bright and attractive, surrounded by greenery, and there are 18 cottages in the grounds. It has an inviting pool.

**Anurag Resort** (☎ 220451; anuragresort@yahoo.com; Ranthambhore Rd; s/d from Rs 500/1000; ❄) Anurag is around 3km from the train station, a terracotta building built in neo-Rajasthani style with scalloping details, set amid lawns. Rooms are plain, marble-floored, nicely decorated, spacious, airy and bright.

**Hotel Ranthambhore Resort** (☎ 221645; Ranthambhore Rd; d Rs 400-700) This place is about 5km from the train station and offers simple but scrubby rooms – the more expensive ones are larger and better kept.

**RTDC Castle Jhoomar Baori** (☎ 220495; Ranthambhore Rd; standard s/d Rs 600/700, with AC 900/1000; ❄) This is a stunningly set hilltop former royal hunting lodge, about 7km from the train station (you can spot it from the train). The multichamber rooms are loaded with character, although they're a bit shabby these days. Open-rooftop areas add appeal.

**RTDC Vinayak Tourist Complex** (☎ 221333; Ranthambhore Rd; s/d Rs 500/650, with AC Rs 800/900; ❄) On the road back into Sawai Madhopur, this complex has bright newly decorated rooms with appealing little sitting areas in alcove windows. There's a nice lawn area, and a campfire is lit in the winter. You're well placed for tour reservations here – the complex also houses the booking office.

**Sawai Madhopur Lodge** (☎ 220541; Ranthambhore Rd; r from US$240, ste US$260; ❄ 🏊) This Taj Group lodge, 3km from the train station, once belonged to the maharaja of Jaipur. It's luxurious, with a pool (Rs 400 for nonguests), a tennis court and more than 4.5 hectares of lovely, well-kept gardens. The simple, restful rooms overlook serene lawns.

**Hotel Ranthambhore Regency** (☎ 221176; Ranthambhore Rd; s/d incl meals US$70/90; ❄ 🏊) This is an efficient place near Ankur Resort. It has attractive, well-appointed rooms and cottages lining a long, private courtyard and a small pool.

**Aman-i-Khás** (☎ 252052; www.amanresorts.com; Ranthambhore Rd; d 3-night packages incl all meals US$2250; 🕐 Oct-Apr; ❄) There are several opulent camp sites here. This splendid place is on the edge of the park in a tranquil rural setting. The 10 tents are each over 100 sq metres, with bedroom, and sitting and lounging areas. The design has an almost Japanese minimalism, relying on space and subtlety to create a sense of grandeur and opulence. Bathrooms have big bathtubs and showers. It has a spa.

**Vanyavilas** (☎ 223999; www.oberoihotels.com; Ranthambhore Rd; tents US$570; ❄ 🏊) Oberoi works its exclusive magic: this is a camp site to die for. Each 240-sq-metre, teak-floored tent has jungle décor and free-standing baths. The resort is set in a private compound amid 8 hectares of beautifully landscaped grounds, including lush gardens, artificial waterways and an orchard.

**Sher Bagh** (☎ 252120; www.sherbagh.com; Ranthambhore Rd; d incl all meals US$250; 🕐 Oct-Apr) Another luxurious camp: here beautiful tents – based on the design for the maharaja of Jodhpur last century – are set on manicured lawns in an isolated woodland spot near the park. Each of the 12 tents has a veranda and gorgeous bathrooms with sunken showers. It's more reasonably priced than the two other wildly luxurious tented camps.

## Shopping

**Dastkar Craft Centre** (☎ 252049; Ranthambhore Rd; 🕐 10am-8pm) About 3km from the train station, this place is worth a visit. The organisation helps to empower low-caste village women, who gain regular income through selling their textile and embroidery work. Many attractive handicrafts are on sale, including saris, scarves, bags and bedspreads.

**Ranthambhore School of Art** (☎ 234813) This place aims to promote conservation through art, and sells signature photo-realistic wildlife prints.

## Getting There & Away

### BUS

Buses include those going to Jaipur (Rs 60, six hours, three daily) and Kota (Rs 45, four hours, four daily). Buses going to these destinations via Tonk leave from the Bundi bus stand near the petrol station close to the overpass. To go via Dausa (on the Jaipur–Bharatpur road), buses leave from the roundabout near the main post office. The train is preferable for most routes. The inquiries number is ☎ 2451020.

Buses to Bundi (Rs 50, 3½ hours) leave from the Bundi bus stand, and go on to Kota (Rs 80, five hours). Travelling to Bharatpur by bus invariably involves a change in Dausa – the train is infinitely preferable.

#### TRAIN

The train station has a **computerised reservation office** (🕑 8am-8pm Mon-Sat, 8am-2pm Sun) for bookings.

The *Golden Temple Mail* (No 2903) leaves Sawai Madhopur at 12.40pm, arriving in Delhi (Rs 91 in 2nd class, 361km) at 7pm. It goes via Bharatpur (Rs 54, 182km), arriving at 3.20pm. From Delhi, it leaves at 7.55am, stopping at Bharatpur at 10.51am and arriving at 1.08pm. To Kota, there are about seven trains daily, the most convenient of which is the *Avadh Express* (Nos 5063/4). It leaves Sawai Madhopur at 9.30am and arrives in Kota (Rs 37, 109km) at 11am. Going the other way, it leaves Sawai Madhopur at 4.50pm, arriving in Agra at 9.40pm.

### Getting Around

Bicycle hire is available in the main bazaar (around Rs 25 per day). Autorickshaws are available at the train station; the journey to Ranthambhore Rd will cost around Rs 25.

## KARAULI

Picturesque Karauli was founded in 1348 and has some important Krishna temples – the city is the home of Shri Madan Mohanji, the deity of Lord Krishna, and attracts many pilgrims. Around 23km from Karauli is the massively popular temple of Kaila Devi – during the Navratri celebrations in

#### KARAULI'S CRIME-RIDDEN RAVINES

The Chambal River valley, straddling Uttar Pradesh and Rajasthan, was once notorious as the territory of Phoolan Devi – the Bandit Queen who later became a politician before being assassinated. Borderlands are popular with dacoits (bandits) – separate policing for each state makes it easier to confuse the law.

Between Bharatpur, Dholpur and Karauli, the evocatively desolate ravines, strewn with bushes and gullies, have more recently housed another notorious bandit Auturi, who has of late been increasing his celebrity status. In 2004 and 2005 the robber began installing huge brass gongs bearing his name and prayers in local temples. Police were unable to stop the dacoit and, on removing the gongs, received such protests from local Gurjar people that they had to be reinstalled. Like the notorious bandit Veerappan, caught and killed by police in 2004, he has become a local folk hero.

It seems the area is criminally disposed. Further intrigue swirls at the ruined fort of Timangarh, in the heart of the dacoits' outback territory, 40km from Karauli. Remote and inaccessible, the fort, dating from 1100, sits above a water lily–filled lake. It seems the fort was abandoned around 300 years ago, according to local lore because of the curse of a Natni (an acrobat). The king challenged the Natni to walk over a 2km tightrope and promised to reward her with half his kingdom if she did so. On her return journey, he panicked and ordered the rope to be cut. The Natni fell and died, but placed a curse on the king that his fort would one day be in ruins.

Once the fort was so impenetrable that treasures – *ashtadhatu* (idols made from eight metals), stone idols and sculptures – were left here for safekeeping. The site remained untouched other than by nature for centuries, but in the 1970s local nawabs are believed to have set up operations to loot the fort for idols and weaponry. Once word got out of the riches within the fort, a large-scale smuggling operation was set in motion, with robbers coming via helicopter to carry away pieces of carving to sell on the international markets.

The fort today is a tragic pile of rubble, as foretold by the acrobat. Elaborate carving on the remaining pieces hints at its onetime glory. It's an evocative place, but there's not much to see now that the building has fallen in on itself. If you do make it here, it's up to the small police camp on guard near the entrance whether you may wander around or not.

March/April and September/October, thousands of devotees flood the town en route to the temple.

Completely off the tourist trail, the area is also famous for its red-sandstone mines and for its lak (resin) bangles. Nearby is the rugged **Kaila Devi Game Sanctuary** (25km away), with some beautiful scenery and assorted wildlife, including chinkaras, wild boars, bluebulls, jackals and leopards. About 40km away is Timangarh, an 11th-century fort ruined by looters.

The mainly 17th-century **old city palace** (Indian/foreigner Rs 50/100; sunrise-sunset) was constructed over different periods; the oldest part has existed for 600 years. The Durbar Hall has some particularly fine paintings. Old-time retainers light rickety lamps to show them to you. Occupied by the Karauli royal family until around the 1950s, the palace is run-down and worn, but atmospheric. It has some great views from the roof. Today it's occupied by naughty monkeys and a gaggle of geese. In the old days geese were used to sound the alert if intruders entered the palace grounds. There's a **Krishna temple** (5-11.30am & 4-8pm) in the compound.

Around 40km from town, along a potholed track, is a tragically ruined fort, **Timangarh**. Built around 1100 and reconstructed in 1244, this once mighty fort overlooks a lake filled with water lilies. It was deserted 300 years ago, but was destroyed by looters over the last 50 years (see the boxed text, p223). You'll need to hire a taxi to get here, and one that can manage the track – the return journey will cost you around Rs 400.

**Bhanwar Vilas Palace** (☎ 07464-20024, 2290763; www.karauli.com; s/d/ste May-Sep Rs 1475/1550/2100, Oct-Apr Rs 2000/2100/2750, garden cottages year-round Rs 700-900; ), owned by Maharaja Krishna Chandra Pal (whose family hail back to Krishna), is closer to a large country manor than a palace. A back-in-time place, it features a billiard room, some shady verandas, rambling grounds and classic cars in the garages. Rooms are comfortable and feel like you've turned up for a country-house weekend, perhaps as part of a shooting party. Excursions to nearby points of interest, including the old city palace, can be organised. There's a pool, but it's grubby.

The town is 182km southeast of Jaipur, situated between Bharatpur (110km) and Sawai Madhopur (104km). There are buses running between Jaipur and Karauli (Rs 60, five hours).

The nearest train stations are Gangapur City (31km) and Hindaun (30km), both on the main Delhi–Mumbai (Bombay) Line, where almost all the trains running between Mumbai and Delhi stop. There are regular services from Sawai Madhopur (Rs 27 in 2nd class, 1¼ hours) to Gangapur.

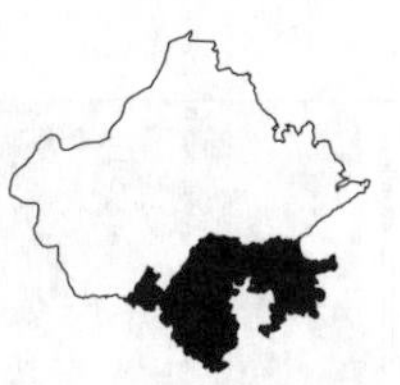

# Southern Rajasthan

Southern Rajasthan holds arguably Rajasthan's most enchanting city, Udaipur, a milk-white confection surrounded by hills and meandering around several lakes. It's the ultimate in Rajput fantasy with its cream-coloured *havelis* (traditional mansions) and palaces, one of which, floating in Pichola Lake, is one of India's most famous hotels, the Lake Palace.

In the south are Rajasthan's two finest forts, Chittorgarh (Chittor), which sprawls over an enormous hilltop plateau, and Kumbalgarh, far from anywhere, perched at 1100m, with awe-inspiring views over the dense Aravalli hills that fade into a pale blue horizon.

Here also are two Jain temple complexes where artistic virtuosity has reached dizzy pinnacles. Ranakpur, deep in an Aravalli valley, has a hall of 1444 pillars, each unique; Dilwara, on a hilltop near Mt Abu, has marble carving so delicate that it's almost transparent in places. Mt Abu is Rajasthan's only hill station; a holiday resort set amid vast hills, it's a world away from the rest of Rajasthan and largely undiscovered by foreign tourists.

Southern Rajasthan is great if you want to get off the beaten track. Bundi is an enchanting town, painted Brahmin blue and overlooked by a palace seemingly built by goblins. Nearby Kota holds one of the state's finest palaces. Jhalawar is really off the trail, with a mighty, forgotten fort and a city of temples nearby. Jaisamand, a vast blue-reflecting hill-ringed expanse, is Asia's biggest artificial lake. The region offers some exhilarating activities too. You can trek or ride around the beautiful countryside near Udaipur, Mt Abu or Kumbalgarh, cycle around Bundi, or take a boat trip down the crocodile-infested Chambal River.

## HIGHLIGHTS

- **Chittorgarh** (p241) and **Kumbalgarh** (p265) – architectural magnificence reflecting noble times
- **Udaipur** (p246), an ice-cream cake of a city, with dreamy lakes overlooked by shadowy hills
- Exquisite, mind-blowing carving in the Jain temples at **Mt Abu** (p272) and **Ranakpur** (p266)
- Endearing **Bundi** (p228), a blue-painted small town, overlooked by a ramshackle fort and a magical palace
- The rolling, unexplored-feeling countryside around **Kumbalgarh** (p265), **Udaipur** (see p264) or **Mt Abu** (p276)

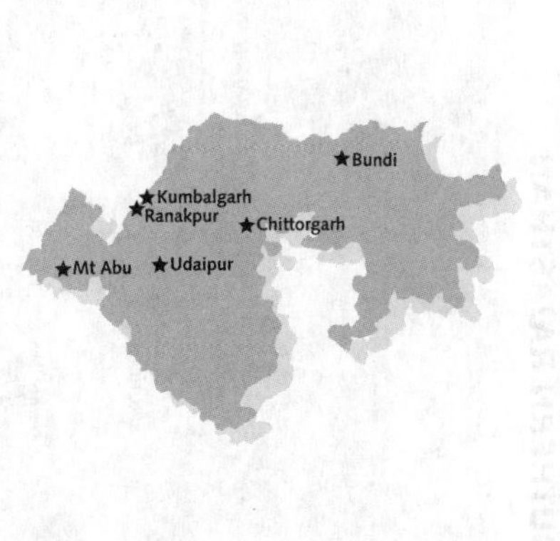

# SOUTHERN RAJASTHAN

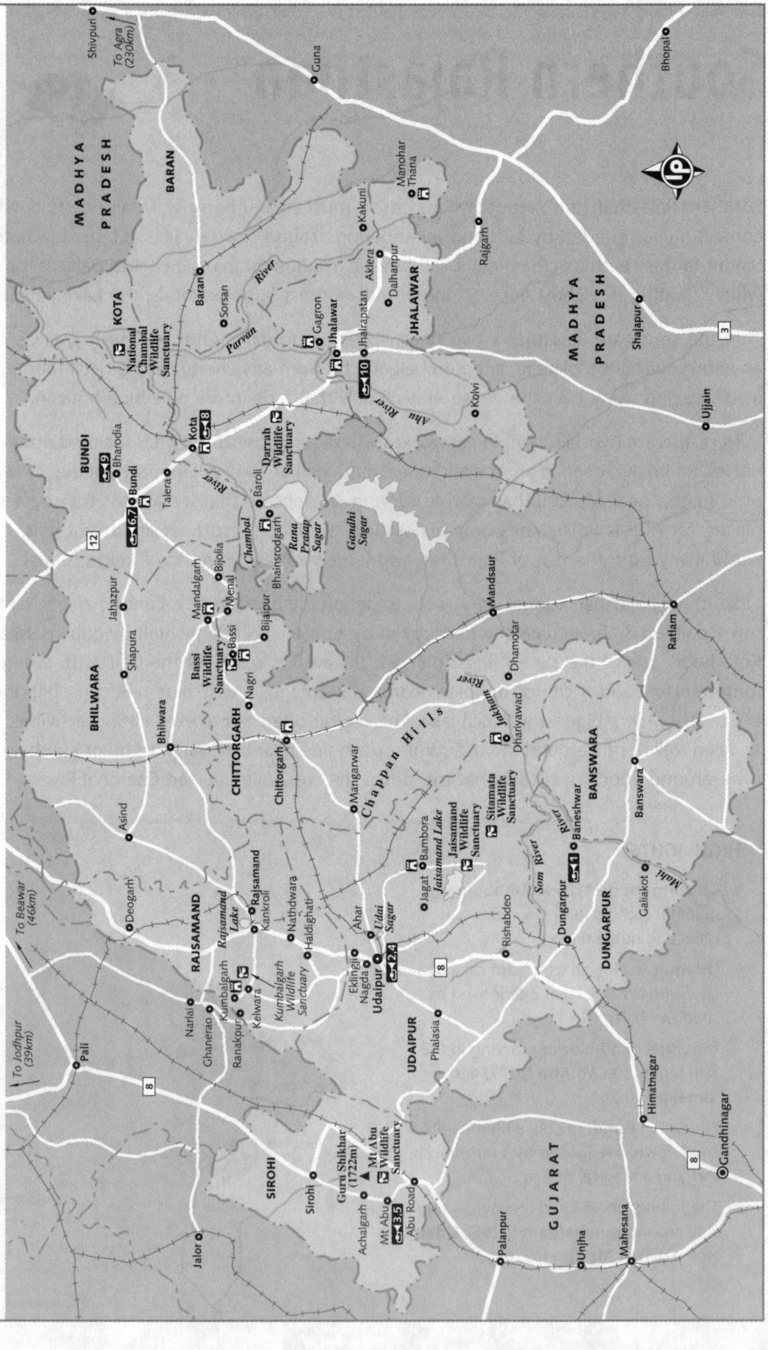

0 60 km
0 40 miles

MADHYA PRADESH
BARAN
KOTA
BUNDI
BHILWARA
CHITTORGARH
RAJSAMAND
UDAIPUR
SIROHI
GUJARAT
DUNGARPUR
BANSWARA
JHALAWAR
MADHYA PRADESH

Shivpuri
To Agra (230km)
Guna
Bhopal
Manohar Thana
Kakuni
Rajgarh
Aklera
Dalhanpur
Shajapur
Baran
Sorsan
Parvan River
Gagron
Jhalawar
Jhalrapatan
National Chambal Wildlife Sanctuary
Kota
Darrah Wildlife Sanctuary
Abu River
Kolvi
Ujjain
Bharodia
Bundi
Talera
Chambal River
Baroli
Bhainsrodgarh
Rana Pratap Sagar
Gandhi Sagar
Jahazpur
Bijolia
Mandalgarh
Menal
Bijaipur
Mandsaur
Ratlam
Shapura
Bassi Wildlife Sanctuary
Bassi
Nagri
Dhamotar
Jakham River
Bhilwara
Chittorgarh
Chappan Hills
Dhariyawad
Mangarwar
Asind
Sitamata Wildlife Sanctuary
Baneshwar
Banswara
Bambora
Jaisamand Lake
Jaisamand Wildlife Sanctuary
Jagat
Som River
Mahi
Galiakot
Deogarh
To Beawar (46km)
Rajsamand Lake
Rajsamand
Kankroli
Nathdwara
Haldighati
Ahar
Udai Sagar
Eklingji
Nagda
Udaipur
Rishabdeo
Dungarpur
Narlai
Kumbalgarh
Kelwara
Ghanerao
Ranakpur
Kumbalgarh Wildlife Sanctuary
Phalasia
Pali
To Jodhpur (39km)
Himatnagar
Gandhinagar
Sirohi
Guru Shikhar (1722m)
Mt Abu Wildlife Sanctuary
Achalgarh
Mt Abu
Abu Road
Jalor
Palanpur
Unjha
Mahesana
3
8
12
8
8

SOUTHERN RAJASTHAN

## FESTIVALS IN SOUTHERN RAJASTHAN

There's a flurry of fantastically colourful festivals in the south, while statewide and nationwide festivals (see p363) are also celebrated with aplomb. Festivals in this boxed text are marked on Map p226.

**Baneshwar Fair** (1; Jan-Feb; Baneshwar, p270) This big tribal event is celebrated by thousands of Bhil people in Baneshwar, Dungarpur district. The fair site is at the confluence of the Mahi, Som and Jakham Rivers. The festival is two fairs combined, one honouring Lord Shiva and the other Vishnu, who is worshipped as Mavji. Festivities include acrobatic performances and cultural programmes, and a silver image of Mavji is paraded through the village on horseback and doused in the river. The river is thought to become holiest at this time, so many people bathe at the same time as the idol.

**Holi** (2; Feb-Mar; Udaipur, p246) This joyful festival is celebrated across India, but Udaipur is the place to be for it. Holi marks the end of winter and the beginning of spring, and it symbolises the victory of divine power over demonic strength. It's also known as the Festival of Colours because of the exuberant throwing of coloured powder and water on the last day. The Udaipur royal family hosts an elaborate function at the City Palace to celebrate Holi. There's an evening procession with decorated horses, as well as a band, local nobility in traditional attire and, of course, the royal family. After performing an ancient religious ceremony, the royal family lights a huge sacred fire, Holika Dahan, signifying the triumph of good over evil. Tribal people then perform a traditional dance. Afterwards you get the chance to rub shoulders with nobility at a cocktail and dinner reception held in the Zenana Mahal at the City Palace. Tickets cost Rs 3000 per person and can be obtained at the Shiv Niwas Palace Hotel (p259) in Udaipur.

**Gangaur** (3; Mar-Apr; Mt Abu, p270) Gangaur is celebrated across Rajasthan but has some interesting adaptations in this region. Essentially a festival for women, it's dedicated to the goddess Gauri (Parvati). Wives pray for their spouses, and unmarried women pray for good husbands. The Garasia tribes of the Mt Abu region celebrate Gangaur for an entire month. An image of Gauri is carried aloft from village to village, accompanied by singing, dancing and proffering of invitations. Young unmarried people are able to meet without social sanction and select marriage partners, with whom they elope. In Bundi (p228), Kota (p233) and Jhalawar (p238), unmarried girls collect poppies from the fields during Gangaur and make them into wreaths for the goddess. In Nathdwara (p264), the Gangaur procession lasts for seven days, and the goddess is dressed differently each day. On the last day she wears black and gold, and the women carrying the image wear similar clothes.

**Mewar Festival** (4; Mar-Apr; Udaipur, p246) Udaipur's colourful take on Gangaur, this festival also welcomes the onset of spring. People dressed in traditional costumes sing and dance in a lively procession that goes through the town to Gangaur Ghat on Pichola Lake. Idols of Gauri and Shiva, who represent the perfect couple, are carried in the procession and then set afloat on the lake in boats. There are also free cultural programmes.

**Summer Festival** (5; Apr-May; Mt Abu, p270) The hill station of Mt Abu registers the coolest temperatures in the state at this scorching time of the year, so this is not a bad place to be in April/May. The festival includes classical and traditional folk-music programmes, as well as boat races on Nakki Lake and fireworks.

**Kajli Teej** (6; Aug-Sep; Bundi, p228) The traditional Rajasthani festival of Teej, which marks the coming of the monsoon, is celebrated somewhat differently in Bundi. Here it's observed on the third day of the month of Bhadra. A palanquin (litter) bearing the goddess Teej is carried through the streets from Nawal Sagar to Azad Park. The celebrations are a good chance to see local artists perform, and they merge with the festival of Janmashtami, Krishna's birthday.

**Bundi Utsav** (7; Oct-Nov; Bundi, p228) This cultural festival showcases the colourful traditions of the region with a procession, classical raga performances, magic and fireworks.

**Dussehra** (8; Oct-Nov; Kota, p233) Kota is the place to be at the end of this festival, when enormous effigies, some around 20m high, are filled with crackers and set alight. The festival – an India-wide celebration – marks the triumph of good over evil in celebrating the story of Rama's victory over Ravana (see p48).

**Ghans Bheru Festival** (9; Oct-Nov; Bharodia, p228) Held on the day after Diwali (see p365) in the little village of Bharodia, about 10km northeast of Bundi, the festival honours the Hindu god Ghans Bheru. While almost unknown to most tourists, this colourful festival attracts thousands of villagers from the Bundi district, who converge on the village to celebrate a prosperous harvest.

**Chandrabhaga Fair** (10; Nov-Dec; Jhalrapatan, p239) The fair takes place on the last day of the Hindu month of Kartika on the banks of the holy Chandrabhaga River near Jhalrapatan, the city of temple bells. A huge cattle fair attracting villagers from Rajasthan and neighbouring states, it includes livestock trading and colourful stalls. The religious element involves pilgrims bathing in a sacred part of the river known as Chandrawati.

### History

The kingdom of Mewar (the area encompassing Chittorgarh and Udaipur) has dominated the history of the south, which is splattered with bloodshed and vast doses of valour.

Chittorgarh, the former Mewar capital, was sacked three times from 1303 to 1568 and each defeat ended in immense carnage, with the impossibly noble Rajputs reliably choosing death before dishonour. While the men died in battle, the women committed *jauhar* (collective sacrifice) by throwing themselves into the flames of huge pyres. After the third attack, Mewar's ruler, Maharaja Udai Singh II, wisely decided to give up Chittorgarh as a bad job and establish his new capital in Udaipur.

Udaipur was shielded by thick forests and the Aravallis, and it was far less vulnerable than exposed Chittorgarh. But this did not stop invaders from trying their luck, and Udaipur also had its share of battles. These power struggles ended in the early 19th century when the British signed an alliance pledging to protect the Mewar rulers.

The rulers of the Mewar region, the illustrious Sisodia Rajput clan, claim descent from the sun, and you'll see the symbol of the sun repeated in their palaces and forts.

As the Sisodia Rajputs have long occupied the top of the Rajput hierarchy, this is historically an important region. The dynasty is believed to be one of the oldest in the world, reigning in unbroken succession for over 1400 years. Staunchly defying foreign domination of any kind, they were the only Hindu princes who refused to intermarry with the once-influential Mughal emperors. For them, honour, heritage and independence were of paramount importance, even if that meant deprivation and suffering.

Other princely states in southern Rajasthan, such as Kota and Bundi, were formed long after the region of Mewar. The remote royal state of Jhalawar was created as recently as 1838.

## BUNDI

☎ 0747 / pop 88,312

A captivating small town with narrow lanes of Brahmin-blue houses, lakes, hills, bazaars and a temple at every turn, Bundi is dominated by a fantastical palace – faded-parchment cupolas and loggias rising from a mighty fortress that's mounted on a crag. The town is the perfect place to relax and write that novel (as Rudyard Kipling did, in a fragile lakeside icing-sugar house).

Bundi was the capital of a major princely state during the Rajputs' heyday. Although its importance dwindled with the rise of Kota during Mughal times, it remained independent until its incorporation into Rajasthan in 1947.

The storybook, crumbling palace houses the famous Bundi murals (see the boxed text, p233), as well as not-so-famous masses of bats and pigeons. Dusk heralds the extraordinary sight of streaming clouds of bats exiting the palace and heading for the woods. From January to March delicate pink poppies fill surrounding fields.

### History

The Hadoti Chauhans, who claim their descent from the sacred fires of Mt Abu, conquered this area of Rajasthan in the 12th century, wresting it from the Mina and Bhil tribes. This occurred after they were pushed south from their stronghold at Ajmer by Mohammed of Ghori. Bundi was chosen to be the capital of the new Hadoti kingdom, and Kota was the land grant of the ruler's eldest son.

In 1624 Kota was made into a separate state at the instigation of the Mughal Emperor Jehangir. Bundi's importance dwindled with the rise of Kota during Mughal times, but it maintained its independence until it was incorporated into the state of Rajasthan after Independence in 1947.

### Orientation

It's easy to find your way to the palace on foot through the bazaar. Once you pass through the city gates there are only two main roads through town, and the palace is visible from many points. The bus stand is at the Kota (southeast) end of town, and the train station is about 2km south of town, across National Hwy 12.

### Information

No banks in Bundi change money, but the small moneychanger south of the palace will change various currencies, and sometimes even travellers cheques, depending on his mood. There's a government hospital in the south of town, near the bus stand.

Mukesh Mehta, at the Haveli Braj Bhushanjee (see p232) is a terrific source of tourist information; his brother's website, www.kiplingsbundi.com, is also useful.

**Ayurvedic Hospital** (☎ 2443708; 🕑 9am-1pm & 4-6pm Mon-Sat, 9am-1pm Sun) Opposite the Haveli Braj Bhushanjee, the hospital prescribes natural plant-based remedies. There are medicines for all sorts of ailments, from upset tummies to arthritis, and many of them are free.

**Cyber Dream** (per hr Rs 60; 🕑 9am-9pm) One of the increasing number of places to check your email.

**SBBJ ATM** (outside Chogan Gate) Accepts international cards.

**Shri Balaji.com** (Nahar ka Chuhata; per hr Rs 60; 🕑 9am-9pm) An alternative to Cyber Dream.

**Tourist office** (☎ 2442697; 🕑 10am-5pm Mon-Fri) Near Raniji-ki-Baori; you can get a free map here.

## Sights

### BUNDI PALACE

An extraordinary, decaying edifice, the **palace** (admission Rs 50, camera/video Rs 50/75; 🕑 8am-5pm) has fabulous, fading turquoise and gold murals. It's reached from the bazaar's northwestern end. Previously shut up and left to the bats, it's been cleaned up, and the entirety is now open to the public. Knowledgeable guides hang around the ticket office.

You enter through the huge elephant gate (1607). From here you can visit the Chhatra Mahal, built in 1644, which has some of Bundi's finest murals: one room features well-preserved paintings of Krishna – one for each month. The Phool Mahal was built in 1607 and shows a huge royal procession.

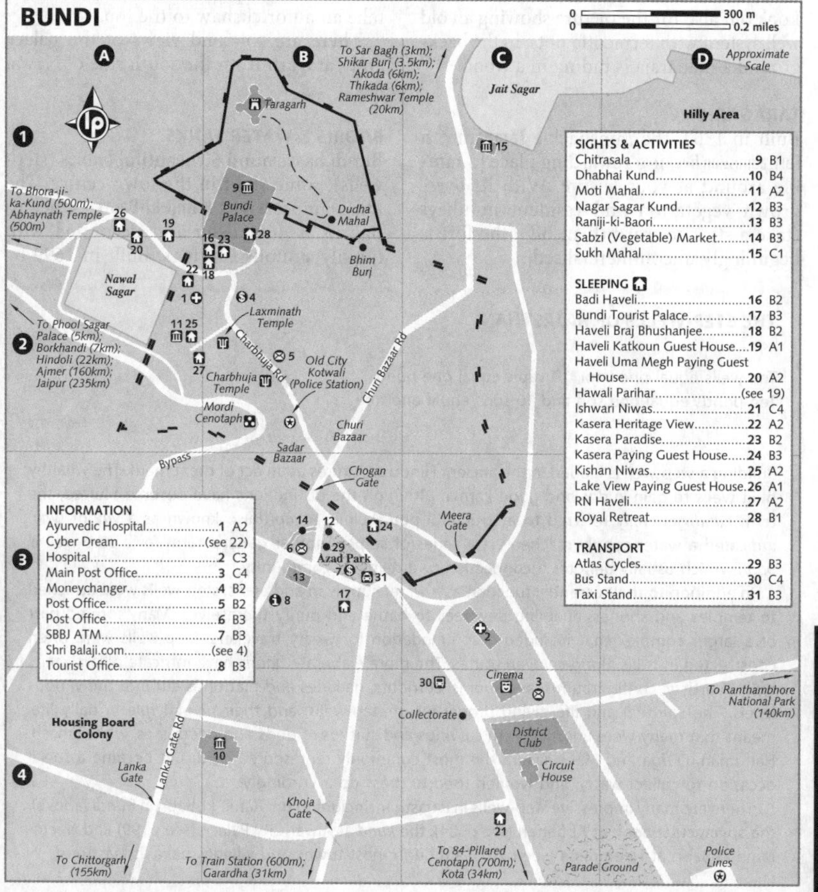


SOUTHERN RAJASTHAN

Of the same date, the Badal Mahal has a wonderful Chinese-inspired ceiling, divided into petal shapes and decorated with peacocks and Krishna (note his Chinese eyes).

To get to the **Chitrasala** (Umed Mahal; admission free; 7am-6pm), built by Rao Umed Singh in the 18th century, you exit through the elephant gate and walk further uphill to the entrance. Above the garden courtyard are several rooms covered in beautiful paintings. There are some great Krishna pieces, including him stealing the clothes of the *gopis* (milkmaids), and one in which he plays the flute while Radha, in a water pot, crosses a river to him. The back room on the right is the Sheesh Mahal, badly damaged but with some beautiful inlaid glass. Back in the main courtyard there's a picture of Bundi itself. Look out also for the picture showing an old well system with terracotta pots; in the background a maharaja is hiding in a wood.

#### TARAGARH

Built in 1354, the ramshackle **Taragarh** (Star Fort; admission free) is a rewarding place to ramble around at your leisure. With its overgrown vegetation and resident monkeys (take a stick to ward them off), the fort is beguilingly uncommercialised.

The views from the top are magical, especially at sunset. Inside the ramparts are huge reservoirs carved out of solid rock, and the Bhim Burj, the largest of the great bastions, on which there is mounted a famous cannon – a trench alongside it provided shelter for the artillery. The least-sensitive-to-heritage award should go to the national broadcaster, Doordarshan, who is responsible for the ugly concrete transmission tower right next to the fort.

Taragarh is reached by a steep road leading up the hillside to its enormous gateway. Take the path up behind the Chitrasala, then go east along the inside of the ramparts and left up the steep stone ramp just before the Dudha Mahal, a small disused building 200m from the palace. It's also possible to take an autorickshaw to the top.

There are splendid views of the palace and Taragarh from the south side of Nawal Sagar.

#### BAORIS & WATER TANKS

Bundi has around 60 beautiful *baoris* (step-wells), some right in the town centre. The most impressive, **Raniji-ki-Baori** (Queen's Baori), is 46m deep and decorated with funkily sinuous carvings. Built in 1699 by

### THE STEP-WELLS OF RAJASTHAN

Ten wells equal one vapi, 10 vapis equal one pond
Ten ponds equal one son and 10 sons equal one tree

*Vedic verse*

Building a step-well is lauded in the ancient Hindu scriptures as an act of great merit. The wealthy built wells to gain kudos and good karma. Although the distinctions have become blurred, the term *kund* generally referred to a structural pond, while a *vapi* (also known as a *vav* or *wav*) indicated a water supply reached via a series of steps. Another generic term for a step-well is *baori*, which usually denotes a connection to a religious community.

In addition to their essential function as a water supply in arid areas, step-wells were attached to temples and shrines, enabling devotees to bathe and purify themselves. Many formed part of a larger complex that included accommodation for weary travellers. Step-wells were often constructed in trails along caravan routes. The more elaborate *baoris* have intricate pillars, steps built in artistic configurations, and rooms, corridors, galleries and platforms cut into the various levels. The spiritual and life-giving properties of step-wells, and their pivotal role in daily life, meant that many were adorned with carvings and statues of gods and goddesses, with Ganesh, Hanuman, Durga and Mahishasura the most commonly represented deities. It became a social occasion to collect water, and women used to dress up accordingly.

There are many impressive step-wells in Rajasthan, including the Raniji-ki-Baori in Bundi (above), the spectacular *baori* at Abhaneri (see p184), the *kund* at Alwar City Palace (see p199) and Neemrama-ki-Baori at Neemrama (see p201), although most towns and villages have at least one.

Rani Nathavatji, it's one of the largest of its kind. The **Nagar Sagar Kund** is a pair of matching step-wells just outside the Chogan Gate to the old city.

Visible from the fort is the square artificial lake of **Nawal Sagar**, which tends to dry up if the monsoon is poor. At its centre is a temple to Varuna, the Aryan god of water.

Opposite the **Abhaynath Temple**, one of Bundi's oldest Shiva temples, is the 16th-century tank **Bhora-ji-ka-Kund**, which attracts a variety of bird life after a good monsoon, including kingfishers and hummingbirds. The Dhabhai Kund, south of the Raniji-ki-Baori, is another imposing tank.

### OTHER ATTRACTIONS

It's great to amble around the bazaars of the old city. Just outside the walls, the **sabzi (vegetable) market**, between Raniji-ki-Baori and Nagar Sagar Kund, is particularly vibrant. There are more than 200 temples here and more than 100 step-wells. At the time of research, Haveli Braj Bhushanjee (see p232) was planning a self-guided heritage walk. Contact the staff to see if they have a map.

Bundi's other attractions are out of town and are best visited by bike or rickshaw. The modern **Phool Sagar Palace** (Flower Palace) has gardens and a beautiful artificial tank that's good for spotting kingfishers. Inside are murals created by Italian prisoners of war. Several kilometres west of town, on the Ajmer road, the palace is closed to the public, but it's due to open in future.

**Jait Sagar**, to the north, is a picturesque lake flanked by hills and strewn with pretty lotus flowers during the monsoon and winter months. The stately **Sukh Mahal** (⏲ 10am-5pm) is a smaller palace surrounded by terraced gardens. Here Rudyard Kipling once stayed and wrote part of *Kim*. On the opposite side of the lake, the nearby, neglected **Sar Bagh** contains 66 royal cenotaphs, some with terrific, intricate carvings – the most spectacular is that of Chattar Sal Singh. **Shikar Burj** is a small former royal hunting lodge (once there were tigers, deer and boars here). Next to a water tank, on the road that runs along the north side of the Jait Sagar, is a good place for a picnic. South of town is the **84-Pillared Cenotaph**, which is set in gardens. Particularly stunning when lit up at night, it was built to honour the son of the maharaja's ayah (nurse) about 600 years ago.

There are some lovely cycle excursions from Bundi – you can visit tiny villages in the pristine countryside. Around 6km north of Bundi are **Akoda**, a merchant's village, and **Thikarda**, which has various potteries. About 20km north are a Shiva cave temple and a waterfall at **Rameshwar**. Around 7km west of Bundi is rural **Borkhandi** village. Twenty-two kilometres towards Jaipur is **Hindoli**, home to a huge lake and a ruined hilltop fort.

About 33km south of Bundi, at the village of **Garardha**, you can see some ancient rock paintings, believed to be about 15,000 years old, flanking the river. There's a curious depiction of a man riding a huge bird, as well as some hunting scenes. There are also some stick figures of people holding hands – this is apparently how villagers crossed rivers long ago and is still practised today in some regions. It's best to come here with a local guide; contact Haveli Braj Bhushanjee (see p232) for more information. A half-day trip in a jeep costs around Rs 500 return.

Back in town, the **Moti Mahal** – a palace in the centre of the old town – is still inhabited by the maharaja, but there's talk of part of it opening as a museum.

## Activities

The **Ayurvedic Hospital** (☎ 2443708; ⏲ 9am-1pm & 4-6pm Mon-Sat, 9am-1pm Sun), opposite the Haveli Braj Bhushanjee, prescribes natural plant-based remedies and offers various Ayurvedic treatments.

## Sleeping & Eating

Bundi's guesthouses (also the best places to eat) are charm packed and family run. They're mainly budget, with some midrange options. There are no five-star hotels.

The commission racket operates here, so don't let your taxi or rickshaw driver pressure you. In this chapter, all rooms have private bathrooms unless otherwise indicated.

### BUDGET

**Haveli Katkoun Guest House** (☎ 2444311; raghunandansingh@yahoo.com; r Rs 250-450) Run by retired Major Singh and his gentle family, this hassle-free place has comfortable, spotless rooms off a calm, leafy garden. The rooms upstairs open onto a communal balcony with views. The restaurant provides good home-cooked food (and beer), and free pick-ups from the bus and train stations are on offer.

**Haveli Uma Megh Paying Guest House** (☎ 244 2191; r Rs 150-350; dishes Rs 25-35) Friendly brothers run this guesthouse, which has a wide range of rooms with wall paintings, alcoves and some lake views. Some pricier rooms are really spacious. It's peaceful and has an excellent lakeside garden restaurant that's just right for candlelit dinners.

**Kasera Heritage View** (☎ 2444679; r Rs 150-450) Popular and operated by a charming young couple, the Kasera has a rooftop restaurant that's perfectly placed for gazing at the palace and a range of rooms in an old *haveli* (nab the one with a palace-view balcony or the one overlooking the mosque).

**Lake View Paying Guest House** (☎ 2442326; dilipparashar@yahoo.com; r with shared bathroom Rs 125, with private bathroom Rs 200; dishes around Rs 30) This guesthouse, set in the modest 200-year-old Meghwahanji Haveli, is overseen by an elderly character and his assorted younger relations. It occupies a lovely lakeside spot. Some rooms have lake views and stained-glass windows – most people prefer the rooms downstairs next to a small garden. Home-cooked meals are available.

**Ishwari Niwas** (☎ 2442414; in_heritage@indiatimes.com; 1 Civil Lines; r Rs 250-600) Family-run Ishwari Niwas has royal associations. The graceful old colonial building has variable rooms with murals – some rooms have high ceilings – all arranged around a large, peaceful courtyard. The location is not the best as it's away from the old city, past the bus stand. Sightseeing excursions can be arranged.

**Kasera Paying Guest House** (☎ 2446630; d with shared bathroom Rs 200, with private bathroom Rs 250; dishes Rs 30-35) The same family from Kasera Heritage View watches over this small-scale guesthouse, near Chogan Gate in the main bazaar. It offers small budget rooms, set in a delightful small *haveli*, and a good little rooftop restaurant.

**Bundi Tourist Palace** (☎ 2442650; s/d with shared bathroom Rs 85/140) This basic place, opposite Azad Park, has undersized rooms but it's clean, friendly and family-run. There are better places to stay, but it's cheap.

**Royal Retreat** (☎ 2444426; royalretreatbundi@yahoo.com; s Rs 150-350, d Rs 300-500) In the palace compound, Royal Retreat has attractive rooms with tiled floors arranged around a hushed, open-air courtyard. However, it's lackadaisically staffed and makes little of its fantastic location.

Family homes operating as guesthouses:

**Hawali Parihar** (☎ 2446675; r Rs 100-200) Opposite Gopal Temple.

**Kishan Niwas** (☎ 2446110; jain_jp@hotmail.com; s Rs 80-100, d Rs 150-200) Near Laxminath Temple, Nahar ka Chohtta.

**RN Haveli** (☎ 2443278; r with shared bathroom Rs 100-150) Behind Laxminath Temple, Rawle ka Chowk.

### MIDRANGE

**Haveli Braj Bhushanjee** (☎ 2442322; www.kiplingsbundi.com; r Rs 400-1850; ❄) This rambling 250-year-old *haveli* has a warren of appealing rooms, directed by the helpful Braj Bhushanjee family (descendants of Bundi's former prime ministers). It's an enchanting place with splendid rooftop views. There's an unrivalled range of accommodation (rooms have views): old and atmospheric or modern, beautifully muralled and decorated with antique furniture and miniatures. The meals and snacks are relatively expensive. Free pick-ups from the bus stand and train station are available. Staff will arrange cycle and walking tours, and even camel safaris.

**Badi Haveli** (☎ 2442322; www.kiplingsbundi.com; r Rs 200-1500; ❄) The Braj Bhushanjee family opened this new hotel in 2004. The centre portion of the converted *haveli* opens on both sides to first-class views. Rooms are of different sizes, but all are white-painted and alcove-filled, and have fresh, tiled bathrooms. The rooftop restaurant has fantastic town and palace views.

**Kasera Paradise** (☎ 2444679; r Rs 400-1500; ❄) The amiable couple at Kasera Heritage View opened this second, smarter hotel in 2004, having renovated a *haveli* that had lain empty for 80 years. The spacious rooms have smartly tiled bathrooms and lots of alcove action, and the décor features coloured glass and dangly chandeliers. There's a fabulous rooftop with city and palace views.

## Getting There & Away

### BUS

Bus journeys to and from Bundi are bone-rattlers. Express buses run to Ajmer (Rs 80, four hours, half-hourly), Kota (Rs 16, one hour, every 15 minutes), Chittorgarh (Rs 72, five hours, four daily), Sawai Madhopur (Rs 45, 4½ hours, five daily), Udaipur (Rs 135, 8½ hours, four daily), Jodhpur (Rs 160, 10 hours, seven daily), Bikaner (Rs 190, 10 hours, three daily), Jaipur (Rs 90, five hours, half-hourly) and Indore (Rs 150, 12 hours, four daily) in Madhya Pradesh. There's a direct bus to Pushkar (Rs 90, five hours) at 8.30am. A private sleeper bus runs to Udaipur from Bundi; inquire near the bus stand.

There are also buses to Bijolia (Rs 24, 1½ hours, 10 daily), Keshraipatan (Rs 16, 1½ hours, 10 daily), Menal (Rs 24, two hours, four daily), and Shivpuri (Rs 125, eight hours, two daily).

#### TRAIN

The train station is about 2km south of the old city. There are rail connections between Bundi and Agra, Chittorgarh and Kota. From Kota you can catch a connecting train to various destinations.

There will be additional express services between here and Udaipur once the long-awaited transfer to broad-gauge track is completed. Check locally for current information – after conversion there should be an express train from New Delhi to Udaipur via Kota, Bundi and Chittorgarh.

### Getting Around

Taxis can be hired at the stand near Raniji-ki-Baori. A rickshaw to the train station costs Rs 40; a half-day city/outside city tour costs Rs 70/125; and a trip out to Akoda and Rameshwar costs around Rs 200 return. For local sightseeing, expect to pay around Rs 50 per hour for an autorickshaw.

Bicycles are an ideal way to get around this area. They are available at **Atlas Cycles** (Azad Park; per hr/day Rs 3/20). You can also hire motorbikes locally – ask around at the guesthouses.

## KOTA

☎0744 / pop 695,899

Busy, clamorous Kota lacks the charm of many Rajasthan towns, and so has remained untouristy – foreign tourists still attract stares on the street. However, it has a spectacular, beautiful palace with an excellent museum and lovely murals. The Chambal River, the state's only permanent river, runs through the town and offers scenic boat trips.

Kota serves as an army headquarters and has the dubious distinction of being Rajasthan's industrial centre (mainly producing chemicals). The nearby nuclear plant made headlines in 1992 when it was revealed that levels of radioactivity were way above 'safe' levels. Kota also has one of Asia's largest fertiliser plants.

Growing industrialisation has led to increased pollution. Black smoke belches into the air from two huge chimneys across the river. Fortunately, leafy parks and an artificial lake provide breaths of fresh air.

Kota is well known for its beautiful saris, which are woven at the nearby village of Kaithoon. Known as *kota doria* saris, they are made of cotton or silk in an assortment of colours, many with delicate golden

#### THE MINI MASTERPIECES OF KOTA & BUNDI

Some of Rajasthan's finest miniature work was produced around the Hadoti region. The Hada Rajputs who ruled Bundi and Kota were keen artistic patrons, and their influence and finance have left an exquisite legacy. The style combined the dominant features of folk painting – intense colour and bold forms – with the influence of the Mughals' concern with naturalism. See p52 for more information on the development of miniature painting.

All the regions of Rajasthan produce paintings of individual character, but here they are even more distinctive. The schools were initially similar, but they developed markedly different styles. In both, however, they usually have a background of thick foliage, cloudy skies and scenes lit by the setting sun. When architecture appears it is depicted in loving detail. The willowy women have round faces, large petal-shaped eyes, a small nose and a receding chin – the forerunners of Bollywood pin-ups. Themes are often passionate, as well as courtly or religious.

The paintings of the Bundi school are notable for their blue hues, with a palette of turquoise and azure that is unlike anywhere else. Bundi Palace (p229) has wonderful examples.

In Kota you'll notice the painters' penchant for hunting scenes, and for depicting the local foliage and fauna. Their dense woodland-packed pictures are unique, providing a vivid and detailed portrayal of hunting expeditions in Kota's once thickly wooded surrounds. Kota City Palace (p234) has some of the best-preserved wall paintings in the state.

thread designs. The miniature paintings of Kota are also famous – check them out in the marvellous City Palace (see right).

## History

Building of the city began in 1264 following the Hadoti Chauhan defeat and beheading of Koteya, a Bhil chieftain who gave the city his name. The foundation stone of the fort was laid on the very spot he lost his head.

Kota didn't reach its present size until well into the 17th century, when Rao Madho Singh, a son of the ruler of Bundi, was made ruler of Kota by the Mughal Emperor Jehangir. Kota remained a separate state until it was integrated into Rajasthan after Independence. Subsequent rulers have all added to the fort and palaces, and each also contributed to making Kota a flourishing centre of art and culture.

## Orientation

Kota is strung out along the east bank of the Chambal River. The train station is well to the north; the RTDC Hotel Chambal, a number of other hotels and the bus stand are in the middle; and Chambal Gardens, the fort and the Kota Barrage are to the south.

## Information

There are numerous ATMs, including HDFC ATMs next to Hotel Phul Plaza, and on platform 1 of the railway station.

**Main post office** (🕓 10.30am-1.30pm & 2-6pm Mon-Sat) Centrally located.

**Shiv Shakti Enterprises** (per hr Rs 5; 🕓 10am-10pm) Internet access, opposite Umed Park.

**State Bank of Bikaner & Jaipur** (Industrial Estate) Opposite Rajasthan Patrika, changes travellers cheques and currency.

**State Bank of India** (Chawni Circle) Changes travellers cheques (Amex only) and currency.

**Tourist Reception Centre** (☎ 2327695; 🕓 10am-5pm Mon-Sat, closed 2nd & 4th Sat of month) In the grounds of the RTDC Hotel Chambal.

## Sights & Activities

### CITY PALACE & FORT

Beside the Kota Barrage, overlooking the river, the **City Palace and fort** make up one of the largest such complexes in Rajasthan.

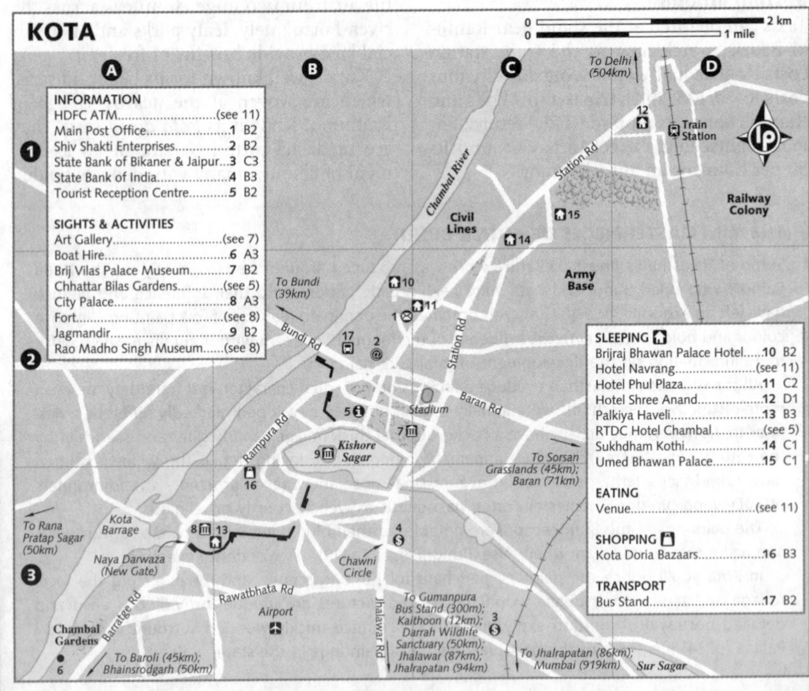

The palace itself was the former residence of the Kota rulers and used to be the centre of power. The treasury, courts, arsenal, soldiers and various state offices were all located here. Some of its buildings are now used as schools. Entry is from the south side through the **Naya Darwaza** (New Gate).

There are several palaces within the fort, including Madho Singh Mahal, Raj Mahal, Bada Mahal, Chhatra Mahal and the ruined Jhala Haveli. Inside is excellent **Rao Madho Singh Museum** (☎ 2385040; Indian/foreigner Rs 10/50, camera/video Rs 50/100; 🕑 10am-4.30pm Sat-Thu). It's on the right-hand side of the complex's huge central courtyard and is entered through a gateway topped by rampant elephants. You'll find all the stuff necessary for a respectable Raj existence – silver furniture, an old-fashioned ice-cream maker, and ingenious, beautiful weapons. The oldest part dates from 1624. Downstairs is an elegant durbar hall with beautiful mirrorwork, while upstairs some of Rajasthan's best-preserved miniatures decorate the elegant small-scale apartments. The upstairs rooms dance with exquisite paintings, particularly the hunting scenes for which Kota is renowned.

The curator may offer to take you around, but try to look around on your own so that you can wander at leisure.

After visiting the museum it's worth exploring the rest of the complex to appreciate how magnificent it must have been in its heyday. The fort ramparts are some of the highest in Rajasthan, with three-level fortifications, six double gates and 25 towers. Unfortunately, a lot of it is falling into disrepair, and the gardens are no more, but there are some excellent views over the old city, the Chambal and the monstrous industrial complex across the river. Pollution is believed to be contributing to the deterioration of the fort. Some of the exterior murals are fading, which is a great pity. There's a small restaurant in the courtyard.

#### JAGMANDIR

Between the City Palace and the Tourist Reception Centre is the picturesque artificial lake **Kishore Sagar**, constructed in 1346. In the middle of the lake, on a small island amid palm trees, is the enchanting little tangerine palace of **Jagmandir**. Built in 1740 by one of the maharanis of Kota, it's a sight that seems to mock the frantic streets on either side of the lake. The palace is closed to the public.

#### BRIJ VILAS PALACE MUSEUM

Near the Kishore Sagar, this small government **museum** (admission Rs 3; 🕑 10am-4.30pm Sat-Thu) is also housed in a palace. It has a collection of miniature paintings, and some interesting 9th- to 12th-century stone idols and other sculptural fragments (mainly from Baroli and Jhalawar), such as Vishnu reclining on a serpent with Lakshmi at his feet.

Next door is a small modern **art gallery** (admission free; 🕑 10am-5pm Mon-Sat) exhibiting works by local artists.

#### BOAT TRIPS

A lovely hiatus from the city is a Chambal River **boat trip**. Once you escape the industry near the town, it's beautiful, with lush vegetation and craggy cliffs on either side, and lots of opportunities to spot birds, crocodiles and gharials (thin-snouted, fish-eating crocodiles) – be sure you don't fall in. It costs Rs 25/50 for a 1½-/3½-hour trip. Boats start from Chambal Gardens.

#### GARDENS

There are several well-maintained, peaceful gardens in Kota that provide a splash of greenery amid the industry. The **Chambal Gardens** are on the riverbank south of the fort, with a murky pond stocked with crocodiles as a centrepiece, which you can walk over on a wobbly suspension bridge. Once common all along the river, by the mid-20th century crocodiles had been virtually exterminated through hunting. There are also some rare gharials.

Next to the Tourist Reception Centre are the **Chhattar Bilas Gardens**, a collection of overgrown but impressive royal cenotaphs interspersed with carved elephants.

### Sleeping & Eating

Budget accommodation in Kota is lacklustre, but the city's well served for top-end hotels (where it's always worth asking for a discount). Most travellers prefer to base themselves in the more atmospheric town of Bundi. Mosquitoes can be a problem at some hotels in Kota, so come armed with a mossie net or repellent.

A few have good restaurants, or try the early-evening snack stalls on the footpath outside the main post office. If you do eat here, select food that has been freshly cooked, not reheated.

#### BUDGET

**Hotel Navrang** (☎ 2323294; s/d from Rs 400/500, with AC Rs 700/900; dishes Rs 35-60; restaurant 11am-11pm; ) Better than the exterior suggests, this is one of Kota's choicer options. Rooms are worn but comfortable, and are arranged around a modern internal courtyard. Some have more character than others, so try to look at a few first. There's a good veg restaurant, Venue, a subdued business-lunch haunt where zigzag decorations add a dash of disco.

**Hotel Phul Plaza** (☎ 2329350; s/d from Rs 325/425, with AC Rs 550/750; ) Next door to Hotel Navrang, this option is a clean, no-nonsense business hotel with ordinary rooms and overpriced suites. Rooms at the front are a bit noisy. There's a good veg restaurant, serving a wide range of dishes.

**Hotel Shree Anand** (☎ 2462473; s/d from Rs 150/200) This place, in a pink building along the street opposite the train station, is useful if you're catching an early-morning train. The rooms are tiny and dingy but pretty clean, though you'll probably need your own sheets. Veg meals are available.

#### MIDRANGE & TOP END

**Palkiya Haveli** (☎ 2327375; Mokha Para; s/d Rs 900/1100; ) This is an exquisite *haveli* that has been in the same family for 200 years. It's a plant-filled oasis with impressive murals and appealing rooms. The family is charming and helpful, and the food is excellent. The *haveli* is near Suraj Pole.

**Brijraj Bhawan Palace Hotel** (☎ 2450529; s/d from Rs 1550/2150) On an elevated site high above the Chambal River, this charismatic hotel is named after the current maharaja of Kota, Brijraj Singh, who lives with his family in part of the palace. Built in 1830 by the British East India Company, this was once the British Residency, and has attractive rooms opening onto riverside terraces. Some rooms, such as No 4, are huge, with dizzyingly high ceilings. Queen Mary chose this for a snooze in 1911. There are well-maintained gardens and an intimate dining room (for guests only) that, unlike in most palaces, is homy rather than grand.

**Sukhdham Kothi** (☎ 2320081; s Rs 560-920, d Rs 680-1200) Sukhdham Kothi is over 100 years old and was once the home of the British Resident's surgeon. It's set in pretty gardens and is a friendly, family-run place. The inviting rooms have antique furniture, and some open onto terraces.

**Umed Bhawan Palace** (☎ 2325262; off Station Rd; s/d deluxe Rs 2023/2472) Surrounded by sprawling gardens, this gracious palace is stuffily Edwardian. Its voluminous rooms make it appear grander than the Brijraj Bhawan, but the rooms are darker, and the overall feel is impersonal. The palace has a restaurant, a bar and a billiard room.

**RTDC Hotel Chambal** (☎ 236527; dm Rs 50, s/d with private bathroom Rs 400/500, with AC Rs 600/700; ) Near Kishore Sagar at Nayapura, this has bland, reasonably comfortable rooms.

## Shopping

The bazaars around Rampura Rd sell a wide range of *kota doria* (gold-woven saris), or you can hunt them down to the source in nearby Kaithoon (12km from Kota, Rs 4 by bus, Rs 100 return in a rickshaw), where you will find the best quality. **Hamid Bihari** (☎ 2844255; Kota Saree Wala, Kaithoon; 10am-7pm), near the police station, opposite Taileyan Mandirwhich, sells exquisite pieces. You can see them being woven upstairs. Prices range from Rs 600 to 2600.

## Getting There & Away

#### AIR

There used to be flights to and from Kota, but these were discontinued a few years back. Flights may be rescheduled in the future, so ask a travel agent or at any airport.

#### BUS

There are plenty of express bus connections (see the table, opposite).

There are also buses for Delhi (11 hours) and Mt Abu (12 hours). For Jaisalmer, you should change buses at Ajmer. Buses leave for Jhalawar (Rs 38, two hours) every half-hour. To get to Madhya Pradesh, several buses a day go to such places as Gwalior, Ujjain, Bhopal and Indore.

#### TRAIN

Kota is on the main Mumbai–Delhi line via Sawai Madhopur, so there are plenty of trains to choose from, including services going to Sawai Madhopur (Rs 37/135 in 2nd/chair class, two hours, 108km, six daily),

| Destination | Fare (Rs) | Duration (hr) | Frequency |
|---|---|---|---|
| Ajmer | 93 | 6 | half-hourly |
| Bikaner | 265 | 12 | 3 daily |
| Bundi | 16 | ¾ | half-hourly |
| Chittorgarh | 86 | 6 | 5 daily |
| Jaipur | 106 | 6 | half-hourly |
| Jodhpur | 176 | 11 | 3 daily |
| Udaipur | 140 | 6 | 6 daily |

Agra (Rs 85 in sleeper, six hours, 333km), Delhi (Rs 176/789/493 in sleeper/2AC/3AC, 6¼ to 10 hours, 469km) and to Mumbai (Rs 284/1277/798 in sleeper/2AC/3AC, 16 hours, 919km). The No 2952 Rajdhani to Mumbai leaves at 8.50pm (Rs 1750/1680 in 2AC/3AC, 12¼ hours).

The No 193 *Kota–Jaipur Passenger* goes to Jaipur (Rs 350/88 in 3AC/sleeper), leaving at 11.35pm and arriving in Jaipur at 4am.

There will be additional express services between Kota and Udaipur once this section of track is converted to broad gauge. Check locally for current information – after conversion there should be an express train from New Delhi to Udaipur via Kota, Bundi and Chittorgarh.

### Getting Around

Minibuses link the train station and bus stand (Rs 4). An autorickshaw should cost Rs 30 for this journey; there's a prepay place at the station. Cycle-rickshaws are, as always, a cheaper option (around Rs 20).

## AROUND KOTA

### Wildlife Sanctuaries

The thickly forested, wildly beautiful 250-sq-km **Darrah Wildlife Sanctuary** (Indian/foreigner Rs 20/100; 10am-5pm) is about 50km from Kota. Once a royal hunting ground, there are spotted deer, wild boars, bears, sambars, leopards, panthers and antelopes. The sanctuary is sometimes closed during the monsoon (usually from early July to mid-September). You need to get permission to visit from the local forest ranger, or contact the **District Forest Office** (☎ 0744-2321263) in Kota. If that all fails, ask at the Kota **Tourist Reception Centre** (☎ 0744-2327695).

Also accessible from Kota is the **National Chambal Wildlife Sanctuary**, which extends into neighbouring Madhya Pradesh. This 549-sq-km reserve is best known for its gharials, which inhabit the Chambal River; blackbucks, chinkaras, wolves and rarely seen caracals can also be found here.

About 45km east of Kota, flanking the main canal of the Chambal and Parvan Rivers, are the **Sorsan grasslands**. Covering 35 sq km, these grasslands are rich with insects during the monsoon and attract a good variety of resident and migratory birds, including the great Indian bustard – a reluctant flier that is more commonly seen stalking through the grasslands on its sturdy legs. Other birds of Sorsan include mynahs, orioles, quails, partridges, bulbuls, chats, drongos, shrikes, robins and weavers. Indian rollers can be seen in early winter. Flocks of migrants, such as warblers, flycatchers, larks, starlings and rosy pastors, winter at Sorsan between October and March. The nearby canal and lakes attract waterfowl, such as bar-headed and greylag geese, common pochards, common teals and pintails.

You can hire a jeep to reach these parks from Kota for Rs 3.50 per km with a minimum of 250km. Ask at the Tourist Reception Centre for details.

### Baroli

One of Rajasthan's oldest temple complexes is at Baroli, 45km southwest of Kota on the way to Rana Pratap Sagar – the second dam on the Chambal River. Set in a peaceful rural area, many of these 9th-century temples were vandalised by Muslim armies, but much remains. The main edifice is the **Ghateshvara Temple**, which features impressive columns and a finely carved sikhara (temple tower). It's one of the best-preserved temples here, with figures including a dancing Shiva, Vishnu and Brahma. Inside it are five Shiva linga – one of which looks like an upturned pot *(ghata)*, hence the temple name. A ruined temple, **Trimurti**, to the southeast contains a three-headed Shiva.

Many of the sculptures from the temples are displayed in the Brij Vilas Palace Museum in Kota (p235).

There are buses from Kota (Rs 20, 1½ hours, hourly) – tell the driver you want to be dropped off at Baroli. The buses leave from the Gumanpura bus stand, near the petrol pump.

### Bhainsrodgarh

Near Baroli is picturesque Bhainsrodgarh. The 14th-century fort was never besieged by enemies. Perched on a ridge overlooking the Chambal River, it's still occupied by descendants of a feudal family. Although you can't go inside, the views are superb. You need permission to visit – inquire at Kota's **Tourist Reception Centre** (☎ 0744-2327695).

Get to Bhainsrodgarh by autorickshaw from Baroli (about Rs 100 return).

## JHALAWAR

**☎ 07432 / pop 48,049**

Jhalawar is a quiet, sprawling town that sees few visitors, but has some charming sights in the surrounding area, part of their appeal being that they are so seldom visited. Seven kilometres to the southeast is Jhalrapatan, the ancient walled City of Temple Bells, which has some beautiful temples, and 10km northeast is Gagron, a forgotten fort towering over the confluence of two rivers.

Jhalawar was once the capital of a small princely state created in 1838 by Zalim Singh, the charismatic regent of Kota. Singh signed a treaty with the British on behalf of the young Kota prince, and in return he received Jhalawar to rule in his own right.

Situated 87km south of Kota, it's at the centre of an opium-producing region. During winter many of the fields are carpeted with picturesque pink and white poppies.

### Information

Carry enough rupees with you as, at the time of writing, no banks in Jhalawar would change money. There's an SBBJ ATM in the Jhalawar Fort building.

**Tourist office** (☎ 230081; 🕑 10am-5pm Mon-Sat) At the RTDC Hotel Chandrawati (see right). It's of limited help, but it has a map, and staff may assist you to find a vehicle.

### Sights & Activities

In the town centre is the **Jhalawar Fort** (admission free; 🕑 10am-5pm Mon-Sat), built by Maharaja Madan Singh in 1838. A sprawling cream-and-terracotta building, today it houses the government offices. It's run-down, the dusty offices filled with piles of ledgers. Try to get a look in the Zenana Khas, which has fine murals and mirrors, and the Aina Mahal, an indication of past glory that's nowadays complete with whirring institutional fans. There's also the small government **museum** (admission Rs 3; 🕑 10am-5pm Mon-Sat), which has a mixed collection including 8th-century sculptures, gold coins, weapons, old paintings, a handwritten copy of the Quran and a leopard-skin coat. The 1920s **Bhawan Natyashala**, inside the fort, was used for Parsi theatre. It has a unique design with special underground construction that allows horses and carriages onto the stage.

Also interesting to visit is the **Government College Library** (🕑 10am-1pm & 2-5pm), around the corner from the Hotel Dwarika. Topped with a *chhatri* (cenotpah, literally 'umbrella'), the great old building houses 70,000 books, and mottoes, such as 'books are the lighthouses erected in the great sea of time', are hung on the walls.

### Sleeping & Eating

Attracting a smattering of tourists, Jhalawar has limited but OK accommodation.

**Hotel Dwarika** (☎ 232626; fax 231187; Hospital Rd; s/d Rs 250/300, deluxe Rs 300/350, with AC Rs 650/750) The best of the lot, here all rooms are the same whatever the standard; the deluxe rooms have hot water. All are freshly painted, and some have balconies (overlooking the sparse hotel grounds and the highway).

**RTDC Hotel Chandrawati** (☎ 512080; Jhalrapatan Rd; s/d Rs 250/300, with AC Rs 500/600; dishes Rs 8-32) Also housing the tourist office, this is a pleasant compound with bare rooms around a leafy courtyard. 'Deluxe' rooms are overpriced. Checkout is a handy 24 hours, and there's a restaurant.

**Purvaj Hotel** (☎ 231355; r Rs 150-450) At Mangalpura, near the clock tower, is this simple, very run-down, 200-year-old *haveli*. Rooms are basic but cheap, and the building has more character than the other hotels in Jhalawar. There are good views from the roof. It's pretty scrubby, however, and not recommended for solo female travellers.

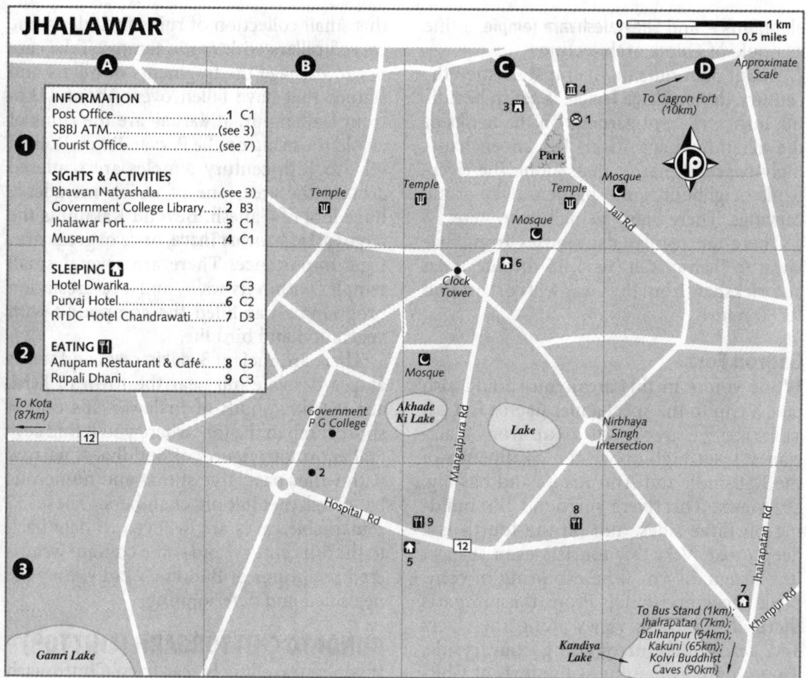


**Rupali Dhani** (Hospital Rd; dishes Rs 15-40; 9am-11pm) Set opposite Hotel Dwarika, this is a friendly restaurant with a garden that has little canopies to sit under. It offers tasty Chinese, South Indian and Indian veg dishes. The sign outside is in Hindi, but 'garden restaurant' is written in English.

**Anupam Restaurant & Café** (Patan Rd; dishes Rs 35-65; 9am-11pm) Another good choice, this offers veg and nonveg food in a small indoor restaurant.

## Getting There & Away

There are regular buses between Jhalawar and Kota (Rs 38, two hours). The bus stand is 1km south of town.

## Getting Around

If you plan to visit the historic sites outside of town, it's best to hire a jeep or taxi. Many of the roads are in a state of bumpy disrepair. Expect to pay Rs 3.50 per kilometre (with a minimum of 250km). The tourist office should be able to arrange jeep or taxi hire for you; otherwise, inquire at your hotel.

To travel anywhere in town by autorickshaw should cost Rs 20.

Bicycle is a good way of making your way around, though finding your way may be a problem. Bicycles are available for hire from near the Purvaj Hotel for Rs 3 per hour.

# AROUND JHALAWAR

## Jhalrapatan

Seven kilometres south of Jhalawar on the Kota road is Jhalrapatan (City of Temple Bells), on the banks of the holy Chandrabhaga River. This walled town once had more than 100 temples, although now far fewer remain. The best known is the huge 10th-century **Surya Temple** (7am-noon & 5-10pm) at the centre, a spacious, high-ceilinged building that contains magnificent sculptures and one of the best-preserved idols of Surya (the sun god) in India. It has a glorious, high, carved stupa with very intricate, almost organic-seeming carving. There's also the 12th-century **Shantinath Jain temple** – colourful, brightly painted and restored with intricately carved statues, an inlaid black-and-white marble floor, and two huge stone elephants – and **Sheetaleshvara Temple**, a fine example of Gupta architecture.

About 3km outside Jhalrapatan, the 7th-century **Chandrabhaga Temple** is set in beautiful, lush, well-kept gardens on the banks of the Chandrabhaga River. It's an enchantingly peaceful place. Ghats along the riverbank neighbour some hidden-away erotic carvings. There's also a small *baori* here.

There are regular daily buses from Jhalawar to Jhalrapatan (Rs 4, 15 minutes). An autorickshaw from Jhalawar will cost around Rs 80 return.

### Gagron Fort

While you're in this area, you should also take a trip to the spectacular **Gagron Fort** (admission free; sunrise-sunset), 10km from Jhalawar. It's set high above the confluence of the Kalisindh and Ahu Rivers and has big, big views. The rivers surround the building on three sides, and on the fourth is a deep moat. Very few tourists even suspect its existence – you'll be exploring in complete peace and quiet. From the ramparts there are fantastic views along the rivers and across the surrounding countryside. Though not as famous as the forts at Chittorgarh, Jodhpur and Jaisalmer, the huge fort occupies a prominent place in the annals of Rajput chivalry and has been fought over for centuries. It was established in the 8th century, changed hands many times, and was the site of a huge *jauhar* in 1443. Later, it was conquered by Akbar.

For the best view of the fort itself, head to Changari, the little village on the outcrop opposite.

Near the fort walls there's the small village of **Gagron** and the **shrine of the Sufi saint Mittheshah**, constructed in 1423. The gate to the shrine was built by Akbar in 1580. Many pilgrims come here during Ramadan.

A rickshaw here would cost around Rs 150 return, but due to the state of the roads it's better to take a car.

### Other Attractions

The Jhalawar region's other attractions are further out of town and difficult to reach without your own transport (a jeep is best as the roads are rough). About 54km (1½ hours) southeast of Jhalawar, at **Dalhanpur**, are some temple ruins believed to be hundreds of years old. Near the Chhapi River, this small collection of ruins includes some carved pillars with erotic figures. Take care not to damage the fragments of pillars and statues that have fallen over. About 11km from Dalhanpur, at **Kakuni**, are the ruins of an old township on the Parvan River. Ruined 9th- to 12th-century temples are scattered around the area, one of which includes a huge idol of Ganesh. Beyond Kakuni is the large **Fort of Manohar Thana**, once of great strategic importance. There are several small temples within its walls, and a reforestation programme has filled the compound with vegetation and bird life.

There are ancient **Buddhist caves** and **stupas** atop a desolate hill near the town of **Kolvi**, about 90km south of Jhalawar. It's only a short climb to the top, where you'll find several enormous figures of Buddha. A narrow path winds past large stupas and numerous bat-filled meditation chambers. These 35 remarkable caves are believed to date back to the 5th century, and some contain weathered sculptures of Buddha – sadly, they are neglected and deteriorating.

## BUNDI TO CHITTORGARH (CHITTOR)

If you're travelling by car from Chittorgarh to Bundi, you can stop at various attractions along the way.

**Bijolia**, a large town 16km from Menal, was once a group of 100 temples and a famous pilgrimage centre. Most of these were destroyed by Mughal invaders, and today only three are left standing. One of them, **Hajaresvara Mahadeva**, is devoted to Shiva, with delicate carving and a high lingam surrounded by lots of small linga.

**Menal**, 48km from Bundi, is a complex of crumbling Shiva temples built in the Gupta period, with some striking statuary and a domed pavilion that affords superb views. Menal was once the retreat of Prithvi Raj Chauhan of Delhi, and there are a few ruined palaces. After a good monsoon, there's an impressive waterfall in the area.

To the west of Menal, **Mandalgarh** is the third fort of Mewar to be built by Rana Kumbha (the others are the great fort of Chittorgarh and the fort at Kumbalgarh). There are good views from the vast, sprawling ruins.

### Bassi

The town of Bassi, about 25km northeast of Chittorgarh and well off the tourist trail,

### KAVADS

The artisans of Bassi are famous for their brightly painted wooden carvings, especially the amazing folding boxes known as kavads. Carved from mango wood, these portable temples – usually painted in traffic-stopping reds or yellows – are made of a number of hinged doors that open outwards, each one covered in colourful pictures that illustrate the great Indian epics. They were the tools of professional bards, known as Kavadia Bhatts, who traditionally travelled from village to village chanting the tales of the Mahabharata (a Vedic epic poem of the Bharata dynasty), a skill that was handed down through the generations. As the stories unfolded, so did the boxes. At the climax of the tale, the last door opened to reveal the supreme deities – usually Rama, Lakshmana and Sita or Krishna. Somewhere near the bottom of the kavad there was always a slot where the audience could show their appreciation by depositing coins. You can buy these magical boxes at the source in Bassi, or in shops in Udaipur.

is famous for its woodcarvers, who create brilliantly coloured religious pieces (see Kavads, above). There's also the **Bassi Wildlife Sanctuary** to explore, with its panthers, antelopes, wild boars and many birds. The hotels can arrange jeep safaris.

Seven kilometres from Bassi, on the Chittorgarh road, is **Nagri**, one of Rajasthan's oldest towns. Hindu and Buddhist remains from the Mauryan to the Gupta periods have been found here. Many old copper coins and sculptures discovered here are now at museums in Chittorgarh and Udaipur.

### SLEEPING & EATING

There are a couple of top-end accommodation options around Bassi, which are far better bets than the dingy Chittorgarh options.

**Bassi Fort Palace** (☎ 01472-225321; www.bassifortpalace.com; s/d Rs 1400/1600, ste Rs 1700/1900, deluxe tents Rs 1100) This glorious meringue of a place is in the town's 450-year-old fort (which was never defeated), set amidst hills. There's a tree, known as *kalp vraksha*, in the grounds that's said to grant wishes. It's a pleasant, peaceful spot with 16 rooms off a garden, or you can stay in a tented camp beside a lake in the wildlife sanctuary.

**Castle Bijaipur** (www.castlebijaipur.com; s/d Rs 1550/1850; ) Castle Bijaipur is a fantastically set 16th-century palace, apparently plucked from Udaipur and dropped in the rural village of Bijaipur. It's a great place to settle down with a good book, do yoga, meditate or just laze around. Rooms are romantic and luxurious. There're a pleasant garden courtyard and an airy restaurant serving Rajasthani food. Reservations should be made through Chittorgarh's Hotel Pratap Palace (see p245). The friendly owners can arrange horse or jeep safaris to places of interest around Bijaipur, such as the nearby Bhil tribal village, or a visit to their cool jungle property, Thanderiberi.

### GETTING THERE & AWAY

Frequent buses travel daily from Chittorgarh to Bassi (Rs 10, 30 minutes), passing through Nagri on the way. A jeep taxi to Bassi costs around Rs 300. There are also buses from Chittorgarh to Bijaipur (Rs 15, 1½ hours), or a return taxi costs around Rs 300.

## CHITTORGARH (CHITTOR)

**☎ 01472 / pop 96,028**

Chittorgarh holds a special place in the hearts of many Rajputs. Its fort is the greatest in Rajasthan and has a history that epitomises Rajput romanticism, chivalry and tragedy. Three times Chittor was under attack from a more powerful enemy. Each time, soldiers realised the odds were impossible and chose death before dishonour, performing *jauhar*. The men donned the saffron martyrs' robes and rode out from the fort to certain death, while the women and children immolated themselves on a huge funeral pyre. Honour was always more important than death.

The only real reason to come to Chittor is to see the fort – the town itself is quite crowded and really not of much interest. An increasing number of industries are based in and around Chittorgarh, scarring the landscape around the fort.

Despite the fort's splendour and impressive location, Chittor is off the main tourist circuit. The town is grotty, but the fort is well worth the detour. It could be squeezed in as a day trip from Udaipur, or as a stop between Bundi and Udaipur.

## History

Chittor is mentioned in the Mahabharata. The story goes that Bhim, one of the Pandava heroes, struck the ground so hard that water gushed out to form a large reservoir. The fort, founded by Bappa Rawal of Sisodia, dates from the 8th century. Chittor's first defeat occurred in 1303, when Ala-ud-din Khilji, the Pathan king of Delhi, besieged the fort, apparently to capture the beautiful Padmini. This all ended in disaster and *jauhar* (see Death Before Dishonour, p244).

In 1535 Bahadur Shah, the sultan of Gujarat, besieged the fort. Once again, the medieval dictates of chivalry determined the outcome, and this time it's thought that some 13,000 Rajput women and 32,000 Rajput warriors died following the declaration of *jauhar*.

The final sacking of Chittor came just 33 years later, in 1568, when the Mughal Emperor Akbar took the town. Once again, the odds were overwhelming. The women performed *jauhar*, and 8000 orange-robed warriors rode out to die. On this occasion, Maharaja Udai Singh II fled to Udaipur, where he re-established his capital. In 1616 Jehangir returned Chittor to the Rajputs. There was no attempt made to resettle, though the fort was restored in 1905.

## Orientation

The fort is roughly fish-shaped, and stands on a 28-sq-km site on top of a 180m-high

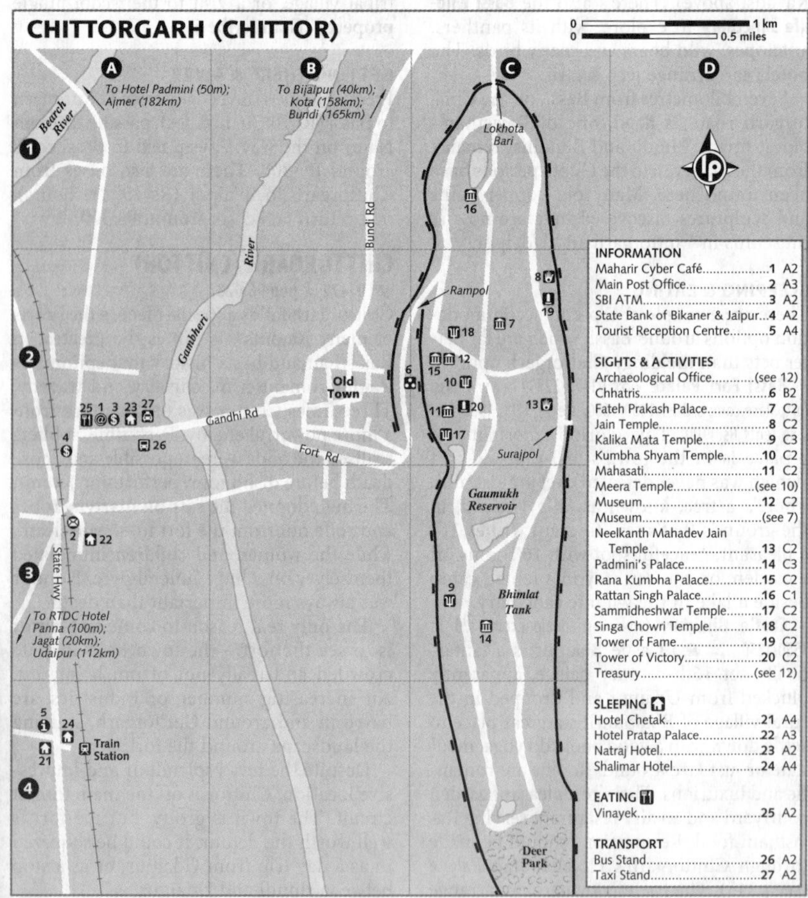

hill that rises abruptly from the surrounding plain. Until 1568 the town of Chittor was within the fort walls, but today's modern town, known as Lower Town, clatters and sprawls to the west of the hill. A river separates it from the bus stand, the railway line and the rest of the town.

## Information

You can change money at the State Bank of Bikaner & Jaipur, which is a short distance north of the post office. There is an SBI ATM in town.

**Maharir Cyber Café** (Collectorate Circle; per hr Rs 25; 9am-10pm) Internet access.

**Main post office** ( 10am-1pm & 2-6pm Mon-Sat) Less than 1km south of the bus stand.

**Tourist Reception Centre** ( 241089; 10am-1.30pm & 2-5pm Mon-Sat) Near the train station.

## Sights

### FORT

All of Chittor's attractions are within the **fort** (Indian/foreigner Rs 5/100; sunrise-sunset). A zigzag ascent of more than 1km leads through seven gateways to the main gate on the western side, the **Rampol** (*pol* means 'gate'; the former back entrance).

On the climb you pass two **chhatris**, memorials between the second and third gates. These mark the spots where Jaimal and Kalla, heroes of the 1568 siege, fell during the struggle against Akbar. Jaimal had been already fatally wounded but was carried out to fight by Kalla. The main gate on the eastern side of the fort is known as the **Surajpol**; it has fantastic views across the empty plains. Within the fort, a circular road runs around the ruins and there's a deer park at the southern end.

There are good views over the town and countryside (and, unfortunately, a huge cement factory) from the western end of the fort; there's even a small village within the walls.

Today, the fort of Chittor is virtually a deserted ruin, but impressive reminders of its grandeur still stand. It's a deserted collection of ruined palaces and around 130 temples. The main sites can all be seen in half a day (assuming you're not walking – see p246), but it's worth spending longer if you like the atmosphere of ancient sites, as this is a vast, mellow place to explore. Guides are available, usually at Rana Kumbha Palace; they charge around Rs 150 for a few hours. Make sure you get a government guide (they carry a guide licence).

#### Rana Kumbha Palace

After entering the fort, turn right and you'll arrive almost immediately at the ruins of this 15th-century **palace**, which include elephant and horse stables and a Shiva temple. Padmini's *jauhar* is said to have taken place in a now-blocked cellar. Across from the palace is the museum and archaeological office, and the treasury building (Nau Lakha Bhandar). The **Singa Chowri Temple**, built in 1448, is nearby.

#### Fateh Prakash Palace

Just beyond Rana Kumbha Palace, this **palace** is more modern (Maharaja Fateh Singh died in 1930). Closed to the public, except for a small, poorly labelled **museum** (admission Rs 3, free Mon; 10am-4.30pm Sat-Thu), it houses a school for local children (around 4000 villagers live within the fort).

#### Tower of Victory

Heading south, you come to the glorious **Tower of Victory** (Jaya Stambha), symbol of Chittor (and a particularly masculine expression of triumph?). Erected by Rana Kumbha between 1458 and 1468 to commemorate his victory over Mahmud Khilji of Malwa in 1440, it rises 37m in nine exquisitely carved storeys, and you can climb the 157 narrow stairs (the interior is also carved) to the 8th floor, from where there's a good view of the area.

Hindu sculptures adorn the outside of the tower. The dome was damaged by lightning and repaired during the 19th century.

Close to the tower is the **Mahasati**, an area where the ranas were cremated during Chittorgarh's period as the Mewar capital. There are many *sati* stones here – 13,000 women committed *jauhar* close by in 1535. The intensely carved **Sammidheshwar Temple**, built in the 6th century and restored in 1427, is nearby.

#### Gaumukh Reservoir

Walk down beyond the temple and at the edge of the cliff, is a deep **tank** where you can feed the fish. The reservoir takes its name from a spring that feeds the tank from a cow's mouth carved in the cliffside.

**DEATH BEFORE DISHONOUR**

History has been kept alive by bards and folk songs in Rajasthan, and historical fact often merges with myth. This is the story that is told of the first sack of Chittor.

By the turn of the 14th century, much of North India had been conquered by the Mughals who ruled from Delhi. However, the rana of Chittor, Rattan Singh, like many Rajput rulers, had managed to resist the invaders.

The jewel of the kingdom was Padmini, Rattan Singh's wife. Although she never left the zenana (women's quarters) uncovered, word had spread of her beauty, and Padmini was admired far beyond the sturdy walls of the fortress, even as far away as Delhi. The rumours aroused the curiosity of the sultan of Delhi, Ala-ud-din Khilji, and he decided to confirm them for himself.

In 1303 Ala-ud-din amassed his armies around Chittorgarh and sent word to Rattan Singh that he wanted to meet Padmini. Knowing that his forces were no match for the sultan's armies, the rana reluctantly agreed, but he set a number of conditions. The sultan was required to enter the fort unarmed. Once inside, Ala-ud-din was not permitted to meet Padmini in person, but was only able to gaze upon her reflection in a mirror, while she sat well out of his reach inside a pavilion built (just to be sure) in the middle of a lotus pool.

But this glimpse was enough. Ala-ud-din was mesmerised and resolved to possess her at any cost. As Rattan Singh escorted him to the gate, Ala-ud-din gave an order to his forces lying in wait. The rana of Chittor was taken hostage and the ransom demanded for his return was Padmini herself.

The court was thrown into panic, until Padmini came up with a plan. She sent word that she agreed to Ala-ud-din's terms and soon a long train of 150 beautiful curtained palanquins, befitting great ladies of the court in purdah (the custom of keeping women in seclusion), trundled slowly out of the fort. The palanquins were Chittor's Trojan Horse – as soon as they entered the sultan's camp, four armed Rajput warriors leaped out of each palanquin and rescued their leader.

The sultan was furious and laid siege to the fort, patiently waiting as the Rajputs slowly starved. It was clear that the sultan could not be defeated, but the Rajputs couldn't consider the dishonour of surrender. Instead, a funeral pyre was lit in an underground tunnel. Padmini and all the ladies of the court put on their wedding saris and threw themselves into the fire as their husbands watched. The men then donned saffron robes, smeared the sacred ashes on their foreheads and rode out of the fort to face certain death.

Although it's clear that Ala-ud-din Khilji did lay siege to Chittor in 1303, and that the Rajput women indeed committed the horrific act of *jauhar*, it's also rumoured that the beautiful Padmini may have been invented by a 16th-century bard.

### Padmini's Palace

Continuing south, you reach **Padmini's Palace**, beside a large lotus pool with a central pavilion. Legend relates that, as Padmini sat in this pavilion, Ala-ud-din saw her reflection in the lake. This glimpse convinced him to destroy Chittor in order to possess her. The bronze gates to this pavilion were carried off by Akbar and can be seen in Agra Fort. Near Padmini's Palace is a small prison where captured invaders were kept; former prisoners include sultans of Malwa and of Gujarat.

Not far away are the former military training grounds for Rajput soldiers. Today the grounds are used as a helipad for visiting dignitaries. Continuing around the ring road, you pass the deer park, Bhimlat Tank, Adhbudhnath Shiva Temple, the Surajpol and the Neelkanth Mahadev Jain temple before reaching the Tower of Fame.

### Tower of Fame

The 22m-high **Tower of Fame** (Kirti Stambha) is older (probably dating from the 12th century) and smaller than the Tower of Victory. Built by a Jain merchant, the tower is dedicated to Adinath, the first Jain *tirthankar* (one of the 24 revered Jain teachers) and is decorated with naked figures of the various *tirthankars*, indicating that it is a Digambara (Sky Clad) monument. (Monks of the Digambara Jain sect go naked.) A narrow stairway leads through the seven storeys to the top. The staircase is usually locked, although the gatekeeper may open the door for some baksheesh.

### Rattan Singh Palace

While Padmini's Palace was the summer abode of the Chittor royals, the **winter palace** takes the name of her husband, Rattan Singh. It overlooks a small lake and, although rundown, is an interesting place to explore.

### Other Buildings

Close to the Fateh Prakash Palace is the **Meera Temple**, built during the reign of Rana Kumbha in the ornate Indo-Aryan style and associated with mystic-poetess Meerabai. She consumed poison sent by an enemy, but survived due to the blessings of Krishna. The larger temple in this same compound is the **Kumbha Shyam Temple** (Temple of Varah).

Across from Padmini's Palace is the **Kalika Mata Temple**, an 8th-century sun temple that was damaged during the first sack of Chittor and then converted to a temple to the goddess Kali in the 14th century. At the fort's northern tip is another gate, the **Lokhota Bari**, while at the southern end is a small opening used for hurling criminals into the abyss.

## Sleeping & Eating

Hotel standards in Chittor are generally disappointing; cleanliness and service are usually below average, and many of the cheaper places have miserable bathrooms. Another option is the Paying Guest House Scheme, which operates in Chittor (ask about it at the Tourist Reception Centre; see p243). If you'd prefer to stay in top-end accommodation you'd be better off staying in Bassi and visiting Chittor on a day trip.

The budget hotels near the train and bus stations are places where lone women may feel uncomfortable.

**Hotel Pratap Palace** (☎ 243563; hpratap@hotmail.com; s/d Rs 660/700, deluxe Rs 935/985, super deluxe Rs 1325/1450; ❄) Deservedly one of the most popular places to stay. The cheaper rooms are OK value, though nothing special, and the more expensive rooms have window seats and leafy outlooks. Top prices get you a big mural as well (room 208). Next to a pleasant garden area there's a restaurant with good food. Village safaris and visits to the owners' castle in Bijaipur (see p241) can be arranged.

**RTDC Hotel Panna** (☎ 241238; dm Rs 50, s/d from Rs 200/300, deluxe Rs 400/500, with AC Rs 600/700; ❄) This hotel is closer to town, meaning it's further from the fort. It's surrounded by some grassy areas, giving it a nicer feel than other cheap options. The ordinary rooms are OK, but the deluxe ones aren't well named. The refurbished AC rooms are quite smart.

**Hotel Padmini** (☎ 241718; hotel_padmini@rediffmail.com; s/d Rs 490/600, with AC Rs 1000/1200; ❄) Out of town near the Bearch River, Padmini has a garden with horses and kids' play equipment. The hotel's owned by a marble magnate, and he's lined his hotel with his favourite stone. Some rooms have balconies looking out to the distant fort. Some customers have found the rooms overpriced and have complained of grubby sheets.

**Natraj Hotel** (☎ 241009; s with shared bathroom Rs 60-125, d with private bathroom Rs 90-250) Near the bus stand, this has cheery reception staff who'll usher you through to small, dark, dank cells with grimy walls – still, it's an adequate option if you're counting the rupees.

**Shalimar Hotel** (☎ 240842; s with shared bathroom Rs 100, s/d with private bathroom Rs 250/300) This hotel has the advantage of being near the train station, but is otherwise unremarkable. Rooms are grim and dull, but cleanish.

**Hotel Chetak** (☎ 241588; s/d Rs 250/350, better r Rs 600/700) Chetak is noisy and shabby. The pricier rooms are smarter, in a vinyl-headboard kind of way. The downstairs restaurant is not recommended.

**Vinayek** (Collectorate Circle; dishes Rs 15-60; ⏰ 7am-11pm) Serves up North Indian veg dishes as well as Chinese and South Indian food. It's a gloomy basement, enlivened by its popularity and sweet counter.

Retiring rooms can be found at the train station. Doubles are Rs 100 or Rs 200 with AC. A simple veg thali is available for Rs 20. Readers have recommended **Shri Amerdeep Guesthouse** (☎ 248610), near Rampol Gate on the fort hill, as unusually clean and welcoming – it's certainly got a great location.

## Getting There & Away

If you're coming from Bundi, it's possible to catch the early morning train to Chittor, spend three or four hours seeing the fort and then catch a bus on to Udaipur, or vice versa.

### BUS

Express buses serve Delhi (Rs 256, 14 hours, two daily), and regularly go to Ajmer (Rs 81, five hours), Jaipur (Rs 135, eight hours), Udaipur (Rs 48/40 express/local, 2½/three hours) and Bundi (Rs 72, five hours), among other places.

#### TRAIN

The No 9770 *Jaipur Express* leaves Chittor at 6.15am and arrives in Jaipur (Rs 83 in 2nd class, 324km) at 2.15pm, travelling via Ajmer (Rs 55, 4½ hours, 189km).

For Udaipur (Rs 38 in 2nd class, 115km), the No 9615 *Chetak Express* leaves at 5.40am, arriving at 9am; heading north, it departs at 9.45pm and arrives in Delhi (Rs 216/968 in sleeper/2AC, 612km) at 11.18am, travelling via Ajmer and Jaipur.

There's a train to Udaipur at 1.45pm, but you'd be better off taking the bus as this is slow. The No 9943 *Ahmedabad Express* leaves at 2pm, arriving in Ahmedabad (Rs 160/720 in sleeper/2AC, 412km) at 4.25am.

Once the track from Udaipur has been converted to broad gauge, there should be an express train between Udaipur and Delhi that calls at Kota, Bundi and Chittorgarh – check locally for the current situation.

There are also regular connections to Kota (see p236).

### Getting Around

It's about 6km from the train station to the fort (less from the bus stand) and 7km around the fort itself, not including the long southern loop out to the deer park. Autorickshaws charge around Rs 150 from the bus or train station to go around the fort, and back (including waiting time). You'll have to haggle, and make sure it's clear that you're going to visit the sights and have time to look around. A rickshaw between the bus and train stations should cost Rs 20.

Bicycles can be hired near the train station (Rs 30 per day), but you may have to walk up the steep hill to the fort. Still, they're great for seeing the fort, and coming back downhill.

## UDAIPUR

☎ 0294 / pop 389,317

> the most romantic spot on the continent of India
>
> *Colonel James Tod*
>
> Annals & Antiquities of Rajasthan

A pale white, grey-rose and cream city, crowned by cupolas, Udaipur sits on Pichola Lake; at the centre lies the Lake Palace, the creamiest, cakiest building of them all. When the lake is full, the palace seems to float, an hallucinated piece of architectural frippery, carved from icing sugar.

The city sits in a valley surrounded by the ochre- and purple-shaded Aravalli hills, dominated by the huge lakeshore City Palace and overlooked by Sajjan Garh (Monsoon Palace), perched high on a peak as if plucked from a miniature painting. Udaipur's at its best if you step from the tourist epicentre into the jumbled streets of the old city, wander around the lake, or find a rooftop to while away the afternoon. It's also surrounded by some dramatic countryside – folded peaks dotted with tiny villages – so it's rewarding to venture outside the city on foot or horseback, or by motorbike.

Udaipur is also a centre for arts, crafts and dance, and has a renowned school of miniature painting. West of the city is Shilpgram, a village specially constructed to showcase the best of the region's arts. You can see puppet shows and whirling dance displays, and hear the best musicians both here and in the city itself.

It's a great place to shop, too. The shops here are so enticing that it can be hard to tear yourself away, with more miniature paintings than probably should be allowed, jewellery shops, textiles in bright colours, wood carvings, puppets and handmade-paper sellers galore.

Although Colonel Tod's description can still be trotted out, Udaipur has suffered in recent years from consecutive poor monsoons. With little rain, the lake dries up into a puddle, leaving the Lake Palace high and dry, its grubby petticoats exposed. Additionally, in the old city around Lal Ghat, rampant commercialism seems to be devouring the very romance that brings people here – every building is a hotel, shop, restaurant, travel agent or (usually) all four. It seems churlish to complain about commercialism when this is just the fallout from long-term tourism, but the city suffers from mountains of plastic waste, ever-taller hotels competing for the best view and endless mediocre restaurants serving up a standard menu. Tourists can do their bit to stop the rot by encouraging environmentally friendly practices – being careful with water, cutting down on plastic and encouraging proper disposal of plastic waste. And boycotting banana porridge?

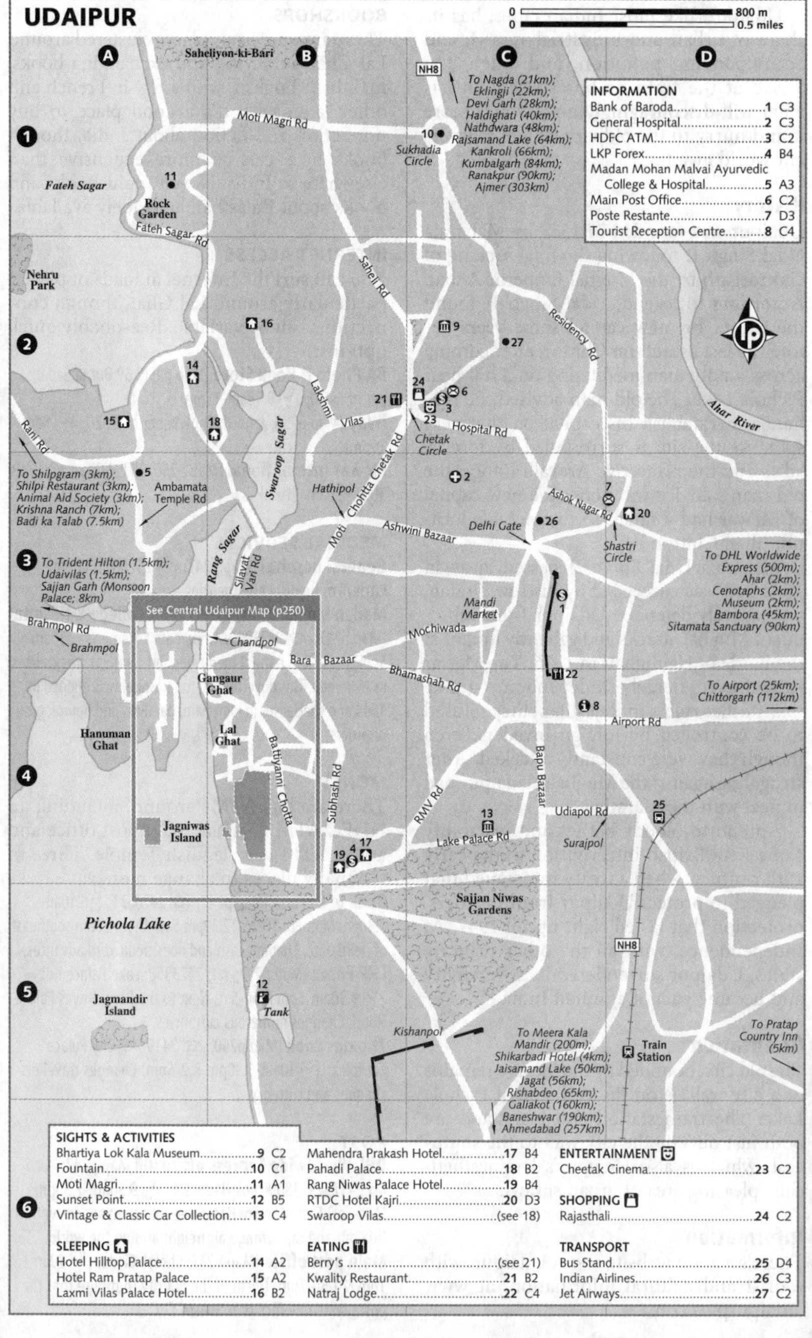
UDAIPUR
0 800 m
0 0.5 miles
INFORMATION
Bank of Baroda 1 C3
General Hospital 2 C3
HDFC ATM 3 C2
LKP Forex 4 B4
Madan Mohan Malvai Ayurvedic College & Hospital 5 A3
Main Post Office 6 C2
Poste Restante 7 D3
Tourist Reception Centre 8 C4
Saheliyon-ki-Bari
NH8
To Nagda (21km); Eklingji (22km); Devi Garh (28km); Haldighati (40km); Nathdwara (48km); Rajsamand Lake (64km); Kankroli (66km); Kumbalgarh (84km); Ranakpur (90km); Ajmer (303km)
Moti Magri Rd
Sukhadia Circle
Fateh Sagar
Rock Garden
Fateh Sagar Rd
Nehru Park
Saheli Rd
Residency Rd
Ahar River
Lakshmi Vilas
Swaroop Sagar
Chetak Circle
Hospital Rd
Rani Rd
To Shilpgram (3km); Shilpi Restaurant (3km); Animal Aid Society (3km); Krishna Ranch (7km); Badi ka Talab (7.5km)
Ambamata Temple Rd
Hathipol
Moti Chohtta Chetak Rd
Ashok Nagar Rd
Rang Sagar
Silavat Vari Rd
Ashwini Bazaar
Delhi Gate
Shastri Circle
To Trident Hilton (1.5km); Udaivilas (1.5km); Sajjan Garh (Monsoon Palace; 8km)
To DHL Worldwide Express (500m); Ahar (2km); Cenotaphs (2km); Museum (2km); Bambora (45km); Sitamata Sanctuary (90km)
See Central Udaipur Map (p250)
Brahmpol Rd
Brahmpol
Chandpol
Mandi Market
Mochiwada
Bara Bazaar
Bhamashah Rd
Gangaur Ghat
To Airport (25km); Chittorgarh (112km)
Airport Rd
Lal Ghat
Hanuman Ghat
Battiyanni Chotta
Subhash Rd
RMV Rd
Bapu Bazaar
Udiapol Rd
Surajpol
Jagniwas Island
Lake Palace Rd
Sajjan Niwas Gardens
Pichola Lake
Jagmandir Island
Tank
Kishanpol
To Meera Kala Mandir (200m); Shikarbadi Hotel (4km); Jaisamand Lake (50km); Jagat (56km); Rishabdeo (65km); Galiakot (160km); Baneshwar (190km); Ahmedabad (257km)
Train Station
To Pratap Country Inn (5km)
SIGHTS & ACTIVITIES
Bhartiya Lok Kala Museum 9 C2
Fountain 10 C1
Moti Magri 11 A1
Sunset Point 12 B5
Vintage & Classic Car Collection 13 C4
SLEEPING
Hotel Hilltop Palace 14 A2
Hotel Ram Pratap Palace 15 A2
Laxmi Vilas Palace Hotel 16 B2
Mahendra Prakash Hotel 17 B4
Pahadi Palace 18 B2
Rang Niwas Palace Hotel 19 B4
RTDC Hotel Kajri 20 D3
Swaroop Vilas (see 18)
EATING
Berry's (see 21)
Kwality Restaurant 21 B2
Natraj Lodge 22 C4
ENTERTAINMENT
Cheetak Cinema 23 C2
SHOPPING
Rajasthali 24 C2
TRANSPORT
Bus Stand 25 D4
Indian Airlines 26 C3
Jet Airways 27 C2

Udaipur, like most Indian cities, has its share of urban and industrial sprawl, and accompanying pollution, and when you arrive at the train or bus station, this is what will discouragingly greet you. Ignore it and hurry to the old city, where a different world awaits.

## History

Udaipur was founded in 1568 by Maharaja Udai Singh II following the final sacking of Chittorgarh by the Mughal Emperor Akbar. According to legend, Udai Singh II found the site of his new capital some years before the last assault on Chittor, after coming across a holy man meditating on a hill near Pichola Lake. The old man advised the maharaja to establish his capital on that very spot. As the site is surrounded by forests, lakes and the protective Aravalli Range, the old man's advice was good: the new capital of Mewar had a much less vulnerable location than Chittor.

Maharaja Udai Singh II passed away in 1572 and was succeeded by his son, Pratap, who bravely defended Udaipur from subsequent Mughal attacks and gallantly fought at the Battle of Haldighati in 1576. The Mewar rulers were fiercely independent; unlike many other rulers in Rajasthan, they refused to be controlled by foreign invaders, even though they were constantly attacked. After struggling against the Mughals, Udaipur had to deal with the Marathas.

An end to bloody battles and instability came with British intervention in the early 19th century, when a treaty was signed that pledged to protect Udaipur from invaders, protection that lasted right up till 1947. At Independence, with all the other princely states, Udaipur surrendered its sovereignty and became part of a united India.

## Orientation

The old city, bounded by the meagre remains of a city wall, is on the east side of Pichola Lake. The train station and bus stand are both just outside the city wall to the southeast, which is also Udaipur's less aesthetically pleasing area of urban sprawl.

## Information

There's a good website about Udaipur, with tourist and cultural information, at www.udaipurplus.com.

### BOOKSHOPS

There are numerous places clustered around Lal Ghat purveying and exchanging books, mainly in English, with a few in French and other languages. It's a good place to buy nonfiction and fiction about India, though books here can be more expensive than elsewhere in India. Novels, guidebooks and books about Rajasthan are widely available.

### INTERNET ACCESS

You can surf the Internet at loads of places, particularly around Lal Ghat, though connections can be variable. Reasonably quick options:

**BA Photo N Book Store** (Map p250; 69 Durga Sadan; per hr Rs 30; ⌚ 9.15am-11pm)

**iWay** (Map p250; Jagdish Chowk; per hr Rs 20; ⌚ 8am-11pm)

**Mewar International** (Map p250; 35 Lal Ghat; per hr Rs 30; ⌚ 9am-11pm)

### MEDICAL SERVICES

**General hospital** (Map p247; ☎ 2528811; Chetak Circle) For medical emergencies.

**Madan Mohan Malvai Ayurvedic College & Hospital** (Map p247; ☎ 2431900; Ambamata Scheme; ⌚ 10am-5pm) Prescribes natural medicines and conducts free courses in Ayurveda. This government-run hospital was opened in 1944 and specialises in joint pain, paralysis and neurological disorders.

### MONEY

There are lots ATMs around, including an HDFC ATM near the main post office and a UTI ATM near Jagdish Temple. Three of the many places to change money:

**Bank of Baroda** (Map p247; ☎ 2420671; ⌚ 10am-2.30pm Mon-Fri, 10am-12.30pm Sat) About 200m southeast of Delhi Gate. Changes cash and does credit-card advances.

**LKP Forex** (Map p247; ☎ 2423358; Lake Palace Rd; ⌚ 9.30am-7pm Mon-Sat) Next to the Rang Niwas Palace Hotel. Changes numerous currencies.

**Thomas Cook** (Map p250; ☎ 2419746; City Palace Complex; ⌚ 10am-1.30pm & 2-5pm) Changes travellers cheques and currency.

### POST

**DHL Worldwide Express office** (Off Map p247; ☎/fax 2412979; 380 Ashok Nagar Rd; ⌚ 9.30am-7.30pm Mon-Sat) East of town. Has a free collection service within Udaipur and can arrange air freight around the world.

**Main post office** (Map p247; Chetak Circle; ⌚ 10am-1pm & 1.30-7pm) North of the old city (but note that the poste restante office is at Shastri Circle).

### TIE THE KNOT WITH AN EXOTIC TWIST

Getting married? If you want to play prince and princess, you couldn't do much better than Udaipur, with its whimsical palaces already dressed in white for the day. The city has become a favourite wedding venue for foreigners – many have travelled thousands of miles to take the plunge in this dreamy destination.

Plum in the middle of Pichola Lake, the gorgeous Lake Palace Hotel was once the exclusive summer residence of Udaipur's maharajas, but today it's accessible to anyone who can afford it. There are several sumptuous venues to choose from within the palace. If you like the thought of celebrating your marriage in a James Bond set, then the Lily Pond may appeal to you – an inner open-air courtyard complete with lily ponds and fountains, the place starred in *Octopussy*. For those who want to get married on the move, there's the Gangaur Boat, a graceful old royal barge belonging to the maharaja of Udaipur.

All arrangements are made by the Lake Palace Hotel. Most types of wedding ceremonies are possible. If you intend to be married by a Christian priest, you must send a 'No Objection Certificate' (issued by a church in your country of residence) to Udaipur at least a month prior to your wedding date. If you opt for a Hindu ceremony, all arrangements can be made by the Lake Palace Hotel, including advice on where to get traditional Rajasthani wedding clothes. You will even get a certificate of marriage.

You're advised to make a reservation at least six months ahead. The best and most pleasant time to get married is during the cooler months between November and March. For prices and further information, contact the food and beverage manager at the **Lake Palace Hotel** (☎ 2528800; lakepalace.udaipur@tajhotels.com; Post Box 5, Udaipur 313001 Rajasthan).

In Udaipur it's also possible to have weddings at the beautiful Shiv Niwas Palace Hotel (see p259), where venues include the poolside, the lawns and the top terrace. For a big bash, there's the grand Durbar Hall (see Durbar Glitz, p253), while the Sunset View Terrace is perfect for more intimate gatherings; both are in the Fateh Prakash Palace Hotel in the City Palace complex. Otherwise, you could go for evocative Jagmandir Island, with its fantastic colonnaded terrace overlooking the lake – here there are places that can accommodate from 30 to 500 people. There are also various courtyards within the City Palace itself. For these venues, you must contact the sales and marketing manager, HRH Group of Hotels at the **City Palace** (☎ 1600-332933; www.hrhindia.com; Udaipur 313001 Rajasthan). Check out more details on the website. If possible, have a look at all the venues before making a choice. Good luck!

**Post office** (Map p250; 10.30am-1pm & 1.30-4.30pm Mon-Sat) Outside the City Palace museum.

#### TOURIST INFORMATION

Apart from the Tourist Reception Centre listed below, smaller tourist information counters operate at the train station and the airport.

**Out & About tourist office** (Map p250; 10am-5pm) In Bagore-ki-Haveli. A fantastic source of information, covering everything from Hindi lessons to pool joints, is *Out & About in Udaipur* (Rs 10), a bimonthly magazine available in most bookshops in Udaipur (or ask at your hotel). It also provides details of worthwhile local projects; donations can be made by contacting the office.

**Tourist Reception Centre** (Map p247; ☎ 2411535; Fateh Memorial Bldg; 10am-5pm Mon-Sat, closed 2nd & 4th Sat of month) Near Surajpol, less than 1km from the bus stand.

#### TRAVEL AGENCIES

Udaipur has scores of small travel agencies (concentrated in the tourist-laden old city), all promising the best deals in town. It's definitely worth shopping around for the best price, as most will try to match or better the prices quoted to you by other agencies.

## Dangers & Annoyances

If you have trouble with hotels or rickshaw drivers (note their registration number), contact the **police** (☎ 2412693) or report it to the **Tourist Reception Centre** (☎ 2411535).

## Sights

#### PICHOLA LAKE

Limpid and large, **Pichola Lake** spreads from the shores of the city, reflecting the cool grey-blue mountains on its rippling mirrorlike surface. It was enlarged by Maharaja Udai

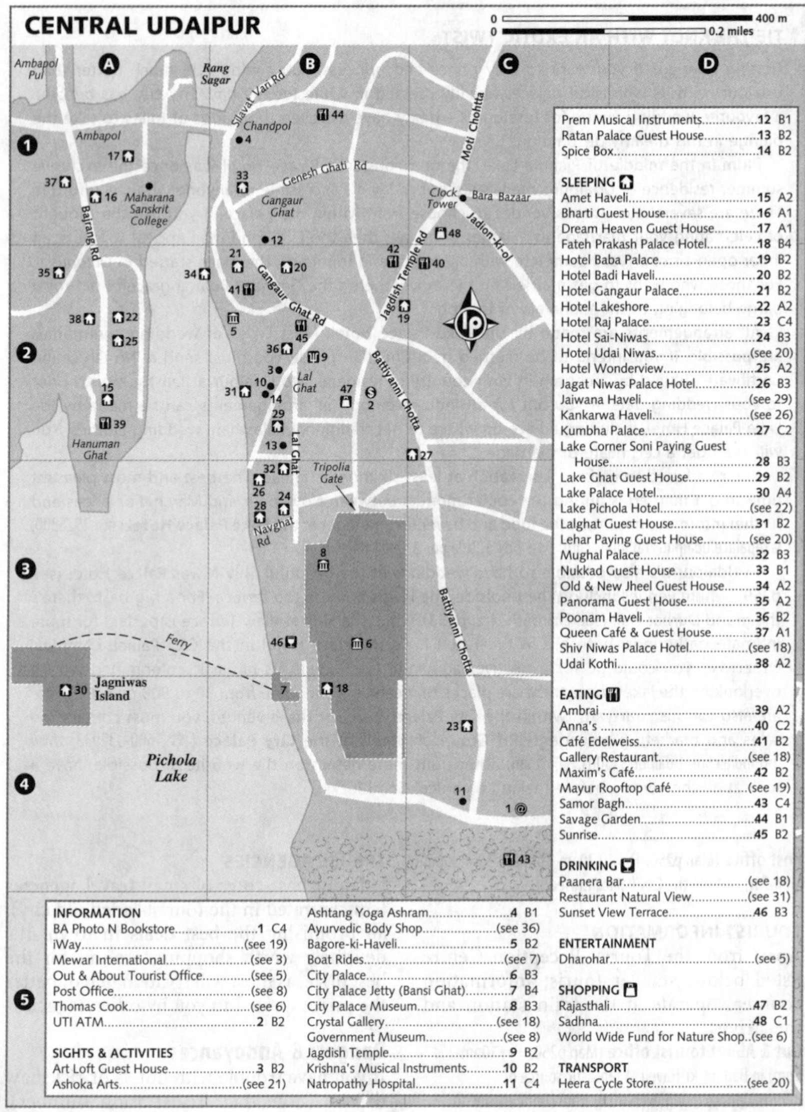




Singh II after he founded the city. He flooded Picholi village, which gave its name to the lake, by building a masonry dam, known as the Badipol. The lake is now 4km long and 3km wide, but it remains shallow and dries up in severe droughts, when you can walk to Jagniwas and Jagmandir, the two major islands on the lake, and camels and buffalo graze around the seemingly shipwrecked Lake Palace.

A handful of crocodiles is believed to inhabit the more remote parts of the lake, near uninhabited sections of the shore. Unfortunately, the lake is occasionally choked with that insidious weed, the water hyacinth. The City Palace extends for a long stretch along the east bank. South of the palace, a pleasant garden runs down to the shore. North of the palace, you can wander along the waterfront to some interesting bathing and *dhobi* (laundry) ghats – the slapping noise made by the dhobi-wallahs (washerpeople) echoes across the lake on all sides.

**Boat rides** (Map p250; adult/child per 30min Rs 100/50, per 1hr Rs 175/100; 9.30am-5pm) leave half-hourly from the City Palace jetty (AKA Bansi Ghat), when the lake is high enough. The longer trip includes a visit to Jagmandir Island.

### Jagniwas Island

The Lake Palace Hotel island of **Jagniwas** is about 1.5 hectares in size and completely covered by the palace built by Maharaja Jagat Singh II in 1754. Once the royal summer palace, it was converted into a hotel in the 1960s by Maharaja Bhagwat Singh and was greatly extended. It is the ultimate in luxury hotels, with courtyards, fountains, restaurants and even a swimming pool. The gleaming white **Lake Palace Hotel** was largely responsible for putting Udaipur on the international tourist map. Its unparalleled location, majestic interior and exquisite architecture have made it one of the world's most famous hotels. It's a magical place, but casual visitors are discouraged. Nonguests can only come over for lunch or dinner (see p261). Hotel launches cross to the island from the City Palace jetty. The Lake Palace, along with the Shiv Niwas Palace and the Monsoon Palace, was used as a set in the James Bond movie *Octopussy*.

Behind Jagniwas is a much smaller island called **Arsi Vilas**, which was built by a former maharaja of Udaipur as a place to watch the sunset. There's a landing attached to this island, which has been used as a helipad in the past.

### Jagmandir Island

The palace on **Jagmandir Island** was built by Maharaja Karan Singh in 1620, and added to by Maharaja Jagat Singh (r 1628–52). It has a restaurant – closed at the time of research because of the dearth of water in the lake. It's said that the Mughal Emperor Shah Jahan (then Prince Kharrim) derived some of his inspiration for the Taj Mahal from this palace after staying here in 1623 and 1624 while leading a revolt against his father, Jehangir. Europeans were sheltered here by Maharaja Sarup Singh during the 1857 Uprising. Flanked by a row of enormous stone elephants, the island has an impressive *chhatri* carved from grey-blue stone, and fantastic views across the lake to the city and its golden palace. There's a small **museum** here detailing the history of the island, as well as frangipani trees, flowers and neat courtyards.

#### THE ULTIMATE SACRIFICE

In Udaipur a sometime royal servant, Panna Dhai, has been immortalised for her extraordinary loyalty to the royal family – the most extreme example you could possibly imagine.

Prince Udai Singh II was just a baby when his father, Vikramaditya, the maharaja of Mewar, was assassinated by a man called Banbir in 1535. Banbir wanted control of the kingdom, and he was determined to eliminate anyone that stood in his way, including the young heir to the throne – Udai Singh. One night, Banbir managed to break into the prince's bedroom, planning to kill the baby boy.

However, Udai Singh's devoted *dhai* (wet nurse), Panna, was one step ahead of him. At the time, Panna was also breastfeeding her own infant son, Chandan. She had already suspected Banbir's wicked intentions and had placed her Chandan in the prince's cradle. When Banbir demanded to know which child was the prince, Panna Dhai pointed to the prince's cradle where her own son slept. Banbir whipped out his sword and slaughtered the child.

Soon after the murder, Panna Dhai hid the prince in a basket and fled to the fort at Kumbalgarh. She told the nobles and people of Mewar what had happened, and the prince was promptly crowned, ensuring the unbroken lineage of the Mewar dynasty.

The current maharaja of Udaipur has honoured the memory of Panna Dhai with a special award at the annual Maharaja Mewar Foundation Awards ceremony. The Panna Dhai Award is given to an individual who 'ventures beyond the call of duty and sets an example in society of permanent value through sacrifice'.

### CITY PALACE & MUSEUMS

The imposing **City Palace** (Map p250), surmounted by balconies, towers and cupolas, towering over the lake, is Rajasthan's largest palace, with a façade 244m long and 30.4m high. A conglomeration of buildings built and extended by various maharajas, it still manages to retain a surprising uniformity of design. Construction was begun by Maharaja Udai Singh II, the city's founder. There are fine views over the lake and the city from the upper terraces.

Enter the museum from the northern side (up the hill from the Jagdish Temple), otherwise there's an extra Rs 25 visitor fee (also payable to get to the Sunset View Terrace, p261). From the north you enter through the Baripol (Great Gate; 1600) and the three-arched Tripolia Gate (1725). To the left, seven arches commemorate the seven times maharajas were weighed here and their weight in gold or silver distributed to the lucky locals. The ticket office is here too.

Guides can be hired near the ticket office. An English-speaking guide costs Rs 100 (maximum of five people). In the winter months (the prime tourist season), the museum can get particularly crowded, so try to visit before 11am to avoid the rush.

In Badi Chowk, which is the large rectangular courtyard set outside the museum, there are pricey handicraft shops, a **World Wide Fund for Nature** (WWF; Map p250; 9.30am-5.30pm) shop, a Thomas Cook office, a post office and banks.

#### City Palace Museum

The main part of the palace is now preserved as the **City Palace museum** (Map p250; adult/child Rs 50/30, camera/video Rs 200/200; 9.30am-4.30pm), housing a large, varied collection of artefacts. Downstairs from the entrance is an armoury section sporting old weapons including a lethal two-pronged sword. Usually after visiting the armoury, most people head straight for the City Palace Museum, which is through the Ganesh Deori, but you can also cross the courtyard to get to the government museum (right).

The Ganesh Deori is the entrance to the museum and leads up to the **Rajya Angan** (Royal Courtyard), the very spot where Udai Singh met the sage who told him to found his city here. The rooms of the museum are extravagantly decorated with mirrors, tiles and paintings. In the **Manak Mahal** (Ruby Palace) there is exquisite glass and mirrorwork, while **Krishna Vilas** has a remarkable collection of miniatures (no photography is permitted here). The **Moti Mahal** has beautiful mirrorwork, and the **Chini Mahal** is covered in ornamental tiles. The **Surya Chopar** has a huge, ornamental sun – the symbol of the sun-descended Mewar dynasty. **Mor Chowk** (Peacock Sq) has beautiful mosaics of peacocks, the favourite Rajasthani bird. **Bhim Vilas** has a striking striped floor. In the **Bari Mahal** there's a fine central garden with good views over the old city.

More beautiful paintings can be seen in the **Zenana Mahal**, which opens onto **Laxmi Chowk**; there's a beautiful white pavilion in the centre of this square. Take note of the large tiger-catching cage, which worked rather like an oversized mousetrap, near the Zenana Mahal entrance; a goat or buffalo would be tied up inside the cage as a tiger-tempting snack, which would lure the tiger into captivity.

Palace ladies once used the gallery to observe the grand **Durbar Hall** (see Durbar Glitz, opposite).

Inside the separate palace enclosure, entered from the south of Badi Chowk, are the Shiv Niwas and Fateh Prakash Palace Hotels (see p259), the Sunset View Terrace (p261), the Gallery Restaurant (p261), the Crystal Gallery (opposite), and the boat wharves for trips out to Jagmandir and the Lake Palace. It costs Rs 25 for nonguests to enter this area. There's another entrance to this enclosure on the southern side of the palace, which is more convenient if you're staying in the Lake Palace Rd area.

#### Government Museum

There's also a **government museum** (Map p250; admission Rs 3, free Mon; 10am-5pm Sat-Thu) within the palace complex. There are inscriptions dating from the 2nd to the 17th centuries, and some wonderful sculpture dating from the 5th century onwards, including pieces from Jagat and Kumbalgarh. It has a splendid collection of jewel-like miniature paintings of the Mewar school. Stranger exhibits include a freaky monkey holding a lamp. There are also regal maharaja portraits in profile, documenting the palace's rulers and the changing fashions of the moustache.

**Crystal Gallery**

Situated at the Fateh Prakash Palace Hotel, the **Crystal Gallery** (Map p250; adult/child Rs 325/165, photography prohibited; 10am-1pm & 3-8pm) houses the rare crystal Maharaja Sajjan Singh ordered from F&C Osler & Co in England in 1877. The maharaja died before it arrived, and all the items stayed packed up in boxes for 110 years. The extraordinary, extravagant, unused collection includes crystal chairs, sofas, tables and even beds. There's an exquisite antique jewel-studded carpet that has to be seen to be believed. The rather exclusive admission fee includes a soft drink, tea or coffee in the Gallery Restaurant (see p261), where high tea is served daily. Admission also includes entry to the grand Durbar Hall (see Durbar Glitz, below).

**JAGDISH TEMPLE**

Only 150m north of the City Palace entrance, this fantastically carved Indo-Aryan **temple** (Map p250; 5am-2pm & 4-10.30pm) was built by Maharaja Jagat Singh in 1651. It enshrines a black stone image of Vishnu as Jagannath, Lord of the Universe. There's a brass image of the Garuda (man-bird vehicle of Vishnu) in a shrine in front of the temple, and the templs steps are flanked by elephants. You can donate money, which is used to feed the hungry, between 11am and noon.

**BAGORE-KI-HAVELI**

This gracious 18th-century **haveli** (Map p250; admission Rs 25; 10am-7pm), set on the water's edge in the Gangaur Ghat area, was built by a former prime minister and has been carefully restored. There are 138 rooms set around courtyards. Some have been arranged to evoke the period during which the house was inhabited, and others house cultural displays, including the world's biggest (and saggiest) turban. The *haveli* also houses an interesting art gallery, which features contemporary and folk art, and world-famous monuments lovingly carved out of polystyrene. The upper courtyard makes an atmospheric setting for fabulous Rajasthani dance performances at 7pm (see p262).

**FATEH SAGAR**

North of Pichola Lake, this **lake** – which dries up if the monsoon has been poor – is ringed by hills and is a hangout for lovestruck locals. Overlooked by a number of hills, it was originally built in 1678 by Maharaja Jai Singh but reconstructed by Maharaja Fateh Singh after heavy rains destroyed the dam. A pleasant drive winds along the east bank. In the middle of the lake is **Nehru Park**, a garden island. An autorickshaw from the old city costs Rs 20 (one way).

**MOTI MAGRI**

Overlooking Fateh Sagar, atop **Moti Magri** (Pear Hill; Map p247), is a statue of the Rajput hero Maharaja Pratap, who frequently defied the Mughals while riding his beloved horse, Chetak (see Haldighati, p264 for more about this noble quadruped).

**DURBAR GLITZ**

Many palaces in India have a durbar hall (royal court). Usually the grandest room in the place, with a good quota of chandeliers and gilt, the durbar hall had to impress – it was used by India's rulers for official occasions, such as state banquets, and to hold meetings.

The restored Durbar Hall at the Fateh Prakash Palace Hotel, in the City Palace complex in Udaipur, is undoubtedly one of India's most impressive, vast and lavish, with some of the country's hugest chandeliers. The walls display royal weapons and striking portraits of former maharajas of Mewar (a most distinguished-looking lot). The illustrious Mewar rulers come from what is believed to be the oldest ruling dynasty in the world, spanning 76 generations.

The foundation stone was laid in 1909 by Lord Minto, the viceroy of India, during the reign of Maharaja Fateh Singh. As a mark of honour to Lord Minto, it was originally named Minto Hall. The top floor of this high-ceilinged hall is surrounded by viewing galleries, where ladies of the palace could watch in veiled seclusion what was happening below. Nowadays, it's the Crystal Gallery museum (above).

The hall still has the capacity to hold hundreds of people and can even be hired for conferences or social gatherings. For details, contact the **Fateh Prakash Palace Hotel** (☎ 2528016; www.hrhindia.com).

The path to the top of the hill traverses some pleasant **gardens** (Map p247; adult/child Rs 15/5; 7.30am-7pm), including a Japanese rock garden. Car/rickshaw/motorcycle/bicycle entry costs Rs 20/10/5/1.

### BHARTIYA LOK KALA MUSEUM

The interesting collection exhibited by this small **museum** (Map p247; ☎ 2529296; Indian/foreigner Rs 15/25, camera/video Rs 20/50; 9am-5.30pm) and foundation for the preservation and promotion of local folk arts includes dresses, turbans, dolls, masks, musical instruments, paintings and – its high point – puppets. One-hour **puppet shows** (Indian/foreigner Rs 30/50) are staged at noon and 6pm.

### SAHELIYON-KI-BARI

The **Saheliyon-ki-Bari** (Garden of the Maids of Honour; Map p247; admission Rs 5; 8am-7pm) is in the north of the city. Built by Sangram Singh II in 1710, this small, quaint ornamental garden was laid out for 48 women attendants who came as part of a princess's dowry. It has well-maintained fountains (water shortages permitting; you may have to pay to see them turned on), kiosks, marble elephants and a delightful lotus pool. There's also a small **museum** ( noon-5pm) here, in which the main attractions are some stuffed cobras.

### SHILPGRAM

A crafts village 3km west of Fateh Sagar, **Shilpgram** (Off Map p247; Indian/foreigner Rs 15/25, camera/video Rs 10/50; 11am-7pm), was inaugurated by Rajiv Gandhi in 1989. Set in dusty, rolling countryside, it's contrived but interesting. There are displays of traditional mud huts with glittering mirrored interiors from Rajasthan, Gujarat, Goa and Maharashtra. Best, though, are the excellent demonstrations by traditional performers and artisans (crafts are on sale). There are always splendid groups ready to perform as you approach, though it can feel deserted of visitors on a regular day. There's a festival in December that's a fantastic spectacle; check with the Tourist Reception Centre (p249) or at Bagore-ki-Haveli (p253) for details.

**Shilpi Restaurant** (Off Map p247; dishes Rs 42-94; 11.30am-10.30pm), next to the crafts village site, is a pleasant open-air restaurant serving good veg and nonveg Indian, Continental and Chinese food. It also has a **swimming pool** (admission Rs 100; 11am-8pm).

Some people walk out to Shilpgram; a return autorickshaw trip (including a 30-minute stop) between the old city and Shilpgram costs Rs 80.

### AHAR

About 2km east of Udaipur, at **Ahar** (Off Map p247), are more than 250 restored **cenotaphs** (Off Map p247) of the maharajas of Mewar, forming a spectacular city of snowy domes built over 350 years. Around 19 former maharajas were cremated here. The most striking cenotaph is that of Maharaja Amar Singh, who ruled from 1597 to 1620. Nearby you can visit the remains of an ancient city – the Sisodias' capital – and a **museum** (Off Map p247; admission Rs 3, photography prohibited; 10am-5pm) housing some accompanying artefacts, where you'll find a limited but very old collection of earthen pottery, sculptures and other archaeological finds. Some pieces date back to 1700 BC, including such homy objects, such as a 1st-century BC skin scrubber and a grain pot, and there's a beautiful 10th-century metal figure of Buddha. Not many tourists make it out here, but the sites are very much worth the trip.

### SAJJAN GARH (MONSOON PALACE)

Perched on the top of a distant mountain range like a fairy-tale castle, this neglected late-19th-century **palace** (Off Map p247) was constructed by Maharaja Sajjan Singh. Originally an astronomical centre, it became a monsoon palace and hunting lodge. Now government owned, it's open to the public after lengthy closure, but there's not much to see but neglect. You pay Rs 80/20 per person/rickshaw at the foot of the hill to enter the Sajjan Garh Wildlife Sanctuary. The main reason to visit is for the breathtaking views, particularly at sunset. Autorickshaw return trips cost Rs 150 (including waiting).

### OTHER ATTRACTIONS

The maharajas' **Vintage & Classic Car Collection** (Map p247; ☎ 2420979; admission Rs 100; 9-11am & 2-6pm) is fascinating. Housed in the former state garage are 22 splendid vehicles, including a 1938 Cadillac complete with purdah system, the beautiful 1934 Phantom Rolls Royce used in *Octopussy*, a homely little Morris Minor Traveller from 1959, and the Cadillac convertible that whisked Queen Elizabeth II to the airport in 1961.

**Sunset Point** (Map p247; admission Rs 5) is a lovely, easy-to-reach sunset spot, with dazzling views over Pichola Lake, Jagmandir Island and the Monsoon Palace. There's a musical fountain here (drought permitting), which plays each evening.

The huge **fountain** (Map p247) in the middle of Sukhadia Circle, north of the city, is illuminated at night. **Sajjan Niwas Gardens** (Map p247), located near the Vintage & Classic Car Collection, has a rose garden, the Gulab Bagh, pleasant lawns (beware of the unfriendly dogs here) and a zoo.

Almost 5km beyond Shilpgram, 7.5km from town, is **Badi ka Talab** (Tiger Lake), a mammoth artificial lake, which is usually full. Flanked by hills, it's a great place to head for some relaxation and a picnic. Crocodiles apparently lurk in parts of the lake, so swimmers beware! Near the lake there's a small **Shiva and Hanuman temple**. An autorickshaw to the lake should cost Rs 100/200 one-way/return (with a one-hour wait).

## Activities

See p251 for information about boat cruises.

### AYURVEDA

**Madan Mohan Malvai Ayurvedic College & Hospital** (Map p247; ☎ 2431900; Ambamata Scheme; ⌚ 10am-5pm) prescribes natural medicines and conducts free courses in Ayurveda.

### HORSE RIDING

Kumbha Palace (see p257) arranges recommended riding excursions around Udaipur. A 2½-hour ride costs Rs 500 (includes mineral water), and a half-/full-day excursion costs Rs 700/1200 (includes water and lunch). You can also stay overnight in the hotel's rural cottages on its **Krishna Ranch** (d Rs 1000-1200), set in beautiful countryside 7km from Udaipur, or arrange much longer trips. A 24-hour safari including accommodation at the ranch costs Rs 2000.

Pratap Country Inn (see p257) also runs horse safaris.

### MASSAGE

The **Ayurvedic Body Shop** (Map p250; ☎ 5120802; 39 Lal Ghat; head massage Rs 100, 15min back massage Rs 200, 45min full-body massage Rs 500; ⌚ 10.30am-9pm) offers Ayurvedic massages and has some good products on sale, such as oils, moisturisers, shampoos and soaps.

You can also indulge in a massage at the **Naturopathy Hospital** (Map p250; ☎ 2422700; cnr Battiyanni Chotta & Lake Palace Rd; 30min massage Rs 50; ⌚ 8am-2pm Mon-Sat, 8-11am Sun), though 'indulge' may be the wrong word. You'll be rubbed down vigorously by one or two masseurs in a room of uncertain cleanliness. It may not be relaxing, but it's invigorating and cheap.

Recommended by several travellers, Raju at **Bharti Guest House** (☎ 2433469; Hotel Lake Pichola Rd), on Hanuman Ghat, also performs massages. He's perhaps the most skilled of the lot, mixing a range of techniques including shiatsu, acupressure and Thai massage. He charges Rs 600/750/1050 per 30 minutes/45 minutes/one hour. Women may not relish being massaged by a man (you have to undress), though female travellers have reported feeling comfortable with him.

### TREKKING

Exploring the surrounding countryside and villages on foot is a fantastic way to see rural and tribal life while taking in some beautiful scenery; guides advertise in *Out & About in Udaipur* (see p249). One recommended guide is **Ganpat Singh** (☎ 2414664; 44 Pandu Wari) at Royal Palace Guesthouse.

## Courses

See left for information on courses in Ayurveda.

### COOKING

**Spice Box** (Map p250; ☎ 5100742; spicebox2001@yahoo.co.in; 38 Lake Ghat) offers recommended cooking lessons (Rs 400 to 500 for four hours), in which you learn a selection of dishes and then eat the results. The cooking lessons at **Art Loft Guest House** (Map p250; ☎ 2420163; jairaj34@yahoo.com; 35 Lal Ghat), which charges Rs 500 for two hours, are also recommended.

### MUSIC

Bablu at **Prem Musical Instruments** (Map p250; ☎ 2430599; 28 Gadia Devra) gives sitar, tabla and flute lessons (Rs 100 per hour). He also sells and repairs those instruments and can arrange performances. Krishna at **Krishna's Musical Instruments** (Map p250; 37 Lal Ghat) also offers recommended lessons.

The family from **Ratan Palace Guest House** (Map p250; ☎ 2561570; 21 Lal Ghat) are musical; the father plays the sitar and the son the tabla. They give lessons and occasional concerts.

#### PAINTING

**Ashoka Arts** (Map p250; Hotel Gangaur Palace) runs painting lessons (Rs 150 for two to three hours, including materials). Art Loft Guest House (see p255) also offers painting lessons (Rs 500 for two hours).

#### YOGA

**Ashtang Yoga Ashram** (Map p250; ☎ 2524872; Raiba House, inside Chandpol) is a friendly hatha yoga centre, with yoga classes every morning at around 8am. The teacher has 20 years' experience, and payment is by donation (proceeds go to the local animal hospital).

### Tours

Five-hour **city tours** (per person excl admission charges Rs 78, minimum 5 people) leave at 8am from the RTDC Hotel Kajri and take in the main sights. There are also **excursions** (per person excl admission charges incl veg lunch Rs 276) to Ranakpur and Kumbalgarh. Contact the Tourist Reception Centre (p249) for more information. See p251 for info about boat cruises.

## Sleeping

Like most big tourist destinations in Rajasthan, there are many more budget than midrange places. However, Udaipur has an unusually wide choice of accommodation in all categories, with some particularly enchanting midrange options.

Staying close to the lakeshore is most romantic. West of Jagdish Temple, the Lal Ghat area, close to the shores of the lake, is crowded with places offering masses of choice. Or you could opt for the quieter and less touristy Hanuman Ghat on the other side of the lake, which often has even better views. Ask for a lake-facing room (usually more expensive).

The commission system is in place with a vengeance, so if you get a rickshaw driver who insists that the hotel of your choice has burnt down or suddenly closed, or the owner has died in a freak accident, politely decline his kind alternative offer. Unless your rickshaw is prepaid, if you're heading for Lal Ghat, ask for the Jagdish Temple when you arrive as it's a good place to start looking for accommodation. An autorickshaw from the bus stand to Jagdish should cost about Rs 25. To bypass rapacious rickshaw drivers, use the police-supervised prepaid autorickshaw stands outside the train and bus stations. Some unscrupulous operators will still try to take you to the hotel of their choice, but remember: they don't get reimbursed until you hand over the receipt at the end of your journey. See Dangers & Annoyances, p249 for info on what to do if you have trouble with hotels or rickshaw drivers. In the low season the prices of budget hotels crumble and midrange places plummet – it's well worth bargaining.

#### BUDGET

Udaipur pioneered the Paying Guest House Scheme in Rajasthan. Expect to pay Rs 100 to 300 per night. The Tourist Reception Centre (see p249) has a list detailing all the places and services offered.

#### Lal Ghat Area

If you're staying in this area, actively encourage your hotel to dispose of rubbish in an environmentally friendly manner to prevent this magnificent place from being spoilt.

**Lalghat Guest House** (Map p250; ☎ 2525301; lalghat@hotmail.com; 33 Lal Ghat; dm Rs 50, s with shared bathroom Rs 75, d with shared bathroom Rs 100-150, s/d with private bathroom Rs 200/250; 💻) This mellow guesthouse by the lake was one of the first to open in Udaipur, and it's still great. The rooftop areas have superb lake views and are a serene place to sunbathe, and there's a back terrace overlooking the ghats. The older part has a lot more character. Accommodation ranges from spruce, end-to-end dorm beds to the best room, which has arched windows and thick walls (Rs 350). All the rooms have fans and mosquito nets, and there's a small kitchen for self-caterers.

**Hotel Udai Niwas** (Map p250; ☎ 5120789; www.hoteludainiwas.com; Gangaur Ghat Rd; r Rs 250-1000; ❄ 💻) A new hotel that has sprung up in a narrow space off Ganguar Ghat, Udai Niwas has excellent, spotless rooms that feel much more luxurious than their price range would suggest. They're painted white and decorated with puppets and wall hangings – the cheapest rooms are a real bargain. Staff are nice and helpful, and there's a good travel agency and Internet café. The hotel claims the highest rooftop in Udaipur – we're unsure if building so high should be encouraged, but this is a very good choice.

**Hotel Gangaur Palace** (Map p250; ☎ 2422303; Gangaur Ghat Rd; r Rs 80-350) This is a whitewashed, elaborate, faded *haveli* around a courtyard.

The pricier rooms are atmospheric, though basic, with wall paintings, window seats and private bathrooms; the cheaper rooms are simple and share a bathroom, but are fine. Rooms with a lake view are the most expensive. The hot water is a bit iffy. There's a palmist working here from 2pm to 5pm, who charges Rs 50 to 100.

**Lehar Paying Guest House** (Map p250; ☎ 2417651; 86 Gangaur Ghat Rd; s/d from Rs 100/150) Run by a redoubtable matriarch, this has some squeaky clean rooms in an old building, some of which (usually the costlier ones) are decorated with wall paintings and coloured glass.

**Lake Corner Soni Paying Guest House** (Map p250; ☎ 2525712; 27 Navghat Rd; s/d with shared bathroom from Rs 80/100, s/d with private bathroom from Rs 100/125) Tucked away close to the City Palace is this simple courtyard-centred guesthouse. It's run by a charming couple and is imbued with a family atmosphere. Mr Soni offers Hindi lessons, the home cooking is excellent, and there's a great view from the rooftop.

**Mughal Palace** (Map p250; ☎ 2417954; mughal palace2001@hotmail.com; 46 Lal Ghat; r Rs 150-400) Also located near the City Palace, Mughal Palace is a modern hotel with traditional flourishes. It's quiet, with good-value rooms and surreal wall paintings. Room 101 has a pretty view and a balcony. There's a very pleasant rooftop restaurant with a great lake view.

**Old & New Jheel Guest House** (Map p250; ☎ 2421352; 56 Gangaur Ghat; d Rs 150-600) Both Old and New Jheel are right down by the ghat. Old Jheel Guest House is in an old *haveli*, and accommodation ranges from basic back rooms to one with a small balcony and three lake-facing windows. Nearby New Jheel has breezy rooms and a brilliant position over the lake (when it's full). Room 201 is the best, with windows on three sides. Both the Jheels get good reviews from readers.

**Nukkad Guest House** (Map p250; 56 Ganesh Ghat Rd; r from Rs 100-150) Staying at the Nukkad means renting rooms in a friendly, family house. There are just a couple of unadorned, homy rooms and a nice rooftop.

**Hotel Badi Haveli** (Map p250; ☎ 2412588; Gangaur Ghat Rd; r Rs 200-450) In an old whitewashed building around a leafy courtyard, the Badi Haveli is well kept but overpriced. Rooms are basic and clean; costlier ones are furnished with wall paintings, coloured glass and alcoves, and some have views. There's a variety of rooms with shared or private bathrooms.

### Hanuman Ghat Area

Directly across the water from Lal Ghat, Hanuman Ghat is a more peaceful place to stay, with its local vibe and handful of excellent choices.

**Dream Heaven Guest House** (Map p250; ☎ 2431 038; 22 Bhim Permashever Rd; r Rs 120-450; veg/nonveg dishes Rs 15-45) An excellent choice and deservedly popular. There are only seven spick-and-span rooms, featuring wall hangings and paintings. Some have views and some have a splendid balcony. The food at the rooftop restaurant, which is overlooking the lake and Udaipur at its best, is fresh and tasty. You can chill out here on a pile of cushions.

**Panorama Guest House** (Map p250; ☎ 2431027; krishna2311@rediffmail.com; Hanuman Ghat; r Rs 80-150) Another divine choice that's smart, well kept and quietly set, overlooking a small local square. The spotless rooms have wall paintings and either a private bathroom or a view, and there's a relaxing rooftop.

**Queen Café & Guest House** (Map p250; ☎ 2430875; 14 Bajrang Rd; r with shared bathroom Rs 100-150; veg dishes Rs 15-35) Run by a Jain family, Queen has two unadorned rooms in a homy and atmospheric family house. The home cooking is excellent, and cooking lessons are offered here.

**Hotel Lakeshore** (Map p250; ☎ 2432480; ashfak_h@yahoo.com; d Rs 250-700; ❄ 💻) Grubby yellow-and-blue rooms have small shutters opening onto the water, and there's a terrace with good views over the lake (if it's full, over a field if it's not). There's only one really good room, full of arches and pillars; it costs Rs 600 (Rs 700 with AC).

### Elsewhere

**Kumbha Palace** (Map p250; ☎ 2422702; Battiyanni Chotta; r Rs 70-350) This excellent place is run by a Dutch-Indian couple. Quietly tucked away, not far from Jagdish Temple, Kumbha Palace has simple rooms (some with shared bathroom, some with private) backed by a lush lawn that's bordered by the City Palace's retainers' quarters. The owners run horse-riding excursions (see p255). Free pick-ups from the bus or train stations are on offer.

**Pratap Country Inn** (Off Map p247; ☎ 2583138; s/d Rs 300/400) This is a serene, though shabby, secluded country retreat at Titaradi village, about 7km outside Udaipur. Horse safaris can be arranged here.

### MIDRANGE

#### Lal Ghat Area

**Jagat Niwas Palace Hotel** (Map p250; ☎ 2420133; mail@jagatniwaspalace.com; 23-25 Lal Ghat; r with AC Rs 1250, deluxe r Rs 1550, ste Rs 2650; ) On the lakeshore, this wonderful hotel consistently receives good reports. In two converted *havelis*, rooms are charming and evocative, with carved wooden furniture and cushioned window seats. Go for a room with a lake view. The hotel has a great rooftop restaurant (see p260).

**Kankarwa Haveli** (Map p250; ☎ 2411457; fax 2521403; 26 Lal Ghat; r Rs 750-1450) This option, in an old *haveli*, is set right next to Jagat Niwas Palace. Whitewashed rooms give a sublime simplicity, but the service isn't always spot-on. Pricier rooms overlook Pichola Lake.

**Poonam Haveli** (Map p250; ☎ 2410303; poonamhaveli@hotmail.com; 39 Lal Ghat; r Rs 400-1050; ) A fairly modern place decked out in traditional style, Poonam gets positive reports from readers. Boasting big beds, the rooms are plain, fresh and large, some decorated with mirrorwork and some with views. The '007' room has arches as elegant as a raised eyebrow.

**Jaiwana Haveli** (Map p250; ☎/fax 2521252; 14 Lal Ghat; r Rs 400-1500; ) Formerly Hotel Caravanserai, this modern, spacious, rather impersonal place has unfussy, well-kept rooms decorated with block-printed fabrics. Views from the rooms are through slightly tinted windows, but there are vast views from the rooftop.

**Lake Ghat Guest House** (Map p250; ☎ 2521636; 4/13 Lal Ghat; d Rs 500-700; veg dishes around Rs 50) Some of the smart, biggish rooms have views, others have balconies, and all are decorated with stained glass. The rooms are set around a small atrium filled with hanging plants. There are splendid views from the summit, and a good restaurant.

**Hotel Baba Palace** (Map p250; ☎ 2427126; www.hotelbabapalace.com; s Rs 300, d Rs 400-600, deluxe r with AC Rs 800-1000; ) This new, somewhat brash hotel has sparkling rooms and an unusual location eye-to-eye with Jagdish Temple. Rooms have remarkable views.

**Hotel Sai-Niwas** (Map p250; ☎ 2421586; 75 Navghat Rd; d Rs 500-1250; ) Just down the hill towards the ghat from the City Palace entrance, this hotel lacks the polish of some midrange places, but certainly has lots of character. The seven double rooms are imaginatively decorated, with psychedelic murals covering the walls. Room 5 is particularly romantic – the bed is in a pillared alcove with tiny windows on all sides.

#### Lake Palace Road Area

**Rang Niwas Palace Hotel** (Map p247; ☎ 2523890; www.rangniwaspalace.com; Lake Palace Rd; s Rs 500-900, d Rs 700-1100, s/d ste Rs 2200/2500; ) A converted 19th-century palace set in scenic gardens, Rang Niwas boasts a tiny pool (Rs 125 for nonguests). Rooms (some are small) have carved wooden furniture, and some feature balconies with swing seats for relaxing on. Note that suites are just bigger rooms. The service receives mixed reports.

**Mahendra Prakash Hotel** (Map p250; ☎ 2419811; r Rs 500-1500; ) Spacious gardens, well-furnished rooms, a cheery atmosphere and friendly staff are the name of the game at Mahendra Prakash. The restaurant overlooks a step-well, and there's a pool (Rs 100 for nonguests).

**Hotel Raj Palace** (Map p250; ☎ 2410364; rajpalaceudr@yahoo.com; 103 Battiyanni Chotta; d Rs 650-850, ste Rs 1250) The Raj Palace is housed in a 300-year-old *haveli* that feels more tired than old. There are comfortable doubles; the more expensive they are, the more cushioned alcoves and pillars you get. There's a leafy courtyard restaurant, which is a great place to chill out with a beer.

#### Hanuman Ghat

**Amet Haveli** (Map p250; ☎ 2431085; regiudr@datainfosys.net; s/d Rs 1650/1850, ste with AC Rs 1850/2150; breakfast Rs 175) A romantic choice in a 350-year-old heritage building on the lakeshore. The beautiful rooms have window seats, and small stained-glass and shuttered windows. One of Udaipur's most scenic restaurants, Ambrai (p260), is next door.

**Udai Kothi** (Map p250; ☎ 2432810; www.udaikothi.com; r from Rs 2000; deluxe r Rs 2500, ste Rs 3000; ) This hotel is in a new building, but designed with lots of traditional froth (cupolas, icing-sugar stucco etc). It has a wonderful rooftop terrace, where you can dine well (see p260) or swim in Udaipur's *only* rooftop pool (Rs 200 for nonguests), and there's a Jacuzzi with a view. Rooms are beautifully appointed and decorated with summery, pretty prints, and the hotel is full of thoughtful touches, such as bowls of floating flowers. However, it's recently had some mixed reports.

**Lake Pichola Hotel** (Map p250; ☎ 2431197; www.lakepicholahotel.com; standard r Rs 975, s/d from Rs 1700/1800; ❄) Dramatic Belgian glass chandeliers line the reception hall, while Pichola Lake offers excellent views. It's worth paying to get a room with a lakeside balcony or a cushioned window seat – standard rooms are overpriced and musty. The restaurant is worthwhile, and you can sit on the narrow terrace overlooking Pichola Lake.

**Hotel Wonderview** (Map p250; ☎ 2432494; 6 Panch Dewari Rd; r Rs 550-950) Wonderview offers more fine views, through scalloped windows arrayed with cushioned seats. Rooms are a bit worn, but still decent.

### Elsewhere

**Hotel Ram Pratap Palace** (Map p247; ☎/fax 2431700; 5B Alkapuri; s/d Rs 1585/1885) An elegantly modern *haveli* in the Fateh Sagar area, Ram Pratap Palace has been lavished with lots of attention to detail. That said, it's rather impersonal and isn't fantastic value. Calmly decorated deluxe rooms face the lake (which may be empty if the monsoon's been poor). There's a fine restaurant on site and there are views from the rooftop terrace.

**Swaroop Vilas** (Map p247; ☎/fax 2431959; 6 Ambargarh; s/d Rs 950/1350, with AC Rs 1600/2200) A new hotel in an out-of-the-way, quiet area, this creamy building has keen management and modern rooms that are smart and clean. The more expensive ones have balconies and views.

**Pahadi Palace** (Map p247; ☎/fax 2433458; 18 Ambargarh; s/d Rs 300/400, deluxe d Rs 700-1100) Next door to Swaroop Vilas, Pahadi Palace is looking rather exhausted, though the better rooms – decorated in inoffensive beige luxury – are very spacious and have generous views. The cheaper ones could do with a fresh lick of paint.

**Hotel Hilltop Palace** (Map p247; ☎ 2432246; hilltop@datainfosys.net; s/d from Rs 1950/2950; ❄ 🏊) This is a modern hotel that, as its name suggests, sits on a hill. It feels a bit sterile, but some rooms are nicely decorated and have swing seats. Those with balconies are best. The rooftop terrace has great 360-degree views.

**Shikarbadi Hotel** (Off Map p247; ☎ 2583201; www.hrhindia.com; s/d Oct-Mar from Rs 2300/2800, Apr-Sep from Rs 1600/1950; 🏊) This option is 4km south of town on the Ahmedabad road. Once a royal hunting lodge, it's set in wilderness in the foothills of the Aravallis, amid relaxing gardens with pristine lawns. Some rooms have exposed stone walls, others are whitewashed, but all have refreshing rural outlooks, and some have balconies. A stud farm on the premises offers short horse rides (Rs 250 for 40 minutes). Sip tea while you watch the wild boars gorge at 4pm each day (not far from the pool area).

> **THE AUTHOR'S CHOICE**
>
> **Devi Garh** (Off Map p247; ☎ 02953-289211; www.deviresorts.com; Delwara; tents US$150, ste US$350-1300; ❄ 🏊) This outstanding hotel is a unique place, 28km northeast of Udaipur amid the dramatic Aravelli hills. It's housed in a beautiful 18th-century palace, but has been decorated in wonderfully contrasting, contemporary style using traditional motifs. The best suites have private pools.

## TOP END

### City Palace

**Lake Palace Hotel** (Map p250; ☎ 2528800; www.tajhotels.com; d US$375, with lake view US$460, ste US$750-1100; ❄ 🏊) This romantic palace, seemingly floating in the lake (drought permitting), is extraordinary, with open-air courtyards, lotus ponds and a small, mango tree–shaded pool. Rooms are hung with silk and filled with carved furniture. The cheapest overlook the lily pond or terrace. Recent renovations (spurred by competition from Udaivilas?) have given it an overdue facelift.

**Shiv Niwas Palace Hotel** (Map p250; ☎ 2528016; www.hrhindia.com; s/d US$125/150, ste with terrace from US$300; ❄ 🏊) Once the maharaja's guest quarters, Shiv Niwas has some incredibly lavish, over-the-top rooms, filled with fountains and silver furniture. The cheapest rooms are unexciting and not really great value – go for a room with a terrace. The marble pool (Rs 300 for nonguests) is gorgeous. It's best to get a room around the pool (No 16 has fine views over the lake). For an all-out splurge there are some lavish suites; the imperial suite even has a small fountain near the dreamy four-poster bed. The hotel has an atmospheric restaurant (see p261), a bar and an Ayurvedic massage centre.

**Fateh Prakash Palace Hotel** (Map p250; ☎ 2528019; www.hrhindia.com; s/d US$170/200, ste with lake view US$250/275; ❄) Built in the early 20th century when Maharaja Fateh Singh reigned, the hotel has palatial suites. The cheapest of the double rooms are not in the main palace wing, but all have a lake view. Far more ornate rooms furnished with traditional pieces are available (some with a lake view). The intimate Gallery Restaurant (see opposite) has brilliant views across the lake.

### Elsewhere

**Udaivilas** (Off Map p247; ☎ 2433300; www.oberoihotels.com; s/d from US$450/475, ste with pool US$1950; ) Lying 1.5km west of Udaipur, Udaivilas' sea of butter-sculpture domes is a recent addition to the Udaipur skyline. It's a luxury boutique hotel that doesn't spare the glitz and gold leaf. Suites come with private pools. The hotel houses two excellent restaurants (see opposite).

**Trident Hilton** (Off Map p247; ☎ 2432200; www.trident-hilton.com; s/d/ste US$120/130/220; ) Also out west, this is one of Udaipur's slickest options when it comes to service. Hidden in the hills, way beyond Chandpol, the Trident offers smart and comfortable, though unspectacular, rooms. The restaurant is excellent, and there's a gorgeous pool.

**Laxmi Vilas Palace Hotel** (Map p247; ☎ 2529711; r US$175; ) This grand hilltop hotel (with requisite hunting trophies) has been recently refurbished, creating a lush, traditional atmosphere. A bar and a good restaurant are on site. Nonguests can use the pool here for Rs 165.

## Eating

Udaipur has scores of sun-kissed rooftop cafés, many with mesmerising lake views, as well as fine dining at the top-end hotels. Indian food is usually a better bet than Western-style dishes. Some restaurants serve bhang lassi; see p365.

Many budget restaurants have nightly screenings of contemporary movies or *Octopussy* – which, as no-one will allow you to forget, was partly filmed in Udaipur.

**Ambrai** (Map p250; dishes Rs 35-120; 12.30-3pm & 7.30-10.30pm) This outdoor restaurant has a superb location, and is a great place for an afternoon drink, as well as a meal. Unique among restaurants in Udaipur, it sits at water level, looking across to the Lake Palace, Lal Ghat and the City Palace. It feels like a French park, with its wrought-iron chairs and dusty ground. The ambience is brilliant, and the food reasonable.

**Udai Kothi** (Map p250; dishes Rs 75-190) The glorious terrace restaurant in the hotel of the same name (p258) has tables and cushioned alcoves around the edge of the pool. It's especially romantic in the evening. Try the delicious fish tandoori. Musicians play in the evenings from October to April.

**Café Edelweiss** (Map p250; snacks Rs 10-50; 7.30am-7.30pm) There's a morning magnetism about Edelweiss, and something rather European that attracts travellers in droves to this bright, open-fronted cubbyhole. You can sit in the comfortable chairs to drink real coffee and eat cakes (the cinnamon whirls deserve special mention) and other snacks (the tuna salad is terrific). The same owners run Savage Garden (opposite).

**Samor Bagh** (Map p250; Lake Palace Rd; dishes Rs 20-110; 9am-11pm) Samor Bagh, a garden restaurant with a well-spaced lawn, is especially charming in the evening, when it's lit by candles and fairy lights and there are traditional musicians playing.

**Maxim's Café** (Map p250; Jagdish Temple Rd; dishes Rs 20-70; 7.30am-11pm) Maxim's has a small, two-level, sparkling terrace overlooking the street. The kitchen is clean and the pure veg food freshly cooked.

**Mayur Rooftop Café** (Map p250; 155 Jagdish Chowk; dishes Rs 25-75; 8am-11pm) Open-air Mayur with *de rigueur* scalloped arches has a great view into Jagdish Temple. The menu of pizza, Chinese and Indian dishes is reasonable, though nothing special, but the café is worth visiting for the location.

**Anna's** (Map p250; 151 Jagdish Temple Rd; dishes Rs 15-45; 7.30am-10pm) Anna's is small and sweet,

**THE AUTHOR'S CHOICE**

**Jagat Niwas Palace Hotel** (Map p250; dishes Rs 50-200; noon-3pm & 6.30-10.15pm) In the striking hotel (see p258) is this delightful, peaceful rooftop restaurant, which has a wonderful position at the edge of the lake, with views over the water and across to the Lake Palace. The best seating (on floor cushions) lines the edge of the restaurant – perfect ringside seats for lounging and enjoying that view. Food is excellent – the fish dishes are particularly good. It's wise to book ahead (especially for dinner, when the candlelight makes it the most romantic choice in town).

offering simple, reasonable food served at little red booths. There's also a rooftop restaurant here.

**Sunrise** (Map p250; cnr Lal Ghat & Gangaur Gat Rd; dishes Rs 10-50; 8am-10pm) Recommended Sunrise, on top of a family house, has delicious home-cooked Indian dishes (and brilliant breakfasts) and is run by a friendly family. The rooftop is good for people-watching.

**Savage Garden** (Map p250; 22 Inside Chandpol; dishes Rs 85-140; 11am-10pm) Savage Garden, tucked away in the backstreets (but well signposted) near Chandpol, continues to receive rave reviews. It's unusually atmospheric, set as it is in a 250-year-old *haveli* with peacock-blue walls, and laid out with bowls of flowers and tables in alcoves or in a pleasant courtyard. Imaginative dishes, such as pasta with Indian sauces, are cooked here.

**Trident Hilton** (Off Map p247; buffet Rs 500) The service and delicious multicuisine buffet at this slick top-end hotel (see opposite) are excellent and much recommended.

**Berry's** (Map p247; Chetak Circle; dishes Rs 35-240; 9am-11.30pm) A calm restaurant with an impressive brass door, Berry's is enhanced by white tablecloths and a burbling fish tank. The cooking is classy veg and nonveg, with pizza, Chinese and Indian food on offer.

**Kwality Restaurant** (Map p247; Chetak Circle; dishes Rs 35-110; 11am-11pm) Kwality is a bizarre retro salon with mood music, groovy stripe-and-check décor, axe-shaped menus and a scary pink art installation on the wall. Beer is available (you may need it), as are 'chicken lollipops' (spicy chicken pieces served on the bone), tandoori and substantial thalis.

**Natraj Lodge** (Map p247; New Bapu Bazaar; thalis Rs 40; 10am-3pm & 6.30-11pm) Famous throughout town for its delicious all-you-can-eat Gujarati thalis, this is permanently busy with locals. It's a bit hard to find as it's in a backstreet. Just ask if you need directions.

**Shiv Niwas Palace Hotel** (Map p250; dishes around Rs 300; 6.30-10.30am, 12.30-2.30pm & 7.30-10.30pm) Most captivating in the evening, this formal restaurant in Shiv Niwas Palace Hotel (p259) has indoor seating, but it's best out in the pleasant open-air courtyard by the pool. Indian classical music is performed nightly. The food gets mixed reports.

**Lake Palace Hotel** (Map p250; ☎ 2528800; 7.30-10.30pm) In the hotel of the same name (see p259), this is Udaipur's most famous dining experience, but it has left many travellers feeling it's overpriced and overhyped. The sumptuous buffet dinner costs a cheeky Rs 1500 (includes boat crossing). Reservations are essential and dress is smart casual. For something different, ask about the tiny floating pontoon on Pichola Lake, which holds lunch/dinner for US$75 per person (maximum four people). If you don't want a waiter hanging around, you can request a cordless phone to be left in case you need anything. Be sure to wear something warm if you're dining at night in winter.

**Surya Mahal** (Off Map p247; dishes around Rs 500; noon-3.30pm & 7-10pm) For a big romantic splash, it's worth heading to Udaivilas (opposite). Surya Mahal is a 1930s-style place serving delicious Continental and Asian cuisine in high-ceilinged opulence.

**Udai Mahal** (Off Map p247; dishes around Rs 500; noon-3.30pm & 7-10pm) Udai Mahal is also in Udaivilas and specialises in the most refined Rajasthani and North Indian food.

**Gallery Restaurant** (Map p250; ☎ 2528019; tea 3-5pm) In the palace enclosure (admission Rs 25), at the Fateh Prakash Palace Hotel (p259), this elegant little restaurant has beguiling views across Pichola Lake. It has the best cream teas in town; proper tea, including sandwiches, biscuits, scones, jam and cream, costs Rs 250.

### UDAIPUR'S TOP FIVE ROMANTIC EATS

**Jagat Niwas Palace Hotel** (opposite) Terrace overlooking the lake; delicious food.

**Ambrai** (opposite) Water-level garden, with wonderful views.

**Udai Kothi** (opposite) Glamorous rooftop terrace with poolside seating.

**Savage Garden** (left) Lashings of flair, deep-blue walls, alcoves and unusual Indo-Western fusion dishes.

**Surya Mahal** (below) Haute cuisine in surroundings of bygone opulence.

## Drinking

**Paanera Bar** (Map p250; 11am-11pm) At the Shiv Niwas Palace Hotel (p259). Plush, poolside and soft sofas.

**Sunset View Terrace** (Map p250; City Palace; admission Rs 25; 11am-11pm) On a terrace overlooking Pichola Lake, this is *the* place to be at sunset – it's perfect gin-and-tonic territory. However, the food is overpriced and nothing special.

**Restaurant Natural View** (Map p250; Lal Ghat; dishes Rs 20-90; 8am-10.30pm) A long-running travellers' favourite, on the roof of the budget guesthouse Evergreen, Natural View has wonderful views across the lake. The food and service aren't up to much, though – stick to a leisurely drink.

## Entertainment

Udaipur offers some excellent opportunities to see traditional dance and music.

**Dharohar** (Map p250; Gangaur Ghat; adult/child Rs 60/30, camera/video Rs 10/50; 7pm) Don't miss out on this: the wonderful backdrop of Bagore-ki-Haveli hosts mesmerising Rajasthani dances, including traditional Mewari, Bhil and western Rajasthani dances, by talented performers who can whirl better than most dervishes.

**Meera Kala Mandir** (Off Map p247; ☎ 2583176; Sector 11, Hiran Magari; admission Rs 60) Has one-hour Rajasthani folk dance and music performances at 7pm Monday to Saturday, from August to April. An autorickshaw from Jagdish costs Rs 30.

**Cheetak Cinema** (Map p247; Chetak Circle) One of a number of cinemas in Udaipur if you feel like taking in the latest Bollywood hit.

## Shopping

Udaipur offers glorious shopping potential, with masses of little shops selling jumbles of things from cloth lanterns to exquisite antique jewellery.

The town is known for its local crafts, particularly miniature paintings in the Rajput-Mughal style: miniature and textile shops line Lake Palace Rd and also cluster around the Jagdish Temple. The miniatures are painted on cloth, marble, wood, paper and even leaves. This is one of the best places to buy them. There are also many leather- and cloth-bound books of handmade paper (from Jaipur) for sale, in every design imaginable. Silver jewellery, carpets, block-printed fabrics, marble items, wooden figures and papier-mâché are other popular buys.

Shops along Lake Palace Rd also sell small, beautiful, brightly painted wooden Hindu gods.

Interesting, less tourist-focused bazaars spread out from the clock tower. Bara Bazaar sells silver and gold, as well as saris and fabrics. Traditional shoes are sold at Mochiwada, and more silver at Battiyanni. Colourful Mandi Market, a sprawling bazaar, is the centre for spices – take your camera.

Be prepared to bargain hard, as most places have ridiculously inflated prices for tourists. For some useful tips on how to bargain, see p371.

**Sadhna** (Map p250; www.sevamandir.org; Mangi Kee Baudi, Kasaron Ki; 10am-7pm) The outlet for Seva Mandir, an NGO set up in 1969 to help rural women. The small shop sells attractive and individual fixed-price textiles such as clothes, cushion covers and bags; profits go to the artisans and towards community development work.

**Rajasthali** Chetak Circle (Map p247; 10.30am-7pm Mon-Sat); Jagdish Temple (Map p250; 10am-6.30pm) The government fixed-price emporium is worth dropping into to gauge handicraft prices.

## Getting There & Away

### AIR

There are **Indian Airlines** (Map p247; ☎ 2410999; Delhi Gate; 10am-1pm & 2-5pm Mon-Sat, 10am-2pm Sun) flights to Delhi (US$115) via Jodhpur (US$75), Jaipur (US$90) and Mumbai (US$138). **Jet Airways** (Map p247; ☎ 2561105; Blue Circle Business Centre, Madhuban, Chetak Circle), near the main post office, has similar flights for similar prices. Alliance Air and Jagson Airlines also offer competitively priced domestic flights serving Jaipur. See p382 for more information on flying within Rajasthan.

You are strongly advised to make flight bookings well in advance during the busy tourist season.

### BUS

Frequent Rajasthan State Road Transport Corporation (RSRTC) buses travel from Udaipur to other regional centres, as well as to Delhi and Ahmedabad. If you use these buses, take an express as the ordinary buses take forever, make innumerable detours to various towns off the main route, and can be very uncomfortable (rattly and crowded). For long-distance travel it's best to use deluxe or express buses, but you'll need to book ahead. The inquiries number is ☎ 2484191. Destinations served by express and deluxe buses are listed in the table, opposite. Where only one price is given, there are only express buses.

Private buses operate to Ahmedabad (Rs 150/200/150 in ordinary/AC/sleeper, six

| Destination | Fare (express/deluxe, Rs) | Approximate duration (hr) |
|---|---|---|
| Agra | 101/120 | 6 |
| Ahmedabad | 120 | 6 |
| Ajmer | 111/145 | 8 |
| Bundi | 135 | 7 |
| Chittorgarh | 40/48 | 3/2½ |
| Delhi | 270/420 | 14 |
| Jaipur | 161/201 | 9 |
| Jodhpur | 113/125 | 8 |
| Kota | 140 | 8 |
| Mt Abu | 82 | 6 |

hours), Mumbai (Rs 400/600 in ordinary/sleeper, 16 hours), Delhi (Rs 200/350 in ordinary/sleeper, 14 hours), Mt Abu (Rs 100 in ordinary, five hours) and Jodhpur (Rs 100/150 in ordinary/sleeper, six hours).

#### TAXI

Many drivers will show you a list of 'official' rates to places such as Mt Abu, Chittorgarh and Jodhpur. You can arrange a car and driver through many travel agencies and hotels around town. Shop around (Rs 3.5 per km is a good starting point) for the most competitive rate. Remember that taxis charge return fares even if you're only going one way. For useful tips on hiring a taxi and driver, see p386.

#### TRAIN

The lines into Udaipur have recently converted from metre to broad gauge, which will revolutionise the journey to and from Udaipur – there will be an express train between New Delhi and Udaipur, calling at Kota, Bundi and Chittorgarh. Check locally for the current situation and news on faster trains available. Until work is finished, however, buses will usually be a faster option. The inquiries number is ☎ 2527390.

The No 9616 *Chetak Express* to Delhi (Rs 268/1131 in sleeper/2AC, 19 hours, 727km) departs at 6.15pm and goes via Chittorgarh (Rs 38 in 2nd class, 3¼ hours, 115km), Ajmer (Rs 78 in 2nd class, eight hours, 304km) and Jaipur (Rs 197/813 in sleeper/2AC, 11 hours, 439km).

The No 9766 *Lake City Express* leaves Udaipur at 8.50pm and arrives in Jaipur at 7.15am, travelling via Chittorgarh and Ajmer.

The No 9943 *Ahmedabad Express* departs at 7.45pm and arrives in the Gujarati capital of Gandhinagar (Rs 122/549 in sleeper/2AC, 297km) at 4.25am.

### Getting Around

#### TO/FROM THE AIRPORT

The airport is 25km east of town. A taxi will cost at least Rs 200; there's no airport bus.

#### AUTORICKSHAW

These are unmetered, so you should agree on a fare before setting off – the standard fare anywhere in town is around Rs 20 to 25. There are prepaid autorickshaw stands at the bus and train stations. It costs Rs 200 to hire an autorickshaw for a day of local sightseeing.

The commission system is in place, so if a rickshaw driver insists that the hotel you are after has burnt down or that the owner has died in a freak accident, ignore his advice and tenaciously pursue your choice.

#### BICYCLE & MOTORCYCLE

A cheap and environmentally friendly way to buzz around is by bike. Motorbikes are great for exploring the surrounding countryside. You can hire bicycles for around Rs 25 per day. **Heera Cycle Store** (Map p250; ☎ 2523525; 7.30am-9pm), which is near Hotel Badi Haveli, hires out bicycles/mopeds/motorcycles for Rs 25/150/300 per day.

## NORTH OF UDAIPUR

### Eklingji & Nagda

The interesting village of Eklingji – only 22km and a short bus ride north of Udaipur – has a fascinating ancient temple complex that attracts lots of pilgrims but few tourists.

The **Shiva temple** (admission free, photography prohibited; 4-6.30am, 10.30am-1.30pm & 5-7.30pm), with its 108 small shrines, was originally built in 734, although its present form dates from the rule of Maharaja Raimal (r 1473–1509). Constructed from sandstone and marble, the walled complex has an elaborately pillared hall under a large pyramidal roof and features a four-faced Shiva image of black marble. Check the opening hours as they change regularly. Avoid the temple on Monday (an auspicious day for devotees), as it can get very crowded. The maharaja of Udaipur pays a private visit to the temple on Monday evening. Guides are available at the temple.

At Nagda, about 1km off the road and 1km before Eklingji, there are some 10th-century temples. The 11th-century **Jain temple of Adbudji** is very fine, though it was much damaged by the Mughals, and contains a 15th-century black-marble idol of *tirthankar* Shanti Nath. About 500m away are a pair of mother-in-law (Sas) and daughter-in-law (Bahu) **temples**, dating from the 9th century. They feature some very fine and intricate carvings, including some erotic figures. You can reach these temples by hiring a bicycle in Eklingji. There are also some small temples submerged in the nearby lake, though after a poor monsoon they're completely exposed.

### SLEEPING & EATING

**Heritage Resorts** (0294-440382; www.heritageresort.com; Bagela Lake; s/d incl all meals Rs 2365/4180; ) Heritage Resorts, at Bagela Lake in Nagda, is a pebblestone building set in a brilliant position high up on a hilltop. Rooms have fantastic views over the surrounding countryside and across to the nearby ruins. It's popular with families from the neighbouring state of Gujarat, so book ahead. Its restaurant (nonguests are welcome) has good views. There's a small pool, and short horse rides are available. Check the website for special offers.

### GETTING THERE & AWAY

Local buses travel from Udaipur (Rs 8, 30 minutes) to Eklingji every hour from 5am to 10pm.

## Haldighati

This **battlefield site**, 40km north of Udaipur, is where Maharaja Pratap defied the superior Mughal forces of Akbar in 1576. The site is marked by a small *chhatri* that commemorates the warrior's horse, Chetak. Although badly wounded and exhausted, this brave horse carried Maharaja Pratap to safety before collapsing and dying. It's for this loyalty and courage that Chetak is honoured. There's not a lot to see, but the historic site attracts many Indian visitors, and there's a **sound-and-light show** (Rs 20; 8am-8pm). Haldighati can be reached by bus from Nathdwara (Rs 12, 30 minutes); the site is 2km from the town.

## Nathdwara

02953

The 18th-century Krishna temple of **Sri Nathji** (admission free, photography prohibited; 5-5.30am, 7.15-7.45am, 9.15-9.45am, 11.30am-noon, 3.30-4pm, 4.30-5pm & 6-6.30pm) stands at Nathdwara, 48km north of Udaipur. It's another place that draws many pilgrims but sees few tourists. The shrine has

### EXPLORING AROUND UDAIPUR

Around Udaipur lie huge, muscular hills, cut through by narrow winding roads across an expansive landscape, which open up to impressive views across the countryside. It makes a fantastic excursion to ramble out into the rural areas, stopping at small villages and little-visited temples. The best way to travel is by motorbike – try to find a local person who'll take you around, though you could chance a rickshaw.

Heading north, you could visit **Madar Lakes**, around 15km from the city; head to Madar village, from where there are two tracks, leading to **Little Madar Dam** or **Great Madar Dam**, each with splendid views across the expanse of water. Going west out of Udaipur, head towards the village of Sisarma, then go towards the tiny village of Dhar, from where the road leads to the **Ubeshwarji**, a revered Shiva shrine that attracts many pilgrims. Leaving Ubeshwarji, the road leads through a remote hill pass – you'll need local help to seek out **Kailashwarji**, a magnificent waterfall that plunges 50m, straight out of *The Jungle Book*. The small villages and temples you hit on the way may not be spectacular, but it's an adventure, and getting there is all part of the fun.

special significance for Vaishnavites (followers of Vishnu or of his incarnations). The black-stone Krishna image that's housed in the temple was brought here from Mathura in 1669 to protect it from the destructive impulses of Aurangzeb. According to legend, the getaway vehicle, a wagon, sank into the ground up to the axles as it was passing through Nathdwara. The priests realised that this was a sign from Krishna – the image did not want to travel any further! Accordingly, the Sri Nathji temple was built on the spot.

Attendants treat the image like a delicate child, getting it up in the morning, washing it, putting its clothes on, offering it specially prepared meals and putting it down to sleep, all at precise times throughout the day. It's a very popular pilgrimage site, and the temple opens and closes around the image's daily routine. It gets very crowded from 3.30pm to 4pm when Krishna gets up after a siesta. Check that the listed temple timings have not changed.

Nathdwara is also very well known for its *pichwai* paintings, which were produced after the image of Krishna was brought to the town in the 17th century. These bright screen paintings, with their rather static images, were usually created on handspun fabric and intended to be hung behind the idol – they usually show Sri Nathji decked out in different outfits. As with many other schools of painting, numerous inferior reproductions of the *pichwai* paintings are created specifically for the lucrative tourist market.

#### SLEEPING & EATING

**RTDC Hotel Gokul** (☎ 230917; Lal Bagh; dm/s/d Rs 50/400/500, superdeluxe d Rs 700) Considering it's an RTDC establishment, this hotel is surprisingly good. It's set in quiet gardens, around 4km from the temple. A bar and a restaurant are on site.

**RTDC Hotel Yatrika Mangla** (☎ 231119; dm/s/d Rs 50/300/400) The Yatrika Mangla is only around 1km from the temple, so it's more convenient than, though not as appealing as, Gokul. It too has a restaurant.

**Shreeji Resort** (☎ 231284; s/d from Rs 890/990, with AC from Rs 990/1090) Offers reasonable rooms in a fairly modern, frilly building with balconies, but the rooms are overpriced and the welcome isn't that friendly. The restaurant serves Indian veg food.

#### GETTING THERE & AWAY

There are frequent daily buses from Udaipur to Nathdwara (Rs 25, one hour). It costs Rs 10 to park a car at the temple.

### Kankroli & Rajsamand Lake

At Kankroli, 66km from Udaipur, there's a beautiful **temple** devoted to Dwarkadhish (an incarnation of Krishna), which is similar to the temple at Nathdwara (opposite); the opening hours are similarly erratic.

Nearby is the large **Rajsamand Lake**, created by a dam constructed in 1660 by Maharaja Raj Singh (r 1652–80). There are numerous ornamental arches and beautifully carved *chhatris* set along the huge bund (embankment), which is 335m long and 13m high. It has several interesting old inscriptions.

There are frequent RSRTC buses from Udaipur (Rs 25, 2½ hours).

### Kumbalgarh

☎ 02954

About 84km north of Udaipur, **Kumbalgarh** (Indian/foreigner Rs 5/100; 🕒 8am-6pm) is a fantastic, remote fort, fulfilling romantic expectations and vividly summoning up the chivalrous, warlike Rajput era. Built by Rana Kumbha in the 15th century, the isolated fort is perched at an amazing 1100m, from where endless views melt into blue distance. The journey there, a trip along twisting roads through the Aravelli mountains, is a highlight in itself.

Kumbalgarh was the most important Mewar fort after Chittorgarh, and the rulers, sensibly, used to retreat here in times of danger. Here a baby prince of Mewar was hidden from an assassin (see The Ultimate Sacrifice, p251). Unsurprisingly, Kumbalgarh was taken only once in its entire history, and even then it took the combined armies of Amber, Marwar and Mughal Emperor Akbar to breach its strong defences, and they only managed to hang onto it for two days.

The thick fort walls stretch some 36km. They're wide enough for eight horses to ride abreast and they enclose around 360 temples, as well as palaces, gardens, *baoris* and 700 cannon bunkers. The fort was renovated in the 19th century by Maharaja Fateh Singh. It's worth taking a leisurely walk in the large compound, which has some interesting ruins and is very peaceful.

If you stay in Kumbalgarh, you can trek from your hotel to the fort, which is a dramatic way to approach and one that reinforces the fort's impenetrability.

It's a steep climb up to the fort entrance, so don't forget to buy your ticket first, near the start of the road from the car park. It costs Rs 25 to park a car.

Nearby there's also the big **Kumbalgarh Wildlife Sanctuary** (Indian/foreigner Rs 10/100; ⌚ sunrise-sunset), known for its wolves. The scarcity of water holes between March and June makes this the best time to see animals. Wildlife includes chowsingha (four-horned deer), leopards, sloth bears and various bird species. You need permission from the forest department in nearby Kelwara to enter (ask at your hotel for advice). All hotels can arrange three-hour horse or jeep safaris. Shivika Lake Hotel (right) in Ranakpur arranges jeep tours at a cost of Rs 500 per person, which covers all admission fees.

### SLEEPING

**Aodhi Hotel** (☎ 242341; crs@udaipur.hrhindia.com; s/d Rs 3000/3500, ste Rs 4000/4500; ) About 5km from the fort is this appealing, blissfully tranquil hotel with an inviting pool and winter campfires. It's an ideal place to read a book or play a leisurely game of cards. Built on the side of a hill, rooms are decorated in a wilderness theme, and the pool is situated amid the hills. Nonguests can dine in the restaurant. A safari from here costs Rs 600, a three-hour visit to the sanctuary is Rs 2000 (maximum of five people), and trekking is around Rs 1000 per day for five people.

**Kumbhal Castle** (☎ 242171; www.kumbhalcastle.com; s/d Rs 800/980, deluxe Rs 1200/1500) The modern Kumbhal Castle, 3km from the fort, has plain white rooms featuring curly iron beds, bright bedspreads and window seats, shared balconies and good views.

**Hotel Ratnadeep** (☎ 242217; dm Rs 100, s/d from Rs 400/500, superdeluxe Rs 750/950; dishes Rs 10-40) In the scrappy settlement of Kelwara, 7km from the fort, is this attractive but simple hotel. Basic rooms, as well as (costlier) spacious and airy ones, are arranged around a garden courtyard, where there's a restaurant. A return taxi to the fort from here will cost around Rs 150 (including waiting charge).

**Thandiberi Forest Guest House** (d Rs 250) is within the sanctuary. Bookings need to be made in advance through the **deputy chief wildlife warden** (☎ 0294-2453686) in Udaipur.

### GETTING THERE & AWAY

There are several RSTC buses going to/from Udaipur (Rs 35, 3½ hours), but not all leave from the bus stand; some go from Chetak Circle. Some services stop in Kelwara, 7km away, and some at the Aodhi Hotel, from where it's a 2km walk. Hiring a taxi from Udaipur means you can visit both Ranakpur and Kumbalgarh in a day. Many travellers ask around to make up a group and share the expense (taxis take four to five people and cost Rs 950).

## Ranakpur

☎ 02934

In a plunging wooded valley, reached down a twisting road, **Ranakpur** (admission free, camera/video Rs 50/100; ⌚ Jains 6am-7pm, non-Jains noon-5pm) is one of India's biggest and most important Jain temples. The main temple is called the **Chaumukha Mandir** (Four-Faced Temple), dedicated to Adinath and built in 1439. It's an incredible building in milk-white marble – a complicated series of 29 halls supported by a forest of 1444 pillars, no two of which are alike. The interior is completely covered in knotted carving. The devotion of its builders is shown in this complex architecture and loving carving, and the pale interior has an unparalleled sense of space and harmony.

Within the complex are two other Jain temples dedicated to **Neminath** and **Parasnath**, and a nearby **Sun Temple**. About 1km from the main complex is **Amba Mata Temple**.

Shoes, cigarettes and all leather articles must be left at the entrance.

The complex is well worth a visit, and it makes a convenient stop between Jodhpur and Udaipur. It's tucked away in a remote, quiet valley of the Aravalli Range, 90km from Udaipur, which is, for those with the time, a great place to kick back for a few days. You can visit Kumbalgarh and its nearby wildlife sanctuary from here, and trek into the hills. One four-hour trek leads to a Parshurama Shiva Temple in a cave. Guided trekking trips cost around Rs 500 for a day.

### SLEEPING & EATING

**Shivika Lake Hotel** (☎ 286625; shivikalake@rediffmail.com; r Rs 400-1200; dishes Rs 40-100; ) Shivika

Lake offers small, cosy cottages with pretty décor, set amid leafy gardens. This is a welcoming, rustic place to stay. Tents with private bathrooms are also available. The warm, knowledgeable family arranges forest safaris (a three-day safari costs around Rs 1950 per person per night, all included) and guides for short or longer treks. The hotel also has a restaurant.

**Maharani Bagh Orchard Retreat** (☎ 285105; balsamand@sify.com; s/d Rs 2400/3000; ) This relaxing place, set in a lush mango orchard 4km from Ranakpur, offers accommodation in modern, comfortable, wood-furnished cottages, which have terraces surrounded by green lawns. Nonguests are welcome in the restaurant.

**Ranakpur Hill Resort** (☎ 286411; www.ranakpurhillresort.com; Ranakpur Rd; s/d Rs 1200/1500; ) This is a typically smart, brash, traditional-style place. The plain white rooms are brightly curtained and have window seats.

**Fateh Bagh** (in Udaipur ☎ 0294-2528008; www.hrhindia.com; Ranakpur Rd; s/d Rs 3000/3500, ste Rs 4000/4500; ) Next to Maharani Bagh Orchard Retreat is Fateh Bagh, a palatial building carved from peachy sandstone. Amazingly, the construction was transplanted: a palace built by Rawla Koshilav near Jodhpur in 1802 was transferred piece by piece and reconstructed here – 65,000 pieces were moved in total. The result is an impressive and opulent yet small hotel, with thematically decorated rooms. Novel features include a swing bed in the honeymoon suite.

**Roopam Restaurant** (mains Rs 30-170; 10am-10pm) Peaceful, friendly Roopam has a laid-back garden restaurant.

#### GETTING THERE & AWAY

A good number of buses run to Ranakpur from Udaipur (Rs 35, three hours, hourly), and stop right outside the temple, but it's hard to visit both Ranakpur and Kumbalgarh by public transport in a day – a taxi taking in both from Udaipur costs around Rs 950.

There are express buses to/from Mt Abu (Rs 80, five hours) and Jodhpur (Rs 85, five hours).

All the accommodation in Ranakpur is too far from the bus stop to walk. Jeeps can sometimes be hired at the bus stop (ask at the shop), or call your hotel and see if you can be picked up.

### Narlai

☎ 02934

Quiet yet spectacular, Narlai is an ideal base for exploring the various attractions around Udaipur. Opposite the Rawla Narlai hotel is a mammoth granite rock that's dotted with caves and temples. Narlai is also home to a good *baori*, several old temples and lots of quiet walks.

**Rawla Narlai** (☎ 282425, in Delhi ☎ 011-26221419; www.ajitbhawan.com; r Rs 2400-2900, ste Rs 3000) was once the hunting lodge of the rulers of Narlai. A well-kept place, its appealing antique-furnished rooms – often decorated with frescoes, stained glass and hanging baubles – lead onto balconies and porches that face the huge granite outcrop opposite.

There are buses from Udaipur (Rs 62, two hours) and Jodhpur (Rs 110, four hours).

### Ghanerao

☎ 02934

About 12km from Narlai is little Ghanerao, which is dominated by a castle that has been converted into another charismatic hotel. **Mahavira Temple**, a 10th-century Jain temple devoted to the founder of Jainism, is also worth visiting. Splendidly set among woodland, it's flanked by two mighty elephants, and its walls are richly carved with warriors, horses and gods riding chariots.

According to legend, the maharaja of Udaipur once visited and, seeing a hair in the saffron paste, laughingly remarked to the priest that the Lord must have a moustache. The priest solemnly said that the Lord takes many forms, but the maharaja continued to insist on the point, saying he'd like to see the Lord with a moustache. Lord Mahavira then appeared with a moustache, as he wanted to reward the priest's belief. There's a statue of the Lord with a moustache at the temple, which is often called Muchhal Mahavir (Moustached Mahavir).

**Ghanerao Royal Castle** (☎ 84035; s/d Apr-Sep Rs 800/1000, Oct-Mar Rs 1400/1800) is another charming castle-hotel. Carved from red sandstone, it looks more like a palace, with a pavilion in a central courtyard where palace musicians used to perform. The whitewashed rooms have arches and tall ceilings. Near the castle are the cenotaphs of former rulers.

Take an RSRTC bus from Udaipur to Sadri (Rs 75) or Desuri (Rs 75), then a jeep taxi (about Rs 80) from there to Ghanerao.

# SOUTH OF UDAIPUR

## Rishabdeo

☎ 02907

The village of Rishabdeo, about 65km south from Udaipur, is a significant pilgrimage centre with a magical atmosphere, making it well worth a visit. The village is home to a 15th-century **Jain temple** (admission free; ⌚ 6am-9.30pm) dedicated to Rishabdeo, a reincarnation of Mahavira, the 24th and last of the Jain *tirthankars*. Mahavira founded Jainism around 500 BC and is also worshipped as a reincarnation of Vishnu. The temple features a beautiful silver image of Rishabdeo and some lovely carvings. Two large, glossy, black stone elephants flank the temple's entrance, two more are beyond them, and another huge one is inside. The interior is multipillared and decorated with carvings in white marble. There are 52 idols around the outside. A short walk through a lane lined with small shops leads you there.

**RTDC Hotel Gavri** (☎ 230145; dm Rs 50, s/d from Rs 400/500, with AC Rs 800/900; ❄) is about 500m from the temple and has the RTDC's signature decrepit air. The rooms aren't too bad, if functional, and there are lawns around the building.

There are buses going to Rishabdeo from Udaipur (Rs 35, 1½ hours).

## Bambora

☎ 0294

About 45km to the southeast of Udaipur, the sleepy village of Bambora has a dramatic 250-year-old fort that has been converted into an impressive hotel.

**Karni Fort** (☎ 2398220; s/d from Rs 2200/3000; ❄ 🏊) is in the middle of nowhere, dramatically plumped on a hilltop. Inside the fort walls the main building rises up like a grand country house. All rooms are smart, but the best room (on the 2nd floor) has a blissfully soft round bed with panoramic views. There're a good restaurant, a secret tunnel, and an alluring swimming pool that has four water-spurting marble elephants and a central pavilion, set in the hilly garden. Staff are very obliging. You can make bookings for Karni Fort at the Karni Bhawan hotel (see p314) in Jodhpur.

## Jagat

At the unassuming small town of Jagat, 56km southeast of Udaipur, is a small, 10th-century, pentagonal **Durga temple** with 17 turrets. There are some elaborate carvings, including a couple of erotic images. Fairies and demons throng the outside walls.

## Jaisamand Lake

☎ 0294

A startlingly huge expanse of water 48km southeast of Udaipur, **Jaisamand Lake** floods between wooded hills, surveyed by Udaipur maharanis' summer palaces. At 88 sq km, the artificial lake is one of Asia's largest. Created by damming the Gomti River, it was built by Maharaja Jai Singh in the 17th century and is today 14km long and 9km wide. There are beautiful marble *chhatris* around the 330m-long, 35m-high embankment, fronted by carved elephants. Today it's busy with a scattering of people waiting for boats and small boys selling fish food. The small hilltop palace is Rothi Rani; the larger, near the dam, is Hawa Mahal. On the day of the dam's inauguration the maharaja went walkabout, distributing his weight in gold.

The lake features a variety of bird life, and the nearby **Jaisamand Wildlife Sanctuary** (Indian/foreigner Rs 10/80, camera Rs 200; ⌚ 10am-5pm) is the home of panthers, leopards, deer, wild boars and crocodiles. However, it's not well set up for visitors – there's no information at the local office. The forests here used to be a favourite hunting ground of the former rulers of Mewar, and elaborate hunting expeditions would frequently take place. It costs Rs 65/3 to take a car/bicycle inside.

There are boats available for lake tours – a small/medium/large circuit of the lake costs Rs 30/50/80. This lake could be great for bird-watching, but if you take a boat out you'll find the engine noise a hindrance.

### SLEEPING

**Jaisamand Island Resort** (☎ 2431401; www.lakend.com; s/d from Rs 1800/2700; ⌚ Oct-Feb; ❄ 🏊) A modern but somewhat shabby hotel in a wonderful, secluded location, 20 minutes by boat across the lake. Rooms are comfortable, but they're run-down and hence overpriced. However, all have great views over the water. The pool has a brilliant setting, but isn't always full. Discounts are often available. A return boat ride to the resort costs Rs 150 (nonguests are welcome to visit).

**Forest Guest House** (r Rs 450) is run by the wildlife sanctuary, and has large double rooms and fantastic views over the lake. The guesthouse has a dilapidated air, though, and the bathrooms are a bit grotty. You must contact the **deputy chief wildlife warden** (☎ 0294-2453686) in Udaipur for reservations.

### GETTING THERE & AWAY

There are frequent buses from Udaipur (Rs 20, 1½ hours, hourly).

## Sitamata Wildlife Sanctuary

If you want to get away from it all, this is the place to visit. Lying 90km southeast of Udaipur, **Sitamata Wildlife Sanctuary** covers 423 sq km of mainly deciduous forest that is known for its ancient teak trees. Wildlife includes deer, sambars, leopards, caracals, flying squirrels and wild boars. Few tourists make it out this way, which is part of its charm. If you're in search of picturesque countryside, peace and plenty of fresh air, this place is ideal. Two very different accommodation options are available, close to remote tribal villages in this region dominated by Bhils.

**Fort Dhariyawad** (☎ 02950-220050; s/d Rs 1540/1650, deluxe Rs 2035/2145) is in the Sitamata sanctuary area, 120km from Udaipur. It's housed in a 16th-century fort founded by Prince Sahasmal, second son of Maharaja Pratap, and offers great creature comforts. The restaurant here serves tasty food. Jeep safaris can be arranged to places of interest in the area. The owners can also arrange tented accommodation for the Baneshwar Fair (see p270).

There are RSRTC buses from Udaipur to Dhariyawad (Rs 55, 3½ hours).

## Dungarpur

☎ 02964

About 110km south of Udaipur, attractive Dungarpur, the City of Hills, was founded in the 13th century when Rawal Veer Singh Dev took over this area from the Bhils. It's set in the foothills of the Aravalli Range, and the landscape is wild and stony, dotted with cactus and hardy trees.

You can visit the wonderful, deserted old palace, **Juna Mahal** (admission Rs 100; ⌚ 9am-5pm). Built in stages between the 13th and 18th centuries, on a 450m rocky peak, this crumbling, seven-storey palace is filled with old frescoes and paintings. The fascinating murals include the Kamasutra, hidden discreetly in a cupboard, and there are even willow-pattern plates embedded in the walls. The Aam Khas (main living room) has impressive mirrorwork and glass inlays. The former royal hunting lodge, on a nearby hilltop, has sensational views over the town and its many temples. Get your ticket to Juna Mahal from Udai Bilas Palace (below).

Also of interest is the **Rajmata Devendra Kunwer State Museum** (admission Rs 3, free Mon; ⌚ 10am-5pm Sat-Thu), near the hospital, which has a sculpture gallery featuring pieces from as far back as the 6th century, including a black-stone Shiva. There are also some interesting old photographs of the area.

**Gaib Sagar**, overlooked by Udai Bilas Palace and surrounded by hills, is a good place for bird-watching, as migratory birds, such as cranes, geese, ducks, cuckoos and weaver birds, visit in winter. There's a shrine to Shrinathji on the bank.

The multilayered **Deo Somnath Temple**, about 25km north of town, dates back to the 12th century and has a structure that combines horizontal and vertical elements to extraordinarily harmonious effect. Note the amazing banyan tree opposite the temple, which must be hundreds of years old.

### SLEEPING

**Udai Bilas Palace** (☎ 230808; www.udaibilaspalace.com; s/d/ste Rs 2750/3500/4000) Set on sparkling Gaib Sagar, the fantastical 18th-century palace (with beautifully carved balconies built of *pareva*, Dungarpur's blue-grey stone) has been partly converted into a hotel by Maharaja Kumar Harshvardhan Singh. It's built around the astonishing Ek Thambia Mahal (One-Pillared Palace), and the rooms retain their original Art Deco and 1940s furnishings (some have balconies facing the lake). Suite 9 has a mirror-floored dressing room. The previous maharaja's penchant for hunting is underlined by the stuffed beasts that watch your progress around the hotel, including in the long dining hall, where the exquisite ceiling is made from Burmese teak. The gorgeous outdoor pool is so designed that, as you swim, it seems to merge with the lake. Bicycle hire and bird-watching excursions can be organised for guests.

**Hotel Pratibha Palace** (☎ 230775; Shastri Colony; d Rs 100-150) This is the best budget hotel in town. It has tiny rooms that are nothing flash, but they aren't bad value for money.

#### GETTING THERE & AWAY

Frequent RSTC buses travel to and from Udaipur (Rs 50, three hours, hourly). There's also a snail's-pace train that runs to and from Udaipur (Rs 21/154 in 2nd/1st class, four to five hours, 114km).

### Galiakot

About 50km southeast of Dungarpur is the important Muslim pilgrimage centre of Galiakot. This small town is famous for the **tomb of the saint Fakruddin**, who spread the word of Mohammed in the 10th century. Each year, thousands of local and international Bohra Muslim pilgrims flock here to pay homage to the saint at his white-marble shrine.

There are daily express buses running from Udaipur (Rs 60, three hours).

### Baneshwar

The town of Baneshwar lies at the confluence of three holy rivers: the Mahi, Som and Jakham. In January/February the week-long **Baneshwar Fair** is held at the Baneshwar Temple, about 80km from Dungarpur. The name comes from the Shiva Lingam kept in the temple – Baneshwar means 'master of the delta'. The fair also honours Vishnu incarnated as Mavji – there's a nearby Vishnu temple believed to have been built where Mavji meditated. The event attracts thousands of Bhil tribal people. Music, dance and fairground rides go on alongside the ritual of the festival.

There are regular buses from Dungarpur (Rs 10, one hour) to Baneshwar.

## MT ABU

**☎ 02974 / pop 22,045 / elev 1200m**

According to one legend, Mt Abu is as old as the Himalaya. It was named after Arbuda, a mighty serpent who saved Shiva's revered bull, Nandi, from plunging into an abyss. Another relates that in Mt Abu, the four Rajput fire clans, the Chauhans, Solankis, Pramaras and Pratiharas, were created from a fire pit by Brahmin priests.

The town is certainly unlike anywhere else in Rajasthan. The state's only hill station, it lies in the south of the region, close to the Gujarat border. It's reached up a winding road through massive wooded hills – the rolling alpine slopes are a revelation after so many baking desert plains. Gujarat and Rajasthan's favourite holiday getaway, Mt Abu is a particular hit with honeymooners and middle-class Gujarati families; you won't find many Western travellers here. The beautiful landscape around the town is well worth exploring, and you can go on short treks from here.

Don't come during Diwali or the following two weeks, when prices soar and the place is packed. Like most hill stations, it's also best to avoid Mt Abu in summer, when hordes of people come to escape the heat. Tourism has greatly altered the natural environment here. Vegetation has been cleared to make way for the many hotels that continue to crop up, and the temperatures are not as cool as they used to be.

However, out of respect for the altitude's drop of a few degrees in temperature, everyone wraps up in shawls and fur hats in the cool season. It does get cold at night in winter, so pack something warm.

### Orientation

Mt Abu sprawls along a 1220m-high plateau that's about 22km long by 6km wide, 27km from the nearest train station (Abu Road). The main part of the town extends along the road from Abu Road and surrounds picturesque Nakki Lake.

### Information

There's an SBBJ ATM near Hotel Samrat International.

**Bank of Baroda** (⏰ 10am-3pm Mon-Fri, 10am-12.30pm Sat) Changes travellers cheques and currency, and does credit-card advances.

**Main post office** (Raj Bhavan Rd; ⏰ 9am-5pm Mon-Sat) At the northern end of town.

**Shree Krishna Telecommunications** (Main Market; per hr Rs 40; ⏰ 8am-10pm) Internet access.

**Tourist Reception Centre** (☎ 235151; ⏰ 10am-5pm Mon-Sat, closed 2nd Sat of month) Opposite the main bus stand and below the railway ticket reservation office. Gives out a free map.

### Sights

#### NAKKI LAKE

Scenic Nakki Lake, the town's focus, is a big attraction. It's so named because, according to legend, it was scooped out by a god using his *nakh* (nails). Some Hindus thus believe it to be a holy lake, but you're more likely to see people pedaloing around it than bathing in it. It's a pleasant stroll around the perimeter – the lake is surrounded by hills, parks and strange rock formations. The best known, **Toad Rock**, looks just like a toad about to hop into the lake. The 14th-century **Raghunath Temple** stands beside the lake.

Nakki Lake is the heart of all activity in Mt Abu. At the edge, by the town centre, there are juice and food stalls, ice-cream parlours, balloon vendors and souvenir shops. You'll probably have to plough through the persistent photographers eager to take a happy snap of you by the water. The honeymoon market is catered for by aphrodisiac vendors, with potions that 'make big difference'.

For a great time, you can hire a **pedalo** (2-/4-person boat for 30min Rs 50/100). If the honeymoon vibe has got to you, try a romantic gondola-like **shikara** (2-person boat for 30min Rs 100).

**VIEWPOINTS**

**Sunset Point** is a popular and lovely place from which to watch the brilliant setting sun. Hordes stroll out here every evening to catch the end of the day, the food stalls and all the usual entertainment. It's a 1km-walk from the road to the viewpoint. Other viewpoints include **Honeymoon Point** – another good sunset point – and **The Crags** (Ganesh Temple). You can follow the white arrows along a path to the summit of **Shanti Shikhar**, west of Adhar Devi Temple, where there are panoramic views.

The best view over the lake is from the terrace of the maharaja of Jaipur's former **summer palace**, which has been converted to Jaipur House (p274).

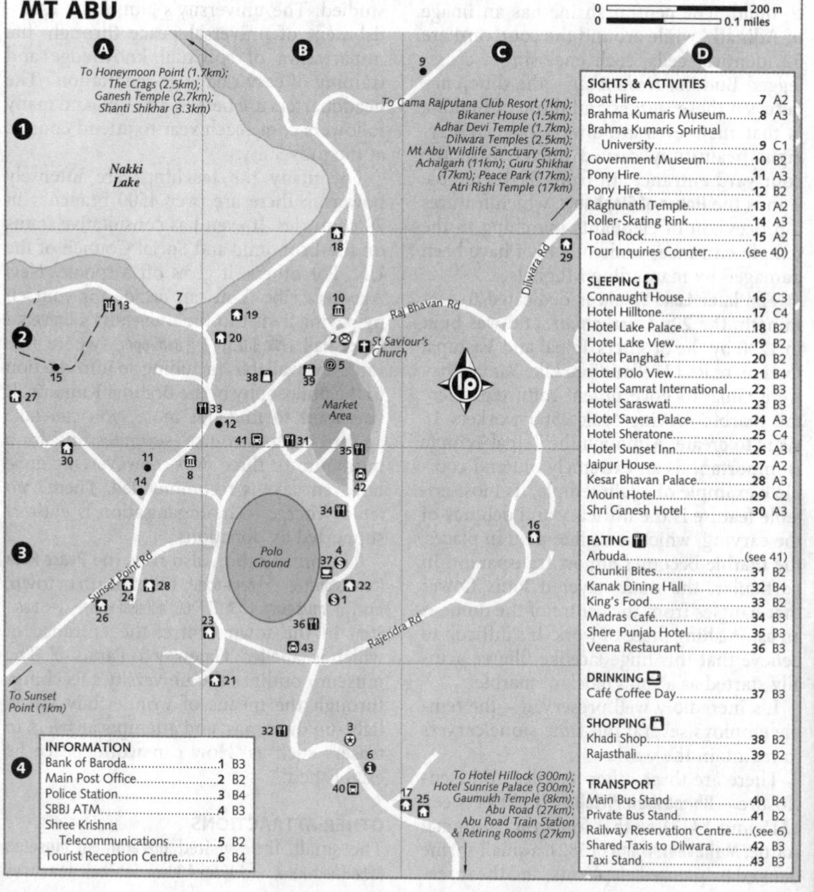

 

### DILWARA TEMPLES

These remarkable **Jain temples** (admission free, photography prohibited; ⏰ Jains sunrise-sunset, non-Jains noon-6pm) are Mt Abu's main attraction and feature some of India's finest temple decoration. It's said that the artisans were paid according to the amount of dust they collected, encouraging them to carve ever more intricately. Whatever their inducement, there are two temples in which the work is dizzyingly intense, a collection of delicate milky kaleidoscopes, with carving so fine it looks like you should break it off and eat it.

The older of the temples is the **Vimal Vasahi**, started in 1031, which was financed by a Gujarati minister named Vimal. It's dedicated to the first *tirthankar*, Adinath. It took 14 years and cost Rs 180.5 million to build. The central shrine has an image of Adinath, while around the courtyard are 52 identical cells, each enclosing a cross-legged Buddha-*tirthankar* – the difference between these statues and those of Buddha is that their eyes are always open. Forty-eight beautifully carved pillars form the courtyard entrance. In front of the temple stands the **House of Elephants**, which features a procession of elephants marching to the temple entrance, some of which have been damaged by marauding Mughals.

The later **Luna Vasahi** is dedicated to Neminath, the 22nd *tirthankar*, and was built in 1230 by the brothers Tejpal and Vastupal for a mere Rs 125.9 million. Like Vimal, they were Gujarati government ministers. Here the marble carving took 2500 workers 15 years to create. Although the Tejpal Temple is important as an extremely old and complete example of a Jain temple, its most notable feature is the intricacy and delicacy of the carving, which is so fine that, in places, the marble becomes almost transparent. In particular, the many-layered lotus flower that dangles from the centre of the dome is an astonishing piece of work. It's difficult to believe that this huge lacelike filigree actually started as a solid block of marble.

It's incredibly well preserved – the temple employs several full-time stone carvers to maintain the work.

There are three other temples in the enclosure – **Bhimashah Pittalhar** (built between 1315 and 1433), with a four-ton five-metal statue, **Mahaveerswami** (1582), a small shrine flanked by painted elephants, and the three-storey **Khartar Vasahi**. But none of them competes with Luna Vasahi and Vimal Vasahi.

As at other Jain temples, leather articles (belts as well as shoes) have to be left at the entrance, and menstruating women are warned away.

You can stroll out to Dilwara from Mt Abu in less than an hour, or take a shared taxi (see p276).

### BRAHMA KUMARIS SPIRITUAL UNIVERSITY & MUSEUM

The white-clad people around town are not just a coincidence, but are studying at **Brahma Kumaris Spiritual University** (www.bkwsu.com). This organisation teaches that all religions lead to God and are equally valid, and that the principles of each should be studied. The university's aim is the establishment of universal peace through 'the impartation of spiritual knowledge and training of easy raja yoga meditation'. The headquarters are here in Mt Abu, and many followers come each year to attend courses at the university.

For many the teachings are intensely powerful; there are over 4500 branches in 70 countries. It even has consultative status on the Economic and Social Council of the UN. For others, it gives off a spooky New Age–sect vibe. You can decide for yourself by paying a visit to the university's **Universal Peace Hall** (☎ 38261; ⏰ 8am-6pm), where free tours are available, including an introduction to the philosophy of the Brahma Kumaris. If you want to find out more, you can take an introductory course (seven lessons) for a minimum of three days, however, a course of seven days is recommended. There's no fee or charge – the organisation is entirely supported by donations.

The organisation also runs the **Peace Park** (admission free; ⏰ 8am-6pm), 17km north of town, and a **museum** (☎ 223260; admission free; ⏰ 8am-8pm) in the town centre, the entrance of which is labelled 'Gateway to Paradise'. The museum outlines the university's teachings through the means of wonderfully kitsch light-up dioramas, and attempts answers to teasers such as 'How can world peace be established?'

### OTHER ATTRACTIONS

The small, little-visited **government museum** (admission Rs 3; ⏰ 10am-4.30pm Sat-Thu) features a diorama to illustrate local tribal life and some hill-dwellers' artefacts; there are also some miniature paintings. The highlight is the sculpture gallery, with works from the ancient town of Chandravati, 7km from Mt Abu, dating from the 6th to the 12th centuries. One sculpture of the snake goddess Vish Kanya shows her breastfeeding a snake.

About 3km north of town, 365 steps lead to the ancient **Adhar Devi temple**, which is built in a natural cleft in the rock. You have to stoop to get through the low entrance to the temple. There are splendid views over Mt Abu from up here.

## Activities

The town has a **roller-skating rink** (9am-10pm), which charges Rs 15/25 per 15/30 minutes, including skate hire.

### TREKKING

Lalit Ganesh at the Shri Ganesh Hotel (right) organises treks into the hills – one in the morning and one to see the sunset. The routes vary and the level of difficulty depends on the fitness of the group. For Rs 20 you can join as many walks as you like. It's common to spot bears as well as other wildlife. Note that it's unsafe to wander unguided in the hills – travellers have been mugged.

### HORSE RIDING

You can hire ponies for rides at various places dotted around the town. One-hour rides cost Rs 50.

## Tours

The RTDC has five-hour tours of the main sites, leaving from the bus stand at 8.30am and 1.30pm (later in summer). Tours cost Rs 37 excluding admission and camera fees. The afternoon tour finishes at Sunset Point. Make reservations at the **inquiries counter** (☎ 235434) at the bus stand.

## Sleeping

Mt Abu mostly consists of hotels, and new ones spring up each year. Most are along or just off the main road through to Nakki Lake. The high season lasts from mid-April to June, during and after Diwali (October to November, when you need to book way ahead, prices become ridiculous, and you can't move for crowds – not a good time to visit) and from Christmas to New Year.

During the low season, discounts of up to 70% are available, and midrange accommodation can be an absolute steal. Most places are definitely open to a bit of bargaining, and the rates get cheaper the longer you stay. Most of the budget hotels have an ungenerous 9am checkout time.

Usually there are touts working the bus and taxi stands. Ignore them in the low season, but at peak times they can save you legwork, as they'll know where the last available room is.

Hot water can be erratic at the budget places, and the service is rather unenthusiastic at most places.

The Paying Guest House Scheme, which gives you the opportunity to live with a local family, operates in Mt Abu. It costs around Rs 100 to 500 per night. Contact the Tourist Reception Centre (see p270) for details.

### BUDGET

**Shri Ganesh Hotel** (☎ 235062; lalit_ganesh@yahoo.co.in; dm Rs 50, r with shared bathroom Rs 60-200, r with private bathroom Rs 150-250; 💻) Up the hill towards the maharaja of Jaipur's old summer palace, this serene place is the most popular spot to stay, and deservedly so. It has a peaceful rooftop, friendly management, loads of helpful local info, a guest kitchen and good home cooking. There's yoga on the roof in the mornings. Lalit Ganesh takes travellers trekking (see left), and his Irish wife, Beverley, offers cooking lessons. If you stay in the dorm, you'll have to pay Rs 50 for a shower.

**Hotel Lake View** (☎ 238659; Nakki Lake Rd; s/d from Rs 200/400, r with lake view Rs 500) This good-value place has snug, simple rooms (those opening onto the lake are much nicer) and pretty views over the lake. Hot water is available from 7am till 11am. There's an agreeable terrace with swing seats, and veg meals are served.

**Hotel Panghat** (☎ 238886; d Rs 300-450) Well-situated close to Lake View, this is in the heart of the action. It has plain rooms but an appealing rooftop overlooking the lake. Some cheaper, claustrophobic rooms are also available.

**Hotel Polo View** (☎ 235487; s/d Rs 200/300) Smallish, well-priced rooms with curly iron beds, white walls and 24-hour hot water.

**Hotel Saraswati** (☎ 238887; r Rs 150-400) Popular and efficient, Saraswati is a reasonably appealing place in a peaceful setting behind the polo ground. There's a range of OK rooms. Prices can rise Rs 200 at the weekend.

**Hotel Vrindavan** (☎ 235147; s/d Rs 250/450) Conveniently located if you don't feel like walking far from the bus stand, medium-sized Vrindavan is set back from the main road and has unexciting but practical rooms opening onto a walkway.

### MIDRANGE

Most places offer low-season discounts of 30% to 50%.

**Hotel Lake Palace** (☎ 237154; s/d from Rs 400/500, r with lake view from Rs 600) In an excellent lakeside situation, spacious, friendly Lake Palace overlooks a small garden. It's classier than most on the lake with appropriately higher prices. Rooms are unfussy and appealing, and some have semiprivate lakeview terrace areas. It's popular with Brahma Kumaris students.

**Mount Hotel** (☎ 235150; Dilwara Rd; s/d Rs 300/600) Once a British army officer's house, this is a lovely, homy, recently renovated place. The seven rooms are outfitted with wooden furnishings that give off a Swedish vibe. It's in a tranquil location with a small lawn.

**Hotel Samrat International** (☎ 235173; s with shared bathroom from Rs 170, r with private bathroom from Rs 400-730) This well-run, central hotel has a bewildering range of rooms from tight-fit doubles to attractive, spacious hideaways with sheltered balconies overlooking the polo ground. The restaurant is good too.

**Hotel Sunset Inn** (☎ 235194; s/d Rs 500/600) On the western edge of Mt Abu, the modern Sunset Inn is efficiently driven and friendly. Its doubles, though good, are rather overpriced. It's set in pleasing small gardens.

**Hotel Savera Palace** (☎ 235354; saverapalace@indiatimes.com; d Rs 500; ) Near Hotel Sunset Inn, this hotel has decent rooms but not particularly good service. There're a restaurant and a swimming pool (not always full).

**Hotel Sheratone** (☎ 238366; d Rs 700) The spelling isn't quite right…a cunning take on a famous name. Rooms here have balconies and views across the trees. Marble staircases add to the general feel of grandeur done on the cheap. The deluxe rooms have more ridiculous curtains than the ordinary rooms.

**Hotel Sunrise Palace** (☎ 243573; www.sunrisepalace-mtabu.co.in; r Rs 1800-3000, ste Rs 3500) At the southern end of Mt Abu is yet another former summer residence of a Rajput maharaja (this time the maharaja of Bharatpur). Although it lacks the panache of Connaught House and the Palace Hotel, it's very tranquil hotel and in a great position. The rooms are subdued yet smart (the more you pay, the bigger they are), and there's a wonderful terrace with excellent views across the hills.

**Hotel Hilltone** (☎ 238391; www.hotelhilltone.com; s/d Rs 1400/1800, with AC Rs 1600/2400, deluxe Rs 1800/3200; ) Hotel Hilltone is a central holiday complex. Rooms are quite swish (some have black marble floors), but it doesn't quite make the grade of its famous namesake. There're a small pool, a sauna, a fine restaurant and a cocktail bar.

**Kesar Bhavan Palace** (☎ 235219; Sunset Point Rd; r Rs 1600-1800, ste Rs 2850; ) This heritage property is perched high up among trees and has appealing leafy views, but it feels a little stark. The well-thought-out, comfortable, marble-floored rooms all have balconies, and the suites are on two levels.

### TOP END

**Connaught House** (☎ 238560; welcom@ndf.vsnl.net.in; d Rs 2600) Owned by the maharaja of Jodhpur and seemingly staffed by Raj retainers, Connaught House is delightful, a stuck-in-time colonial bungalow on the southeastern edge of town. It's more like an English cottage than a hotel, with lots of sepia photographs, dark wood, slanted ceilings, gorgeous shady gardens and marmalade for breakfast. Attractive newer rooms in a separate block have great views, though less character. Delicious meals are available but should be ordered in advance.

**Jaipur House** (☎ 235176; www.royalfamilyjaipur.com; s/d junior ste Rs 2000/2800, other ste Rs 3500-4000) Perched on a hilltop overlooking the lake, this was built by the maharaja of Jaipur in 1897. Opulent suites overlook the town from a suitably lofty height. If you're not really a suite person, there are rooms in the former servants' quarters that verge on the simple (but aren't any cheaper). The restaurant and bar are open to nonguests and are great places to drink in the views while sipping a G&T.

**Palace Hotel** (Bikaner House; ☎ 238673; Delwara Rd; s/d deluxe Rs 2000/2650, ste Rs 3000/3500) Near the Dilwara temples is this huge palace, built in

1893 by Sir Swinton Jacob. Once the summer residence of the maharaja of Bikaner, it resembles a Scottish stately manor, with tree-shaded gardens, a private lake, tennis courts and a restaurant. There are 35 well-decorated rooms; the ones in the old wing have the most character – some are huge and feel very much like you've stepped into a British country house.

**Hotel Hillock** (☎ 238463; s/d from Rs 2990/3990; ❄ 🏊) South of town, this is a swanky, comfortable place – don't be put off by the bland exterior. Staff here are more welcoming than at some top-end places, and the rooms are well appointed, and offer good views. Checkout is at noon.

**Cama Rajputana Club Resort** (☎ 238205; www.camahotelsindia.com; d Rs 2550, with AC Rs 3050, deluxe with AC Rs 3300; ❄ 🏊) North of town, this resort was once the British private club, built in 1895. Set in landscaped gardens, it's a classy place with nice views over the hills. Rooms are extremely comfortable but otherwise ordinary. The surroundings are stunning and the pool is fun.

## Eating

Most holidaymakers here are Gujarati – tough customers when it comes to cuisine, hence the profusion of good-quality places to eat in the town.

**Jaipur House** (snacks Rs 60-150, dishes Rs 100-235; 🕒 noon-3pm & 7-11pm) From its open terrace this has divine views over the hills, the lake and the town's twinkling lights. Happily, the food measures up to the setting. In the hotel of the same name (see opposite), it's also a brilliant place for a drink.

**Kanak Dining Hall** (dishes Rs 25-45; 🕒 8am-11pm) A popular option. The excellent all-you-can-eat Gujarati thalis (Rs 45) are contenders for Mt Abu's best. Sit indoors in the busy dining hall or outside under a canopy.

**Veena Restaurant** (veg dishes Rs 15-50; 🕒 7am-11pm) Veena, near the taxi stand, also draws crowds for its excellent Gujarati thalis. As at Kanak, you can eat outside.

**Arbuda** (Arbuda Circle; dishes Rs 25-75; 🕒 6am-11pm) Set on a sweeping, curved, open-air terrace that's filled with chrome chairs, Arbuda specialises in Punjabi and South Indian food, and offers snacks.

**Madras Café** (Lake Rd; dishes Rs 15-60; 🕒 7am-11pm) The laid-back Madras Café has pleasant indoor, outdoor and rooftop seating. It's a pure-veg place serving an assortment of South Indian and Punjabi dishes, as well as pizzas. Try the delicious, substantial mixed-fruit lassi. You can watch bread being baked in the outside oven.

**King's Food** (dishes Rs 25-90; 🕒 7.30am-11.30pm) A busy, open-to-the-street fast-food joint that's good for a light bite. It has the usual have-a-go menu, including Chinese, Punjabi and South Indian food, and good lassis.

**Chunkii Bites** (Shopping Complex, Lake Rd; dishes Rs 25-70; 🕒 7am-11.30pm) Across the road from Arbuda is this place (catchphrase 'bite to live long'), a good spot to grab a cheap snack. Grubby but cheery, it has loud music and regional delicacies such as *bhelpuri* (a popular Mumbai snack) and Delhi *chaat* (snacks such as samosas and potato patties seasoned with spices and served with chutney).

**Shere Punjab Hotel** (dishes Rs 25-200; 🕒 8am-midnight) Shere Punjab, in the market, has bargain Punjabi and Chinese food. For the devil-may-care carnivorous, there's brain fry or brain masala, but also some more conventional options, such as chicken curry.

## Drinking

**Café Coffee Day** (Hotel Maharaja International; snacks Rs 15-60; 🕒 8.30am-11pm) You probably didn't come to India to hang out in Western-style coffee bars, but every now and then you may be gasping for a latte or a cup of unadulterated Darjeeling tea. This also serves lurid cakes, and has armchairs and little tables.

**Jaipur House** (☎ 235176) The outdoor terrace of this heritage hotel has superlative views across Mt Abu, Nakki Lake and the surrounding countryside, and is the perfect place for a sunset tipple.

**Hotel Hilltone** (☎ 238391) This rather more down-market hotel also has a serene cocktail bar if you're eager for a drink.

## Shopping

Around Nakki Lake there are lots of bright little shops and stalls flogging all sorts of kitsch curios. In the evening the town comes to life, and this is a fine time to do some leisurely browsing and people-watching.

There's an expensive branch of **Rajasthali** (Raj Bhavan Rd; 🕒 9.30am-9pm), the government crafts emporium, which has some very eager sales staff. Alternatively, you may like to try the fixed-price **khadi shop** (Raj Bhavan Rd; 🕒 10am-1pm & 3.30-9pm), which sells all things woven.

## Getting There & Away

As you enter Mt Abu there's a toll gate – bus and car passengers are charged Rs 10, plus Rs 10 for a car (keep change handy).

#### BUS

From 6am to 9pm, buses make the 27km climb from Abu Road station up to Mt Abu (Rs 16, one hour, half-hourly). You never know quite what to expect as the bus spirals up the mountain. Buses leave from outside the main bus stand, next to the ticket booth. Some RSTC buses go all the way to Mt Abu, while others terminate at Abu Road.

The bus schedule from Mt Abu is extensive, and for many destinations you will find a direct bus faster and more convenient than going down to Abu Road and waiting for a train.

**RSTC buses** (☎ 235434) go to Jaipur (Rs 230/250 in express/deluxe, 12 hours, two daily), Ajmer (Rs 175/192 in express/deluxe, 10 hours, two daily), Udaipur (Rs 82 in express, 4½ hours, six daily), Jodhpur (Rs 126 in express, seven hours, one daily), and Ahmedabad (Rs 104 in express, 6½ hours). Buses belonging to private bus companies leave from the private bus stand.

There are lots of travel agencies around town, which also sell bus tickets. Shop around for the best price.

#### TAXI

A taxi for up to six people into town from Abu Road costs about Rs 200. Some drivers claim that this is only as far as the bus stand and ask an extra fee (as much as Rs 50) to take you to your hotel. To hire a jeep for sightseeing costs about Rs 400/800 per half-day/day (bargain hard and you may bring it down). Many hotels can arrange jeep hire, or they can be hired in the town centre.

#### TRAIN

Abu Road, the railhead for Mt Abu, is on the broad-gauge line between Delhi and Mumbai via Ahmedabad. In Mt Abu, above the tourist office, there's a **railway reservation centre** (🕑 8am-2pm), which has quotas on most of the express trains.

The No 9106 *Ahmedabad Mail* leaves at 1.10pm and reaches Ahmedabad (Rs 54 in 2nd class, 185km) at 5.30pm. The No 9105 *Delhi Mail* leaves Abu Road at 2.20pm, arriving in Jaipur (Rs 104 in 2nd class, 440km) at 11.10pm and Delhi (Rs 306/1241/807 in sleeper/2AC/3AC, 749km) at 5.20am. The No 9111 *Tawi Express* to Jodhpur (Rs 72 in 2nd class, five hours, 269km) leaves at 3.22pm. For Bhuj and the rest of the Kathiawar peninsula in Gujarat, change trains at Palanpur, 53km south of Abu Road.

## Getting Around

Buses from the main bus stand go to the various sites in Mt Abu, but it takes a little planning to get out and back without too much hanging around. It's easier to take the five-hour tour (see p273). For Dilwara you can take a shared taxi (jeep). These leave when full from opposite the Madras Café (Rs 4 per person, or Rs 40 all to yourself). Alternatively, you could walk the 4km to the temples.

There are no autorickshaws in Mt Abu, but it's easy to get around on foot. Unique to the town is the *baba-gari*, a porter-pulled handcart. They cart your luggage for Rs 15 or even one/two people for Rs 20/30.

# AROUND MT ABU

## Achalgarh

The fascinating, atmospheric Shiva temple of **Achaleshwar Mahandeva**, 11km north of Mt Abu in Achalgarh, boasts a number of diverse features, including what's said to be a toe of Shiva, as well as a brass Nandi bull (Shiva's vehicle). Where the Shiva lingam would normally be, there's a deep hole, said to extend all the way down to the underworld.

Just outside the temple, beside the car park, three stone buffaloes stand around a tank, while the figure of a king shoots at them with his bow and arrows. A legend tells that the tank was once filled with ghee, but demons, in the form of the buffaloes, came down and polluted the ghee – until the king shot them. A path leads up the hillside to the hilltop group of colourful Jain temples, which have fantastic views out over the plains.

## Guru Shikhar

At the end of the plateau, 15km north of Mt Abu, is 1721m **Guru Shikhar**, Rajasthan's highest point. A road goes almost all the way to the summit and the **Atri Rishi Temple**, complete with a priest and fantastic, huge views. A popular spot, it's visited as part of the RDTC tour. Otherwise, a jeep will cost Rs 350 return.

### Mt Abu Wildlife Sanctuary

This 290-sq-km **sanctuary** (Indian/foreigner/jeep Rs 10/40/100; 8am-5pm), 5.5km northeast of Mt Abu, on a large plateau, is home to panthers, sambars, foxes, wild boars, bears, crocodiles and bird life. It's about a 1km walk from the Dilwara temples. You can walk around the sanctuary, which is set in beautiful countryside.

### Gaumukh Temple

Down on the Abu Road side of Mt Abu, 8km from the town, a small stream flows from the mouth of a marble cow, giving the shrine its name (*gaumukh* means 'cow's mouth'). There's also a marble figure of the bull Nandi. The tank here, Agni Kund, is said to be the site of the sacrificial fire, made by the sage Vasishta, from which four of the great Rajput clans were born. An image of Vasishta is flanked by figures of Rama and Krishna.

To reach the temple you must take a path of 750 steps down into the valley (and then climb those 750 steps back out again!).

## ABU ROAD

This station, on the plains 27km down the hill from Mt Abu, is the rail junction for Mt Abu. (A 'road' is a railway town that serves as a communication point to a larger town off the line.) The train station and bus stand are conveniently located right next to each other on the edge of town.

Although there are RSRTC buses from Abu Road to other cities, such as Jodhpur, Jaipur, Udaipur and Ahmedabad, there's little point in catching them from here as these services are all available from Mt Abu itself. Alternatively, private bus companies also operate their services from Mt Abu to several destinations.

There's a sprinkling of cheap hotels along Abu Road and most are only a short walk from the train station. These places are satisfactory for a night's stay, but the accommodation available in Mt Abu is the better choice in terms of comfort and price.

The **retiring rooms** (d Rs 150) at the Abu Road train station are convenient if you're catching an early train.

# Northern Rajasthan (Shekhawati)

The extraordinary Shekhawati region is famous for its painted *havelis*. These grand houses are unique, smothered with dazzling murals that are part cartoon, part meandering decoration. What makes the region all the more astonishing is that these works of art are found in small towns, connected to each other by single-track roads that run through the flat, dry countryside where women seem to flicker like beacons as they move across the fields.

Today it seems curious that such attention was lavished on these out-of-the-way houses, but from the 14th century these towns were important trading posts on the caravan routes from Gujarati ports. The name of the region and its inhabitants can be traced to a 15th-century Rajput Kachhwaha chieftain by the name of Rao Shekha. Most of the buildings date from the 18th and 19th centuries, when the local merchants moved to places with richer pickings, but sent all their money back to build grand homes for their families.

Part of the fascination of the artwork is that the artists combined traditional subjects, such as mythology, religion and family, with contemporary concerns, such as new inventions and historic events, which they rendered from their imagination. As a whole these present a document of life at that time, with all its grandeur and innocence.

Exploring the region is like a magical mystery tour crossed with a treasure hunt. You can go in search of a particular *haveli*, or wander the towns at random. There's no chance of getting lost, and there are surprises around every corner. It's impossible to detail all the beautiful homes you may stumble across, so this chapter includes a selection of highlights. There are also forts, *baoris* (step-wells), *chhatris* (cenotaphs) and mosques to discover.

## HIGHLIGHTS

- Glorious technicolour **havelis**, especially in Fatehpur (p297), Nawalgarh (p284), Mandawa (p299) and Parsurampura (p288)
- A **tour** (p286) around Nawalgarh, exploring narrow rural back roads
- **Khetri Mahal** (p291) in Jhunjhunu – arches, columns and architectural whimsy
- **Sone ki Dukan Haveli** (p295), featuring lavish paintings using real gold, in sleepy, back-in-time Mahansar
- Churu's crumbling **Malji ka Kamra** (p302), and the treasure hunt to find it

## History

A rich but lawless land on the trade route between the ports of the Arabian Sea and the fertile Ganges valley, this region was, in its early history, dominated by the Shekhawats, with portions (principally Jhunjhunu and Fatehpur) held by the Muslim Kayamkhani nawabs (Muslim ruling princes or landowners). The Shekhawat *thakurs* (noblemen), like other Rajasthani rulers, once were most noted for their indulgence in arguing among themselves. Unlike other areas of Rajasthan though, the region was never combined into a single principality, but remained a bunch of separate, quarrelsome feudal domains – mainly run by the same family.

As the Mughal empire declined after the death of Aurangzeb in 1707, the descendants of Rao Shekha, who had already installed themselves in the area to the east of the Aravalli Range, encroached to the north and west.

The *thakurs* of the region retained a nominal loyalty to the Rajput states of Jaipur and Amber, which in turn honoured them with the hereditary titles of *tazimi sardars* (hereditary nobles entitled to be received at a ceremonial reception held by the chief). The Rajputs, however, never really trusted the *thakurs* – for example, when Jaipur was built in the 18th century, the Shekhawats were offered land *outside* the city walls to build their houses. Despite not being allowed in the inner circle, it was probably exposure to the courts of Jaipur and Amber that encouraged the *thakurs* to commission the first murals to decorate their *havelis*.

By 1732, two of these *thakurs* Sardul Singh and Shiv Singh had overthrown the nawabs of Fatehpur and Jhunjhunu and carved up their territories. Their descendants, particularly the sons of Sardul Singh, installed themselves in surrounding villages, filling their pockets via heavy taxes imposed on the poor farmers of the area and duties levied on caravans carrying goods from the ports of Gujarat. The merchants travelled via Shekhawati as a cheap option – the Rajput states on either side imposed even greater levies. The arid region of Shekhawati was thus busy with trade, attracting more and more merchants. The riches also attracted dacoits (bandits), and there was an atmosphere of lawlessness in the area.

The rise of the British Raj could have sounded the death knell for Shekhawati. The British ports in Bombay (Mumbai) and Calcutta (Kolkata) were able to handle a higher volume of trade than those in Gujarat. Pressure by the British East India Company compelled Jaipur state to reduce its levies, and it was no longer necessary for traders to travel via Shekhawati. But Shekhawat merchants had received a good grounding in the practices and principles of trade, and were reluctant to relinquish a lucrative source of income.

Towards the end of the 19th century, men emigrated en masse from their desert homes to the thriving trading centres emerging on the ports of the Ganges. Their business acumen was unparalleled, and some of the richest merchants of Calcutta hailed from the tiny region of Shekhawati. Some of India's wealthiest industrialists of the 20th century, such as the Birlas, were originally Marwaris (as the people of Shekhawati became known).

## Responsible Travel

The tourist boom has not quite caught up here. There's an infrastructure (more developed in some towns than others) to accommodate the increasing number of foreign

### FESTIVALS IN NORTHERN RAJASTHAN

Shekhawati has a couple of festivals to its name, but also celebrates statewide and nationwide festivals with fervour (see p363). Festivals in this boxed text are marked on Map p280.

**Shekhawati Festival** (1; 10-11 Feb, statewide) Promoted by the Rajasthan Tourism Development Corporation (RTDC). At present the official programme includes safaris, tours of the region, competitions and fireworks, but none of these events have significant roots in local culture and it fails to attract many tourists. Given Rajasthan's propensity for spectacle, it may become more colourful in time.

**Bissau Festival** (2; Sep or Oct, Bissau, p294) Ten days before the festival of Dussehra, Bissau hosts dramatic mime performances of the Ramayana. The actors wear costumes and locally made masks, and the performances take place in the bazaar at twilight.

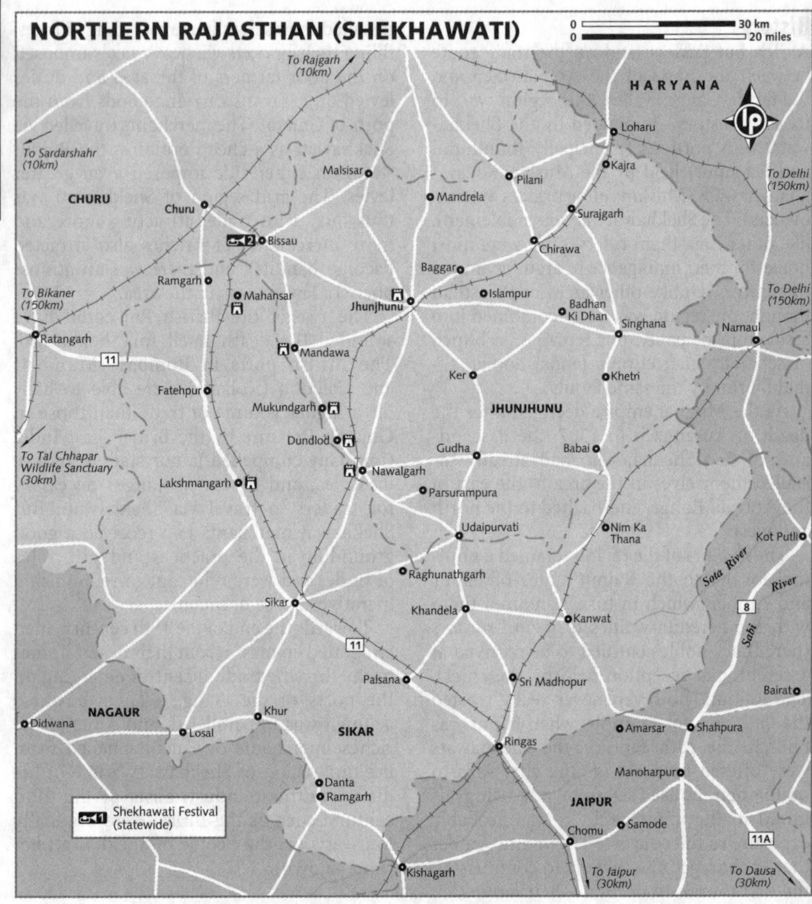


visitors but tourism is still in its infancy. So as not to damage the region, visitors should try to be culturally sensitive and preserve the region's environment. Tourism can also play a positive role in promoting interest in Shekhawati's great legacy of beautifully painted buildings and so generating the political will to preserve them.

Only a few *havelis* are open as museums or for display, and consequently many are either totally or partially locked up. While the caretakers and tenants are often tolerant of strangers wandering into their front courtyard, be aware that these are private places, and that tact should be used. Some people may ask for a little baksheesh to let you in. Local custom dictates that shoes should be removed when entering the inner courtyard of a *haveli*.

A couple of towns have antique shops that are chock-a-block with items ripped from *havelis* – usually doors and window frames, although anything that can be carted away is fair game. Avoid investing in any of these antiques – you will encourage this desecration.

Flashes from cameras can damage the paintings. In many instances, there may not be an express prohibition on flash photography, but don't do it!

Water is a critical issue in Shekhawati and every drop is precious (see p71). Consider washing with a bucket rather than using the shower, even if your hotel has one installed.

Camel safaris are a popular way to visit the local villages. If you take a safari, ensure that your rubbish is carried away and insist on kerosene fires instead of using already scarce sources of wood. It's also possible to stay in village homes: Ramesh Jangid from Nawalgarh has some interesting homestay programmes (see p286).

Ramesh is also the president of Les Amis du Shekhawati (Friends of Shekhawati) – to read more information about the society and its endeavours to protect the paintings of Shekhawati, see p376. In 2004, Ramesh opened a Shekhawati chapter with the Indian National Trust for Art and Cultural Heritage (Intach), which runs local workshops to raise awareness of the need to preserve the region's heritage. He has also initiated some visionary ecological measures at his resort, Apani Dhani (p287), located in Nawalgarh.

Another good source of information on the painted *havelis* of Shekhawati is Laxmi Kant Jangid at Hotel Shiv Shekhawati (p293) in Jhunjhunu.

French artist Nadine Le Prince's restored *haveli* (p297) in Fatehpur is now a cultural centre. Local and French artists work there, and the centre publicises the plight of the *havelis*.

## Information

### BOOKS

For a full rundown on the history, people, towns and buildings of the area, it's well worth buying a copy of *The Guide to the Painted Towns of Shekhawati* by Ilay Cooper. This publication gives details of the buildings of interest in each town, precise locations of interesting paintings and fine sketch maps of the larger tours of the area. *Shekhawati: Rajasthan's Painted Homes* by Pankaj Rakesh is an impressive coffee-table book with some fine photographs. Both of these can be bought in Delhi or Jaipur, or try www.amazon.com.

Another good book, available locally, is *Shekhawati Painted Townships* by Kishore Singh, which is well photographed and has lots of background information.

Apani Dhani (p287) in Nawalgarh has a good reference library of books on the region, in English and French, available for use by guests and those dropping by for a meal.

## Activities & Tours

A number of operators offer camel or horse-riding safaris in the Shekhawati region. These are a relaxing way to see rural and bird life, fitting in well with the pace of life outside the towns. In Nawalgarh you have a choice of trekking, horse riding, camel safaris or tours by bicycle (see p286). In Dundlod experienced riders can go horse riding (see p289) on fine Marwari horses, or you can take a camel or jeep safari. Camel safaris are on offer at Mahansar (p295) and camel and jeep safaris at Mukundgarh (p290), while you have the choice of camel, jeep or horse trips at Mandawa (p300), or camel, jeep or bicycle trips at Jhunjhunu (p293).

There are also several places where, inspired by all this artwork, you can undertake courses in painting or local crafts. In Jhunjhunu you can also do a 10-day cooking course. See p286 and p293 for more details.

## Getting There & Away

Access to the region is easiest from Jaipur or Bikaner. The towns of Sikar (gateway to the region, but with no notable *havelis*) and Fatehpur are on the main Jaipur to Bikaner road and are served by many buses. Churu is on the main Delhi to Bikaner train line, while Sikar, Nawalgarh and Jhunjhunu have train links with Jaipur and Delhi. For more details, see the Getting There & Away sections under each town entry.

## Getting Around

The Shekhawati region is crisscrossed by narrow bitumen roads and all towns are served by government or private buses and jam-packed shared jeeps. Old 1950s snub-snouted Tata Mercedes buses ply the routes, with turbaned villagers riding 'upper class' (on the roof). Buses may be busy but they are less crowded than jeeps, and safer. Many of the roads are in poor condition, so be prepared for an occasionally bumpy journey.

Several of the towns are served by trains. Passenger trains (Nos 488/6, two daily) stop at Bissau, Mahansar, Ramgarh, Fatehpur and Lakshmangarh. These are slow, often late, and the stations are often some way out of town – buses are a better bet.

To cover ground more speedily and in greater comfort, it's well worth hiring a taxi for the day to take you around the area. This is easy to arrange in the towns that have

## AN OUTDOOR GALLERY

In the 18th and 19th centuries, Marwari merchants lived frugally while piling up money far from home in India's new commercial centres. They sent the bulk of their vast fortunes back to their families in Shekhawati to construct grand *havelis* (traditional, ornately decorated mansions) – to show their neighbours how well they were doing and to compensate their families for their long absences. Merchants competed with one another to build ever more grand edifices – homes, temples, step-wells – and these were richly decorated, both inside and out, with painted murals.

The artists belonged to the caste of *kumhars* (potters) and were both the builders and painters. Known as *chajeras* (masons), many were commissioned from beyond Shekhawati – particularly from Jaipur, where they had been employed decorating the new capital's palaces – and others flooded into the region to offer their skills. There was a cross-pollination of ideas and techniques, with local artists learning from the new arrivals.

*Haveli* walls, particularly at the entrance, the courtyards, and sometimes some of the rooms, are painted from the ground to the eaves. Often the paintings mix depictions of the gods and their lives with everyday scenes featuring modern inventions, such as trains and aeroplanes, painted by artists who had never seen them. So Krishna and Radha are seen in flying motorcars.

As well as the *havelis*, the temples (for example Gopinathji Mandir, p288, at Parsurampura) are sometimes painted, and the characteristic village or town *chhatri* (for example, the one at Dundlod, p289) and its adjacent quadruple-towered and domed well may be painted too.

These days most of the *havelis* are still owned by descendants of the original families, but not inhabited by their owners, for whom small-town Rajasthan has lost its charm. Many are occupied just by a single *chowkidar* (caretaker), while others may be home to a local family. They are pale reflections of the time when they accommodated the large households of the Marwari merchant families. A few *havelis* have been restored, but many lie derelict, crumbling slowly.

### Architecture

The Persian term *haveli* means 'enclosed space', but the architecture of the *haveli* did much more than this – it divided the space so as to promote an entire way of life.

Most *havelis* have as their main entrance a large wooden gate (usually locked). In this gate is a smaller doorway that gives access to the outer courtyard. Often a huge ramp leads to the entrance, up which a prospective groom could ascend in appropriate grandeur on horse- or elephantback. Above the entrance you can usually see one or more small shield-shaped devices called *torans*. These are wrought of wood and silver, and often feature a parrot – the bird of love. In a mock show of conquest, the groom was required to pierce the *toran* with his sword before claiming his bride. Each *toran* represents the marriage of a woman from the household.

The doorway leads into an outer courtyard where to one side there's usually a *baithak* (salon) in which the merchant could receive guests. In order to impress visitors, this room was generally the most elaborately crafted and often featured marble or mock-marble walls. Here the merchant and his guests reclined against bolsters and were fanned by punkahs (cloth fans) as they discussed their business. Opposite the *baithak* is often a stable and coach house, called a *nora*.

Between the outer and inner courtyards is a vestibule, traversed by a blank wall with a small window. Through this window the women of the household, kept in strict purdah (isolation), could peep at prospective guests. Entry into the inner courtyard was restricted to women, family

accommodation, although finding a driver who speaks English is more of a challenge. The usual rate for a non-AC taxi is Rs 3.5 per kilometre with a minimum of 250km per day. Around four or five people can travel in a car, so having a larger group will keep costs down.

Another means of getting around the area is by bicycle – you can hire bikes in most of the major places – but be prepared for a bumpy, dusty ride.

The best way to explore the towns themselves is on foot. Bring a hat and water to stave off the heat, and a compass is handy for finding your way around. Some of the larger towns offer transport in autorickshaws and tongas (two-wheeled horse carriages) – you're most likely to want a members and, occasionally, privileged male guests. Access was gained on either side of the partitioning wall. This courtyard was the main domestic arena – the walls were often smoke-stained by countless kitchen fires. Rooms off this courtyard served as bedrooms or store rooms, and staircases led to galleries on upper levels, mostly comprised of bedrooms – some of which were roofless, for hot nights. The separation of male and female domains has long been a common arrangement in households across India, in Morocco, Turkey and many other countries, where it serves male-dominated families and sets a premium on female privacy and security. The *haveli* provided everything for the women and there was no need for them to venture out into the outside world. And in Shekhawati their cages were spectacularly gilded.

The arrangement of courtyards, together with the thick walls, also provided deep shade to cool the inner rooms, a vital necessity in this sun-scorched land. The largest of the mansions had as many as eight courtyards and were up to six storeys high.

### Paintings

Shekhawati's colourful paintings were a vivid response to the arid landscape, serving to educate, entertain and depict the concerns of the day.

Originally the colours used in murals were all ochre based. Apparently yellow ochre was obtained from the urine of cows fed on mango leaves – a practice discontinued as it was found to be cruel to cows. In the 1860s artificial pigments were introduced from Germany. The predominant colours were blue and maroon, but other colours were also featured.

Artists used the fresco technique to remarkable effect. It was painstaking: the wall was covered in several layers of plaster (the clay often gathered from ant hills), with different additives such as lime and hessian. The final layer was of lime dust mixed with buttermilk and jaggery (coarse brown sugar made from the sap of the date palm). The painters worked on the plaster while it was still wet, which accounts for the brilliance of the colours. Once completed the works were polished with agate and rubbed with dry coconut to seal them. After about 1900 the artists began to paint on dry plaster instead, allowing greater intricacy but losing the original urgency.

The early paintings are strongly influenced by Mughal decoration, with floral arabesques and geometric designs (according to the dictates of Islam, the Mughals never created a representation of an animal or human). The Rajput royal courts were the next pervading influence. Scenes from Hindu mythology were prevalent – usually featuring Krishna and Rama – and used as moral teachings in which good prevailed over evil. Other major themes were history, folk tales, animals, landscapes and eroticism (many of these works have been prudishly defaced or destroyed). With the European arrival, walls were embellished by paintings of new technological marvels the Shekhawat merchants had been exposed to in centres such as Calcutta. Pictures of trains, planes, telephones, gramophones and bicycles appeared – often painted from the artist's imagination.

The advent of photography and exposure to European art had a dramatic influence on Shekhawati art. Previously, subjects were depicted two-dimensionally, with little emphasis on anatomical accuracy or shading for perspective, and more emphasis on the imagination. With the influence of photography, artists sought a more faithful rendering of their subjects.

The paintings of Shekhawati are thus an extraordinary synthesis of Eastern and Western influences, the cultural collision perfectly illustrated in paintings showing Krishna playing a gramophone for Radha, or the two of them flying off in a Rolls Royce.

rickshaw in Jhunjhunu, the region's largest town.

## NAWALGARH

☎ 01594 / pop 56,482

Nawalgarh is a quiet town that makes an excellent base. It has a fine bunch of *havelis*, a colourful bazaar and some smashing accommodation options.

The town was founded in 1737 by Nawal Singh, one of the five sons of the Rajput ruler Sardul Singh. The arrival of merchants from Jaipur increased the town's prosperity, and some of India's most successful merchants, such as the wealthy Goenka family (which built many *havelis*), hailed from Nawalgarh. The town is built in a depression where a number of rivers terminate. The accumulated silt carried by these rivers was used to make the bricks (some of the best-preserved in Shekhawati) for local *havelis*.

## Orientation & Information

Nawalgarh is a small town with *havelis* spread throughout its confusing web of streets. You can reach most of them on foot. The train station is at the western end of town and accommodation is concentrated in the north and west.

There are several Internet cafés around town, as indicated on the map. The **State Bank of Bikaner & Jaipur** (SBBJ; Bala Quila complex) changes currency and travellers cheques, and there's an SBBJ ATM near the post office, though don't count on it working.

The best sources of information on Nawalgarh and its painted *havelis* are Ramesh Jangid at Apani Dhani (p287) and his son Rajesh at Ramesh Jangid's Tourist Pension (p287). They are involved in the preservation of Shekhawati's *havelis* and in educational programmes to raise local awareness about their rich cultural legacy. Ramesh can speak Hindi, English, French and German. They also run ecologically minded tours through their agency Alternative Travels, mainly in Rajasthan but also to Gujarat, Uttar Pradesh, Madhya Pradesh, Tamil Nadu, Kerala and Karnataka. See the website (www.apanidhani.com) for more details.

## Sights

### BALA QILA

The fort of Bala Quila was founded in 1737, but today its modern additions largely obscure the original building, and it houses a fruit-and-vegetable market and two banks. One room in the southeastern quarter of the fort retains mirrorwork and beautiful paintings on its ceiling, which depict street scenes of both Jaipur and Nawalgarh from the mid-19th century. To find it, climb a small greenish staircase in the southeast corner of the fort to the 2nd floor. The room is hidden behind a sweet shop, where you will be asked for Rs 10 to let you through.

### HAVELIS

To the west of Bala Qila is a group of six *havelis*, known as the **Aath Havelis**, erected around 1900. *Aath* means 'eight'; they are so-named because originally eight *havelis* were planned. The paintings are not technically as proficient as some others in this town, but they illustrate the transition in painting styles over the decades. As you approach the group through the gate from the road, the first *haveli* to the left is a case in point: there are older paintings on the front of the side external wall, while newer paintings, with synthetic colours, are at the rear. The front section depicts a steam locomotive, while the back section features some monumental pictures of elephants, horses and camels. There are lots of lively subjects, such as barbers, trains and false windows.

Opposite this group of *havelis* is the **Murarka Haveli**, which has some fine paintings, including miniatures above the entrance depicting the Krishna legends. The *haveli* is no longer inhabited, but is hired out for marriage celebrations. Unfortunately, unless a function is taking place, the richly painted inner courtyard is usually locked.

About 10 minutes' walk to the north is the **Hem Raj Kulwal Haveli**, built in 1931. Above the entrance are portraits of the Kulwal family, and of Mahatma Gandhi and Jawaharlal Nehru. Kaleidoscopic architraves surround the windows, and the outer courtyard features a triumphant train. An ornate silver door leads to the inner courtyard, which features paintings depicting mostly religious themes. The *chowkidar* will ask Rs 20 to let you in. Opposite is the household's guesthouse, built in the same year, which looks as if it's strayed from Brighton (England).

Nearby is the **Khedwal Bhavan**, which features beautiful mirrorwork above the entrance to the inner courtyard, and fine blue tilework. A locomotive is depicted above the archway, and a frieze along the north wall shows the Teej festival (spot the women on swings). On the west wall is a large locomotive crossing a bridge and underneath are portraits of various English people. On the outside north wall is the story of Dhola Maru, painted in two frames. (See the boxed text, p287.) In the first frame, soldiers chase the fleeing camel-borne lovers. Maru fires arrows at the assailants while Dhola urges the camel on. Above this is a smaller painting of an English woman with an infant. The lane between the Hem Raj Kulwal Haveli and the Khedwal Bhavan leads to three more beautifully painted *havelis* that are worth checking out.

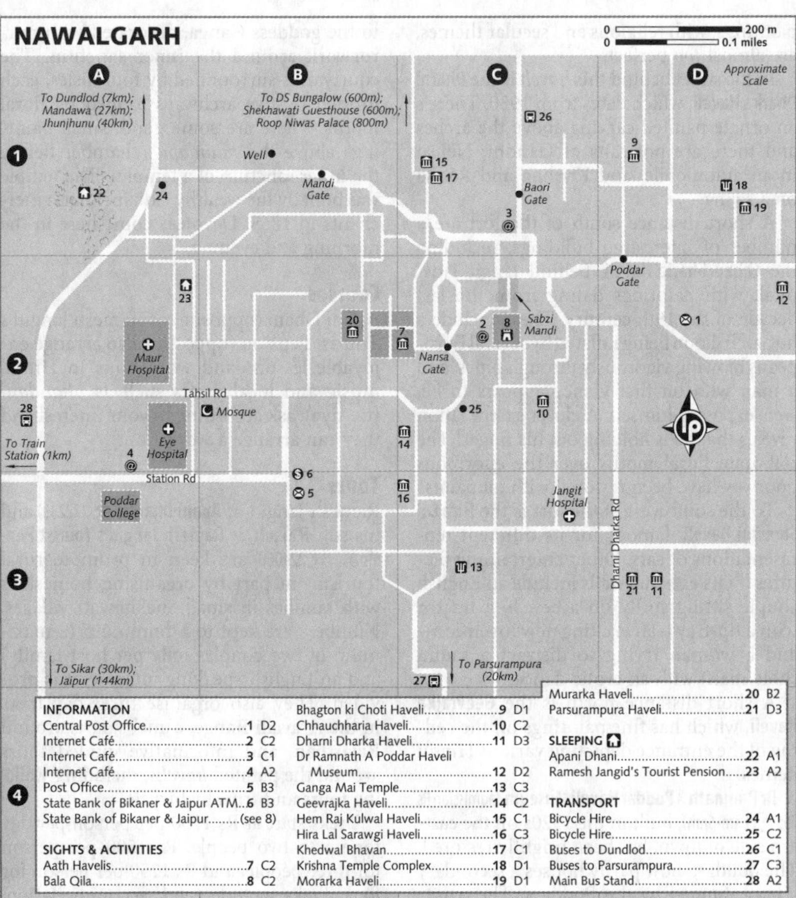


To the northeast of the Baori Gate is **Bhagton ki Choti Haveli**, where you need to pay around Rs 10 to 20 to be allowed in. On the external west wall is a locomotive and a steamship. Above them, elephant-bodied *gopis* (milkmaids) dance. Adjacent to this women dance during the Holi festival.

Above the doorway to the inner courtyard is a detailed picture of the marriage of Rukmani. Krishna cheated the groom Sisupal of his prospective wife by touching the *toran* first, thus claiming her for himself. The walls of the salon resemble marble, painted black with decorative incisions. The inner chamber upstairs contains the family quarters, also elaborately painted. A room on the west side has a picture of a European man with a cane and pipe and a small dog on his shoulder. Adjacent, a melancholy English woman plays an accordion.

About 200m east is the **Morarka Haveli** (admission Rs 20). This has well-presented original paintings, preserved for decades behind doorways blocked with cement. On the western external wall, under the eaves, is a picture of Jesus Christ. The inner walls depict scenes from the Ramayana. Across the road are a Krishna temple complex and a well.

On Dharni Dharka Rd is the **Parsurampura Haveli**, which dates from the early 20th century and belongs to a merchant from Parsurampura. Demonstrating the change in style that came with the influence of magazines and Western art, the grandiose paintings, with religious and secular themes, are almost *too* perfect.

In the street behind this *haveli* is the **Dharni Dharka Haveli**, which dates from 1930. There's an ornate painted carving above the arches and there are portraits of Gandhi, Nehru in an automobile, and Krishna and Radha on a swing.

A short distance south of the fort are a number of interesting buildings, including the **Chhauchharia Haveli**, behind Jangit Hospital, with paintings dating from the last decade of the 19th century. These include a hot-air balloon being inflated by several Europeans blowing vigorously through pipes, and a man who on first glance appears to be, well, exposing himself. A closer examination reveals that he is holding out his finger! The elaborate floral motifs over the enormous doorway have been restored with oil paints.

To the southwest of the fort is the **Hira Lal Sarawgi Haveli**, famous for its different representations of cars. Other entertaining pictures on its external walls include an English couple sitting stiffly on a bench, a tractor with a tip-tray – an exciting new invention – and a woman trying to distract a sadhu (holy man) with an erotic dance.

A short distance north is the **Geevrajka Haveli**, which has fine paintings on the ceiling of the entrance depicting various Hindu deities.

**Dr Ramnath A Poddar Haveli Museum** (admission Rs 75; 🕒 8am-6pm), built in the 1920s on the eastern side of town, has been brightly restored. The building now partly houses a secondary school, funded by the Poddars. The paintings of this *haveli* are now defined in strong colours, as they must have looked when new. New additions have also been made – they represent some of the few actively preserved paintings in Nawalgarh. Note the trompe l'oeil windows on the façade, giving a convincing illusion of reality. Fresco subjects include religious scenes, trains, cars and the British. On the ground floor there are several displays, including one room with examples of different schools of Rajasthani painting and one with dolls in the wedding dress of different castes. Lessons for the school are held on the floor above.

### GANGA MAI TEMPLE

Several hundred metres to the south of the Nansa Gate is this fine temple, dedicated to the goddess Ganga, decorated with mirrorwork around the inner sanctum. The courtyard's surrounded by four aisles, each formed by five archways topped by floral motifs. There are some good, small paintings above the *mandapa* (chamber before the inner sanctum of a temple). The temple was built by the wealthy Chhauchharia merchants in 1868. Devotees come here in the morning and evening.

## Courses

Apani Dhani (opposite) or Ramesh Jangid's Tourist Pension (opposite) also arrange enjoyable lessons and workshops in Hindi, music and local crafts such as *bhandani* (tie-dye); ask according to your interest and they can arrange a workshop.

## Tours

Ramesh Jangid at **Apani Dhani** (☎ 222239) and his son Rajesh at **Ramesh Jangid's Tourist Pension** (☎ 224060) are keen to promote rural tourism, in part by organising homestays with families in small Shekhawati villages. Numbers are kept to a minimum (a maximum of two couples only per host family) and an English-speaking interpreter is provided. They also organise three-day treks in the Aravalli Range, camel safaris around Rajasthan, and informative guided tours around the painted *havelis*, including walking tours and trips by bicycle.

Treks start at Rs 1750 per person per day for up to two people, Rs 1500 per person for three people, and Rs 1250 per person for four. Treks include food, accommodation, transfers and a guide, and involve such excursions as walks along a dried-up nadi (you can have your luggage carried for you between picnics and nightly encampments), and visits to ashrams and temples en route.

Prices for jeep tours to the villages of Shekhawati from Nawalgarh are as follows: a three-hour trip taking in Dundlod and Parsurampura is Rs 1200 for up to four people; a five-hour trip taking in Mandawa, Dundlod and Fatehpur is Rs 1500 for up to four people; a seven- to eight-hour trip visiting Bissau, Churu, Ramgarh and Mahansar is Rs 1800. Guided walking tours of Nawalgarh cost Rs 250, and take two to three hours.

The Roop Niwas Palace (opposite) provides English-speaking guides for two-hour/full-day walking tours of the painted

### THE LEGEND OF DHOLA MARU

One of the most popular paintings to be seen on the walls of the Shekhawati *havelis* depicts the legend of Dhola Maru, Shekhawati's answer to *Romeo and Juliet*.

Princess Maru hailed from Pugal, near Bikaner, and Dhola was a young prince from Gwalior. When Maru was two years old there was a bad drought in her homeland, so her father, the maharaja, shifted to Gwalior where his friend, Dhola's father, ruled. He stayed for three years, returning to Pugal when he learned that the drought was over. Before he left, as a token of friendship between the two rulers, a marriage alliance was contracted between their children. After 20 years, however, the promise was forgotten and Maru was contracted to marry someone else.

Wedding plans would have proceeded but a bard, who'd travelled from Pugal to Gwalior, sang at the royal court of the childhood marriage of Dhola and Maru. In this way Dhola came to hear of the beautiful and virtuous Maru, with whom he immediately, sight unseen, fell in love and resolved to meet. Of course, when Maru laid eyes on her champion she returned his affections and they decided to elope at once.

Her betrothed, Umra, heard of their flight and set chase with his brother, Sumra. They pursued the camel-borne lovers on horseback and it was the brave Maru who fired at them with arrows, although they proved of little use against the brothers, who had guns. They were able temporarily to elude the brothers and took shelter in a forest. But Dhola was bitten by a snake and succumbed on the spot. Maru, thus thwarted by death, proceeded to weep for her lost lover and her lamentations were heard by Shiva and Gauri (Parvati) who were luckily walking nearby. Parvati beseeched Shiva to restore the dead Dhola to life and the couple was reunited.

walls of Nawalgarh. It also specialises in horse and camel excursions, and even has a dedicated website: www.royalridingholidays.com. Horse rides cost Rs 450 for one hour, or Rs 1450/2900 for a half/full day. Camel rides cost Rs 400/800/1600 for one hour/half day/full day.

## Sleeping & Eating

**Apani Dhani** (☎ 222239; www.apanidhani.com; s/d from Rs 600/750) This is a groundbreaking, award-winning ecofarm, as well as a delightful and relaxing place. Rooms are in traditional, cosy mud huts, enhanced by thatched roofs and comfortable beds, around a bougainvillea-shaded courtyard. The adjoining organic farm supplies delicious ingredients, and alternative energy is used wherever possible, including solar cookers and water heaters, compost toilets and biogas. It's near the TV tower on the west side of the Jaipur road. Multilingual Ramesh Jangid runs the show, and is also president of Les Amis du Shekhawati, an organisation aiming to preserve the *havelis*. Tours around the area, via bicycle, car or foot, are available (see opposite).

**Ramesh Jangid's Tourist Pension** (☎ 224060; s/d from Rs 300/350) Near the Maur Hospital, this pension is well known, so if you get lost, just ask a local to point you in the right direction. This guesthouse, now run by genial Rajesh, Ramesh's son, offers homely, clean accommodation in spacious rooms with big beds. Some rooms have furniture carved by Rajesh's grandfather. Scrumptious meals (made with organic ingredients) are available (vegetable thali Rs 70). The family also arranges all sorts of tours around Shekhawati (see opposite).

**DS Bungalow** (☎ 222703; s/d Rs 250/350, bigger r Rs 350/450) Run by a nice couple, this is a quiet, comfortable place with simple rooms, a little out of town on the way to Roop Niwas Palace. It's backed by a garden with a pleasant outdoor mud-walled restaurant. The home cooking is excellent.

**Shekhawati Guesthouse** (☎ 224658; www.shekhawatirestaurant.com; s/d/tr Rs 400/500/600) Next door to DS Bungalow, this is a clean, family-run place with six rooms and a lovely garden restaurant in a thatched bungalow, which offers home cooking made from organic produce. Free pick-up from the bus or train station can be arranged.

**Roop Niwas Palace** (☎ 222008; www.roopniwaspalace.com; s/d from Rs 1700/1900; 🏊) About 1km north of the fort is this converted palace, with a back-to-the-Raj feel, grand grounds, and comfortable old-fashioned rooms that are eclectically decorated. This was the rural retreat of the *thakur* of Nawalgarh, Nawal Singh (1880–1926). See opposite for information about camel and horse excursions.

## Getting There & Away

### BUS

There are buses between Nawalgarh and Jaipur (Rs 52, 3½ hours, half-hourly), and several services each day to Delhi (Rs 130, seven hours) and to Jodhpur (Rs 160, nine hours, six daily).

Buses for destinations in Shekhawati leave every few minutes and shared jeeps leave according to demand (Rs 10 to Sikar, Rs 15 to Jhunjhunu). Private buses run to Fatehpur (Rs 22, hourly) and Mandawa (Rs 12, every 45 minutes).

There are private services that go to Ajmer (Rs 85, six hours). For buses to Ahmedabad (15 hours), Chittorgarh (10 hours) and Udaipur (12 hours), you'll need to go to Sikar first.

### TRAIN

There are rail connections to several destinations in Shekhawati. The 9734 *Shekhawati Express* leaves Nawalgarh at 9.24pm, arriving in Delhi at 5.06am (Rs 573/140 in 2AC/sleeper). To Jaipur, the 9733 *Shekhawati Express* leaves Nawalgarh at 6.14am, reaching Jaipur at 10.20am (Rs 428/121 in 2AC/sleeper).

## Getting Around

Bicycles can be hired from various places on the Dundlod Rd and near Bal Quila, as marked on the map, for around Rs 25 per day. If you're staying at Ramesh Jangid's Tourist Pension (p287), bicycle hire can also be organised there.

A shared autorickshaw from the train or bus station to the main market costs Rs 5; you can wave them down anywhere along this route. To hire an autorickshaw or a horse-drawn tonga from either the bus or train station to the fort costs about Rs 30.

# PARSURAMPURA

This little village, 20km southeast of Nawalgarh, has some of Shekhawati's best-preserved and oldest paintings. The **Shamji Sharaf Haveli**, just south of the bus stand, dates from the end of the 18th century and is decorated with a mixture of Hindu gods and Europeans. Pictures include a grandmother having her hair dressed, a woman spinning and an English woman in shiny patent-leather shoes carrying a parasol. A frieze shows a celebration, probably of a marriage – on one side is a priest presiding over the ceremony. The opposite wall depicts Europeans in a car. Above the lintel are some well-preserved portraits, and below, portrayals of Ganesh, Vishnu, Krishna and Radha. Saraswati is riding a peacock in the right-hand corner.

Beautiful paintings, featuring the lives of the gods, ring the interior of the dome of the **Chhatri of Thakur Sardul Singh**, 50m to the south, which dates from the mid-18th century. The exquisite work here is reminiscent of miniature painting and the antiquity of the work is evident in the muted, russet colours used – these are natural rather than artificial pigments. Pictures include those of the *thakur* and his five sons, graphic battle scenes from the Ramayana, and the love story of Dhola Maru, a common theme employed by the painters of Shekhawati. To visit the cenotaph you must obtain the key from the caretaker, Sri Banwari Lal (nicknamed Maharaj), who sits in the little booth under the peepul tree outside the gate of the Shamji Sharaf Haveli. Maharaj is a Brahmin priest, and it's almost entirely through his efforts that the *chhatri* is so well maintained. He is responsible for the pretty flower beds of roses and jasmine that surround the *chhatri*, and there's a toilet here. A small donation would be welcome – it'll be put to good use.

Also found in Parsurampura is the small **Gopinathji Mandir**, on the left just before you leave the village on the road to Nawalgarh. The temple was built by Sardul Singh in 1742 and it's believed that the same artist responsible for the paintings on the Chhatri of Thakur Sardul Singh executed the fine paintings here. According to local lore, the artist had half completed the work when the son of Sardul Singh chopped his hands off because he wanted the artist's work to be exclusive to his father's *chhatri*. Not to be deterred, the valiant artist completed the work with his feet! Perhaps this accounts for some of the subject matter, which includes a vision of hell.

## Getting There & Away

There are numerous buses to Parsurampura from Nawalgarh, which depart from the Parsurampura bus stand. The trip can take up to one hour (due to multiple stops en route) and costs Rs 10. You'll probably have to fight for a seat (or roof space!). The road is dusty and corrugated, and crosses a dry riverbed just before the village.

## DUNDLOD

☎ 01594

Dundlod is a sleepy, back-in-time village lying about 7km north of Nawalgarh. Its small fort was built in 1750 by Keshri Singh, the fifth and youngest son of Sardul Singh. Major additions were made in the early 19th century by his descendant Sheo Singh, who resettled in the region despite attempts on his life by Shyam Singh of Bissau (Shyam Singh murdered his father and brother in an attempt to claim the region for himself). Members of the wealthy Goenka merchant family also settled here, and their prosperity is evident in their richly painted *havelis*.

### Sights

The **Dundlod Fort** (admission Rs 20; ⏰ sunrise-sunset) was added to over 200 years, and features a blend of Rajput and Mughal art and architecture. Inside it combines a fashionable mix of European and Rajput decorative elements. The Diwan-i-Khas (Hall of Private Audience) has a mustard-coloured colonnade, stained-glass windows, fine Louis XIV antiques and an impressive collection of rare books. Above the Diwan-i-Khas is the *duchatta* (women's gallery) from where the women in purdah could view the proceedings below, through net curtains. The zenana features walls of duck-egg blue, and opens out onto the reading room of the *thakurani* (noblewoman). This room has a hand-carved wooden writing table, which bears Oriental dragon motifs. You can stay in the fort (see p290) or take horse-riding, camel or jeep tours from here (see right).

The beautiful **Chhatri of Ram Dutt Goenka** and the adjacent well were built by Ram Chandra Goenka in 1888. They lie about five minutes' walk to the southeast of the fort. If there's no caretaker in sight, borrow the key from the Ram Chandra Goenka Haveli. The interior of the dome has floral motifs extending in banners down from its centre, and is encircled by a frieze depicting Krishna dancing with the *gopis*, interspersed with peacocks and musicians. Paintings around the inner base of the dome illustrate a battle scene from the Mahabharata, a marriage celebration and Vishnu reclining on a snake.

**Bhagirath Mal Goenka Haveli** is often locked, but you can see some fine mirrorwork above the windows on the upper courtyard walls. Portraits in round frames nestle under the eaves. The *haveli* opposite is interesting, as the work is unfinished, so it's possible to see how the artist sketched the drawings before adding colour. Pictures include an elephant, camel and rider, and a horse.

In a small square to the right just before the fort entrance is **Satyanarayan Temple**, which was built by Hariram Goenka in 1911. On the temple's west wall is a long frieze, with endearing pictures showing Europeans on sturdy bicycles and in cars, and a long train, with telegraph lines above it (all very cutting-edge). The portraits under the eaves show nobles at leisure, smelling flowers and reading. One fine moustached and turquoise-turbaned fellow has a bird in his hand, and another painting shows a woman admiring herself in a mirror.

A short distance to the south of the temple is the stunning **Seth Arjun Das Goenka Haveli** (1875-85; admission Rs 20; ⏰ 7am-7pm). As with all restored *havelis*, the bright colours are something of a shock. The interior offers a good illustration of the merchants' lives, starting in their reception room, which is cooled by huge fans swinging from ropes. Above the window arches, mirrors are arranged in florets.

Well-preserved paintings can be seen on the east wall of nearby **Jagathia Haveli**, with an animated train station scene – in one carriage, a man appears to be in a passionate embrace with his wife, but look closer and you can see he is furiously beating her. A man hurries along on a bicycle, parallel to the train, and is pursued by a dog.

Just south, the **Ram Chandra Goenka Haveli** is painted a soft yellow colour, featuring florets and birds in the outer courtyard.

### Tours

Dundlod Fort (p290) has around 60 horses stabled at its Royal Equestrian and Polo Centre – India's largest Marwari horse-breeding centre. They organise upmarket horse safaris, which cost Rs 8500 per person per day, for experienced riders only. You can ride for three to 12 days, covering about 25km to 30km per day and along various routes, for example, around Shekhawati, to local fairs, in the Aravalli hills, or to other areas of Rajasthan such as Pushkar or Nagaur. It's also possible to hire a camel and an English-speaking guide to visit the *havelis* of Dundlod, or to arrange jeep safaris (minimum of four people) for a half or full day.

### Sleeping & Eating

**Dundlod Fort** (☎/fax 252519, in Jaipur ☎/fax 0141-2211276; www.dundlod.com; s/d Rs 2200/2400) Still run by the family of Dundlod's founder, who are descended from Sardul Singh. The building is grand, but the rooms are variable. All have character but some can be a bit shabby.

### Getting There & Away

It's possible to walk all the way from Nawalgarh to Dundlod, although it's a hot walk along a busy, dusty road. For just a few rupees, you can catch one of the many local buses that ply the route every 15 minutes. Catch one at the bus stand in Nawalgarh.

## MUKUNDGARH

☎ 01594

Mukundgarh is a crafts centre, renowned for its textiles, brass and iron scissors and betel-nut cutters. It's a charming, quiet town with little tourist development and some interesting painted *havelis*, including Kanoria, Ganriwal, and Saraf Havelis. It's about 5km north of Dundlod.

**Saraf Haveli** (admission Rs 30) is open when there's a caretaker around. The atmospheric house took eight years to build, starting in 1909. The main entrance is on an elevated platform almost 3m high, and is big enough for an elephant. One of the biggest *havelis* in Shekhawati, it has eight courtyards, though not all may be open for viewing. Rooms retain old family pictures and swing ceiling fans. The paintings in the main courtyard are fine though faded; the second courtyard features religious stories. The *haveli* across the road has some beautifully carved doors.

**Mukundgarh Fort** (☎7252397, in Delhi ☎011-6372565; fax 011-6814954; s/d from Rs 1000/2000, Maharaja ste Rs 6000; 🏊) is an impressive fort dating from the 18th century, although it is a little run-down and some of the 46 rooms are beset by damp patches. Newer rooms are better but less atmospheric. The Maharaja suite can accommodate up to eight people. Prices include breakfast. Camel or jeep safaris can be arranged (a two-hour trip on a camel cart costs Rs 300 per person).

## JHUNJHUNU

☎ 01592 / pop 100,476

Jhunjhunu, Shekhawati's most important commercial centre, has a different atmosphere to the smaller towns, with lots of traffic and hustle and bustle, as befits the district headquarters.

The town was founded by the Kaimkhani nawabs in the middle of the 15th century, and remained under their control until it was taken by the Rajput ruler Sardul Singh in 1730. It was in Jhunjhunu that the British based their Shekhawati Brigade, a troop formed in the 1830s to try to halt the activities of the dacoits – largely local petty rulers who had discovered that an easy way to become wealthy was to pinch other people's money.

Due to the town's long importance, it has numerous impressive *chhatris*, as well as some remnants of forts and a palace. Unfortunately many of the fine frescoes that once adorned the architecture have been whitewashed out of existence.

Jhunjhunu is also notorious for its Rani Sati Temple – enormously popular and dedicated to a young bride who burned to death on her husband's funeral pyre.

### Information

Laxmi Kant Jangid (owner of the Hotel Shiv Shekhawati and Hotel Jamuna Resort, see p293) is a knowledgeable, government-approved guide. He provides free guided tours around Jhunjhunu, or can arrange car tours of surrounding towns.

Useful businesses:

**Cyber World** (per hr Rs 30; 🕒 9am-8pm Mon-Sat, 11am-8pm Sun) A cramped place near Nehru Bazaar.

**SBBJ ATM** (Paramveer Path) Don't rely on it working. No banks in Jhunjhunu change money.

**Tourist Reception Centre** (☎ 232909; 🕒 10am-5pm Mon-Sat) Out of the centre at the Churu Bypass, Mandawa Circle. It's of limited help but can provide a basic map of the town and region.

### Sights

#### RANI SATI TEMPLE

In the northeast corner of town is the enormous multistorey **Rani Sati Temple** (admission free, photography permitted; 🕒 4am-10pm), notorious and hugely popular for commemorating an act of *sati* (self-immolation) by a merchant's wife in 1595. Rani Sati Temple has long been embroiled in a national debate about *sati* (p43), especially since the 19-year-old widow Roop Kanwar committed *sati* in nearby Sikar district in 1987. It's fronted by two courtyards, around which 300 rooms offer shelter to pilgrims. The main hall is of marble with elaborate silver repoussé work before the inner sanctum.

There's a tile-and-mirror mosaic on the ceiling of the *mandapa* depicting Rani Sati, with Shiva, Ganesh and Durga watching over her. A relief frieze on the north wall shows her story. Her husband is killed by the nawab's army; Rani Sati mounts the funeral pyre; she is consumed by flames while Durga sends her power to withstand the pain. In the next panel Rani commands a chariot driver to place her ashes on a horse, and to build a temple over the spot where the horse halts. The final panel shows the ostentatious temple built in her honour. Rani Sati is the patron goddess of the merchant class, which is believed to hold 60% of the wealth in India and control all the major newspapers. The temple apparently receives the second-highest number of donations of any in India.

### KHETRI MAHAL

At the western end of Nehru Bazaar, a series of small laneways, a short rickshaw drive north of the bus station, leads to the **Khetri Mahal**, a small palace dating from around 1770. Although run-down, it's one of Shekhawati's most sophisticated and beautiful

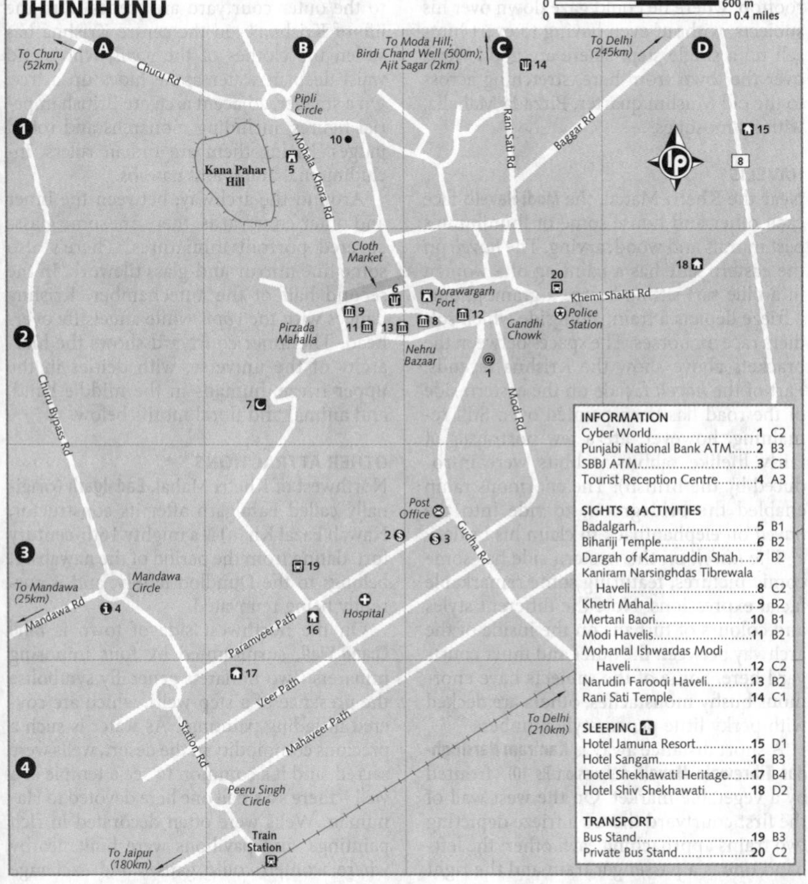

buildings. It's believed to have been built by Bhopal Singh, Shardul Singh's grandson, who founded Khetri. Unfortunately it's now overrun with goats and has a desolate, forlorn atmosphere, but the architecture is superb. There are no doors or windows in the palace. Wherever possible, walls have been replaced by sandstone columns, and the rooms are connected by an intricate series of arches and columns. The unpainted lime plaster has a rosy cast.

In the private chamber of the *thakur* are two small alcoves that retain fragments of paintings in natural earth pigments. The various levels of the palace are connected by a series of ramps (big enough for a horse) along which the *thakur* and *thakurani* could be pulled – the *thakur* could reach the rooftop, where he could gaze down over his subjects, without even having to exert himself up a single step. There are good views over the town from here, stretching across to the old Muslim quarter, Pirzada Mahalla, with its mosques.

#### HAVELIS

Near the Khetri Mahal, the **Modi Havelis** face each other and house some of Jhunjhunu's best murals and woodcarving. The *haveli* on the eastern side has a painting of a woman in a blue sari sitting before a gramophone; a frieze depicts a train, alongside which soldiers race on horses. The spaces between the brackets above show the Krishna legends. Part of the *haveli* façade on the eastern side of the road has been painted over. Still remaining, however, are a few portrayals of fairly lifelike rabbits (rabbits were introduced by the British). The enormous ramp enabled the bridegroom to ride into the *haveli* on elephantback to claim his bride.

The *haveli* on the western side has some comic pictures, featuring some remarkable facial expressions. Note the different styles and colours of turbans on the inside of the archway between the outer and inner courtyard here. Some of the subjects have enormous bushy moustaches, others are decked with perky little pencil-style numbers.

A short distance away is **Kaniram Narsinghdas Tibrewala Haveli** (admission Rs 10), fronted by a vegetable market. On the west wall of the first courtyard there's a frieze depicting two trains approaching each other: the left-hand one is a passenger train and the right a goods train filled with livestock – these trains look like they have come straight from the artist's imagination. On the north wall, a man ties his turban while another man holds a looking glass. Close by, a man and woman pass a child between them.

A short distance west is **Narudin Farooqi Haveli**, close to the Noor Mosque. In usual Islamic style, only floral motifs are depicted (there are no animal or human representations) and blue is the dominant colour. Unfortunately, the arches leading to the salons off the first courtyard have been sealed off with concrete.

On the north side of Nehru Bazaar is **Mohanlal Ishwardas Modi Haveli** (admission Rs 10), which dates from 1896. A train runs merrily across the front façade. Above the entrance to the outer courtyard are scenes from the life of Krishna – in the centre Krishna has stolen the clothes of the *gopis*, who stand waist-deep in water as he hides up a tree. On a smaller, adjacent arch are British imperial figures, including monarchs and robed judges. Facing them are Indian rulers, including maharajas and nawabs.

Around the archway, between the inner and outer courtyards, there are some glass-covered portrait miniatures. There's also some fine mirror-and-glass tilework. In the second half of the antechamber, Krishna dances with the *gopis* while angels fly overhead. The inner courtyard shows the hierarchy of the universe, with deities in the upper frieze, humans in the middle band, and animal and floral motifs below.

#### OTHER ATTRACTIONS

Northwest of Khetri Mahal, **Badalgarh** (originally called Fazalgarh after its constructor, Nawab Fazal Khan) is a mighty 16th-century fort, dating from the period of the nawabs. It belongs to the Dundlod family, and is currently being renovated.

On the northwest side of town is **Birdi Chand Well**, surmounted by four imposing minarets (two minarets generally symbolise the presence of a step-well), which are covered in fading paintings. As water is such a precious commodity in the desert, wells were sacred, and it's common to see a temple at a well – there's a small one here devoted to Hanuman. Wells were often decorated in rich paintings, and pavilions were built nearby where women could gather and exchange news. These served as important social centres. As at this well, you will often find a neem tree nearby, the twigs from which are used to clean the teeth.

To the west of the well is an old inn where caravans would once have halted.

A couple of kilometres further north is the picturesque lake **Ajit Sagar**, built by Jitmal Khaitan in 1902.

The **Mertani Baori**, to the northwest of the fort, is named after the woman who commissioned it, Mertani, the widow of Sardul Singh. Built in 1783, it has been restored and is Shekhawati's most impressive step-well. It's about 30m deep, and its sulphuric waters are said to cure skin diseases. An English official reported in 1930, however, that the water here was so poisonous, anyone who drank it died a couple of hours later. On either side of the well, steps lead to a series of cool resting rooms for visitors.

To the south of Kana Pahar hill is the **Dargah of Kamaruddin Shah**, a complex consisting of a madrasa (Islamic college), a mosque and a *mehfilkhana* (concert hall) at which religious songs are sung. Fragments of paintings depicting floral motifs remain around the courtyard, particularly on the eastern and northern sides (although many have been whitewashed). Blue – a favourite colour of the Muslims – is the predominant colour used.

A short distance northwest of Jorawargarh Fort is the fine **Bihariji Temple**, which dates from approximately 1776 and is dedicated to Krishna. It has some fine, though worn, murals. On the inside of the dome, Krishna and the *gopis* are rendered in natural pigments – their dance, called the *rasalila*, suits the circular form of the dome and so is a popular theme here.

### Courses

For tuition in traditional Shekhawati painting, contact Laxmi Kant Jangid at the Hotel Shiv Shekhawati or Hotel Jamuna Resort (see right). Laxmi can organise lessons with a local artist in traditional Shekhawati painting, and offers accommodation by donation at the Hotel Shiv Shekhawati for anybody who studies painting and stays at least 16 days (two months is ideal).

He also runs cookery packages at Hotel Jamuna Resort. The cooking course (€950, all-inclusive apart from flights) lasts for 10 days, and includes visits to Jaipur and to local families. One-day decorative-art workshops are also available, which cover henna painting, textiles (including *bandhani* – tie-dye) and fresco painting.

### Tours

Camel and jeep safaris can be arranged at Hotel Shiv Shekhawati or Hotel Jamuna Resort (below). A packed lunch or snacks can be organised. The hotel also arranges three- to five-day bicycle packages around the region. The tours cost US$70 per person per day (including all accommodation, meals and jeep transfers), cover 90km to 110km and start and end in Jhunjhunu. Routes include Alsisar–Malsisar–Bissau, Mandawa–Fatehpur–Ramgarh–Mahansar, and also Mukandgarh–Nawalgarh–Dundlod–Churi.

### Sleeping & Eating

**Hotel Jamuna Resort** (☎ 232871; s/d Rs 500/600, with AC Rs 700/800; ❄ 🏊) Operated by Laxmi Kant Jangid (who also runs Hotel Shiv Shekhawati), Jamuna Resort has AC rooms either vibrantly painted or decorated with traditional mirrorwork. There's a pool (Rs 50 for nonguests), also set in the serene garden. You can stay here by donation if you study painting and help decorate the rooms. The hotel also has a large meeting hall and brand-new kitchens – all set up for the cooking courses (see left).

**Hotel Shekhawati Heritage** (☎ 237134; Paramveer Path; shekhawati_heritage@yahoo.com; s/d from Rs 400/500) Near Hotel Sangam, this place, with kindly management, is the pick in this area. The bright rooms are well decorated, with leafy outlooks.

**Hotel Shiv Shekhawati** (☎ 232651; www.shivshekhawati.com; d Rs 400-800; ❄) East of the centre, Shiv Shekhawati is a modern place built around a central inner courtyard, with squeaky-clean, plain rooms. It's 2km from the private bus stand in a quiet area on the eastern edge of town. The affable owner, Laxmi Kant Jangid (usually at Hotel Jamuna Resort), is a wealth of knowledge on the villages of Shekhawati (see p290).

**Hotel Sangam** (☎ 232544; s/d from Rs 250/300) This impersonal hotel, in the bus stand area, has reasonable, large doubles tiled in grey and blue; singles are small but still OK. Check-out is 24 hours. Budget rooms are at the front and could be noisy.

### Getting There & Away

#### BUS

There are regular buses between Jhunjhunu and Jaipur (Rs 70, five hours), Churu (Rs 18/25 in local/express, around 1½ hours, hourly) and Bissau (Rs 15, 1½ hours, hourly). There are numerous buses to Mandawa (Rs 10, one hour) from 6.30am and to Nawalgarh (Rs 15, one hour).

Buses leave for Delhi from 5am (Rs 116, six hours, half-hourly). There are also buses to Jodhpur (Rs 160, 10 hours), Ajmer (Rs 131, seven hours) and Bikaner (Rs 87, five hours). The Roadways inquiries number is ☎ 27232664.

There's a private bus stand on Khemi Shakti Rd.

#### TRAIN

The *Shekhawati Express* runs between Jhunjhunu and Delhi (Rs 529/128 in 2AC/sleeper, seven hours). It also serves Jaipur (Rs 51 in 2nd class, 5¼ hours). There are also several daily passenger trains to Jaipur.

### Getting Around

For local sightseeing, you'll pay about Rs 40 per hour for an autorickshaw. A rickshaw from the train or bus station to the Hotel Shiv Shekhawati costs about Rs 25.

## BAGGAR

This small, peaceful village has few *havelis* to nose around, but it's a great place to stay, about 15km from Jhunjhunu.

**Piramal Haveli** (☎ 01592-221220; www.neemranahotels.com; r Rs 1500-2000) has just eight rooms so advance bookings are essential. This is a gorgeous, colonial-style, grand old 1920s house, built by a merchant who traded in opium, cotton and silver in Bombay. The house is appointed with original furniture and kitsch paintings featuring gods in motorcars.

## BISSAU

☎ 01595 / pop 21,133

Pint-sized Bissau lies about 32km northwest of Jhunjhunu. Founded in 1746 by Keshri Singh, the last of Sardul Singh's sons, it has one of Shekhawati's fiercest histories. The town prospered under Keshri, but fell into brigandry during the rule of his grandson Shyam Singh. It's said that the merchants of Bissau, who had been encouraged to set up in the town by Keshri, packed up and left when Shyam extracted vast sums of mone[y] from them. The *thakur* then resorted t[o] brigandry, embarking on raids with dacoit[s] to neighbouring regions. The British calle[d] on the Shekhawati Brigade to restore orde[r] in the anarchic town, although by the tim[e] the expedition was mounted, Shyam Singh had expired and his heir, Hammir Singh had driven out the brigands and encourage[d] the merchants. The British were impresse[d] by the town's prosperity and left without a single shot being fired.

### Sights

On the façade of the **Chhatri of Hammir Singh** (1875), near the private bus stand, you ca[n] see British folk in fancy carriages, including one shaped like a lion and another lik[e] a hybrid lion-elephant. The *chhatri* is no[w] multipurpose, being both a primary school with lessons held under the dome and eve[n] in the sandy courtyard, and a storage plac[e] for fodder. On the external back wall is a portrayal of Dhola Maru (see the boxed text p287), and unusually, the bard who feature[s] in the love story is also depicted. On th[e] southern wall, a man on a horse dispatches a lion with a sword. The paintings on the fou[r] corner pavilions are badly deteriorated.

If you walk north from the bus stand an[d] take the first right, on the left-hand side a[t] the next intersection is the **Haveli of Girdarila[l] Sigtia**. The paintings on the external wall[s] have been destroyed, but the rooms retai[n] some vibrant murals in bright orange[s,] blues, reds and greens. A room in the northeast corner of the *haveli* shows Shiva (wit[h] the unusual addition of a moustache) wit[h] the Ganges flowing from his hair. There'[s] also a woman nursing a tiny child. Note th[e] orange handprints on the outer courtyar[d] wall; these are a custom peculiar to Shekhawati, signifying the birth of a male child.

On the opposite side of this lane is th[e] **Motiram Jasraj Sigtia Haveli**, which is now [a] junior school. On the north wall, Krishn[a] has stolen the *gopis'* clothes. The maiden[s] have been modestly covered by the artis[t] in the coils of snakes, although one reptil[e] can be seen slinkily emerging from betwee[n] a *gopi's* legs.

### Getting There & Away

There are daily buses from Bissau to Jhunjhunu (Rs 15, 1½ hours) every 30 minute[s] and to Mahansar (Rs 4, 20 minutes), Mandawa (Rs 12, 1½ hours) and Churu (Rs 7, 30 minutes).

Bissau is also served by the *Bikaner Jaipur Express*, which runs to Bikaner (Rs 491/121 in 2AC/sleeper, 4½ hours) and Jaipur (Rs 491/121 in 2AC/sleeper, five hours), and by local passenger trains.

### Getting Around

Bicycles can be hired for Rs 25 per day (bargain hard) from the shops near the Chhatri of Hammir Singh. Bicycles are an excellent way to tour this region, and are particularly good for the 6km trip to Mahansar.

## MAHANSAR

A turn-off to the left as you leave Bissau on the Churu road leads 6km to the quaint, slow-moving, untouristy village of Mahansar, a dusty place with lots of rural charm where donkeys outnumber motorised vehicles. There are a few gemlike *havelis*, all financed by the wealthy Poddar clan.

Mahansar was founded by Nawal Singh in 1768, and the town prospered for several decades until one of the Poddars lost his livelihood when two shiploads of opium sank without trace.

The town is also famous for homemade liquor, known as *daru*, which resembles Greek ouzo.

### Sights

The **Raghunath Mandir**, dating from the mid-19th century, is a temple that resembles a *haveli* in its architecture. It has fine floral arabesques beneath the arches around the courtyard and a grand façade. There are good views across the small town from the *chhatri*-ringed upper floor.

A short distance to the northeast of the Raghunath Mandir is **Sone ki Dukan Haveli** (admission Rs 100; 7am-5pm). The name means 'gold shop' and it was so named due to the striking paintings, which use a shimmering amount of gold leaf – unusual for Shekhawati. The scenes from the Ramayana in the southern section of the ceiling in the first chamber are particularly intense, with their glorious quantities of gold leaf. The lower walls are richly adorned with floral and bird motifs, creating a Utopian fantasy of butterflies, trees laden with fruit, and flowers. Painted in gold script on panels on the west wall of this chamber are the names of the gods. Carved wooden beams divide the ceiling into three sections. On the north side, the life of Krishna is portrayed. A golden river connects the holy cities of Vrindavan, where Krishna spent his childhood, and Mathura, where he lived as a king. Lakshmi, goddess of wealth, is also featured, as are portraits of women playing different instruments.

About 10 minutes' walk from the bus stand, past the fort on the right-hand side of Ramgarh Rd, is the **Sahaj Ram Poddar Chhatri**. Some archways have been bricked in, but there are still some well-preserved paintings on the lower walls of this well-proportioned and attractive building.

### Sleeping & Eating

**Narayan Niwas Castle** ( 01595-264322; r from Rs 600-900) In the old fort, about 100m north of the bus stand, Narayan Niwas Castle is the only place to stay in this remote village. This is a proper creaky Rajasthani castle dating from 1768 that feels evocatively uncommercial. Rooms are dusty but characterful, some with antique furniture and paintings covering the walls. It's run by the down-to-earth *thakur* of Mahansar and his wife, an elderly couple who know lots about the local area and can tell interesting stories about bygone days. Ask to see several rooms before checking in, as some are better than others (room No 5 is atmospheric). There are some smaller, cheaper rooms in a separate portion of the castle. The food gets excellent reports and the hotel offers guided tours, as well as camel safaris into the local sand dunes.

### Getting There & Away

There are regular bus services that go between Mahansar and Ramgarh (Rs 5), Churu (Rs 10), Fatehpur (Rs 15) and Bissau (Rs 4, 20 minutes). Change at Bissau for buses to Jhunjhunu.

## RAMGARH

Sixteen kilometres south of Churu and 20km north of Fatehpur is Ramgarh, which was founded by a disaffected group from the wealthy Poddar family in 1791, and has the biggest concentration of painted *havelis* in the region. The Poddars defected from nearby Churu in a fit of pique after the local *thakur* imposed an extortionate wool levy. They set about building extravagant homes for themselves, and Ramgarh thus has a splendid, albeit uncared for and faded, artistic legacy. It prospered until the late 19th century. It's pretty snoozy today.

The town is easy to explore on foot. The bus stand is at the western edge of town. In the northern section, about 600m from the bus stand, there's a concentration of *havelis*, as well as the main Shani Temple and the Ganga Temple. There's nowhere to stay in Ramgarh.

### Sights

The imposing **Ram Gopal Poddar Chhatri**, to the south of the bus stand, was built in 1872. The main dome of the *chhatri* is encompassed by a series of smaller domes. On the west side of the outer rim of the main dome, one of the projecting braces bears a picture of a naked woman stepping into her *lenga* (skirt), while another woman shields her from the eyes of a man with the hem of her skirt. The drum of the main dome is brightly painted and has well-preserved paintings in blues and reds depicting the battle from the Ramayana. The building on the north side of the *chhatri* was where family members paying homage to their dead ancestor could rest. Unfortunately, the *chhatri* is in a sorry state – the northeast corner of the building is badly water damaged. To enter the compound, you will need to find the caretaker, who'll ask for about Rs 50.

Just a short distance to the north of the town wall, on the east side of the road, is the fine **Ganga Temple**. It was built by one of the Poddar clan in 1845, and is an imposing building with large elephant murals on its façade. The right side of the façade is deteriorating – the foundations are crumbling. The temple only opens for morning and evening *puja* (prayers). Other paintings depict religious themes, including local favourite Krishna.

About 20m further north, on the left-hand side, is a **Ganesh Temple**. It has a densely painted forecourt and a series of interesting paintings between the brackets under the eaves, mostly featuring birds and religious themes.

From here, a road heads east to the spectacular tiny **Shani Mandir** (Saturn Temple). This was built in 1840, and features some crude paintings on its façade. The exterior, however, belies the temple's richly ornate interior, which is completely covered in fantastic mirrorwork. There are some fine murals, worked in gold, in the chamber before the inner sanctum. The overall effect is dazzling. Subjects include Krishna and Radha and events from the Mahabharata. To the south (left) of the inner sanctum there's a painting on the ceiling featuring the marriage of Shiva and Gauri. Unfortunately, the ceiling in the chamber on the right-hand side of the inner sanctum is badly damaged by dampness.

If you go back to the main Churu Gate, continue past the gate for about 50m, then turn left, you'll come to a group of **Poddar havelis**. Popular motifs include soldiers, trains, and an unusual design, peculiar to Ramgarh, of three fish arranged in a circle. One *haveli* has a painting of women carrying water in pitchers, and there's a novel portrayal of the Dhola Maru legend (see the boxed text, p287) on the west wall of another: while Maru fires at the advancing assailants, Dhola nonchalantly smokes a hookah!

### Getting There & Away

There are buses to Nawalgarh (Rs 25, 2½ hours), Bissau (Rs 8, 45 minutes), Fatehpur (Rs 8, 45 minutes) and Mandawa (Rs 16, 1½ hours). Ramgarh is on the narrow-gauge line that runs between Sikar and Churu; daily services connect these towns.

## FATEHPUR

☎ 01571 / pop 78,471

A scrappy, busy small town, Fatehpur is chock-full of wonderful but slowly disintegrating *havelis* on either side of the main street. The lack of good tourist facilities means that it's a better place to stop off than stay the night. It's hoped that the grand restoration of Haveli Nadine Prince, now a gallery and cultural centre, may rescue the area's other beautiful buildings by focusing attention on the area.

Established in 1451 as a capital for Muslim nawabs, Fatehpur was their stronghold for centuries before it was taken over by the Shekhawati Rajputs in the 18th century. It was even ruled by an Irishman George Thomas in 1799 before he lost it to the maharaja of Jaipur. You can see that the merchant community here (which included the rich Poddar, Choudhari and Ganeriwala families) was enormously wealthy by the number of vibrant, grandiose *havelis*, fine *chhatris*, wells and temples.

Mahesh Yogi is a government-approved guide based in Fatehpur. To find him, ask at the RTDC Hotel Haveli (p298), or in the town centre along the Churu–Sikar Rd.

## Sights

At the first intersection to the north past the intersection of the Mandawa road and the Churu–Sikar road, turn right and you'll soon come to **Haveli Nadine Prince** (☎ 231479; www.cultural-centre.com; adult/child Rs 100/50; 9am-5pm), an 1802 *haveli* that has been brightly restored to its former glory. There's a finely carved lintel with Ganesh sculpted over the centre (Ganesh, the protector of households, is often depicted here).

French artist Nadine Le Prince spent three years having the *haveli* restored (it had been empty for nearly 40 years), and has turned it into a gallery and cultural centre. Inside, the grand hall has a ceiling lined with real gold and retains the original woodcarving. Charming features include a couple's winter room with specially designed steep steps to deter children, and niches for musicians in the dining room.

There's a gallery displaying art by French artists working here, as well as a tribal art gallery, which shows some beautiful, delicate work from local artists. Its Art Café (p299) has appealing snacks.

Just south of this *haveli* is the small **Chauhan Well**, which dates from the early 18th century and was built by the Rajput wife of a Muslim nawab. There's some painting around the windows and a couple of the pavilions, and the minarets retain fragments of geometric and floral designs.

Return to the Haveli Nadine Prince, and from there, retrace your steps back to the main Churu–Sikar road. Cross this and continue along the same road, then turn right up the first lane. On the right-hand side is the Jagannath Singhania Haveli, dating from 1855. It has a fantastic ornately painted interior, but is often locked. There are some interesting paintings on its façade, including of Krishna and Radha framed by four elephants, and above this, some British men with guns.

On the south of the Mandawa road, about 50m east of the main intersection with the

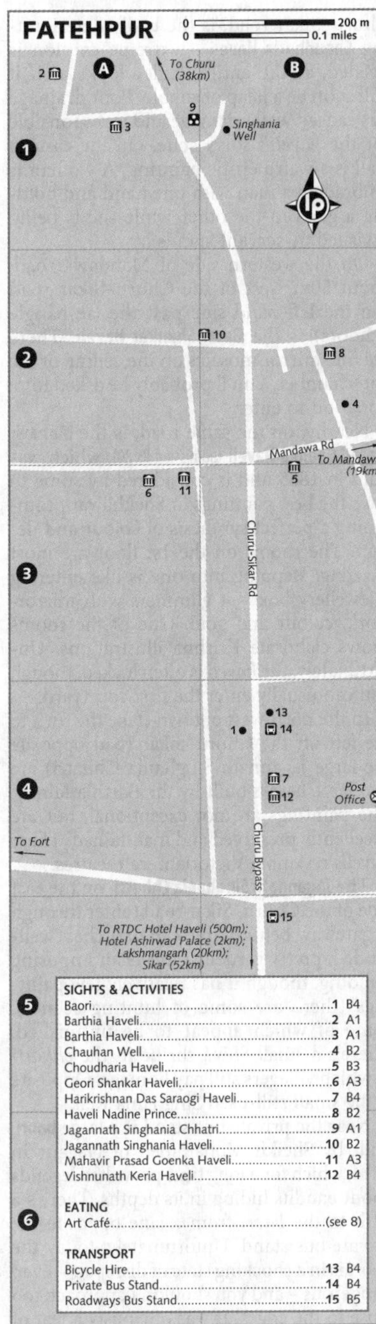

Churu–Sikar road, is the badly deteriorating **Choudharia Haveli** – extreme caution is needed, as the entire edifice looks as if it will soon be a heap of rubble. Poor drainage has caused water damage and is responsible for the *haveli's* sorry state. On the eastern wall is a weird erotic painting. A woman is embracing a man with one hand and holding a glass in the other while she is being ravished. A servant stands by.

On the western side of Mandawa road, about 50m west of the Churu–Sikar road (on the left-hand side past the lac bangle vendors) is the **Geori Shankar Haveli**. There are fine mirror mosaics on the ceiling of the antechamber. You'll probably be asked for a donation to enter.

Nearby, on the same road, is the **Mahavir Prasad Goenka Haveli** (admission Rs 20), which was built in 1885 and is considered by some to have the best paintings in Shekhawati, combining a perfect synthesis of colour and design. The rooms on the 1st floor are most dazzling: stepping into one is like entering a jewellery box – it glimmers with mirrorwork, colour and gold. One of the rooms shows elaborate Krishna illustrations. Unfortunately, the *haveli* is often locked, though you can usually enter the first courtyard.

In the northwest of town (take the turn to the left off the Churu–Sikar road opposite the large Jagannath Singhania Chhatri) are two large **havelis** built by the Barthia family. The paintings are not exceptional, but are excellently preserved and maintained. These *havelis* resemble Victorian-era theatres.

The **Jagannath Singhania Chhatri**, on the east side of the Churu–Sikar road (enter through a gateway behind the *chhatri*), has well-tended, pretty gardens. This is an imposing building, though it has relatively few paintings (there are some of hunting scenes), some of which appear to be unfinished. There's a small Shiva shrine in the *chhatri* at which villagers still pay homage. Opposite is the small still-used Singhania well.

Near the private bus stand is a large **baori**, built by Sheikh Mohammed of Nagaur in 1614, which for a long time provoked legends about bandits hiding in its depths. There's a path to the *baori* from a lane opposite the private bus stand. Unfortunately, today the *baori* is in a shocking state of disrepair – even dangerous – and you shouldn't approach too close to the edges. It was obviously a feat of some magnitude to dig to this depth, and around the sides there's a series of arched galleries, mostly collapsed. The *baori* now has a new career as a rubbish dump. On the south side of it a *haveli* has half fallen into the well, and its courtyard paintings are exposed. The minarets of the *baori* stand as sad testament to its former grandeur.

Diagonally opposite the *baori*, on the south side of the private bus stand, the **Harikrishnan Das Saraogi Haveli** features a colourful façade with iron lacework on the upper verandas and shops at street level. There's a vibrantly coloured outer courtyard. Spot the woman smoking a hookah and, in the inner courtyard, a camel-drawn cart juxtaposed with a motorcar.

Adjacent to this *haveli* (to the south) is the **Vishnunath Keria Haveli**. The outer courtyard has some wonderful pictures on either side of the inner courtyard door that show the marriage of religion and technology. Radha and Krishna can be seen in strange gondola-like flying contraptions, one with an animal's head, the other with the front part of a vintage car, and both featuring angel-like wings. On the north wall of the outer courtyard is a portrait of King George and Queen Victoria. The paintings in the southeast corner of the inner courtyard have been badly damaged by smoke from the kitchen fire. In this courtyard, the sun god Surya is seen in a carriage being drawn by horses. On the southern external wall, pictures include Queen Victoria, a train, a holy man and Krishna playing a gramophone to Radha.

## Sleeping & Eating

Fatehpur has an unfortunate lack of good hotels.

**RTDC Hotel Haveli** (☎ 230293; dm Rs 50, s/d from Rs 200/300, with AC Rs 600/700; dishes Rs 10-75; ❄) The best of a bad bunch, about 500m south of the bus stand on the Churu–Sikar road. Rooms are nothing special but it's friendly. There's the requisite gloomy dining hall serving reasonable food.

**Hotel Ashirwad Palace** (☎ 223347; Churu Bypass; r Rs 350-900; ❄) A better option than the RTDC, but it's even further out of town. It's welcoming, however, and has a restaurant and clean rooms around a peaceful, grassy courtyard. The more deluxe rooms have grander furniture and fancy names, such as the 'Maharani Bedroom'.

**Art Café** (Haveli Nadine Prince; dishes Rs 25-80) You'll have to pay to get into the *haveli*, but this is a good option for a light lunch. It's a cosy arched place with low tables, serving food such as omelettes, toast and rum-blazed bananas, as well as some Indian snacks.

### Getting There & Around

At the private bus stand, on the Churu–Sikar road, buses leave for Jhunjhunu (Rs 17, one hour), Mandawa (Rs 8/12 in local/express, one hour), Churu (Rs 15, one hour), Ramgarh (Rs 8, 45 minutes) and Sikar (Rs 18/21 in local/express, one hour/45 minutes).

From the Roadways bus stand, which is further south down this road, buses leave for Jaipur (Rs 68, 3½ hours, every 15 minutes), Delhi (Rs 128, seven hours, six daily) and Bikaner (Rs 73, 3½ hours, hourly).

Bicycles (Rs 5/25 per hour/day) can be hired near the private bus stand.

## MANDAWA

☎ 01592 / pop 20,717

Mandawa is an excellent base, a subdued but bustling little market town with some gorgeous painted *havelis*. Settled in the 18th century, and fortified by the dominant merchant families, today it's the most touristed place in Shekhawati, with alarming numbers of antique shops, but it's still pretty relaxed. The fort was built by Sardul Singh's youngest son in 1760, though inhabited much later, and has some fine frescoes, though it's now an upmarket hotel.

### Information

There's slow Internet access at a few places, which charge Rs 40 per hour.

**State Bank of Bikaner & Jaipur** (⌚ 10am-4pm Mon-Fri, to 1pm Sat) In Binsidhar Newatia Haveli; changes travellers cheques and currency.

### Sights

**Binsidhar Newatia Haveli**, on the northern side of the Fatehpur–Jhunjhunu road, now houses the State Bank of Bikaner & Jaipur. The interior paintings have been whitewashed, but there are fantastically entertaining paintings on the external eastern wall (accessible through the bank). These include a European woman in a car driven by a chauffeur; a man on a bicycle; the Wright brothers evoking much excitement in their aeroplane as women in saris, among others, point with astonishment; a boy using a telephone; and a bird-man flying by in a winged device. The paintings date from the 1920s.

Continue west and turn right at the bus stand and then left. About 50m along are several *havelis* belonging to the Goenka family. To the right of the entrance to **Hanuman Prasad Goenka Haveli** is a composite picture that shows either Indra on an elephant or Shiva on his bull, depending on which way you look at it. Across the road is the **Goenka Double Haveli**, which has two entrance gates and monumental pictures, including of elephants and horses, on the façade.

Adjacent is the 1930s **Murmuria Haveli** – here you can see how European art, magazines and prints were beginning to influence local artists. From the sandy courtyard in front of this *haveli*, you can get a good view of the southern external wall of the adjacent double *haveli*: it features a long frieze depicting a train, with a crow flying above the engine and much activity at the railway crossing. Nehru is depicted on horseback holding the Indian flag. Above the arches on the south side of the courtyard are two paintings of gondolas on the canals of Venice.

From here a road leads south, and 50m along you can take a short detour to the right to see the impressive **Harlalka well**, marked by four pillars and its old pulley and camel ramp. Back on the road heading south, you come to a T-junction; turn left. On the next corner is the **Jhunjhunwala Haveli** (admission Rs 20), which has an impressive gold leaf–painted room to the right of the main courtyard.

About 50m southeast is the **Mohan Lal Saraf Haveli**. On the south wall, a maharaja is depicted grooming his bushy moustache. There's fine mirror- and mosaicwork around the door to the inner courtyard, and Surya, the sun god, can be seen over the lintel.

Further south on the same street is the **Lakshminarayan Ladia Haveli**. The west wall features a faded picture of a man enjoying a hookah, and a good procession frieze. Between the wall brackets, *gopis* emerge from the tentacles of a sea monster upon whose head Krishna dances. Other pictures include that of Rama slaying Ravana.

Unfortunately, many of the erotic images in the **Gulab Rai Ladia Haveli**, a short distance to the east, have been systematically defaced by prudish souls. In the last pair of brackets on the first half of the southern

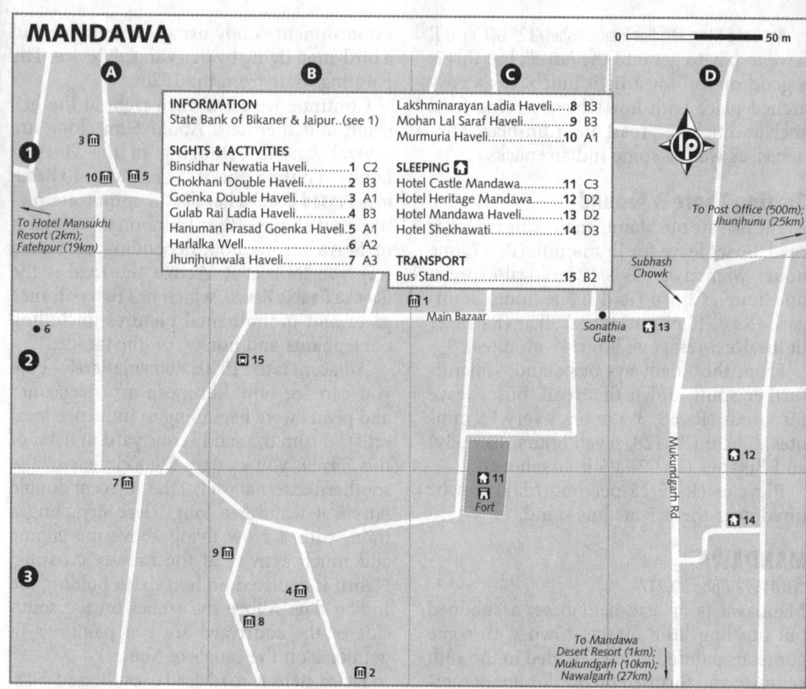


wall a woman is seen giving birth, attended by maidservants. There's an erotic image in the fifth niche from the end on this wall, but don't draw too much attention to it, or it may suffer the same fate as the other erotic art. There's also something untoward happening in a train carriage on this wall.

About 150m south past this *haveli* is the **Chokhani Double Haveli**. This dates from 1910, by which time the quality of painting was beginning to deteriorate as themes and coverage were reduced. The building, however, is rather grand. The paintings inside include floral arabesques and peacocks above the archways, as well as the Krishna legends.

## Activities

You can organise camel and horse rides at the Hotel Castle Mandawa (opposite) or the Mandawa Desert Resort (opposite). A one-hour camel ride costs Rs 500 and a half-/full-day trip is Rs 800/1100. Both can also organise horse and jeep safaris on request.

Another possibility is the Hotel Heritage Mandawa (opposite), which organises half-/full-day camel rides and longer safaris, as well as jeep hire or guide hire for around the same prices.

## Sleeping & Eating

**Hotel Mandawa Haveli** (☎ 223088; r from Rs 900, ste around Rs 2000) Close to Sonathia Gate, this hotel is in a glorious, restored 19th-century *haveli*, with rooms surround a painted courtyard. Cheaper rooms are small, so it's worth splashing out on a suite, filled with arches, window seats and countless small windows.

**Hotel Mansukhi Resort** (☎ 223657; r Rs 300-500, with AC Rs 700; ) This excellent-value place is about 2km from Mandawa. A handful of romantic round huts are well spaced out on a lawn and there are a couple of charming rooms on several levels in its main building. Bathrooms are big and clean. Free pick-up from the town is offered – contact its office on the road to the fort.

**Hotel Shekhawati** (☎ 223036; hotelshekwati@sify.com; near Mukundgarh Rd; r Rs 200-600; ) The only real budget choice in town is run by a retired bank manager and his son (who's also a registered tourist guide). Bright naive, somewhat lurid murals painted by artistic former guests give the rooms a splash of colour. Tasty meals are served on the peaceful rooftop.

**Hotel Heritage Mandawa** (☎ 223742; r Rs 400-2000; ❄) Near the Subhash Chowk is this gracious old *haveli*. The somewhat dark, sometimes clashingly decorated rooms are set around tranquil courtyards. Best are the rooms with small upstairs areas, but the cheaper rooms are good for those who want a *haveli* experience on a budget.

**Hotel Castle Mandawa** (☎ 223124; www.castlemandawa.com; s/d from Rs 2050/2650, deluxe Rs 3300/4400, ste Rs 6600-10,000; ❄) Mandawa's big upmarket hotel in a converted castle has a contrived medieval atmosphere. The building is fantastic, but the rooms are not that special – some have more charm than others, so look at a few. Staff are uninterested.

**Mandawa Desert Resort** (☎ 252519; in Jaipur ☎ 0141-2371194; www.castlemandawa.com; s/d Rs 2050/2650, cottages Rs 3300/4400, ste Rs 6600-10,000; ❄ 🏊) A top-end resort, also run by Castle Mandawa, this is laid out in the style of a Rajasthani village. The spacious rooms, in mud-walled huts decorated with twinkling mirrorwork, are a lot plusher than your average village home and have big bathrooms. If hut life is not for you, there are suites in a traditional-style *haveli*. It's in a pretty spot too, but all a bit unreal.

### Getting There & Away

There are buses to Nawalgarh (Rs 10, 45 minutes), Fatehpur (Rs 8/12 in local/express, one hour), Bissau (Rs 12, 1½ hours) and Ramgarh (Rs 16, 1½ hours). There are also direct buses to Jaipur (Rs 67, four hours) – change at Fatehpur – and Bikaner (Rs 60, 3½ hours). A taxi between Mandawa and Fatehpur costs Rs 250 (one way), or you can take a crammed share jeep for Rs 10.

## LAKSHMANGARH

**☎ 01573 / pop 47,288**

Off the tourist track, 20km south of Fatehpur, this is an unusual town, laid out in an easy-to-explore grid pattern, with a main north–south oriented bazaar dissected at intervals by three busy *chaupars* (town squares formed by the intersection of major roads).

The most imposing building here is the small fortress, which looms over the township to its west. The fort was built by Lakshman Singh, the raja of Sikar, in the early 19th century after the prosperous town was besieged by Kan Singh Saledhi.

### Sights

About 50m north of the bus stand through the busy bazaar, a wide cobblestone path wends its way up to the eastern side of the **fort**. A sign warns that the fort is private property, but there's a good view from the top of the ramp before you get to the main entrance. From here you can see the layout of the double Char Chowk Haveli, below and to the northeast. Head for this when you descend the ramp.

Beneath the eaves on the northern external wall of the **Char Chowk Haveli**, there's a picture of a bird standing on an elephant with another elephant in its beak. The large paintings on the façade of the northern *haveli* have mostly faded, and the paintings in the outer downstairs courtyard are covered by blue wash. The murals in the inner courtyard, however, are well preserved, and the walls and ceiling of a small upstairs room on the east side of the northern *haveli* are completely covered with paintings. It has some explicit erotic images, but it's ill-lit, so you'll need a torch to see them properly.

In the same building, a room in the northwest corner retains floral swirls and motifs on the ceiling with scenes from the Krishna legends interspersed with inlaid mirrors. The black-and-white rectangular designs on the lower walls create a marbled effect. No-one lives in the *haveli*, but the caretaker may open it for you (for baksheesh). The front façade is disintegrating at the lower levels, with the plaster crumbling and the bricks exposed. The southern *haveli* is still inhabited by about 30 people.

About 50m east of this *haveli* is the large **Radhi Murlimanohar Temple** (1845), which retains a few paintings beneath the eaves and some sculptures of deities around the external walls.

If you take the road west from the temple, on the corner of the second laneway on the right is the **Chetram Sanganeeria Haveli**. The lower paintings on the west wall are badly damaged; the plaster has peeled away and concrete rendering has been applied. But you can spot a woman on a swing suspended from a tree, a woman spinning, a man dancing on a pole while balancing some knives, people enjoying a ride on a Ferris wheel, a man ploughing fields with oxen, and men sawing timber.

A little to the south of the temple is the busy **bazaar**, flanked by shops whose overhanging balconies have three scalloped open arches between two blank arches, which have lattice friezes. The shops were constructed during the mid-19th century by a branch of the Poddar family known as the Ganeriwala, who hailed from the village of Ganeri.

On the northeast corner of the clock tower square, about 100m south of the temple via the busy bazaar, is the **Rathi Family Haveli**. On the west wall, a European woman in a smart red frock sews on a treadle machine. The European influence is much in evidence here, with painted roses and a Grecian column effect. On the south side of this *haveli* are ostentatious flourishes and the British crown flanked by unicorns. On the east side are some blue-eyed British soldiers and a railway station (with a sign saying 'a railway station' in case it wasn't clear enough).

There's a busy set of chai stalls on the west side of the *haveli*, a good place to sit down and admire these extraordinarily over-the-top paintings.

### Getting There & Away

There are many buses between Lakshmangarh and both Sikar (Rs 12) and Fatehpur (Rs 10), as well as Nawalgarh (Rs 10).

### Getting Around

A bicycle shop just to the south of Radhi Murlimanohar Temple hires out bikes for a nominal price.

## CHURU

☎ 01562 / pop 97,627

Churu is not technically part of Shekhawati, being over the border in Bikaner district, but it has a Shekhawat heart. It was a centre of trade and commerce, and the many rich merchant families who hailed from here left a legacy of fine painted *havelis*. About 95km to the southwest of Churu is the small Tal Chhapar Wildlife Sanctuary (opposite), home to a substantial population of blackbucks and other mammals and birds.

### Sights

You'll need help (ask a local) to find the **Malji ka Kamra**, to the north of the bus stand, down a lane on the west side of the main bazaar. It's worth the effort to find this place: it's an extraordinary edifice covered in pale-blue stucco and perched on green pillars like a minty baroque wedding cake, nowadays splattered in pigeon pooh and housing rubbish-grazing cows. Statues on the façade include a bored-looking woman dressed in a sari (with a handbag and wings), turbaned men, and angels. Built in 1925, its days of glory are long gone.

A short distance to the northwest (within easy walking distance) is the five-storey **Surana Double Haveli**, packed with hundreds of rectangular windows and achieving something of a Georgian effect. On the lower levels of the west wall are fragments of paintings, including processions and peacocks. The *haveli* is beyond an archway at the end of a narrow laneway.

A further 100m to the northwest is the **Surajmal Banthia Haveli**, which was built in the 1920s. It's best known for its infamous picture of a laconic Christ enjoying a cigar, on the external north wall, rather incongruously juxtaposed beside a British lady. Across the lane to the north is a **haveli** with what may well be the most bizarre paintings on any of the *havelis* of Shekhawati – beneath the eaves on the eastern side is a series of inverted paintings of naked men fondling rabbits!

### Sleeping & Eating

Not many travellers choose to stay in Churu, but if you do find yourself here for a night there's one reasonable hotel, although English can be a problem.

**Hotel Deluxe** (☎ 251114; d Rs 250) Faces the private bus stand and offers small, grimy rooms. There's a restaurant downstairs that cooks up unassuming veg fare at modest prices.

### Getting There & Away

The Roadways bus stand is 500m west of the private one. Regular services to destinations in Shekhawati from the private bus stand include Fatehpur (Rs 15, one hour), Jhunjhunu (Rs 18/25 in local/express, around 1½ hours) and Sikar (Rs 30, two hours). From the Roadways bus stand there are services to Delhi (Rs 125, six hours) and Jaipur (Rs 85, five hours).

The train station is 100m north of the private bus stand. To get to Bikaner, the train takes approximately four hours (Rs 31 in 2nd class). There are trains to Delhi (Rs 421/145 in first class/sleeper, eight to nine hours) and to Jaipur (Rs 495/121 in 2AC/sleeper, 5½ hours).

## AROUND CHURU

### Tal Chhapar Wildlife Sanctuary

This little-known, small grassland sanctuary, which lies about 95km southwest of Churu and 210km northwest of Jaipur, covers 70 sq km. It has healthy populations of blackbucks, elegant creatures with long spiralling horns, as well as fast, graceful chinkaras (Indian gazelles), wolves, and smaller mammals such as desert foxes. The sanctuary lies on the migration route of a number of bird species, most notably harriers, which descend here during September. Other wintering birds include various types of eagle (tawny, imperial, short-toed, steppe), and the demoiselle crane. Throughout the year there are populations of crested larks, ring and brown doves and skylarks.

It's best to visit the sanctuary between November and March. There's a forest rest-house at Chhapar. For more information, contact the **tourist office** (☎ 0141-2375466) in Jaipur.

# Western Rajasthan

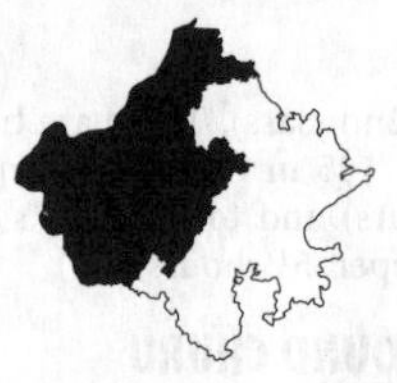

Rama, hero of the Ramayana, fuming with incandescent rage with the sea god who policed the straits between India and Lanka (Sri Lanka), resolved to fire a destructive arrow at the god. However, in the nick of time the sea god apologised to Rama, so Rama switched the arrow's aim and fired it off into the northwest. Thus arose the desolate wastelands of western Rajasthan, which encompass Jodhpur, Jaisalmer, Barmer and Bikaner.

Here is the vast Great Thar Desert, its barren sandy scrub extending into the Punjab, Haryana and Gujarat, and into Pakistan. It's India's only desert, and the world's most populous arid zone. Desert culture, elemental struggles and mighty forts make up part of western Rajasthan's unique atmosphere, and the region contains some powerfully evocative towns. It's as if the glory of the great caravan trade routes has been preserved in the dryness of the air. Jaisalmer, the Golden City, rears up from the blank, flat plains of the Thar like a huge sand castle. Jodhpur, the Blue City, spreads out from beneath the shadow of mighty Meherangarh – a fort of dizzying splendour. Bikaner has no allotted colour, but the narrow medieval streets of its old city are a dusty, dirty red. Its fort, Junagarh, has some of Rajasthan's most luxurious interiors.

The west is where you can take a desert safari on camelback, see brilliantly clothed villagers mark the landscape like daubs of paint, and ride through strange, dry, warped landscapes, deserted villages and night skies swarming with stars.

**HIGHLIGHTS**

- Soaring, magnificent **Meherangarh** (p309), overlooking Jodhpur's crazy blue maze
- **Havelis** (p331) in Jaisalmer – like lace carved from sand
- Fairy-tale, ancient **Jaisalmer Fort** (p328) – the closest architecture gets to a sand castle
- **Camel safaris** from Jaisalmer (p334), Khuri (p342), Bikaner (p348) and Osiyan (p322) – the best way to bump around Rajasthan's desert, and you get to sleep under the stars
- Holy rats! – rodents eat sweets, drink milk and run over your feet at **Karni Mata Temple** (p353) in Deshnok
- **Demoiselle cranes** (p323) filling the skies over Khichan

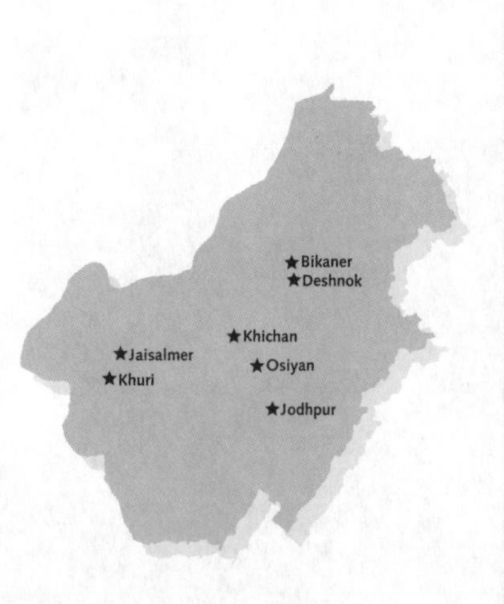

## History

The district of Jodhpur was for a long time the ancient kingdom of Marwar, the largest kingdom in Rajputana and the third largest in India, after Kashmir and Hyderabad.

The region's history is hazy until the 3rd century BC. The indigenous inhabitants were subjugated by the Aryans during their invasion of northern India between 1500 and 200 BC. In 231 BC Chandragupta Maurya's empire came to power, spreading across northern India from its capital at present-day Patna, in Bihar. Subsequent centuries saw a bit of pass the parcel until the Rathore Rajputs, who hailed from Kannauj in present-day Uttar Pradesh, came out on top, ousting the local tribal leaders. This is when the state of Marwar emerged. The Rathores originally settled at Pali, southeast of present-day Jodhpur, shifting to Mandore in 1381. In 1459 Rao Jodha, the Rathore leader, moved the capital about 9km to the south and founded the city of Jodhpur.

Jaisalmer was founded in the 12th century, after the Bhati Rajput capital at Lodharva had been destroyed by Mohammed of Ghori. After experiencing great unrest in the medieval period, Jaisalmer enjoyed a heyday from the 16th century to the 18th century, when it was a stop on an important international trade route.

Meanwhile, the Muslims were entrenched at Nagaur. Mohammed Bahlim, the governor of Sind, erected a fort there in 1122,

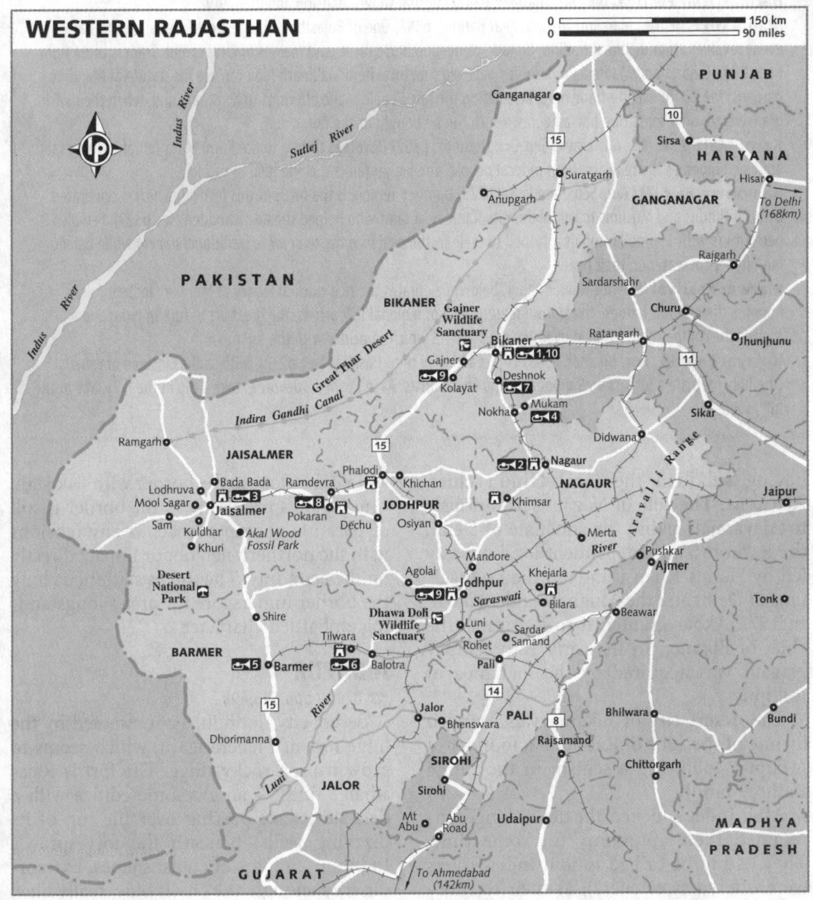

## FESTIVALS IN WESTERN RAJASTHAN

Western Rajasthan's festivals, usually starring camels, splash colour against the desert. (For details of statewide and nationwide festivals, see p363.) Festivals in this boxed text are marked on Map p305.

**Bikaner Camel Festival** (❶; Jan-Feb; Bikaner, p343) Organised by the Department of Tourism, this festival sees dressed-up camels and best-breed competitions, camel dances and tugs-of-war, processions, and races.

**Nagaur Fair** (❷; Jan-Feb; Nagaur, p321) A week-long cattle and camel fair – more about serious trading and thus more authentic than most. The fair attracts thousands of rural people from far and wide – and, this being Rajasthan, it does have its share of song, dance, camel fashion and trinket traders.

**Jaisalmer Desert Festival** (❸; Jan-Feb; Jaisalmer, p325) Everything is even more light-hearted and tourist focused at this festival, which has camel races and dances, folk music, traditional ballads, puppeteers, turban-tying contests and the famous Mr Desert competition. Many events take place on the Sam sand dunes, which provide a spectacular, undulating sandy backdrop for the mayhem.

**Jambeshwar Fair** (❹; Feb-Mar; Mukam, Bikaner, p343) This honours the founder of the Bishnoi sect (see p319) and draws pilgrims from many states. At Guru Jambhoji's temple in Mukam people offer grain, which is used to feed birds on special platforms around the temple.

**Barmer Thar Festival** (❺; Mar; Barmer, p342) Cultural shows, dancing and puppetry.

**Mallinath Fair** (❻; Mar-Apr; Tilwara, near Barmer, p342) One of Rajasthan's biggest cattle fairs, this 14-day event revolves around animal trading, bullock, camel and horse races, and masses of local colour. Traders come from Rajasthan, Gujarat and Madhya Pradesh. It's believed that local hero Mallinath (you can see his statute at Mandore gardens; see p318) used to trade here, originating the fair. People make offerings to his shrine and, when their wish is answered, offer miniature horse figures, which can be bought at the fair.

**Karni Mata Fair** (❼; Apr-May & Sep-Oct; Deshnok, p352) Devotees throng to the Karni Mata Temple, where rats are worshipped as the reincarnations of local people. The bigger fair is the one held in spring.

**Ramdevra Fair** (❽; Aug-Sep; Ramdevra, p323) Ramdev Temple is the focus of this festival, which is celebrated by both Hindus and Muslims to commemorate Ramdev, a saint who helped the downtrodden (see p323). Female performers with 13 small cymbals attached to their costumes dance the *terahtal* (a traditional dance) while balancing pitchers of water on their heads.

**Marwar Festival** (❾; Oct-Nov; Jodhpur, below) Celebrates the rich cultural legacy of Marwar (Jodhpur) and honours the region's heroes. The festival features lots of regional folk artists, the great art of turban tying and a moustache competition. It's held over two days, one of which coincides with the full moon.

**Kolayat Fair** (❿; Nov; Bikaner, p343) This is a kind of mini-Pushkar (see p212), with sadhus instead of camels (the holy men are a lot less well groomed) and few tourists. As in Pushkar, devotees take a dip in the holy lake at the full moon.

having subdued the local Hindu chief, Ajayaraja. The rule of Nagaur fell variously to Ajayaraja (again), the sultanate of Delhi, the Rathores, an independent local dynasty led by Shams Khan Dandani, the Lodi sultans of Delhi and the Mughals under Akbar. In 1572 Akbar granted it to Raisimha, the chief of Bikaner. In the early 18th century Nagaur was acquired by the maharaja of Jodhpur.

The desert city of Bikaner was founded by one of the sons of Rao Jodha, founder of Jodhpur, following a schism in the ruling Rathore family.

After Independence, the desert kingdoms retained their autonomy for some time. They had to be bribed to join India (rulers were offered sweeteners), as their territory was vital – close to the border with Pakistan. The region's proximity to the border is still of paramount importance, as any tensions with the northern neighbour impact directly on the economy. The forces stationed along the border underscore the area's longstanding embattled character.

## JODHPUR

**☎ 0291 / pop 846,408**

A desert city, Jodhpur is dominated by the huge fort of Meherangarh, which seems to grow from a rocky ridge. The fort is Rajasthan's finest – an awesome edifice with a delicate palace peering over the top of its dizzying walls. Beneath the fort sprawls Jodhpur – a mass of cubist shapes. Extraordinarily enough, the city is blue, really blue, with many of its buildings painted as though to reflect the colour of a hot sky.

Jodhpur is at its bluest in the old city, surrounded by a 10km-long, 16th-century wall, a tangle of winding, glittering streets, scented by incense, roses and sewers, with shops selling everything from trumpets and temple decorations to snuff and saris. Traditionally, blue signified the home of a Brahmin, but non-Brahmins have got in on the act, too. As well as glowing with a mysterious light, the colour is thought to repel insects.

A very hectic place cluttered with traffic, Jodhpur feels poorer and less developed than the cities of the east. Be prepared for some hassle, particularly around the clock tower and up to the fort. You can escape this by diving into the heart of the old city (west of the clock tower), with its jewel-like, back-in-time bazaars.

## History

Driven from their homeland of Kannauj by Afghans serving Mohammed of Ghori, the Rathores fled west to the region around Pali, a short distance to the south of Jodhpur. An expedient marriage between the Rathore Siahaji and the sister of a local prince enabled the Rathores to take root in the region. They prospered to such a degree that they managed to oust the Pratiharas of Mandore, 9km to the north of present-day Jodhpur.

By 1459 it became evident that more secure headquarters were required. The rocky ridge 9km to the south of Mandore was an obvious choice for the new city of Jodhpur. The natural fortifications afforded by its steep flanks were greatly enhanced by a fortress of staggering proportions (see p309).

Founded by Rao Jodha, from whom it takes its name, the city lay on the vital trade route between Delhi and Gujarat. It grew out of the profits of opium, sandalwood, dates and copper, and controlled a large area. Rathore kingdom was once cheerily known as Marwar (the Land of Death) due to its harsh topography and climate.

A war for independence and struggles for succession dominated the 17th and 18th centuries, which saw much unrest. However, the 19th century saw the commencement of competent rule by Sir Pratap Singh (of Jodhpurs fame – see Jodhpur's Jodhpurs, below), followed by Maharaja Umaid Singh. Thus Jodhpur – Rajasthan's largest kingdom – was reasonably stable when it came to Independence in 1947.

## Orientation

The Tourist Reception Centre, train stations and bus stand are all outside the old city. High Court Rd runs from Raika Bagh train station, past the Umaid gardens, and round beside the city wall towards the main train station and the main post office. Trains from the east stop at the Raika Bagh station before heading on to the main station, which is handy if you're staying at a hotel on the eastern side of town.

Watch out in Jodhpur for similarly named places – some businesses take on remarkably unoriginal names, closely resembling a thriving local business, in order to confuse travellers (this doesn't only happen in the hotel business – check out the number of clone-named spice and even omelette shops around the clock tower).

## Information

There's a UTI ATM near LKP Forex, and there are ICICI and IDBI ATMs on Airport Rd.

**Bank of Baroda** (Map p308; Sojati Gate) Issues cash advances against Visa and MasterCard.

**International Tourists Bureau** (☎ 2439052; ⏰ 5am-11.30pm Mon-Sat) At the main train station, the bureau provides help for foreign passengers. It's a handy place to hang around while waiting for a train. There are comfortable armchairs and a shower and toilet here. Unattended luggage must be deposited in the train station cloakroom (Rs 10 per piece for 24 hours).

### JODHPUR'S JODHPURS

Jodhpurs are baggy-tight aristocratic riding breeches – a fashion staple, worn by self-respecting horsey people all around the world. Usually a pale cream colour, they're loose above the knee and tapered from knee to ankle. It's said that Sir Pratap Singh, a virtuoso horseman, designed the breeches for hunting and polo, and also brought them to a wider public by wearing them on trips abroad.

JODHPUR
0 1 km
0 0.5 miles
A
B
C
D
1
2
3
4
5
6
To Maha Mandir (2km); Balsamand Lake (7km); Mandore (7km); Osiyan (65km); Khimsar (95km); Nagaur (135km)
Nagauri Gate
See Meherangarh Map (p310)
Meherangarh
Navchokiya
Sadar Market
Nai Sarak
Umaid Gardens
Raika Bagh Train Station
To Ajmer (205km); Jaipur (336km)
High Court Rd
Sojati Gate
Mohanpura Overbridge
Circuit House
Palace Rd
Gavshala Rd
Siwanchi Gate
Ranchodji Temple
Jalori Gate
Pal Link Rd
Station Rd
Jodhpur Train Station
Chopasani Rd
Ratanada Rd
Old Loco Shed Rd
Airport Rd
Umaid Bhawan Rd
To Dhawa Doli Wildlife Sanctuary (40km); Barmer (150km)
To Rohet (40km); Sardar Samand (66km); Bhenswara (130km); Udaipur (260km); Mt Abu (326km)
Residency Rd
Bhatia Circle
Ratanada Circle
To Devi Bhawan (150m); Airport (3km)
To Madho Niwas (150m); Newtons Manor (800m); Sadar Club (1.3km)
INFORMATION
Bank of Baroda 1 B3
ICICI ATM 2 D4
IDBI ATM 3 D4
LKP Forex 4 D3
Main Post Office 5 B3
Rathi's Media Centre 6 B3
Reliance Webworld 7 B3
Sarvodaya Bookstall 8 B3
State Bank of India 9 C2
Tourist Reception Centre 10 C3
UTI ATM (see 1)
SIGHTS & ACTIVITIES
Clock Tower 11 B2
Jaswant Thada 12 B1
Rajasthan Sangeet Natak Akademi Folk Art Museum 13 C3
Sadar Government Museum 14 C3
Umaid Bhawan Palace & Museum 15 D4
Zoo 16 C3
SLEEPING
Ajit Bhawan 17 D3
Blue House 18 B3
Cosy Guest House 19 A2
Durag Niwas Guest House 20 C3
Durag Villas Guest House (see 20)
Durjan Niwas Hotel 21 B4
Govind Hotel 22 B3
Haveli Guest House 23 B2
Hotel City Palace 24 B3
Hotel Kalinga 25 B3
Inn Season 26 B4
Karni Bhawan 27 D5
Pal Haveli 28 B2
Ranbanka 29 D3
Ratan Vilas 30 B4
Shivam Paying Guest House 31 B2
Singhvi's Haveli 32 A2
Taj Hari Mahal Palace 33 B4
Tourist Guest House 34 C3
EATING
Agra Sweets 35 B3
Garden Restaurant 36 D3
Hotel Priya & Restaurant 37 B3
Jodhpur Coffee House (see 40)
Kalinga Restaurant (see 25)
Mid Town 38 B3
Omelette Shop 39 B2
On the Rocks (see 17)
Pokar Sweets (see 37)
Poonam Restaurant 40 B3
Pushpa Bhojnalya Dining Hall 41 A3
Shri Mishrilal Hotel 42 B2
Sweet Shops 43 A3
SHOPPING
Antique Shops 44 D3
Handloom House 45 B3
Khadi Shop 46 B3
MV Spices 47 B2
TRANSPORT
Indian Airlines 48 C4
Railway Booking Office 49 B3
Roadways Bus Stand 50 D2
Taxi Stand 51 B4

**LKP Forex** (Map p308; ☎ 2512066; shop No 1, Mahareer Palace) Opposite Circuit House. Changes currencies and travellers cheques.

**Main post office** (Map p308; Station Rd; ⏰ 10am-5pm Mon-Fri, 10am-1pm Sat) Less than 500m north of the main train station.

**Rathi's Media Centre** (Map p308; Mohanpura Overbridge; ⏰ 7am-9pm) Stocks a reasonable range of books in English, including novels and recent releases, and lots of magazines.

**Reliance Webworld** (Map p308; Nai Sarak; per hr Rs 30; ⏰ 10.30am-11pm) The best of many cheap Internet places (usually Rs 20 per hour, and usually slow) around town. Offers broadband.

**Sarvodaya Bookstall** (Map p308; ⏰ 8.30am-10.30pm) Off Station Rd, opposite Ranchodji Temple. Sarvodaya has English-language newspapers and magazines, a good range of books on India and a few Western novels. It also stocks some good maps of Rajasthan.

**State Bank of India** (Map p308; ☎ 2543649; ⏰ 10am-4pm Mon-Fri, 10am-1pm Sat) Changes currency and travellers cheques.

**Tourist Reception Centre** (Map p308; ☎ 2545083; ⏰ 8am-8pm Mon-Sat) In the RTDC Hotel Ghoomar compound. Offers a free map.

## Sights

### MEHERANGARH

Still run by the maharaja of Jodhpur, **Meherangarh** (Majestic Fort; Map p310; Indian admission/camera/audio guide Rs 20/50/150, foreigner incl camera & audio guide Rs 250; ⏰ 9am-5pm) is a captivating place to visit. Following the lines of a 125m hill, the fort's height becomes apparent as you approach. It's a mesmerising, formidable feat of construction. The battlements are 6m to 36m high. As the building materials were chiselled from the rock on which the fort stands, the structure seems to merge with and grow from its base. The fort was added to over the centuries by reigning Jodhpur maharajas. A winding road leads up to the entrance from the city, 5km below.

Cast off your audio-tour prejudices, as this tour (in multiple languages) is terrific. The mix of history, information and anecdote make it really entertaining. It's a real treat to wander around at your leisure, taking a fix of information when you feel like it. However, if you prefer a real person, guides are available for around Rs 100.

The fort's seven *pols* (gates) include the **Jayapol**, built by Maharaja Man Singh in 1806 following his victory over the rulers of Jaipur and Bikaner. This is the main entrance to the fort. Beyond it is the ticket office, where there's a lift (Rs 15) that will whisk disabled or weary travellers to the top of the fort. The walls at the entrance are still scarred by cannonball hits, showing that this was a fort that earned its keep. To the left, just beyond the ticket office, is the **Chhatri of Kiratsingh Sodha**. This cenotaph was built over the site where a soldier fell defending Jodhpur against Jaipurians in 1806.

Built in the 16th-century, **Imritiapol** is arranged at the top of a slope, after a sharp turn, in order to stop onslaughts by an enemy's elephants. The **Fatehpol** (Victory Gate), at the southwestern side of the fort, was erected by Maharaja Ajit Singh to commemorate his defeat of the Mughals.

The next gate is the **Lohapol** (Iron Gate), again built at the top of the slope, just beyond a bend. Its iron spikes were a further elephant deterrent. Beside the gate are 15 tiny handprints, the *sati* (self-immolation) marks of Maharaja Man Singh's widows, who threw themselves on his funeral pyre in 1843 – the last *sati* widows of the Jodhpur dynasty. The handprints still attract devotional attention, and are usually covered in red powder and paper-thin silver.

Inside the fort is a terracotta-latticed network of courtyards and palaces, all beautiful examples of the asymmetry and symmetry that mark Rajput buildings. **Surajpol** leads to the museum. Through the gate you'll find **Singhar Chowk**, where coronations take place. The small marble seat was used for coronations from the 17th century.

The **museum** holds a splendid collection Indian royal trappings, showing the wealth and power of the Marwars, including Rajasthan's best collection of elephant howdahs (seats for carrying people on elephants' backs – essential for glittering processions). Some feature the most exquisite repoussé (raised relief) silverwork. There are also maharajas' palanquins, including covered palanquins for the women in purdah (seclusion). Apparently one of these sent the British media into a frenzy when the maharajas visited – the press were all desperate to get a picture of the hidden queen. One photographer caught a picture of her foot, but there was such an outcry when it was published that all the newspapers in which it was printed had to be recalled. Perhaps the finest palanquin is that presented to

Jaswant Singh I by the Emperor Shah Jahan; it's exquisitely worked in silver and gold, and has a natty little umbrella to beat the heat. The museum also has some splendid miniatures and, as you might expect, the armoury is impressive – each weapon is a work of art, its beauty sitting strangely alongside its deadliness. Also on display is some wonderful ephemera, such as 19th-century ivory-inlaid ladies' dumbbells and camel-bone carpet weights.

Within the complex are numerous small palaces with evocative names, such as the Sukh Mahal (Pleasure Palace). Upstairs is the **Phool Mahal** (Flower Palace), in which traditional dances were performed. It was also used as a durbar hall (see p253) by former maharajas. The fine paintings adorning the walls of this palace were executed by a single artist, who took 10 years to create them using a curious concoction of gold leaf, glue and cow's urine. The artist passed away before the work was finished, which is evident in the bare patch to the left of the hallway. The gold ceiling is embellished with over 80kg of gold plate, and around it the various maharajas of Jodhpur are depicted. Stained glass further adds to the room's opulence.

## MEHERANGARH

0 – 200 m
0 – 0.1 miles

**SIGHTS & ACTIVITIES**

| | | |
|---|---|---|
| Astrologer | (see 8) | |
| Chamunda Devi Temple | 1 | A4 |
| Chhatri of Kiratsingh Sodha | 2 | B3 |
| Fatehpol | 3 | A4 |
| Imritiapol | 4 | B3 |
| Jayapol | 5 | B3 |
| Lift | 6 | B3 |
| Lohapol | 7 | B3 |
| Moti Mahal | 8 | B3 |
| Museum | 9 | B3 |
| Phool Mahal | 10 | B3 |
| Singhar Chowk | 11 | B3 |
| Surajpol | 12 | B3 |
| Thakhat Vilas | 13 | B3 |
| Zenana | 14 | B3 |

**SLEEPING**

| | | |
|---|---|---|
| Hill View Guest House | 15 | B3 |
| Yogi's Guest House | 16 | B4 |

**EATING**

| | | |
|---|---|---|
| Café Mehran | 17 | B3 |
| Mehran Terrace | 18 | B3 |

Also on view is **Thakhat Vilas**, the private chamber of Maharaja Thakhat Singh (r 1843–73), who had no less than 30 maharanis and numerous concubines. The beautiful ceiling is distractingly adorned with lac painting and hung with Christmas baubles.

Nearby, in the zenana (women's apartments), the **Zhanki Mahal** has cradles of infant princes, including that of the current maharaja – a motorised version. From the zenana the women would peep at palatial goings-on through the latticed windows, the screens of which are said to feature over 250 different designs.

Next is an impressive marble-floored courtyard called **Holi Chowk**, as this is where the maharaja and friends would celebrate Holi. On its right is the early-17th-century **Moti Mahal** (Pearl Palace), where royal women would hold meetings. The walls are coated with seashell dust. The five alcoves along the western wall and the other tiny alcoves were for oil lamps. The gold-painted ceiling is embellished with glass tiles.

At the southern end of the fort, cannons look out from the ramparts over the sheer drop to the old town beneath. There are magical, stupendous views, and you can clearly hear the voices and city sounds swept up by the air currents. Aldous Huxley noted this in *Jesting Pilate – An Intellectual Holiday* (George H Doran Co, 1926):

> From the bastions of the Jodhpur Fort one hears as the Gods must hear from Olympus – the Gods to whom each separate word uttered in the innumerable peopled world below, comes up distinct and individual to be recorded in the books of omniscience.

The peaceful **Chamunda Devi Temple**, dedicated to the goddess Durga (the Inaccessible, a form of Devi) in her wrathful aspect, stands at this end of the fort. This is a lovely place to sit in the window alcoves and overlook the city below.

Just near Surajpol is classy eatery **Café Mehran** (Map p310; 9am-5pm), offering snacks and some simple meals. A restaurant spectacularly situated on the fort ramparts is open in the evenings (see p315).

### JASWANT THADA

This milk-white marble **memorial** (Map p308; Indian/foreigner Rs 10/20, camera Rs 25; 9am-5pm) to Maharaja Jaswant Singh II is an array of whimsical domes about 1km from the fort. It's a welcome peaceful spot after the hubbub of the city, and the view across to the fort is superb. The cenotaph, built in 1899, was followed by the royal crematorium and the three other cenotaphs that stand nearby. There are carved wooden doors and marble jali (lattice) work over the windows. Brought 240km from Makrana, the marble used to build the monuments is now translucent in places. Look out for the memorial to a peacock that flew into a funeral pyre.

The cenotaph is fronted by a little garden of flowering shrubs. It's the definitive tomb with a view.

### CLOCK TOWER & MARKETS

The **clock tower** (Map p308) is an old city landmark, surrounded by the vibrant Sardar Market. The market's lines of shops are an impressive example of 19th-century town planning and a wonderful place to ramble around. Narrow alleys bustle with commerce and tiny cubbyhole outlets. Heading westwards from here, you go deep into the old city's commercial heart, with alleys leading to bazaars selling vegetables, spices, sweets, silver and handicrafts.

### RAJASTHAN SANGEET NATAK AKADEMI FOLK ART MUSEUM

This academy, established in 1938, has the gigantic task of preserving the traditional folk art, dance, drama and music of Rajasthan. You might need to rustle someone up to open the little **museum** (Map p308; ☎ 2544090; www.sangeetraj.org; Town Hall, High Court Rd; admission Rs 5; 10am-5pm Tue-Sun), but it's well worth the effort. There are beautiful puppets, an amazing array of rare traditional instruments and other exhibits on the performing arts. Unfortunately, there's not much information in English. The academy also organises regular performances of music, dance and theatre (call for details).

### UMAID GARDENS & SADAR GOVERNMENT MUSEUM

The pleasant **Umaid gardens** contain the **Sadar Government Museum** (Map p308; admission Rs 3; 10am-4.30pm Sat-Thu), which feels charmingly frozen somewhere in the 19th century. The ill-labelled exhibits in dusty cabinets include weapons and 6th- to 10th-century sculptures, as well as the obligatory motheaten stuffed animals. The military section includes wooden biplane models.

There's also a desultory **zoo** (Map p308; admission Rs 3; 10am-5pm Sat-Thu) in the grounds.

### UMAID BHAWAN PALACE & MUSEUM

Sometimes called the Chittar Palace, because local Chittar sandstone was used to build it, this immense pink-and-white **palace** (Map p308) was begun in 1929. The 365-room monster was designed by the British Royal Institute of Architects president for Maharaja Umaid Singh, and took 3000 workers 15 years to complete, at a cost of around Rs 11,000,000. The building is mortarless, and incorporates Italian marble and Burmese teak in the interior. It was built surprisingly close to Independence, after which the maharajas and their grand extravagances were a thing of the past. Apparently the construction was motivated as a royal job-creation programme during a time of severe drought – very philanthropic.

Umaid Singh died in 1947, four years after the palace was completed; the current maharaja, Maharaja Gaj Singh II (known as Bapji), still lives in part of the building. The rest has been turned into a suitably grand hotel (see p315).

Most interesting in the **museum** (Indian/foreigner Rs 15/50) are the photos showing the strange Art Deco/1970s-gangster-chic design of the palace interior. The museum also has beautifully crafted weapons; an array of stuffed leopards; an enormous banner presented by Queen Victoria to Maharaja Jaswant Singh Bahadur in 1877; human-sized Chinese urns and other fine china; and a fantastic clock collection, including specimens shaped like windmills and lighthouses. Attendants will ensure that you don't stray into the hotel, but you can peer at the soaring domed central hall. Alternatively, you can visit the hotel to eat at one of its restaurants (see p316).

## Activities

### ASTROLOGY

Astrologer **Mr Sharma** (Map p310; ☎ 2548790, ext 39; ⏰ 9am-1pm & 2-5pm) has been studying astrology for over 30 years. Don't wear nail polish if you intend to get a reading, as the nails are used to ascertain your state of health. Mr Sharma charges Rs 150/300 for a basic 15-minute/detailed 30-minute consultation at his office in the Moti Mahal section of the fort. He can also offer a private consultation, for which you'll need a booking.

### GOLF

There's a golf course at **Sadar Club** (Off Map p308; ⏰ 1-11pm), south of Jodhpur in Ratanada. The brown grounds offer some challenging shots for golfers. Expect to pay Rs 100 for 18 holes, including equipment. A caddie costs Rs 20 and equipment is Rs 50. Popular with the British during the Raj, the club is about 100 years old, but has been revamped over the last few years. However, it still has a sense of history: you can see the damage inflicted on part of the building when it was bombed during the first war between India and Pakistan.

## Tours

The Tourist Reception Centre runs **city tours** (Rs 90, admission fees extra; ⏰ 9am-1pm & 2-6pm), taking in the Umaid Bhawan Palace, Meherangarh, Jaswant Thada and Mandore gardens (see p318).

Jodhpur is known for its interesting village safaris, which visit the nearby villages of the Bishnoi, a people whose belief in the sanctity of the environment and the need to protect trees and animals dates from the 15th century. See p318 for more information.

It's a well-worn trail, visiting potters and *dhurrie* (carpet) weavers, so it can feel touristy – it depends how good your guide is. However, you have the chance to meet the local people as they go about their daily lives, have a traditional lunch at one of the villages and stop at a few crafts outlets. Visitors are sometimes invited to share *amal* (an opium preparation), which is traditionally offered to guests. Just about every hotel can organise these excursions; all charge around Rs 350 to 450 per person for a half-day tour, including lunch. Recommended places include **Singhvi's Haveli** (Map p308; ☎ 2624293), **Durag Niwas Guest House** (Map p308; ☎ 2512385), **Durag Villas Guest House** (Map p308; ☎ 2512298) and **Govind Hotel** (Map p308; ☎ 2622758).

**Shivam Paying Guest House** (Map p308; ☎ 2610688) arranges recommended trips to villages around Osiyan (see p321), 65km north of Jodhpur, where you can take a camel or jeep safari and stay overnight in a village.

**Cosy Guest House** (Map p308; ☎ 2612066) and the **Govind Hotel** (Map p308; ☎ 2622758) can also arrange trips out to Osiyan.

## Sleeping

As usual, if a rickshaw driver is clamouring to take you somewhere, it's because he is going to receive a juicy commission. For anywhere near the clock tower, you can avoid this by getting dropped at the tower and walking the rest. When you ask this, some rickshaw drivers ask 'Which clock tower?' to confuse you. There's only one.

Staying around the clock tower is convenient for the fort and shopping district, and there's a cluster of mainly budget guesthouses here, but it's also where you'll encounter the most hassle. The places around Navchokiya in the old city are quieter.

Prices everywhere fluctuate according to how many tourists are around. If it's busy, prices will often go up, while at quiet times you can get big discounts.

Like most tourist centres in Rajasthan, there are far more budget choices than midrange options. However, the quality of accommodation in all categories is good, with an excellent range of characterful options. Rates for all places listed in this chapter include private bathrooms unless otherwise stated.

A number of families are registered with the Paying Guest House Scheme in Jodhpur. Costs per night range from Rs 200 to 1000. Inquire at the Tourist Reception Centre (see p307).

### BUDGET

**Shivam Paying Guest House** (Map p308; ☎ 2610688; shivamgh@hotmail.com; s/d with shared bathroom Rs 125/150, s with private bathroom from Rs 175, d with private bathroom Rs 200-450) Near the clock tower is this cosy option where you'll get no hassles. Run by a gentle, helpful family, it has comfortable rooms on several floors, reached by steep staircases, and a lovely rooftop restaurant, where the home-cooking is excellent. The pasta dishes are particularly good, if you want a break from Indian food.

**Cosy Guest House** (Map p308; ☎ 2612066; cosyguesthouse@yahoo.com; Navchokiya; rooftop Rs 60, tents Rs 150, s/d with shared bathroom Rs 200/250, d with private bathroom Rs 350) Formerly known as Joshi's Blue House, this is a great, unpretentious choice in the heart of the old city. It's a 500-year-old blue house, with several levels of higgledy-piggledy rooftops and a genial owner. Options include rooms with bathroom, a single room without bathroom but with a fantastic view from the doorway and its own flight of steps, and tents on the roof. Ask the rickshaw for Navchokiya Rd, from where the guesthouse is signposted.

**Tourist Guest House** (Map p308; ☎ 2541235; Ral-laram Bldg, High Court Rd; s/d Rs 150/250) This is a good choice outside the old city and thus outside the tourist scene. Don't be put off by the battered exterior, as this is a really nice place to stay. Run by a lovely family, it has simple, clean rooms.

**Govind Hotel** (Map p308; ☎ 2622758; www.govindhotel.com; dm Rs 60, r Rs 200-700) This is a friendly, unfussy place, well set up for travellers and with helpful management. Opposite the main post office, it's just a five-minute walk from the main train station, which is great if you've got an early-morning train departure. The rooms at the back are the quietest, though some have no external window. Otherwise, rooms range from basic to smart, and there's a rooftop restaurant with fort views (an oasis in this area). The owners don't pay commissions.

### THE AUTHOR'S CHOICE

**Singhvi's Haveli** (Map p308; ☎ 2624293; Navchokiya, Ramdevji ka Chowk; r Rs 150-700; dishes Rs 20-70) In the oldest part of the city, this is a wonderful place to stay – a beautiful, family-run, red-sandstone *haveli* with exquisitely carved jalis. Rooms are all atmospheric, ranging from basic, good-value options to the magnificent maharani suite with 10 windows and a fort view. The romantic rooftop restaurant is decorated with sari curtains and floor cushions, and serves home-cooked dishes.

**Yogi's Guest House** (Map p310; ☎ 2643436; s/d with shared bathroom Rs 200/250, r with private bathroom Rs 650) At the base of the fort walls is Yogi's, a chilled-out travellers' hangout that's gone upmarket and refurbished many of its rooms in recent years, though there are still a few budget options. Set in the 500-year-old Rajpurohitji-ki-Haveli, the rooms are smart, spacious and clean. However, the service is erratic and lacks attention, and the ticket-booking service is best avoided. There's a lovely rooftop restaurant with a fort view and good food. The guesthouse is well signposted off the lanes leading to the fort.

**Durag Niwas Guest House** (Map p308; ☎ 2512385; www.durag-niwas.com; 1 Old Public Park; s/d from Rs 150/250; ⊠) This is a recommended, friendly, family-run place with very helpful owners who do their utmost to make travellers feel welcome and well informed. One enormous room here (Rs 500) sleeps up to eight people. Good home-cooked veg dishes are available, and there's a cushion-floored, sari-curtained area on the roof for hanging out.

**Durag Villas Guest House** (Map p308; ☎ 2512298; 1 Old Public Park; r Rs 250-600; ⊠) Next door to Durag Niwas, this is run by the same family and is a nice place with simple, good-value rooms – the more expensive rooms are better. It's a quiet and relaxed, and set around a small, tranquil, leafy courtyard.

**Haveli Guest House** (Map p308; ☎ 2614615; www.haveliguesthouse.net; Makrana Mohalla; r Rs 250-850; dishes Rs 30-60; ⊠ 💻) This 250-year-old building inside the walled city is a popular, efficient and friendly place. Many rooms have semi-balconies and fort views. It's one of those concerns that relies on rickshaws to keep hauling in the punters, so if you come in a rickshaw, your room will be pricier. This business ethic is obviously working, as the management has rented a building across the road (with equally pleasant rooms) to take the overflow. The rooftop veg restaurant has tasty food and excellent views. Rickshaws sometimes take travellers to copycat places, so note that the Haveli Guest House we recommend faces a stagnant step-well.

**Hill View Guest House** (Map p310; ☎ 2441763; d Rs 150; thalis Rs 30-40) A family house on the way up to the fort, this is very enthusiastically run (you'll be made to feel part of the family). Rooms are basic, clean and simple the rooftop has a great view over th Home-cooked food is on offer.

**Madho Niwas** (Bhenswara House; Off Map p308; ☎ 2512486; New Airport Rd, Ratanada; s/d Rs 750/900, deluxe Rs 1185/1485; ) This place, a stately, rambling house built in the 1940s, is run by Dalvir Singh and is a cosy place to stay, with a quiet lawn area. It's around 2km from the centre of town, but it's good value, with comfortable rooms and tasty food. The Marwari-style barbecue chicken with a squeeze of lemon is delicious. The hotel can also arrange a stay at Ravla Bhenswara (p320), outside Jodhpur.

**Blue House** (Map p308; ☎ 2621396; Moti Chowk; bluehouse36@hotmail.com; r from Rs 100, s/d Rs 200/250) This has a nice position in the old city, but rooms are quite ordinary. However, two facing the fort with shared bathroom, thatched roofs and a small seating area are good. The management directs visitors to various local shops, but remember that you'll be paying commission if you buy from them.

Reasonable rooms are available at the main train station. Dorms are Rs 75, doubles Rs 150 and doubles with AC Rs 350.

### MIDRANGE

**Pal Haveli** (Map p308; ☎ 2439615; www.palhaveli.com; Gulab Sagar; r Rs 1500) This central *haveli* ranged around a courtyard was built by the Thakur of Pal in 1847. There are 12 charming, mostly large rooms, decorated in traditional heritage style. The family still lives here, and can show you their small museum in the sitting room.

**Ratan Vilas** (Map p308; ☎ /fax 2614418; ratanvilas_jod@rediffmail.com; Old Loco Shed Rd, Ratanada; r Rs 1275-1500; ) The staff are exceptional at this lovely, quiet, colonial villa. Fronted by a serene lawn, the place has a bygone-days atmosphere and a family vibe. Wonderful home-cooked meals are available. If you're interested in getting authentic jodhpur trousers made, ask here – allow at least a week for your jodhpurs to be stitched.

**Ranbanka** (Map p308; ☎ 2512801; www.ranbankahotels.com; Circuit House Rd; s/d Rs 1995/3000, ste Rs 4500) In a beautiful, domed sandstone building, built for Maharajadhiraj Ajit Singh (younger brother of Maharaja Umaid Singh), this is right next to Ajit Bhawan (see opposite). Rooms have old colonial furniture and mostly have wooden floors. Decoration is very calm and cool, but the place is comfortable rather than charismatic. The hotel has a lovely pool, and a good restaurant.

**Newtons Manor** (Off Map p308; ☎ 2430686; www.newtonsmanor.com; 86 Jawahar Colony, Ratanada; r from Rs 995) Newtons Manor, 800m southeast of town, has elegant rooms, with lots of antique furniture, in a fussy, old-colonial style. It's crammed with kitsch knick-knacks, and there are just five doubles, one of which is a bigger room with a bathtub. The rooms are clean, the outdoor area is pleasant, with a fish tank and a huge birdcage. Scrumptious home-cooked meals are available.

**Karni Bhawan** (Map p308; ☎ 2512101; Palace Rd; s/d Rs 1425/1625; lunch/dinner Rs 250/275; ) This place is a remodelled colonial bungalow that feels modern and thus a little bland. However, it has smart, themed rooms (such as one based on Holi) with dark wooden, traditional furnishings, a sense of calm, and appealing lawns and a pool.

**Devi Bhawan** (Off Map p308; ☎ 2511067; devibhawan@satyamonline.com; 1 Ratanada Area; s/d/ste Rs 800/900/1200; veg thali Rs 120) Devi Bhawan is a recommended, delightful green oasis, with appealing rooms and a cottage. It's great value, though a bit out of the way (150m southeast of town), but you'll have no hassles here whatsoever. There's a good restaurant.

**Inn Season** (Map p308; ☎ /fax 2616400; r Rs 1200, ste Rs 1800; ) Near the taxi stand, this is a fine, modernish choice, with well-kept rooms and a lovely suite. There's a pool, and the restaurant serves Indian and Continental food. Check out the old German record player and eclectic collection of classic records, including Louis Armstrong and Ella Fitzgerald.

**Durjan Niwas Hotel** (Map p308; ☎ 2616994; fax 2616991; Daspan Vihar, Old Loco Shed Rd; s/d Rs 1200/1500) This is a big white building, with spacious, ordinary, vaguely 1970s rooms that have balconies. It was built by Thakur Dujan Singh in 1920, but feels more modern.

**Hotel Kalinga** (Map p308; ☎ 2627338; www.kalingahotel.com; s/d Rs 800/900) This hotel is convenient, as it's close to the main train station. It's an ordinary place, with dull but comfortable and spacious rooms. The hotel offers 24-hour checkout, and there's a good restaurant (see opposite).

**Hotel City Palace** (Map p308; ☎ 2431933; 32 Nai Sarak; s/d with AC Rs 990/1190; ) Near Sojati Gate, this is a reasonable choice if you want to be in the heart of the hubbub of the shopping district (a short walk from the clock tower). The rooms are characterless, though, and the building's a boring block.

### TOP END

**Ajit Bhawan** (Map p308; ☎ 2511410; www.ajitbhawan.com; Airport Rd; r incl breakfast Rs 3500-4500; ) This is a great place to stay, and it's deservedly popular with travellers. Despite its location on a dusty main road, the hotel is a city oasis; the building is set well back from the road, amid gardens. Behind the gracious main heritage building are stone cottages with wood furnishings. There're a restaurant, a sensational swimming pool (Rs 250 for nonguests) and a gift shop. Baby-sitting services are available, and you can rent a vintage car from a wonderful collection that includes a 1939 Chevrolet convertible. There are also several nearby restaurants.

**Umaid Bhawan Palace** (Map p308; ☎ 2510101; www.jodhpurheritage.com; r US$150-200, ste US$275-500; ) This hulking 20th-century palace, also home to a museum (see p311), is carved from red sandstone and feels rather like a grand parliament building or a university – that is, it's not that cosy. It has a tennis court, an indoor swimming pool, lush lawns and several restaurants (see p316). If you can stretch to it, opt for a suite; the cheaper rooms are run of the mill.

**Taj Hari Mahal Palace** (Map p308; ☎ 2439700; fax 2624451; 5 Residency Rd; s/d from US$170/180; ) Run by the Taj Group, this is a hugely flash and luxurious modern place built in traditional style. It has most conceivable mod cons, and is centred on a courtyard with a big, lush swimming pool. Cheaper rooms look out on the garden, while the pricier ones have a pool view. Prices drop by up to two-thirds in the low season.

## Eating

While you're in Jodhpur, try a glass of *makhania lassi*, a filling saffron-flavoured variety of that most refreshing of drinks.

### RESTAURANTS

**On the Rocks** (Map p308; dishes Rs 50-260; 10am-2am, lunch noon-3pm, dinner 7.30-11pm) This leafy place next to the Ajit Bhawan hotel is popular. The garden restaurant has a small playground and is candlelit in the evening. It serves tasty Indian cuisine, with lots of barbecue options. There's also a partly open-air bar, Rocktails, which is Jodhpur's funkiest, but not many women hang out here. The excellent bakery (pastries Rs 15) makes birthday cakes with sufficient notice.

**Hotel Priya & Restaurant** (Map p308; 181-182 Nai Sarak; dishes Rs 15-50; 7am-midnight) Partially open to the hubbub of Nai Sarak, this popular, friendly eatery has a cheerful sense of chaos. It's usually packed with locals, has good service, and serves reliable North and South Indian cuisine. The thalis are tasty, and there are sweets, too.

**Garden Restaurant** (Map p308; dishes Rs 85-170; noon-3pm & 7.30-10.30pm) Near Ajit Bhawan, this is a large, lovely garden restaurant, candlelit at night, with well-spaced tables, and excellent Indian and Continental dishes.

**Pushpa Bhojnalya Dining Hall** (Map p308; dishes Rs 6-45; 10am-10.30pm) This place could be mistaken for an oversized shoebox, but it's indeed a restaurant and does tasty Rajasthani food, such as hearty *dal batti* (baked balls of wholemeal flour served with dhal). The Kashmiri *paneer* with apple, cashew and banana is nice, too.

**Kalinga Restaurant** (Map p308; Station Rd; dishes Rs 50-160; 8am-11pm) This restaurant, at the hotel of the same name (see opposite), is smart and popular, with a dim ambience and yellow, segmented walls. Offering tasty veg and nonveg Indian, Chinese and Continental food, it's a good place to kill time while waiting for a train.

**Mid Town** (Map p308; Station Rd; dishes Rs 18-70; 7am-11pm) Clean, cheery Mid Town has downstairs and rooftop eating areas, and good veg food, including Rajasthani specialities, some particular to Jodhpur, such as *chakki-ka-sagh* and roti (wheat dumpling cooked in rich gravy), *bajara-ki-roti pachkuta* (*bajara* wheat roti with local dry

### THE AUTHOR'S CHOICE

**Mehran Terrace** (Map p310; ☎ 2549790; Meherangarh; veg/nonveg thalis Rs 300/350, other dishes Rs 80-150; 7.30-10pm) Dining on one of the fort's terraces is unsurpassably romantic. Perched 140m above the city, the open-air restaurant is overlooked by lacy palace buildings that resemble an opera set. When you look over the wall, the city is spread out below you – an amazing sight. Sit at one of the well-spaced, candlelit tables and enjoy the rich Rajasthani thalis and other very palatable choices – all appropriate to the setting, if not as spectacular a[s] the view. You'll need to book.

vegetables) and *kabuli* (vegetables with rice, milk, bread and fruit).

**Jodhpur Coffee House** (Map p308; High Court Rd; dishes Rs 26-36, thalis Rs 30; 9am-10.30pm) This stuck-in-time place has been going since 1954, and feels like it might not have changed much in that time. A calm contrast after the busy street, the pale-green restaurant is on two levels with a utility-furniture feel, and offers South Indian food.

**Poonam Restaurant** (Map p308; High Court Rd; dishes Rs 12-50, thalis Rs 35-50; 9am-11pm) In a dark-brown environment with (that Indian restaurant favourite) brown-booth seating, Poonam offers South Indian and veg 'delights' (its description). The food is reasonably priced and reasonably good.

Umaid Bhawan Palace (p311) has four restaurants, including the very grand Marwar Hall (although the buffet is fairly average), which is a bit like eating in a grandiose, echoing railway station. Overlooking the back lawn and with a view of the fort is the Pillars, a breezy informal eatery with sublime lawn views. There are also the more formal Jodhpur Lancers, specialising in Continental cuisine, and Kebab Konner, a casual open-air restaurant that's especially popular with the locals, serving moderately priced barbecued Indian food (dinner only). Main dish prices cost Rs 200 to 600. Or you could just have a drink at the Trophy Bar.

### QUICK EATS

**Omelette Shop** (Map p308; Sadar Market) Just through the gate (by the inner arch – don't be fooled by imitations) on the northern side of the square, this shop claims to go through 1000 eggs a day – the egg man has been doing his thing for over 30 years. Two tasty, spicy boiled eggs cost Rs 5, and a two-egg omelette with chilli, coriander and four pieces of bread is Rs 12.

**Shri Mishrilal Hotel** (Map p308; clock tower) This place is nothing fancy, but whips up the best lassis in town. A delicious glass of impossibly thick, creamy *makhania lassi* costs Rs 13 and will do you for lunch.

**Agra Sweets** (Map p308; opposite Sojati Gate) There are good lassis (Rs 12), as well as delectable Jodhpur specialities, such as *mawa ladoo* (a milk sweet made with sugar, cardamom and pistachios wrapped in silver leaf; Rs 10) and the baklava-like *mawa kachori* (Rs 10).

**Pokar Sweets** (Map p308; cnr Nai Sarak & High Court Rd) This place has a huge selection of sweet treats. You can pick out a box of five or six for around Rs 20.

The cool, quiet refreshment room on the 1st floor of the train station has a strangely timeless ambience and has surprisingly palatable food. Veg/nonveg thalis are Rs 20/25.

There's an inviting cluster of sweet shops (Map p308) in the old city, on the way to Cosy Guest House.

## Shopping

Take care while shopping in Jodhpur. If a rickshaw driver, friendly man on the street, guesthouse or hotel recommends a shop to you, it's almost certain that they're getting a commission. Local smooth-talking salesfolk also love to wax lyrical about the big international stores or designers they export to. Take this with a pinch of salt.

The usual Rajasthani handicrafts are available, with shops selling textiles and other wares clustered around the clock tower (you'll need to bargain hard). However, Jodhpur is famous for antiques. The greatest concentration of showrooms is along Palace Rd, near Umaid Bhawan Palace. These shops are well known to Western antique dealers, who come here with wallets stuffed with plastic cards. As a result, you'll be hard-pressed to find any bargains. Also remember that the trade in antique architectural fixtures is contributing to the desecration of India's cultural heritage (beautiful old *havelis* are often ripped apart for their doors and window frames). Most of these warehouse-sized showrooms also deal in antique reproductions, catering for a growing number of overseas export houses, and can make you a piece of antique-style furniture; the prices aren't bad. The showrooms are fascinating places to wander around, and they're definitely the spot to head if you want a life-size wooden giraffe or two.

Make sure you find out how much customs charges will be in your home country. Certain restrictions apply to the export of Indian items over 100 years old; see p370.

Around the clock tower are various spice shops, but these are mainly for tourists, with prices to match, and there have been complaints about quality. However, **MV Spices** (Map p308; ☎ 5109347; www.mvspices.com; 209B Vegetable Market; 10am-9pm) still gets good reports from travellers for its genuine spices and excellent service. If you would like to buy spices at more normal prices, head westwards from the clock tower towards Navchokiya. You'll pass a square overlooked by a temple; beyond are some small spice shops, where chilli powder will cost around Rs 80 per kilogram and real saffron around Rs 45 to 55 per gram. Heading this way into the old city you'll come across little cubbyhole shops selling such things as hand-carved wooden printing blocks, miniature gods, musical instruments and *bandhani* (tie-dye) saris.

**Handloom House** (Map p308; Nai Sarak) Back on the main drag is this huge department store, thronged with locals. Alongside some questionable clothes are mountains of good-quality fixed-price *bandhani*, silk saris and woollen shawls.

**Khadi Shop** (Map p308; Station Rd; 10.30am-7.30pm Mon-Sat) This dowdy shop, not far from the main train station, has fixed-priced hand-woven goods, such as shawls and shirts. It's worth a look in case you turn up a bargain.

## Getting There & Away

### AIR

The office for **Indian Airlines** (Map p308; ☎ 2510757; Airport Rd; 10am-1.15pm & 2-4.30pm) is south of the city centre. Flights go to Delhi (US$120) via Jaipur (US$90) and also to Mumbai (US$160) via Udaipur (US$90). **Jet Airways** (☎ 5102222) also flies to Delhi (via Jaipur) and Mumbai (via Udaipur).

Jodhpur **airport** (☎ 2512617) is just 5km from the city centre.

### BUS

Rajasthan State Road Transport Corporation (RSRTC) buses leave from the Roadways bus stand. There are RSRTC buses regularly to, such places as Jaisalmer (Rs 60, 5½ hours, half-hourly), Udaipur (Rs 60, 5½ hours, seven daily), Jaipur (Rs 140/163 in express/deluxe, 7½ hours, half-hourly), Ajmer (Rs 99, 4½ hours, half-hourly), Bikaner (Rs 100, 5½ hours), Delhi (Rs 262/363 in express/deluxe, 12½ to 14 hours, five daily) and Ahmedabad (Rs 180/210 in express/deluxe, 10 to 12 hours, six daily). There's a **Roadways inquiry number** (☎ 2544686).

Private buses have offices opposite the main train station and in the street leading to the Ranchodji Temple. Deluxe buses with 2 x 2 (two seat by two seat) pushback seats run to destinations such as Agra, Ahmedabad, Ajmer, Delhi, Jaipur, Jaisalmer and Udaipur. Some sleepers are available.

The main highway between Jodhpur and Jaisalmer goes via Agolai, Dechu and Pokaran, but it's more interesting to go on the less frequently travelled route via Osiyan and Phalodi (for Khichan), which meets the main route at Pokaran.

### TAXI

There's a taxi stand outside as you exit the main train station. The usual rules apply – a good price to aim for is Rs 3.5 per kilometre (for a non-AC car), with a minimum of 250km per day. The driver will charge you for his return journey.

### TRAIN

The computerised **booking office** (Map p308; Station Rd; 8am-8pm Mon-Sat, 8am-1.45pm Sun) is between the main train station and Sojati Gate. Demand for tickets is heavy, so come here soon after you arrive. There are tourist quotas on trains from here. Reserve your tickets at window 788. At the main train station there's an International Tourist Bureau (see p307).

The *Jodhpur–Jaisalmer Express* (No 4810) departs every night at 11.15pm, arriving in Jaisalmer (Rs 157/411 in sleeper/3AC, 294km) at around 5.15am; the No 4809 from Jaisalmer also leaves at 11.15pm, arriving in Jodhpur at 5.15am.

The *Mandore Express* (No 2462) leaves Jodhpur at 7.30pm, arriving in Delhi (Rs 273/1092/713 in sleeper/2AC/3AC, 623km) at 6.30am. The *Intercity Express* (No 2466) to Jaipur (Rs 180/450 in sleeper/3AC, 313km) leaves at 5.45am, arriving at 10.35am.

There are several daily trains to Bikaner (Rs 148/594 in sleeper/2AC, five hours), including services at 10.15am and 8.35pm. There are also services to Agra, Varanasi and Mumbai.

## Getting Around

### TO/FROM THE AIRPORT

The journey to/from the airport costs about Rs 60/150 in an autorickshaw/taxi.

### AUTORICKSHAW

Most autorickshaw journeys in town should cost no more than Rs 25. A day's sightseeing costs around Rs 200.

#### BICYCLE

It's possible to hire a bike from several places near the Kalinga Restaurant, though be warned that two-wheel travel will be bumpy, dusty and traffic-plagued.

#### TAXI

There's a taxi stand near the main train station. To hire a taxi for sightseeing in Jodhpur, expect to be quoted around Rs 500/750 per half-/full day. To Mandore, a taxi costs about Rs 200, including a one-hour wait. To Osiyan the fare is Rs 600 return, including a three-hour stay there.



## AROUND JODHPUR

### Maha Mandir & Balsamand Lake

About 2km northeast of the city is the **Maha Mandir** (Great Temple), which is quite an adventure to seek out. This edifice is supported by 100 pillars and protected by defensive bastions. There's a splendid altar in the centre of the temple, covered by a golden canopy. On the walls are pastel paintings of fantastic yoga contortions. The temple also houses a local school.

The picturesque **Balsamand Lake** is 5km further north. A refreshing escape from Jodhpur, this artificial lake is the oldest in Rajasthan – it was built in 1159 – and has a picturesque summer palace on its banks.

Striking **Balsamand Palace** (☎ 2572321; s/d/ste Rs 2500/3000/7000; ), a deep-red sandstone building with elaborately carved balconies, sits at the edge of the lake. It offers comfort in a lush and serene setting not too far from Jodhpur. The attractive rooms are in the former stables. All have a private terrace with exposed stone walls and serene views.

### Mandore

Situated 9km north of the centre of Jodhpur, Mandore was the capital of Marwar prior to the founding of Jodhpur. It was founded in the 6th century, and passed to the Rathore Rajputs in 1381. Few traces of the ancient seat of power remain, but the lush gardens and *chhatris* (cenotaphs, literally 'umbrellas') make the place an appealing and relaxing excursion from Jodhpur (it's thronged with Indian tourists at weekends).

Its **gardens**, stepped with rock terraces, contain a mixture of dark-red stupas and domes – the cenotaphs of Jodhpur rulers. These include the soaring **Chhatri of Maharaja Dhiraj Ajit Singh** (1793), which combines Buddhist and Jain elements in its architecture. It's an enormous edifice with carved elephants, a pillared forechamber, fine sculpture and *amalaka* (disk-shaped flourishes with fluted edges). You can climb to the third storey up a peculiar set of staircases. The memorial also marks the spot where 64 queens and concubines committed *sati* on Ajit Singh's death in 1724.

Opposite is the 1720 **Chhatri of Maharaja Dhiraj Jaswant Singh I**, an enormous octagonal pavilion with a vast dome. It achieves a remarkable symmetry, with a gallery supported by huge pillars, and sculptures of Krishna and the *gopis* (milkmaids). The rest of the cenotaphs all date to the 17th century.

At the rear of the complex is the small **government museum** (admission Rs 5; 🕐 10am-4pm Sat-Thu), which is housed in the Abhay Singh Palace and shows relics of Mandore, including sculpture and inscriptions.

To the left is the 18th-century **Hall of Heroes**. This is a fantastically bright array of 15 solemn Hindu deities and local Rajput heroes carved out of a rock wall, coated with fine plaster and luridly painted. The **Shrine of 33 Crore Gods** is painted with figures of deities and spirits (one crore equals 10 million).

#### SLEEPING

**Mandore Guest House** (☎ 0291-2545210, 2571620; www.mandore.com; s/d Rs 400/650, with AC Rs 550/850; ) Delightful rounded mud-walled cottages are set in a leafy garden. There's good home-cooked food. The guesthouse is also connected with a local NGO working to address drug addiction and provide medical services. The NGO has short-term volunteer programmes (see p375).

#### GETTING THERE & AWAY

There are many buses throughout the day between Jodhpur and Mandore (Rs 6), which is on the main road between Jodhpur and Nagaur. Catch one on High Court Rd. Mandore is also included on the Tourist Reception Centre's city tours (see p312). You could get a rickshaw to take you there and back for around Rs 120.

### Bishnoi Villages

A number of Bishnoi and other traditional villages are strung along and off the Pali road, to the southeast of Jodhpur. Various operators, including the RTDC in Jodhpur, conduct jeep safaris to the villages – see p312 for details. A tour is essential to visit this region. Some of these villages are tiny, and they're reached along tracks that can barely be made out in the sand (and that you'll be hard-pressed to find on any maps).

Many villagers live in handmade thatched huts, in the traditions of their ancestors. Tours usually include a meal cooked over the fire in one of the villages. Unfortunately, the increase in tourism is starting to cause tension in some villages. Remember that you are visiting a private community, and make sure you ask before taking photographs.

Many visitors are surprised by the density, and fearlessness, of the wildlife around the Bishnoi villages. The relationship between the villagers and the animals has been carefully nurtured for hundreds of years. The 1730 sacrifice of 363 villagers to protect the khejri trees (see Village Activists, below) is commemorated in September at **Khejadali** village, where there is a memorial to the victims fronted by a small grove of khejri trees.

At **Guda Bishnoi**, the locals are traditionally engaged in animal husbandry. There's a small artificial lake where migratory birds and mammals, such as blackbucks and chinkaras, can be seen, particularly at

**VILLAGE ACTIVISTS**

*Sar santey rookh rahe to bhi sasto jaan.* (A chopped head is cheaper than a felled tree.)

*Bishnoi saying*

The Bishnoi are among the world's most dedicated conservationists. They hold all animal life sacred, in particular the endangered blackbuck (Indian antelope). The Bishnoi sometimes bury dead blackbuck and mark their graves with stones, and the women are said to suckle blackbuck fawns that have been orphaned. They believe that they will be reincarnated as deer. They also have a long history of protecting the sacred khejri tree – sometimes with their lives. The men are recognisable by their large white turbans, while women usually wear earth colours and a large nose ring, a skirt with a white dot and a red dupatta with a green border.

The sect was founded in the 15th century, when a severe drought was crippling the desert regions near Jodhpur. A villager named Jambeshwar had a vision that the drought had been caused by humans meddling with the natural order. He laid down 29 tenets for conserving nature, including not killing animals, not felling trees and not using wood for funeral pyres. Other commandments include taking early morning baths, not taking opium or cannabis or drinking alcohol, not indulging in unnecessary discussions, and not wearing blue (it's thought this was to save the indigo plant). Jambeshwar became known as Guru Jambhoji, and his followers became known as the Bishnoi (meaning 29) after the principles they followed.

In 1730 the most famous Bishnoi act of self-sacrifice occurred. The maharaja of Jodhpur sent woodcutters into Bishnoi villages to cut down khejri trees for his lime kilns. A woman named Amritdevi clung to one of the trees and refused to be removed, crying 'A chopped head is cheaper than a felled tree'. The axeman cut her head off. One by one, other Bishnoi villagers followed Amritdevi's lead, and each in turn was killed by the axemen until 363 people lay dead. The maharaja, hearing of the carnage, declared a conservation zone around the Bishnoi villages, prohibiting tree felling or poaching in the area.

Today the site at Khejadali is a quiet grove of khejri trees, and a temple commemorates the sacrifice. The Bishnoi continue to live by their strict code and to defend native wildlife. In 1996 a Bishnoi villager named Nihal Chand Bishnoi was shot and killed by poachers near Bikaner as he tried to save the lives of some chinkaras (Indian gazelles). In October 1998 Bollywood superstar Salman Khan was arrested for killing two blackbucks near a Bishnoi village. The authorities were allegedly alerted to the crime by the villagers, who chased Khan from the scene and presented the dead blackbucks as evidence. Today around 90% of the blackbucks in India live under Bishnoi protection.

A festival near Bikaner celebrates Jambeshwar, the sect's founder, in around January or February (see Festivals in Western Rajasthan, p306).

dusk, when they come to feed. The lake is full only after a good monsoon (July and August). There are plans to shift Jodhpur's airport here within the next decade.

The village of **Salawas** is a centre for weaving *dhurries*, though many villages also practise this craft. Today a cooperative of 48 weavers runs the efficient **Roopraj Dhurry Udyog** (☎ 0291-2896658; rooprajdurry@sify.com) in Salawas, through which all profits go to the artisan. A beautiful 1.3m x 2m *dhurrie* can take about one month to complete, depending on the intricacy of the design and the number of colours used, and costs Rs 2500 to 3000. The coordinator, Roopraj, will happily answer any questions you may have about this craft.

These days, chemical rather than natural dyes are used. *Dhurries* are usually of cotton, but sometimes camel or goat hair, or silk, is used. After the weaving is completed, the *dhurries* are sometimes stonewashed to give an antique effect. The *dhurrie* weavers can arrange post by sea or air (shipping costs around Rs 1200 for one piece).

Also in Salawas, several families, mostly of the Muslim community, are engaged in block printing. The hand-woven, block-printed cloth is known as *fetia*. A single bed sheet costs around Rs 300, and a double sheet is about Rs 450, depending on the design.

At the villages of **Zhalamand**, **Salawas** and **Kakani**, potters can be seen at work, using hand-turned wheels.

## Sardar Samand Lake

The route to this charming and remote wildlife centre, located about 66km southeast of Jodhpur, passes through a number of colourful little villages. Blackbucks, chinkaras and bird life, including flamingos, pelicans, ducks, cranes, egrets and kingfishers, may be spotted.

Built in 1933 as the maharaja of Jodhpur's summer palace and hunting lodge, **Sardar Samand Palace** (☎ 02960-245003; s/d Rs 2500/3000; 🏊) is a grey-stone building with a single domed turret. Rooms are comfortable and have great views. There are a restaurant and a gorgeous lakeside swimming pool to enjoy, and it's a world away from the clamour of Jodhpur. Village safaris are available. You can also book accommodation at Sardar Samand through **Umaid Bhawan Palace** (☎ 0291-510101) in Jodhpur.

## Rohet

In this small village, 40km south of Jodhpur, the former local ruler has converted his 350-year-old manor into a heritage hotel. **Rohet Garh** (☎ 02936-268231; s/d from Rs 1450/2000, ste Rs 3000; ❄ 🏊) is a heritage hotel with lots of character and relaxing gardens. Bruce Chatwin wrote *The Songlines* here, and William Dalrymple began *City of Djinns* in the same room (No 15). It's surprising that they were so diligent, as there's a gorgeous colonnaded pool and the rooms are lovely. The hotel can also organise village safaris and horse rides.

From Jodhpur, there are local daily buses to Rohet (Rs 15), or you can get a taxi for around Rs 650.

## Bhenswara

Bhenswara, which translates as 'the place where buffaloes were kept', is about 130km south of Jodhpur, on the banks of the Jawai river.

**Ravla Bhenswara** (☎ 02978-222080; s/d from Rs 800/950, deluxe Rs 995/1395; ❄ 🏊), an unpretentious rural manor, is perfect if you want a respite from travelling. This place is run by a nice young couple, Shiv Pratap Singh and Uma Kumari, who give the hotel a cosy appeal. The quaint rooms are decorated with lots of personality. Jeep village safaris and village bullock cart rides can be organised (there's a minimum of two people). The hotel owners can arrange a visit to the nearby **Jalor Fort**. The climb up to the fort takes about 45 minutes (carry water, as the ascent can be a hot one).

The closest bus route goes to Jalor (Rs 75 from Jodhpur), where you should catch a taxi to Bhenswara.

## Dhawa Doli Wildlife Sanctuary

This sanctuary is about 40km southwest of Jodhpur, on the road to Barmer, and has populations of blackbucks, partridges, desert foxes and nilgais. There's no accommodation here, but it's possible to take a half-day tour from Jodhpur for Rs 600, or if you have your own transport you could stop en route to Barmer. The forest office is in a small group of village huts – you'll have to ask on the way – and the family there will help you look for wildlife. It's best to visit before about 11am or a few hours before sunset.

### Khejarla

This 400-year-old **fort** (☎ 02930-258311; s/d Rs 1185/1485) is 85km east of Jodhpur en route to Ajmer. Its extraordinary carved window frames, made of deep-red sandstone, are bunched on the front of its stern fortifications. Rooms are whitewashed and rustic rather than swish.

Village safaris can be arranged, as well as a visit to an old step-well (ask Dalip Singh about the ghost).

### Khimsar

About 95km northeast of Jodhpur, **Khimsar Fort** (☎ 01585-262345; www.khimsarfort.com; s/d Rs 3500/3900, ste Rs 3900/4500; ) dates back to 1523. The zenana was added in the 18th century, and a new wing built in the 1940s. The palatial building has been converted into an upmarket hotel, with lush, well-appointed rooms. The hotel also boasts a sauna, yoga centre, pool (with nearby hammock to laze away the day), a good restaurant and pleasant gardens. It's possible to arrange a jeep safari, or a horse or camel ride. Ayurvedic massage costs around Rs 825 for one hour.

A local bus from Jodhpur costs Rs 50, while a taxi costs about Rs 800.

## NAGAUR

☎ 01582 / pop 88,313

Lying 135km northeast of Jodhpur, Nagaur is home to the massive 12th-century ruins of **Ahhichatragarh** (Fort of the Hooded Cobra; Indian/foreigner Rs 15/50, camera/video Rs 25/100; 9am-1pm & 2-5pm), which have been beautifully restored (the project was partly financed by the Getty Foundation). The fort is protected by vast double walls that encompass a richly painted Rajput-Mughal palace complex and a unique water system that recycles every drop. Within the walls of the old city are several **mosques**, including one commissioned by Akbar for a disciple of the Sufi saint Khwaja Muin-ud-din Chishti (see p206).

Nagaur also hosts a colourful fair, which is a smaller and even more camel-focused version of Pushkar Camel Fair – see Festivals in Western Rajasthan, p306. During this time a tourist information office is set up at the festival grounds.

### Sleeping

**Hotel Mahaveer International** (☎ 243158; Vijai Vallabh Chowk; s/d from Rs 250/350, with AC Rs 400/500; ) About 1km from the fort, this hotel has uninspiring but comfortable rooms aimed at business travellers. There're also a restaurant and a bar.

**Hotel Sujan** (☎ 240283; Nakash Gate; s/d Rs 200/300) Near the fort, the Hotel Sujan has gloomy hallways, but the rooms are fine.

**Hotel Bhaskar** (☎ 240100; Station Rd; s/d from Rs 200/250) This friendly place has bright but run-down rooms. It's conveniently near the train station.

Fabulous, 4-sq-metre royal tents are available in the fort grounds from November to March. Tents with private bathroom cost US$95 to $US125 and go up to US$250 during fair time. Bookings are essential; contact **Balsamand Palace** (☎ 0291-2571991).

During Nagaur's fair, the RTDC also has tents (singles/doubles Rs 2000/2500) and opens a hotel. For details, contact the general manager at **Central Reservations** (☎ 0141-2202586; RTDC Hotel Swagatam Campus, Jaipur, 302006). The office is near the train station in Jaipur.

### Getting There & Away

Nagaur is connected by express buses to Jodhpur (Rs 60, three hours) and Bikaner (Rs 65, 2½ hours).

## JODHPUR TO JAISALMER

The most direct route by road to Jaisalmer is the southern route via Agolai, Dechu and Pokaran. But, if you have time, it's more rewarding to take the lesser-travelled northern route, which goes via Osiyan and Phalodi and meets up with the main route at Pokaran. The exquisite temples at Osiyan, the spectacular demoiselle cranes at Khichan and the important pilgrimage site of Ramdevra all lie on or just off this southern route, which numerous buses ply every day.

### Osiyan

This ancient Great Thar Desert town, 65km north of Jodhpur, was an important trading centre between the 8th and 12th centuries. Known as Upkeshpur, it was dominated by the Jains, whose wealth left a legacy of exquisitely sculptured, well-preserved temples. Today it receives lots of pilgrims at certain times, but not that many tourists, and it's a good place for a taste of the desert if you can't make it to Jaisalmer. The village of Osiyan is inhabited mostly by Brahmins – most of the houses here are painted blue (traditionally a Brahmin practice), as in Jodhpur.

### SIGHTS

#### Temples

The finely carved ancient temples of Osiyan rival the Hoysala temples of Karnataka and the Sun Temple of Konark in Orissa.

About 200m north of the bus stand is the hilltop **Sachiya Mata Temple** (6am-7.15pm) – Sachiya Mata is the ninth and last incarnation of the goddess Durga. This temple receives crowds of pilgrims, both Hindu and Jain. People usually come here after the marriage of their children, but crowds come for *navratra* (nine nights of worship in March or April and October or November). A long flight of steps, under fancifully decorated arches, takes you to the forechamber. Before the *mandapa* (chamber before the inner sanctum), and beyond the impressive *torana* (gateway), are sandstone statues of various incarnations of Durga that were excavated by archaeologists and installed here. The main temple is flanked by nine smaller temples, each dedicated to an incarnation of the goddess. Abutting the sides of the main temple is a series of ancient temples contemporary with this one.

Five minutes' walk from Sachiya Mata Temple is **Mahavira Temple** (admission Rs 5, camera/video Rs 30/100; 6am-8.30pm), which was dedicated to the last of the Jain *tirthankars* (great teachers). This is a more spacious temple than Sachiya Mata, featuring an open-air pavilion-style *mandapa* supported by carved pillars. As at the Sachiya Mata Temple, the drum of the dome features sculptures of *apsaras* (celestial maidens). There is also a beautiful *torana* before the temple, decorated with very intricate sculptural work.

The image of Mahavira is quite difficult to make out in the dimly lit inner sanctum. According to legend it's over 2000 years old, was found buried underground, and is made of sand and milk and coated in gold. In the right-hand corner there's an ancient frieze, which retains fragments of colour.

Among the other temples in Osiyan are those dedicated to Surya, Shiva and Harihara. The temples are ruined, but they have some beautiful carving. The damaged 9th-century Katan *baori* (step-well) has more fine, worn sculptural work.

### TOURS

**Gemar Singh** (☎ 0291-2619688; gemar@rediffmail.com), at Jodhpur's Shivam Paying Guest House (p312), arranges homestays, camping, desert walks and camel safaris from Jodhpur to Osiyan and surrounding Rajput and Bishnoi villages. It costs around Rs 700 per person per day, with a minimum of two people.

### SLEEPING & EATING

Few travellers overnight in Osiyan, which accounts for the lack of accommodation.

**Camel Camp** (in Jodhpur ☎/fax 0291-2437023; tents with private bathroom Rs 2500-7000) Offers upmarket but rather overpriced tent accommodation perched on a secluded sand dune overlooking Osiyan. Camel safaris can be arranged. Bookings are essential.

Prakash Bhanu Sharma, a personable Brahmin priest, has an echoing **guest house** (☎ 02922-274296; d Rs 300), geared for pilgrims, near Mahavira temple. Prakash can arrange jeep excursions and camel rides, and is also a knowledgeable guide to the temples. You can usually find him sitting at the gateway to the temple, or ask any of the village children, who will happily track him down for you.

### GETTING THERE & AWAY

There are regular buses from Jodhpur (Rs 30, 1½ hours, half-hourly), and buses also serve Phalodi (for Khichan; two hours). There's also a train to/from Jodhpur (Rs 27 in 2nd class, 1½ hours, 65km). A return taxi from Jodhpur costs Rs 600.

## Khichan

Morning and evening in the winter months, the tiny village of Khichan hosts a fabulous feast for huge swarms of beautiful demoiselle cranes (see the boxed text, opposite). The village also has beautiful red-sandstone *havelis* (some around 100 years old), an attractive Jain temple and a crumbling fort. A series of sand dunes affords a stunning desert panorama. Your hotel can organise a guide to take you to Khichan.

Khichan is about 10km east of Phalodi, a town about 135km from Jodhpur and 165km from Jaisalmer. Phalodi is nondescript, but it has a lovely hotel.

### SLEEPING & EATING

Note that both the options listed here are in Phalodi.

### THE DEMOISELLE CRANES OF KHICHAN

From late August or early September to the end of March you can witness the extraordinary sight of over 7000 demoiselle cranes *(Anthropoides virgo)* wintering near Khichan. The birds circle overhead, then make a dramatic descent for the grain Khichan's villagers spread for them. Brought to France from the Russian steppes, the cranes were tagged 'demoiselle' by Marie Antoinette because of their grace. Here they're known as kurjas.

Brown-grey birds with a black chest and throat, demoiselle cranes stand about 76cm high, and have a long neck and a short beak. In traditional Marwari songs, women beseech the cranes to bring back messages from their loved ones when they return from distant lands. The flock consumes a phenomenal 600kg of grain each day, which is distributed at the Birds Feeding Home. All the grain is funded by (very welcome) donations.

The feeding of the cranes dates back some 150 years, and the number of cranes is increasing by about 10% to 15% each year. The grain is spread at night, ready for the birds to feed at sunrise (about 7am), and again around 5pm, in time for the birds' return in the afternoon. The sight of these wonderful birds in such large numbers descending on the feeding ground is truly awe-inspiring – the noise of the assembly is amazing. It shouldn't be missed if you're in the area. Please keep a distance from the birds and refrain from making a noise, so as not to scare them.

The demoiselle cranes also winter in Pakistan and Africa. To migrate they must cross the Himalayas from their breeding range, which extends over a wide belt spanning eastern Europe, Central Asia and eastern China.

For more information about the demoiselle cranes and the feeding programme at Khichan, contact the **International Crane Foundation** (☎ 608-3569462; fax 3569465; www.savingcranes.org; PO Box 447, E-11376 Shady Lane Rd, Baraboo, WI 53913-0447, USA).

**Lal Niwas** (☎ 02925-223813; s/d Rs 1600/1800, ste 1900/2100; 🏊) This is a splendid, carved, deep-terracotta *haveli* in the old part of town, with balconies, courtyards and a tangle of passages. All the rooms are different, decorated in the traditional style with wooden furniture. The family suite is fantastic, especially if you have kids, as it has a number of rooms divided by carved arches. A restaurant and a bar are on site.

**Hotel Sunrise** (☎ /fax 02925-222257; s/d with shared bathroom Rs 100/150, s/d with private bathroom Rs 200/250) Directly opposite the Roadways bus stand, this place has basic but acceptable rooms and a restaurant.

#### GETTING THERE & AWAY

There are regular buses to/from Jodhpur (Rs 60, 3½ hours), Jaisalmer (Rs 65, 3½ hours) and Bikaner (Rs 65, 3½ hours).

Phalodi is on the broad-gauge line and has rail connections with Jodhpur (Rs 121 in sleeper, 3¼ hours, two daily) and Jaisalmer (Rs 121 in sleeper, 2½ hours, two daily).

#### GETTING AROUND

There are daily buses between Phalodi and Khichan (Rs 4, 15 minutes). A return autorickshaw to Khichan will cost Rs 50.

## Ramdevra

This desolate and windswept desert village lies 10km north of Pokaran. While it's not the most salubrious place to stay, it has an important, fascinating temple dedicated to deified local hero Ramdev, who lived in the Middle Ages.

#### SIGHTS

##### Ramdev Mandir

Ramdev was born in Tanwar village to a Rajput family and was opposed to all forms of untouchability, believing that all human beings are equal. He took samadhi (an ecstatic state involving conscious exit from the body) in 1458. The 1931 **temple** built in his honour has a brightly coloured façade, but isn't especially thrilling architecturally. However, the devotional activities of the hundreds of pilgrims who pay homage here are enthralling (Ramdev is worshipped by both Hindus and Muslims). The temple's at its busiest during the festival devoted to the saint in August or September (see the boxed text, p306). The streets outside are lined with tea shops and souvenir-wallahs.

Devotees place model horses in the temple in honour of the holy man's trusty steed, who carried him around when he was doing

### NUCLEAR SABRE-RATTLING

In May 1998 India detonated five nuclear devices in the Pokaran area. These included miniature devices to be used for missile warheads and a 43-kiloton device that was almost three times more powerful than the Hiroshima bomb. India also conducted its first nuclear test here, in 1974.

The 1998 tests led to poisonous tension between India and neighbouring Pakistan – rivals since Partition in 1947. The crux of the contention between the two countries has long been the disputed territory of Kashmir, which is claimed by both India and Pakistan. Hundreds of thousands of Hindu loyalists celebrated Prime Minister Atal Behari Vajpayee's controversial decision to hold the tests with fireworks and parties in the street. The US was less impressed, immediately imposing sanctions, suspending aid and recommending the freezing of international development loans. Japan withdrew its ambassador. Pakistan also swiftly responded to India by detonating its own nuclear devices, igniting global concern about a nuclear arms race in south Asia. The rupee plummeted and the military tensions really killed the holiday atmosphere – visitors were scared away, and Jaisalmer was rendered a virtual ghost town.

It was only in late September 2001 that the US lifted the sanctions against India that were imposed after the nuclear tests. Analysts saw this as a reward for India's support in the 'war against terror' after the 9/11 attacks on the United States.

The underground explosions have left a huge crater that's strictly off limits. Local villagers have complained of skin rashes and nose bleeds since the blasts, but it's uncertain if these are a result of the tests (doctors say that they're likely to be a result of the intense summer temperatures, which can reach up to 50°C).

Worth seeking out is director Anand Patwardhan's award-winning 2002 documentary *War & Peace*. This fascinating, dark and funny film examines the nuclear standoff, the patriotism that followed and the human cost. It was banned in India for two years.

Less controversial missiles continue to be tested at the site.



his good works. There are sometimes hundreds of embroidered horses, like the ones for sale all over Rajasthan.

You'll probably be assailed by people with receipt books demanding donations, both as you enter the temple complex and within the temple itself, even by men who 'guard' your shoes.

### SLEEPING

**Hotel Sohan Palace** (☎ 02996-237025; s/d Rs 150/200) Near the temple and the bus stand, Hotel Sohan is not much of a palace, but it has simple rooms if you must stay. No meals are available here.

### GETTING THERE & AWAY

Most buses between Phalodi and Pokaran pass through Ramdevra – the trip from Phalodi to Ramdevra costs Rs 20. Jeep taxis leave when full and travel along the main street to Pokaran (Rs 5, 20 minutes).

## Pokaran

☎ 02994

At the junction of the Jaisalmer, Jodhpur and Bikaner roads, 110km from Jaisalmer, is this desert town, site of another fort – a grand edifice the colour of dusty berries. Potters in the town make terracotta animals and red-and-white pottery.

Pokaran became notorious in 1998 as the site of India's controversial nuclear tests (see Nuclear Sabre-Rattling, above).

The bus stand is on the Jodhpur road at the southern edge of town. The fort is 1.5km to the northeast of the bus stand. There is nowhere to change money in Pokaran, so bring enough rupees.

### SIGHTS

#### Pokaran Fort & Museum

The red-sandstone **Pokaran Fort** (admission Rs 50, camera/video Rs 30/30; 7am-7pm) is an evocative place overlooking a tangle of narrow streets lined by balconied houses. Built from the 14th to the 17th century, it once had charge of 108 villages. Part of it is now a heritage hotel. There's a small museum with an assortment of weaponry, some brocaded clothes, old wooden printing blocks and various games belonging to former rulers of Pokaran, including dice and dominoes. There's also a small shrine to Durga.

A stop at Pokaran breaks the long journey between Jodhpur and Jaisalmer, but there's not a huge amount to see, so most travellers stop here for lunch rather than overnight.

### SLEEPING & EATING

Most travellers don't stay here, but there are a couple of reasonable choices.

**Fort Pokaran** (☎ 222274; r Rs 1100, ste Rs 2000; ❄) Within the fort, this place offers faded, characterful rooms that have been refurbished but are not particularly luxurious. It's a peaceful place to stay, and jeep safaris can be arranged from here.

**RTDC Motel Godawan** (☎ 222275; s/d Rs 400/500) About 3km west of the bus stand, this offers rooms and huts. A lot better than many other RTDC hotels, it also has a restaurant.

### GETTING THERE & AWAY

There are regular RSRTC buses to Jaisalmer (Rs 35, two hours). There are also buses to Bikaner (Rs 88, five hours) and to Jodhpur (Rs 60, three hours).

Trains were not serving Pokaran station (connected with Jodhpur and Jaisalmer) at the time of research. Check locally for the current situation.

## JAISALMER

☎ 02992 / pop 58,286

A giant, gleaming sand castle rising from 80m-high Trikuta (Three-Peaked) Hill, Jaisalmer is a breathtaking sight. Known as the Golden City, it's a mirage in the middle of a barren desertscape. It seems to have sprung from a chivalrous tale, a storybook or an overly imaginative miniature illustration. No place better evokes ancient desert splendour and exotic trade routes.

Ninety-nine huge bastions encircle the narrow streets of the fort, which is still inhabited. Elaborate houses, splendid temples, magnificent gateways and a beautiful palace are all carved out of the same warm-yellow sandstone. Once the inhabitants worked for the maharajas, but today they mainly run guesthouses, or shops and stalls swaddled in the kaleidoscopic mirrors and embroideries of Rajasthani cloth. Despite the commercialism of the Italian restaurants, Internet cafés and camel-safari culture, it's impossible not to be bewitched.

There's still a sense of community within the straitened streets, with families pouring out of the close-knit web of houses, and cows blocking the narrowest corners. Spreading from the fort is the old city, containing lavish sandstone *havelis*, and all around lie the scrub, dunes and villages of the Great Thar Desert.

### History

Jaisalmer history since it was founded in 1156 has been derived from the tales and songs of the bards. The succession of maharajas of Jaisalmer trace their lineage back to a ruler of the Bhatti Rajput clan, Jaitasimha.

#### ARRIVAL IN JAISALMER

If you're arriving in Jaisalmer by bus, you'll notice that the number of passengers suddenly swells about an hour before arrival. Your new companions are touts, not wanting to miss the chance of a captive audience.

In the past few years, local authorities have introduced policies designed to keep the touts at bay. Most carriages on the overnight train carry at least a couple of soldiers to try to ensure you get a good night's sleep, and soldiers also patrol the train-station platforms in Jodhpur with varying degrees of vigilance. Perhaps the most surreal experience is stumbling out of the train in the predawn light to find a small army of hotel owners kept behind a barricade about 20m from the station exit, holding up their signs and champing at the bit. Once you cross that line, you're on your own.

Don't believe anyone who offers to take you 'anywhere you like' for just a few rupees, and take with a fistful of salt claims that the hotel you want to stay in is 'full', 'closed' or 'no good any more', or has suffered some other inglorious fate. Also watch out for hotel representatives who offer you amazingly cheap rooms. They often just want you to join their camel safari and will throw you out if you don't fancy it – some even become aggressive. If the hotel of your choice has a representative waiting for you, by all means accept the free ride. Alternatively, take a rickshaw and hope you get an honest driver (they do exist) – pay no more than Rs 30.

The Bhatti Rajputs trace *their* lineage back to Krishna.

The 13th and 14th centuries were a tempestuous time, as rulers relied on looting for want of other income, and Jaisalmer was repeatedly attacked as those looted sought revenge. In the 14th century the emperor of Delhi, Ala-ud-din Khilji, mounted an expedition to Jaisalmer to retrieve treasure that the Bhattis had taken from a caravan train en route to the imperial capital. He laid siege to Jaisalmer Fort for nine years. When defeat was imminent, *jauhar* (ritual mass suicide) was declared: the women of Jaisalmer committed themselves to the flames, while the men donned saffron robes and rode out to certain death. Jaitasimha's son Duda, a hero of the Bhattis, perished in the battle.

Duda's descendants continued to rule over the desert kingdom. In 1541 Lunakarna of Jaisalmer fought against Humayun when he passed through Jaisalmer en route to Ajmer. The relationship between the Jaisalmer rulers and the Mughal empire was not always hostile, and various marriages were contracted between the two parties to cement their alliance. Later Jaisalmer notables include Sabala Simha, who won the patronage of the Muslim Emperor Shah Jahan (r 1627–58) when he fought with distinction in a campaign at Peshawar. Although not the legitimate heir to the *gaddi* (throne), Shah Jahan invested Sabala Simha with the power to rule Jaisalmer, and he annexed areas that now fall into the administrative districts of Bikaner and Jodhpur.

The Jaisalmer rulers continued to line their coffers with illicit gains won through cattle rustling as well as through more orthodox methods, such as imposing levies on the caravans that passed through the kingdom on their way to Delhi. They were renowned for their valour in battle and for their treachery, as they fought to enlarge and secure their territories.

Religion and the fine arts flourished under the rulers of Jaisalmer. Although professing Hinduism, they were tolerant of Jainism, encouraging the construction of the beautiful temples that now grace the old city within the fort walls. Sculptural depictions of both Hindu and Jain deities and holy men stand side by side on the walls of these fine edifices. The visionary rulers commissioned scholars to copy precious sacred manuscripts and books of ancient learning that may otherwise have been lost during Muslim raids.

From the 16th to the 18th century Jaisalmer's strategic position on the camel-train routes between India and Central Asia brought it great wealth. The merchants and townspeople built magnificent houses and mansions, all carved from wood and golden-yellow sandstone. These merchant *havelis* can be found elsewhere in Rajasthan (notably in Shekhawati), but nowhere are they quite as exquisite as in Jaisalmer. Even the humblest of shops and houses display something of the Rajput love of the decorative arts in its most whimsical form.

The rise of shipping trade and the port of Mumbai saw the city decline. At Independence, Partition and the cutting of trade routes through to Pakistan seemingly sealed the city's fate, and water shortages could have pronounced the death sentence. However, the 1965 and 1971 wars between India and Pakistan revealed Jaisalmer's strategic importance, and the Indira Gandhi Canal to the north is restoring life to the desert.

Today tourism rivals the military base as the pillar of the city's economy. The presence of the Border Security Force means that the occasional sound of war planes disturbs the tranquillity of this desert gem. Being so reliant on the tourist dollar, Jaisalmer is in a vulnerable position. When tensions run high along the border, the city suffers. In 2002, when tourists stayed away following India's decision to conduct nuclear tests, Jaisalmer was deserted.

## Orientation

This old city was once completely surrounded by an extensive wall, much of which has, sadly, been torn down in recent years for reuse as building material. Some of it remains, however, including the city gates and, inside them, the massive fort that rises above the city and is the essence of Jaisalmer. The fort is entered via the First Fort Gate. Within its walls is a warren of narrow, paved streets complete with Jain temples and the old palace of the former ruler – it's small enough that you'll never get lost for long.

The main market, Bhatia Market, and most of the city's attractions and important offices surround the fort to the north.

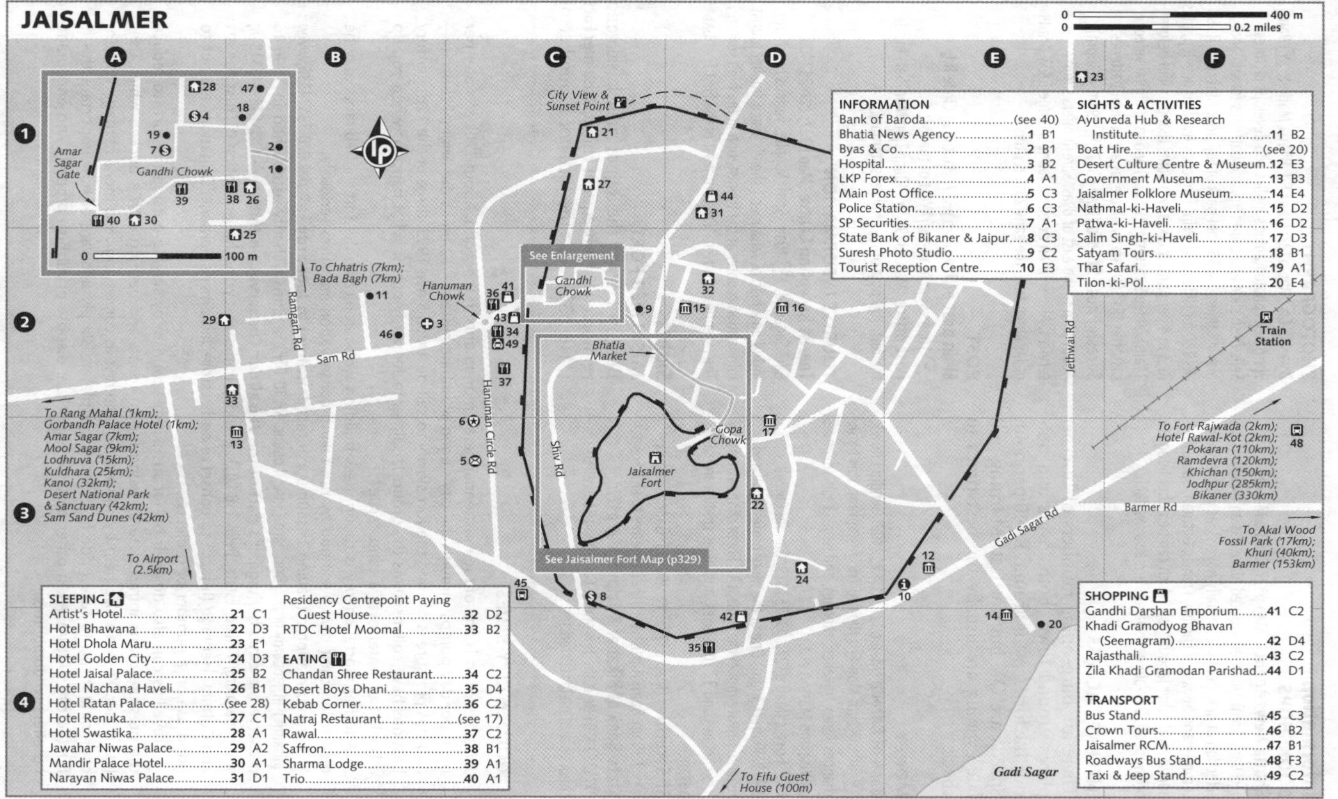
JAISALMER
0 400 m
0 0.2 miles
INFORMATION
Bank of Baroda....(see 40)
Bhatia News Agency....1 B1
Byas & Co....2 B1
Hospital....3 B2
LKP Forex....4 A1
Main Post Office....5 C3
Police Station....6 C3
SP Securities....7 A1
State Bank of Bikaner & Jaipur....8 C3
Suresh Photo Studio....9 C2
Tourist Reception Centre....10 E3
SIGHTS & ACTIVITIES
Ayurveda Hub & Research Institute....11 B2
Boat Hire....(see 20)
Desert Culture Centre & Museum....12 E3
Government Museum....13 B3
Jaisalmer Folklore Museum....14 E4
Nathmal-ki-Haveli....15 D2
Patwa-ki-Haveli....16 D2
Salim Singh-ki-Haveli....17 D3
Satyam Tours....18 B1
Thar Safari....19 A1
Tilon-ki-Pol....20 E4
SLEEPING
Artist's Hotel....21 C1
Hotel Bhawana....22 D3
Hotel Dhola Maru....23 E1
Hotel Golden City....24 D3
Hotel Jaisal Palace....25 B2
Hotel Nachana Haveli....26 B1
Hotel Ratan Palace....(see 28)
Hotel Renuka....27 C1
Hotel Swastika....28 A1
Jawahar Niwas Palace....29 A2
Mandir Palace Hotel....30 A1
Narayan Niwas Palace....31 D1
Residency Centrepoint Paying Guest House....32 D2
RTDC Hotel Moomal....33 B2
EATING
Chandan Shree Restaurant....34 C2
Desert Boys Dhani....35 D4
Kebab Corner....36 C2
Natraj Restaurant....(see 17)
Rawal....37 C2
Saffron....38 B1
Sharma Lodge....39 A1
Trio....40 A1
SHOPPING
Gandhi Darshan Emporium....41 C2
Khadi Gramodyog Bhavan (Seemagram)....42 D4
Rajasthali....43 C2
Zila Khadi Gramodan Parishad....44 D1
TRANSPORT
Bus Stand....45 C3
Crown Tours....46 B2
Jaisalmer RCM....47 B1
Roadways Bus Stand....48 F3
Taxi & Jeep Stand....49 C2
Amar Sagar Gate
Gandhi Chowk
0 100 m
To Chhatris (7km); Bada Bagh (7km)
Hanuman Chowk
City View & Sunset Point
See Enlargement
Bhatia Market
Gopa Chowk
Jaisalmer Fort
Shiv Rd
Sam Rd
Ramgarh Rd
Hanuman Circle Rd
Jethwai Rd
Barmer Rd
Gadi Sagar Rd
Gadi Sagar
Train Station
See Jaisalmer Fort Map (p329)
To Rang Mahal (1km); Gorbandh Palace Hotel (1km); Amar Sagar (7km); Mool Sagar (9km); Lodhruva (15km); Kuldhara (25km); Kanoi (32km); Desert National Park & Sanctuary (42km); Sam Sand Dunes (42km)
To Airport (2.5km)
To Fort Rajwada (2km); Hotel Rawal-Kot (2km); Pokaran (110km); Ramdevra (120km); Khichan (150km); Jodhpur (285km); Bikaner (330km)
To Akal Wood Fossil Park (17km); Khuri (40km); Barmer (153km)
To Fifu Guest House (100m)
WESTERN RAJASTHAN

## Information

### BOOKSHOPS

**Bhatia News Agency** (Map p327; Bhatia Market; 9am-9pm) This well-stocked place has an excellent selection of new books (especially novels), as well as some second-hand books (in English, French, German, Spanish and several other languages), which can be either bought or swapped. Day-old newspapers are also available.

### INTERNET ACCESS

There are burgeoning numbers of Internet places around town, both inside and outside the fort. Cost is around Rs 40 per hour. Speeds are OK but not fast. Morning and late evening are usually the best times to check.

### MONEY

**Bank of Baroda** (Map p327; ☎ 252402; Gandhi Chowk; 10am-2pm Mon-Fri) Next to Trio restaurant, this bank changes Amex travellers cheques, and issues cash advances on Visa and MasterCard.

**LKP Forex** (Map p327; ☎ 253679; Gandhi Chowk; 9.30am-9.30pm) One of the more professional and reliable private moneychangers, LKP Forex changes travellers cheques and 32 currencies, and gives credit-card cash advances.

**SP Securities** (Map p327; ☎ 250025; Gandhi Chowk; 9.30am-8pm) A trustworthy alternative to LKP Forex.

**State Bank of Bikaner & Jaipur** (Map p327; ☎ 252430) Near the bus stand. Can change travellers cheques and major currencies.

### PHOTOGRAPHY

**Byas & Co** (Map p327; Court Rd, Bhatia Market; 9am-9pm) Sells photographic supplies and develops pictures. Sells fresh slide and print film, and batteries for still and movie cameras. A 36-shot pack of Fuji print film costs Rs 90 (Rs 180 for slide film). Print film costs Rs 15 to develop, plus Rs 3 to 4 per print. It takes two hours (hand in film before 11am). Video 8 cassettes (Rs 250) and mini digital video cassettes (Rs 300) are available, as are lithium batteries.

**Suresh Photo Studio** (Map p327; 9am-8.30pm) About 50m to the east of Byas, Suresh offers similar services. Also sells an excellent range of large B&W prints of Jaisalmer from the early 20th century.

### POST

**Main post office** (Map p327; Hanuman Circle Rd; 10am-5pm Mon-Sat) West of the fort.

**Post office** (Map p329; 10am-3pm Mon-Sat) Inside the fort, this post office only sells stamps.

### TOURIST INFORMATION

**Tourist Reception Centre** (Map p327; ☎ 252406; Gadi Sagar Rd; 10am-5pm) Supplies various brochures, including a map of Jaisalmer. (There's also a smaller tourist information counter at the train station in the high season.) The reception centre is 1km southeast of the First Fort Gate.

## Sights

### JAISALMER FORT

Built in 1156 by the Rajput ruler Jaisala and reinforced by subsequent rulers, **Jaisalmer Fort** (Map p329) was the focus of a number of

#### GOLDEN CITY BLUES

Jaisalmer's fort is one of the most endangered monuments in the world. About 120L of water per head per day pumps through the city's aged plumbing system – 12 times the original capacity – and this pressure is causing the fort slowly to self-destruct. Since 1993, three of the 12th-century bastions have collapsed. As the group Jaisalmer in Jeopardy puts it, what happens when you tip a bucket of water over a sand castle?

Another mortal enemy is thoughtless building work. Ironically, the fort's inhabitants may be destroying their own livelihood by not taking conservation measures seriously.

For information on saving Jaisalmer, contact **Jaisalmer in Jeopardy** (☎/fax 020-73524336; www.jaisalmer-in-jeopardy.org; 3 Brickbarn Close, London SW10 0TP), a British charity established in 1996 to preserve the city's heritage. It's part of the **Jaisalmer Conservation Initiative** (☎ 011-24631818; www.intach.org; 71 Lodi Estate, Delhi 110 003), a wider initiative by the Indian National Trust for Art and Cultural Heritage (Intach) to conserve and restore Jaisalmer's heritage. Donations are put to good use on a number of projects.

Travellers can also do their bit for sustainable tourism by staying outside the fort (to reduce the pressure on its infrastructure), using Indian toilets and bathing with a bucket, which uses less water. You can also help by showing an interest in conserving Jaisalmer's heritage and encouraging locals to take pride in it. Many people are simply unaware of how important this is for the city's future. As in other parts of Rajasthan, dispose of rubbish properly and encourage hoteliers to do so, too.

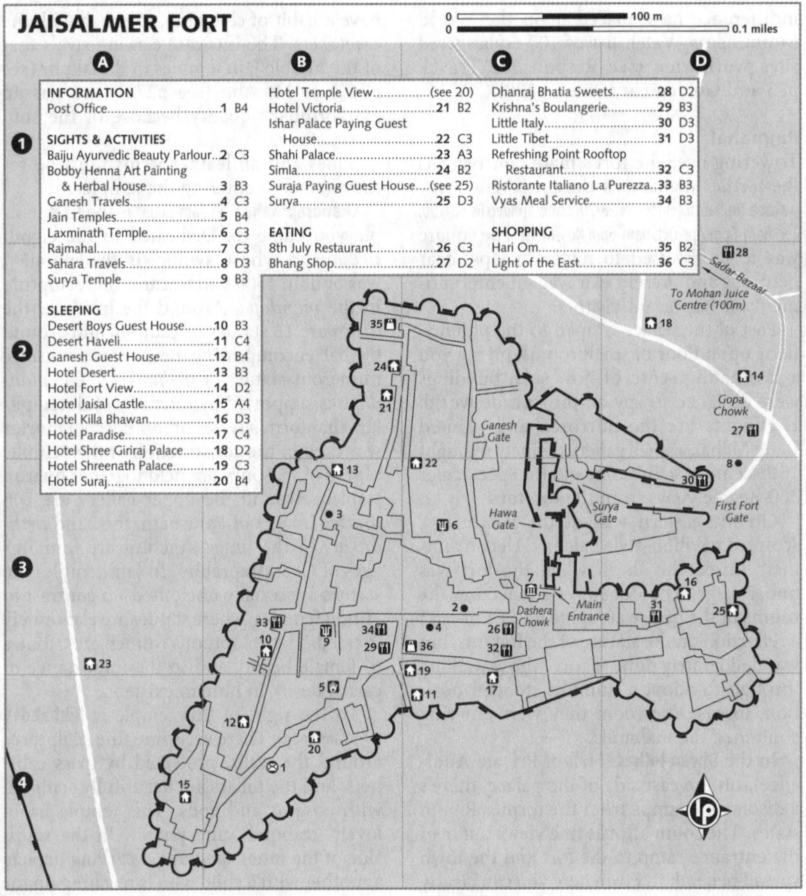


battles between the Bhattis, the Mughals of Delhi and the Rathores of Jodhpur. The lower of the fort's three layers of wall is composed of solid stone blocks, which reinforce the loose rubble of Trikuta Hill. The second wall snakes around the fort, and between this and the third, or inner, wall, the warrior Rajputs hurled boiling oil and water, and massive round missiles on their unwitting enemies below.

The Jaisalmer standard, which features a *chhatri* against a red-and-yellow background, flies above the structure.

You enter the fort through a forbidding series of massive gates leading to a large courtyard, and it's inside the walls that Jaisalmer's unique quality becomes clear: it is a living fort – about 25% of the old city's population resides within its walls. It's an extraordinary, resonant experience to wander around the lanes inside this animated museum. It's packed with houses, temples, handicraft shops and beauty parlours, and honeycombed with narrow, winding lanes, all of them paved in stone. It's also quiet – vehicles cannot drive beyond the main courtyard. The fort walls provide superb views over the old city and surrounding desert – it's fantastic to stroll around the outer fort ramparts at sunset. The fort looks especially magical when it's lit up at night under a clear sky full of stars.

Sadly, the tourist trade is threatening the fort. Tourist numbers and government indifference have placed it on the World Monuments Watch list of 100 endangered sites worldwide (see Responsible Travel, p75 and Golden City Blues, p328).

### Rajmahal

Towering over the fort's main courtyard is the former maharaja's elegant seven-storey **palace** (Indian/foreigner Rs 20/70, camera/video Rs 50/150; 8am-6pm Apr-Oct, 9am-6pm Nov-Mar). The square was formerly used to review troops, hear petitions and present extravagant entertainment for important visitors.

Part of the palace is open to the public – floor upon floor of small rooms, giving you a fascinating sense of how such buildings were designed to spy on the outside world. Highlights are the mirrored and painted Rang Mahal, a small gallery of finely wrought 15th-century sculptures, and the spectacular 360-degree views from the rooftop.

On the eastern wall of the palace is a sculpted pavilion-style balcony. Here drummers raised the alarm when the fort was under siege. The doorways connecting the rooms of the palace are quite low – this isn't a reflection on the stature of the Rajputs, but was deliberately done to force those walking through to adopt a humble, stooped position, in case the room they were entering contained the maharaja.

In the **Diwan-i-Khas** (Hall of Private Audience), on the east side of the palace, there's a display of stamps from the former Rajput states. The room affords fine views out over the entrance ramp to the fort and the town spread beneath it. From here you can clearly see the numerous round rocks piled on top of the battlements, ready to be rolled onto advancing enemies. There's a small **Diwan-i-Am** (Hall of Public Audience), with lower walls lined with porcelain tiles.

The adjacent room is lined with blue and white tiles. Upstairs, close to the maharaja's private chamber on the east side of the palace, is a room with some exquisite stone-panel friezes that on first glance appear to have been carved from wood.

### Jain Temples

Within the fort walls is a maze-like, interconnecting treasure trove of seven beautiful yellow-sandstone **Jain temples** (Map p329; admission Rs 10, camera/video Rs 50/100), dating from the 12th to the 16th century. Opening times have a habit of changing, so check with the caretakers. The intricate carving rivals that of the marble Jain temples in Ranakpur (see p266) or Mt Abu (see p272), and has an extraordinary quality because of the soft, warm stone.

Shoes and all leather items must be removed before entering the temples.

**Chandraprabhu** ( 7am-noon) is the first temple you come to. Dedicated to the eighth *tirthankar*, whose symbol is the moon, it was built in 1509 and features fine sculpture in the *mandapa*. Around the inside of the drum are 12 statues of Ganesh, and around the hall encompassing the inner sanctum are numerous statues of *tirthankars*. The *mandapa* is supported by intensely sculpted pillars that form a series of *toranas*. No mortar was used in the construction of this temple; blocks of masonry are held together by iron staples. Around the upper gallery are 108 marble images of Parasnath, the 22nd *tirthankar*. In the inner sanctum are four images of Chandraprabhu. In Jain temples the statues are usually unclothed – a contrast to Hindu temples, where statues are elaborately dressed. The voluptuous women are tributes to female beauty and to the importance of carnal desire in human existence.

To the right of this temple is **Rikhabdev** ( 7am-noon). There are some fine sculptures around the walls, protected by glass cabinets, and the pillars are beautifully sculpted with *apsaras* and gods. This temple has a lovely, tranquil atmosphere. On the south side of the inner sanctum, a carving depicts a mother with a child who is reaching up for the fruit she is holding just out of reach. Behind the sanctum is a depiction of the Hindu goddess Kali, flanked by a Jain sculpture of an unclothed woman – a chance to compare the elaborately garbed Hindu statue with its less prim Jain equivalent.

Behind Chandraprabhu temple is **Parasnath** ( 11am-noon), which you enter through a beautifully carved *toran* culminating in an image of the Jain *tirthankar* at its apex. There is a voluptuous carving of an *apsara* balancing sets of balls on her raised forearm. The temple interior has a beautiful, brightly painted ceiling.

A door to the south leads to small **Shitalnath** ( 11am-noon), dedicated to the 10th *tirthankar*. The depiction of Shitalnath enshrined here is composed of eight precious metals. A door in the north wall leads to the enchanting, dim chamber of **Sambhavanth** (11am-noon) – in the front courtyard, Jain priests grind sandalwood in mortars for devotional use. Steps lead down to the **Gyan Bhandar** (10-11am), a fascinating, tiny library founded in 1500 by Acharya Maharaj Jin Bhadra Suri. This small underground vault houses priceless ancient illustrated manuscripts, some dating from the 11th century. Other exhibits include astrological charts and the Jain version of the Shroud of Turin: the Shroud of Gindhasuri, a Jain hermit and holy man who died in Ajmer. When his body was placed on the funeral pyre, the shroud remained miraculously unsinged. In a small locked cabinet are images of Parasnath that are made of ivory and various precious stones, including emerald and crystal. The remaining two temples are **Shantinath**, and **Kunthunath** (11am-noon), below the library, both built in 1536. They each have plenty of sensual carving. The enclosed gallery around Shantinath is flanked by hundreds of images of saints, some made of marble and some of Jaisalmer sandstone.

Guides are available outside the temples for around Rs 50.

### Laxminath Temple

This **Hindu temple** (Map p329), in the centre of the fort, is simpler than the Jain temples and has a brightly decorated dome. Devotees offer grain, which is distributed before the temple. There're a repoussé silver architrave around the entrance to the inner sanctum, and a heavily garlanded image enshrined within.

There's also a small Hindu temple devoted to Surya, the sun god, inside the fort.

## HAVELIS

Outside the fort walls, Jaisalmer has some incredibly fine sculpted sandstone buildings built by wealthy merchants in the 19th and 20th centuries; some are in excellent condition. An admission fee is charged at some of the *havelis*, but most of them reserve their most stunning decoration for the outside – showing that building was much about status for these merchants.

### Patwa-ki-Haveli

The biggest fish in the *haveli* pond is **Patwa-ki-Haveli** (Map p327; admission Rs 20, camera/video Rs 20/20; 9am-6pm), which towers over a narrow lane, its stonework like craggy, honey-coloured lace. It was built between 1800 and 1860 by five Jain brothers who made their fortunes in brocade and jewellery. It's most impressive from the outside, but inside there are remnants of paintings in vibrant red and gold, as well as fine mirrorwork. The interior has been set up to evoke 19th-century life, with old furnishings and household items. There's a superb view of the fort from the roof.

### Salim Singh-ki-Haveli

This 300-year-old private **haveli** (Map p327; admission Rs 15, camera/video Rs 10/50; 8am-7pm May-Sep, 8am-6pm Oct-Apr) has an amazing, distinctive shape. It's narrow for the first floors, and then the top storey spreads out into a mass of carving, with graceful arched balconies surmounted by pale blue cupolas. The beautifully arched roof has superb carved brackets in the form of peacocks. There are stone elephants before the *haveli* – a traditional sign of welcome commonly found in front of all respectable palaces and grand mansions. Amazingly, the building is constructed with no mortar or cement – the stones are connected with tongue-and-groove joints.

Salim Singh was a notorious prime minister of Jaisalmer. His father had been prime minister before him, but was murdered. When Salim Singh was old enough, he took revenge on the perpetrators of his father's death by murdering them in turn. His was a stern, unpleasant rule, and his ill treatment of the local Paliwal community led them to abandon their 84 villages in the Jaisalmer region and move elsewhere. You can visit Kuldhara, one of the deserted villages – see p341. Salim Singh was eventually murdered on the orders of the maharaja.

The admission fee to Salim Singh-ki-Haveli includes a free guided tour, although language can be a bit of a problem.

### Nathmal-ki-Haveli

This late-19th-century **haveli** (Map p327; admission free; 8am-7pm) also used to be a prime minister's house and it's still partly inhabited. It has an extraordinary exterior dripping with carving, and the beautiful paintings on the 1st floor used 1.5kg of gold. A doorway is surrounded by 19th-century British postcards, and there's a picture of Queen

Victoria. The left and right wings were the work of two brothers, whose competitive spirit apparently produced this virtuoso work – the two sides are similar, but not identical. Sandstone elephants keep guard out the front.

### GADI SAGAR

This stately **tank**, south of the city walls, was once the water supply of the city and, befitting its importance in providing precious water to the inhabitants of this arid place, it is surrounded by many small temples and shrines. The tank was built in 1367 by Maharaja Gadsi Singh, taking advantage of a natural declivity that already retained some water. It's a waterfowl favourite in winter. Between 8am and 9pm you can hire a boat for Rs 10 to 100 for 30 minutes.

The attractive **Tilon-ki-Pol** (Map p327) gateway that straddles the road down to the tank is said to have been built by a famous prostitute. When she offered to pay to have it constructed, the maharaja refused permission on the grounds that he would have to pass under it to go down to the tank, and he felt that this would be beneath his dignity. While he was away, she built the gate anyway, adding a Krishna temple on top so the king could not tear it down.

### MUSEUMS

Next to the Tourist Reception Centre is the **Desert Culture Centre & Museum** (Map p327; ☎ 252188; admission Rs 10; ⏰ 10am-5pm), which has interesting information on Rajasthani culture, as well as textiles, old coins, fossils, traditional Rajasthani musical instruments and a *karal* (opium-mixing box), among other things. Its aim is to preserve cultural heritage and conduct research on local history. There's a nightly one-hour **puppet show** (admission Rs 30, camera/video Rs 20/50) at 6.30pm.

Admission to the Desert Culture Centre includes entry to the small **Jaisalmer Folklore Museum** (Map p327; camera/video Rs 20/50; ⏰ 8am-6pm), which has everything from camel ornaments to opium bottles. Both museums were founded by NK Sharma, a local historian and folklorist. The hill nearby is a tremendous place to soak up the sunset.

Close to the RTDC Hotel Moomal is the small **government museum** (Map p327; admission Rs 3, free Mon, photography prohibited; ⏰ 10am-4.30pm Sat-Thu), which has a limited but well-captioned collection of fossils, some dating back to the Jurassic era (160 to 180 million years ago). Other exhibits include examples of ancient script, coins, religious sculptures (some from the 11th century), puppets and textiles. There's even a stuffed great Indian bustard, the state bird of Rajasthan, which thrives in the Great Thar Desert but is declining in numbers elsewhere.

## Activities

### MASSAGE

After a long camel trek you can soothe your jangled body with a spot of Ayurvedic massage and herbal healing. Most people come to the **Ayurveda Hub & Research Institute** (Map p327; ☎ 254692; drprathmeshvyas@yahoo.co.in; 62 CV Singh Colony, off Sam Rd; ⏰ 9am-6.30pm) for a massage. One-hour ordinary massages cost Rs 400, and one-hour fresh-leaf massages with herbs, powders and oils are Rs 600. A 20-minute steam bath costs Rs 150. For the more adventurous, the centre offers a wide range of other Ayurvedic treatments to cure everything from asthma to arthritis. A full day of detoxification therapy costs Rs 1800, which includes around six different treatments and takes three to four hours.

There are loads of other places offering Ayurvedic massage and henna painting, including **Baiju Ayurvedic Beauty Parlour** (Map p329; ☎ 255730; ⏰ 10am-8pm), located near Rajmahal in the fort, which offers facials (Rs 200) and Ayurvedic massage (Rs 400), as well as manicures, pedicures and waxing. It's female run, so women will feel comfortable here.

**Bobby Henna Art Painting & Herbal House** (Map p329; ☎ 254468; ⏰ 10am-8pm), another women-only show, is a good place to get your hands decorated with henna (Rs 50 to 100). Massage (full body Rs 250, Ayurvedic Rs 300) is also on offer – as is some unusual sex-therapy advice, apparently.

## Courses

The **Ayurveda Hub & Research Institute** (Map p327; ☎ 254692; drprathmeshvyas@yahoo.co.in; 62 CV Singh Colony; ⏰ 9am-6.30pm), off Sam Rd, offers courses in Ayurveda, which last from seven days to six months. A seven-day course costs Rs 4500, including free treatments. Longer courses are free, but you must volunteer at the institute.

## Tours

Few travellers visit Jaisalmer without venturing into the desert on a camel. For details, see Jaisalmer Camel Safaris, p334.

The Tourist Reception Centre runs sunset tours to the Sam sand dunes (Rs 130 per person) at 3pm, returning after sunset. On request, the tours to Sam may stop at Kanoi, 5km before the dunes, from where it's possible to get a camel to the dunes in time for sunset (around Rs 200).

## Sleeping

Staying within the fort is romantic, but authorities are urging tourists to make an ethical choice and stay outside the walls, as pressure on the fort infrastructure is contributing to subsidence (see p328).

Motorised traffic is not permitted beyond the main square at most times, but anywhere further into the maze is a 10-minute walk at most.

Rates fluctuate a lot. If there's a festival on, rooms are expensive and scarce, but at slow times most places offer big discounts. You'll get massive discounts between April and August, but you'd also be crazy to come during this time, as Jaisalmer becomes hellishly hot. Often guesthouses here are rented by the management, so they can alter in quality from one year to the next according to who's in charge.

Like many Rajasthan tourist centres, there are a lot more budget choices than midrange options, but some of the budget choices are of a very decent standard. (Unfortunately, a few budget hotels are really into the high-pressure selling of camel safaris; see Arrival in Jaisalmer, p325.) This being such an important stop on the tourist route, there's also an unusually large choice of top-end hotels.

Many hotels in Jaisalmer have a stingy 9am checkout time.

### BUDGET

There are plenty of budget hotels to choose from. Most of the rock-bottom places are pretty similar in standard – clean and reasonable, but watch out for the hard-sell safari. The Paying Guest House Scheme has only a few participating families in Jaisalmer. Expect to pay Rs 150 to 300 – contact the **Tourist Reception Centre** (Map p327; ☎ 252406; Gadi Sagar Rd; 10am-5pm) for details.

#### Town Area

**Hotel Renuka** (Map p327; ☎ 252757; hotelrenuka@rediffmail.com; r Rs 100-250) Renuka has bright, clean rooms – the best have balconies and bathrooms. The hoel has a roof terrace with great fort views and a restaurant.

**Hotel Ratan Palace** (Map p327; ☎ 253615; s/d Rs 100/250) The same family runs the Hotel Renuka. Ratan Palace is a newer building, with the same friendly approach and large, bright rooms.

**Hotel Swastika** (Map p327; ☎ 252483; s/d from Rs 80/120, larger from Rs 120/150) This place is well run, efficient and clean, and you'll receive no hassles. Rooms are simple and unfussy with no frills; some have balconies.

**Hotel Golden City** (Map p327; ☎ /fax 251664; hotelgoldencity@hotmail.com; off Gadi Sagar Rd; rooftop Rs 25, r Rs 145-525; ) This hotel is in the southern section of the walled city, and has a range of clean, modern rooms from smaller budget options to bigger plush ones with balcony and satellite TV. You can also sleep on the roof for a small charge. Readers have reported some safari hassles. Nonguests can use the pool for Rs 50.

**Artist's Hotel** (Map p327; ☎ 251498; artisthotel@yahoo.com; Artist Colony, Suly Dungri; r Rs 250) Austrian-owned, this helps local musicans with school fees and emergency money. The surrounding colony gives it a village atmosphere, and there are great fort views from the roof (where there are regular concerts). Rooms are ordinary but comfortable.

**Hotel Bhawana** (Map p327; ☎ 250116; loisemason@hotmail.com; r Rs 150-300) Run by a nice Indian-Kiwi couple, this recommended small guesthouse is tucked away near the First Fort Gate. It has five pleasant, simple rooms. At the time of research there were plans to move to a new building at Sunset Point, near the *chhatris*, sometime in the next few years, so ring ahead to check the location (prices will remain similar).

**Hotel Fort View** (Map p329; ☎ 252214; r Rs 100-200) Close to the fort entrance is this friendly option, though some of the rooms are tiny. The best room has a great fort view and balcony. There's a popular top-floor fort-facing restaurant.

**Hotel Shree Giriraj Palace** (Map p329; ☎ 252268; r with shared bathroom from Rs 80, with private bathroom Rs 125) Just off Bhatia Market, this hotel has cheap-and-cheerful rooms in an old building. The upstairs restaurant has fort views.

**Residency Centrepoint Paying Guest House** (Map p327; ☎/fax 252883; s/d Rs 350/400) Near the Patwa-ki-Haveli, this friendly, family-run guesthouse has five clean, spacious doubles. Room No 101 has a lovely antique balcony. The rooftop restaurant has superb fort views and offers home-cooked food.

The retiring rooms at the train station aren't bad at all. Dorm beds are Rs 75, and doubles with private bathroom are Rs 150. Try to get one of the thatched huts, which are set back from the station. No meals are available.

### Fort

**Simla** (Map p329; ☎ 253061; simlahaveli@yahoo.co.in; Kund Para; r Rs 65-300) In the north corner of the fort is this clean, charming place, built from light golden sandstone. It has a range of rooms with some good furniture and carving. There's a restaurant on the roof.

**Ganesh Guest House** (Map p329; ☎ 253119; ganeshguesthouse@yahoo.com; Vyas Para; r Rs 250-450) A new guesthouse, run by camel-safari agency Ganesh Travels (see Jaisalmer Camel Safaris, below), this is a new sandstone building and an appealing, hassle-free place to stay. It's built in traditional style, and has attractive, spick-and-span rooms with satin-cushioned window seats. Room 104 has great temple-top views.

**Hotel Desert** (Map p329; ☎ 250602; ajitdeserthotel@hotmail.com; r Rs 150-450) Relaxed, hassle-free

## JAISALMER CAMEL SAFARIS

Trekking around Jaisalmer by camel is the most evocative and fun way to sample desert life. The best time to go is from October to February.

### Before You Go

Competition between safari organisers is cut-throat, and standards vary. None of the hotels have their own camels – these are independently owned – so the hoteliers and the travel agencies are just go-betweens.

Hotel owners pay the camel drivers around Rs 175 per camel per day, so if you're offered a safari at Rs 250 per day, this leaves only a small margin for food and profit, and corners are obviously going to be cut somewhere. Beware of operators who claim (and charge for) three-day safaris when you return after breakfast on the third day – this is hardly value for money.

The realistic minimum price for a safari is about Rs 400 to 450 per person per day. For this you can expect breakfasts of porridge, tea and toast, and lunches and dinners of rice, dhal and chapatis. Blankets are also supplied. Usually you must bring your own mineral water. Of course, you can pay for greater levels of comfort, such as tents, stretcher beds, better food and beer, but take care: some travellers have paid extra for promised upgrades, only to find out afterwards that their safari was much the same as for people who paid less.

However much you decide to spend, ensure you know where you'll be taken and check that what has been promised is in place before leaving Jaisalmer. Attempting to get a refund for services not provided is a waste of time. Take care of your possessions, particularly on the return journey. It's wise to look after your own bag rather than have drivers keep an eye on it. Any complaints you do have should be reported, either to the **Superintendent of Police** (☎ 252233) or the **Tourist Reception Centre** (☎ 252406).

If you're on your own, it's worth getting a group together. Organisers will make up groups, but four days – or even two – are a lot to spend with a stranger you don't get on with. Usually each person is assigned their own camel, but check this, as some agencies might try to save cash by hiring fewer camels. This means you'll find yourself sharing your camel with a camel driver – definitely not an advisable option for women travellers, and not much fun for men either.

### What to Take

Women should consider wearing a sports bra, as a trotting camel is a bumpy ride. A wide-brimmed hat (or I-am-Lawrence-of-Arabia turban), long trousers, toilet paper, sunscreen and a water bottle (with a strap) are also recommended. It can get cold at night, so if you have a sleeping bag, bring it along even if you're told that lots of blankets will be supplied.

and good value, Hotel Desert has simple rooms with great views. The pricier ones upstairs are smart, with window seats and balconies. There's a perfect view from the rooftop restaurant.

**Ishar Palace Paying Guest House** (Map p329; ☎ 253062; isharpalace@hotmail.com; dm Rs 50, d Rs 80-250) Near the Laxminath Temple, this guesthouse gets good reports and has a nice owner. It's a bit run-down and rooms are basic, but it was the home of a 19th-century prime minister, Ishar Singh – as evidenced by the statues of elephants in front of the building – and has lots of character. Rooms range from one with a shared bathroom and tented ceiling, to the PM's own modest room, with a balcony from which he used to address petitioners.

**Desert Haveli** (Map p329; ☎ 251555; r Rs 200-400) A laid-back place that's undergone a few changes of management in recent years. It's housed in a lovely, reputedly haunted, old *haveli*. The best room is lined with pillars and has windows looking onto the street.

**Hotel Temple View** (Map p329; ☎ 252832; s/d with shared bathroom Rs 175/200, with private bathroom from Rs 250/300) This has simple, small but decent enough rooms – pricier ones have views over the temple tops – and the rooftop view is great.

**Surya** (Map p329; ☎ 250647; d with shared bathroom Rs 50-200) This good-value place is an ancient

WESTERN RAJASTHAN

### Which Safari?

Several independent camel safari agencies have been recommended. **Ganesh Travels** (Map p329; ☎ 250138; ganeshtravel45@hotmail.com), inside the fort, is owned by camel drivers and is a well-thought-out operation that gets good reports. **Sahara Travels** (Map p329; ☎ 252609; www.mrdesertjaisalmer.com), by the First Fort Gate, also gets good reviews. It's run by Mr Bissa, alias Mr Desert, who graces lots of Rajasthan Tourism posters.

**Satyam Tours** (Map p327; ☎ 250773; ummedsatyam@yahoo.com; Gandhi Chowk) and **Thar Safari** (Map p327; ☎ /fax 252722; Gandhi Chowk) offer variations on the usual circuit.

Remember that no place is perfect – recommendations here should not be a substitute for doing your own research. The best way to go about this is to ask other travellers who've recently been desert-bound. Many hotels run good safaris, but it's advisable to ask around about these, too.

Whoever you go for, insist that all rubbish is carried back to Jaisalmer.

### In the Desert

Don't expect dune seas: the Great Thar Desert is mostly barren scrub, sprinkled with villages and ruins. You often see tiny fields of millet, and children herding flocks of sheep or goats, whose neckbells tinkle in the desert silence. It's a nice change from the sound of farting camels.

Camping out at night, huddling around a tiny fire beneath the stars and listening to the camel drivers' songs, is magically romantic.

The reins are fastened to the camel's nose peg, so the animals are easily steered. Stirrups make the journey a lot more comfortable. At resting points, the camels are unsaddled and hobbled. They limp away to browse on nearby shrubs while the camel drivers brew chai or prepare food. The whole crew rests in the shade of thorn trees.

Most safaris last three to four days; if you want to get to the most interesting places, this is a bare minimum unless a significant jeep component is included.

The traditional circuit takes in Amar Sagar (see p340); Lodhruva (see p340); Mool Sagar (see p340); Bada Bagh (see p340); and the Sam sand dunes (see p341), as well as various abandoned villages along the way.

However, more and more travellers are opting for 'nontouristic' safaris on offer by agencies and hotels. You are driven in a jeep for around 30km or so, and then head off on your steed, avoiding the major sights and other groups.

If you're really pressed for time, you could opt for a half-day camel safari (which involves jeep transfers).

The camel drivers will expect a tip or gift at the end of the trip; this tops up their meagre wage, so don't neglect to give them one (unless you're heartily dissatisfied, of course).

For a more off-the-beaten-track safari option, see Bikaner Camel Safaris, p348.

building tucked away in the southeast corner of the fort. It's quiet, and the atmospheric rooms often have good views. The restaurant is charming, with lots of loungeable floor cushions.

**Suraja Paying Guest House** (Map p329; ☎ 253836; d Rs 100-1000) Next to Surya in the southeast corner, this guesthouse has a good range of rooms in the fort wall, some with balconies, and views from the rooftop. The most expensive room is the ramshackle but grand 'honeymoon suite'.

**Hotel Paradise** (Map p329; ☎ 252674; hotelparadise_jsm2001@yahoo.co.in; r with shared bathroom from Rs 200, with private bathroom Rs 400-750) Popular Hotel Paradise has a mixed bag of rooms, including a poky one with shared bathroom, an atmospheric one with a view in the old part of the building and a modern one with mock-wood paint. The hotel surrounds a leafy courtyard. However, it gets mixed reports from travellers, who have found it impersonal and the staff unhelpful.



### MIDRANGE

#### Town Area

**Shahi Palace** (Map p329; ☎ 255920; www.shahipalacehotel.com; Shiv Rd; r 250-650) Stunning value, Shahi Palace is a brilliant, peaceful place to stay. It has lovely rooms with window seats, sandstone walls and bathrooms, and carved stone or wooden beds. The elegant rooftop is also fantastic, with a fort view. The hotel is opposite SBBJ Bank.

**Fifu Guest House** (Off Map p327; ☎ 252656; www.fifutravel.com; Bera Rd; r from 400) Set 250m south of town a little bit away from the hubbub, but not too far from the action, this has comfortable, bright sandstone rooms and a wonderful rooftop with a stunning fort view. It gets good reviews. The management also run a guesthouse in Khuri.

**Hotel Nachana Haveli** (Map p327; ☎ 252538; nachana_haveli@yahoo.com; Gandhi Chowk; d Rs 900-2200; ❄) Housed in a charming 280-year-old *haveli*, this hotel has a reasonable ambience and comfortable rooms located around a courtyard. The décor consists of grandiose, atmospheric Rajput–high camp furnishings, such as bearskins.

**Hotel Jaisal Palace** (Map p327; ☎ 252717; hoteljaisalpalace@yahoo.com; s/d from Rs 500/600) Near the Nachana Haveli is this clean, well-run place with smallish rooms. Those on the south side have fort-facing balconies. The chair-swing on the roof terrace is a great place to soak up the view.

**Mandir Palace Hotel** (Map p327; ☎ 252788; mandirpalace@hotmail.com; Gandhi Chowk; r Rs 1500; ❄) Just inside the town walls is this royal palace – the erstwhile royal family still lives here. It's so named because it contains many mandirs (temples). The intricate stone latticework is exquisite. Some rooms are atmospheric, with antique furnishings, but the newly built ones are characterless. The building feels deserted, and service has had bad reports.

**Narayan Niwas Palace** (Map p327; ☎ 252408; www.narayanniwas.com; s/d from Rs 1650/2750; ❄ 🏊) North of the fort, this grand 19th-century building counts among its former guests Britain's Princess Anne. Rooms are reasonable, and there's an appealing indoor swimming pool. The rooftop has a superb view of the fort and the old city. However, the hotel is impersonal and geared towards groups.

**RTDC Hotel Moomal** (Map p327; ☎ 252392; dm Rs 50, s/d Rs 450/500, with AC Rs 900/1000, huts Rs 600/700; ❄) West of the walled city, the exterior here is more impressive than the interior. There are ordinary (and musty) rooms in the main complex and air-cooled thatched huts in the grounds. There are a bar and a restaurant.

#### Fort

**Hotel Shreenath Palace** (Map p329; ☎ 252907; shreenath52907@hotmail.com; d with shared bathroom Rs 450-1050) Near the Jain temples is this family-run hotel, set in a beautiful 450-year-old *haveli*. Some rooms are better than others – the best are ringed with pillars and have little alcoves and balconies on all sides; some have magnificent sunset views over the temples. The inlaid ceiling in room No 4 is particularly nice.

**Desert Boys Guest House** (Map p329; ☎ 253091; desert_p@yahoo.com; d Rs 300-1000) This popular guesthouse isn't far from Surya Temple. Rooms vary vastly, but many are nicely furnished. The most expensive are beautifully decorated and have sweeping views, attractive furniture and window seats. The good rooftop restaurant serves Italian food.

**Hotel Suraj** (Map p329; ☎ 251623; r Rs 450-950) Near Hotel Temple View is another popular, family-run, atmospheric *haveli* featuring fine sculpture on the façade and good views from the roof. Rooms vary. Some have beautiful architecture, but they're a bit rough around the edges.

**Hotel Victoria** (Map p329; ☎ 252150; hotelvictoria@rediffmail.com; r Rs 450-650) This charming small *haveli* is an excellent choice, with appealing sandstone-walled rooms, some with a view, and smart bathrooms.

**Hotel Jaisal Castle** (Map p329; ☎ 252362; jaisalcastle@yahoo.com; s/d Rs 1500/2000) Another restored *haveli*, this is in the southwest corner of the fort. Its biggest attraction is its position, high on the ramparts overlooking the desert. The rooms are run-down and overpriced, but spacious.

### TOP END

Most of the top-end hotels are inconveniently located a few kilometres from town.

**Hotel Killa Bhawan** (Map p329; ☎ 251204; www.killabhawan.com; 445 Kotri Para; r Rs 2000, with AC 2700; ) This is an exception, lying within the fort walls. It's a gorgeous, atmospheric place – very *World of Interiors*. It's beautifully decorated and romantic with wooden furniture, dazzling bright silks and wall hangings. The cheaper rooms don't have attached bathrooms but are still luxurious. It may be within the fort, but its plumbing and waste disposal systems are irreproachable.

**Fort Rajwada** (Off Map p327; ☎ 253233; r Rs 3900, ste Rs 6500-8500; ) About 3.5km east of the old city, this modern place was built according to the ancient Indian design principles of *vaastu*, which is similar to feng shui. All materials in the hotel are natural. An opera designer created the traditional interior, so it's suitably dramatic. Carved sandstone balconies, taken from royal *havelis* in Jaisalmer, have been installed in the foyer.

**Jawahar Niwas Palace** (Map p327; ☎ 252208; Bada Bagh Rd; s/d Rs 2000/2750; ) About 1km west of the fort is this stunning sandstone palace, standing rather forlornly in its own sandy grounds. Rooms are elegant and spacious. Those upstairs at the front have the best (if distant) fort views. And it has a fabulous pool.

**Rang Mahal** (Off Map p327; ☎ 250907; www.hotelrangmahal.com; r from Rs 3000, ste Rs 4500; ) About 2.5km west of the fort is this dramatic traditional-style building with big bastions and impressive rooms. The deluxe suites are divine, and there's a spectacular pool (Rs 150 for nonguests).

**Gorbandh Palace Hotel** (Off Map p327; ☎ 253801; crs@udaipur.hrhindia.com; Sam Rd; s/d from Rs 2000/2500, ste Rs 3500; ) Near Rang Mahal is a grand modern hotel with traditional design elements. Constructed of local sandstone, the friezes around the hotel were sculpted by local artisans. You won't be writing home about the rooms, but they are comfortable, and there's a superb pool (Rs 200 for nonguests).

**Hotel Rawal-Kot** (Off Map p327; ☎ 251874; www.tajhotels.com; r US$90; ) Next to Fort Rajwada is another good choice. It's a grand, impressively carved sandstone hotel surrounding a large courtyard, with well-kept gardens. The large rooms are decorated in traditional style, but they're a bit bland.

**Hotel Dhola Maru** (Map p327; ☎ 252863; Jethwai Rd; s/d Rs 2000/2500; ) This option, to the northeast of the walled city, is a few kilometres from the fort entrance. It's a popular choice, although the location is not great and it lacks the polish of the other top-end hotels – some readers have been disappointed. There's an extraordinary little bar, which has incorporated tree roots and saddle-shaped bar stools into its décor, and there's a restaurant.

## Eating

With so many tourists visiting Jaisalmer, you may find standards and service at some restaurants sloppy. Nonetheless, there are plenty of excellent choices, places where you can kick back and lovely rooftops to hang out on. Inside the fort there's an embarrassment of Italian restaurants – as if everyone got the same recipe book for Christmas.

### TOWN AREA

**Desert Boys Dhani** (Map p327; Seemagram Campus; dishes Rs 35-80; 11am-4pm & 6.30-11pm) A serene walled-garden restaurant, tables scattered across its lawns, this is a lovely place to eat excellent, good-value Indian veg dishes.

**Trio** (Map p327; ☎ 252733; Gandhi Chowk; dishes Rs 40-150; noon-3pm & 6.30-10.30pm) With a romantic setting under a tented roof, this popular, upmarket, long-running Indian and Continental restaurant offers reliably good veg and nonveg dishes. It has a lot more atmosphere and swank than most places in town. Traditional musicians play in the evening, and there's a great fort view.

**Saffron** (Map p327; dishes Rs 40-140; 7am-3pm & 7-10.30pm) Now taken over by the family who run Nanchana Haveli below, the veg and nonveg food here gets excellent reports. The restaurant has a great setting on a sandstone terrace overlooking the comings and goings on Gandhi Chowk.

**Kebab Corner** (Map p327; Hanuman Chowk; dishes Rs 30-140; 11am-11pm) Previously the Slow Food restaurant, this has changed its name – presumably because it's not slow at all. The personable chef remains the same. Specialising in tandoori, Kebab Corner offers some great veg and nonveg sizzling dishes. The location is a surprisingly peaceful tent by a busy junction, and there's a campfire in winter.

**Natraj Restaurant** (Map p327; dishes around Rs 50; 8am-11pm) This is an excellent place to eat, and the rooftop has a satisfying view of the upper part of the Salim Singh-ki-Haveli next door, and across the south of town. The food is consistently excellent, the service is good and the prices are very reasonable.

**Rawal** (Map p327; Hanuman Chowk; dishes Rs 25-190; 6.30pm-midnight) A bit out of the way, by the fort, bastion-shaped Rawal has a good fort view from the roof. It whips up interesting Indian dishes, such as tandoori thali (containing tandoori chicken), chicken *tikka*, vegetable kebab, *paneer tikka* (spiced unfermented cheese), butter naan and pappadam.

**Chandan Shree Restaurant** (Map p327; dishes Rs 15-70, thalis Rs 30; 7am-11pm) Always busy, this is a popular dining hall, usually packed with locals, churning out tasty, spicy, all-you-can-eat Gujarati, Rajasthani, Punjabi and Bengali thalis.

**Sharma Lodge** (Map p327; thalis Rs 30; 5.30am-10.30pm) This simple eatery beneath the Top Deck restaurant offers equally simple thalis.

### Quick Eats

**Mohan Juice Centre** (Off Map p329; Bhatia Market; lassis Rs 7-16) Near the fort, this has a little sitting area – in the style of a dingy ice-cream parlour – at the back. It sells assorted interesting lassis, such as honey and *makhania*.

**Bhang Shop** (Map p329; lassis Rs 30-35) Outside the First Fort Gate, this place offers lassis of different strengths. Bhang cookies, cakes and candy (including special camel-safari packs) can also be produced with notice. Note that bhang doesn't agree with everyone (see Beware of Those Bhang Lassis!, p365).

**Dhanraj Bhatia Sweets** (Map p329; Sadar Bazaar) This place in Bhatia Market has been churning out traditional sweet treats for 10 generations. It's renowned in Jaisalmer and beyond for its local specialities, such as *ghotua ladoos* (sweetmeat balls made with gram flour) and *panchadhari ladoos* (made with wheat flour), which cost Rs 5 each. This simple little shop is worth visiting just to watch the sweetmakers ply their trade. There's no English sign, but you can recognise it by the small wooden platform out the front and the many locals stopping in to buy sweets.

#### THE AUTHOR'S CHOICE

**Little Italy** (Map p329; dishes Rs 50-100; 8am-11pm) Set right next to the First Fort Gate, Little Italy is a stately new restaurant, housed in a section of the old fort wall. The interior is decorated with floor cushions, mirrorwork, terracotta lamps and a satin-tented ceiling, or you can sit outside on the rooftop, overlooking the old town and the fort walls. It's romantic, and the bruschetta is fantastic. The pasta is pretty good, too (mysteriously, this has the same menu as several other restaurants in town).

### FORT

**Krishna's Boulangerie** (Map p329; dishes Rs 30-100; 6am-10.30pm) A popular café with a relaxed atmosphere and cheery music, this is open to the sky and has great cakes and pastries, as well as tea and real coffee. It also serves pizza, pasta and salads.

**Little Tibet** (Map p329; dishes Rs 25-60; 10am-10pm) East of the main square, with wicker chairs out on a calm, sheltered, makeshift-feeling terrace, airy Little Tibet has friendly service and large servings, and is a popular place for an evening beer (there's also rooftop seating). The extensive menu includes hearty soups and tasty *momos* (Tibetan dumplings).

**Ristorante Italiano La Purezza** (Map p329; dishes Rs 50-100; 10am-11pm) This rooftop restaurant has a bamboo roof, mirror-patterned mud walls and great views (excellent at sunset). It serves authentic pizza and pasta, good bruschetta and real coffee.

**Vyas Meal Service** (Map p329; dishes Rs 8-50, thalis Rs 50-200; 10am-10pm) Vyas, close to the Jain temples, is a brilliant place for homemade food. It offers traditional veg cuisine, including wholesome thalis, breakfasts of *paratha* (bread) with honey or apple curd with honey, and good masala tea.

**8th July Restaurant** (Map p329; Dashera Chowk; dishes Rs 35-55; 8am-10.30pm) and **Refreshing**

**Point Rooftop Restaurant** (Map p329; Dashera Chowk; dishes Rs 15-70; 7am-11.30pm), both above the main square in the fort, are ideal places to watch the passing human and bovine traffic, but the food (which dabbles in a wide range of cuisines) is variable.

## Shopping

Jaisalmer has a particularly stunning array of mirrorwork wall hangings – the best in Rajasthan – and is also famous for embroidery, rugs, blankets, bedspreads, oil lamps, old stonework and antiques. Watch out when buying silver items; the metal is sometimes adulterated with bronze.

**Hari Om** (Map p329; ☎ 255122; 10am-9pm) This silversmith makes beautiful, delicate silver rings and bracelets featuring places and Hindu gods. Visitors have commissioned personalised wedding rings here and been delighted with the results. There's a shop inside the fort, or you can contact the jeweller at home: house 275, Taloti Vyaspara.

**Light of the East** (Map p329; 8am-9pm) On the laneway leading up to the Jain temples within the fort, this is an enthralling little shop selling crystals and rare mineral specimens, including zeolite, which fetch up to Rs 5000 depending on the quality. Ask the owner to show you the amazing apophyllite piece that's ceremoniously displayed behind a fetching pink curtain. Don't set your heart on it – unfortunately, it's not for sale.

There are several good *khadi* shops around town selling fixed-price carpets, shawls and woven garments. These include Zila Khadi Gramodan Parishad (Map p327), **Khadi Gramodyog Bhavan (Seemagram)** (Map p327; Dhibba; 10am-6pm Mon-Sat) and **Gandhi Darshan Emporium** (Map p327; Gandhi Chowk; 11am-7pm Fri-Wed). You can also pop into **Rajasthali** (Map p327; Gandhi Chowk; 10am-8pm Mon-Sat) to check out prices – this is the government handicraft emporium, which sells all sorts of products from cushion covers to wooden ornaments.

## Getting There & Away

### AIR

The airport, 2.5km south of town, has been closed for the last few years due to border tensions with Pakistan. When it is open, it's only during high season (October to March). If it reopens, the Indian Airlines agent is **Crown Tours** (Map p327; ☎/fax 251912), about 350m west of Amar Sagar Gate.

### BUS

The main **Roadways bus stand** (Map p327; ☎ 251 541) is near the train station. Fortunately, all buses start at a more convenient bus stand southwest of the fort.

There are buses to Jodhpur (Rs 60/135 in express/deluxe, 5½ hours, hourly) and express buses to Bikaner (Rs 142, seven hours, four daily), Jaipur (Rs 194 in deluxe, 12 hours, one daily) and Barmer (Rs 66, three hours, hourly).

You can book private buses through most travel agencies. If you can't get a ticket, check with a few agencies, as sometimes people tell you a bus is full when it's not. Bus routes to go Bikaner (Rs 110/130 in express/deluxe), Jaipur (Rs 180/190 in express/deluxe), Jodhpur (Rs 70/90/110 in express/deluxe/sleeper), to Mt Abu (Rs 220/240 in express/deluxe) to Ahmedabad (Rs 200/300 in deluxe/sleeper) and elsewhere. Most private buses (except those going to Bikaner) require a change at Jodhpur. Buses also run to Ajmer (Rs 180 in express, 12 hours) and Udaipur (Rs 200 in express, 10 hours). Some travellers have found themselves in Jodhpur with a useless onward ticket, so make sure you clarify what you're getting.

### TRAIN

There's a **reservation office** ( 8am-8pm Mon-Sat, 8am-2pm Sun) at the train station.

There are numerous trains going to/from Jodhpur, including the *Jodhpur Express* (No 4809), which leaves Jaisalmer at 11.15pm, arriving in Jodhpur (Rs 157/411 in sleeper/3AC, 294km) at 5.15am. The *Jaisalmer Express* (No 4810) leaves Jodhpur at 11.15pm and arrives in Jaisalmer at 5.15am. The *Jaisalmer–Delhi Express* (No 4060) leaves at 4.15pm, calls at Jodhpur (Rs 97/322 in 2nd/chair class) at 10pm, at Jaipur (Rs 256/690 in sleeper/3AC, 313km) at 5.15am and at Delhi (Rs 322/877 in sleeper/3AC, 623km) at 10.43am. Going the other way, the express (No 4059) leaves Delhi at 6.15pm and arrives in Jaisalmer 19 hours later.

From Jodhpur you can get train connections to other destinations (see p317).

## Getting Around

### AUTORICKSHAW

Bargain hard. An autorickshaw ride to Gadi Sagar costs about Rs 20 one way from the fort entrance.

#### BICYCLE

A good way to get around is by bicycle. There are a number of hire places, including one near Gandhi Chowk called **Jaisalmer RCM** (Map p327; per hr Rs 5, per day Rs 25; 8am-7pm).

#### JEEP

It's possible to hire jeeps from the stand (Map p327) on Gandhi Chowk. To Khuri or the Sam sand dunes expect to pay Rs 450 return with a one-hour wait. For Lodhruva, you'll pay Rs 200 return with a one-hour stop. A full day of sightseeing around Jaisalmer will cost around Rs 1000. To cut the cost, find other people to share with you (there's a maximum of six people per jeep).

## AROUND JAISALMER

There are many fascinating places to visit in the desolate, ancient landscape around Jaisalmer, although beyond the major sights, the barren sand-dune desert stretches across the lonely border into Pakistan.

Due to the alleged arms smuggling across that border, most of Rajasthan west of National Hwy No 15 is a restricted area. Special permission is required from the **district magistrate** (☎ 02992-252201) in Jaisalmer to go there, and is usually only issued in exceptional circumstances. Places exempted are Amar Sagar, Bada Bagh, Lodhruva, Kuldhara, Akal, Sam, Ramkund, Khuri and Mool Sagar.

### Bada Bagh

About 7km north of Jaisalmer, Bada Bagh is a fertile oasis with a huge old dam. It was built by Maharaja Jai Singh II and completed after his death by his son.

Above the gardens (closed to visitors) are picturesque royal **chhatris** (admission Rs 20, camera Rs 2; 6am-7pm), with beautifully carved ceilings and equestrian statues of former rulers. On the memorial of Maharaja Jeth Singh it is inscribed that on his death his queen and 10 concubines committed *sati*. Bada Bagh is now surrounded by windmills used to generate electricity.

### Amar Sagar

This once pleasant formal garden, 7km northwest of Jaisalmer, has fallen into ruin. The lake usually dries up several months into the dry season. According to locals, the step-wells here were built by prostitutes.

Nearby is a finely carved 19th-century **Jain temple** (Indian/foreigner free/Rs 10, camera/video Rs 50/100; sunrise-sunset) that's well worth a look. Restoration commenced on the structure in the 1970s – craftspeople were brought from Agra in Uttar Pradesh.

### Lodhruva

About 15km northwest of Jaisalmer are the deserted ruins of Lodhruva, the ancient capital before the move to Jaisalmer. It was probably founded by the Lodra Rajputs, and passed to the ruler of Devagarh, Bhatti Devaraja, in the 10th century. In 1025 Mahmud of Ghazni laid siege to the town, and it was sacked various times over subsequent decades, prompting Jaisala to shift the capital to a new location – Jaisalmer.

The **Jain temples**, rebuilt in the late '70s, are the sole reminders of the city's former magnificence. The **main temple** (admission Rs 10, camera/video Rs 50/100; sunrise-sunset) enshrines a finely wrought silver image of Parasnath, the 23rd *tirthankar*, surrounded by fine sculptures.

The ornate rosette in the centre of the drum of the dome over the *mandapa* was carved from a single piece of stone, and before the temple is a beautiful *torana*. The small sculptures around the lower course of the inner sanctum are badly damaged, and still bear the scars of Muslim raids. Behind the inner sanctum is a 200-year-old carved Jaisalmer stone slab that bears carvings of the *tirthankars'* feet in miniature.

The temple has its own resident cobra, which is said to be 1.5m long and over 400 years old. It lives in a hole on the north side of the main temple. It's supposed to be very auspicious to see the cobra, but probably as close as you'll get is viewing the photograph of it, which is housed separately inside the temple. The small temple to the right is dedicated to Adinath, the first *tirthankar*.

There is nowhere to stay in Lodhruva – the *dharamsala* (pilgrims' lodging) beside the temple is for Jains only.

There are buses from Jaisalmer to Lodhruva (Rs 5, 20 minutes, three daily).

### Mool Sagar

Situated 9km west of Jaisalmer, this is another pleasant, but rather neglected, small **garden and tank** (admission Rs 5; 8am-7pm). It belongs to the royal family of Jaisalmer and was originally built as a cool summer retreat.

In the lemon grove there's a small Shiva temple carved from two pieces of sandstone.

## Kuldhara

This small **village** (admission Rs 10, vehicle Rs 50; sunrise-sunset) is 25km west of Jaisalmer. Around 400 years ago, all the inhabitants of the 84 villages in the area left after a dispute with the prime minister, Salim Singh, whose *haveli* you can visit in Jaisalmer (see p331). The prime minister had taxed the Paliwals heavily, they had been looted and a daughter of one family had been kidnapped, but there was no response to their complaints, so the entire community upped and left. According to legend, they couldn't carry all their gold and silver, so they buried it. Several years ago some Westerners armed with metal detectors arrived at Kuldhara on motorcycles and found some valuable silver coins. Local villagers became suspicious and called the police, and the treasure hunters were apprehended and divested of their booty.

Some of the houses appear in remarkable condition, as they have been heavily restored for use as film sets – this is a popular movie location.

Kuldhara is included on some of the extended camel treks. If you don't want to pay Rs 50 to bring in a car or a jeep, you can cover the 500m from the gate on foot. Restoration work is being done here.

## Desert National Park & Sanctuary

This **national park** (Indian/foreigner Rs 5/10, guide Rs 200, vehicle Rs 100), 42km southwest of Jaisalmer, was established in 1980 to preserve the desert ecosystem and thus protect the range of drought-resistant species that inhabit it, including the critically endangered Indian bustard *(Choriotis niergceps)*, known locally as godawan. It encompasses an area of 3162 sq km, an arid zone of sand dunes, thorn forest, scrub and sandy wastelands between Jaisalmer and Barmer, including the areas around Sam and Khuri. It will be of interest to visitors with an interest in desert wildlife – to the layperson it's not that exciting.

The park should be avoided during summer months, when temperatures soar to over 50°C. You need to bring a good supply of drinking water at any time. For more information, contact the Desert National Park's **deputy director** (☎ 02992-2522201) in Jaisalmer – you need permission to visit the park.

## Sam Sand Dunes

The silky **Sam sand dunes** (admission Rs 3, vehicle Rs 20, camel admission Rs 80) lie on the edge of the Desert National Park, and are one of the most popular excursions from Jaisalmer. The dunes are 42km from the city, along a very good sealed road (which is maintained by the Indian army).

This is Jaisalmer's nearest real Sahara-like desert. It's best to be here at sunrise or sunset, and many camel safaris spend a night at the dunes. Just before sunset jeep loads of day-trippers arrive from Jaisalmer to be chased across the sands by tenacious camel owners offering short rides, dressed-up dancing children and young boys selling soft drinks. Yes, this place has become a massive tourist attraction, so don't set your heart on a solitary desert sunset experience. The hordes of people here at sunset lend the place something of a carnival atmosphere. If you want a less touristy sand-dunes experience, Khuri is a much more peaceful and pristine alternative (see p342).

Despite the tourist hype, it's still a magical place – the fat swell of the sand is impossible to corrupt – and it's possible to frame pictures of solitary camels against lonely dunes. An awesome sight on a smaller scale is the desert dung beetle. Study a dune close up to spot these industrious little creatures rolling lumps of dung twice their size.

One tragic consequence of dune-hungry hordes is the debris and rubbish they leave behind. Visitors are now charged a fee to visit the dunes, money which could be put to good use to clean them up, but is more likely lining the pocket of some local official. If you feel strongly about the rubbish here, a letter to the **Chief Tourism Officer** (RTDC Tourism, Swagatam Campus, near train station, Jaipur 302006, Rajasthan) might have some effect. For further information, contact the Desert National Park's **deputy director** (☎ 02992-252201) in Jaisalmer.

### SLEEPING & EATING

There are quite a few places to stay at while visiting the dunes – mostly upmarket camps with luxury tents. However, most travellers prefer to visit the dunes on a day trip from Jaisalmer or as part of a camel safari. There's a straggling line of restaurants and tea shops at the dunes.

**RTDC Hotel Sam Dhani** (huts with private bathroom Rs 500) This hotel has good, though by no means luxurious, rooms and is in an appealing spot overlooking the dunes. It's a good idea to book ahead, through RTDC Hotel Moomal (☎ 02992-252392) in Jaisalmer, as the manager isn't always around.

**Dune Safari Camp** (☎ 02992-254463; contact@dunesafaricamp.com; d Rs 3000) The spacious camp has comfortable Swiss tents with bathrooms, and is located close to the dunes. The price quoted here is a package, including meals and entertainment, but you could probably get a cheaper price if you booked locally.

#### GETTING THERE & AWAY

There are three daily buses to Sam (Rs 22, 1½ hours) from Jaisalmer.

### Khuri

☎ 03014

Khuri is a small village 40km southeast of Jaisalmer, with its own desert sand dunes. People in Jaisalmer like to gossip that Khuri has become commercial and is best avoided, but it's likely they have a vested interest in your going elsewhere. Khuri remains a peaceful place (apart from during holiday periods, as it's popular with Indian holidaymakers), with houses of mud and straw decorated like the patterns on Persian carpets. There are plenty of camps of mud huts and camel drivers eager to take you on the dunes, but no shop-lined streets or pancake restaurants. Once the excitement of sunset is over, you have desert solitude and the brilliant star-studded sky to look forward to.

#### SLEEPING & EATING

Places to stay in Khuri are mostly basic, fan-less thatched mud huts with wall paintings, set around a campfire area, though some have improved their facilities in recent years. All places listed here provide meals and can arrange camel safaris.

**Badal House** (☎ 274120; huts or r with shared bathroom incl meals Rs 125) Here you can stay in a family compound with a few charming small huts and freshly painted rooms. Former camel driver Badal Singh is a lovely, gentle man who charges Rs 300 for a camel safari with a night on the dunes. Don't let touts warn you away. The phone number given here belongs to his brother Amal Singh, who can pass on a message.

**Khuri Resort** (☎ 274044; r Rs 300-700) This was the Khuri Guest House, but has expanded into something of a complex. It's a friendly place, with cheap, basic, scrubby rooms and huts, more expensive freshly painted new rooms with private bathroom, and tents that are right among the dunes (overnight package around Rs 1000).

**Mama's Guest House** (☎ 274042; gajendra_sodha2003@yahoo.com; huts with shared bathroom incl dinner & breakfast per person Rs 350) This is a long-running place, with a circle of cosy whitewashed huts. A basic/luxurious overnight camel safari costs Rs 350/600.

**Gangaur Guest House** (☎ 274056; hameersingh@yahoo.com; huts with shared bathroom per person Rs 200, with private bathroom Rs 250) This is a small place with yet another circle of snug huts. It offers packages, including one with a camel ride, dinner with traditional dance entertainment and breakfast for Rs 500. It's closest to the dunes.

#### GETTING THERE & AWAY

There are several buses to Khuri from Jaisalmer (Rs 25, one hour).

### Akal Wood Fossil Park

About 1km off the road to Barmer, 17km from Jaisalmer, are the amazing fossilised remnants of a 180-million-year-old **forest** (Indian/foreigner Rs 5/20, car Rs 10, bike Rs 2; 🕒 8am-5pm Apr-Oct, 8am-6pm Nov-Mar). The remains are amazing when you think about them rather than when you look at them. They're a collection of broken partial logs – tree bones – protected by strange little corrugated-iron huts. The largest fossil is 13.4m long and 0.4m wide. The climate here must have once been hot and humid – a stark contrast with today's dry desert, which is particularly parched around here. The fossil park is apparently 108 hectares, of which only 18 have been excavated. Near the entrance is a small display, where you get the chance to stroke an ancient red wood tree trunk fossil. One of the foresters will show you around.

A return taxi will cost around Rs 200.

## BARMER

☎ 02982 / pop 83,517

Barmer is famed for woodcarving, carpets, embroidery, block printing and other handicrafts, and it's a great place to hunt for bargains. The small shops in the colourful

Sadar Bazaar are a good place to start – exploring the narrow backstreets, you'll find artisans at work. Otherwise this desert town, 153km south of Jaisalmer, isn't very interesting, and few travellers make the trek out here. The best part is the journey through peaceful, small villages, their mud-walled houses decorated with geometric designs. There's a particularly interesting village south of Barmer (see below).

### Sleeping & Eating

Barmer's accommodation options are strictly at the budget end of the scale.

**Hotel Krishna** (☎ 220785; s/d with shared bathroom from Rs 110/200, r with private bathroom Rs 200-500; ❄) This is Barmer's best option: on the main street leading from the train station, it's friendly and has acceptably clean rooms.

**Kailash Sarover Hotel** (☎ 230030; Station Rd; r with AC Rs 700; ❄) Further away from the station and on the opposite side of Station Rd (with a spillover building nearby), this hotel offers OK but overpriced rooms. Hotel Krishna is a better bet.

**RTDC Hotel Khartal** (☎ 222956; s/d Rs 300/400) Out of the town centre, this hotel is a basic option. It's nothing flash, but it has adequate rooms. Meals are available.

**Raj Restaurant** (Station Rd; dishes Rs 15-60; 7.30am-11.30pm) Between the train station and Hotel Krishna, Raj Restaurant is a jolly, if slightly grubby, little place that's open onto the street. It offers veg dishes at reasonable prices.

### Getting There & Away

From Barmer there are frequent buses to/from Jaisalmer (Rs 65, 2½ hours) and Jodhpur (Rs 86, four hours). There's a train station, and work is underway to reopen this line, which forms a link with Pakistan. Buses leave from the main bus stand, which is about 1km north of the train station.

The *Dee Jaisalmer Express* (No 4059) goes to Barmer (Rs 76/125 in 2nd class/sleeper, four hours). The rail link between Munabao in Barmer district and Khokhraparkar in Pakistan (via Barmer), closed since 1965, is due to be reopened when works have finished. Check locally for the current status.

## AROUND BARMER

About 35km from Barmer, the 10th- to 11th-century, remote-feeling **Kiradu Temples** feature some very fine sculpture. These five temples conform to a style of architecture known as Solanki, and the most impressive is **Someshvara Temple**, which has a multiturreted spire and beautiful sculpture. However, it's located in the sensitive border region near Pakistan, so you'll first need to contact the **district magistrate** (☎ 02982-220003), who will obtain the necessary permission from the superintendent of police for you to visit. You'll need to fill out an application form and submit a photocopy of your passport – usually if you ask for permission in the morning it will be granted by the afternoon.

South of Barmer the road leads 67km to **Dhorimmana**, a small, dusty market town with no specific sights, but which is a busy meeting point for villagers living in the area. It's a chance to see some wonderful traditional tribal dress, with lots of Bishnoi people. The colourful villages along the route are also very traditional, consisting of huddles of mud huts among the desert scrub. This is an interesting, unexplored route to take if you have your own transport – few tourists come this way.

## BIKANER

**☎ 0151 / pop 529,007**

A dust-swirling desert city, Bikaner's finest sight is its fort, Junagarh, with its dazzlingly rich interiors. Close to the fort lies the old city, surrounded by a high crenellated wall. Within the walled city the streets feel medieval (despite the motorbike and rickshaw traffic) – narrow, dark and uneven, complete with open sewers, rubbish heaps, dark-red sandstone *havelis* and some exquisitely painted Jain temples.

Bikaner feels far less set up for tourism than other Rajasthan cities, though there are a lot of hotels here and a busy camel-safari scene.

Many travellers come here to visit the notorious Karni Mata Temple, 30km south, where pilgrims worship thousands of holy rats. Less Brothers Grimm, but still fairytale, is the small temple town of Kolayat, with its holy lake, 54km to the south.

More and more visitors are opting to take desert camel safaris from Bikaner, thus avoiding the Jaisalmer hustle.

The city is also known for its traditional fire dances, performed by members of a Hindu religious sect called the Jas Naths.

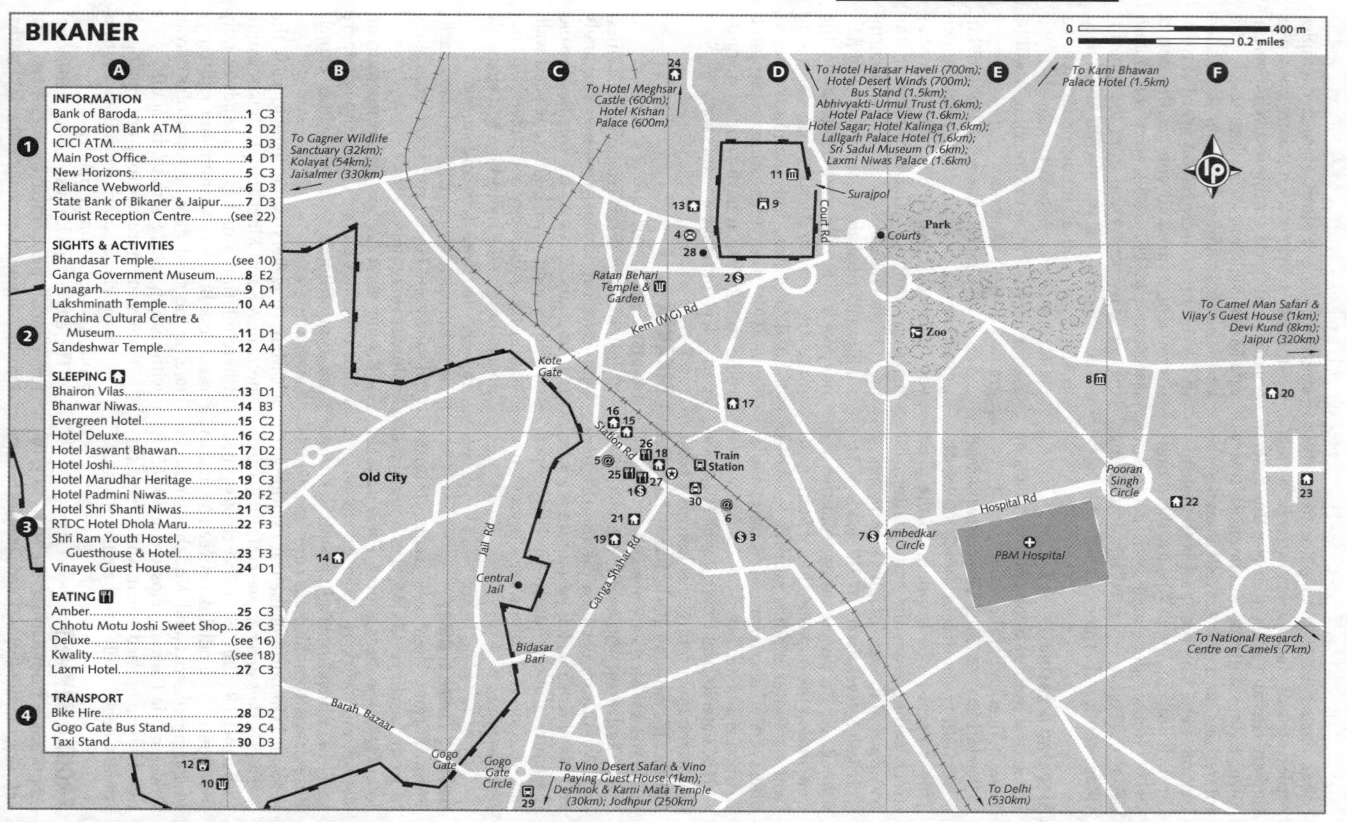
BIKANER
0 400 m
0 0.2 miles
A
B
C
D
E
F
1
2
3
4
INFORMATION
Bank of Baroda......1 C3
Corporation Bank ATM......2 D2
ICICI ATM......3 D3
Main Post Office......4 D1
New Horizons......5 C3
Reliance Webworld......6 D3
State Bank of Bikaner & Jaipur......7 D3
Tourist Reception Centre......(see 22)
SIGHTS & ACTIVITIES
Bhandasar Temple......(see 10)
Ganga Government Museum......8 E2
Junagarh......9 D1
Lakshminath Temple......10 A4
Prachina Cultural Centre & Museum......11 D1
Sandeshwar Temple......12 A4
SLEEPING
Bhairon Vilas......13 D1
Bhanwar Niwas......14 B3
Evergreen Hotel......15 C2
Hotel Deluxe......16 C2
Hotel Jaswant Bhawan......17 D2
Hotel Joshi......18 C3
Hotel Marudhar Heritage......19 C3
Hotel Padmini Niwas......20 F2
Hotel Shri Shanti Niwas......21 C3
RTDC Hotel Dhola Maru......22 F3
Shri Ram Youth Hostel, Guesthouse & Hotel......23 F3
Vinayek Guest House......24 D1
EATING
Amber......25 C3
Chhotu Motu Joshi Sweet Shop......26 C3
Deluxe......(see 16)
Kwality......(see 18)
Laxmi Hotel......27 C3
TRANSPORT
Bike Hire......28 D2
Gogo Gate Bus Stand......29 C4
Taxi Stand......30 D3
To Gagner Wildlife Sanctuary (32km); Kolayat (54km); Jaisalmer (330km)
To Hotel Meghsar Castle (600m); Hotel Kishan Palace (600m)
To Hotel Harasar Haveli (700m); Hotel Desert Winds (700m); Bus Stand (1.5km); Abhivyakti-Urmul Trust (1.6km); Hotel Palace View (1.6km); Hotel Sagar; Hotel Kalinga (1.6km); Lallgarh Palace Hotel (1.6km); Sri Sadul Museum (1.6km); Laxmi Niwas Palace (1.6km)
To Karni Bhawan Palace Hotel (1.5km)
Surajpol
Court Rd
Courts
Park
Zoo
Ratan Behari Temple & Garden
Kem (MG) Rd
Kote Gate
Station Rd
Train Station
Old City
Jail Rd
Central Jail
Ganga Shahar Rd
Hospital Rd
Ambedkar Circle
Pooran Singh Circle
PBM Hospital
Bidasar Bari
Barah Bazaar
Gogo Gate
Gogo Gate Circle
To Camel Man Safari & Vijay's Guest House (1km); Devi Kund (8km); Jaipur (320km)
To National Research Centre on Camels (7km)
To Vino Desert Safari & Vino Paying Guest House (1km); Deshnok & Karni Mata Temple (30km); Jodhpur (250km)
To Delhi (530km)

Today it's only possible to see this dance during the Bikaner Camel Festival (see p306), in the village of Katriyasar, 40km from Bikaner on the Jaipur road.

The Ganga Canal, built between 1925 and 1927, irrigates a large area of previously arid land around Bikaner.

## History

The city was founded in 1488 by Rao Bika, a descendant of Jodha, Jodhpur's founder, and was another important staging post on the great caravan trade routes. Being closer to Delhi, Bikaner spent more time fighting the Mughals than other Rajasthan cities, but its harsh desert surroundings helped to defeat many of its enemies. Post Mughals, the city declined, though its geography excused it the attacks from the Marathas that plagued many other cities. By the 19th century the province was markedly backward, but managed to turn its fortunes around by trading camels with the British during the Afghan War. In 1886 it was the first desert princely state to install electricity.

Maharaja Ganga Singh (r 1898–1944) was one of Rajasthan's most notable and accomplished rulers. His clever diplomacy and canny economic sense (he promoted the Ganga Canal) helped develop Bikaner. He later led the Indian delegation to the League of Nations.

## Orientation

The old city is encircled by a 7km-long wall with five entrance gates that was constructed in the 18th century. The fort and palace, built of the same reddish-pink sandstone as Jaipur's famous buildings, are outside the city walls.

## Information

For an online guide to Bikaner, check out www.realbikaner.com.

**Bank of Baroda** (☎ 2545453; ⏰ 10am-2pm Mon-Fri, 10am-12.30pm Sat) Changes travellers cheques only.

**ICICI ATM** (Station Rd) There's also Corporation Bank ATM opposite the fort. Note that ATMs here can be unreliable.

**Main post office** (⏰ 10am-1pm & 2-3pm Mon-Fri, 10am-1pm Sat) Near Junagarh.

**New Horizons** (Biscuit Gali; per hr Rs 20; ⏰ 8am-9pm) Off Station Rd, this is one of several Internet places in Bikaner (an increasing number of hotels have Internet access, too).

**Reliance Webworld** (Station Rd; ⏰ 10am-7pm) An alternative to New Horizons. Broadband is available.

**State Bank of Bikaner & Jaipur** Ambedkar Circle (☎ 2544361; ⏰ noon-4pm Mon-Sat); public park, near Junagarh (☎ 2544034; ⏰ 10am-2pm Mon-Fri, 10am-noon Sat) Changes cash and travellers cheques.

**Tourist Reception Centre** (☎ 2226701; ⏰ 10am-5pm Mon-Sat) Near Pooran Singh Circle, in the RTDC Hotel Dhola Maru compound, about 1km from the city centre. It has various brochures (including a good map of Bikaner for Rs 2) and a toilet that can be used by tourists.

## Sights

### JUNAGARH

This most impressive **fort** (adult/child Rs 100/50, camera/video Rs 30/100; ⏰ 10am-4.30pm) was constructed between 1588 and 1593 by Raja Rai Singh, a general in the army of the Mughal Emperor Akbar. Palaces and luxurious suites were added by subsequent maharajas. Unlike many Rajasthan forts, Junagarh doesn't command a hilltop position. However, it's no less imposing for that and – a credit to its planners and architects – it has never been conquered.

It's protected by a 986m-long wall with 37 bastions, and was once surrounded by a moat (now dry). The sandstone **Surajpol** (Sun Gate) is the main entrance. The palaces within the fort are on the southern side, and make a picturesque ensemble of courtyards, balconies, *chhatris*, towers and windows, with superb stone carving.

The handprints that can be seen close to the Daulatpol commemorate the wives of Rajput soldiers lost in battles, who committed *sati* on their husbands' funeral pyres.

You may be besieged by 'guides' offering tours before you arrive at the ticket counter. Unless you want an individual tour, this is unnecessary, as the ticket price includes a group tour with an official guide. The one-hour tours leave every 15 to 20 minutes. To visit at a leisurely pace, ask for your own guide, as larger groups rush around.

The gold-painted ceiling of the beautiful **Diwan-i-Khas** (Hall of Private Audience) was executed in 1631, and the silver *gaddi* of the maharajas can still be seen here. There's a courtyard paved with Italian tiles; through the fine lattice screens surrounding it, the women of the zenana could watch the activities below. Beside the **Phool Mahal** (Flower Palace), built during the reign of Maharaja Gaj Singh, is a marble statue of Surya, the sun god. Around the upper edges of the walls are paintings depicting Hindu gods.

The beautiful **Anup Mahal** was commissioned by Maharaja Karan Singh (r 1631–69). According to local lore, the maharaja was camping at Golkonda, in southern India, in his capacity as a general in the Mughal army, when an artist showed him fine works in gold. The artist told the maharaja that he was originally from Jaisalmer, but had migrated to southern India when a famine swept over his homeland. The maharaja was inspired by the proficiency and great beauty of the work he had been shown, and so he invited the artist to return to Bikaner, where the artist was given royal patronage.

The work of this artist and of his students features in the **Karan Mahal** and the **Anup Mahal**. Three types of work can be seen here: the *sonakin* style features white plaster decorated with delicate patterns and painted with gold leaf; the *jangali sunthari* style features plaster with a green backing that depicts floral motifs; and the *manovat* style features a pillar of clay that is embossed on plaster, the entire work painted with gold leaf.

In the **Badal Mahal** (Cloud Palace), the walls are painted with blue cloud motifs, and there's a statue here of Vishnu and Lakshmi. The large pillars beside the Karan Mahal were installed with the aid of elephants nearly 400 years ago.

The **Gaj Mandir** formed the private chambers of Maharaja Gaj Singh. The maharani's chamber is decorated with mirror tiles and gold painting, and there's wooden lac painting on the ceiling. The maharaja's chamber has a beautiful painted wood ceiling featuring florets and geometric motifs, and carved ivory doors.

In the **Hawa Mahal** (Palace of the Winds – used in the summer), there's an ingenious device said to have alerted the maharaja to potential enemies. A mirror positioned over the bed enabled Maharaja Dunga Singh to see the reflections of people walking across the courtyard below (this is the purpose of the mirror according to the official fort guides, but other motives might be suspected). The ceiling features floral arabesques and scenes of Krishna dancing. The decorative blue tiles were imported from both Europe and China.

There's an interesting museum exhibition (included in the ticket price), housed in several of the newer rooms of the palace. In the armoury are enormous bore guns that were used for shooting from the backs of camels, as well as the usual collection of sinister-looking pistols and swords.

In the **Diwan-i-Khas** of Ganga Singh are three massive, intricately carved arches and a throne of sandalwood. Here also can be seen a 56kg suit of armour, including chain mail, and sculptures of Krishna dancing and stealing the clothes of the *gopis*. Beautiful if deadly weapons, each an exquisite work of art – swords with ivory and crystal handles, some in the shape of lions – can also be seen here. In a separate chamber are the royal vestments of Maharaja Ganga Singh, as well as items from his office, including a paperweight and his briefcase. There's also an old biplane that was presented to Ganga Singh by the British government during WWI. This is one of only two models of this kind of plane in the world.

### PRACHINA CULTURAL CENTRE & MUSEUM

The **museum** (admission Rs 25, camera Rs 20; ⏲ 9am-6pm), across the main courtyard from Surajpol, is fascinating and well labelled. It focuses on the Western influence on the Bikaner royals before Independence, including crockery from England and France and menu cards from 1936, as well as some exquisite Rajasthani costumes, jewellery and textiles, and intriguing everyday ephemera.

There are a small shop and café at the museum, and a reference library containing a limited collection of books on Rajasthan, which is open to the public.

### JAIN TEMPLES

Two Jain temples just inside the walled city are well worth seeking out. **Bhandasar Temple** (admission free; ⏲ 6am-7pm) is particularly beautiful, with yellow-stone carving and dizzyingly vibrant paintings. It's dedicated to the fifth *tirthankar*, Sumtinath, and the building was commissioned in 1468 by a wealthy Jain merchant Bhandasa Oswal. It was completed after his death, in 1514.

The interior of the temple is stunning. The pillars bear floral arabesques and depictions of the lives of the 24 Jain *tirthankars*. It's said that 40,000kg of ghee was used instead of water in the mortar, which locals insist seeps through the floor on hot days.

On the 1st floor of the three-storey temple are beautiful miniatures of the sentries of the gods. There are fine views over the city from the 3rd floor, with the desert stretching behind it to the west.

The second Jain temple here is **Sandeshwar Temple** (admission free, camera/video Rs 20/30; 6am-noon & 6-7pm). It's smaller than Bhandasar Temple, and has good carving around the door architraves and columns, and ornately carved, painted pillars. Inside the drum of the *sikhara* (spire) are almost ethereal paintings, and the sanctum itself has a marble image of Sandeshwar, flanked by smaller marble statues of other Jain *tirthankars*.

### LAKSHMINATH TEMPLE

Behind Bhandasar Temple, to the right, is the splendid Hindu **Lakshminath Temple** (admission free, photography prohibited). It was built during the reign of Rao Lunkaran between 1505 and 1526. Lakshminath was the patron god of the rulers of Bikaner, and during major religious festivals a royal procession led by the maharaja paid homage at the temple. The elaborate edifice was maintained with tributes received from five villages and several shops, which were granted to the temple by Maharaja Ganga Singh (1887– 1943).

### LALLGARH PALACE

About 3km north of the city centre, this red-sandstone **palace** was built by Maharaja Ganga Singh (1881–1942) in memory of his father, Lal Singh. It's out-and-out grandeur, with overhanging balconies and delicate latticework. The 1st floor contains the **Sri Sadul Museum** (Indian/foreigner Rs 10/20, camera/video Rs 20/50, photography prohibited; 10am-5pm Mon-Sat). It has fascinating old B&W photographs and some evocative maharaja accessories reflecting the former royals' privileged lifestyles. Artefacts include (empty) wine and sherry bottles, menu cards, European crockery and a brass vessel known as a *tokna* (used to collect revenue that was transported by camel to the Bikaner state treasury). There's even a funky old film projector made in New York in 1921. Other more pedestrian exhibits include Maharaja Karni Singh's golf tees, roller skates, typewriters and pink-shaded sunglasses. There's also a disturbing pictorial display of tiger carnage, including a shot of the five tigers shot in three minutes by Maharaja Ganga Singh in 1937.

In front of the palace is a carriage from the maharaja's royal train (you can stay in the train; see p350).

### GANGA GOVERNMENT MUSEUM

This **museum** (admission Rs 3, free Mon; 9.30am-5pm Sat-Thu), on the Jaipur Rd, houses a well-displayed, interesting collection.

Exhibits include terracotta ware from the Gupta period, a range of Rajasthani traditional musical instruments, rich gold paintings by local Usta artisans, miniature wooden models of the Gajner and Lallgarh palaces, and a miniature of the Royal Bikaner train with the roof folded back to reveal its comfortable amenities. There's a separate exhibition hall with antique carpets and royal vestments.

Other interesting exhibits include decrees issued by the Mughals to the maharajas of Bikaner, including one advising Rai Singh to proceed to Delhi 'without any delay and with utmost expedition and speed, travelling over as great a distance as possible during the day time as well as by night' as 'Emperor Akbar is dying'. It was issued by Crown Prince (who would shortly become Emperor) Jehangir.

There are also some fine oil paintings, including one entitled *Maharaja Padam Singh avenging...the death of his brother, Maharaja Mohan Singhji by killing the Emperor's brother-in-law...He drew his sword, rushed upon his enemy...and severed him in two with a blow which also left a mark upon the pillar*.

The sculptures include a beautiful, busty image of Devi, and a marble Jain sculpture of Saraswati dating from the 11th century.

Only still cameras (no videos) are permitted (no charge). The entrance to the museum is at the back of the building on the left-hand side.

## Tours

The Tourist Reception Centre (see p345) can arrange English-speaking guides (Rs 300 per day, with a maximum of four people).

Bhairon Vilas (see p349) offers various tours, including a range of camel safaris, village tours, a jeep tour to Deshnok via a couple of the desert villages, and a tour to Kolayat (see p352) and Gajner Wildlife Sanctuary (see p351). Most of the tour options cost around Rs 600 to 1000 per day, including transport, a guide and (sometimes) food. The trip to Gajner includes jeep transport into the sanctuary for wildlife spotting.

### BIKANER CAMEL SAFARIS

Bikaner is an excellent, offbeat alternative to the Jaisalmer safari scene, and this less-touristed city is becoming increasingly popular with travellers. There are fewer organisations running safaris here, so you're unlikely to encounter much hassle. However, the Bikaner version of the safari tends to involve more travel in a camel cart – less tiring but also less fun. There are also fewer sights than around Jaisalmer, but it's great if you want to ride in empty desert scrub, sleep on dunes and see life in desert villages.

Recommended operators are Vino Desert Safari (see Vino Paying Guest House, below), south of the city, opposite the Gopeshwar Temple, which offers two- to seven-day trips (Rs 400 to 800 per day, depending on how much luxury you require and how much you use a jeep). The friendly, enthusiastic Vinod speaks English, French and German.

Then there's Camel Man (Vijay Singh Rathore; see Vijay's Guest House, below), another friendly chap, who operates basic safaris for Rs 550, and more upmarket excursions (beds with sheets are provided) for Rs 800 to 1100 per day. Safaris range from half-day jaunts to 14-day trips all the way to Jaisalmer.

There are many different camel-trek routes, including trips to Khichan, home of the demoiselle cranes, and to the rat temple at Deshnok.



## Sleeping

As elsewhere in western Rajasthan, Bikaner is big on budget accommodation, while good midrange places are a bit more scarce. There are some fine top-end options. The **Tourist Reception Centre** (☎ 2544125) at the RTDC Hotel Dhola Maru has a list of families registered with Bikaner's Paying Guest House Scheme. Rates cost Rs 150 to 400 per night.

### BUDGET

The cheapest budget options are along the clatteringly noisy Station Rd. The better budget options are to the north or south of town.

**Hotel Meghsar Castle** (☎ 2527315; www.hotelmeghsarcastle.com; 9 Gajner Rd; r Rs 300-800; ❄ 💻) North of town, this hotel has clean, old-fashioned rooms with subdued tiling, some echoingly large. The front rooms can cop a bit of traffic noise. It's a well-run place, with meals available in the garden.

**Hotel Kishan Palace** (☎ 2527762; fax 2522041; 8B Gajner Rd; r Rs 250/300, d Rs 300-650; ❄) Next door to Meghsar Castle, Kishan Palace is a reasonable place, with spacious, airy, comfortable rooms. Meals are available, and there's free pick-up from the bus station.

**Shri Ram Youth Hostel, Guesthouse & Hotel** (☎ 2522651; www.yhaindia.org, www.hotelshriram.com; YHA dm Rs 100, s/d from Rs 100/200, guesthouse r Rs 200-600, hotel r from Rs 300) In a quiet area east of town, this is an accommodation multiplex comprising a youth hostel, guesthouse and hotel. Despite its diversity, it retains a family atmosphere. Rooms are spotless.

**Vino Paying Guest House** (☎ 2270445; vino_desertsafari@yahoo.com; s Rs 80-90, d Rs 100-200) This guesthouse in a family home south of town is a cosy choice. Rooms are excellent value, and the family is enthusiastic, helpful and welcoming. Vinod plans huts in the garden, too, and runs recommended safaris. His family gives free cooking lessons.

**Hotel Desert Winds** (☎ 2542202; s/d Rs 150/200, AC Rs 450/600; ❄) This nice little place is next to Hotel Harasar Haveli (ask rickshaw drivers for the latter and get a cheap ride; see opposite). Meals are available and the owner, a retired deputy director of tourism with the RTDC, can give you info about the city.

**Vinayek Guest House** (☎ 2202634; r Rs 150-200) Offers three spacious rooms in a quiet family house owned by the secretary of the Urmul Trust. There's no sign outside, but it's near Sher Singh's Flour Mill and Old Pugal House.

**Vijay's Guest House** (☎ 2231244; www.camelman.com; Jaipur Rd; s/d/tr Rs 200/300/400) Camel safari organiser Vijay also has a guesthouse. West of town, opposite Sophia School, it has a family atmosphere and vast rooms.

**Hotel Marudhar Heritage** (☎ 2522524; hmheritage2000@yahoo.co.in; Ganga Shahar Rd; s Rs 250-900, d Rs 350-999; ❄ 💻) This is a great, friendly choice, well kept and well run, with rooms to suit most budgets. Rooms are plain, comfortable and good value. There are nice views from the roof.

**Hotel Harasar Haveli** (☎ 2209891; r Rs 200-1500) Most people you meet will want to bring you here – it's notorious for its commission-paying tactics. If you don't mind encouraging such behaviour, it's a great choice – big and efficient with clean, uncluttered rooms and better deluxe rooms. Room prices can be bargained down if things are quiet. There's a pleasant rooftop restaurant with swing chairs. Camel safaris are available.

Reasonably priced retiring rooms are available at the train station. It's Rs 100 for a room with private bathroom, and Rs 200 for a room with AC. Other belt-tighteners:

**Evergreen Hotel** (☎ 2542061; Station Rd; s/d Rs 175/210) Not a bad choice. The green-tiled rooms are fine, though expect some mustiness and noise.

**Hotel Deluxe** (☎ 2528127; Station Rd; d Rs 90-150) Dingy, bare, usually clean rooms. Has 24-hour checkout.

**Hotel Shri Shanti Niwas** (☎ 2521925; shrishanti@vsnl.com; s Rs 175-225, d Rs 250-300) Opposite the train station. A clean, budget business-traveller place.

**RTDC Hotel Dhola Maru** (☎ 2529621; fax 2522109; s/d from Rs 200/300, with AC Rs 600/700; ❄) Bland but OK rooms.

### MIDRANGE

**Bhairon Vilas** (☎ /fax 2544751; hbhairon@rediffmail.com; r Rs 500-1000) Bikaner's prime minister once lived here (he had three wives, hence the 120-year-old building's four parts). The hotel is run by the prime minister's great-grandson, Harsh Singh, who's made it by far Bikaner's funkiest place to stay. Rooms are eclectically decorated with antique clothes, bearskins and old family photographs. Superb traditional musicians sometimes play in the evening, and there's a new restaurant with trees growing through the walls (stick to Indian dishes, and be warned that service can be slow). There's an interesting, if pricey, shop here called Vichitra Arts (see p351). Free pick-up from the bus or train station is available.

**Hotel Palace View** (☎ 2543625; opnain_jp1@sancharnet.in; s Rs 300-650, d Rs 450-800) This friendly place is north of town, close to Lallgarh Palace. You've guessed it – it has palace views. It's pleasant, small and efficient, in a very peaceful spot, with good-value, spotless rooms.

**Hotel Padmini Niwas** (☎ 2522794; 148 Sadul Ganj; s/d from Rs 450/750; ❄ 🏊) Padmini Niwas has clean, pleasant rooms. The owner is relaxed, and the small lawn area is very nice, with the town's only outdoor pool (Rs 100 for nonguests).

**Hotel Jaswant Bhawan** (☎ /fax 2548848; jashwant@sanchar.web; r Rs 400-700; 💻) This is a pleasant, quiet, welcoming place with a small garden. The pricier rooms are spacious and airy. It's handy for the train station without the noise of Station Rd, and you can use the excellent kitchen for self-catering.

**Hotel Joshi** (☎ 2527700; Station Rd; r Rs 350-775) Clean and efficient, though unexciting, rooms await at this place. It's conveniently near the train station and has 24-hour checkout.

**Hotel Sagar** (☎ 2520677; fax 2201877; www.sagarhotelbikaner.com; r Rs 300-1100; ❄) This hotel, north of town, is a large salmon-pink building – it's the first place to the left of the driveway as you approach the palace. It offers a range of rooms, from thatched huts set in the garden to overfurnished grand rooms set in the main building, which surrounds a courtyard. The cheapest rooms belong to another hotel that's accessed through the same building, and are reasonable for the price.

**Hotel Kalinga** (☎ 209751; s/d Rs 200/300, with AC Rs 400/500; ❄) North of town, opposite the Hotel Sagar, this choice offers spartan but reasonable rooms around a balding grassy courtyard.

### TOP END

**Bhanwar Niwas** (☎ 2529323; www.bhanwarniwas.com; s/d Rs 1999/3000; ❄) This place, in the beautiful Rampuri Haveli, near the *kotwali* (police station) in the old city, has 26 large, solemnly decorated rooms, each different, with hand-painted wallpaper, arranged around an internal courtyard. Turn left at the Kote Gate, and take the first right at Lady Elgin School. The hotel is close to a community of kitemakers, who can be seen practising their craft. The 26 atmospheric rooms are all different, and are set around a graceful courtyard. The *haveli* was completed in 1927 for Seth Bhanwarlal Rampura, heir to a textile and real-estate fortune. In the foyer is a stunning blue 1927 Buick with a silver horn in the shape of a dragon, and an immaculate 1942 Indian Ambassador.

**Laxmi Niwas Palace** (☎ 2202777; s/d/ste Rs 4500/5500/8000; ❄) Beside Lallgarh Palace, north of town, this is a beautifully restored building with some lovely carving. Rooms are enormous, elegant and evocative, with painted walls. The courtyard is overlooked by the old zenana, and there's a charming restaurant (see below).

**Lallgarh Palace Hotel** (☎ 2540201; www.lallgarhpalace.com; s/d from Rs 2500/3000; ) Some 3km north of the city centre, this hotel is part of the maharaja's palace, dating from 1902, and has well-appointed, old-fashioned rooms around a courtyard. The pricier ones are huge, with high ceilings. There are an indoor pool (Rs 250 per hour for nonguests), a billiard room, croquet facilities, and a resident masseur and astrologer. You can even stay in the Royal Saloon train carriage (Rs 2000). The hotel can organise three-hour camel safaris.

**Karni Bhawan Palace Hotel** (☎ 2524701; www.mewarindia.com; Gandhi Colony; s/d/ste Oct-Mar Rs 2000/2500/3500, s/d/ste Apr-Sep Rs 1400/1750/2450) This hotel is about 800m east of the Lallgarh Palace Hotel and was briefly the residence of Maharaja Karni Singh. It's an ugly but splendid red-and-white flourish of a building, cosy and well run. Huge suites are furnished in grand Art Deco style. A visit to stunning Gajner Palace Hotel outside Bikaner can be arranged (see opposite).

## Eating

### RESTAURANTS

**Deluxe** (Station Rd; dishes Rs 15-30; 6am-10pm) This has an ice cream–striped interior, and veg South Indian and Chinese dishes, as well as breakfast.

**Amber** (Station Rd; dishes Rs 40-95; 10am-3pm & 6-10pm) Amber, with brown walls and mirrors and a staid, no-nonsense look, is well regarded and popular for veg fare. South Indian snacks are also available, and there's a variety of Indian sweets, including delicious *gulab jamuns* (deep-fried balls of dough soaked in a rose-flavoured syrup).

**Laxmi Hotel** (Station Rd; dishes Rs 15-40; 10am-10pm) This is a simple place, open onto the street, with tasty fresh veg dishes – you can see the roti being flipped in front of you.

**Hotel Laxmi Niwas** (☎ 2202777; dishes around Rs 200-250, buffet Rs 600; noon-3pm & 7.30-10.30pm) In Laxmi Niwas Palace (see p349), this excellent garden restaurant is a lovely place to eat. (Note that there are different prices for Indians and foreigners.) There's music in the evenings.

**Bhanwar Niwas** (☎ 2529323; set lunch/dinner Rs 350/350) A splendid place to eat, this hotel (see p349) welcomes nonguests to its veg dining hall (notice is essential). You can have a drink before dinner in the courtyard.

**Lallgarh Palace Hotel** (☎ 2540201; meals Rs 300-400) A majestic option, this hotel (see left) also opens its restaurant up to nonguests. There's a good range of veg and nonveg dishes, or you may just prefer to sip a beer in the bar, with stuffed beasts peering down at you. Snacks, such as vegetable pakoras, are also available.

### QUICK EATS

Bikaner is noted for the *bhujiya*, which is a special kind of *namkin* (spicy snack), sold in the shops along Station Rd among other places.

**Chhotu Motu Joshi Sweet Shop** (Station Rd) This is Bikaner's best-loved sweet stop, with an assortment of Indian treats. Try milk-sweet *rasmalai* (ricotta dessert with cardamom, nuts and sugar; Rs 12) and saffron *kesar cham cham* (Rs 6 for two). The latter is a sausage-shaped sticky confection of milk, sugar and saffron; when bitten, it oozes a sweet sugar syrup. Fresh samosas are available out the front in the mornings, and *bhujiya* costs Rs 5 per plate.

**Kwality** (Station Rd; ice cream Rs 10-15) Next door to Hotel Joshi, Kwality has quality ice cream.

## Shopping

**Abhivyakti** (Ganganagar Rd; 8.30am-6.30pm) Run by the Urmul Trust, a local NGO supported by Urmul Dairy (which has an outlet next door), Abhivyakti sells high-quality textiles produced by skilled artisans from local villages. The profits go directly to the producers, and to health and education projects in the surrounding villages, such as a girls' college. Take care, as rickshaw drivers and touts have taken visitors to other, commercial shops, claiming that they're run by the Urmul Trust.

The trust, founded in 1986, aims to provide primary health care and education to the people of the remote villages of Rajasthan, raise awareness of poor women's rights and promote the handicrafts of rural artisans, thus cutting out middlemen and commissions. You can pick up *pattus* (lovely handloom shawls) from Rs 310 to 2000, cushion covers (Rs 65 to 575), ladies' kurtas (shirts; Rs 500 to 700) and men's kurtas

(Rs 350 to 375). It sells jootis (traditional, pointy-toed Rajasthani shoes), hand-printed cotton garments, puppets and more.

The Urmul Trust welcomes volunteers (see p376).

Go to Usta St in the old city to see artisans making *usta* (gold-painted camel leather) products.

Vichitra Arts, located at Bhairon Vilas (p349), is a shop selling beautiful antique clothes, including magnificently heavy wedding skirts. It's pricey (newer items are definitely overpriced) but interesting. There's an adjoining workshop with a resident artist painting miniatures. He'll paint one on your fingernail given half a chance.

## Getting There & Away

### BUS

The bus stand is 3km north of the city centre, almost opposite the road leading to Lalgarh Palace. If your bus is coming from the south, ask the driver to let you out closer to the city centre. Express buses run to various places, including Udaipur (Rs 224, 12 hours, 6.30pm), Ajmer (Rs 113, seven hours, 15 daily), Jaipur (via Fatehpur and Sikar; Rs 115, seven hours, 15 daily), Jodhpur (Rs 104, 5½ hours, 15 daily), Jaisalmer (Rs 110, eight hours, three daily), Agra (Rs 227, 12 hours, 5am) and Delhi (Rs 190/207 in ordinary/express, 11/10 hours, six daily) sometimes via Jhunjhunu (Rs 87, five hours, three daily).

Private buses run to Jaipur (Rs 100/150 in express/sleeper), Jodhpur (Rs 100/120), Udaipur (Rs 210/250), Mt Abu (Rs 260/280), Delhi (Rs 170/200), Agra (Rs 200/250) and Ajmer (Rs 100 in express).

### TRAIN

To Jaipur, there's the *Bikaner Howrah Superfast* (No 2308A), leaving at 3.55pm (Rs 201/510 in sleeper/3AC, seven hours, 175km) or the *Jaipur–Bikaner Express* (Nos 4737/8), departing at 9.45pm (Rs 158/731 in sleeper/2AC, 10¼ hours). The *Ranakpur Express* (No 4707) leaves for Jodhpur at 9.45am (Rs 148 in sleeper, five hours, 569km). To Delhi, the *Bikaner Mail* (No 4792) leaves at 7.50pm and arrives in the capital at 6am (Rs 200/827 in sleeper/2AC, 449km).

## Getting Around

An autorickshaw from the train station to the palace should cost Rs 20, but you'll probably be asked for more. Bicycles can be hired near Bhairon Vilas for Rs 25 a day.

# AROUND BIKANER

## Devi Kund

The marble and red-sandstone royal **cenotaphs** of the Bika dynasty rulers, with some fine frescoes, are 8km east of Bikaner. The white-marble *chhatri* of Maharaja Surat Singh is among the most imposing.

It costs Rs 100 return by rickshaw to get to this quiet spot.

## National Research Centre on Camels

This government-managed station, 8km away from Bikaner, is probably unique in Asia. There are about 230 camels at the **National Research Centre on Camels** (☎/fax 0151-2230183; admission free, camera Rs 10; 🕒 3-5pm), and three different breeds are reared here. The British Army had a camel corps drawn from Bikaner during WWI. There's not a great deal to see, unless you have a camel fetish, but you can visit the baby camels and look around the small museum.

The round trip, including a half-hour wait at the camel farm, is around Rs 100 for an autorickshaw or Rs 200 for a taxi.

## Gajner Wildlife Sanctuary

The lake and forested hills of this **reserve** (admission per jeep Rs 1000), 32km from Bikaner on the Jaisalmer road, are inhabited by wildfowl, hares, wild boar, desert foxes, and a number of deer and antelopes, including blackbucks and bluebulls. It was once a royal hunting ground – many British luminaries, including Lord Elgin, Lord Mountbatten and the Prince of Wales, have shot down animals here. There are no authorised guides at the sanctuary and, apart from the Gajner Palace Hotel (see below), no accommodation or infrastructure for visitors. The reserve is only accessible by Gajner Palace Hotel vehicles (which may be hired by non-guests). Jeeps can take a maximum of six people.

### SLEEPING & EATING

**Gajner Palace Hotel** (☎ 01534-255065; fax 255060; www.hrhindia.com; s/d Oct-Mar Rs 3000/3600, ste Rs 4500/5500, s/d Apr-Sep Rs 2100/2450, ste Rs 3150/3850) Right on the edge of a beautiful lake, is the magnificent erstwhile royal winter palace and hunting lodge, set in 2400 hectares. The

WESTERN RAJASTHAN

fantastic, busily carved red-sandstone building is set in serene, lush surroundings – ideal for some serious rest and relaxation. The suites are very grand. Some of the rugs in the main palace were woven by prisoners of the Bikaner jail. There's a restaurant, and you can eat indoors or outdoors as you watch the birds bobbing on the calm lake. Bookings for Gajner Palace can also be made through Karni Bhawan Palace Hotel in Bikaner (☎ 0151-2524701).



### GETTING THERE & AWAY

There are frequent daily buses (Rs 22) running to Gajner village, about 1km away from the hotel. A return taxi from Bikaner should cost around Rs 500, including the two hours' waiting time.

## Kolayat

Set around a temple-ringed lake, Kolayat is a beautiful, untouristed town, around 54km to the south of Bikaner. Adding to its sleepy air are stoned sadhus emerging from temples and shrines around the lakes as if rehearsing for Michael Jackson's *Thriller* video. Kolayat is a very holy place, with 52 ghats surrounding its holy lake. Visiting here is a very worthy pilgrimage, and spending one day here can equal up to 10 years at another sacred place. Like Pushkar, it has a Brahma temple – rare in India.

There are a number of *dharamsalas*, but most won't accept tourists. **Bhaheti Dharamsala** (r with shared bathroom Rs 30), on the main ghat by the lakeside, is a good place with simple rooms (you'll need to rent a bed for Rs 5). Otherwise Kolayat is a good day trip from Bikaner.

The **Kapil Muni Mela** (fair) is held here in October-November, around the same time as the Pushkar Camel Fair (minus the camels and cattle, but with plenty of sadhus). The main temple at Kolayat is **Kapil Muni Temple** (closed 3-5pm).

There are regular buses from Bikaner (1½ hours), or there's a train at 8.30am (1½ hours), returning at 4pm.

## Deshnok

Most travellers coming to Bikaner make a beeline for the extraordinary **Karni Mata Temple** (www.karnimata.com; admission free, camera/video Rs 20/50; 4am-10pm) at this village 30km south of Bikaner (see The Temple of Rats, opposite). The holy rodents of Karni Mata are considered to be incarnations of storytellers, and they run riot over the temple complex.

Two special festivals take place at the Karni Mata Temple around April/May and October/ November. Ask at the **Tourist Reception Centre** (☎ 0151-2544125) in Bikaner for the exact dates.

There are at least two buses hourly from Bikaner or Gogo Gate bus stand to Deshnok (Rs 10, 40 minutes). A return taxi costs Rs 350.

### GET TO KNOW YOUR CAMEL

The camels reared at Bikaner's National Research Centre on Camels are of three breeds. The long-haired camels with hair in their ears are local camels from the Bikaner district; they are renowned for their strength. The light-coloured camels are from the Jaisalmer district, and are renowned for their speed – up to 22km/h. The dark-coloured camels are from Gujarat, and the females are renowned for the quantity of milk they produce – an average of 4L to 6L at each milking. The milk tastes a little salty and is reputedly good for the liver. If you have a cup of chai in a small desert village, you're quite possibly drinking camel milk. The stout of heart might even like to try fresh, warm camel milk at the farm. The camels on the farm are crossbred so, in theory, they should be the strongest, fastest and best milk-producing camels you'll find anywhere. Breeding season is from around December to March, and at this time the male camels froth disconcertingly at the mouth.

This is also a stud farm; locals bring their female camels here to be serviced free of charge. Female camels give birth every one and a half years, depending on their age and health, following a long (13-month) gestation period. A male camel can inseminate up to five cows per day.

Adult camels consume about 16kg of fodder in summer, and drink around 30L of water per day; in winter, they drink about 20L per day. In winter a healthy camel can work up to one month without food or water, and in summer up to one week.

### THE TEMPLE OF RATS

The Karni Mata Temple at Deshnok is one of India's more challenging temples for Westerners – its resident mass of holy rodents isn't for the squeamish. Karni Mata lived in the 14th century and performed many miracles during her lifetime. When her youngest son, Lakhan, drowned, Karni Mata ordered Yama, the god of death, to bring him back to life. Yama replied that he was unable to do this, but that Karni Mata, as an incarnation of Durga, could restore Lakhan's life. This she did, decreeing that members of her family would no longer die but would be reincarnated as *kabas* (rats), and that these *kabas* would return as members of her family. Around 600 families in Deshnok claim descent from Karni Mata and that they will be reincarnated as *kabas*.

The temple is an important place of pilgrimage; pilgrims are disgorged from buses every few minutes. Once at the village, they buy *prasad* (holy food offerings) in the form of sugar balls to feed to the rats. Eating *prasad* covered in holy rat saliva is also claimed by believers to bring good fortune, although most travellers are willing to take their word for it.

The pilgrims are anointed with a tikka made with ash from a holy fire in the inner sanctum, while the objects of their devotion run over their toes (sorry, no shoes permitted). Before the temple is a beautiful marble façade with solid silver doors, donated by Maharaja Ganga Singh. Across the doorway to the inner sanctum are repoussé silver doors – one panel shows the goddess with her charges at her feet. An image of the goddess is also enshrined in the inner sanctum. There are special holes around the side of the temple courtyard to facilitate the rats' movements, and a wire grille has been placed over the courtyard to prevent birds of prey and other predators consuming the holy rodents.

It's considered highly auspicious to have a *kaba* run across your feet – you'll probably find you'll be inadvertently graced in this manner whether you want it or not. White *kabas* are quite rare, although there are one or two at the temple, and sighting one augurs well for your spiritual progress.

The temple is an important pilgrimage site, and what may seem unusual to Western eyes is devoutly believed by pilgrims – remember that this isn't a sideshow but a place of worship. And don't conveniently forget to remove your shoes!

### SIGHTS

#### Shri Karni Centenary Auditorium

The pictorial display in this **auditorium** (admission Rs 2; 7am-7pm), across the square from the temple, is worth a look. It tells the story of Karni Mata's life, with descriptions in English and Hindi.

### GETTING THERE & AWAY

Buses from the main or Gogo Gate bus stands in Bikaner depart hourly for Deshnok (Rs 10, 30 minutes). A slow return rickshaw from the train station can be arranged for Rs 100, but Rs 150 is more common. A taxi (Rs 250) is better and safer.

# Directory

## CONTENTS



## ACCOMMODATION

Accommodation in Rajasthan ranges from simple whitewashed cells to glorious palaces and forts that have been converted into some of India's most luxurious, atmospheric and extraordinary hotels.

Throughout this book accommodation listings appear under a Sleeping heading, and may be divided into budget, midrange and top-end categories. Recommendations within these listings are in descending order of preference. Roughly, the budget breakdown in this book is from around Rs 75 to 600 for a budget room, from around Rs 600 to 3000 for midrange and from around US$100 upwards for the top end. However, this is a loose guide; sometimes places fall into categories for their presentation rather than their price, and sometimes places have rooms covering a variety of categories – their upper-priced rooms are midrange, lower-priced ones are budget. Prices also vary depending on the season, whether it's a tourist hot spot, and whether you are bedding down in the town or country.

Although most prices quoted here are for single and double rooms, many hotels will put an extra bed in a room to make a triple for about an extra 25%.

During the peak tourist season, which falls from mid-November to February (the main season is from October to March, but these are the months in which it gets really busy) and some festivals, hotel rates can skyrocket and it can also be tough finding a bed – advance reservations are advisable.

Room quality can sometimes vary dramatically within properties so try to inspect a few rooms first. For a bathroom lowdown see Get to Know Your Bathroom, p356.

Some hotels operate on a 24-hour system (ie your time starts when you check in), while others have fixed checkout times – it pays to ask.

Credit cards are accepted at most top-end hotels and many midrange ones; however, few budget places will take them. Some hotels may request an upfront payment. If you're asked to sign a blank impression of your credit card, refuse to do so. If they insist, fill in an amount less than your estimated expenditure.

In some towns, notably Jodhpur, some hotels 'borrow' the name of a thriving competitor to confuse travellers. To avoid landing up at an inferior copycat, make sure that you know the *exact* name of your preferred hotel, and before paying the driver double-check that you're at the right place, as some cheeky chaps will try to off-load you at hotels where they receive fat commissions. Also see About Touts, p357.

**PRACTICALITIES**

- The electrical current is 230V to 240V, 50Hz AC and sockets are the three round-pin variety. Blackouts are more common during the hotter months.
- Officially India uses the metric system for weights and measures. Terms you're likely to hear are lakhs (one lakh = 100,000) and crores (one crore = 10 million).
- Major English-language dailies include the *Hindustan Times, Times of India, Indian Express, Pioneer, Asian Age, Hindu, Statesman, Telegraph* and *Economic Times*. In Delhi there are several listings and general information guides: *Delhi Cityinfo* and *First City*. Jaipur also has a couple of listings and tourist guides: *Jaipur Vision* and *Jaipur City Guide*. In Udaipur look out for *Out and About in Udaipur*.
- Read incisive current affairs in *Frontline, India Today*, the *Week, Sunday* and *Outlook*. For India-related travel articles get *Outlook Traveller*.
- The national (government) TV broadcaster is Doordarshan. More widely watched are satellite and cable TV; channels include BBC, CNN, Discovery, Star Movies, HBO and MTV. TV (and radio) programme/frequency details appear in most major English-language dailies.
- Government-controlled All India Radio (AIR) nationally transmits local and international news. There are also private channels broadcasting news, music, current affairs, talkback and more.

## Accommodation Options

### BUDGET & MIDRANGE HOTELS

These options range from squalid dives to lovely, excellent-value budget haunts and well-kept midrange places. Most hotels in this category come with ceiling fans. Shoestring travellers may like to consider bringing their own sheets and pillowcases, as some of the cheaper places have bed linen that even the most ferocious dhobi-wallah (washerperson) couldn't whiten.

Midrange hotels offer you more comfort than their budget brothers, but they can be a mixed bag: some have dreary, boxlike rooms while others ooze character. Some of these hotels have 'air-cooled' rooms that are one step up from a ceiling fan and one step below air-conditioning (AC). An air-cooler is a large (usually notoriously noisy) device built into a frame within a wall. Being water-filled, it's doesn't help much in humid conditions.

Some budget and midrange hotels lock their gates at night and remain unmanned on the outside, so let someone know if you intend coming back late.

#### Camping

There are few camping options in Rajasthan, though a couple of hotels allow you to camp in their grounds, as detailed in the Sleeping sections of regional chapters. Some budget hotels let travellers sleep on their rooftop (usually providing a mattress and some bedding) for a nominal charge.

#### Paying Guest House Scheme (Homestays)

Rajasthan pioneered the Paying Guest House Scheme, so it's well developed in the state. Staying with a local family can be a refreshing change from dealing only with tourist-oriented folk and the scheme enables you to do just that. Prices range from budget to upper midrange – contact the local Rajasthan Tourism Development Corporation (RTDC) tourist offices for details (for contact information, see the individual regional chapters).

#### Railway Retiring Rooms

These are at train stations, and you can technically only stay here if you possess an ongoing train ticket. The rooms, which can range from substandard to surprisingly nice, are handy if you have an early morning train departure although they can be noisy if it's a busy station. Most are let on a 24-hour basis, and usually offer dormitories and private rooms.

#### RTDC Accommodation

Tourist bungalows are run by the RTDC; their facilities and service are not usually up to much, though there are some exceptions. They offer cheap dorm beds (Rs 50 per person per night), and there are also usually three types of rooms available, all with private bathroom: ordinary, deluxe and superdeluxe. These vary in standard, often the ordinary rooms are a lot better value than the pricier ones. The local branch of the RTDC tourist office is often on the premises.

### PALACES, FORTS & CASTLES

Rajasthan is famous for its wonderful palace, fort and castle hotels, most famous being the Lake Palace (p259) in Udaipur, Devi Garh (p259) near Udaipur, Rambagh Palace (p171) in Jaipur and Umaid Bhawan Palace (p315) in Jodhpur. But there are hundreds of others, and it often doesn't cost a fortune: some are the height of luxury and priced accordingly, but many are simpler, packed with character and in stunning locations.

As palaces and forts were not originally designed for tourism, the size and quality of rooms can vary wildly. If possible, try to look at a few rooms before choosing one.

Throughout Rajasthan there are many finely appointed historical buildings that have been converted into tourist accommodation. They are known as 'heritage hotels' and include *havelis* (traditional mansions), forts and former royal hunting lodges. Many of the RTDC tourist offices have a brochure that lists heritage hotels, or you can check out the website http://heritagehotels.com.

### TOP-END HOTELS

As major tourist centres, Rajasthan, Delhi and Agra have a bevy of top-end hotels, ranging from swanky five-star chains such as the Oberoi, Taj and Welcomgroup (affiliated to Sheraton), to less-glamorous four-starrers. Despite the level of luxury, top-end hotel staff are often appallingly paid, and can be downright apathetic.

Note that US dollar rates usually apply to foreigners, including to Nonresident Indians (NRIs).

If you're interested in staying at a top-end hotel, it's sometimes cheaper to book them through a travel agent in your home country, who may be able to swing you a good-value package deal.

## Additional Costs

### SEASONAL VARIATIONS

Most hoteliers in Delhi, Agra and Rajasthan crank up their high-season prices to around two to three times the low-season price – the process is gradual, so as the high season approaches, prices will creep up. The prices quoted in this book are high-season rates.

High season begins about a month before Christmas and includes the two months following. Some hotels charge higher rates for the brief Christmas and New Year period, or over major festivals such as Diwali (p365) and the Pushkar Camel Fair (see

### GET TO KNOW YOUR BATHROOM

All top-end and most midrange hotels in India have sit-down flush toilets with toilet paper. Some midrange and many budget hotels have a choice of squat and sit-down flush toilets. In the rock-bottom category squat toilets are the norm and toilet paper is rarely provided.

Some hoteliers refer to squat toilets as 'Indian-style' and sit-down flush toilets as 'Western-style'. In some places you may discover the curious hybrid toilet, which is a sit-down toilet with footpads on the edge of the bowl.

Throughout India, there's various terminology for hotel bathrooms: 'common bath', 'without bath' or 'shared bath' means communal bathroom facilities. 'Attached bath', 'private bath' or 'with bath' indicates that the room has its own bathroom.

'Running', '24-hour' or 'constant' hot water indicates that there's hot water around the clock (not always the case in reality). At the cheapest level, some hotel bathrooms only have cold tap water so hot water is provided in buckets, sometimes only within certain hours and at a small charge.

Hotels that advertise 'room with shower' can be misleading. Even if a bathroom has a shower, check that it works before accepting the room. Some hotels surreptitiously disconnect showers to cut costs, while showers at other places render a mere trickle of water.

Some budget and midrange hotels have small hot-water tanks in the bathroom, which need to be switched on anywhere up to an hour before use.

In this book, hotel rooms have private bathroom unless otherwise stated.

Pushkar Camel Fair, p212). Conversely, in the low season (from around April to September), prices at even normally expensive hotels can drop dramatically, creating some amazing bargains. Between low and high season there's usually a shoulder season when prices rise to somewhere between the low- and high-season rates. It's always worth asking for a better rate if the hotel doesn't seem busy.

### TAXES & SERVICE CHARGES

At most rock-bottom places you won't have to pay any taxes. Once you get into the top end of budget places, and certainly in midrange and top-end accommodation, you will usually have to pay a 10% 'luxury' tax – officially on rooms over Rs 1000.

On top of taxes, many midrange and upmarket hotels have a 'service charge' (usually around 10%). This may be restricted to room service and telephone use, or may be levied on the total bill. Rates quoted in this book exclude taxes unless otherwise indicated.

Many hotels raise their tariffs annually, some raise them when business is good, and some raise rates with an increase of popularity (often because they have had a good write-up in Lonely Planet!) – be prepared for increments on the rates quoted here.

## ACTIVITIES

From exploring the desert on camelback, to being covered in Ayurvedic oils, Rajasthan has an exhilarating range of activities on offer.

Remember that travel agents often take a cut of what you pay and sell you on as clients to someone else. The end provider gets only part of what you paid and so you may get poor equipment, insufficient food or poor safety standards. If you are using an agent, try to deal with companies that are the end provider and ask if they're registered with the state government. Then ask if they're members of an accredited association such as the Travel Agents Association of India, Indian Association of Tour Operators or the Adventure Tour Operators Association of India – ask to see their accreditation. Ask official tourist offices for government-approved operators or, best of all, get recommendations from fellow travellers.

For information on camel, horse, jeep and wildlife safaris, see p374.

#### ABOUT TOUTS

Rajasthan, Delhi and Agra are magnets for touts, all vying for your cash. Their natural habitats are airport terminals and bus/train stations, waiting to snare the fresh (most vulnerable) arrivals. Often they're rickshaw- or taxi-wallahs. Some try to gauge your vulnerability by inquiring whether it's your first trip to India – say it isn't. Their goal is to divert you to a hotel where they earn commission. Some hotels refuse to pay touts and you'll more often than not hear stories about those places being 'full', 'under renovation', 'closed' or whatever. Nine times out of 10 they'll be just that – stories. Think twice before agreeing to stay in any hotel recommended by a tout, as you'll be paying through the nose for your accommodation.

### Ayurveda

Massages, treatments and assessments are available at various places, including Ashtaang, in Delhi (p109), and Kerala Ayurveda Kendra and Chakrapania Ayurveda in Jaipur (p164). There are also Ayurvedic hospitals in Udaipur (p255) and Bundi (p231) offering treatment, and the Ayurveda Hub & Research Institute (p332) in Jaisalmer.

### Bird-Watching

Rajasthan contains some splendid bird-watching sites, including World Heritage–listed Keoladeo Ghana National Park (p191) in Bharatpur, Ranthambhore National Park (p218), Khichan (see the boxed text, p323), near Phalodi, Sariska Tiger Reserve (p201) and Dungarpur (p269).

### Boating

In southern Rajasthan, boats can be hired at Nakki Lake (p270) in Mt Abu, at Chambal Gardens (p235) in Kota, and on Pichola Lake (water-level permitting; p249) in Udaipur. At Jaisalmer, in western Rajasthan, you can hire boats at Tilon-ki-Pol (p332).

### Cycling

Ramesh Jangid, from Apani Dhani (p287) in Nawalgarh, Shekhawati, can organise cycling tours around the villages of Shekhawati, including informative commentaries on the region's remarkable paintings. Hotel

Jamuna Resort (p293) in Jhunjhunu, Shekhawati, can also arrange cycling tours. Butterfield & Robinson offers more-upmarket organised bicycle tours (see p382 for more information).

### Golf

It's possible to play golf in Jaipur (p164) and Jodhpur (p312; equipment is available for hire).

### Swimming

Quite a few of the upmarket hotels allow nonguests to use their swimming pools. Expect to pay anywhere from Rs 100 to 300 for this privilege, which should include a towel.

### Trekking

Various operators can organise treks in the Aravalli Range. Ramesh Jangid (see p287) organises treks that include a guide, all meals, transport and accommodation in village homes, tents and *dharamsalas* (pilgrims' rest houses).

You can also make short treks in the marvellous Aravalli hills around Mt Abu (p273). Other places worth exploring are around Udaipur (p255), Ranakpur (p266) and Kumbalgarh (p266), which have stunning scenery.

## BUSINESS HOURS

Official business hours are from 9.30am to 5.30pm Monday to Friday. Unofficially they tend to be from 10am to 5pm.

Most major banks are open from 10am to 2pm (some from 9am to 1pm and 1.30pm to 4pm) on weekdays, and from 10am to noon on Saturday – there are often variations, so it pays to check. In the bigger cities and tourist centres there are invariably foreign-exchange offices that stay open for longer.

In most cities, the main post office is open from around 10am until 5pm on weekdays (some close for lunch any time between 1pm and 2pm) and on Saturday until noon (and occasionally on Sunday).

Shop hours vary regionally, but most tend to open from around 10am to 6pm and close once a week (often on Sunday).

In the more popular tourist areas, such as Udaipur, Jaisalmer and Pushkar, many shops open at around 9am and don't close until about 7pm, and half close on Sunday.

Restaurant hours vary – unless otherwise mentioned in Eating reviews, restaurants are open from around 11am till 10.30pm.

## CHILDREN

Being a family-oriented society, India is a child-friendly destination. But travelling with kids in India can be hard work, requiring constant vigilance – be especially cautious of roads, as traffic can be erratic. Any long-distance road travel should include adequate stops, as rough roads can make travel more tiring than usual, especially for little ones. Train is usually the most comfortable mode of travel, especially for long trips. Always carry sufficient clean drinking water.

Health risks, such as diarrhoea, can be much more of a threat to children than adults – see p392. If your child takes special medication, bring along an adequate stock in case it's not easily found locally.

For helpful hints, see Lonely Planet's *Travel with Children*, and the Lonely Planet website (www.lonelyplanet.com), which has a subdirectory on travelling with children, as well as the Thorn Tree travel forum, which can connect you with people who have travelled with young ones.

### Practicalities

Many hotels have 'family rooms' or will happily provide an extra bed, and the more upmarket hotels may offer baby-sitting facilities and/or kid's activity programmes – inquire in advance. The more upmarket hotels have cable TV featuring children's channels such as Cartoon Network.

Regarding restaurants, it's usually the more upmarket ones (or those at popular family destinations) that supply high chairs. Restaurants rarely have dedicated nappy-changing rooms. For more information on eating, see p84.

Standard baby products such as nappies (diapers) are available in larger towns, where nappies start at Rs 63 (pack of 10) and baby milk powder costs Rs 140 (500g); these can be considerably pricier beyond big cities.

### Sights & Activities

Allow several days for children to acclimatise to India's explosion of sights, smells, tastes and sounds. Start with short outings and include child-friendly attractions (generally more prevalent in bigger cities), such as the sound-and-light show of Delhi (p100), and fun museums such as Delhi's doll museum (p108). Chokhi Dhani (p174), near Jaipur, is a great place for children, and they'll love the elephants at Amber Fort (p179).

Wildlife and camel safaris are also worth considering (see p374), and horse safaris (p374) can be another child-pleaser.

Travelling is usually much better out of the larger towns – without the hectic traffic and hassle children will be safer, and find it much easier to adapt. Bear in mind, however, that you won't find the facilities and comforts of the cities.

## CLIMATE CHARTS

The climate of Rajasthan can be neatly divided into four seasons: premonsoon, monsoon, postmonsoon and winter. *Kharif* (monsoon) and *rabi* (winter) are the two main crop-growing seasons. For comprehensive details, see p17.

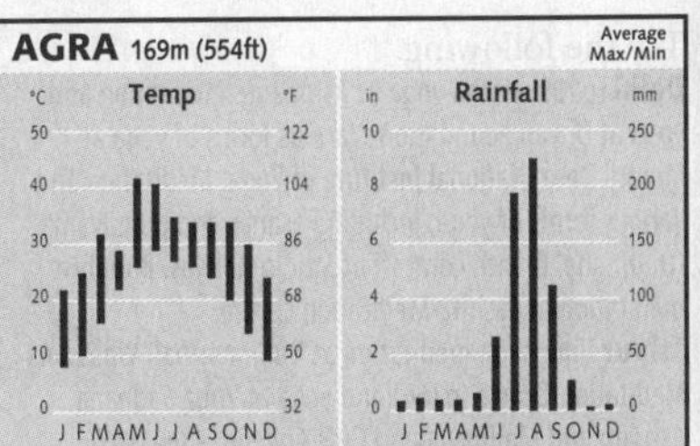


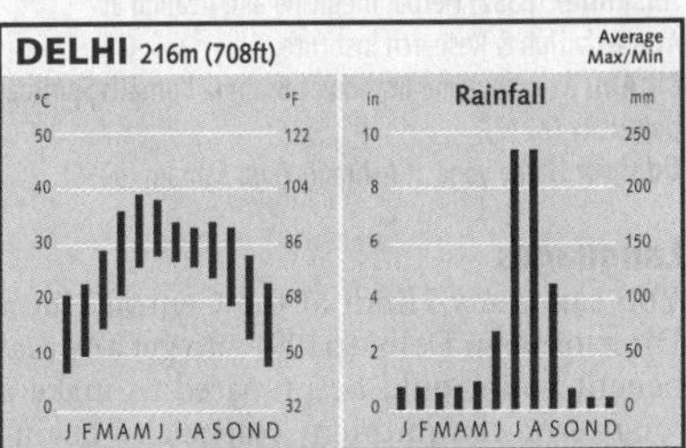


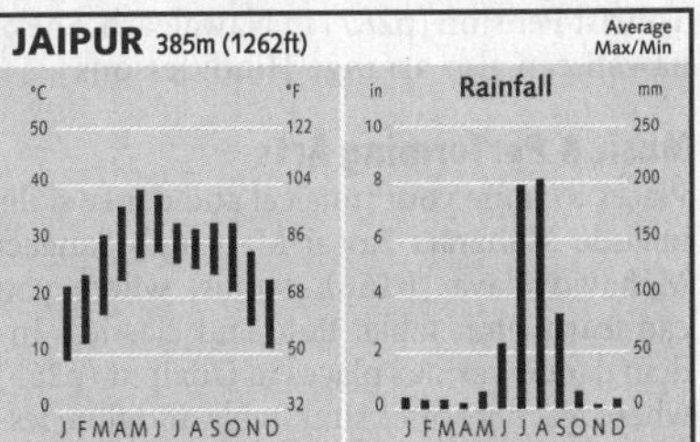


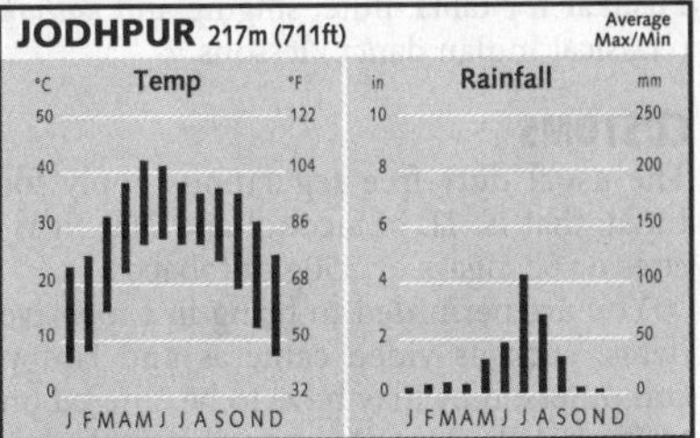


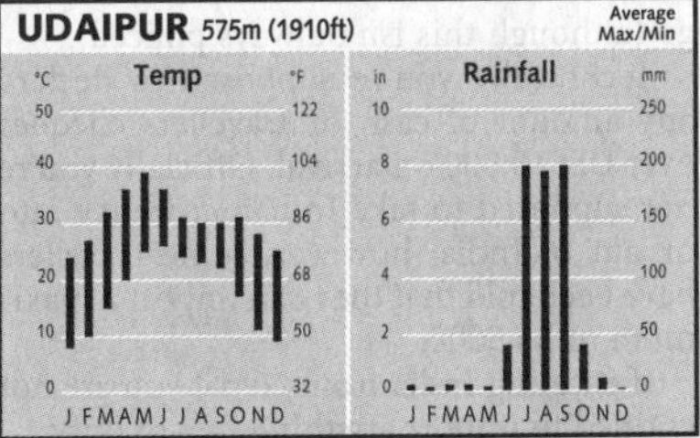


## COURSES

To find out about new courses that may now be on offer, inquire at tourist offices, ask fellow travellers and check local newspapers and magazines. For information on cooking courses, see p86.

### Arts & Crafts

There are myriad arts and crafts courses available in Rajasthan.

**Jaipur** Painting and ceramics offered by Mr Kripal Singh (p166). Block printing and blue pottery at Sakshi (p166), about 12km south of Jaipur in Sanganer village.

**Jhunjhunu** Tuition in local Shekhawati painting is offered at and Hotel Jamuna Resort – see (p293).

**Nawalgarh** *Bandhani* (tie-dye) and other crafts are offered at Apani Dhani (p286).

**Udaipur** Painting lessons are offered at Art Loft and Ashoka Arts – see p256.

### Astrology

Those fascinated by the future can take lessons in astrology at the Rajasthan Astrological Council & Research Institute (p166) in Jaipur.

### Ayurveda, Meditation & Yoga

There are many places in Rajasthan, Agra and Delhi offering meditation and yoga courses – ask around for recommendations. For places that don't levy a charge, donations are much appreciated.

Try the following:
**Delhi** (p109) Hatha yoga at Ashtaang. Meditation and yoga at Dhyan Foundation. Various forms of yoga at Morarji Desai National Institute of Yoga. Meditation and various forms of yoga, including asanas and pranayama (traditional breath control) at Studio Abhyas. Buddhist meditation at Tushita Meditation Centre.
**Jaipur** Vipassana meditation at Dhammathali Vipassana Meditation Centre (p166) and yoga at Yoga Sadhana Ashram and Madhavanand Girls College – see p167.
**Jaisalmer** (p332) Herbal medicine and healing at Ayurveda Hub & Research Institute.
**Mt Abu** Raja Yoga meditation at Brahma Kumaris Spiritual University (p272).
**Udaipur** Hatha yoga at Ashtang Yoga Ashram (p256).

### Languages

You can study Hindi at the Central Hindi Directorate in Delhi (p109) – to get any real benefit you should be prepared to make a long-term commitment (especially beginners). Apani Dhani and Ramesh Jangid's Tourist Pension (p287) in Nawalgarh, Shekhawati can also arrange Hindi lessons.

### Music & Performing Arts

Places to hone your musical and dance skills include Maharaja Sawai Mansingh Sangeet Mahavidyalaya (p166), Jaipur, where you can learn sitar, tabla, flute and classical Indian dance; various places in Udaipur (p255) where teachers offer sitar, tabla and flute lessons; and Saraswati Music School (p213) in Pushkar for tabla, flute, singing and *kathak* (classical Indian dance) lessons.

## CUSTOMS

The usual duty-free regulations apply for India; that is, 1L of alcohol and 200 cigarettes or 50 cigars or 250g of tobacco.

You are permitted to bring in expensive items, such as video cameras and laptop computers; they may have to be entered on a 'Tourist Baggage Re-export' form to ensure you take them out with you when you go (although this isn't always policed).

Technically you're supposed to declare any amount of cash or travellers cheques over US$10,000 on arrival. Officially you're not supposed to take Indian currency into or out of India; however, some travellers have been told that they can import a maximum of Rs 5000.

If entering India from Nepal you are not entitled to import anything free of duty.

There are certain restrictions about what you can take out of India – see p370.

## DANGERS & ANNOYANCES

Like anywhere else in the world, common sense and caution are your best weapons against theft or worse. Chat with other travellers and tourism officials in order to stay abreast of the latest potential hazards. Also see the India branch of **Lonely Planet's Thorn Tree forum** (www.lonelyplanet.com) where travellers often post warnings about problems they've encountered. Women travellers should see p377.

### Contaminated Food & Drink

In past years, some private medical clinics have provided patients with more treatment than is necessary in order to procure larger medical insurance claims – get several opinions where possible. Worse still, a serious food scare erupted in north India in 1998, principally in Agra and Varanasi, when numerous travellers became sick and two died after eating at local establishments where the food had been purposely contaminated. This scam has thankfully been quashed, but there's always the chance it could reappear.

The water (see Drinking Water, p398) can also be a potential problem. Always ensure the seal is intact on bought mineral water and check that the bottom of the bottle hasn't been tampered with. Crush plastic bottles after use to eradicate them being misused later. Better still, bring along water-purification tablets to avoid adding to India's plastic waste problem – see p74.

### Druggings & Theft

Never leave important valuables (passport, tickets, money) in your room (see p368) and always keep luggage securely locked. On trains, keep your gear near you; padlock bags to luggage racks or loops found under some train seats. Thieves tend to target popular tourist train routes, such as Delhi to Agra. There have been reports of backpacks being slashed. Be extra alert during train departure times, when the confusion and crowds are at their worst. Airports are another place to exercise caution, as after a long flight you're unlikely to be at your most alert.

Occasionally tourists (especially those travelling solo) are drugged and robbed on train or bus journeys. Unwary travellers are

**A WARNING**

If you believe any stories about buying anything in India to sell at a profit elsewhere, you'll simply be proving (once again) that old adage about separating fools from their money. Precious stones and carpets are favourites for this game. Merchants will tell you that you can sell the items back home for several times the purchase price, and will even give you the (often imaginary) addresses of dealers who will buy them. You may also be shown written statements from other travellers documenting the money they have made, even photographs of the merchants shaking hands with their so-called business partners overseas – besuited Westerners standing outside big stores in Europe and America. Don't be taken in, it's all a scam. The stones or carpets you buy will be worth only a fraction of what you pay. Often the gem scams involve showing you real stones and then packing up worthless glass beads to give you in their place. Don't let greed cloud your judgment.

These scams can be elaborate productions and can begin when touts strike up conversations in excellent English while you're waiting for a bus or eating in a restaurant, until you develop a friendly relationship with them. It might be several hours (or even days if they know where you hang out and can organise to see you again) before any mention is made of reselling items.

Tip: beware of anyone who wants to become your best friend in areas that see a lot of tourist traffic, eg hotel and shopping strips and transport hubs. You don't need to avoid and ignore all the locals, but go to a less-touristy area if you're interested in a genuine conversation.

befriended, offered a spiked drink (to send them to sleep) and their valuables are then stolen. It's wise to politely decline drinks or food offered by relative strangers (use your instincts), particularly if you're alone.

Unfortunately some travellers make their money go further by helping themselves to other people's – take care. For stolen/lost travellers cheques, contact the Amex or Thomas Cook office in the closest capital city – to locate nationwide branches contact their Delhi offices (p96).

## Holi Festival

Although the Holi festival (p365) is mostly good fun, there have been incidences of people being doused with toxic substances mixed in water, sometimes leaving them with scars. During Holi, there's also a tradition of guzzling alcohol and consuming cannabis-derived bhang in the form of lassis, pakoras and cookies. Female travellers have been groped by spaced-out blokes – particularly in touristy areas. Officials advise women to avoid venturing onto the streets alone during Holi.

## Other Important Warnings

Gem scams are a major problem in Rajasthan, especially Jaipur (see p156) and in Agra (see p137) and many people have been conned by dealers who convince them to part with large sums of money for gems to resell at home. The gems are usually overpriced, and often valueless.

Be careful using credit cards when shopping. If you're told that the merchant won't forward the credit slip for payment until you've received the goods, don't believe a word of it. No trader will send you as much as a postcard until they have received the full amount for the goods. Don't let your credit card be taken out the back to be processed – make sure transactions take place in front of you, to avoid multiple imprints of your card by unscrupulous traders.

Delhi is one of the worst places in India for scamming travellers, as scamsters prey on new arrivals. See p97 for some handy avoidance tips.

## Precautions

A good travel-insurance policy is essential. If you have something stolen, immediately report it to the police. Ensure you get a statement proving you have done so – essential if you want to make an insurance claim. Note that some policies require you to report a theft to the police within a certain amount of time after you realise you've been robbed.

It's a good idea to keep photocopies of your important documents (passport, insurance documents etc) in a separate place, in case they do get pinched.

Always keep an emergency cash stash in case you lose your travellers cheques, and in that same place (ie separate from your travellers cheques) keep a record of the cheques' serial numbers, proof-of-purchase slips, encashment vouchers and your photocopied passport details (data and visa pages).

To rapidly replace lost travellers cheques you need the proof-of-purchase slip and the numbers of the missing cheques (some places require a photocopy of the police report and a passport photo). If you don't have the cheque numbers, Amex (or whichever company has issued them) will contact the place where you bought them.

## DISABLED TRAVELLERS

India's crowded public transport, crush of people in urban areas and variable infrastructure can test the hardiest traveller. If you have a physical disability or are vision impaired, these pose a greater challenge. However, seeing the way the mobility-impaired locals whiz through traffic in modified bicycles proves that nothing is impossible.

India has limited wheelchair-friendly hotels (mostly top end), restaurants and offices. Staircases are often steep. Footpaths, where they exist, are often riddled with holes, littered with debris and packed with pedestrians, severely hindering movement.

Try to prebook ground floor hotel rooms and if you use crutches, bring along spare rubber caps for the tips as they can wear down quickly in India.

If your mobility is considerably restricted you may like to consider travelling with an able-bodied companion. Additionally, hiring a car with driver will make moving around a whole lot easier (see p385).

Organisations that may offer further advice include the **Royal Association for Disability and Rehabilitation** (RADAR; ☎ 020-7250 3222; www.radar.org.uk; 12 City Forum, 250 City Rd, London EC1V 8AF, UK) and **Mobility International USA** (MIUSA; ☎ 541-3431284; www.miusa.org; PO Box 10767, Eugene, OR 97440, USA).

## DISCOUNT CARDS

### Senior Cards

For those aged over 65, Jet Airways offers a 25% discount on domestic air travel. Discounts on other air carriers may emerge as competition among airlines increases (ask travel agents). If you're over 60 you're entitled to a 30% discount on train travel and a 50% discount on flights operated by Air Sahara.

### Student & Youth Cards

Student cards are of limited use nowadays – many student concessions have either been eliminated or replaced by 'youth fares' or other age concessions. Hostels run by the Indian Youth Hostels Association are part of the Hostelling International (HI) network; an HI card entitles you to standard discount rates. Members of YMCA/YWCA are also entitled to standard discounts on accommodation.

Foreigners aged below 30 receive a 25% discount on domestic air tickets.

## EMBASSIES & HIGH COMMISSIONS

### Indian Embassies & High Commissions

The following represent just some of India's missions around the world. For comprehensive contact details see www.meaindia.nic.in (click on the 'Missions and Posts Abroad' link).

Apart from the main mission, there are Indian consulates in many countries – inquire locally for these (as well as for relevant fax/email details).

**Australia** (☎ 02-6273 3999; 3-5 Moonah Place, Yarralumla, ACT 2600)

**Bangladesh** (☎ 02-9889339; House 2, Rd 142, Gulshan I, Dhaka)

**Bhutan** (☎ 02-322162; India House Estate, Thimphu)

**Canada** (☎ 613-744 3751; 10 Springfield Rd, Ottawa, Ontario K1M 1C9)

**France** (☎ 01 40 50 70 70; 15 Rue Alfred Dehodencq, 75016 Paris)

**Germany** (☎ 030-257950; Tiergartenstrasse 17, 10785, Berlin)

**Ireland** (☎ 01-497 0843; 6 Leeson Park, Dublin 6)

**Israel** (☎ 03-5291999; 140 Hayarkon St, Tel Aviv - 61033)

**Italy** (☎ 064 88 46 42; Via XX Settembre 5, 00187 Rome)

**Japan** (☎ 0332 622 391; 2-2-11 Kudan Minami, Chiyoda-ku, Tokyo 1020074)

**Myanmar** (Burma; ☎ 01-240633; 545-547 Merchant St, Yangon)

**Nepal** (☎ 014 410900; 336 Kapurdhara Marg, Kathmandu)

**The Netherlands** (☎ 0703 46 97 71; Buitenrustweg 2, 2517 KD, The Hague)

**New Zealand** (☎ 04-473 6390; 180 Molesworth St, Wellington)

**Pakistan** (☎ 0512 206950; G5, Diplomatic Enclave, Islamabad)

**Sri Lanka** (☎ 012 421605; 36-38 Galle Rd, Colombo 3)

**Thailand** (☎ 0 2258 0300; 46 Soi Prasarnmitr, Soi 23, Sukhumvit Rd, Bangkok 10110)

**UK** (☎ 020-7836 8484; India House, Aldwych, London WC2B 4NA)

**USA** (☎ 202-939 9806; 2536 Massachusetts Ave NW, Washington DC 20008)

## Embassies & High Commissions in India

Most missions operate from 9am to 5pm Monday to Friday (some close between 1pm and 2pm).

If your country's mission is not listed below, that doesn't necessarily mean it's not represented in India – see the local phone directory or call one of the missions listed here for relevant contact details.

The following missions are located in Delhi.

**Australia** (Map pp102-4; ☎ 011-51399900; 1/50G Shantipath, Chanakyapuri)
**Bangladesh** (Map pp92-4; ☎ 011-24121389; EP39 Dr Radakrishnan Marg, Chanakyapuri)
**Bhutan** (Map pp102-4; ☎ 011-24121389; Chandragupta Marg, Chanakyapuri)
**Canada** (Map pp102-4; ☎ 011-51782000; 7/8 Shantipath, Chanakyapuri)
**France** (Map pp102-4; ☎ 011-26118790; 2/50E Shantipath, Chanakyapuri)
**Germany** (Map pp102-4; ☎ 011-26871831; 6/50G Shantipath, Chanakyapuri)
**Ireland** (☎ 011-24626741, 230 Jor Bagh)
**Israel** (Map pp102-4; ☎ 011-23013238; 3 Aurangzeb Rd)
**Italy** (Map pp102-4; ☎ 011-26114355; 50E Chandragupta Marg, Chanakyapuri)
**Japan** (Map pp102-4; ☎ 011-26876581; 50G Shantipath, Chanakyapuri)
**Malaysia** (Map pp102-4; ☎ 011-26111291; 50M Satya Marg, Chanakyapuri)
**Myanmar** (Burma; Map pp102-4; ☎ 011-6889007; 3/50F Nyaya Marg, Chanakyapuri)
**Nepal** (Map pp102-4; ☎ 011-23327361; Barakhamba Rd)
**The Netherlands** (Map pp102-4; ☎ 011-26884951; 6/50F Shantipath, Chanakyapuri)
**New Zealand** (Map pp92-4; ☎ 011-26883170; 50N Nyaya Marg, Chanakyapuri)
**Pakistan** (Map pp102-4; ☎ 011-24676004; 2/50G Shantipath, Chanakyapuri)
**Singapore** (Map pp92-4; ☎ 011-26877939; E6 Chandragupta Marg, Chanakyapuri)
**South Africa** (Map pp92-4; ☎ 011-26149411; B18 Vasant Marg, Vasant Vihar)
**Sri Lanka** (Map pp102-4; ☎ 011-23010201; 27 Kautilya Marg, Chanakyapuri)
**Switzerland** (Map pp102-4; ☎ 011-26878372; Nyaya Marg, Chanakyapuri)
**Thailand** (Map pp102-4; ☎ 011-26118103; 56N Nyaya Marg, Chanakyapuri)
**UK** (Map pp102-4; ☎ 011-26872161; Shantipath, Chanakyapuri)
**USA** (Map pp102-4; ☎ 011-24198000; Shantipath, Chanakyapuri)

# FESTIVALS & EVENTS

Rich in religions and traditions, Rajasthan has scores of vibrant holidays and festivals.

Most holidays and festivals follow either the Indian lunar calendar (a complex system determined chiefly by astrologers) or the Islamic calendar (which falls about 11 days earlier each year; 12 days earlier in leap years), and therefore change annually relative to the Gregorian calendar. The India-wide holidays and festivals listed here are arranged according to the Indian lunar (and Gregorian) calendar which starts in Chaitra (March or April) – contact local tourist offices for exact festival dates, as many are variable.

Many festivals in India occur during *purnima* (full moon), which is traditionally auspicious.

The 'wedding season' generally falls between the cooler months of November and March (the dates revolve around auspicious timings set by astrologers). During this period you're likely to see at least one wedding procession on the street, which will be a merry mix of singing, dancing and a loud brass band.

The following represent major national festivals – for more details about regional ones see the Festivals in… boxed texts at the beginning of individual chapters.

## Chaitra (March/April)

**Mahavir Jayanti** A Jain festival commemorating the birth of Mahavira, the founder of Jainism.
**Ramanavami** Hindu temples all over India celebrate the birth of Rama. In the week leading up to Ramanavami, the Ramayana is widely read and performed.
**Easter** This Christian holiday marks the Crucifixion and Resurrection of Christ.

## Vaisakha (April/May)

**Muharram** This 10-day Muslim festival commemorates the martyrdom of Imam Hussain, the Prophet Mohammed's grandson.
**Baisakhi** A Sikh festival commemorating the day that Guru Gobind Singh founded the Khalsa, the Sikh brotherhood, which adopted the five *kakkars* (means by which Sikh men recognise each other) as part of their code of behaviour. The Guru Granth Sahib, the Sikh holy book, is read through at gurdwaras (Sikh temples). Feasts and dancing follow in the evening.

### REGIONAL FESTIVAL CALENDAR

Look at the Festivals in… boxed texts at the beginning of each regional chapter for detailed coverage. A quick reference for dates of the major regional fairs and festivals up to the year 2009:

| Festival & location | 2006 | 2007 | 2008 | 2009 |
|---|---|---|---|---|
| Nagaur Fair (p306), Nagaur | 2-4 Feb | 25-28 Feb | 13-16 Feb | 2-5 Feb |
| Baneshwar Fair (p227), Baneshwar | 4-7 Feb | 29 Jan-2 Feb | 17-21 Feb | 5-9 Feb |
| Desert Festival (p306), Jaisalmer | 8-12 Feb | 31 Jan-2 Feb | 19-21 Feb | 7-9 Feb |
| Brij Festival (p187), Bharatpur | 10-12 Feb | 2-4 Feb | 2-4 Feb | 2-4 Feb |
| Elephant Festival (p151), Jaipur | 14 Mar | 3 Mar | 21 Mar | 10 Mar |
| Kaila Devi (p187), Karauli | 26 Mar | 21-22 Mar | 8-9 Apr | 29-30 Mar |
| Shri Mahavirji Fair (p187), Mahaveerji | 1-2 Apr | 27 Mar-2 Apr | 14-20 Apr | 3-9 Apr |
| Gangaur Fair (p151), Jaipur | 1-3 Apr | 21-23 Mar | 8-10 Apr | 29-31 Mar |
| Mewar Festival (p227), Udaipur | 7-13 Apr | 16 Mar | 3 Apr | 23 Mar |
| Summer Festival (p227), Mt Abu | 11-13 May | 30 Apr-2 May | 18-20 May | 7-9 May |
| Teej (p151), Jaipur | 28-29 Jul | 15-16 Aug | 4-5 Aug | 24-25 Jul |
| Kajli Teej (p227), Bundi | 11-12 Aug | 30-31 Aug | 18-19 Aug | 8-9 Aug |
| Ramdevra Fair (p306), Ramdevra | 2-3 Sep | 21-22 Sep | 9-10 Sep | 29-30 Aug |
| Dussehra (p227), Kota | 30 Sep-2 Oct | 19-21 Oct | 7-9 Oct | 26-28 Sep |
| Marwar Festival (p306), Jodhpur | 6-7 Oct | 25-26 Oct | 13-14 Oct | 3-4 Oct |
| Pushkar Camel Fair (p212), Pushkar | 29 Oct-5 Nov | 17-24 Nov | 5-13 Nov | 25 Oct-2 Nov |
| Chandrabhaga Fair (p227), Jhalrapatan | 4-6 Nov | 23-25 Nov | 12-14 Nov | 1-3 Nov |
| Kolayat Fair (p306), Kolayat | 1-9 Nov | 20-29 Nov | 9-18 Nov | 29 Oct-7 Nov |

**Buddha Jayanti** This 'triple-blessed festival' falls on the full moon (usually in May, sometimes in late April or early June) and celebrates Buddha's birth, enlightenment and attainment of nirvana.

**Eid-Milad-un-Nabi** An Islamic festival celebrating the birth of the Prophet Mohammed.

## Jyaistha (May/June)

No major festivals currently fall during this period.

## Asadha (June/July)

No major festivals currently fall during this period.

## Sravana (July/August)

**Naag Panchami** This Hindu festival is dedicated to Ananta, the serpent upon whose coils Vishnu rested between universes. Snake charmers do a roaring trade, despite protests by animal-rights activists, who say the snakes suffer ill-treatment (possibly even death). Snakes are believed to have power over the monsoon rainfall and keep evil away from homes.

**Raksha Bandhan (Narial Purnima)** On the full-moon day girls fix amulets known as *rakhis* to the wrists of their (not necessarily blood-related) brothers to protect them in the coming year. The brothers reciprocate with gifts. Some people also worship the Vedic sea god Varuna.

## Bhadra (August/September)

**Independence Day** This public holiday on 15 August marks the anniversary of India's Independence in 1947.

**Drukpa Teshi** Celebrates the first teaching given by Buddha.

**Ganesh Chaturthi** This joyful festival marks the birth of the popular elephant-headed god, Ganesh. On the last day of the festival clay idols of Ganesh, the god of good fortune, are paraded through the streets before being ceremoniously immersed in a river, sea or tank.

**Janmastami** The anniversary of Krishna's birth is celebrated with happy abandon – in tune with Krishna's own mischievous moods. Devotees fast all day until midnight.

**Shravan Purnima** On this day of fasting, high-caste Hindus replace the sacred thread that they wear looped over their left shoulder.

**Pateti** Parsis celebrate their new year at this time.

## Asvina (September/October)

**Navratri (Festival of Nine Nights)** For nine happy nights, this Hindu festival leading up to Dussehra is dedicated to the goddess Durga who valiantly beheaded a menacing demon. Goddesses Lakshmi and Saraswati, of wealth and learning respectively, also get special praise. During the day Hindus take part in rituals, fasting and prayer. Then after sundown there's often tabla-accompanied *dandiya raas* (folk dancing with sticks). Some regions also have nightly *garbas* (folk dances without the sticks).

**Dussehra (Durga Puja)** This festival celebrates Durga's victory over the buffalo-headed demon Mahishasura. In many places it culminates with the burning of huge images of the demon king Ravana and his accomplices, symbolic of the triumph of good over evil. In Delhi (and elsewhere) it's also known as Ram Lila (Life Story of Rama), with fireworks and reenactments of the Ramayana. It's particularly spectacular in Kota.
**Gandhi Jayanti** This public holiday is a solemn celebration of Mohandas (Mahatma) Gandhi's birth anniversary on 2 October with prayer meetings at the Raj Ghat in Delhi where he was cremated.

## Kartika (October/November)

**Diwali (Deepavaali)** This is the happiest festival of the Hindu calendar, celebrated on the 15th day of Kartika. At night decorative oil lamps are lit to show Rama the way home from his period of exile. The festival is also dedicated to Lakshmi and to Kali. In all, it lasts five days. On the first day, houses are thoroughly cleaned and doorsteps are decorated with intricate *rangolis* (chalk/powder designs). Day two is dedicated to Krishna's victory over Narakasura, a legendary tyrant. Day three is spent worshipping Lakshmi. Traditionally this is the beginning of the new financial year for companies. Day four commemorates the visit of the friendly demon Bali whom Vishnu put in his place. On the fifth day men visit their sisters to have an auspicious tikka put on their forehead. Giving sweets has become as much a part of Diwali as the lighting of oil lamps and firecrackers.
**Govardhana Puja** A Hindu festival dedicated to the holy cow.
**Ramadan (Ramazan)** This 30-day dawn-to-dusk fast marks the ninth month of the Islamic calendar, the month during which the Prophet Mohammed had the Quran revealed to him in Mecca. This festival moves forward 11 days each year and is due to begin in late September in 2006 and mid-September in 2007.
**Eid al-Fitr** This feast celebrates the end of Ramadan; festivities continue for three days. In 2006 it's scheduled to fall in October.

## Aghan (November/December)

**Nanak Jayanti** The birthday of Guru Nanak, the founder of Sikhism, is celebrated with prayer readings and processions.

## Pausa (December/January)

**Christmas Day** Christians celebrate the anniversary of the birth of Christ on 25 December.
**Eid al-Adha** This Islamic occasion commemorates the Prophet Ibrahim's readiness to obey God even to the point of sacrificing his son.

## Magha (January/February)

**Republic Day** This public holiday on 26 January celebrates the anniversary of India's establishment as a republic in 1950. Celebrations are held in Jaipur, but it's most spectacular in Delhi, where there's a military parade along Rajpath. As part of the same celebration, three days later a Beating of the Retreat ceremony takes place in Delhi.
**Vasant Panchami** Heralds the onset of spring. People worship Saraswati, goddess of wisdom and knowledge, on this day, and make floral offerings, dress in yellow, cook yellow rice and exchange yellow sweets – yellow represents the ripening of the spring crops. It's held on the 5th day of Magha.

## Phalguna (February/March)

**Holi** This is one of the most exuberant Hindu festivals, when people celebrate the beginning of spring by throwing coloured water and *gulal* (powder) at one another. Don't wear good clothes, be ready to duck, and expect to look like a *gulab jamun* (a red, sticky sweet) at the end of the day (women see also p361). Udaipur and Jaisalmer are both excellent venues to celebrate Holi. On the night before Holi, bonfires are built to symbolise the destruction of the evil demon Holika.
**Muharram** An Islamic festival commemorating the martyrdom of the Prophet Mohammed's grandson, Imam.
**Shivaratri** This day of Hindu fasting is dedicated to Shiva, who danced the *tandava* (cosmic dance) on this day. Temple processions are followed by the chanting of mantras and anointing of linga (phallic symbols).

# FOOD

Sampling India's amazing cuisine is an adventure in itself. In some sections of this book, eateries are listed under 'Restaurants' and 'Quick Eats' subheadings: The Quick Eats sections cover street stalls, snack joints, market vendors, takeaway counters, sweet shops and the like; they're generally open from early morning (or lunchtime) to late at night. Restaurants cover pretty much everything else.

For comprehensive coverage of Rajasthan's culinary scene see p77.

**BEWARE OF THOSE BHANG LASSIS!**

Although it's rarely printed in menus, some restaurants in Rajasthan clandestinely whip up bhang lassi, a yogurt and iced-water beverage laced with bhang, a derivative of marijuana. Commonly dubbed 'special lassi', this often potent concoction doesn't agree with everyone. Some travellers have been stuck in bed for several miserable days after drinking it; others have become delirious.

## GAY & LESBIAN TRAVELLERS

As with relations between heterosexual Western couples travelling in Rajasthan – both married and unmarried – gay and lesbian travellers should exercise discretion and refrain from displaying overt affection towards each other in public. For more information see p42.

The Mumbai publication *Bombay Dost* is a gay and lesbian magazine available at a limited number of bookshops and newsstands in Delhi.

For further information about India's gay scene, there are some excellent websites including **Gay Bombay** (www.gaybombay.org), **Humsafar** (www.humsafar.org) and the Delhi-based **Humrahi** (www.geocities.com/WestHollywood/Heights/7258).

## HOLIDAYS

In India there are three national public holidays: Republic Day (26 January), Independence Day (15 August) and Gandhi Jayanti (2 October). There are usually also holidays during major festivals (sometimes only followed by certain religious denominations), which include Diwali, Dussehra and Holi (all three are Hindu), Nanak Jayanti (Sikh), Eid al-Fitr (Islamic), Mahavir Jayanti (Jain), Buddha Jayanti (Buddhist) and Easter and Christmas (Christian). For dates see p364.

Most businesses (offices, shops etc) and tourist sites close on public holidays. Public transport tends to remain unaffected and can even be beefed up during some festivals. Remember that accommodation at festival destinations can be difficult to get and room rates increase dramatically. It's wise to make reservations well in advance if you intend visiting during major festivals. You'll also need to book train tickets well in advance.

## INSURANCE

A travel insurance policy to cover theft, loss and medical problems is wise – health insurance is vital (see p392). Be aware that some policies specifically exclude dangerous activities, which can include trekking. There is a wide variety of policies available, so check the small print.

If you have to make a claim later, ensure you keep all documentation. Check that the policy covers an emergency flight home. Note that it is crucial to get a police report if you've had anything stolen, as insurance companies may refuse to reimburse you without one.

## INTERNET ACCESS

Internet outlets in Rajasthan are spreading fast – most medium-sized towns have email facilities, even if it's just a computer in a cramped back office. In bigger towns there are usually a few broadband places, but connections at less cutting-edge cafés can be very slow. Connections and speed are usually superior in the morning and early afternoon (peak demand seems to fall between 5pm and 9pm making this a slow period).

It usually costs around Rs 10 to 60 per hour. Some places enforce a minimum time of 15 minutes.

If you're thinking of travelling with a notebook or hand-held computer, be aware that your modem may not work once you leave your home country. The safest option is to buy a reputable 'global' modem before you leave home, or buy a local PC-card modem if you're spending an extended time away. An essential is a universal AC adaptor, which will enable you to plug in without frying the innards of your machine. You'll also need a plug adaptor for India. For more information on travelling with a portable computer see www.teleadapt.com.

See also p21.

## LAUNDRY

Unless a hotel has its own in-house laundry, your clothes will be washed by a dhobi-wallah. You hand over your dirty clothes in the morning and you'll usually get them back washed and pressed that same evening for a minimal cost (around Rs 5 to 10 per item; often a little more in touristy places). If you don't think your gear will stand up to being thrashed clean, then hand wash them yourself or give them to a drycleaner. Washing powder can be bought cheaply in small sachets all over the place.

## LEGAL MATTERS

If you find yourself in a sticky legal predicament, contact your embassy (see p362). Travellers are subject to Indian laws and in the Indian justice system it can often seem that the burden of proof is on the accused.

You should carry your passport at all times, and the less you have to do with local police the better.

### Drugs

India has long been known for its smorgasbord of illegal drugs, but would-be users should be aware of the severe risks. Apart from opening yourself up to being taken advantage of, if convicted on a drugs-related charge, sentences are for a *minimum* of 10 years and there is no remission or parole. Cases can take several years to appear before a court while the accused waits, locked up. In addition, there's usually a hefty monetary fine. The police have been getting particularly tough on drugs-related issues involving foreigners so you should take the risk seriously.

### Smoking

The Indian government has banned smoking in public places in Delhi and prohibited all forms of tobacco advertising. The ban, now extended to other parts of India, doesn't cover snuff and chewing tobacco, which account for the bulk of tobacco consumption in India. Transgressors face a mere Rs 100 fine, which probably accounts for the ban's limited success.

## MAPS

There's a dearth of high-quality maps in India. Some of the better possibilities include TTK's Discover India series, which has a number of state, regional and city maps. Eicher produces an excellent *Delhi* street atlas, as well as useful foldaway city maps. The Survey of India publishes decent city, state and country maps, while the Indian Map Service has a *Rajasthan* road atlas (based on Survey of India maps). There's also the *Rajasthan Road Atlas*, published by Anada Sahitya Prakashan and Gyan Vigyan Prakashan, which has 1:600,000 maps of each district. Nelles Maps publishes a *Western India* map, which has pretty good coverage of Rajasthan, but it can be hard to find. All these maps are stocked at good bookshops and some modern petrol stations.

Throughout Rajasthan, state government tourist offices stock local maps, which are often dated and lacking in essential detail, but they're still reasonably useful for general orientation.

## MONEY

The rupee (Rs) is divided into 100 paise (p). There are coins of five, 10, 20, 25 and 50 paise and Rs 1, 2 and 5, and notes of Rs 10, 20, 50, 100 and 500. There is a Rs 1000 note but this is not always easy to get.

Whenever you change money, take your time and check each note even if the wad appears to have been stapled together. Some bills look quite similar, so check them carefully. Don't accept any filthy, ripped or disintegrating notes, as you'll have difficulty in getting people to accept these (you can change them at the Reserve Bank of India as a last resort). Remember, you must present your passport whenever changing currency and travellers cheques.

It can be difficult to use large denomination notes because of a seemingly perpetual lack of change in shops, taxis etc, so it's a good idea to maintain a constant stock of smaller currency.

For information about costs read p19. See the front cover flap for exchange rates.

Outside Rajasthan's main cities, the State Bank of Bikaner & Jaipur (SBBJ) or the State Bank of India (SBI) are usually the places to change money. In the more remote regions (such as parts of Shekhawati), few banks offer exchange facilities, so use banks in the main tourist centres before heading out into the desert – although you'll have no trouble changing money at Bikaner or Jaisalmer.

### ATMs

Twenty-four hour ATMs linked to international networks are common in many places in Rajasthan. This means that travellers can now rely on debit cards as a primary cash source. A cash or travellers cheque back-up is recommended in case you lose or break your card, or if ATMs are temporarily out of order – a fairly regular annoyance, especially in smaller towns. You shouldn't rely on ATMs as your sole source of cash if you're planning to travel beyond the larger towns or away from tourist centres, as they either won't be available, or may not accept foreign cards. Alternatively, ensure you withdraw adequate cash from ATMs in big cities before striking out into the outback.

ATMs usually accept Cirrus, Maestro, MasterCard, Plus and Visa (but not always all cards). Banks in India that currently accept foreign cards include Citibank, HDFC, ICICI, UTI, HSBC, SBI, Standard Chartered, IDBI, State Bank of Bikaner & Jaipur and Corporation Bank.

Your bank is likely to impose higher charges on international transactions, so once in India it's generally more economical to withdraw big amounts of money at once than to make lots of small transactions. *Always* check in advance with your home bank whether your card can indeed access banking networks in India and if so, what the charge per transaction is and whether they have schemes to minimise these.

Several travellers have reported ATMs snatching back money if you don't remove it within around 30 seconds. Conversely, some people have said that machines can take more than 30 seconds to release cash, so don't hastily abandon the ATM assuming something has gone wrong.

The ATMs listed in this book's regional chapters all accept foreign cards (but not necessarily all types of cards).

### Cash

It's no problem changing money in bigger towns. However, it's advisable to have some US dollars or pounds sterling (the most widely accepted currencies) in cash in case you're unable to change travellers cheques or use a credit card, especially in smaller places.

### Credit Cards

Most major cities and tourist centres accept credit cards, with MasterCard and Visa being the most widely accepted. Cash advances on major credit cards can be made at various banks (although rarely in smaller towns). For details about whether you can access home accounts in India, inquire at your bank before leaving.

Credit cards are accepted at almost all top-end hotels and at some midrange ones, however, it's rare that budget hotels, restaurants or shops accept them.

### Encashment Certificates

By law, foreign currency must be changed at official moneychangers or banks, which give you an encashment certificate (these money-exchange receipts are valid for three months). They are required to re-exchange rupees exceeding Rs 10,000 into foreign currency when departing India (see right). Encashment certificates are also needed for tax clearance certificates (see opposite). Some shipping agents may request them as well.

Note that money-exchange receipts are required when paying for tourist quota train tickets in rupees – these are usually only demanded in Delhi.

### International Transfers

Naturally it's preferable not to run out of money, but if you do, you can have money transferred in no time at all (at a charge of course) via Thomas Cook's Moneygram service or at Western Union, which both have branches throughout India. To collect cash, you need to bring along your passport and the name and reference number of the person who sent the funds.

### Moneychangers

Usually open for longer hours than the banks, private moneychangers are a convenient option and they are virtually everywhere. However, it pays to check the bank rates first, and as with anywhere, check you are given the correct amount.

### Re-exchange

Before leaving India you can change rupees back into foreign currency. Note that some airport banks only do so if you change a minimum of Rs 1000. You can change up to Rs 10,000 into foreign currency without money-exchange receipts. Any amount exceeding this requires the presentation of encashment certificates (see left) that cover the rupee amount and are less than three months old. You may also have to show your passport and airline ticket.

You can convert rupees back to major currencies at some city banks and moneychangers and at international airports, although these may only do so within 48 hours of leaving the country.

Note that cash withdrawals from ATMs do not provide encashment certificates, and that most banks and moneychangers won't change rupees back into foreign currency from plastic transactions; however, most international airports will (on presentation of your ATM slip).

### Security

The safest place for your money and your passport is next to your skin, in a moneybelt or pouch. Never, ever carry these things in your luggage or a shoulder bag. Bum bags are not recommended either, as they advertise that you have a stash of goodies. Never leave your valuable documents and travellers cheques in your hotel room (including under your mattress). If the hotel is a reputable one, you should be able to use the hotel safe.

It's wise to peel off at least US$100 and keep it stashed away separately from your main horde, just in case.

Finally, separate your big notes from your small ones so you don't display large wads of cash when paying for things.

### Tax Clearance Certificates

If you have a visa enabling you to stay in India for more than six months, you must technically get a tax clearance certificate to leave the country. This is to prove that you financed your stay in India with your own money rather than through working in the country. For details contact a local Foreigners' Regional Registration Office (in Delhi or Jaipur). You'll need to show your passport, visa extension form, any other appropriate paperwork and a bunch of bank encashment certificates.

### Tipping, Baksheesh & Bargaining

In tourist restaurants or hotels, where a service fee (amounts vary regionally) is usually already added on to your bill, tipping is optional. In smaller places, where there is no service fee, a tip is appreciated. Hotel and train porters expect around Rs 20 to carry bags, and hotel staff also expect around the same to provide services above and beyond the call of duty. It's not mandatory to tip taxi or autorickshaw drivers.

Baksheesh can be defined as a 'tip'. Baksheesh also refers to giving alms to beggars. Many Indians implore tourists not to hand out sweets, pens or money to children, as it's positive reinforcement to beg. Instead you may prefer to donate to a school or charitable organisation (see p375).

Apart from at fixed-price shops, bargaining is the norm in India – see The Art of Haggling, p371.

### Travellers Cheques

All major brands are accepted in India, with Amex and Thomas Cook being the most widely traded. Pounds sterling and US dollars are the safest bet, especially beyond the major cities. Not all places take all brands – which means it pays to carry more than one flavour. Charges for changing travellers cheques vary from place to place and bank to bank.

If you lose your cheques, contact the Amex or Thomas Cook office in the closest capital city – to find details of branches nationwide contact their offices in Delhi (see p96).

## PHOTOGRAPHY

For useful tips and techniques on travel photography, read Lonely Planet's *Guide to Travel Photography, Travel Photography: Landscapes* and *Travel Photography: People & Portraits*.

### Digital

Modern digital processing and memory cards are currently only available from photographic shops in the larger cities (eg a 128MB Sony memory stick costs around Rs 2000), however, the availability of digital services and products is set to escalate over the coming years. More widespread are shops/Internet centres that will download images onto CD (for between Rs 50 and 100) – many travellers use this system, keeping CDs as a backup or for emailing shots home. For digital processing at photographic shops, the charge is roughly Rs 6 per print plus Rs 15 for developing.

### Print & Slide

Colour print film-processing facilities are readily available in most Indian cities. Film is relatively cheap and the quality is usually good. You'll only find colour slide film in the major cities and tourist centres. On average, to develop 4x6 colour prints costs around Rs 6 per print plus Rs 15 for processing. Passport photos are terrific value at about Rs 60/100 for four/10 shots (ready in around 10 minutes).

Always check the use-by date on local film and slide stock. Make sure you get a sealed packet and ensure you're not handed a roll that's been sitting in a glass cabinet in the sunshine for the last few months: heat and humidity can play havoc with film, even if it isn't past the use-by date. Be wary of street hawkers who have been known to load old/damaged film into new-looking canisters. The hapless tourist only discovers this when the film is developed. It's best to only buy film from reputable stores – and preferably film that's been refrigerated.

### Restrictions

India is touchy about photographs being taken of places of military importance – this can include train stations, bridges, airports, military installations and sensitive border regions.

Places of worship (temples and mosques) may prohibit photography. If in doubt, ask.

#### PHOTOGRAPHING PEOPLE

Some people are more than happy to be photographed, but care should be taken in pointing cameras, especially at women. Again, if in doubt, ask. A zoom is a less intrusive means of taking portraits – even when you've obtained permission to take a portrait, shoving a lens in your subject's face can be disconcerting. A reasonable distance between you and your subject will help reduce your subject's discomfort, and will result in more natural shots.

## POST

Indian postal and poste restante services are generally good. Expected letters almost always arrive and letters you send do invariably reach their destination, though they may take up to three weeks. Even though the Indian postal system is fairly reliable, don't count on a letter or package getting through if there's anything of market value inside it. Amex in major city locations offers an alternative to the poste restante system for holders of Amex cards.

Some cities have courier services (such as DHL) that can reliably arrange speedy air freight around the world; from Delhi to the UK or France DHL charges Rs 2299/2656 for 500g/1kg and to Australia it's Rs 2224/2643 for 500g/1kg.

### Receiving Mail

Request senders to address letters to you with your surname in capital letters and underlined, followed by poste restante, main post office, and the city or town in question. Many 'lost' letters are simply misfiled under given (first) names, so always check under both your names. Ask senders to provide a return address, just in case you don't collect your mail. Letters sent via poste restante are generally held for one month before being returned. To claim mail, you'll need to show your passport. It's best to have any parcels sent to you by registered post.

### Sending Mail

Posting aerogrammes/postcards overseas costs Rs 8.50/8 and for airmail letters the cost is Rs 15. For postcards, it's not a bad idea to stick on the stamps *before* actually writing on them. This is because post offices can give you as many as four stamps per card, which can cover up your carefully composed missive.

Posting parcels is quite straightforward and prices vary depending on the weight. The parcel counter usually closes in the early afternoon, so if you want to send something, it's best to go to the post office in the morning. In the main cities, there's usually a person at the post office who sews parcels up in cheap linen. The post office will have the necessary customs declaration forms. To avoid paying duty at the delivery end, specify that the contents are a 'gift' under the value of Rs 1000.

Express post has a maximum of 35kg and charges to various destinations follow:

**Australia** The first kilogram is Rs 700, each additional kilogram is Rs 300.

**Europe and the UK** The first kilogram is Rs 950, each additional kilogram is Rs 300.

**USA** The first kilogram is Rs 775, each additional kilogram is Rs 400.

Books or printed matter can go by bookpost (maximum 5kg), which is considerably cheaper than parcel post, but the package must be wrapped a certain way: make sure that the package can be opened for inspection along the way, or that it's wrapped with the two ends exposed so that the contents are visible. A customs declaration form is usually not necessary. The overseas bookpost rates vary depending on the weight; Rs 127/260/478/940 for 500g/1kg/2kg/4kg.

Be cautious with places that offer to mail things to your home address after you have bought them. Government emporiums are usually fine but in most other places it pays to do the posting yourself.

## SHOPPING

Rajasthan really is one of the easiest places to spend money, with its busy bazaars, colourful arts and crafts, gorgeous fabrics, miniature paintings, and much more. The cardinal rule is to bargain and bargain hard.

Be careful when buying items that include delivery to your home country. You may well be given assurances that the price includes all charges, but this is not always the case.

Beware that sellers often claim that miniature paintings are antiques; this is rarely the case. For other important warnings also read p137.

Avoid buying products that further endanger threatened species and habitats. It's illegal to export ivory products or any artefact made from wild animals. Articles over 100 years old are not allowed to be exported from India without an export clearance certificate. If you have doubts about any item and think it could be defined as an antique, you can check with branches of the Archaeological Survey of India. In Delhi, contact the Director of Antiquities, **Archaeological Survey of India** (Map pp102-4; ☎ 011-23017443; Janpath; ⏰ 9.30am-1.30pm & 2-6pm Mon-Fri), next to the National Museum.

Detailed information on what is best to buy in each region is given in the regional chapters. For information on buying Rajasthani arts and crafts, see the Rajasthani Handicrafts chapter, p58.

## SOLO TRAVELLERS

Perhaps the most significant issue facing solo travellers is cost. Single-room rates at guesthouses and hotels are sometimes not much lower than rates for a double; some midrange and top-end places don't even offer a single tariff, though you can try to bargain down the double rate.

If you tire of your own company, never fear: Rajasthan, Delhi and Agra are tourist hubs, so it's easy to meet other travellers – head for popular hotels and restaurants.

Although most solo travellers experience no major problems in India, remember that some (locals and travellers alike) may view lone tourists as an easy target for theft. Don't be paranoid, but, like anywhere in the world, it's wise to stay on your toes in unfamiliar surroundings.

For important information specific to women, see p377.

## TELEPHONE

Even in the tiniest towns you'll find private call booths with direct local, interstate and international dialling (PCO/STD/ISD); these are invariably cheaper than calls made from hotels. A digital meter means you can keep an eye on what the call costs, and you get a print-out when the call is finished.

### THE ART OF HAGGLING

Haggling is a must in most parts of India. Shopkeepers in tourist hubs are accustomed to travellers who have lots of money and little time to spend it. It's not unusual to be charged at least double, or even triple the 'real' price.

So how do you know if you're being overcharged and need to strike back with some serious haggling? Well, you're safe in government emporiums, cooperatives and modern shopping complexes, where the prices are usually fixed. But in most other shops that cater primarily to tourists, be prepared to don your haggling hat. The kind of places that usually fall into this category include handicraft, carpet, painting, souvenir and clothing shops.

The first 'rule' to haggling is never to show too much interest in the item you want to buy. Secondly, don't buy the first item that takes your fancy. Wander around and price things, but don't make it obvious. Otherwise if you return to the first shop the vendor will know it's because they are the cheapest.

Decide how much you would be happy paying and then express a casual interest in buying. If you have absolutely no idea of what something should really cost, start by slashing the price by half (even more in touristy spots). This is usually completely unacceptable to the vendor but it works as a good starting point to haggle for a happy compromise. You'll find that many shopkeepers lower their so-called 'final price' if you proceed to head out of the shop saying you'll 'think about it'.

Haggling is a way of life in India, but it should never turn ugly. Keep in mind exactly how much a rupee is worth in your home currency so you don't lose perspective, and if a vendor seems to be charging an unreasonably high price and is unwilling to negotiate, simply look elsewhere.

Throughout most of India, interstate calls from booths (not hotels) charge the full rate from around 9am to 8pm. After 8pm the cost slides, with the cheapest time to call being between 11pm and 6am. Interstate calls are half rate on Sunday.

India's White Pages are found at www.indiawhitepages.com, and the Yellow Pages at www.indiayellowpages.com.

### Domestic Calls

Telephone numbers in Rajasthan have an annoying tendency to change. Call ☎197 for local telephone-number inquiries. Collect-call operators can be reached on ☎186.

### International Calls

Direct international calls from call booths (not hotels) cost an average of Rs 22 to 40 per minute depending on the destination. The cheapest international calls can be made through Internet cafés using Net2phone or a similar service. Calls cost from as little as Rs 5 per minute to the USA, Rs 7 to Australia and Rs 10 to Europe.

In some centres PCO/STD/ISD booths may offer a 'call-back' service – you ring your folks or friends, give them the phone number of the booth and wait for them to call you back. The booth operator charges about Rs 5 to 10 per minute for this service, plus the cost of the preliminary call.

### Mobile Phones

If you bring your mobile phone to India, local mobile networks are cheap to use and getting hooked up to the mobile phone network is straightforward. Calls (even international) are delightfully cheap by world standards.

In most towns you simply buy a prepaid mobile phone kit (SIM card and phone number) from any phone shop or other outlet such as PCO/STD/ISD booths, Internet cafés and grocery stores. The most popular (and reliable) companies are Airtel, Hutch, BPL and Idea.

The SIM card itself costs about Rs 100 but you usually pay for an additional amount of credit to get started. You then buy recharge cards (top-ups) from any phone shop for between Rs 100 and 3400. Credit usually must be used (or topped up) within a fixed period (ie 15 to 60 days) and remember that the amount you pay for a credit top-up is not the amount you get on your phone – state taxes and service charges come off first, so for a Rs 500 top-up you'll get around Rs 375 worth of calls. Note that with some networks, recharge cards are being replaced by direct credit, where you pay the vendor and the credit's deposited straight to your phone – ask which system is in use before you buy.

Calls made within the state/city where you bought the SIM card are cheap – less than Rs 1 per minute – and you can call internationally for less than Rs 25 per minute. SMS messaging is even cheaper. The more credit you have on your phone, the cheaper the call rate.

The downside to the whole thing is that the prepaid system is not truly national – major cities and all states have their own networks, which means your SIM card will work fine in the city/state you bought it, and you only pay for calls you make. If you move outside that network area you'll have to ensure it has roaming capabilities. Call rates are a little higher and you will be charged for incoming calls as well as outgoing calls – in some cases the incoming charges are higher than the outgoing.

Some travellers have reported difficulties in using their mobile even within states (either no coverage at all or frequent cut offs). In addition, international texting is reliable on some days and not others – you can normally receive text messages but sometimes can't send replies for days at a time.

As the mobile phone industry is an evolving one, mobile rates, suppliers and coverage are all likely to develop over the life of this book.

### Phone Codes

To make a call *to* India from overseas, dial the international access code of the country you're in, then ☎91 (international country code for India), then the area code (drop the initial 0; this zero only applies for calls made within India), then the local number. See this book's regional chapters for area codes.

To make an international call *from* India, dial ☎00 (international access code from India), then the country code (of the country you are calling), then the area code, then the local number.

Also available is the Home Country Direct service, which gives you access to the international operator in your home country. For the price of a local call, you can then make reverse-charge (collect) or phonecard calls. Some countries and their numbers:

| Country | Number |
|---|---|
| Australia | ☎ 0006117 |
| Canada | ☎ 00016788 |
| Germany | ☎ 0004917 |
| Japan | ☎ 0008117 |
| The Netherlands | ☎ 0003117 |
| Singapore | ☎ 0006517 |
| Spain | ☎ 0003417 |
| UK | ☎ 0004417 |
| USA | ☎ 000117 |

## TIME

India is 5½ hours ahead of GMT/UTC, 4½ hours behind Australian Eastern Standard Time (EST) and 10½ hours ahead of American EST. The local standard time is known as IST (Indian Standard Time), although many affectionately dub it 'Indian Stretchable Time'.

## TOILETS

Public toilets are generally confined to tourist sites (eg museums), upmarket shopping complexes and cinemas, but they can be scarce and cleanliness is variable.

When it comes to effluent etiquette, it's customary to use your left hand and water, not toilet paper. A strategically placed tap, usually with a little plastic jug nearby, is available in most bathrooms. If you can't get used to the Indian method, bring your own toilet paper (widely available in towns). However, paper, sanitary napkins and tampons are going to further clog an already overloaded sewerage system. Often a bin is provided so that you can dispose of such items – use it.

## TOURIST INFORMATION

### Local Tourist Offices

There are RTDC tourist offices (often called Tourist Reception Centres) in most places of interest in Rajasthan (for details see the regional chapters). Staff range from extraordinarily helpful to useless and grumpy, but almost always can supply glossy brochures and maps.

There is a **Rajasthan tourist office** (☎ 011-3381884; Tourist Reception Centre, Bikaner House, Pandara Rd, Delhi) in Delhi, and **Government of India tourist offices** (Delhi India Tourism Delhi; Map pp106-7; ☎ 011-23320005; 88 Janpath, Delhi; Jaipur Map pp152-3; ☎ 0141-2372200; ⏲ 9am-6pm Mon-Fri) in Delhi and Jaipur.

### Tourist Offices Abroad

The **Government of India** (Ministry of Tourism; www.incredibleindia.org) maintains a string of tourist offices in other countries where you can attain brochures and leaflets. These often have high-quality information about Rajasthan, so they are worth obtaining. However, some of these foreign offices are not always as useful as those within Rajasthan.

India tourist offices abroad include the following:

**Australia** Sydney (☎ 02-9264 4855; goitosyd@next century.com.au; Level 2, Piccadilly, 210 Pitt St, Sydney, NSW 2000)

**Canada** Toronto (☎ 416-962 3787; indiatourism@bellnet.ca; 60 Bloor St, West Suite 1003, Toronto, Ontario, M4W 3B8)

**France** Paris (☎ 01 45 23 30 45; intourpar@aol.com; 11-13 Blvd Haussmann, F-75009, Paris)

**Germany** Frankfurt am-Main (☎ 069-2429490; info@india-tourism.com; Basolar Strasse 48, D-60329, Frankfurt am-Main 1)

**Italy** Milan (☎ 028 053 506; info@indiatourismmilan.com; Via-Albricci 9, Milan 20122)

**The Netherlands** Amsterdam (☎ 0206 208 991; info.nl@india-tourism.com; Rokin 9/15, 1012 KK Amsterdam)

**UK** London (☎ 020-7437 3677; info@indiatouristoffice.org; 7 Cork St, London W1S 3LH)

**USA** Los Angeles (☎ 213-380 8855; goitola@aol.com; Room 204, 3550 Wiltshire Blvd, Los Angeles, CA 900102485); New York (☎ 212-586 4901; ny@itonyc.com; Suite 1808, 1270 Ave of the Americas, NY 100201700)

## TOURS

The RTDC offers a range of package tours covering various destinations in Rajasthan, including transport, accommodation (usually at RTDC hotels), sightseeing and guide; entry charges are extra. For more information, contact the **RTDC Tourist Reception Centre** (☎ 011-3381884, 3383837; www.rajasthantourismindia.com; Bikaner House, Pandara Rd, Delhi, 110011).

Many travel agencies offer excursions in Rajasthan. One of the few outfits in Rajasthan that promotes sustainable tourism is **Alternative Travels** (☎ 01594-222239; Apani Dhani, Nawalgarh, Shekhawati). Ramesh Jangid of Alternative Travels can organise camel and cycling trips around the painted towns of

Shekhawati, treks in the Aravalli Range and homestays with villagers, as well as tours elsewhere in India. For more details on his Rajasthan tours, see p286.

Other agencies:

**Indo Vacations** (Map pp152-3; ☎ 0141-9414312872; www.indien-reise.com in German; 312-6 Valmiki Rd, Raja Park, Jaipur)

**Rajasthan Travel Service** (Map pp152-3; ☎ 0141-2365408; www.rajasthantravelservice.com; ground fl, Ganpati Plaza, MI Rd, Jaipur)

**Sita World Travels** (Map pp152-3; ☎ 0141-5103434; Jaipur Towers, MI Rd)

## Safaris

### CAMEL SAFARIS

It's possible to take a camel safari lasting from an hour up to several weeks. Camel-safari central is Jaisalmer (see Jaisalmer Camel Safaris, p334), in western Rajasthan, and prices vary according to what is provided. Basic safaris start at about Rs 450 per person per day, which includes meals, but you pay more for greater comfort. You can also take safaris from Khuri (p342), near Jaisalmer. Bikaner (see Bikaner Camel Safaris, p348) is another centre, and many travellers head here to avoid the Jaisalmer hype (note you're more likely to travel by camel cart here, rather than on camelback). A less-visited area for camel trekking is that around Osiyan (p322), 65km from Jodhpur.

The Pushkar area (p214) is also popular, and a couple of operators in Shekhawati (see p281) offer camel treks into the countryside, around towns full of interesting painted *havelis*.

### HORSE & JEEP SAFARIS

Some hotels can arrange horse safaris – the best options are in Udaipur at the Kumbha Palace and Pratap Country Inn (see p255). The Dundlod Fort (p289), in Shekhawati, can arrange horse safaris for experienced riders – on spectacular Marwari horses – around the Shekhawati region and further afield.

For most horse safaris, you are required to bring your own riding hat and boots – call ahead to check. The best time to ride is during the cooler months (between mid-October and mid-March).

Quite a few hotels, particularly in western Rajasthan, offer jeep safaris, also usually available at palace hotels in remote regions. One-day jeep safaris to the Bishnoi villages (p318) around Jodhpur are another popular option.

### WILDLIFE SAFARIS

The state's major wildlife sanctuaries are in eastern Rajasthan. Wildlife safaris are available by jeep at Sariska Tiger Reserve (p201) and at Ranthambhore National Park (p218). Another option at Ranthambhore is a trip in a canter (open-topped truck). At Keoladeo Ghana National Park (p191), motorised vehicles are prohibited, but you can see the park by cycle-rickshaw or bicycle.

# TRAVEL PERMITS

Due to the hostilities between India and Pakistan, foreigners are prohibited from going within 50km of the India–Pakistan border. Special permission is required from the **District Magistrate** (☎ 02992-252201) in Jaisalmer to travel to most of Rajasthan west of National Highway No 15, and is only issued in exceptional circumstances. Places exempted are Amar Sagar, Bada Bagh, Lodhruva, Kuldhara, Akal, Sam, Ramkund, Khuri and Mool Sagar.

Permission is required from the **District Magistrate** (☎ 02982-220003) in Barmer to travel to Kiradu, which is about 35km from Barmer near the border with Pakistan.

# VISAS

You must get a visa *before* arriving in India. Six-month multiple-entry visas (valid from the date of issue) are issued to nationals of most countries (check visa options with the Indian embassy in your country) regardless of whether you intend staying that long or re-entering the country. Visas cost A$75 (an extra A$15 service fee applies at consulates) for Australians, US$60 for US citizens and UK£30 for Britons.

You won't be issued a visa to enter India unless you hold an onward ticket, which is taken as sufficient evidence that you intend to leave the country.

Extended visas (up to five years) are possible for people of Indian descent (excluding those in Pakistan and Bangladesh) who hold a non-Indian passport and live abroad. A special People of Indian Origin (PIO) card is also possible (valid for 15 years). Contact your embassy (see p362) for more details.

### Visa Extensions

Fourteen-day extensions are possible under exceptional circumstances from Foreigners' Regional Registration Offices (FRROs) in Jaipur and Delhi, but it's rare that you'll get an extension on a tourist via.

In Delhi, the **FRRO** (Map pp92-4; ☎ 011-26711443; Level 2, East Block 8, Sector 1, RK Puram; 9.30am-1.30pm & 2-3pm Mon-Fri) is behind the Hyatt Regency hotel. Come here for visa extensions or replacement visas (if you've had your lost/stolen passport replaced).

For those with a good reason, the FRRO issues 14-day visa extensions, free for nationals of all countries except Japan (Rs 390), Sri Lanka (Rs 235), Russia (Rs 1860) and Romania (Rs 500). Bring your confirmed air ticket, one passport photo and a photocopy of your passport (the information and visa pages). Applying for a (maximum) one-month extension (all nationalities Rs 1860) on a six-month visa entails shuttling between the FRRO and Ministry of Home Affairs. For this longer extension you need an exceptionally good reason. The long-term visa extension form is available from the Foreigners Division of the **Ministry of Home Affairs** (Map pp102-4; ☎ 011-23385748; 26 Jaisalmer House, Man Singh Rd; 10am-noon Mon-Fri). Be prepared to wait. Then take the form and three passport photos to the FRRO. If the extension is authorised, the authorisation has to be taken *back* to the Ministry of Home Affairs, where the visa extension is issued.

For visas beyond six months, you technically need to register at the FRRO (within 14 days of arriving in India) and get a tax clearance certificate before departure. For the certificate, go to the Foreign Section of the **Income Tax Office** (Map pp102-4; ☎ 011-23379161; Indraprastha Estate; 10am-1.30pm & 2.30-6pm Mon-Fri).

You can only obtain another six-month tourist visa by leaving the country.

## VOLUNTEER WORK

Numerous charities and aid agencies have branches in India and, although they're mostly staffed by locals, there are some opportunities for foreigners. It's advisable to write in advance and, if you're needed, you'll be of far more use if you can commit enough time to be of help. A week on a hospital ward may salve your conscience, but you may do little more than get in the way of the people who work there long term.

Flexibility in the work you are prepared to do is also really vital. Some charities are inundated with requests from foreign volunteers who want to help babies in an orphanage, for instance, but few are willing to work with adults who have physical or mental disabilities.

### Overseas Volunteer Placement Agencies

For long-term posts, the following organisations may be able to advise:

**Action Without Borders** (☎ 212-8433973; www.idealist.org; Suite 1510, 360 West 31st St, New York, NY 10001, USA)

**AidCamps International** (☎ 020-8291 6181; www.aidcamps.org; 5 Simone Ct, Dartmouth Rd, London SE26 4RP, UK)

**Australian Volunteers International** (☎ 03-9279 1788; www.ozvol.org.au; PO Box 350, Fitzroy VIC 3065, Australia)

**Co-ordinating Committee for International Voluntary Service** (☎ 01 45 68 49 36; www.unesco.org/ccivs; Unesco House, 31 Rue Francois Bonvin, 75732 Paris Cedex 15, France)

**Global Volunteers** (☎ 651-407 6100; www.globalvolunteers.org; 375 East Little Canada Rd, St Paul, MN 55117-1628, USA)

**Voluntary Service Overseas** (VSO; ☎ 020-8780 7200; www.vso.org.uk; 317 Putney Bridge Rd, London SW15 2PN, UK)

**Working Abroad** (France office ☎ /fax 04-68 26 41 79; www.workingabroad.com; PO Box 454, Flat 1, Brighton, BN1 3ZS, East Sussex, UK)

Other useful sites:

- www.volunteerabroad.com
- www.studyabroad.com
- www.volunteerabroad.com
- www.responsibletravel.com

### Programmes in Delhi & Rajasthan

Following are details of some of the programmes operating in Delhi and Rajasthan that may have volunteering opportunities; contact them in advance rather than just turning up. Donations of money or clothing from travellers may also be warmly welcomed. Some Non-Governmental Organisations (NGOs) may also offer you volunteer work – for details visit www.indianngos.com.

Note that unless otherwise indicated, volunteers are always expected to cover their own costs, including accommodation, food and transport.

## DELHI

There are two branches of Mother Teresa's Kolkata- (Calcutta-) based Missionaries of Charity in the Civil Lines area that welcome volunteers: **Shishu Bhavan** (Map pp92-4; ☎ 011-23950181; 12 Commissioners Lane) looks after infants (female volunteers only) while **Nirmal Hriday** (Map pp92-4; ☎ 011-23952180; 1 Magazine Rd) cares for the sick, destitute and dying.

**Concern India Foundation** (☎ 011-26210997, delhi@concernindia.org; A-52 1st fl, Amar Colony, Lajpat Nagar 4) may be able to link volunteers with current projects – contact it in advance to ascertain possibilities.

**SOS Children's Village** (Map pp102-4; ☎ 011-24359734; www.soscvindia.org; A7 Nizammudin West) assists orphaned, abandoned and destitute children. Volunteers may be needed to teach English. You must apply in advance and a minimum three-month commitment is requested. See right for more information about SOS.

## RAJASTHAN

**Animal Aid Society** (☎ 0294-3111435; www.animalaidsociety.org; Chota Hawala Village, Udaipur) is an animal hospital that rescues and treats injured and destitute animals and sterilises street dogs. For more details see Animal Aid Society, p70.

The first organisation in Rajasthan to provide services under one roof for people living with cerebral palsy and other neural conditions, **Disha – Centre for Special Education, Vocational Training and Rehabilitation** (☎ 0141-2393319, 2391690; disha_jaipur@hotmail.com; 450 AB Nirman Nagau, Kings Rd, Jaipur) has worked with more than 600 families through its services, including a centre for special education, home management, staff training, counselling and advocacy. Volunteers from the fields of physiotherapy, speech therapy, special education, sports, arts and crafts and vocational counselling are welcomed. Contact Mrs PN Kavoori or Mrs Deepak Kalva.

The animal hospital **Help in Suffering** (HIS; Map pp152-3; ☎ 0141-2760803; hisjpr@datainfosys.net; Jaipur) is funded by the World Society for the Protection of Animals (WSPA) and Animaux Secours, Arthaz, France, and welcomes qualified voluntary vets (three-/six-/12-month commitments). Write to: Help in Suffering, Maharani Farm, Durgapura, Jaipur 302018, Rajasthan. Visitors are welcome at the shelter in Jaipur, and donations are also gratefully accepted. For more information see Help in Suffering, p183.

The Jaipur branch of the **Indian National Trust for Art and Cultural Heritage** (Intach; ☎ 0141-2228275; www.intach.org; B14/A Bhawani Singh Rd, Jaipur, 302001, Rajasthan) and Jaipur Virasat, a local heritage organisation linked to it, are working to preserve the vast cultural and physical heritage of Rajasthan's capital, and to increase local awareness of heritage issues. You can volunteer to work in various capacities. The focus is on restoration and conservation work, but you can also help if you have skills in promotion, art or administration. You need to stay for a minimum of one month – email with details of your skills a few weeks in advance.

**Les Amis du Shekhawati** (Friends of Shekhawati; contact through ecofarm Apani Dhani ☎ 01594-222239; www.apanidhani.com; Nawalgarh, 333042, Rajasthan) aims to preserve Shekhawati's rich artistic heritage. The society's work includes educating local villagers about the importance of the paintings, as well as promoting the region. You can be involved in painting restoration, promotion or teaching English or French to trainee guides. Architects who can help with creating a record of the *havelis* in Shekhawati will also be welcomed.

The NGO **Marwar Medical & Relief Society** (c/o Mandore Guest House; ☎ 0291-2545210, 2571620; www.mandore.com; Mandore, Jodhpur) works to address drug-addiction problems and provide medical services in the Jodhpur district. It welcomes short-term volunteers for its Village Project.

**Missionaries of Charity** (☎ 0141-2365804; Vardhman Path, C-Scheme, Jaipur), a branch of Mother Teresa's Kolkata-based order, provides a refuge for the destitute, many of whom are mentally ill or disabled.

**Seva Mandir** (☎ 0294-2450960; Old Fatehpura, Udaipur) develops natural resources, health promotion and literacy programmes. Volunteers can observe or participate in development work for a minimum of two weeks at this NGO.

SOS Worldwide runs more than 30 programmes across India. In Jaipur **SOS Children's Village** (☎ 0141-2280262; opposite Petal Factory, Jhotwara Rd, Jaipur) looks after orphaned, destitute and abandoned children, who are cared for by unmarried women, abandoned wives and widows. Volunteers teach English and help the children with their homework.

SOS also educates children (particularly girls) who come in for the day. The organisation only accepts volunteers prepared to commit for one year. You can also sponsor a child for Rs 500 per month; or Rs 1200 is enough to educate a child for a year.

**Urmul Trust** (☎ 0151-2523093; Ganganagar Rd, Bikaner) provides primary health care and education to the people of around 500 villages in Rajasthan; raises awareness among the women of the desert of their rights and privileges in society; and promotes the handicrafts of rural artisans with its profits going directly back to them. There is volunteer work (minimum one month) available in social welfare, teaching English, health care, or possibly helping with implementation and overseeing of projects.

## WOMEN TRAVELLERS

### Attitudes Towards Women

India is a largely conservative country, and the clothing and culturally inappropriate behaviour of some travellers (not to mention Western TV programmes) seems to have had a ripple effect on the perception of foreign women in general. An increasing number of female travellers have reported some form of sexual harassment (predominantly lewd comments and groping) despite making a concerted effort to act and dress conservatively. While there's no need to be concerned to the point of paranoia, you should be aware that your behaviour and dress code is under scrutiny.

Rajasthan is usually a perfectly safe place for women travellers, even those travelling alone, but you will have to put up with some aggravation. Getting constantly stared at is, unfortunately, something you'll have to get used to. Just be thick-skinned and don't allow it to get the better of you. It's best to refrain from returning stares, as this may be considered a come-on; dark glasses can help. A good way to block out stares in restaurants is to take along a book or postcards to write home. Other harassment women have encountered include provocative gestures, jeering, groping and being followed. Exuberant special events (such as the Holi festival, see p361) can be notorious for this.

Women travelling with a male partner are less likely to be harassed. However, a foreign woman of Indian descent travelling with a non-Indian male may cop disapproving stares; having a non-Indian partner is still not condoned in parts of India.

Ultimately, there are no sure-fire ways of shielding yourself from harassment, even for those who do everything 'right'. You're essentially going to have to use your judgment and instincts as there isn't a blanket rule that applies to every case. If the warnings here make travel in India seem a little daunting, remember that most men are not out to bother you, and the problems mentioned here are just things to be aware of.

### Clothing

Warding off sexual harassment is often a matter of common sense and culturally appropriate behaviour. What you wear helps enormously. Baggy clothing that hides the contours of your body is the way to go.

Wearing Indian dress makes a positive impression and, although we've had a few reports of women still being groped, most find it curtails harassment. The *salwar kameez* (the tunic and trouser combination), widely worn by Indian women, is practical, comfortable, cool in hot weather and shows respect for the Indian dress code. The dupatta (long scarf) worn with this outfit is handy if you visit a shrine that requires your head to be covered.

Going into public wearing a choli (small blouse worn under a sari) or a sari petticoat (which many foreign women mistake for a skirt) is like strutting around half dressed, so best avoided.

You can read fellow women travellers' experiences at www.journeywoman.com, which has a section devoted to dress.

### Staying Safe

To keep discussions short, get to the point as quickly and politely as possible. Getting involved in inane conversations with men can be misinterpreted as a come-on. Statements such as 'do you have a boyfriend?' or 'you are looking beautiful' should start alarm bells ringing. Some women wear a pseudo wedding ring, or announce early on in the conversation that they are married or engaged (whether they are or not). This often proves effective in putting men off, though it may provoke questions on how you're coping during this sexual hiatus.

If, despite your efforts, you still get the feeling that a man's encroaching on your space, he probably is. A firm request to keep away is usually enough to take control of the situation, especially if it's loud enough to draw the attention of passers-by. Alternatively, the silent treatment can be a remarkably good way of getting rid of unwanted male company.

When interacting with men on a day-to-day basis, adhere to the local practice of not shaking hands – instead, relay respect by saying *namaste*, which is a traditional Hindu greeting.

Female film-goers will probably feel more comfortable (and decrease the chances of harassment) by going to the cinema with a companion.

Lastly, it's wise to arrive in towns before dark and always avoid walking alone at night, especially in isolated areas.

### Taxis & Public Transport

Officials recommend that solo women prearrange an airport pick-up from their hotel if their flight is scheduled to arrive late at night. If that's not possible, catch a prepaid taxi and make a point of (in front of the driver) writing down the car registration and driver's name and giving it to one of the airport police. In 2004 a prepaid-taxi driver (from Delhi's international airport) was charged with the murder of an Australian woman and although authorities have assured travellers that the prepaid system is now safer, most solo women (especially to Delhi) still prefer to prearrange an airport pick-up or wait until daybreak before leaving the airport.

Whenever you catch a taxi, avoid doing so late at night (when many roads are deserted) and never agree to more than one man (the driver) in the car. The driver will invariably try to convince you that it's 'just his brother' or 'for more protection' etc, but authorities warn against it, so heed their advice. Women are also advised against wearing expensive-looking jewellery as it can make them a target for assault.

On extended train and bus travel, being a woman has some advantages. You go to the front of the ticket queue, and on trains there are special ladies-only carriages. Solo women have reported less hassle in the more expensive classes on trains, especially for overnight trips. When travelling overnight, try to get the uppermost berth, which will give you more privacy (and distance from potential gropers).

On public transport, sit next to a woman; if you can't, don't hesitate to return any errant limbs, put some item of luggage in between you and, if all else fails, move. You're also within your rights to tell him to shove off – loudly enough to shame the guy into leaving you alone.

# Transport

CONTENTS



## GETTING THERE & AWAY

### ENTERING THE COUNTRY

Entering India by air or land is relatively straightforward, with standard immigration and customs procedures. For customs information see p360.

#### Passport

To enter India you must have a valid passport, visa (see p374) and onward/return ticket. Once in India, if your passport is lost or stolen, immediately contact your country's representative (see p363). It's wise to keep photocopies of your passport and airline ticket.

### AIR

#### Airports & Airlines

Most travellers fly into Delhi or Mumbai for Rajasthan. A few international flights serve Jaipur – for details, inquire at travel agencies and see www.indianairports.com.

**Delhi** (DEL; Indira Gandhi International Airport; www.delhiairport.com; ☎ 011-25652011)

**Mumbai** (BOM; Chhatrapati Shivaji International Airport; www.mumbaiairport.com; ☎ 022-26829000)

India's national carrier is **Air India** (www.airindia.com), which also carries passengers on some domestic sectors of international routes. **Indian Airlines** (www.indian-airlines.nic.in), India's major domestic carrier, also flies to 20 neighbouring countries. The safety records of Air India and Indian Airlines can be viewed on www.airsafe.com/index.html. For details about India's domestic airlines see p382.

> **THINGS CHANGE...**
>
> The information in this chapter is particularly vulnerable to change. Check directly with the airline or a travel agent to make sure you understand how a fare (and ticket you may buy) works and be aware of the security requirements for international travel. Shop carefully. The details given in this chapter should be regarded as pointers and are not a substitute for your own careful, up-to-date research.

The major airlines servicing India are listed below (see their websites for contact details):

**Aeroflot** (code SU; www.aeroflot.org) Hub: Sheremetyevo International Airport, Moscow.

**Air Canada** (code AC; www.aircanda.com) Hub: Vancouver Airport.

**Air France** (code AF; www.airfrance.com) Hub: Charles de Gaulle, Paris.

**Air India** (code AI; www.airindia.com) Hub: Indira Gandhi International Airport, Delhi.

**Alitalia** (code AZ; www.alitalia.com) Hub: Fiumicino International Airport, Rome.

**American Airlines** (code AA; www.aa.com) Hub: Dallas Airport.

**Austrian Airlines** (code OS; www.aua.com) Hub: Vienna International Airport.

**Biman Bangladesh Airlines** (code BG; www.bangladeshonline.com/biman/) Hub: Zia International Airport, Dhaka.

**British Airways** (code BA; www.british-airways.com) Hub: Heathrow Airport, London.

**Cathay Pacific Airways** (code CX; www.cathaypacific.com) Hub: Hong Kong International Airport.

**Druk Air** (code KB; www.drukair.com.bt/) Hub: Paro Airport.

**El Al Israel Airlines** (code LY; www.elal.co.il/) Hub: Ben Gurion, Tel Aviv.

**Emirates** (code EK; www.emirates.com) Hub: Dubai International Airport.

**Gulf Air** (code GF; www.gulfairco.com) Hub: Bahrain International Airport.

**Indian Airlines** (code IC; www.indian-airlines.nic.in) Hub: Indira Gandhi International Airport, Delhi.

**Iran Air** (code IR; www.iranair.nl) Hub: Tehran International Airport.
**Japan Airlines** (code JL; www.jal.com) Hub: Narita Airport.
**Kenya Airways** (code KQ; www.kenya-airways.com) Hub: Jomo Kenyatta International Airport, Nairobi.
**KLM – Royal Dutch Airlines** (code KL; www.klm.com) Hub: Schiphol Airport, Amsterdam.
**Kuwait Airways** (code KU; www.kuwait-airways.com) Hub: Kuwait International Airport.
**Lufthansa Airlines** (code LH; www.lufthansa.com) Hub: Frankfurt International Airport.
**Malaysia Airlines** (code MH; www.malaysiaairlines.com) Hub: Kuala Lumpur International Airport.
**Pakistan International Airlines** (code PK; www.piac.com.pk) Hub: Jinnah International Airport, Karachi.
**Qantas Airways** (code QF; www.qantas.com.au) Hub: Kingsford Smith Airport, Sydney.
**Royal Jordanian Airlines** (code RJ; www.rja.com) Hub: Amman Airport.
**Royal Nepal Airlines Corporation** (code RA; www.royalnepal.com) Hub: Kathmandu Airport.
**Saudia Arabian Airlines** (code SV; www.saudiairlines.com) Hub: Ar-Riyadh International Airport.
**Scandinavian Airlines** (code SK; www.scandinavian.net) Hub: Copenhagen Airport.
**Singapore Airlines** (code SQ; www.singaporeair.com) Hub: Changi Airport, Singapore.
**Sri Lankan Airlines** (code UL; www.srilankan.aero) Hub: Bandaranaike International Airport, Colombo.
**Swiss International Airlines** (code LX; www.swiss.com) Hub: Zurich International Airport.
**Syrian Arab Airlines** (code RB; www.syriaair.com) Hub: Damascus Airport.
**Thai Airways International** (code TG; www.thaiair.com) Hub: Bangkok International Airport.
**United Airlines** (code UA; www.united.com) Hub: Chicago Airport.
**Virgin Atlantic** (code VS; www.virgin-atlantic.com) Hub: Heathrow Airport, London.

Many international airlines are represented by the following agencies, which are located in Jaipur Towers in Jaipur:
**Interglobe Air Transport** (Map pp152-3; ☎ 0141-2360532; Jaipur Towers, MI Rd; 🕑 9.30am-6pm Mon-Sat) Represents United Airlines, SAS, Syrian Arab Airlines and Virgin.
**Jetair Ltd** (Map pp152-3; ☎ 0141-2368640; Jaipur Towers, MI Rd; 🕑 9.30am-1pm & 1.30-6pm Mon-Sat) Represents American Airlines, Royal Jordanian Airlines, Austrian Airlines, Gulf Air, Biman Bangladesh and Kenya Airways.

## Tickets

As travellers aren't generally issued a tourist visa to India unless they have an onward/return ticket, few visitors buy international tickets in India itself. For those who do require a ticket, international schedules and fares are available from travel agents in India.

> **DEPARTURE TAX**
>
> The departure tax of Rs 500 (Rs 150 for most south and Southeast Asian countries) is included in the price of most airline tickets – check with your travel agency.

International fares to India fluctuate according to the low, shoulder and high seasons. The fares we've given in this section represent the average fares of various carriers servicing India. Individual carriers have not been specifically mentioned as their routes and fares are subject to change over the life of this book. Contact your travel agent or check out the Internet to get up-to-the-minute ticket prices and schedules.

Online ticket sales are handy for straightforward trips with few or no connecting flights. However, travel agencies are recommended for special deals, sorting out tricky connections and organising insurance and Indian visas. Here are a few reputable international online ticket sites:
**Expedia** (www.expedia.com)
**Flight Centre International** (www.flightcentre.com)
**Flights.com** (www.tiss.com)
**STA Travel** (www.statravel.com)
**Travelocity** (www.travelocity.com)

### AFRICA

**Rennies Travel** (www.renniestravel.com) and **STA Travel** (www.statravel.co.za) have offices throughout Southern Africa. Check their websites for branch details.

Return fares to Mumbai are around US$550 from Nairobi and around US$800 from Johannesburg.

### ASIA

**STA Travel** (Hong Kong ☎ 27361618; www.statravel.com.hk; Japan ☎ 0353-912 922; www.statravel.co.jp; Singapore ☎ 6737 7188; www.statravel.com.sg; Thailand ☎ 0 2236 0262; www.statravel.co.th) has branches all around Asia. Another resource in Japan is **No 1 Travel** (☎ 0332-056 073; www.no1-travel.com); in Hong Kong try **Four Seas Tours** (☎ 2200 7760; www.fourseastravel.com/english).

### Nepal

A return flight from Kathmandu is about US$340 to Delhi and US$550 to Mumbai.

### Pakistan

Be aware that flights between Pakistan and India are often suspended when relations between the two countries turn sour. At the time of writing, flights were operating. It costs around US$180 for a return flight from Lahore to Delhi, US$280 between Karachi and Delhi and US$220 between Karachi and Mumbai.

### Thailand

Bangkok is the most popular departure point from Southeast Asia into India. Various flights go from Bangkok, including to Delhi (from around US$580) and Mumbai (around US$700). These are all return fares.

## AUSTRALIA

**STA Travel** (☎ 1300 733 035; www.statravel.com.au) and **Flight Centre** (☎ 133133; www.flightcentre.com.au) have offices throughout Australia. For online bookings, try www.travel.com.au.

There's usually at least one stop in a Southeast Asian city en route to India, though Qantas has direct flights to Mumbai. The return fares to Delhi and Mumbai from Australian cities are all fairly similarly priced – expect to pay anywhere between A$1200 and A$1700, depending on the season.

## CANADA

**Travel Cuts** (☎ 800-667 2887; www.travelcuts.com) is Canada's national student travel agency. For an online booking try www.expedia.ca and www.travelocity.ca.

From Canada, most flights to India are via Europe but a number of reasonably priced fares are also available from Vancouver via one of the major Asian cities.

The return fare from Vancouver to Delhi or Mumbai is from around C$1750.

## CONTINENTAL EUROPE

Flight options from Europe are similar to those from the UK, with many of the cheaper flights from major European cities via the Middle East. There is a plethora of deals so shop around.

For fares from European destinations to the various Indian hubs, try the agencies below or peruse the Internet.

### France

Some recommended agencies:

**Anyway** (☎ 08 92 89 38 92; www.anyway.fr in French)
**Lastminute** (☎ 08 92 70 50 00; www.lastminute.fr in French)
**Nouvelles Frontières** (☎ 08 25 00 07 47; www.nouvelles-frontieres.fr in French)
**OTU Voyages** (www.otu.fr in French) Specialises in student and youth travellers.
**Voyageurs du Monde** (☎ 01 40 15 11 15; www.vdm.com in French)

### Germany

Some recommended agencies:

**Expedia** (www.expedia.de in German)
**Just Travel** (☎ 089-747 33 30; www.justtravel.de)
**Lastminute** (☎ 01805 284 366; www.lastminute.de in German)
**STA Travel** (☎ 01805 456 422; www.statravel.de in German)

### Italy

One recommended agent is **CTS Viaggi** (☎ 064 62 04 31; www.cts.it in Italian), which specialises in student and youth travel.

### Netherlands

One reputable agency is **Airfair** (☎ 0206 20 51 21; www.airfair.nl in Dutch).

### Spain

Well-regarded agencies:

**Barcelo Viajes** (☎ 902 11 62 26; www.barceloviajes.com in Spanish)
**Nouvelles Frontières** (☎ 902 17 09 79)

## NEW ZEALAND

Both **Flight Centre** (☎ 0800 243 544; www.flightcentre.co.nz) and **STA Travel** (☎ 0508 782 872; www.statravel.co.nz) have country-wide branches. For online bookings try www.travel.co.nz.

Flights between India and New Zealand all go via Southeast Asia. Return fares from Auckland to Delhi start at about NZ$1600.

## UK & IRELAND

Discount air travel is big business in London so always check the latest deals on offer. Advertisements for many travel agencies appear in the travel pages of the weekend broadsheet newspapers, in *Time Out*, the *Evening Standard* and in the free magazine *TNT*.

Good places to start hunting for competitive quotes:

**Bridge the World** (☎ 087-0444 7474; www.b-t-w.co.uk)
**Flightbookers** (☎ 087-0010 7000; www.ebookers.com)

TRANSPORT

**Flight Centre** (☎ 087-0890 8099; www.flightcentre.co.uk)
**North-South Travel** (☎ 012-4560 8291; www.northsouthtravel.co.uk)
**Quest Travel** (☎ 087-0442 3542; www.questtravel.com)
**STA Travel** (☎ 087-0160 0599; www.statravel.co.uk)
**Trailfinders** (www.trailfinders.co.uk)
**Travel Bag** (☎ 087-0890 1456; www.travelbag.co.uk)

### USA



Discount travel agencies in the USA are known as consolidators (although you won't see a sign on the door saying 'Consolidator'). San Francisco is the ticket consolidator capital of America, although some good deals can be found in Los Angeles, New York and other big cities. As fares are so variable, consult travel agents and scan the Internet to nail the best deal.

For online bookings try the following websites:

- www.cheaptickets.com
- www.expedia.com
- www.itn.net
- www.lowestfare.com
- www.orbitz.com
- www.sta.com
- www.travelocity.com

# GETTING AROUND

## AIR

Within Rajasthan, there are airports in Jaipur, Jodhpur and Udaipur. There's also an airport in Jaisalmer, that's open from 1 October to 31 March. However, this is closed throughout the year when tensions are high along the Pakistan border, as was the case at the time of writing.

As of 2005 a flurry of new low-cost airlines emerged, including Kingfisher Airlines. None of these served Rajasthan at the time of writing, but the new carriers have forced established carriers to keep prices competitive. To stay abreast of the latest situation consult travel agents and browse the Internet.

A nifty booklet containing updated domestic air schedules and fares is *Excel's Timetable of Air Services Within India* (Rs 40; published monthly). It's available at various city newsstands and bookshops.

At the time of writing, the airlines listed below offered domestic services to various Indian destinations (see their websites for these). These airlines have offices in major Indian cities (for contact details see the websites and the Getting There & Away sections of some regional chapters):

**Air Deccan** (www.airdeccan.net) Offers competitive fares and flies between Delhi and Jaipur (one way Rs 780) and Mumbai (one way Rs 3100).
**Air India** (www.airindia.com) The national carrier flies between Delhi and Mumbai. Note that most of these flights leave from international terminals (check in advance).
**Air Sahara** (www.airsahara.net) Flies between Delhi and Jaipur (one way US$73) and Mumbai (one way US$195).
**Indian Airlines** (www.indian-airlines.nic.in) India's major domestic carrier, and its subsidiary Alliance Air, offer flights to 57 destinations within India and to 20 neighbouring countries. They are the major player in Rajasthan, serving Agra, Delhi, Jodhpur, Jaisalmer (when the airport is open), Udaipur and Mumbai (see Getting There & Away in the relevant city for prices). The service gets mixed reports and their safety record is not as good as other domestic carriers.
**Jagson Airlines** (www.jagsonairline.com) Flies between Delhi, Jaipur (one way US$40) and Udaipur (one way US$112).
**Jet Airways** (www.jetairways.com) Rated by many as India's best airline, with efficient staff and a modern fleet, serving Delhi, Jaipur, Jodhpur, Mumbai and Udaipur. For prices see the Getting There & Away sections of individual cities.

## BICYCLE

Rajasthan offers an immense array of experiences and challenges for a long-distance cyclist. Nevertheless, long-distance cycling is not for the faint of heart or weak of knee. You'll need physical endurance to cope with the roads, traffic and climate.

Try to read some books on bicycle touring, such as Bicycling Magazine's *Guide to Bike Touring: Everything You Need to Know to Travel Anywhere on a Bike*. Cycling magazines provide useful information and their classifieds sections are good places to look for a riding companion. Also have a look at the **Cyclists Touring Club** (www.ctc.org.uk) and the **International Bicycle Fund** (www.ibike.org). Your local cycling club may also be a handy information source.

If you're a serious cyclist or amateur racer and wish to get in touch with counterparts while in India, there's the **Cycle Federation of India** (☎/fax 011-23392578; Yamuna Velodrome, IGI Sports Complex, Delhi; 🕑 10am-5pm Mon-Fri & 10am-2pm Sat). For anything bicycle-related in Delhi, head for Jhandewalan Cycle Market (Map pp92–4), which has imported and domestic new and second-hand bikes and spare parts.

## Bicycle Tours

If you want to splash out, **Butterfield & Robinson** (☎ 416-864 1354; www.butterfield.com; 70 Bond St, Toronto M5B 1X3, Canada) offers biking expeditions through Rajasthan starting and ending in Delhi, returning via Agra. The all-inclusive tours last for 11 days, which are divided into walking and riding days. Expect to pay at least US$6295 per person (US$7395 for singles).

## Bring Your Own Bike

Most travellers prefer to buy a bike in India, but by all means consider bringing your own. Mountain bikes are especially suited to India – their sturdier construction makes them more manoeuvrable and less prone to damage, and allows you to tackle rocky, muddy roads unsuitable for lighter machines. Inquire in your home country about air transport and customs formalities. When transporting your bike, remove pedals, all luggage and accessories, turn the handlebars, cover the chain and let the tyres down a bit.

It may be hard to find parts, especially wheels, for touring bikes with 700C wheels. Parts for bicycles with 66cm wheels (of variable standards) are available.

Carry a good lock and use it. Consider wrapping your bicycle frame in used inner tubes – this not only hides fancy paint jobs, but protects them from knocks.

## Hire & Purchase

Even in the smallest towns there is usually at least one outlet that hires out bikes but they tend to be rickety bone-rattlers that are only good for short distances. Charges tend to be around Rs 3 to 5 per hour, or around Rs 25 to 35 per day. You may like to buy a bike in India and your best bet is to shop around to get a feel for brands and prices. There are many brands of Indian clunkers, including Hero, Atlas, BSA and Raleigh. Raleigh is considered the finest quality, followed by BSA, which has many models including some sporty jobs. Hero mountain-style bicycles are on sale in larger towns.

Once you've decided on a bike you have a choice of luggage carriers – mostly the rat-trap type varying only in size, price and strength. There's a plethora of saddles available but all are equally bum-breaking. Consider bringing you own saddle, rack and good-quality panniers. Get a machine fitted with a stand and bell.

Reselling is usually a breeze. Count on getting about 60% to 70% of what you paid, if it was a new bike. A local bicycle-hire shop will probably be interested, or simply ask around to find potential buyers.

## Repairs & Maintenance

For Indian bikes, there are plenty of repair 'shops' (some are no more than a puncture-wallah with his box of tools under a tree), which makes maintenance delightfully straightforward. The puncture-wallahs will patch tubes for a nominal cost. Check the tyres regularly for bits of glass or other sharp objects and dig them out before they make it through to the tube.

If you bring your own bicycle to India, you will need to be prepared for the contingencies of part replacement or repair. Several travellers have warned that it is not at all easy locating foreign parts. Ensure you have a working knowledge of your machine. Bring all necessary tools with you as well as a compact bike manual with diagrams – Indian mechanics can work wonders, and illustrations help overcome the language barrier. Roads don't often have paved shoulders and are very dusty, so keep your chain lubricated, and bring a spare.

## Roads & Distances

It's obviously more pleasurable to ride on quieter roads – avoid big cities where the chaotic traffic can be a real hazard for cyclists. National highways can also be a nightmare with speeding trucks and buses. Always make inquiries before venturing off-road.

Avoid leaving anything on your bike that can easily be removed when it's unattended. You may like to bring along a padlock and chain. However, don't be paranoid – your bike is probably safer in India than in many Western cities.

If you've never cycled long distances, start with 20km to 40km a day and increase this as you gain stamina and confidence. Be warned that asking directions can send you on a wild-goose chase.

For an eight-hour pedal an experienced cycle tourist will average 70km to 100km a day on undulating plains, or 50km to 70km in mountainous areas on sealed roads; cut this by at least one-third for unsealed roads. The distance you cycle may be dictated by available accommodation; not all villages have a place to stay. If you're cycling in a hot climate, try to get your cycling done by noon as the sun may be too strong in the afternoon. Hotels also fill up in the afternoon and it's usually dark by 6pm, so these are additional reasons to get an early start.

## BUS

The state government bus service is **Rajasthan Roadways** (www.rajtrans.com), otherwise known as the Rajasthan State Road Transport Corporation (RSRTC). Often there are privately owned local bus services as well as luxury private coaches running between major cities. These can be booked through travel agencies.

Although the bus network is comprehensive and reliable, many travellers prefer to travel by train, as it's a smoother ride and doesn't involve the nerve-wracking zigzagging of road travel. Buses are best suited to short journeys; if you've got a long trip, particularly overnight, opt for a train if there's a choice. The big advantage of buses over trains is that they travel more frequently and getting one usually involves less pre-departure hassle. It's best to avoid night travel when driving conditions can be more hazardous.

The condition of buses largely affects the comfort of the journey – private buses are often the most comfortable option, though some of the deluxe RSRTC buses are now very good as well. Choose a seat between the axles, as this generally minimises the bumpiness of a trip.

Your luggage is usually stored in an enclosed compartment at the back of the bus – the company may charge a few rupees for this. Alternatively, baggage is carried for free on the roof and if this is the case, it's worth taking some precautions. Firstly, ensure your bag is adequately padlocked. Make sure it's tied on securely and that nobody dumps a heavy tin trunk on top of your gear. Theft can be a problem so keep an eye on your bags during any stops en route (which are ideal times to stretch your legs anyway).

### ROAD DISTANCES (KM)

| | Agra | Ahmedabad | Ajmer | Alwar | Bharatpur | Bikaner | Bundi | Chittorgarh | Delhi | Jaipur | Jaisalmer | Jodhpur | Kota | Mt Abu | Mumbai | Udaipur |
|---|---|---|---|---|---|---|---|---|---|---|---|---|---|---|---|---|
| Agra | --- | | | | | | | | | | | | | | | |
| Ahmedabad | 889 | --- | | | | | | | | | | | | | | |
| Ajmer | 388 | 526 | --- | | | | | | | | | | | | | |
| Alwar | 172 | 798 | 272 | --- | | | | | | | | | | | | |
| Bharatpur | 56 | 658 | 332 | 116 | --- | | | | | | | | | | | |
| Bikaner | 665 | 754 | 233 | 462 | 497 | --- | | | | | | | | | | |
| Bundi | 438 | 485 | 163 | 347 | 382 | 396 | --- | | | | | | | | | |
| Chittorgarh | 579 | 364 | 191 | 463 | 523 | 424 | 121 | --- | | | | | | | | |
| Delhi | 195 | 916 | 392 | 163 | 251 | 470 | 465 | 583 | --- | | | | | | | |
| Jaipur | 232 | 657 | 138 | 143 | 174 | 354 | 205 | 345 | 259 | --- | | | | | | |
| Jaisalmer | 853 | 296 | 490 | 762 | 822 | 333 | 653 | 657 | 882 | 543 | --- | | | | | |
| Jodhpur | 568 | 511 | 205 | 477 | 537 | 243 | 368 | 372 | 597 | 317 | 285 | --- | | | | |
| Kota | 453 | 522 | 200 | 383 | 418 | 432 | 36 | 158 | 504 | 242 | 690 | 405 | --- | | | |
| Mt Abu | 737 | 221 | 375 | 647 | 707 | 569 | 418 | 297 | 767 | 465 | 572 | 326 | 455 | --- | | |
| Mumbai | 1204 | 554 | 1071 | 1343 | 945 | 1299 | 1041 | 928 | 1461 | 1202 | 1341 | 1056 | 1005 | 766 | --- | |
| Udaipur | 637 | 252 | 274 | 551 | 581 | 506 | 233 | 112 | 664 | 347 | 545 | 260 | 270 | 185 | 797 | --- |

On long-distance bus trips, chai stops seem to be either far too frequent or agonisingly infrequent. Toilet facilities for women are often inadequate. It's worth taking earplugs (or headphones), as some bus drivers love to crank up bus stereos or videos.

Local city buses, particularly in the larger cities, are fume-belching, human-stuffed, mechanical rattletraps that travel at breakneck speed, except when they are stuck in traffic. Within cities it's more convenient and comfortable to opt for an autorickshaw or taxi rather than a bus.

### Bus Types

On the main routes in Rajasthan you have a basic choice of ordinary, express and deluxe. Express and deluxe buses make fewer stops than ordinary buses – they're still usually crowded though. The fare is marginally higher than ordinary buses, but worth every rupee.

The RSRTC also operates some divisions in the deluxe category: on selected routes there are Gray Line (sleeper) buses – these have beds and make overnight trips more comfortable. Beds have a bunk-bed arrangement, with rows of single beds, each of which has a curtain for privacy, so they are usually fine even for women travelling alone.

Silver Line are superdeluxe services and get good reports for comfort – if one is available on your route, book it. Air-conditioned (AC) Pink Line buses serve the routes between Jaipur and Delhi, Agra and Udaipur.

Private buses also operate on most Rajasthan routes; apart from often being quicker and more comfortable, the booking procedure is much simpler than for state-run buses. However, some private companies can tend to change schedules at the last minute to get as many bums on seats as possible. They can be cheaper than the RSRTC buses. They often offer sleeper buses on overnight trips too.

### Costs

Fares and journey times differ according to the transport provider, class and distance. The fares with private operators can be influenced by the time of year, the condition of the bus and sometimes by your bargaining skills. On state buses, a deluxe bus from Delhi to Jaipur costs around Rs 281 (Rs 425 in AC), an express from Udaipur to Mt Abu costs around Rs 82, and an express from Jodhpur to Jaisalmer costs around Rs 60 (Rs 135 in deluxe).

Journey times quoted in this guide are approximate – a multitude of factors can influence how long it takes to get from A to B, from traffic jams and accidents to the fearlessness of the driver. This is India.

### Reservations

Advance reservations are often not possible on 'ordinary' buses, so it pays to arrive a bit early to bag a seat. Other bus services do usually take advance reservations and it's wise to book ahead as seats can fill up fast, especially on popular routes.

Many bus stations have a separate women's queue, although this isn't always obvious because the relevant sign (where it exists) is rarely in English and there may not be women queuing. More often than not, the same ticket window will handle the male and the female queue so women travellers should sharpen their elbows and make their way to the front, where they will get almost immediate service.

## CAR

### Hire

#### CAR & DRIVER

Long-distance car hire that includes a driver is an increasingly popular way to get around Rajasthan. Spread among, say, four people it's not overly expensive and you have the flexibility to go where you want when you want.

Most local taxis will quite happily set off on a long-distance trip in Rajasthan. Inquiring at a taxi rank is the cheapest and easiest way to organise this. Alternatively, you can ask a travel agency or your hotel to book one for you, but remember that they'll take their cut for this service.

Rates with the Rajasthan Tourism Development Corporation (RTDC) are from Rs 4.50/6 per kilometre for a non-AC/AC car, with the usual 250km minimum per day and an overnight charge of Rs 100.

Expect to pay around Rs 3.50 per kilometre if you arrange a non-AC car directly with a taxi driver, or if you haggle hard with an agency – with a Rs 100 overnight charge and a minimum charge for 250km per day. If you're hiring for several days, try to negotiate a better deal.

If you're only going one way, remember that you have to pay for the driver to return to your starting point. Your driver may ask you for an advance of a few hundred rupees at the start of the trip to pay for petrol. To hire a car with driver for use only within one city (eg Delhi) expect to pay Rs 500 to 600 per day for a non-AC vehicle, around Rs 600 to 750 for an AC vehicle. There's usually an eight hour, 80km limit per day (additional charges apply if you exceed these).

### SELF-DRIVE

Currently there are no agencies in Rajasthan offering self-drive vehicles. Self-drive hire is possible in Delhi, but given the hair-raising driving conditions most travellers opt for a car with driver. Major car-hire companies in India include Budget and Hertz.

Expect to pay around Rs 1700 per day plus 10% tax (minimum three days; unlimited mileage) for a small AC vehicle. You have to leave an insurance deposit (refundable) of Rs 20,000.

You'll also need an International Driving Licence from your national motoring organisation. In some cities, such as Delhi, it's possible to hire or buy motorcycles, and you'll often need to produce a driving licence of some sort (see p388). An International Driving Licence can also come in handy for other identification purposes, such as bicycle hire.

Because of extreme congestion in cities and narrow bumpy roads in the country, driving is a slow, stop-start process – hard on you, the car and fuel economy. Service is so-so; parts and tyres are not always easy to obtain, though there are plenty of puncture-



### TIPS FOR HIRING A CAR & DRIVER

Try to get a driver who speaks at least some English and who is knowledgeable about the region(s) you intend visiting. Night travel is best avoided.

More than a few travellers have shelled out much more money than is reasonable, paying for the driver's accommodation and meals (even booze!), completely unaware that his lodging/meal cost has already been factored into the fee. Make sure you understand the accommodation/meal arrangement for the driver *before* paying the car-hire company and ensure this is made clear to the driver *before* you set off. The charge that's quoted should include an allowance for the driver's daily living expenses (ie food and lodging) as well as petrol (hire rates may fluctuate in tune with petrol prices). Note that there's often a vehicle entry fee into other states, which costs extra. You also have to pay extra for any car-parking/car-entry fees you may incur.

For longer trips, when it comes to where the driver stays overnight, this is for him to decide and should never be your headache (many choose to sleep in the back seat of the car thus pocketing their accommodation allowance).

Be aware that many hotels in Rajasthan don't permit drivers onto their premises (to sleep or eat), even if you're paying. That's because the commission racket has created all sorts of headaches for hotels and, while your intentions may be warm-hearted, the hotel owners are the ones who may face problems with demanding drivers long after you've departed India. Although some places don't mind drivers joining guests at hotel restaurants, respect those that refuse entry – if in doubt, ask. If you want to shout your driver a meal, there are good independent restaurants not attached to hotels that welcome one and all.

Finally, and very importantly, it's imperative to set the ground rules from day one. Many travellers have complained of having their holiday completely dictated by their driver – one couple was bullied into having meals only when it suited the driver. Another set of travellers could only stay at hotels decided by their driver (where he received commission). Politely, but firmly, let the driver know at the very onset that you're the boss – it can make the difference between a carefree journey and a strained one.

Shop around to find the best deal and before paying anything, get in writing what you've been promised to avoid 'misunderstandings' later. Before setting off it's wise to inspect the car and meet the driver.

A tip is in order at the conclusion of your journey; anything from Rs 75 per day is reasonable (more if you're happy with the service).

repair places. All in all, it's not that much fun (especially for longer trips) except in rural areas where there's little traffic.

## HITCHING

Hitching in India isn't a realistic option, as you're likely to only be offered rides by truck drivers (not private cars). You're then stuck with the quandaries of: 'Will the driver expect to be paid?', 'Will they be unhappy if I don't offer to pay or will they want too much?' Women are strongly advised against hitching.

## LOCAL TRANSPORT

Although there are comprehensive local bus networks in most major towns, unless you have time to familiarise yourself with the routes, you're better off sticking to taxis, autorickshaws or cycle-rickshaws, or hiring bicycles.

A basic rule applies to any form of transport where the fare is not ticketed, fixed or metered: agree on the fare beforehand. If you fail to do that you can expect enormous arguments and hassles when you get to your destination. And agree on the fare clearly – if there is more than one of you make sure it covers all of you (the price quoted should be per vehicle, not per person). If you have baggage make sure there are no extra charges, or you may be asked for more at the end of the trip. If a driver refuses to use the meter, or insists on an extortionate rate, simply walk away – if he really wants the job the price will drop. If you can't agree on a reasonable fare, find another driver.

Other useful tips when catching taxis/rickshaws:

- Always have enough small change, as drivers rarely do, which can be a real hassle, especially at night.
- If you are staying or dining at a top-end venue and you need to catch a rickshaw, try walking a few hundred metres down the road to avoid the drivers who hang outside assuming you're a cash cow.
- Finally, it's a good idea to carry around a business card of the hotel in which you are staying, as your pronunciation of streets, hotel names etc may be incomprehensible to drivers. Some hotel cards even have a nifty little sketch map clearly indicating their location.

Fares are often steeper (as much as double the day fare) at night and some drivers charge a few rupees extra for luggage. Many autorickshaw drivers are right into the commission racket – see About Touts, p357.

### Autorickshaw & Tempo

An autorickshaw is a noisy three-wheel device powered by a two-stroke motorcycle engine with a driver up front and seats for two (or sometimes more) passengers behind. They don't have doors and have just a canvas top. They are also known as scooters or autos.

They're generally about half the price of a taxi, are usually metered and follow the same ground rules as taxis. Because of their size, autorickshaws are often faster than taxis for short trips and their drivers are decidedly nuttier. Hair-raising near-misses are guaranteed and glancing-blow collisions are not infrequent; thrill seekers will love them!

Tempos are somewhat like large autorickshaws. These ungainly looking three-wheel devices operate like minibuses or share taxis along fixed routes (at fixed fares). Unless you're spending a lot of time in one city, they're impractical.

### Cycle-rickshaw

Cycle-rickshaws are effectively three-wheeler bicycles with a seat for two passengers behind the driver. You'll find them in parts of Delhi, in Jaipur and in many smaller towns.

As with taxis and autorickshaws, fares must be agreed upon in advance. A typical ride in a cycle-rickshaw is between one and three kilometres and costs roughly between Rs 20 and 40. It's extremely strenuous work, so a tip is appreciated.

### Share Jeep

Share jeeps supplement the bus service in many parts of Rajasthan, especially in areas off the main road routes, such as many of the towns in Shekhawati.

Jeeps leave when (very) full, from well-established 'passenger stations' on the outskirts of towns and villages; locals should be able to point you in the right direction. They are usually dirt cheap and jam-packed. The average fare for a one-hour trip is around Rs 10. They tend to be more dangerous than buses (drivers are even crazier), and travellers may find them too crowded and claustrophobic for longer trips.

### Taxi

Most towns have taxis, and most of them (certainly in the major cities) are metered. Getting a metered fare, however, is rather a different situation. First of all the meter may be 'broken'. Threatening to get another taxi will often miraculously 'fix' it. Opt for prepaid taxis where available.

Another problem with taxis is that their meters may be outdated. Fares are adjusted upwards so much faster and more frequently than meters are recalibrated that drivers often have 'fare adjustment cards' indicating what you should pay for your trip compared to what the meter indicates. This is, of course, open to abuse. You have no idea if you're being shown the right card or if the taxi's meter has actually been recalibrated and you're being shown the card anyway.

The only answer to all this is to get an idea of what the fare should be before departure (ask airport information desks, hotels etc). You'll soon develop a feel for what the meter says, what the cards say and what the two together should indicate.

### Other Transport

In some towns, tongas (horse-drawn two-wheelers) and victorias (horse-drawn carriages) still operate. Delhi's Metro system is partly operational (see p129). Delhi also has suburban trains. See the regional chapters for further details.

## MOTORCYCLE

Cruising solo around India by motorcycle offers the freedom to go when and where you desire. There are also some excellent motorcycle tours available (see right), which take the hassle out of doing it alone.

Helmets, leathers, gloves, goggles, boots, waterproofs and other protective gear are best brought from your home country, as they're either unavailable in India or are of variable quality. You'll also need a valid International Driving Licence.

### Hire

Organised tours provide motorcycles, but if you're planning an independent trip, bikes can be hired at negotiable prices. You'll probably have to leave a cash deposit (refundable) and/or your air ticket.

In Delhi, Inder Motors (opposite) rents out Enfields (minimum three weeks); a 500cc machine for three/eight weeks costs Rs 13,000/22,000. There are burgeoning numbers of hire (or purchase) places in Pushkar in eastern Rajasthan.

### On the Road

Given the overall road conditions in India, motorcycling is not without hazards and ideally should only be undertaken by experienced riders. Hazards range from goats crossing the road to defunct abandoned trucks and of course the perpetual potholes and unmarked speed humps. Rural roads sometimes have grain crops strewn across them to be threshed by passing vehicles – it can be a real hazard for bikers.

Avoid covering too much territory in one day. A lot of energy is spent simply concentrating on the road, making long days exhausting and potentially dangerous. On the busy national highways expect to average 50km/h without stops; on smaller roads, where conditions are worse, as little as 10km/h is not an unrealistic average. On the whole, on good roads you can easily expect to cover a minimum of 100km a day (up to or over 300km with minimal stops). Night riding should be avoided.

For long hauls, putting the bike on a train can be a convenient option. You'll pay about as much as a 2nd-class passenger fare for the bike. The petrol tank must be empty, and there should be a tag in an obvious place detailing name, destination, passport number and train details. When you pack the bike, remove the mirrors and loosen the handlebars to avoid damage.

### Organised Motorcycle Tours

Motorcycle tours usually operate with a minimum number of people and some can be tailor-made. Below are some reputable options (see websites for contact details, itineraries and prices):

**Ferris Wheels** (www.ferriswheels.com.au)
**H-C Travel** (www.hctravel.com)
**Indian Motorcycle Adventures** (http://homepages.ihug.co.nz/~gumby/)
**Indian Shepherds** (www.asiasafari.com)
**Moto Discovery** (www.motodiscovery.com)
**Saffron Road Motorcycle Tours** (www.saffronroad.com)

TRANSPORT

## Purchase

Buying a second-hand machine is a matter of asking around and a good place to start is with mechanics. Do your homework thoroughly and shop around to get an idea of the latest models on the market and their costs. Also try to speak to other bikers – they're a goldmine of information.

In Delhi the area around Hari Singh Nalwa St in Karol Bagh is full of places buying, selling and hiring out motorcycles. The reputation of many places is variable, but Lonely Planet consistently receives good reports about **Inder Motors** (Map pp92-4; ☎ 011-25728579; lallisingh@vsnl.com; 1740-A/55 Basement, Hari Singh Nalwa St, Karol Bagh Market). Run by the knowledgeable Lalli Singh, this place deals only in sales (second-hand and new bikes), hiring, spares and servicing of Enfields only. It also offers other services such as arranging motorbike transport in India and collecting your bike from your final destination if it's not Delhi (for a charge). Pushkar is also a popular place to buy, with numerous outlets – ask around for recommendations.

Prices for new Enfield models at the time of writing are given below. See also www.royalenfield.com.

| Model | Cost (Rs) |
|---|---|
| 350cc (standard) | 61,700 |
| 350cc (Electra) | 65,800 |
| A350cc (Thunderbird) | 71,600 |
| 500cc (Electric Start) | 85,000 |

For a new bike, you'll also have to pay Rs 4500 for comprehensive one-year insurance and lifetime road tax and registration. You may like to invest a little more to get extras such as a luggage rack, protection bar, backrest, rear-view mirrors, lockable fuel tap, petrol filter, complete tool kit and loud horn (you're looking at an extra Rs 3000 to 4500 for all of these). An Enfield 500cc gives about 25km/L. Their tanks hold 14L, or you can get a customised 18L to 20L tank at an extra cost of between Rs 1500 and 3000.

A second-hand Enfield 500cc (two to three years old, without servicing) costs Rs 35,000 to 55,000 (depending on the condition). It's advisable to get it serviced before you set off (around Rs 10,000 to 15,000 for a 500cc).

When the time comes to sell your bike, expect to get around Rs 30,000 for a second-hand Enfield 500cc (in reasonable condition) and about Rs 35,000 to 45,000 if it's a new machine.

You'll pay around Rs 16,000 to ship motorbikes to Australia, Europe and the UK, which includes the crate, packing, customs and shipping agents charges, the freight cost to the destination and insurance. To export a second-hand bike, Indian customs requires you to obtain a No Objection Certificate from the office the bike was registered at.

An obvious tip perhaps, but don't part with your money until you have the ownership papers, receipt and affidavit signed by a magistrate authorising the owner (as recorded in the ownership papers) to sell the machine.

Ownership papers are much more straightforward for a new bike than for a second-hand one. Each state has a different set of ownership-transfer formalities – inquire locally about current requirements.

It takes about a week (up to two weeks for second-hand machines) to get the paperwork done if you wish to buy a new Enfield; you can contact some dealers such as Inder Motors in advance so that the paperwork will be ready by the time you arrive in India.

## Repairs & Maintenance

Original spare parts from an 'authorised dealer' can be expensive compared to copies available from your spare-parts–wallah. Delhi's Karol Bagh Market (p124) is a good place for parts for all Indian and imported bikes. If you're going to remote regions, take basic spares with you (valves, piston rings etc) as they may not be readily available.

For all machines (particularly older ones), make sure you regularly check and tighten all nuts and bolts, as Indian roads and engine vibration tend to work things loose quickly. Check the engine and gearbox oil level regularly – with the quality of oil it's advisable to change it and clean the oil filter every couple of thousand kilometres.

### PUNCTURES

Given the road conditions, the chances are you'll make at least a couple of visits to a puncture-wallah. These phenomenal fix-it men are found almost everywhere, but it's good to have the tools to at least remove your own wheel. It's worth buying new tyres if you purchase a second-hand bike with worn tyres; a new rear tyre for an Enfield costs around Rs 650.

## TRAIN

To take a train is to ride in India's bloodstream. **Indian Railways** (www.indianrail.gov.in) runs over 14,000 trains a day, and moves 14 million passengers daily to any of 6856 stations. At first the system can seem complex, however, it's straightforward once you get used to it and train travel is generally more comfortable than bus travel, especially for long trips. Delhi has a suburban train network, which is usually fine during the day, but it is often unbearably crowded during peak hours.

There are tourist quotas for many express trains, and special offices or counters for foreigners in major cities and tourist centres (you are supposed to bring money-exchange receipts or ATM slips if paying for tickets with rupees, but these are only demanded in Delhi). Many stations have left-luggage rooms with nominal daily charges – see the Information sections of regional chapters.

Train services to certain destinations are often increased during major festivals or other peak travel periods. Be especially careful during these times as there have sometimes been reports of passengers being crushed to death on overcrowded platforms. Other things to beware of (at all times) are passenger drugging and theft of your belongings – see p360.

We've listed major trains throughout this book but there are many more. If you intend on doing a lot of train travel, it's worth getting the national *Trains at a Glance* booklet (Rs 45; available at various train stations or at city bookshops and newsstands). It contains extensive details and there are timetables covering each regional zone. It often takes a bit more than a glance to work these out.

For comprehensive online information about the Indian railway system, a valuable resource is www.seat61.com/India.htm.

### Classes

Shatabdi express trains are same-day services between major and regional cities. These are the fastest and most expensive trains, with only two classes; AC executive chair and AC chair. Shatabdis are comfortable, but the glass windows cut the views considerably compared to non-AC classes on slower trains, which have barred windows and fresh air.

Rajdhani express trains are long-distance express services running between Delhi and the state capitals, and offer AC 1st class (1AC), 2-tier AC (2AC), 3-tier AC (3AC) and 2nd class. Two-tier means there are two levels of bunks in each compartment, which are a little wider and longer than their counterparts in 3-tier. Costing respectively a half and a third as much as 1AC, 2AC and 3AC are perfectly adequate for an overnight trip.

### PALACE ON WHEELS

To travel maharaja-style, try the RTDC *Palace on Wheels* service.

This special train operates weekly tours of Rajasthan, departing from Delhi every Wednesday (September to April). The itinerary covers Jaipur, Jaisalmer, Jodhpur, Ranthambhore National Park, Chittorgarh (Chittor), Udaipur, Keoladeo Ghana National Park and Agra. It's a mammoth stretch in seven days, but most of the travelling is done at night. This train once used the maharajas' original carriages, but these became so ancient that new carriages were refurbished to look like the originals. The train has two dining cars and a bar, and each coach, containing four doubles with private bathroom, is attended by a splendidly costumed captain and attendant.

If you can't afford to do the trip for real, go for a virtual chug on the website: www.palaceonwheelsindia.com. From October to March daily rates per person are US$485/US$350/US$285 for single/double/triple occupancy. In September and April it costs US$395/US$295/US$240. The price includes tours, admission fees, accommodation and all meals. Bookings must be made in advance at the **RTDC Tourist Reception Centre** (☎ 011-23381884; Bikaner House, Pandara Rd, Delhi 110011) or at the **RTDC Central Reservations Office** (Map pp152-3; ☎ 0141-2202586; MI Rd; 🕑 10am-5pm Mon-Sat) in Jaipur. Toll-free numbers for international bookings are given on the website, and you can also book online.

TRANSPORT

Other express and mail trains have 2AC coaches, chair car, non-AC sleeper (bring your own bedding), non-AC 2nd class, and finally there's unreserved tickets. A sleeper costs around a quarter as much as 2-tier AC. For more details see *Trains at a Glance*, or big stations often have English-speaking staff at inquiry counters who can help with picking the best train. At smaller stations midlevel officials, such as the deputy station master, usually speak English.

For an excellent description of the various train classes (including pictures) see the website **Train travel in India...** (www.seat61.com/India.htm); scroll down to the 'What are Indian trains like?' heading.

## Costs

Fares are calculated by distance. For a full rundown on fares see www.indianrail.gov.in or *Trains at a Glance*. On most trains, if your journey is longer than 500km, you can take one break (for two days maximum) but you must have your ticket endorsed by the station master or ticket collector at the station you stop at.

Bedding is free in 1AC, 2AC and 3AC sleepers, but you'll need your own for ordinary sleepers. Meals are free on Rajdhani and Shatabdi trains, and cheap meals are available on other trains.

The major stations have accommodation called 'retiring rooms', which are a possibility if you have a valid ticket – for details see p355.

Tickets are refundable (as late as 12 hours after train departure) but a fee applies; there are no refunds on lost tickets.

Seniors over 60 years of age are entitled to a 30% discount on train tickets.

## Reservations

To make a reservation you must fill out a form stating which class you want and the train's name and number. For overnight journeys it's best to reserve your place a couple of days in advance. If there's no special counter or office for foreigners at the station, you'll have to adopt local queuing practices, which range from reasonably orderly lines to mosh pits. There are sometimes separate ladies' queues, but usually the same window handles men and women. Women should simply proceed to the front of the queue, next to the first male.

If you don't want the hassle of buying a ticket yourself, many travel agencies and hotels are in the business of purchasing train tickets for a small commission. But watch out for small-fry travel agents who promise express-train tickets and deliver tickets for obscure mail or passenger trains, *or* get you a waiting list reservation rather than a seat or bunk. Only leave a small deposit, if any, and check the ticket carefully before paying.

Reserved tickets show your berth and carriage number. Efficient railway staff will also stick lists of names and berths on each reserved carriage, as well as writing the carriage number in chalk.

If you can't buy a reserved seat, ask if there's a waiting list. If you are on the waiting list, it will say 'wl' on your ticket followed by a number, which gives the number of your position in the queue. You can ask when you buy what the likelihood is that you will get a seat.

Alternatively, you could buy unreserved tickets – which go on sale about an hour before departure – and try to upgrade it. Find a reserved-class carriage and a spare seat, and seek out the conductor (officially the Travelling Ticket Examiner – TTE). Explain you could only buy an unreserved ticket and ask about vacancies. With luck, the conductor will be happy to oblige. You pay the difference between the ordinary fare and the fare of whichever class you're in, plus a small excess charge of around Rs 30.

### ONLINE RESERVATIONS

It's possible to book train tickets online at www.irctc.co.in. Helpful tips on making online bookings are available at the website **Train travel in India...** (www.seat61.com/India.htm); scroll down to the 'How to book – from outside India' heading.

### REFUNDS

Tickets are refundable but fees apply. If you present more than one day in advance, a fee of Rs 20 to 50 applies. Steeper charges apply if you seek a refund less than four hours prior to departure, but you can get some sort of refund as late as 12 hours afterwards.

When refunding your ticket you officially have a magic pass to go to the front of the queue, as the next person may require the spot you're surrendering. We've never seen if this works in practice.

# Health

Dr Trish Batchelor

CONTENTS





While the potential dangers of travelling in India can seem quite ominous, in reality few travellers experience anything more than an upset stomach. Hygiene is generally poor throughout the country, so food- and water-borne illnesses are common. Travellers tend to worry about contracting infectious diseases, but infections are a rare cause of *serious* illness or death in travellers. Pre-existing medical conditions such as heart disease, and accidental injury (especially traffic accidents), account for most life-threatening problems.

Fortunately, most travellers' illnesses can either be prevented with some common-sense behaviour or be treated easily with a well-stocked traveller's medical kit. The following advice is a general guide only and does not replace the advice of a doctor trained in travel medicine.

## BEFORE YOU GO

Pack medications in their original, clearly labelled containers. A signed and dated letter from your physician describing your medical conditions and medications, including generic names, is very useful. If carrying syringes or needles, be sure to have a physician's letter documenting their medical necessity. If you have a heart condition, bring a copy of your ECG taken just prior to travelling.

If you take any regular medication, bring double your needs in case of loss or theft. You'll be able to buy many medications over the counter in India without a doctor's prescription, but it can be difficult to find some of the newer drugs, particularly the latest antidepressant drugs, blood-pressure medications and contraceptive pills.

### INSURANCE

Even if you're fit and healthy, don't travel without health insurance – accidents do happen. Declare any existing medical conditions you have, as the insurance company WILL check if your problem is pre-existing and will not cover you if it is undeclared. You may require extra cover for adventure activities, such as rock climbing. If you have health insurance at home that doesn't cover you for medical expenses abroad, consider getting extra insurance. If you're uninsured, emergency evacuation is expensive; bills of over US$100,000 are not uncommon.

Ask in advance if your insurance plan will make payments directly to providers or reimburse you later for overseas health expenditures. (In many countries doctors expect payment in cash.) Some policies offer lower and higher medical-expense options; the higher ones are chiefly for countries that have extremely high medical costs, such as the USA. You may prefer to take out a policy that pays doctors or hospitals directly to avoid having to pay on the spot and claim later. If you have to claim later, make sure you keep all documentation. Some policies ask you to call (reverse charges) a centre in your home country, where an immediate assessment of your problem is made.

### VACCINATIONS

Specialised travel-medicine clinics are your best source of information; they stock all available vaccines and will be able to give specific recommendations for you and your trip. The doctors will take into account factors such as past vaccination history, the length of your trip, activities you may be undertaking and underlying medical conditions, such as pregnancy.

Most vaccines don't give immunity until at least two weeks after they're given, so visit a doctor four to eight weeks before departure. Ask your doctor for an International Certificate of Vaccination (otherwise known as the yellow booklet), which will list all the vaccinations you've received.

## Recommended Vaccinations

The World Health Organization (WHO) recommends travellers to India be up to date with measles, mumps and rubella vaccinations. Other vaccinations it recommends:

**Adult diphtheria and tetanus** Single booster recommended if none in the previous 10 years. Side effects include sore arm and fever.

**Hepatitis A** Provides almost 100% protection for up to a year; a booster after 12 months provides at least another 20 years' protection. Mild side effects such as headache and sore arm occur in 5% to 10% of people.

**Hepatitis B** Now considered routine for most travellers. Given as three shots over six months. A rapid schedule is also available, as is a combined vaccination with Hepatitis A. Side effects are mild and uncommon, usually headache and sore arm. In 95% of people lifetime protection results.

**Polio** In 2004 polio was still present in India. Only one booster is required as an adult for lifetime protection. Inactivated polio vaccine is safe during pregnancy.

**Typhoid** Recommended for all travellers to India, even if you only visit urban areas. The vaccine offers around 70% protection, lasts for two to three years and comes as a single shot. Tablets are also available; however, the injection is usually recommended as it has fewer side effects. Sore arm and fever may occur.

**Varicella** If you haven't had chickenpox, discuss this vaccination with your doctor.

Immunisations recommended for long-term travellers (those going away for more than one month) or those at special risk:

**Japanese B Encephalitis** Three injections in all. Booster recommended after two years. Sore arm and headache are the most common side effects. Rarely an allergic reaction comprising hives and swelling can occur up to 10 days after any of the three doses.

**Meningitis** Single injection. There are two types of vaccination. The quadrivalent vaccine gives two to three years' protection, and the meningitis group C vaccine gives

### MEDICAL CHECKLIST

Recommended items for a personal medical kit:

- antifungal cream, eg Clotrimazole
- antibacterial cream, eg Muciprocin
- antibiotic for skin infections, eg Amoxicillin/Clavulanate or Cephalexin
- antihistamine – there are many options, eg Cetrizine for daytime and Promethazine for night
- antiseptic, eg Betadine
- antispasmodic for stomach cramps, eg Buscopa
- contraceptive method
- decongestant, eg Pseudoephedrine
- DEET-based insect repellent
- diarrhoea medication – consider an oral rehydration solution (eg Gastrolyte), diarrhoea 'stopper' (eg Loperamide) and antinausea medication (eg Prochlorperazine); antibiotics for diarrhoea include Norfloxacin and Ciprofloxacin, for bacterial diarrhoea Azithromycin, and for giardia or amoebic dysentery Tinidazole
- first-aid items such as scissors, Elastoplasts, bandages, gauze, thermometer (but not mercury), sterile needles and syringes, safety pins and tweezers
- Ibuprofen or another anti-inflammatory
- indigestion tablets, eg Quick Eze or Mylanta
- iodine tablets (unless you are pregnant or have a thyroid problem) to purify water
- laxative, eg Coloxyl
- migraine medication if you suffer from them
- paracetamol
- permethrin to impregnate clothing and mosquito nets
- steroid cream for allergic/itchy rashes, eg 1% to 2% hydrocortisone
- sunscreen and hat
- throat lozenges
- thrush (vaginal yeast infection) treatment, eg Clotrimazole pessaries or Diflucan tablet
- ural or equivalent if prone to urine infections

around 10 years' protection. Recommended for long-term backpackers aged under 25.

**Rabies** Three injections in all. A booster after one year will then provide 10 years' protection. Side effects are rare – occasionally headache and sore arm.

**Tuberculosis (TB)** A complex issue. Adult long-term travellers are usually advised to have a TB skin test before and after travel, rather than vaccination. Only one vaccine given in a lifetime.

### Required Vaccinations

Yellow fever is the only vaccine required by international regulations. Proof of vaccination will only be required if you have visited a country in the yellow-fever zone within the six days prior to entering India. If you are travelling to India from Africa or South America you should check to see if you require proof of vaccination.

## INTERNET RESOURCES

There's a wealth of travel-health advice on the Internet. **LonelyPlanet.com** (www.lonelyplanet.com) is a good place to start. Some other suggestions:

**Centers for Disease Control and Prevention** (CDC; www.cdc.gov) Good general information.

**MD Travel Health** (www.mdtravelhealth.com) Provides complete travel-health recommendations for every country; updated daily.

**World Health Organization** (WHO; www.who.int/ith/) Its superb book *International Travel & Health* is revised annually and available online.

## FURTHER READING

Lonely Planet's *Healthy Travel – Asia & India* is pocket sized and packed with useful information about pretrip planning, emergency first aid, immunisation and disease information, and what to do if you get sick on the road. Other recommended references include *Traveller's Health*, by Dr Richard Dawood, and *Travelling Well*, by Dr Deborah Mills – check out the website of **Travelling Well** (www.travellingwell.com.au).

> **HEALTH ADVISORIES**
>
> It's usually a good idea to consult your government's travel-health website before departure, if one is available:
>
> **Australia** (www.dfat.gov.au/travel/)
> **Canada** (www.travelhealth.gc.ca)
> **New Zealand** (www.mfat.govt.nz/travel)
> **South Africa** (www.dfa.gov.za/consular/travel_advice.htm)
> **UK** (www.doh.gov.uk/traveladvice/)
> **USA** (www.cdc.gov/travel/)

# IN TRANSIT

## DEEP VEIN THROMBOSIS

Deep vein thrombosis (DVT) occurs when blood clots form in the legs during flights, chiefly because of prolonged immobility. The longer the flight, the greater the risk. Though most blood clots are reabsorbed uneventfully, some may break off and travel via the blood vessels to the lungs, where they may cause life-threatening complications.

The chief symptom of DVT is swelling or pain of the foot, ankle, or calf, usually but not always on just one side. When a blood clot travels to the lungs, it may cause chest pain and difficulty in breathing. Travellers with any of these symptoms should immediately seek medical attention.

To prevent the development of DVT on long flights you should walk about the cabin, perform isometric compressions of the leg muscles (ie contract the leg muscles while sitting), drink plenty of fluids, and avoid alcohol and tobacco.

## JET LAG & MOTION SICKNESS

Jet lag is common when crossing more than five time zones; it results in insomnia, fatigue, malaise or nausea. To avoid jet lag drink plenty of (nonalcoholic) fluids and eat light meals. Upon arrival, seek exposure to natural sunlight and readjust your schedule (for meals, sleep etc) as soon as possible.

Antihistamines such as dimenhydrinate (Dramamine), promethazine (Phenergan) and meclizine (Antivert, Bonine) are usually the first choice for treating motion sickness. Their main side effect is drowsiness. A herbal alternative is ginger, which works like a charm for some people.

# IN INDIA

## AVAILABILITY OF HEALTH CARE

There are plenty of English-speaking doctors in urban centres. Most hotels have a doctor on call – if you're staying at a budget hotel and they can't help, try contacting an upmar-

HEALTH

ket hotel to find out which doctor they use. Some cities now have clinics catering specifically to travellers and expats. These are usually more costly than local facilities, but are worth it, as they will offer a superior standard of care. Additionally, they understand the local system, and are aware of the safest local hospitals and best specialists. They can also liaise with insurance companies should you require evacuation. It is difficult to find reliable medical care in rural areas.

If you're seriously ill, contact your country's embassy (see p363), which usually has a list of recommended doctors and dentists.

Treatment at public hospitals is generally reliable, though private clinics offer the advantage of shorter queues. However, there have been reports that some private clinics have bumped up the level of treatment to higher than is necessary in order to procure larger medical-insurance claims.

In even the smallest Rajasthani town you will find at least one well-stocked pharmacy (selling everything from malaria medication to nail-polish remover). Many are open until late. Many pharmaceuticals sold in India are manufactured under licence from multinational companies, so you'll probably be familiar with many brand names. Before buying medication over the counter, always check the expiry date and ensure the packet is sealed. Don't accept items that have been poorly stored (eg lying in a glass cabinet exposed to the sunshine).

## INFECTIOUS DISEASES

### Coughs, Colds & Chest Infections

Around 25% of travellers to India will develop a respiratory infection. This usually starts as a virus and is exacerbated by environmental conditions such as pollution in the cities, or cold and altitude in the mountains. Commonly a secondary bacterial infection will intervene – marked by fever, chest pain and coughing up discoloured or blood-tinged sputum. If you have the symptoms of an infection seek medical advice or commence a general antibiotic.

### Dengue

This mosquito-borne disease is becoming increasingly problematic in the tropical world, especially in the cities. As there is no vaccine available it can only be prevented by avoiding mosquito bites. The mosquito that carries dengue bites day and night, so use insect avoidance measures at all times. Symptoms include high fever, severe headache and body ache (dengue was previously known as 'breakbone fever'). Some people develop a rash and experience diarrhoea. There is no specific treatment, just rest and paracetamol – do not take aspirin as it increases the chance of haemorrhaging. See a doctor to be diagnosed and monitored.

### Hepatitis A

A problem throughout the region, this food- and water-borne virus infects the liver and causes jaundice (yellow skin and eyes), nausea and lethargy. There is no specific treatment for hepatitis A; you need to allow time for the liver to heal. All travellers to India should be vaccinated against hepatitis A.

### Hepatitis B

The only sexually transmitted disease that can be prevented by vaccination, hepatitis B is spread by body fluids (eg by sexual contact). The long-term consequences can include liver cancer and cirrhosis.

### Hepatitis E

Hepatitis E is transmitted through contaminated food and water. It has similar symptoms to hepatitis A but is far less common. It is a severe problem in pregnant women and can result in the death of both mother and baby. There is currently no vaccine, and prevention is by following safe eating and drinking guidelines.

### HIV

HIV is spread via contaminated body fluids. Avoid unsafe sex, unsterile needles (including in medical facilities) and procedures such as tattoos. The growth rate of HIV in India is one of the highest in the world.

### Japanese B Encephalitis

This viral disease is transmitted by mosquitoes and is rare in travellers. Like most mosquito-borne diseases, it's becoming a more common problem in affected countries. Most cases occur in rural areas, and vaccination is recommended for travellers spending more than one month outside cities. There is no treatment, and a third of infected people will die, while another third will suffer permanent brain damage.

## Malaria

Considering it's such a serious and potentially deadly disease, there is an enormous amount of misinformation about malaria. You must get expert advice as to whether your trip actually puts you at risk. For most rural areas, the risk of contracting malaria far outweighs the risk of any tablet side effects. Before you travel, seek medical advice on the right medication and dosage for you.

Malaria is caused by a parasite transmitted by the bite of an infected mosquito. The most important symptom of malaria is fever, but general symptoms such as headache, diarrhoea, cough or chills may also occur. Diagnosis can only be made by taking a blood sample.

Two strategies should be combined to prevent malaria – mosquito avoidance and antimalaria medications. Most people who catch malaria are taking inadequate or no antimalarial medication.

Steps travellers are advised to take to prevent mosquito bites:

- Use an insect repellent that contains DEET on exposed skin. Wash this off at night, as long as you're sleeping under a mosquito net. Natural repellents such as citronella can be effective but must be applied more frequently than products containing DEET.
- Sleep under a mosquito net impregnated with permethrin.
- Choose accommodation with screens and fans (if not air-conditioned).
- Impregnate clothing with permethrin in high-risk areas.
- Wear long sleeves and trousers in light colours.
- Use mosquito coils.
- Spray your room with insect repellent before going out for your evening meal.

A variety of medications are available. The effectiveness of the Chloroquine and Paludrine combination is now limited in many parts of South Asia. Common side effects include nausea (40% of people) and mouth ulcers.

The daily tablet Doxycycline is a broad-spectrum antibiotic with the added benefit of helping to prevent a variety of tropical diseases such as leptospirosis, tick-borne disease and typhus. The potential side effects include photosensitivity (a tendency to sunburn), thrush in women, indigestion, heartburn, nausea and interference with the contraceptive pill. More serious side effects include ulceration of the oesophagus – you can help prevent this by taking your tablet with a meal and a large glass of water, and never lying down within half an hour of taking it. It must be taken for four weeks after leaving the risk area.

Lariam (Mefloquine) has received much bad press, some of it justified, some not. This weekly tablet suits many people. Serious side effects are rare but include depression, anxiety, psychosis and fits. Anyone with a history of depression, anxiety, any other psychological disorder or epilepsy should not take Lariam. It is considered safe in the second and third trimesters of pregnancy. Tablets must be taken for four weeks after leaving the risk area.

The new drug Malarone is a combination of Atovaquone and Proguanil. Side effects are uncommon and mild, most commonly nausea and headache. It is the best tablet for scuba divers and for those on short trips to high-risk areas. It must be taken for one week after leaving the risk area.

## Rabies

Around 30,000 people die from rabies in India each year. This uniformly fatal disease is spread by the bite or lick of an infected animal – most commonly a dog or monkey. You should seek medical advice immediately after any animal bite and commence postexposure treatment. Having pretravel vaccination means the postbite treatment is greatly simplified. If an animal bites you, gently wash the wound with soap and water, and apply iodine-based antiseptic. If you are not prevaccinated you will need to receive rabies immunoglobulin as soon as possible, and this is almost impossible to obtain in much of India.

## STDs

Sexually transmitted diseases most common in India include herpes, warts, syphilis, gonorrhoea and chlamydia. People carrying these diseases often have no signs of infection. Condoms will prevent gonorrhoea and chlamydia but not warts or herpes. If after a sexual encounter you develop any rash, lumps, discharge or pain when passing urine seek immediate medical attention. If you have been sexually active on your travels, have an STD check when you return home.

### Tuberculosis

While TB is rare in travellers, those who have significant contact with the local population (eg medical and aid workers and long-term travellers) should take precautions. Vaccination is usually only given to children under the age of five, but adults at risk are advised to undergo pre- and post-travel TB testing. The main symptoms are fever, cough, weight loss, night sweats and tiredness.

### Typhoid

This serious bacterial infection is also spread via food and water. It gives a high and slowly progressive fever and a headache, and may be accompanied by a dry cough and stomach pain. It is diagnosed by blood tests and treated with antibiotics. Vaccination is recommended for all travellers spending more than a week in India. Be aware that vaccination is not 100% effective, so you must still be careful with what you eat and drink.

## TRAVELLER'S DIARRHOEA

Traveller's diarrhoea is the most common problem that affects travellers – between 30% and 70% of people will suffer from it within two weeks of starting their trip. In over 80% of cases, traveller's diarrhoea is caused by a bacteria (there are numerous potential culprits), and therefore responds promptly to antibiotics. Treatment with antibiotics will depend on your situation – how sick you are, how quickly you need to get better, where you are etc.

Traveller's diarrhoea is defined as the passage of more than three watery bowel actions within 24 hours, plus at least one other symptom such as fever, cramps, nausea, vomiting or feeling generally unwell.

Treatment consists of staying well hydrated; rehydration solutions like Gastrolyte are the best for this. Antibiotics such as Norfloxacin, Ciprofloxacin or Azithromycin will kill the bacteria quickly.

Loperamide is just a 'stopper' and doesn't get to the cause of the problem. It can be helpful though, for example if you have to go on a long bus ride. Don't take Loperamide if you have a fever, or blood in your stools. Seek medical attention quickly if you do not respond to an appropriate antibiotic.

### Amoebic Dysentery

Ameobic dysentery is rare in travellers but is often misdiagnosed by poor-quality labs. Symptoms are similar to bacterial diarrhoea: fever, bloody diarrhoea and generally feeling unwell. You should always seek reliable medical care if you have blood in your diarrhoea. Treatment involves two drugs: Tinidazole or Metroniadzole to kill the parasite in your gut and then a second drug to kill the cysts. If left untreated, complications such as liver or gut abscesses can occur.

### Giardiasis

Giardia is a parasite that is relatively common in travellers. Symptoms include nausea, bloating, excess gas, fatigue and intermittent diarrhoea. The parasite will eventually go away if left untreated, but this can take months. The treatment of choice is Tinidazole, with Metronidazole being a second-line option.

## ENVIRONMENTAL HAZARDS

### Air Pollution

Air pollution, particularly vehicle pollution, is an increasing problem in most of India's major cities. If you have severe respiratory problems speak with your doctor before travelling to any heavily polluted urban centres. This pollution also causes minor respiratory problems such as sinusitis, dry throat and irritated eyes. If troubled by the pollution leave the city for a few days and get some fresh air.

### Food

Eating in restaurants is the biggest risk factor for contracting travellers' diarrhoea. Ways to avoid it include eating only freshly cooked food, and avoiding shellfish and food that has been sitting around on buffets. Peel all fruit, cook vegetables and soak salads in iodine water for at least 20 minutes (avoid iodine if you are pregnant or have thyroid problems). Eat in busy restaurants with a high turnover of customers. For more on safe eating, see the boxed text, p84.

### Heat

With temperatures hitting 45°C and over in the summer months, heatstroke and heat exhaustion are serious dangers for travellers used to cooler climes; for most people it takes at least two weeks to adapt. Swelling of the feet and ankles is common, as are muscle cramps caused by excessive sweating. Prevent these by avoiding dehydration and excessive activity in the heat. Take it easy when you first arrive. Don't eat salt tablets (they aggravate the gut), but it helps to drink rehydration solution or eat salty food. Treat cramps by stopping activity, resting, rehydrating with double-strength rehydration solution and gently stretching.

Dehydration is the main contributor to heat exhaustion. Symptoms include a feeling of weakness, headache, irritability, nausea or vomiting, sweaty skin, a fast, weak pulse, and a normal or slightly elevated body temperature. Treatment involves getting the sufferer out of the heat and/or sun, fanning the sufferer and applying cool wet cloths to the skin, laying the sufferer flat with their legs raised, and rehydrating with water containing a quarter of a teaspoon of salt per litre. Recovery is usually rapid. It's common to feel weak for some days afterwards.

Heatstroke is a serious medical emergency. Symptoms come on suddenly and include weakness, nausea, a hot, dry body with a body temperature of over 41°C, dizziness, confusion, loss of coordination, fits, and eventually collapse and loss of consciousness. Seek medical help, and commence cooling by getting the person out of the heat, removing their clothes, fanning them, and applying cool wet cloths or ice to their body, especially to the groin and armpits.

Prickly heat is a common skin rash caused by excessive perspiration getting trapped under the skin. The result is an itchy rash of tiny lumps. Treat by moving out of the heat and into an air-conditioned area for a few hours and by having cool showers. Creams and ointments clog the skin, so they should be avoided. Locally bought prickly-heat powder can be helpful.

### Insect Bites & Stings

Bedbugs don't carry disease, but their bites are very itchy. They live in the cracks of furniture and walls, and then migrate to the bed at night to feed on you. You can treat the itch with antihistamines. Lice inhabit various parts of your body but most commonly your head and pubic area. Transmission is via close contact with an infected person. Lice can be difficult to treat, and you may need numerous applications of an antilice shampoo such as permethrin. Pubic lice are usually contracted from sexual contact.

Ticks are contracted after walking in rural areas. They're commonly found behind the ears, on the belly and in the armpits. If you have had a tick bite and experience symptoms such as a rash at the site of the bite or elsewhere, fever or muscle aches you should see a doctor. Doxycycline prevents tick-borne diseases.

Bee and wasp stings mainly cause problems for people who are allergic to them. Anyone with a serious bee or wasp allergy should carry an injection of adrenaline (eg an Epipen) for emergency treatment. For others, pain is the main problem – apply ice to the sting and take painkillers.

### Skin Problems

Fungal rashes are common in humid climates. Two common rashes affect travellers. The first occurs in the moist areas that get less air, such as the groin, the armpits and between the toes. It starts as a red patch that slowly spreads and is usually itchy. Treatment involves keeping skin dry, avoiding chafing and using an antifungal cream such as Clotrimazole or Lamisil. *Tinea versicolor* is also common – this fungus causes small, light-coloured patches, most commonly on the back, chest and shoulders. See a doctor.

Cuts and scratches easily become infected in humid climates. Take meticulous care of

#### DRINKING WATER

- Never drink tap water.
- Bottled water is generally safe – check the seal is intact at purchase.
- Avoid ice.
- Avoid fresh juices – they may have been watered down.
- Boiling water is the most efficient method of purifying it.
- The best chemical purifier is iodine. It should not be used by pregnant women or those with thyroid problems.
- Water filters should also filter out viruses. Ensure your filter has a chemical barrier such as iodine and a small pore size, eg less than four microns.

HEALTH

any cuts and scratches to prevent complications such as abscesses. Immediately wash all wounds in clean water and apply antiseptic. If you develop signs of infection (increasing pain and redness), see a doctor. Divers and surfers should be particularly careful with coral cuts, as they easily become infected.

### Sunburn

Even on a cloudy day sunburn can occur rapidly. Always use a strong sunscreen (at least factor 30), making sure to reapply after a swim, and always wear a wide-brimmed hat and sunglasses outdoors. Avoid spending too much time in the sun during the hottest part of the day (10am to 2pm). If you become sunburnt stay out of the sun until you have recovered, apply cool compresses and take painkillers for the discomfort. A 1% hydrocortisone cream applied twice daily is also helpful.

## WOMEN'S HEALTH

Pregnant women should receive specialised advice before travelling. The ideal time to travel is in the second trimester (between 16 and 28 weeks), when the risk of pregnancy-related problems is at its lowest and when pregnant women generally feel at their best. Always carry a list of quality medical facilities available at your destination and ensure you continue your standard antenatal care at these facilities. Avoid rural travel in areas with poor transportation and medical facilities. Most of all, ensure travel insurance covers all pregnancy-related possibilities, including premature labour.

Malaria is a high-risk disease in pregnancy. The WHO recommends that pregnant women do NOT travel to areas with Chloroquine-resistant malaria. None of the more effective antimalaria drugs are completely safe in pregnancy.

Traveller's diarrhoea can quickly lead to dehydration and result in inadequate blood flow to the placenta. Many of the drugs used to treat various diarrhoea bugs are not recommended in pregnancy. Azithromycin is considered safe.

In a lot of places, supplies of sanitary products (pads, rarely tampons) are readily available. Birth-control options may be limited, so bring adequate supplies of your own form of contraception. Heat, humidity and antibiotics can all contribute to thrush. Treatment is with antifungal creams and pessaries such as Clotrimazole. A practical alternative is a single tablet of Fluconazole (Diflucan). Urinary tract infections can be precipitated by dehydration or long bus journeys without toilet stops; bring suitable antibiotics.

# Language

## CONTENTS



The huge number of languages spoken in India helps explain why English is still widely spoken more than 50 years after the British left, and why it's still the official language of the judiciary. There are 18 languages recognised in the constitution, and over 1600 minor languages spoken according to the last census. While the locals in Rajasthan, Agra and Delhi may be speaking Punjabi, Urdu, Marwari, Jaipuri, Malvi or Mewati to each other, for you Hindi will be the local language of choice.

Despite major efforts to promote Hindi as the national language of India, phasing out English, many educated Indians speak English as virtually their first language. For the large number of Indians who speak more than one language, it's often their second tongue. Although you'll find it very easy to get around India with English, it's always good to know at least a little of the local language.

## HINDI

Hindi is written from left to right in Devanagari script. While the script may be unfamiliar, English speakers will recognise many of Hindi's grammatical features.

For a far more comprehensive guide to Hindi, get a copy of Lonely Planet's *Hindi, Urdu & Bengali Phrasebook*.

### PRONUNCIATION

Most Hindi sounds are similar to their English counterparts, but there are a few tricky ones. There's a difference between 'aspirated' and 'unaspirated' consonants – the aspirated ones are pronounced with a strong puff of air, like saying 'h' after the sound. There are also 'retroflex' consonants, where the tongue is curled up and back to 'colour' the sound. The simplified transliterations we've used in this language guide, however, don't include these distinctions.

It's important to pay attention to the pronunciation of vowels, and especially their length – **a** compared to **aa**. The combination **ng** after a vowel indicates that it's 'nasalised' (pronounced through the nose).

Pay attention to the consonant sounds listed below. All others are the same as in English.

#### Vowels

| | |
|---|---|
| **a** | as the 'u' in 'sun' |
| **aa** | as in 'father' |
| **ai** | as in 'hair' before a consonant; as in 'aisle' at the end of a word |
| **au** | as in 'haul' before a consonant; as the 'ou' in 'ouch' at a word's end |
| **e** | as in 'they' |
| **ee** | as in 'feet' |
| **i** | as in 'sit' |
| **o** | as in 'shot' |
| **oo** | as in 'fool' |
| **u** | as in 'put' |

#### Consonants

| | |
|---|---|
| **ch** | as in 'cheese' |
| **g** | always as in 'gun', never as in 'age' |
| **r** | slightly trilled |
| **y** | as in 'yak' |

### ACCOMMODATION

**Where is the (best/cheapest) hotel?**
*sab se (achaa/sastaa) hotal kahaang hai?*
**Please write the address.**
*zaraa us kaa pataa lik deejiye*
**Do you have any rooms available?**
*kyaa koee kamraa kaalee hai?*
**I'd like to share a dorm.**
*maing dorm me teharnaa chaahtaa/ee hoong* (m/f)

LANGUAGE

| | |
|---|---|
| **I'd like a ...** | *mujhe ... chaahiye* |
| **double room** | *dabal kamraa* |
| **room with a bathroom** | *gusalkaanevaalaa kamraa* |
| **single room** | *singal kamraa* |

**How much for one night/week?**
*ek din/hafte kaa kiraayaa kitnaa hai?*
**May I see it?**
*kyaa maing kamraa dek saktaa/ee hoong?* (m/f)
**Is there any other room?**
*koee aur kamraa hai?*
**Where's the bathroom?**
*gusalkaanaa kahaang hai?*

| | |
|---|---|
| **bed** | *palang* |
| **blanket** | *kambaal* |
| **key** | *chaabee* |
| **shower** | *shaavar* |
| **toilet paper** | *taailet pepar* |
| **water (cold/hot)** | *paanee (tandaa/garam)* |
| **with a window** | *kirkeevaalaa* |

## CONVERSATION & ESSENTIALS

The word 'please' is usually conveyed through the polite form of the imperative, or through other expressions. This book uses polite expressions and the polite forms of words.

| | |
|---|---|
| **Hello.** | *namaste/namskaar* |
| **Goodbye.** | *namaste/namskaar* |
| **Yes.** | *jee haang* |
| **No.** | *jee naheeng* |
| **Thank you.** | *shukriyaa/danyavaad* |
| **You're welcome.** | *koee baat naheeng* |
| **Excuse me/Sorry.** | *kshamaa keejiye* |
| **How are you?** | *aap kaise/kaisee haing?* (m/f) |
| **Fine, and you?** | *maing teek hoong aap sunaaiye?* |
| **What's your name?** | *aap kaa shubh naam kyaa hai?* |

## DIRECTIONS

| | |
|---|---|
| **Where's a/the ...** | *... kahaang hai?* |
| **bank** | *baink* |
| **consulate** | *kaungnsal* |
| **embassy** | *dootaavaas* |
| **Hindu temple** | *mandir* |
| **mosque** | *masjid* |
| **post office** | *daakkaanaa* |
| **public phone** | *saarvajanik fon* |
| **public toilet** | *shauchaalay* |
| **town square** | *chauk* |

**Is it far from/near here?**
*kyaa voh yahaang se door/nazdeek hai?*

## EMERGENCIES

| | |
|---|---|
| **Help!** | *mada keejiye!* |
| **Stop!** | *ruko!* |
| **Thief!** | *chor!* |
| **Call a doctor!** | *daaktar ko bulaao!* |
| **Call an ambulance!** | *embulains le aanaa!* |
| **Call the police!** | *pulis ko bulaao!* |
| **I'm lost.** | *maing raastaa bhool gayaa/gayee hoong* (m/f) |

| | |
|---|---|
| **Where is the ...?** | *... kahaang hai?* |
| **police station** | *taanaa* |
| **toilet** | *gusalkaanaa* |

**I wish to contact my embassy/consulate.**
*maing apne dootaavaas ke sebaat katnaa logõ chaahtaa/chaahtee hoong* (m/f)

## HEALTH

| | |
|---|---|
| **Where is a/the ...?** | *... kahaang hai?* |
| **clinic** | *davaakaanaa* |
| **doctor** | *daaktar* |
| **hospital** | *aspataal* |

| | |
|---|---|
| **I'm sick.** | *maing beemaar hoong* |

| | |
|---|---|
| **antiseptic** | *ainteeseptik* |
| **antibiotics** | *ainteebayotik* |
| **aspirin** | *(esprin) sirdard kee davaa* |
| **condoms** | *nirodak* |
| **contraceptives** | *garbnirodak* |
| **diarrhoea** | *dast* |
| **medicine** | *davaa* |
| **nausea** | *gin* |
| **syringe** | *sooee* |
| **tampons** | *taimpon* |

## LANGUAGE DIFFICULTIES

**Do you speak English?**
*kyaa aap ko angrezee aatee hai?*
**Does anyone here speak English?**
*kyaa kisee ko angrezee aatee hai?*
**I understand.**
*maing samjhaa/ee* (m/f)
**I don't understand.**
*maing naheeng samjhaa/ee* (m/f)
**Please write it down.**
*zaraa lik deejiye*

## NUMBERS

Where English numbers are counted in tens, hundreds, thousands, millions and billions, the Hindi numbering system uses tens, hundreds, thousands, hundred thousands and ten millions. A hundred thousand is one lakh *(laak)*, and 10 million is one crore *(kror)*. These words are almost always used over their English equivalents.

Once into the thousands, written numbers have commas every two places, not three.

| | |
|---|---|
| **1** | *ek* |
| **2** | *do* |
| **3** | *teen* |
| **4** | *chaar* |
| **5** | *paangch* |
| **6** | *chai* |
| **7** | *saat* |
| **8** | *aat* |
| **9** | *nau* |
| **10** | *das* |
| **11** | *gyaarah* |
| **12** | *bara* |
| **13** | *terah* |
| **14** | *chaudah* |
| **15** | *pandrah* |
| **16** | *solah* |
| **17** | *satrah* |
| **18** | *attaarah* |
| **19** | *unnees* |
| **20** | *bees* |
| **21** | *ikkees* |
| **22** | *baaees* |
| **30** | *tees* |
| **40** | *chaalees* |
| **50** | *pachaas* |
| **60** | *saat* |
| **70** | *sattar* |
| **80** | *assee* |
| **90** | *nabbe/navve* |
| **100** | *sau* |
| **1,000** | *hazaar* |
| **100,000** | *ek laak* (written 1,00,000) |
| **10,000,000** | *ek kror* (written 1,00,00,000) |

## SHOPPING & SERVICES

**Where's the nearest ...?**
*sab se karib ... kah hai?*

| | |
|---|---|
| **bookshop** | *kitaab kee dukaan* |
| **chemist/pharmacy** | *davaaee kee dukaan* |
| **general store** | *dukaan* |
| **market** | *baazaar* |
| **washerman** | *dobee* |

**Where can I buy (a/an) ...?**
*maing . . . kah kareed sakta hoong?*
**I'd like to buy (a/an) ...**
*mujhe ... karidnaa hai*

| | |
|---|---|
| **clothes** | *kapre* |
| **colour film** | *rangin film* |
| **envelope** | *lifaafaa* |
| **handicrafts** | *haat kee banee cheeze* |
| **magazines** | *patrikaae* |
| **map** | *nakshaa* |
| **newspaper (in English)** | *(angrezee kaa) akbaar* |
| **paper** | *kaagaz* |
| **razor** | *ustaraa* |
| **soap** | *saabun* |
| **stamp** | *tikat* |
| **toothpaste** | *manjan* |
| **washing powder** | *kapre done kaa saabun* |

| | |
|---|---|
| **a little** | *toraa* |
| **big** | *baraa* |
| **enough** | *kaafee* |
| **more** | *aur* |
| **small** | *chotaa* |
| **too much/many** | *bahut/adik* |

**How much is this?**
*is kaa daam kyaa hai?*
**I think it's too expensive.**
*yeh bahut mahegaa/i hai* (m/f)
**Can you lower the price?**
*is kaa daam kam keejiye?*
**Do you accept credit cards?**
*kyaa aap vizaa kaard vagairah lete ha?*

**SIGNS**

| | |
|---|---|
| प्रवेश/अन्दर | Entrance |
| निकार/बाहर | Exit |
| खुला | Open |
| बन्द | Closed |
| अन्दर आना [निषिद्ध/मना] है | No Entry |
| धूम्रपान करना [निषिद्ध/मना] है | No Smoking |
| निषिद्ध | Prohibited |
| गर्म | Hot |
| ठंडा | Cold |
| शोचालय | Toilets |

## TIME & DATES

**What time is it?**
*kitne baje haing?*
**It's (ten) o'clock.**
*(das) baje haing*
**It's half past two.**
*daaee baje haing*

| | |
|---|---|
| **When?** | *kab?* |
| **now** | *ab* |
| **today** | *aaj* |
| **tomorrow/yesterday** | *kal* (*kal* is used for both, but the meaning is clear from context) |

| | |
|---|---|
| **day** | *din* |
| **evening** | *shaam* |
| **month** | *maheenaa* |
| **morning** | *saveraa/subhaa* |
| **night** | *raat* |
| **week** | *haftaa* |
| **year** | *saal/baras* |

| | |
|---|---|
| **Monday** | *somvaar* |
| **Tuesday** | *mangalvaar* |
| **Wednesday** | *budvaar* |
| **Thursday** | *guruvaar/brihaspativaar* |
| **Friday** | *shukravaar* |
| **Saturday** | *shanivaar* |
| **Sunday** | *itvaar/ravivaar* |

## TRANSPORT

| | |
|---|---|
| **When's the ... bus?** | *... bas kab jaaegee?* |
| **first** | *pehlaa/pehlee* (m/f) |
| **next** | *aglaa/aglee* (m/f) |
| **last** | *aakiree* |

**What time does the ... leave?**
*... kitne baje jaayegaa/jaayegee?* (m/f)
**What time does the ... arrive?**
*... kitne baje pahungchegaa/pahungchegee?* (m/f)

| | |
|---|---|
| **boat** | *naav* (f) |
| **bus** | *bas* (f) |
| **plane** | *havaaee jahaaz* (m) |
| **train** | *relgaaree* (f) |

**How do we get to ...?**
*... kaise jaate haing?*
**I'd like a one-way/return ticket.**
*mujhe ek ektarafaa/dotarafaa tikat chaahiye*

| | |
|---|---|
| **1st class** | *pratam shreni* |
| **2nd class** | *dviteey shreni* |

# Glossary

This glossary is a sample of words and terms you may encounter on your travels through Rajasthan, Delhi and Agra. For definitions of food and drink, see p86.

**agarbathi** – incense
**Agnikula** – 'Fire Born', name of the mythological race of four *Rajput* clans who were manifested from a sacred fire on Mt Abu; one of the three principal races from which *Rajputs* claim descent
**ahimsa** – nonviolence and reverence for all life
**angrezi** – foreigner
**apsara** – celestial maiden
**Aryan** – Sanskrit word for 'noble'; people who migrated from Persia and settled in northern India
**ashram** – spiritual community or retreat
**autorickshaw** – a noisy three-wheeled device with a motorbike engine and seats for two passengers behind the driver
**Ayurveda** – the ancient and complex science of Indian herbal medicine and healing
**azan** – Muslim call to prayer

**bagh** – garden
**baithak** – salon in a *haveli* where merchants received guests
**baksheesh** – tip, donation (alms) or bribe
**bandh** – general strike
**bandhani** – tie-dye
**Banjaras** – nomadic tribe, believed to be the ancestors of Europe's Gypsies
**baori** – well, particularly a step-well with landings and galleries
**betel** – nut of the betel tree; chewed as a stimulant and digestive in a concoction know as *paan*
**bhang** – dried leaves and flowering shoots of the marijuana plant
**Bhils** – tribal people of southern Rajasthan
**bhojanalya** – basic restaurant or snack bar; known elsewhere in India as a *dhaba*
**bidi** – small, hand-rolled cigarette, really just a rolled-up leaf; also spelt as beedi
**bindi** – forehead mark
**Bishnoi** – tribe known for their reverence for the environment
**Bodhi Tree** – Ficus religiosa, under which Buddha attained enlightenment
**bor** – forehead ornament; also known as a *tikka* or *rakhadi*
**Brahmin** – member of the priest caste, the highest Hindu caste
**Buddha** – Awakened One; the originator of Buddhism; also regarded by Hindus as the ninth incarnation of Vishnu
**bund** – embankment, dyke
**bunti** – wooden block used in block printing fabric; also known as a *chhapa*

**cantonment** – administrative and military area of a *Raj*-era town
**chajera** – mason employed by Marwari businessmen of Shekhawati to build *havelis*
**chakki** – handmill used to grind grain
**chappals** – sandals
**charpoy** – simple bed made of ropes knotted together on a wooden frame
**chaupar** – town square formed by the intersection of major roads
**chhan** – see *dogla*
**chhapa** – wooden block used in block printing fabric; also known as a *bunti*
**chhatri** – cenotaph (literally 'umbrella')
**chitera** – painters of *havelis* in Shekhawati
**choli** – sari blouse
**chowk** – town square, intersection or marketplace
**chowkidar** – caretaker
**chudas** – bangles worn by Rajasthani women
**chureil** – evil spirit; also known as a *dakin*
**crore** – 10 million
**cycle-rickshaw** – three-wheeled bicycle with seats for two passengers behind the rider

**dacoit** – bandit
**dakin** – evil spirit
**Dalit** – preferred term for India's *Untouchable* caste
**dalwar** – sword
**dargah** – shrine or place of burial of a Muslim saint
**darshan** – offering or audience with someone; viewing of a deity
**darwaza** – gateway or door
**dhaba** – hole-in-the-wall restaurant or snack bar; boxed lunches delivered to office workers
**dharamsala** – pilgrims rest house
**dhobi ghat** – place where clothes are washed
**dhobi-wallah** – person who washes clothes
**dhoti** – length of fabric worn by men, which is drawn up between the legs
**dhurrie** – cotton rug
**Digambara** – 'Sky Clad'; a Jain sect whose monks show disdain for worldly goods by going naked
**Diwan-i-Am** – hall of public audience
**Diwan-i-Khas** – hall of private audience

**dogla** – building adjacent to a village dwelling in which livestock and grain are kept; also known as a *chhan*
**dupatta** – long scarf for women often worn with the *salwar kameez*
**durbar** – royal court; also a government

**gaddi** – throne of a Hindu prince
**ganja** – dried flowering tips of marijuana plant
**gaon** – village
**garh** – fort
**ghat** – steps or landing on a river, range of hills or road up hills
**ghazal** – Urdu song derived from poetry; sad love theme
**ghoomer** – dance performed by women during festivals and weddings
**gopis** – milkmaids; Krishna was very fond of them
**gram panchayat** – government at the village level
**Gujjars** – people traditionally engaged in animal husbandry
**gurdwara** – *Sikh* temple
**guru** – teacher or holy person

**Harijan** – name (no longer considered acceptable) given by Gandhi to India's *Untouchables*, meaning 'children of god'
**hathi** – elephant
**hathphool** – ornament worn on the back of the hand by Rajasthani women
**haveli** – traditional mansion with interior courtyards
**hijra** – eunuch
**hookah** – water pipe
**howdah** – seat for carrying people on an elephant's back

**IMFL** – Indian Made Foreign Liquor; beer or spirits produced in India
**Induvansa** – 'Race of the Moon' (Lunar Race); one of the three principal races from which *Rajputs* claim descent

**jagirdari** – feudal system of serfdom imposed on the peasants of Rajasthan
**Jagirdars** – feudal lords of Rajasthan
**jali** – carved marble lattice screen; also refers to the holes or spaces produced through carving timber
**Jats** – traditionally people engaged in agriculture; today Jats play a strong role in administration and politics
**jauhar** – ritual mass suicide by immolation, traditionally performed by *Rajput* women after military defeat to avoid dishonour
**jhonpa** – village hut with mud walls and thatched roof
**jogi** – priest
**jootis** – traditional leather shoes of Rajasthan; men's jootis often have curled-up toes; also known as *mojdis*
**Julaha** – weaver caste

**kabas** – the holy rats believed to be the incarnations of local families at Karni Mata Temple at Deshnok
**Kalbelias** – nomadic tribal group associated with snake charming
**karma** – Hindu, Buddhist and *Sikh* principle of retributive justice for past deeds
**kashida** – embroidery on *jootis*
**kathputli** – puppeteer; also known as a *putli-wallah*
**khadi** – homespun cloth; Mahatma Gandhi encouraged people to spin khadi rather than buy English cloth
**khadim** – Muslim holy servant or mosque attendant
**kharfi** – *monsoon*
**kheis** – shawl; also known as a *pattu*
**kot** – fort
**kotwali** – police station
**Kshatriya** – caste of soldiers and governors, second in the caste hierarchy; *Rajputs* claim lineage from the Kshatriyas
**kuldevi** – clan goddess; every Hindu family pays homage to one
**kund** – lake or tank
**kundan** – type of jewellery featuring *meenakari* on one side and precious stones on the other
**kurta** – long cotton shirt with either a short collar or no collar

**lakh** – 100,000
**lingam** – phallic symbol; symbol of Shiva
**loharia** – form of *bandhani* that gives a ripple effect
**lungi** – worn by men, this loose, coloured garment (similar to a sarong) is pleated by the wearer at the waist to fit snugly

**madrasa** – Islamic college
**Mahabharata** – Vedic epic poem of the Bharata dynasty; describes the battle between the Pandavas and the Kauravas
**mahal** – house, palace
**maharaj kumar** – son of a *maharaja*; prince
**maharaja** – literally 'great king'; princely ruler; also known as maharana, maharao and maharawal
**maharani** – wife of a princely ruler or a ruler in her own right
**Mahavir** – the 24th and last *tirthankar*
**mahout** – elephant rider/master
**mandana** – folk paintings in red chalk on village dwellings
**mandapa** – chamber before the inner sanctum of a temple
**mandir** – temple
**mantra** – sacred word or syllable used by Buddhists and Hindus to aid concentration; metric psalms of praise found in the *Vedas*
**Marathas** – warlike central Indians who controlled much of India at times and fought against the *Mughals* and *Rajputs*
**marg** – major road
**masjid** – mosque
**Marwar** – kingdom of the Rathore dynasty that ruled from Mandore, and later from Jodhpur

**mataji** – female priest; also a respectful form of address to a mother or older woman
**meenakari** – type of enamelwork used on ornaments and jewellery
**mehfilkhana** – Islamic building in which religious songs are sung
**mehndi** – henna; intricate henna designs applied by women to their hands and feet
**mela** – fair, festival
**Mewar** – kingdom of the Sisodia dynasty; ruled Udaipur and Chittorgarh
**Moghul** – see *Mughal*
**mojdis** – see *jootis*
**moksha** – release from the cycle of birth and death
**monsoon** – rainy season; June to October
**moosal** – pestle
**mosar** – death feast
**Mughal** – Muslim dynasty of Indian emperors from Babur to Aurangzeb (16th to 18th centuries)

**namaz** – Muslim prayers
**nawab** – Muslim ruling prince or powerful landowner
**nilgai** – antelope
**niwas** – house, building
**NRI** – Non-Resident Indian

**odhni** – headscarf
**okhli** – mortar; bowl for grinding grain with a *moosal*
**Om** – sacred invocation that represents the essence of the divine principle

**paag** – turban; also called *pagri* and *safa*
**paan** – chewable preparation made from *betel* leaves, nuts and lime
**pagri** – see *paag*
**pahar** – hill
**panchayat sammiti** – local government representing several villages
**panghat poojan** – ceremony performed at a village well following the birth of a child
**pattu** – shawl; also known as a *kheis*
**payal** – anklet worn by Rajasthani women
**PCO** – public call office
**pida** – low folding chair featuring decorative woodcarving, traditionally made in Shekhawati and Bikaner
**pitar** – soul of a dead man
**pitari** – soul of a woman who has died before her husband
**pol** – gate
**prasaad** – sacred food offered to the gods
**puja** – literally 'respect'; offering or prayer
**purdah** – custom among some conservative Muslims (also adopted by some Hindus, especially the *Rajputs*) of keeping women in seclusion; veiled
**putli-wallah** – puppeteer; also known as a *kathputli*

**Rabaris** – nomadic tribe from Jodhpur area
**raga** – any conventional pattern of melody and rhythm that forms the basis for free composition
**raj** – rule or sovereignty; British Raj (sometimes just Raj) refers to British rule before 1947
**raja** – king; also *rana*
**Rajputs** – 'Sons of Princes'; Hindu warrior caste, former rulers of western India
**rakhadi** – forehead ornament; also known as a *bor* or *tikka*
**rana** – see *raja*
**rani** – female ruler; wife of a king
**rawal** – nobleman
**reet** – bride price; opposite of dowry
**Road** – railway town that serves as a communication point to a larger town off the line, eg Mt Abu and Abu Road
**RSRTC** – Rajasthan State Road Transport Corporation
**RTDC** – Rajasthan Tourism Development Corporation

**sadar** – main
**sadhu** – ascetic, holy person, one who is trying to achieve enlightenment; usually addressed as 'swamiji' or 'babaji'
**safa** – see *paag*
**sagar** – lake, reservoir
**sahib** – respectful title applied to a gentleman
**sal** – gallery in a palace
**salwar kameez** – traditional dresslike tunic and trouser combination for women
**sambar** – deer
**sapera** – snake charmer; traditionally associated with the *Kalbelias* tribe
**sati** – suicide by immolation; banned more than a century ago, it is still occasionally performed
**Scheduled Tribes** – government classification for tribal groups of Rajasthan; the tribes are grouped with the lowest casteless class, the *Dalits*
**shikar** – hunting expedition
**Sikh** – member of the monotheistic religion Sikhism, which separated from Hinduism in the 16th century and has a military tradition; Sikh men can be recognised by their beards and turbans
**sikhara** – temple spire
**silavat** – stone carvers
**singh** – literally 'lion'; a surname adopted by *Rajputs* and *Sikhs*
**Sufi** – Muslim mystic
**Suryavansa** – 'Race of the Sun' (Solar Race); one of the three principal races from which *Rajputs* claim descent

**tabla** – pair of drums
**tempo** – noisy three-wheeled public transport; bigger than an *autorickshaw*
**thakur** – nobleman
**tikka** – a mark devout Hindus put on their foreheads with tikka powder; also known as a *bor* or *rakhadi*

**tirthankars** – the 24 great Jain teachers
**tonga** – two-wheeled passenger vehicle drawn by horse or pony
**toran** – shield-shaped device above a lintel, which a bridegroom pierces with his sword before claiming his bride
**torana** – elaborately sculpted gateway before temples
**tripolia** – triple gateway

**Untouchable** – lowest caste or 'casteless', for whom the most menial tasks are reserved; the name derives from the belief that higher castes risk defilement if they touch one; formerly known as *Harijan*, now *Dalit*

**Vaishya** – merchant caste; the third caste in the hierarchy
**Vedas** – Hindu sacred books; collection of hymns composed during the 2nd millennium BC and divided into four books: Rig-Veda, Yajur-Veda, Sama-Veda and Atharva-Veda

**wallah** – man; added onto almost anything, eg *dhobi-wallah*, chai-wallah, taxi-wallah

**yagna** – self-mortification

**zenana** – women's quarters
**zila parishad** – government at district level

# Behind the Scenes

## THIS BOOK

This 1st edition of *Rajasthan, Delhi & Agra* was written by Abigail Hole, with contributions by Sarina Singh (Delhi) and Martin Robinson (Agra). This book was adapted from the 3rd edition of *Rajasthan*, which was written by Monique Choy; Sarina Singh wrote the 2nd edition. The Health chapter of this book was written by Dr Trish Batchelor.

## THANKS from the Authors

**Abigail Hole** Enormous thanks to Sumeet, Jyoti and Niranjan Desai; to the inimitable Hemant Pradhan; to Mona in Jaipur; to Vinod Bhojak in Bikaner; to Ajit Singh and Bhupendra in Bharatpur; to fantastically helpful Piers in Udaipur; to wonderfully efficient Mukesh Mehta and his brother in Bundi; to Lalit and Beverley Ganesh in Mt Abu; to Ramesh Jangid in Shekhawati; to Gemar Bhati in Barmer; to darling most Luca in Jaipur, Ajmer and Pushkar; to intrepid researchers Mum and Ant in Jodhpur, Shekhawati and Mt Abu; to Dad for great office support; and to dearest Gabriel for coming along for the ride and making this trip so memorable. Also huge gratitude to Janine Eberle, all those who worked so hard in production, and the travellers who wrote with suggestions and advice.

**Martin Robinson** Thanks to S Chandola and Anil Gupta in Dehra Dun; Neelambar Badoni, Punit Jasani and Hari Singh in Mussoorie; Akash, Kiwi Sue, Sanjeev Mehta, Subhash Dutta and RB Raturi in Haridwar; Arvind Bhardwoj and Jai Singh Rawat in Rishikesh; S Bindra in Govindghat; Ramesh the Mule in Ghangaria; Mahendra Badwal in Mana village; Manish in Kausani; Mr Khan and Um Ashankar in Varanasi; Harinder and Himanshu in Sirhind; all the chefs and chai makers who kept me going; Origin Pacific for rescuing me when Qantas stranded me in Brisbane; and special thanks to Marie who ensured I wasn't a lonely Lonely Planet researcher.

**Sarina Singh** I'm very grateful to the many people in India who so generously proffered advice and pointed me in the right direction. Thanks also to the numerous readers who wrote to Lonely Planet with their feedback. In Delhi, special thanks to Mamta and Anup Bamhi for allowing me to sift through their massive book collection, and to Padmini Brahma at India Tourism Delhi for being dedicated to accuracy. Thanks also to Surinder Mohan and Rajinder Kumar Budhraja, and to Avnish and Ushi for so kindly chasing up bits and pieces once I was back in Melbourne. At Lonely Planet, a big thank you to everyone who worked on this edition, with special acknowledgement to Janine Eberle and Helen Christinis.

## CREDITS

This guidebook was commissioned in Lonely Planet's Melbourne office and produced by:
**Commissioning Editor** Janine Eberle
**Coordinating Editor** Helen Christinis
**Coordinating Cartographer** Emma McNicol
**Coordinating Layout Designer** Jim Hsu
**Managing Cartographer** Shahara Ahmed
**Project Manager** Celia Wood

### THE LONELY PLANET STORY

The story begins with a classic travel adventure: Tony and Maureen Wheeler's 1972 journey across Europe and Asia to Australia. There was no useful information about the overland trail then, so Tony and Maureen published the first Lonely Planet guidebook to meet a growing need.

From a kitchen table, Lonely Planet has grown to become the largest independent travel publisher in the world, with offices in Melbourne (Australia), Oakland (USA) and London (UK). Today Lonely Planet guidebooks cover the globe. There is an ever-growing list of books and information in a variety of media. Some things haven't changed. The main aim is still to make it possible for adventurous travellers to get out there – to explore and better understand the world.

At Lonely Planet we believe travellers can make a positive contribution to the countries they visit – if they respect their host communities and spend their money wisely. Every year 5% of company profit is donated to charities around the world.

**Assisting Editors** Sarah Bailey, Kristin Odijk, Laura Gibb, Thalia Kalkipsakis
**Assisting Cartographer** Malisa Plesa
**Cover Designer** Pepi Bluck
**Colour Designer** Sonya Brooke
**Language Content Coordinator** Quentin Frayne

**Thanks to** Brigitte Ellemor, Melanie Dankel

## THANKS from Lonely Planet

**Many thanks to the hundreds of travellers who wrote to us with helpful hints, useful advice and interesting anecdotes.**

**A** Meg Abdy, Tina & Jack Adams, Itagaki Akiko, Marina Alberti, GW Albury, Simon Alderson, Mark Aldulaimi, Brooke Alexander, Elke Allenstein, John Anderson, Emma Nora Andersson, Gurumurthy Anjanappa, Graeme Archer, Andrew Ashman, Maggie Atherton, Jennifer Atkinson, Jean-Paul Aubert, Claire Awramenko, Stuart Ayres **B** Jack Backen, Ingrid Bal, Roman Bansen, Einat Bareli, Jake Barr, Michelle Bateman, John Beevers, Hayden JA Bellenoit, Marisa Besmer, John Betts, Fran Bigman, Corine Binnekamp, Dimitri Blomme, Horst Bluemel, Tania Borg, Kelly Boucher, Christoph Bratzler, Holger Braun, Ciaran Breen, Johannes Bronkhorst, Marit Brook-Kothlow, Jacqueline Bryan, Vilasinee Bunnag, Liz Burke **C** Eric Calder, Hannah Marie Campion, Hannah Castro, Tanguy Ceulemans, Jason Chan, Barrie Chapman, Tim Chauvel, Rune Christoffer, Andrea Clark, Esther Clark, Gail Clark, Joe Clark, Morelle Codile, Joanne Coffey, Francois Coheur, Simon Colvin, Joy Cook, Cousturer Courey, David Cowe, Andrew Cox, Conor Creane, Amanda Cunningham **D** Nick Dalton, Fiona Darcy, Geraldine Davies, Martine Davis, Eugen de Boer, Yvonne de Haas, Ben de Viaris, Chantal Demaire, Michelle Dermody, Elena Dervetzi, Michelle Dolbear, Ruth Doodson, Rachel Douglas, Pilar Ducci, Kareb Dujardin, Gisela Durand **E** Lisa Edmonds, Jessica Edwards, Sue Elderkin, David Elias, Jamie Elliott, Clarissa Endean, Alaric Everett **F** Elisabetta Fabris, Fin Farrelly, Russell Farrow, Klaus Fehlker, Anthony Finlay, Sandra Fischli, Robert Fleming, Jonathan Fookes, Ray Forster, V Franklin, Marius & Hemma Fuchs, James Fulford-Talbot, Roderick Furness, Barbara Furrer **G** Chau Shien Gan, Martial Gaunay, Jay Geller, Probal K Ghosh, Steffen Goehlert, Nikolene Gomnesen, Roberto Gonzalez, Sophie Gooch, Katja Gorlitz, Benjamin Gorner, Shansi M Grabfelder, Stephanie Graf, Karl Graham, John Grierson, Chloe Griffiths, Gabrielle Griffiths, Martin & Gabriele Grüger, Katharina Gsaenger, Sandhya Gupta, Sanjay Gupta, Thomas Gutersohn, Fabian Gutscher **H** Chris Habetler, Lea Habif, Nataly Ben Hamo, Layla Hancock-Piper, Tom Harland, Nick Harper, Theon Harrichand, Norman Harris, Sam Harrison, Rowan Harvey, Rob & Karen Hayward, Robert Heathwood, Tony Helper, Janet Hewitt, Tanya Hirst, Owen Hitchens, Karen Ho, Klaus Hoffmann-Hoock, Paul R Hogan, Robin Hogg, David Holland, Robert Housley, Jason & Brian Howard, Ben Humphreys, Makke Hussen, Robert Hutcheson **I** Andrea Irace **J** Johanna Jaghagen, Shailesh Jain, Alice & Justin Jamieson, Mariken Janssen, Gayatari Jayaraman, Peter Jensen, June Jolley, Joe Joseph **K** Jennifer Kagan, Andy Karl, Marnix Kasper, Amy Keatch, Anne-Marie Kleijberg, Verlinden Koen, Gauri & Sanjay Kothari, Akhilesh Kumar, Christin Kyle **L** Simone Laarmans, Isabelle Lafortune, Regina Lally, Sandrine Laloubere, Efrat Laor, Maria J Lara, Sari Lehtola, Ian Lindley, Susan Lindsay, Nicola Liney, Antoinette Llinas, Katie Love, Marco Lovisolo, Arwinder Luther, Susan Luxford, Tara Lynch, Py Lystrup **M** Junaidy McKenzie, Kevin & Cathy Mageau, David Main, Erika Malitzky, Eswar Mani, Alexis Marsden, Vicki Marshall, Simon Martindale, Linda Martini, Michele Matthews-Potter, Stacey Mayle, Susan Mc Daniel, Leone McDermott, Lewis McFadyen, Keith McGowan, W M Mckay, Kelli & Mike McSherry, Eveline Meier, Marieke Meijer, Markus Meyer, Sarah Michael, Moons Mieke, Ann Mievis, Monika Milewska, Shefali Milizanek-Desai, Kim Miller, Steven Mills, Linda Minoo, Bethany Mitchell, Lee Mitchell, Hamblin Mitt, Francesca Molendini, Kate Moore, Marcelo Morales, Jakobsen More, Nicolas Moroz, Jaume Cusido Morral, Claire Morrison, Tudor Morrow, Suz-Anne Moss, Dennis Muldoon, Carlos Mundy, Beatriz Munoz, Michael Murphy, Richard Murray **N** Oksana Nagayets, Claire Neillands, Nadine Neilson, Jenny Nelson, Tony Netting, Russell Newberry, Patrick Newman, Ann Newton Holmes, Monika Niehot, Motti Nissim, Laura Norman, Hannah Norrgard **O** Denis & Lisa O'Connor, Bryne Oerstavik, Megan O'Grady Greene, Ted Olsen, Sean O'Reilly, Vera Ottoni, Jerome Ovion **P** Karishma Pais, Priya Palsule-Desai, Dimitris Pantelides, Margie Parikh, Joanne Parry, Margie Parsons, Lorina Pellach, Andrew Pendleton, Marion Penelas, Marijn Penson, Elvina Carlos Pereira, Igor Petricek, Tim Pettit, Lauren Picard, Jana Plesnikova, Stephanie Pollet, David Polo, Manuela Pop, Sarah Porter, Victoria Pritchard, Carlos Pueo Crespo **Q** Brian Quirk **R** Sushil Kumar Rachuri, Sage Radachowsky,

### SEND US YOUR FEEDBACK

We love to hear from travellers – your comments keep us on our toes and help make our books better. Our well-travelled team reads every word on what you loved or loathed about this book. Although we cannot reply individually to postal submissions, we always guarantee that your feedback goes straight to the appropriate authors, in time for the next edition. Each person who sends us information is thanked in the next edition – and the most useful submissions are rewarded with a free book.

To send us your updates – and find out about Lonely Planet events, newsletters and travel news – visit our award-winning website: **www.lonelyplanet.com/feedback**.

Note: We may edit, reproduce and incorporate your comments in Lonely Planet products such as guidebooks, websites and digital products, so let us know if you don't want your comments reproduced or your name acknowledged. For a copy of our privacy policy visit www.lonelyplanet.com/privacy.

Sonali Ramchandani, Melanie Randall-Coles, Bill & Noelle Rathmell, Merkurios Redis, Yves Reichmuth, Amber Reijnaerdts, Jesse Reynolds, Elly Rice Cleary, Paul Richardson, Patrick Ritzen, Elizabeth Robinson, Mark Rochester, Christoph Roellig, Yael Rohner, C Roice, John Rose, Birgitte & Steve Rucquoy **S** Sargio Sabadi, Ranpreet Sachdeva, Sonja Salkowitsch, Benedicte Salomon, Roberto Sanchez, Veronica Sapiano, Jon Sawyer, Michael Saxe, Margaret Scaramellini, Falk Schleicher, Karin & Manuel Schneider-Gujer, Albert Scholz, Tristan Schulze, Edwin Schuurman, Stefan Schuurman, Stefan Schweiger, Adrian Scicluna, Julian Scott, Zoe Scott, Carine Segers, Marie-Luise Seisenbacher, Luis Sfeir-Younis, Charles & Katie Shively, Rosemarie & Peter Shorten, Sam Shortland, Roni Shouval, Baljit Sihan, Tushar Singh, Jeroen Slikker, Fiona Smith, Nicole Smith-Bertram, Lana Snook, Alex Sohel, Alex Sohelonly, Melissa Spectre, Jamie Spurway, Anusha Srinivasan, Einav Srugo, Fiona & Ian Stafford, Marianne Stam, Jim Stancombe, Natasa Stankovic, Celis Stefan, Debbie Stefanac, Alexander Stein, Cecilia Stenqvist, Luckos Stevens, Marsha Stewart, Andrew Strhubach, Jacob Stringer, Carla Stroecken, Donna Strong, Jannis Stuertz, Geraldine Sumpter, Maria Svensson, Rachel & Zach Swede, Oliver Sweet **T** Catherine Tapp, Susanne Tayfoor, Ed Templeton, Gavin Terblanche, Anita Thorn, Leonie Tijdink, Janet Timbol, Emma Tiplady, Sabine Trautmann, Teresa Trippenbach, Olivier & Marie Trouille **U** Cornelia Uebscher **V** Leon van Beurden, Stephane van Cauwenberghe, Bastiaan van de Ven, Frans van der Sommen, Hans van Nierop, E van Roosendaal, Jan-Diederik van Wees, Erik van de Wiel, John Velick, Laurent Vezignol, Fotis Vlachos, Jan Vonk, Daniela Vyas, Kamlesh Vyas **W** Steve & Fe Ward, Mark Watson, Averil Way, Jane Wells, George Werlberger, Mark A Westgate, Fraser Williams, Peter & Fay Williams, Andrew Wilson, Christianne Wisdom, Alex Wright, Sarah Wright **Z** Paolo Zevi, Anke Zindler, Harry Zinho

## ACKNOWLEDGMENTS

Many thanks to the following for the use of their content:

Excerpt from *City of Djinns* © William Dalrymple 1993. Reprinted by permission of HarperCollins Publishers Ltd.

# Index

## C



**000** Map pages
**000** Location of colour photographs

**G**



**000** Map pages
**000** Location of colour photographs

INDEX

## N



## O



## P

**000** Map pages
**000** Location of colour photographs

## Y



## Z

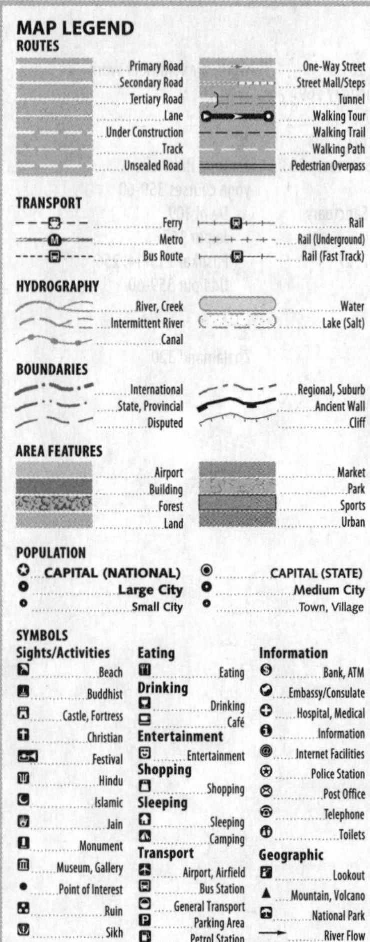


## LONELY PLANET OFFICES


### Australia

Head Office
Locked Bag 1, Footscray, Victoria 3011
☎ 03 8379 8000, fax 03 8379 8111
talk2us@lonelyplanet.com.au

### USA

150 Linden St, Oakland, CA 94607
☎ 510 893 8555, toll free 800 275 8555
fax 510 893 8572, info@lonelyplanet.com

### UK

72–82 Rosebery Ave,
Clerkenwell, London EC1R 4RW
☎ 020 7841 9000, fax 020 7841 9001
go@lonelyplanet.co.uk

**Published by Lonely Planet Publications Pty Ltd**

ABN 36 005 607 983





Cover photographs: One of the world's longest moustaches, India, Frans Lemmens/Getty Images (front); The Taj Mahal - Agra, Uttar Pradesh, Richard I'Anson/Lonely Planet Images (back).





Printed by SNP Security Printing Pte Ltd, Singapore